CHINA
and
CHRISTIANITY

The Ricci Institute for Chinese and Western Cultural History of the University of San Francisco

Named after the Italian Jesuit Matteo Ricci, the Institute was founded in 1984 as a non-profit interdisciplinary research center. Dedicated to studying the history of religious, philosophical, scientific, educational, and cultural exchange between China and the West with emphasis on the Jesuit missions of the Ming and Qing dynasties, the Ricci Institute supports visiting scholars, publishes books and articles, sponsors symposia and seminars, and cooperates with friends and colleagues worldwide.

The Center for the Pacific Rim of the University of San Francisco

The Center for the Pacific Rim was founded in 1988. It promotes understanding, communication, and cooperation among the cultures and economies of the Pacific Rim and provides leadership in strengthening the position of the San Francisco Bay Area as a preeminent gateway to the Pacific. The Center fulfills its mission through offering academic programs, outreach services, research, publication, and a visiting fellows program.

CHINA AND CHRISTIANITY
Burdened Past, Hopeful Future (2000)
Edited by Stephen Uhalley, Jr. and Xiaoxin Wu

CHRISTIANITY IN CHINA
A Scholars' Guide to Resources in the Libraries and Archives of the United States
(revised and expanded edition) (forthcoming)
Original edition edited by Archie R. Crouch, Steven Agoratus,
Arthur Emerson, and Debra E. Soled
Revised edition edited by Xiaoxin Wu

DESCRIPTIVE CATALOGUE OF CHINESE MATERIALS
IN THE JESUIT ARCHIVES IN ROME
(forthcoming)
By Albert Chan, S.J.

CHINA
and
CHRISTIANITY

Burdened Past,
Hopeful Future

Stephen Uhalley, Jr. and Xiaoxin Wu
editors

AN EAST GATE BOOK

M.E. Sharpe
Armonk, New York
London, England

An East Gate Book

Library of Congress Cataloging-in-Publication Data

China and Christianity : burdened by past, hopeful future / edited by Stephen Uhalley, Jr.
and Xiaoxin Wu.
    p. cm.
    "An East gate book"
    Includes bibliographical references and index.
    ISBN 0-7656-0661-5 (alk. paper)—ISBN 0-7656-0662-3 (pbk. : alk paper)
    1. Christianity—China. I. Uhalley, Stephen. II. Wu, Xiaoxin.

BR1285.C523 2000
275.1—dc21   00-059590
CIP

Printed in the United States of America

To Edward J. Malatesta, SJ,
for his passionate goodness and
deep commitment to Christianity in China

Table of Contents

III. China and Christianity in Modern and Contemporary
    History and Beyond

Foreword

This volume consists, for the most part, of selected edited papers that were presented at the "China and Christianity: Burdened Past, Hopeful Future: An International Conference of Reflections for the New Millennium" that was held in San Francisco, October 17–19, 1999 under the sponsorship of the Ricci Institute for Chinese-Western Cultural History and the Center for the Pacific Rim of the University of San Francisco (USF). Accordingly, they represent the considered thinking of particularly outstanding specialists who were personally invited from many countries around the world. These leading scholars hail from "greater" China (i.e., the People's Republic, the Hong Kong Special Autonomous Region, and Taiwan), from Europe (including Western and Central Europe and Russia), and from North America. The forty-seven speakers and panelists at the conference included prominent Protestants, Catholics, Russian Orthodox Christian, and non-Christian scholars. Most of them had already made genuinely outstanding contributions to our understanding of Chinese history, of Sino-Western historical cultural relations, and of the Christian experience in China. Their papers and the responses and discussions that they evoked greatly enhanced the dignity and significance of the occasion.

The conference was held in memory of Father Edward J. Malatesta, SJ, the founding director of the Ricci Institute of the Center for the Pacific Rim, University of San Francisco, until his untimely death in Hong Kong the previous year. This motive facilitated the cooperation of so many top scholar-specialists on such relatively short notice just as it elicited such quality presentations and discussions. There was from the outset no pretension to cover completely the entire range of the exceedingly rich historical experience or to do so on anything approaching a truly systematic and comprehensive basis. Instead, it was necessary to make do with the chronological subdivision of the historical record into, respectively, the deeper "traditional" past, then the more modern period, followed by the experience of recent decades and years, and, finally, likely future prospects. It was left to the individual paper presenters to determine what his or her specific topic would be under each of these general chronological divisions. This approach precluded the possibility of a really tight thematic cohesiveness for the conference but did enable each scholar to present what he or she believed to be particularly germane and significant. It was an unparalleled opportunity for informed personal "reflections" on this grand relationship "for the new millennium," as billed in the conference subtitle.

This volume follows the layout of the conference itself rather faithfully. However, some conference presentations have not been included here. The conference featured two luncheon addresses by David W. Vikner and H. Christopher Luce. Their fine presentations, entitled respectively "Chinese Higher Education and the United Board for Christian Higher Education" and "The Henry Luce Foundation: A Century of Service to Christianity and Higher Education in China", were published in the USF *Pacific Rim Report*, Number 12 (March 2000). Excluded were very good papers that dealt with higher education, a rich area that deserves fuller coverage in another conference and volume. One new, more general paper in this category from one of the conference participants has been added. The excellent paper on church architecture has been omitted, as was the conference's featured roundtable on the future. This session, necessarily speculative, had made for a lively discussion. Unfortunately, space limitation precluded the inclusion of these papers and discussions. Except, that is, to the extent that our distinguished and able conference/volume summarizer, Philip Wickeri, has made apt references to them. Non-specialist coeditor Stephen Uhalley's introductory piece is provided as a perspective setting essay rather than an initial review of the papers included in the volume.

As conference organizers, cochairmen, and coeditors of this volume, we are grateful to all of the participants of the conference as well as to the invited observers, all of whom contributed to the vitality of the proceedings and some of whom early on gave advice that helped make for a successful project. They, and the particular instances, are too numerous to identify individually in this foreword but all of the participants are included in a list near the end of the volume. Of course, to some we are especially indebted. Financial support was generously made available from the EDS-Stewart Chair for Chinese-Western Cultural History at the Ricci Institute and the Kiriyama Chair for Pacific Rim Studies at the Center for the Pacific Rim. Also, the United Board for Christian Higher Education in Asia provided partial travel funding for some of the participants, while Paul Torrens provided funding toward this publication in Father Ed's memory. We are grateful for this assistance. Moreover, in organizing the conference we gained greatly from the very beginning from the advice of John W. Witek,

SJ, who subsequently accepted the invitation to give the conference keynote address, which is included in the Introduction section of this volume.

The leadership of Barbara K. Bundy, executive director of the Center for the Pacific Rim, to which the Ricci Institute is subordinate organizationally, has been priceless. Her wise counsel, great energy, and infectious enthusiasm assured that this project was brought to fruition on a timely basis. We are especially grateful to Monica K. Chang and to Mark S. Mir, who, in truth, should be considered the third and fourth coeditors of this volume. Monica worked with the successive editions of papers and manuscripts from beginning to end and was more intimately involved with each word of the project than anyone else, transferring as she did each version to the master copies including the finished product. Mark is primarily responsible for the compilation of the glossary and the bibliography, those two invaluable scholarly aids to this volume, and he had a hand in the editing as well. Special gratitude goes to Elisabeth Rochat de la Vallée for her editorial assistance in the French language. We appreciate the excellent work of the two conference rapporteurs, Eriberto P. Lozada and Eugenio Menegon.

It has been an honor to be involved in this project and a genuine pleasure to have worked with so many able and thoughtful individuals. Although we owe so much to so many for bringing this volume to completion, any shortcomings that are found remain our responsibility exclusively.

Stephen Uhalley, Jr. and Xiaoxin Wu
San Francisco, June 1, 2000

I

Introduction

Burdened Past, Hopeful Future

STEPHEN UHALLEY, JR.

All of the outstanding scholars who participated in the historic international ecumenical "China and Christianity: Burdened Past, Hopeful Future: An International Conference of Reflections for the New Millennium" including those who contributed to this volume, are engaged one way or another, directly or indirectly, in a longstanding and continuing drama of epic proportions. I hasten to add that I myself am a non-specialist on this specific historical relationship and but a lay person. But, however fortuitously this has come about, it is my good fortune and high honor to be involved with such illustrious company on such an important project and to be asked to write this perspective setting essay. With this understood, let me continue.

As far as the Christian experience is concerned, the very heart of the drama, after all, is the message of the Gospel. For Christians this is a matter of the greatest significance and they know the importance of sharing the message with others. However, many also know that whether those who hear the message accept it or not is something that is ultimately out of the hands of Christians as messengers. Acceptance is, in the end, a matter of whether the hearers are disposed to hear and to listen, of whether they are also provided with the gift of faith and act upon it. This is the province of the Holy Spirit, not the messenger. For Christians it is sufficient to share the message and then, most important, to behave like Christians ... which, for many, it seems, would be quite novel and, in any case, is not easy.

Faith itself, though, seems to be a key element here. Those who have it and those who do not have it do not see this grand subject in quite the same light. This helps account for the great variety of approaches to and interpretations of the encounter.

Still, the power of the message itself, whether it is accepted or not, is astonishing. Speaking of the dogma that encompasses the Christian message, novelist-theologian Dorothy Sayers wrote that "it is this dogma itself that is the drama—not beautiful phrases, nor comforting sentiments, nor vague aspirations to loving kindness and uplift, nor the promise of something nice after death—but the terrifying assertion that the same God who made the world lived in the world and passed through the grave and gate of death. Show that to the heathen," said Sayers, "and they may not believe it; but at least they may realize that here is something that a man might be glad to believe."[1]

The Christian message *is* dynamite material, whether one accepts it with faith or only has an inkling of its enormous evocative power. Hence, the story of its extension around the world is such a fascinating one. This is particularly so where, as in China, a centuries long political-cultural antipathy to organized religion results in crippling regulations and recurrent persecution. Yet, even here, there can be an appreciative response to the congenial and constructive features of Christianity. Any wonder then, that this is such an absorbing and fit subject for serious ongoing contemplation! A subject with a rich history of multiple intriguing crosscurrents, interesting sidelights, and differing interpretations . . . all occasioned, in the end, by the simple but powerful Gospel message . . . especially as it is shared in this case, over time, among the many beautiful and talented people of China.

This conference volume, which highlights nearly four hundred years of contact and engagement between Chinese and Christian traditions, represents astute thinking on the subject at the turn both of a new century and a new millennium, a noteworthy moment of history on this account alone. However, at least as important as the coincidental occurrence of such infrequent major calendar markers is that this also happens to be a transitional moment in history with exceptionally strong distinguishing characteristics. These are the truly great changes now taking place in the world and in all our lives. Changes that are all the more remarkable because they are accelerating at an historically unprecedented pace, hurling us into the unknown future amidst, unfortunately, seriously frayed social and cultural fabrics and a new post–Cold War world order that is yet to be worked out.

It is important to recognize that China, too, is caught up in the fast developing ubiquitous changes and is similarly affected by the widely shared uncertainty that they engender. But in the case of China this universal uncertainty is anything but ameliorated by China's own unique mix of exceedingly difficult and perplexing circumstances. Remember, too, that China is completing a century that has been especially traumatic, leaving one generation after another of its intellectuals reeling. It was only just one hundred years ago that China was beset by the infamous scramble for concessions. Taiwan had already been alienated four years earlier, the Boxer Rebellion was simmering, and the intervention of a foreign international military force was still to unfold in the months ahead. The man who would emerge as the father of the modern Chinese revolution, Sun Yat-sen, seriously worried whether the Chinese race itself would survive!

As it turned out, the Chinese did survive the very troubled twentieth century and did so with a population that is the largest of any country on earth, a distinction which presents problems of its own. Moreover, China is the only major nation that has managed, despite all the problems of the period, to retain as a modern nation-state its empire configuration of a century ago. This is no mean accomplishment in the course of a century that has been distinguished by the dissolution of empires. And the strain shows. But despite such tension, China is in a seriously reintegrating mode as former constituencies return to the fold. The return of Hong Kong in July 1997 and of Macau in December 1999 nearly complete this process, and great attention and much propaganda is now directed at the one remaining constituency, Taiwan.

It is in this heady and problematical environment that the conferees met to share reflections on the overall experience of Christianity in China. The "burdened past" of the conference subtitle refers to problems that are part of the historical record, including disconcerting instances of disunity within Christianity, including within Roman Catholicism itself, and of the unfortunate association at times of Christianity with Western Imperialism. Sometimes, it has been a consequence of Christians themselves not adequately living their faith.

On the other hand, some of the burden is attributable to cultural and ideological dispositions on the part of elites in China that have made life more difficult for Christians. Indeed, Christian achievements in China, in the light of all such burdens, are all the more impressive. Perhaps foremost among the achievements as seen in recent times have been the remarkable self-reliance, staying power, and impressive growth of a distinctively indigenous Chinese Christianity.

In fact, it is this enduring and expanding Chinese Christianity itself that may provide the base for the "hopeful future" of the conference subtitle. It is an essential element to be taken into account in China's journey into modernity at this juncture. Additionally, there has been in recent years China's refreshing opening to the world, accompanied as it has been by spectacular sustained economic growth, by generally increased societal relaxation and greater mobility, and by an encouraging, if selective absorption of new ideas. October 1999, the month of the conference, saw the celebration of the fiftieth anniversary of the People's Republic of China, bringing to our attention many of the positive accomplishments of the Chinese people in this turbulent period. But, it is also worth noting that controls over the media and education stand in the way of a full and fair assessment of these fifty years, revealing instead a disquieting amnesia regarding a tragic past that so many Chinese can remember personally. Meanwhile, the party/state remains sluggish and evasive in implementing even its own program of planned structural political reforms, reforms that were announced more than a dozen years ago.

We do not need to go into the number of serious problems that beset China at present, some of which are abetted by this political delay, including the inordinate corruption that threatens the legitimacy of the party. But it may be helpful to consider one of them as an important and timely example. After two full decades of enjoying the benefits derived from the most easily implemented economic reforms, the Chinese government finally finds itself confronting painful measures that can no longer be postponed. This is such an urgent matter that in the month preceding the China and Christianity conference an important party meeting, the Fourth Plenum of the ruling Fifteenth Central Committee, addressed the situation almost exclusively. This was about the reform of the state-owned enterprises. The country is at present in the midst of a three-year program to try to break the back of this key problem; although rather timid efforts have already been essayed over several years. This sounds like a prosaic and routine technical matter for economists and administrators to resolve. It is much more than that.

This is a perilous undertaking for the party leadership because the changes involved are fraught with extraordinary dangers for the party. This is because the changes deleteriously affect a core constituency of the party itself ... the rather privileged worker in the state enterprises. Moreover, the changes provocatively challenge the very essence of the regime's ideology. This is the line that the party is the vanguard of the workers and the workers themselves, the masters of the enterprises. The reforms court the possibility of serious social instability, particularly as more workers are turned out of comfortable jobs to join the ranks of the numerous unemployed and underemployed. This is a very critical moment for the party/state. We may be on the edge of things happening very quickly in China. In any case, there is enough uncertainty about the outcome of these unavoidable measures that a deep sense of insecurity among the leaders is evident.

And this insecurity is abetted by genuine national security concerns arising from separatist movements that have been threatening for some time particularly in the Northwest. That these separatist tendencies have religious organizational connections is worth keeping in mind. Such security concerns explain China's opposition to NATO and UN military interventions in territories that Chinese leaders argue, sometimes correctly, are those of sovereign states, revealing an anxiety about China's own vulnerability. Unfortunately, such concern was compounded and a patriotic outcry ignited by the May 1999 feckless NATO bombing of the Chinese Embassy in Belgrade. This, of course, merely strengthened suspicions already festering about the United States because of the latter's ambiguous stance regarding China's crowning national integration aspiration—the absorption of Taiwan.

This overall sensitivity and insecurity also helps account for the anxiety over the celebration of the regime's anniversary in October 1999, that it be successful and undisturbed. Hence the arrests and sentencing of political dissidents and general cleanup of unwanted elements from public places during the year. The continued and, in fact, intensified persecution of vulnerable Chinese Christians may in part be a product of the atmosphere created by such social tightening. It helps explain the action against the relatively new *Falun gong* sect, whose peaceful demonstration earlier in the year had caught the party by such surprise. This clampdown would intensify in the months that followed and extend to at least one other *qigong*-related sect as well. It is worth noting that this celebrated campaign against sects has also afforded an opportunity for the state to pointedly reaffirm the official commitment to Marxist materialism and atheism.

In the month just before the China and Christianity conference the American State Department issued its first annual report on religious freedom, which contained a condemnation of China's record in this regard. In rebuttal, China accused Congress of using religious freedom as an excuse to interfere in Chinese domestic affairs. The Chinese authorities hold that Chinese law provides full guarantees of religious freedom and that the Chinese government protects religious activity as long as it is regulated by the state and is within what officials deem "normal religious activity."[2] Only a couple of months after the China and Christianity conference came startling news that would further embarrass Beijing's policy regarding religious freedom, and in this case, Tibet as well. The seventeenth Karmapa, a 14-year-old monk who heads one of most important sects of Tibetan Buddhism, eluded his Chinese guards at his monastery in Tibet and made a dramatic escape across the Himalayas, arriving unannounced in early January 2000 at the Dalai Lama's home in exile in Dharmsala, India.

In this context, China's relations with the West, and with the United States in particular, are very brittle at present. There is a heated discourse within China about the United States and within the United States about China, while meaningful dialogue between the two countries often languishes. While ups and downs in the mutual relationship have occurred many times since the early 1970s, it is a matter of concern this time around that some of the rhetoric on both sides is deteriorating, reaching levels not experienced since the 1950s and 1960s. There are many scurrilous pieces about the United States in the Chinese media. While on the other side, outdoing Chinese claims of U.S. hegemonism is talk of a "China threat." The latter apprehension does seem overblown when one considers the many imponderable domestic difficulties that beset China. Suggesting some sense of the atmospherics, the leading American foreign affairs magazine, in its quarterly issue at the time of the China and Christianity conference, published a lead essay provocatively entitled "Does China Matter?" Its author argued, in effect: Not that much, really.[3]

Shortly after the China and Christianity conference, an American agreement with China on the terms of the latter's entry into the World Trade Organization and the subsequent settlement on reparations both for the Chinese Embassy in Belgrade and for damage done to the American Embassy and consulates in China helped sooth feelings. Even so, the Taiwan issue promised to test even further the U.S.-China relationship in the months ahead. Exacerbating the issue were impending presidential elections both in Taiwan in March 2000 and in the United States later in the year. That Taiwan then did come to elect a new president that represented Beijing's least-preferred candidate would underscore the continued seriousness of the cross–Taiwan Strait situation. Meanwhile, it was understood that continued serious division between the executive and legislative branches of the American government regarding support for Taiwan would complicate matters. The conferees in October 1999 were very much aware of the strained relations with China and the problematical prospects ahead.

These brief comments, intended to place the conference in a broader perspective while taking into account the wider contemporary political situation that prevailed in the weeks immediately surrounding the conference, may seem pessimistic. Perhaps they are and more so than may be warranted. After all, there *are* grounds for hope, too. Whatever the difficulties of the current situation, China will surely survive. We needn't be as disheartened as was Sun Yat-sen a century ago. The Chinese economy, as a whole, still looks quite good. Hopefully, appropriate political reforms will come about in good time. The country is gifted with marvelous political cultural traditions that should yet serve it well. China has many amazingly talented leaders, many within the Communist Party itself, and some in the higher echelons of the party, who, it may be hoped, will get the upper hand decisively. Political accountability and genuine freedom of expression would help mightily to clear the air.

Such genuine openness would greatly facilitate the search that is underway in China for a new foundation for positive values, an undertaking that is so much needed in a time of such runaway materialism. It is also needed in order to complement any real political restructuring that may take place. The architects of this noble undertaking could then more easily draw upon Christian values among other sources. For their part, Chinese Christians would be truly free to practice their faith and to share their message with those who may hear. This grand story of such an exceptional and historic intercultural encounter, featuring as it does such a provocative religious cutting edge, remains one of epic proportions.

Christianity and China:
Universal Teaching from the West

JOHN W. WITEK, SJ

"For all its grave defects, the project of the Chinese revolution (which must not be confused with Maoism) can be thought of as a prophetic judgment on a certain form of Christianity and on its claim to be universal."[1] This statement in the introductory section of a collection of essays published twenty years ago offers a point of departure for considering Christianity's claim of universality, the foundations on which it is based, and in particular, how these perspectives have been applied to China over many centuries.

The Christian viewpoint of universality is rooted in the New Testament. Of several pertinent texts one can cite St. Paul, the Apostle of the early Church, who pointed out to the Galatians, "There does not exist among you, Jew or Greek, slave or freeman, male or female. All are one in Christ Jesus."[2] Whether the Gospel was intended for the Jews alone or for all people is a well-known disagreement in the history of early Christianity. The settlement favored the second part, that is, the Christian message was meant for all men and women. The universality of that message had a specific meaning for the then known world. The statement of St. Paul reflected the events at Pentecost when those present heard various tongues, e.g., those of the Parthians, Medes, Elamites, Mesopotamians, Egyptians, those from Pontus, the province of Asia, etc. Yet all of this occurred within the confines of the Roman Empire that extended from today's England, France, Spain, the northern coast of Africa and over to the Middle East, including Palestine. A few scholarly leaders in that Empire knew something about India, yet far less about China. In the Church itself there was the tradition that St. Thomas the Apostle had reached India, but any connection with China was unknown.

The underground catacombs in Rome and the Colosseum are extant witnesses of the continuing trials and persecutions that the Christians faced in the Roman Empire. Not until the Edict of Milan (312 A.D.) was a modus vivendi reached. St. Paul's words to the Galatians were still the dominant viewpoint for the Christians who, in many ways, tried to convince the non-believers among whom they lived that the universal message of Christianity was still true. Among the Christians competing ideas concerning the nature of Christ arose so that an array of disputed theological points led to the Council of Nicaea (325 A.D.) and other subsequent councils. The removal of the Roman gods from their pedestals, nonetheless, did not mean that the Latin vocabulary was also discarded. Christians adopted a number of terms and phrases from the then contemporary Latin and Greek lexicon and turned them to Christian usage, not the least of which was the term for God, Θεος and Deus. During the next two centuries the Church of the East and the Church of the West were engaged in several major controversies over doctrine and practice so that by 1017 A.D. a split occurred, with Rome becoming the dominant member of the two sides.

The fall of the Roman Empire, the invasions of the Visigoths, Ostrogoths and others, the growth of monasticism, and the rise of Charlemagne—all had an impact upon the Church in Rome which became more self-centered and defensive. The splendor of medieval churches and cathedrals arose within the framework of the papacy engaged against the growth of the temporal power of the state in France and England. By the time the Magna Carta was signed in 1215 the second attempt to plant Christianity in China was still underway, although few in Western Europe were aware of those efforts in that far away land.

This conference entitled "Christianity in China: Burdened Past, Hopeful Future " centers on a range of topics with an overview of the wide spectrum of the Christian presence in the vast and densely populated country of China. Only a few years ago several of us were here at the University of San Francisco exploring aspects of the Chinese Rites Controversy held in commemoration of the 300th anniversary of the Edict of Toleration of 1692. This year is also the sixtieth anniversary of the abrogation of the ban on those same rites which the Catholic Church announced in 1939. In the Chinese cycle of sixty years it is fitting that the past and future status of Christianity in China is under examination today.

To pursue this investigation, five principal stages of the development of Christianity in China can be reviewed in terms of the universal message that Christianity consistently presented as part of the larger dialogue between the West and the Chinese. In terms of Chinese history the stages occurred during the Tang dynasty, the Yuan dynasty, the late Ming and early Qing, then the late Qing to 1949, and lastly China under the control of the Chinese Communist Party for the last fifty years. In all of these periods the universal message of Christianity was offered, but for a variety of reasons only relatively few Chinese accepted it.

Tang Dynasty

During the early Tang dynasty the impact of Buddhism was quite pronounced. Buddhism entered China along the Silk Road, a path that Christianity similarly followed. The Church of the East or more specifically the Syro-Oriental Church (incorrectly at times called the Nestorian Church) had come from Syria through Persia.[3] One thread of its complex history that is being studied to a greater extent is its spread from Persia to China. Known in Chinese as *Jingjiao* it is also called, albeit incorrectly, Nestorianism. In 635 A.D., the leader of the Syro-Oriental Church, Alopen, brought this form of Christianity to Chang'an, then the capital of the Tang dynasty ruled by the Taizong Emperor (627–649). Three years after the arrival of Alopen, the emperor issued the edict allowing the diffusion of Christianity in China and also permitted the first Syro-Oriental monastery to be built in the capital.[4] This imperial approval resulted from the emperor's reading in that same year the first Christian book in China, the *Xuting mishi suojing* (Jesus Messiah Sutra) which Alopen wrote. There is no question but that he stressed the universality of the Christian message presented with some Confucian, Daoist, and Buddhist terms adapted for this purpose. In doing so Alopen underlined that Christ was the Messiah for all men and women. He put this within the context that loyalty to the state and filial piety to one's parents were not only not contrary to Christianity, but indeed every Christian supported both propositions. The Christian message was not a challenge against, but a buttress of the state.

This first opening of Christianity allowed the Church of the East to develop until the years of 698–699 when the Buddhists arose in opposition, and indeed, a little over a decade later, in 713 the Daoists followed suit. This did not stop the Christians in Persia from seeking to rejuvenate the presence of Christianity in China, a policy they carried out by accompanying Arab embassies entering China for diplomatic and trade exchanges. It was at least in part due to this resurgence of Christianity in China that led to the erection in 781 of the *Jingjiao beiwen* (Stele of the Luminous Religion) in Changan. Frequently, but again incorrectly called "The Nestorian Monument," this stele describes the history of Christianity in China in that period. When juxtaposed against the background of the An Lushan Rebellion of 755 and its concomitant social and political upheaval, as well as the renascence of Confucianism and Daoism reclaiming their position in the Chinese tradition, that the Stele was even erected is more than a surprise. The subsequent persecution of Manichaeism in 843 and that of Buddhism in 845 entwined the Christian leaders in Changan so that the imperial edicts against the other two groups uprooted Christianity from the capital.[5] The Christians fled to southern China, but without contacts for support with the church in the Middle East, they were unable to continue for long.

Yuan Dynasty

The second major thrust of Christianity into China occurred during the reign of the Yuan dynasty under the Mongols. At first, that entry from Rome was a diplomatic approach that over time became a religious one. To reach China the Franciscan and the Dominican missionaries had to cross the steppes of Inner Asia, although at times they went first to India and then traversed land routes to China. King Louis IX of France, while on a crusade to recover the Holy Land, sent the Dominican, André de Longjumeau in 1249 and then the Franciscan, Guillaume de Ruysbroek in 1253 as envoys to the Mongol khan in an attempt to create a Mongol alliance with the Christian Franks against the Muslims. Neither envoy was successful in achieving such a goal.[6]

It was in Inner Asia that the nomadic horsemen of the steppes comprised "the finest light cavalry in the world."[7] In his early rise to power Temüjin (1162?–1227) was allied with the Kereit people, a tribe then dominating Outer Mongolia. In fact, he had been a vassal of Toghril, the khan of the Kereit. He moved against the neighboring Mongol tribes and eventually overwhelmed the Tartars of eastern Mongolia. These events were part of the pattern that led to his being proclaimed emperor under the name of Genghis Khan in 1206. Engaged in an offensive war against northern China that began five years later, he was not victorious for another two decades. His seizure of Beijing in 1215 led to his extension of Mongol rule over most of northern China and Manchuria. His defeat of the Khorezm, the great Muslim power in Inner Asia by 1223, along with his destruction of the Tibetan kingdom of the Tangut that was based principally in Gansu province, were stunning news in that part of the world.

For Europeans this news was a shock, since Europe at that time was moving against Islam. Suddenly, the Mongols had appeared along the southeast border of Russia. Successes in battle led to the withdrawal of Mongols from the area for about fifteen years, but eventually they took Kiev on December 6, 1240, and went on to defeat the Magyars on April 11 the next year. The death of Ögödei later that same year of 1241 led to internal dissensions about the choice of his successor. Just a few years earlier in 1238 the kings of France and England received proposals from the Ismailians of Syria—known as the Assassins—who sought an alliance of

Christians and Muslims against what the Muslims said were the common enemies of civilization—the Mongols. Neither France nor England acceded to this request. In fact the bishop of Winchester wrote to King Henry III (1216–1272): "Let these dogs destroy one another and be utterly exterminated and then we shall see the universal Catholic Church founded on their ruins and there will be one fold and one shepherd."[8]

Pope Innocent IV (1243–1254) understood that as soon as the succession dispute among the Mongols was settled, the Christian West had to prepare for an onslaught. To prevent such a threat, he sent the Franciscan, Giovanni da Pian del Carpine (1190–1252) as his envoy to the Great Khan Güyüg (1240–1248) at Karakorum in Mongolia. Of the two letters he sent through his envoy, the pope was quite forthright in his second missive in which he asked that "for the future you desist entirely from assaults of this kind, and especially from the persecution of Christians."[9] Such persecution was in fact a violation of the law of Genghis Khan who stipulated that all religions were to be respected, and above all, their leaders were to be given deferential treatment. Carpine's mission provided information about the overland route and the peoples contacted en route, but failed in its objective of getting the Mongols to stop their threats against Europe. With the fall of Baghdad in 1258, Hülegü, the founder of the Ilkhan dynasty in Persia, showed favor to the Syro-Oriental Church which in turn led to good relations with Kublai Khan (r. 1257–1294) in China. The Syro-Oriental Church reorganized its hierarchy led by the patriarch, Mar Denha (1265–1281), so that "Nestorian" extended from the Persian Gulf and the Indian Ocean to the Caspian and the Pacific. Western interest in the Mongol empire was revived by the return of Maffeo and Nicolò Polo in 1269 with letters from Kublai Khan asking for one hundred missionaries. Meanwhile, a Syro-Oriental (or "Nestorian") archbishopric was set up in 1275 at Kublai Khan's new capital of Khanbaliq (Beijing) and, with churches founded by Christian officials and merchants in several principal cities of China.

When Rabban Sauma (1230?–1294), a Mongolian Turk born in Beijing and bearing a Syrian name, came to Rome in 1287, he visited Philip IV, Edward I, and the newly elected pope, Nicholas IV. Sauma created quite a stir by celebrating the Syrian liturgy in the presence of the pope and the cardinals. He later repeated this at Bordeaux for Edward I. The cardinals in Rome had been more than a little surprised to learn that a Christian priest, a member of the patriarchate's hierarchy, had come as an envoy from the "King of the Tartars." Rabban Sauma pointed out that " . . . many of our fathers in times past entered the lands of the Turks, Mongols and the Chinese and have instructed them in the faith. Today many Mongols are Christians."[10] Rabban Sauma's proposal of a Mongol alliance with the Christian West against the Muslims did not win any supporters, except for Edward I, who showed some interest in that type of crusade. The Egyptian capture of Acre on May 18, 1291 turned the tide so that the Mongol leader of Persia, Öljeitü, son of Argun, who had been baptized as Nicholas in honor of Pope Nicholas IV, became a Muslim. Not long afterwards the Mongols in Persia also became Islamic converts.

In this scenario, Nicholas IV sent letters to Kublai Khan by way of Giovanni da Montecorvino, who traveled through India, disembarked at Quanzhou in Fujian and reached Khanbaliq after the death of Kublai Khan. His successor, Temür (1294–1307), welcomed the papal envoy cordially. Giovanni da Montecorvino was alone for twelve years and is recognized for his remarkable achievement in establishing an active center of Roman Catholicism in Khanbaliq, part of present-day Beijing. It was not until 1307 that Rome, learning of his existence there, appointed him archbishop of Khanbaliq and patriarch of the East. Rome also sent him six missionaries as bishops, three of whom arrived in Khanbaliq where they consecrated Giovanni da Montecorvino bishop. For the next twenty years, the Chinese Mongol mission continued to flourish under his leadership. His discussions with Prince George, the leader of the Öngüt Turks, led the prince and many of his people to change allegiance from the Syro-Oriental Church to the Roman Catholic Church. Giovanni da Montecorvino, translated the New Testament into Uighur and provided copies of the Psalms, the Breviary, and liturgical hymns for the Öngüt. He was instrumental in teaching boys Latin chant, probably for a choir in the liturgy and with the hope that some of them might become priests. Even after the death of Giovanni da Montecorvino the mission in China endured for the next forty years. Perhaps the most significant account of this development is that of Odorico da Pordenone (1265?–1331) who journeyed to China by way of India in 1321 and returned to Europe by an overland route through Inner Asia about seven or eight years later. The Franciscans had established a cathedral and two residences at Quanzhou, the great medieval port near Xiamen (Amoy), and also at Yangzhou, which also had three Syro-Oriental churches.

The Alans, from the region of the Black Sea, converted by Giovanni da Montecorvino, dispatched an embassy to Rome in 1338 to ask for a bishop. Rome's reply was to the send Giovanni de Marignolli who, accompanied by fifty fellow Franciscans, left Avignon that same year and reached Khanbaliq in 1342. He brought a gift of a Western warhorse to the emperor as recorded in the Yuan dynasty annals.[11] Giovanni de Marignolli left China in 1347 and reached Avignon in 1353. Not long after, the Yuan dynasty began to decline. In 1362 the last Catholic bishop of Quanzhou, Giacomo da Firenze, was killed by the Chinese who seized control of the city. By 1369 all Christians, whether Roman Catholic or Syro-Oriental, were expelled by the Ming dynasty founded by the Chinese. But it must be pointed out that Franciscan success was principally with the Turco-Mongols and foreigners, not with the Chinese. This is not surprising since the Chinese in the capital as well as elsewhere resented the Mongol domination of China. For the Chinese, the conquerors of 1279 might embrace or at least favor those who adopted Christianity, but even the Syro-Oriental Church that had translated a significant body of literature into Chinese was considered too close to the ruling regime.

The Late Ming and Early Qing Period

To enter the Middle Kingdom now controlled by the Chinese who cut off contacts with the West was a goal of the Franciscans, Dominicans, and the Jesuits in the Philippines and in Macau. Short visits that some of them achieved by accompanying merchants to Guangzhou (Canton) only increased the desire of making even more attempts for a permanent arrangement. Michele Ruggieri (1572–1607), arrived in Macau, replacing Bernardino de Ferrariis (1537–1584), whom Alessandro Valignano (1539–1606) had originally asked for. This, and Ruggieri's later suggestion to Valignano to have Matteo Ricci (1552–1610) work with him in the initial stages of learning the Chinese language and thus facilitate their entry into China on September 10, 1583, have been recounted in various studies during the conferences honoring Ricci in 1982–1983 and in later symposia.[12] A major step in clarifying to the Chinese the universal message of Christianity, Ricci explained orally even before he published his well-known catechism, *Tianzhu shiyi* (The True meaning of the Lord of Heaven) in 1603. In his introduction he indicated:

> Every state or country has [its own] lord; is it possible that only the universe does not have a lord? A country must be united under only one [lord]; is it possible that the universe has two lords? Therefore, a superior man cannot but know the source of the universe and the creator of all creatures, and then raise his mind [to Him].[13]

In a later section of his introduction he added:

> All men who do good believe that there must exist a SUPREMELY HONORED ONE who governs this world. If this Honored One did not exist, or if He exists but does not intervene in human affairs, would this not be to shut the gate of doing good and to open the road of doing evil?[14]

Discussing filial piety, one of the cardinal characteristics of Chinese society, Ricci pointed out that he himself and the supreme head of any nation were in a relationship of subject and ruler. This was also found in the analogue of the mutual relationship of father and son when he considered himself and the head of his household. Admitting that human beings use such distinctions of sovereign and subject, and of father and son, Ricci went on to emphasize that when such distinctions were viewed in relationship to the common fatherhood of the Lord of Heaven, "they all become brothers with an equal standing."[15] For Ricci this was a fundamental message for all Chinese.

Other Jesuits further outlined the characteristics of a universal teaching of Christianity in pursuing this theme in their scientific and religious writings. From the many writers, only one can be singled out in this presentation: the *Wanwu zhenyuan* (True Origin of All Things) of Giulio Aleni (1582–1649). This 1628 essay in natural theology became a significant guidepost for the missionaries in those days, so that the Chinese would learn how man, by using his natural powers and in light of his natural reason, could come to a knowledge of God. In the opening chapter called "All Things Have a Beginning," Aleni addressed the claim of some *literati* that the Chinese Classics did not record anything about the beginning of heaven and earth. This was an incorrect view, Aleni stated, since the Classics indicated that in the time of Fu Xi, Shen Nong, and Huangdi (Yellow Emperor) all things came into existence. The ancients knew the period before their own era, and thus they realized that the beginning of heaven and earth could not be far from their own day. While not denigrating the Chinese references to heaven as father and earth as mother, and also to the kindness (*en*) of heaven and earth, Aleni indicated that neither of them, nor both combined spontaneously, produced men and all things. This argumentation led Aleni into a discussion of the creator of heaven, earth, and all things who not only makes, but also preserves them in their existence. This is the Lord of Heaven (*Tianzhu*), maker of heaven and earth, and the origin of all of creation, though he himself has no origin.

Such discussions by Ricci, Aleni, and others attempted to affect all levels of Chinese society, and especially found resonance through the development of what Nicolas Standaert has called the "Neo-Confucian-Christian Orthodoxy" of the Three Pillars of the Church. That is, Xu Guangqi, Li Zhizao, and Yang Tingyun in the late Ming era.[16] As a Confucian scholar who was also well versed in Buddhist ideas, Yang, as other Chinese before and after him, found it difficult to acknowledge *Tianzhu* as the unique Lord who was the source and foundation of all moral values in contrast to late Ming Neo-Confucianism, particularly the school of Wang Yangming (1472–1529), which insisted on the individual's heart (*xin*) as the locus of all truth and morality.[17] The Neo-Confucians sought a way to reformulate and to reestablish the ethos of peace and morality of China's past. Christianity could be considered equivalent to original Confucianism so that by becoming Christians they and others like them could use Christianity as a support system with Confucianism to achieve that harmony.

Perhaps one of the clearest examples of the universal role of Christianity Johann Adam Schall von Bell (1592–1666) outlined in his *Zhujiao yuanqi*, (The Origins and Progress of Christianity) and especially the *zonglun* (Summary), a catechism presented to the Chongzhen Emperor (1611–1644), the last of the Ming dynasty. A number of points reflected ideas that Aleni propounded, but Schall made additional observations for the monarch. In the opening pages of the *Zhujiao yuanqi* Schall indicated that the ten thousand things (*wanwu*) must have a beginning and were incapable of existing independently. By considering these ten thousand things, man can deduce that there is a Creator (*zaowuzhe*) of them. Moreover, from the key fact that man did not bring himself into existence, he has an additional way of coming to the knowledge that he was created by that same Creator. This section on God is followed by others on the soul, religion, and salvation. More pointedly are Schall's comments directed specifically to the emperor in the Summary (*zonglun*) that was composed in the spring of 1642. Noting that laws and ordinances are the basis for a government of Great Peace, Schall explained that one can find as many laws as there were rulers in various countries even though there is also a distinction between public and private laws. Nor was it to be forgotten that to achieve peace, there was the important distinction between those who issue laws, that is, "the Lord of Heaven and the rulers of the world."[18] In considering the three teachings of China (Buddhism, Confucianism, and Daoism), Schall did not extensively discuss "the misconceptions of Buddhism and Daoism" which could not be possible foundations for a government of Great Peace, since most followers of the Buddha and Laozi "never do reach the Way." The laws of either of the latter were not applicable to millions of people. While praising the *Da Ming huidian* (Institutions of the Great Ming) and its laws that governed China as exemplifying Confucian values, Schall said that Confucianism was practiced in a wider area, e.g., in Korea and Vietnam, yet it was still "not a universal law." He also stated that during the Zhen'guan period (627–649) of the Tang dynasty, scholars from Syria came to the court with books and statues to explain this teaching of the Lord of Heaven, which spread throughout China as the *Jingjiao beiwen* explained. But when the teaching had become extinct, almost a thousand years had passed so that Matteo Ricci and others presented the teaching of the Lord once more.[19] Schall realized that some Chinese complained about the practice in Christian teaching of not allowing vengeance on one's enemies nor harboring resentment and hate of one's neighbor, was difficult. He pointed out that even if he wanted to make it easily practicable, this would be against the "correct instructions of the Lord of Heaven." Schall insisted that this would result in the people no longer referring to this as the teaching of the Lord, but as "the teaching of the West." Instead, he argued, the teaching of the Lord surpassed either direction of the compass and was truly universal.[20]

During the Kangxi period (1662–1722) the universality of Christianity was attacked, although it also found respect among Chinese officialdom. The opposition of Yang Guangxian versus Schall and his assistant, Ferdinand Verbiest (1623–1688) was not only against their Western astronomy and calendar making, but also against the claim of one of their converts in the Bureau of Astronomy, Li Zubai (d. 1665/1666), who said in his *Tianxue chuangai* (Summary of the Spread of the Heavenly Teaching) that the ancient emperor Fu Xi descended from Adam and came from Judea. It is not possible in this essay to review the recent literature on this calendar controversy, but as Zhang Dawei has sagely observed, the science that the Jesuits brought to China was no longer a "regional but a universal one," and that the nature of the conflict by Yang against Schall was a "struggle between Catholicism and Chinese traditional values."[21]

The respect for Christianity occurred twice during the Kangxi reign, though later events were to tarnish that image. In 1692 in the aftermath of the persecution in Zhejiang, the Board of Rites (*Libu*) prompted by the emperor himself, issued the Edict of Toleration, whereby Chinese could embrace the Catholic faith. Another positive sign occurred at the height of the Chinese Rites Controversy in 1700, when the Jesuits at the imperial court asked the Kangxi Emperor to determine whether or not the rites to Confucius and to one's ancestors were civil and political acts. Along with their memorial they included copies of Ricci's *Tianzhu shiyi* and Aleni's *Wanwu zhenyuan*. After reading the original Chinese texts, the emperor ordered that they should be translated into Manchu. The court official responsible for the translation commented that although Aleni's essay lacked the depth of knowledge of Chinese antiquity found in Ricci's work, it reflected an elegant style and a mastery of writing equal to the best leading authors in China.[22]

During this episode in 1700, the emperor learned much more clearly the relevance of Christianity's claim of universality and its linkage to Chinese customs and society. What became worrisome to him within a few years was not the Christian teaching itself, but the implications of the request of Charles Maillard Cardinal de Tournon (1668–1710), the first papal legate, for permission to have a papal representative reside permanently in Beijing.

The emperor rejected this proposal as unwarranted. This was not a minor element in the Rites Controversy that resulted in the imperial orders that missionaries henceforth needed a certificate (*piao*) to remain in China and the legate's reply with his Edict of Nanjing. As Vincent Cronin, referring to the Kangxi Emperor in this confrontation with Tournon indicated, "Christianity appeared to the outraged Tartar no longer a universal religion adaptable to all peoples but a swashbuckling, narrow, prejudiced local cult."[23]

What is striking, however, is that the refusal of the emperor apparently had no impact in Rome. In the preparations for the mission of the second legate, Carlo Ambrogio Mezzabarba (1685–1741), the members of Propaganda Fide insisted that he repeat the same request for a papal delegate in the capital. Mezzabarba did so in an audience with the emperor, who again turned down the request. Presenting the "Eight Permissions" as a way of ameliorating some of the issues in the Controversy proved insufficient to mollify the emperor who had made several diplomatic approaches to Rome through his own envoys.

At the death of the Kangxi Emperor and the ascension of the Yongzheng Emperor (1722–1735) to the throne, Christianity was proscribed and missionaries, except for the few employed at court, were exiled. No positive change, in fact at times more repression, occurred under his successor, the Qianlong Emperor (1736–1795). Efforts to sustain Christianity now moved underground. The continuity of the Christian mission in Sichuan and in a few other parts of China was impossible to duplicate. In the eyes of the government Christianity was a threat to the state and the stability of Chinese society.

Russian Ecclesiastical Mission

An aspect of the Christian presence in China, all too often overlooked, is the Russian Ecclesiastical Mission in Beijing. The meeting of the Manchu and Russian empires occurred in the seventeenth century along a frontier that was delineated at the Treaty of Nerchinsk in 1689. The Ambassadorial Department (Posol'skii Prikaz) until then was entwined in Mongol terminology and had sent its envoys to "Kitai" (Cathay) under Mongol guides to "Khanbalik" (the name of China's capital under the Yuan dynasty). About one hundred Albazinians were still in China at the time of the treaty, which stipulated that Russian subjects then in China would remain there and the same was true of the Chinese subjects in Russia. The Albazinians became a Russian company in the service of the Kangxi Emperor, that was allowed to settle in the northeast corner of the Tartar City.

There the Nikolskii church was opened in 1683 and ten years later was discovered by a Russian diplomat who was dissatisfied with that church and continued to ask for Chinese permission to build another in the city. By 1730, only two years after the Treaty of Kiakhta of 1728 and its increased diplomatic understanding between Russia and China, the mission reported that there were more than fifty baptized persons among the Chinese and the Manchus, excluding women. The following year the report stated that nine Chinese had been baptized, with eight more about to follow suit, and with the anticipation that two natives per month would become converts.[24] Up to 1860, about 150 priests worked in the mission. After the 1858 Treaty of Tianjin, the status of the mission changed in that its diplomatic activities on behalf of Russia became obsolete. In 1916 there were thirty-two mission churches in various provinces with 5,587 Chinese followers. Within twenty years that number was estimated at ten thousand.[25] In Beijing, Shanghai, and Harbin, there were ten Russian Orthodox journals in the Russian language before World War II. While the fate of their adherents was similar to that of other Christians after the 1949 Communist ascendancy to power, the Sophia Orthodox church in Harbin was closed during the Cultural Revolution, and only recently was reopened.

Nineteenth Century: Changes in the Presence of Christianity in China

Under the Jiajing regime (1776–1820) one of the most severe persecutions against Christianity took place, but did not lead to its obliteration from the hearts and minds of the approximately 200,000 Christians. Martyrdoms of foreign missionaries in Sichuan and Guizhou occurred and churches were confiscated with some razed or put to other uses. In the opening years of the nineteenth century, the foreign missionaries (Franciscans, Dominicans, Missions Etrangères de Paris, and the Congrégation de la Mission) were less than forty in number with the native Chinese clergy not exceeding that figure. This minimal data is important to stress lest there be the impression, as has occurred in the past, that Christianity was, for all practical purposes totally wiped out before the First Opium War in 1839. In fact, just two years earlier, several Chinese Catholics wrote to the Pope and to the Superior General of the Jesuits. The Christians had learned about the restoration of the Jesuit Order and asked that some Jesuits come to China as soon as possible.

There is no doubt that the universal message of Christianity was put under a different focus after the First Opium War. The opening of five ports for commerce that year laid the basis for more change. An additional treaty in 1844 allowing the United States and Great Britain to construct churches and hospitals in those ports was quickly followed later that year by France gaining the same rights. At the insistence of Théodore Lagrené (1800–1862), the French plenipotentiary, an imperial decree allowed missionaries to preach and to construct churches and permitted the Chinese to profess Catholicism. Moreover, it ordered that church property confiscated in the past was to be returned and that local officials who persecuted Catholics were to be punished. This last measure became a point of friction. While Christianity had a universal message for all Chinese and others in the empire, today one can question the wisdom of including such a clause in the treaty. Although a treaty is ipso facto part of a nation's legal system, it does not necessarily follow that the foreign contracting party should stipulate precise measures or practices to be followed in carrying out its provisions.

The resumption of Roman Catholic missions in China had its counterpart in the development of the Protestant missions there. As early as 1805, the London Missionary Society had drawn plans to send a mission to the Chinese by working among the overseas Chinese in the islands of Southeast Asia under the control of European powers. This was undertaken by Robert Morrison and the Anglo-Chinese College at Malacca. Soon the names of Walter Henry Medhurst, Karl Friedrich August Gutzlaff, Elijah C. Bridgman, Peter Parker, and others were part of the roster of missionaries laying the groundwork for the Protestant missionary effort before the Opium War and especially afterwards.

Alongside the external pressure of the foreign powers in the Opium Wars was the rise of that strange phenomenon, the Taiping Heavenly Kingdom. Influenced by several aspects of Christian doctrine and the Bible that were recently translated into Chinese, Hong Xiuquan became convinced that he was the younger brother of Jesus Christ with a special calling from God the Father to overthrow the Manchus and lead the Chinese as a "chosen people" to a paradise on earth.[26] This millenarian movement based on an apocalyptic vision led to a gathering of faithful followers in the 1840s and the creation of the Taiping Heavenly Army in 1850. Its seizure of Nanjing in 1853 transformed the former Ming capital into the base of operations for a decade. Whether China would have changed differently had this remained a spiritual movement is open to speculation. But with the military battles and the dislocation and starvation of thousands, the loss of twenty million lives is not seen as an exaggeration. Uprisings by followers of what the government considered were the White Lotus teachings had occurred in China in past dynasties. These disturbances of the cosmic and earthly order had been put down somewhat readily. The Taiping Movement, however, was different in that, having originated in the mountains of Guangxi province, it spread to central China and attracted those who lived in destitute conditions and thus proposed egalitarian programs that the Chinese state, based on hierarchy, could not endorse. The overthrow of the Taiping Heavenly Kingdom left a negative impact on the growth of Christianity and engendered suspicion and distrust of Christians, Protestant or Catholic, among officials at the Beijing court as well as in the provinces. Overcoming such attitudes took time as other events such as the Tianjin Massacre of 1870 delayed the process. The Boxer Rebellion of 1900 was a turning-point of Chinese popular and elite opposition to the foreign imperialist presence, including the Christian missionary enterprise.

Against the backdrop of China's defeat in the Sino-Japanese War of 1894–1895 and the attempts at reform in 1898, the Confucian order was in decline. Through a modern educational system, Christian missionaries provided new ideas such as democracy and individualism to younger Chinese *literati*. The overthrow of the Boxers led to the imperial government's reassessment of its leadership of society and the need for some changes, such as the abolition of the examination system. There was a considerable lessening of activities against the Christians and the missionaries to such an extent that by 1911, the revolutionary leaders adopted a policy of not disturbing, as much as possible, any Christian institution. To some degree this was a recognition of the universality of Christianity, albeit quite different from the earlier half of the Qing dynasty, for the Western powers might again come to the aid of the Christian missionary enterprise, even by force.

Revolution of 1911

In China's struggle to identify its own nationalism after the Revolution of 1911, the role of Christianity had to be considered. This became part of the paradox of China in the 1920s and 1930s. An anti-Christian movement prevailed even as Chinese Christian churches—either with no ties to foreigners or beginning to break such bonds—were responding to this outgrowth of national consciousness. Such anti-Christian agitation occurred chiefly in the urban sector of central and south China with sporadic impact on the countryside. The other part of the paradox is that despite the anti-Christian movement, China in that period had a number of prominent Christian leaders. Included among them were Sun Yat-sen, and his son, Sun Fo, T. V. Soong, H. H. Kung, and Chiang Kai-shek. Since Sun Yat-sen is considered the "Father of the Country" (*Guofu*) it may be instructive to reflect on his attitudes towards Christianity. His first exposure occurred in Honolulu and continued in Hong Kong where, at the age of eighteen, he was baptized and became a member of the London Missionary Society. During his captivity in London he related that he prayed every day and credited his release when Shangdi had heard his petition. In addressing a group of Protestants meeting in Beijing on September 5, 1912, Sun declared, "If the Chinese Republic is an accomplished fact today, the merit of this achievement should revert not to me but to the Church."[27] In March of that year the Provisional Constitution of the new Republic expressly stated, "The people have liberty of religion." In 1924 Sun reiterated this concept of liberty among the political tenets of the Guomindang Party as he emphasized "People enjoy complete freedom of conscience." In the lectures that comprise the *Sanmin zhuyi* (Three principles of the people), there are only a few references to religion and to Christianity. Recognizing that religion is one of the "most important elements in the formation of a race," Sun also noted that, in primitive ages, man had sought to avoid calamities and to achieve happiness through forms of prayer. He considered Jesus Christ as a revolutionary leading a religious cause.[28] According to his son, Sun Fo, Sun Yat-sen said the day before he died in 1925 that as a Christian he had been fighting the devil for more than forty years, and to his followers he indicated, "You too have to fight in the same way, and what is still more, you have to believe in Shangdi."[29] Within the context of the Guomindang support of the First United Front from 1923 to 1927, these statements of Sun Yat-sen, the "Father of the Country," are quite pertinent towards understanding his views on religion and the state, especially for the future context of Christianity in China.

The commitment of Mao Zedong to Marxism and then Communism within those years of the First United Front and later need not be rehearsed since his opposition to religion, whether Buddhism or Christianity or any other form, is too well known. His ascent to power in 1949 and his leadership of the nation that at first tolerated, then sought to control religious groups, are basic elements of the history of the regime. The Patriotic Associations of the 1950s, whether Catholic or Protestant, were considered measures of state control that left a number of adherents unwilling to follow the directives of the government and the Party. The "Three-Self" Movement of that era was set on pursuing an approach for Christianity free from any outside interference and financial support. The underlying assumption was that Communism as an ideology was to be accepted by the world and thus was to confront the universal message of Christianity. The Cultural Revolution or the "Ten Lost Years" (1966–1976) banned everything old, including all religious institutions with foreign or domestic origins. However, the opening of China to the outside world under Deng Xiaoping by the 1980s generated a changed governmental attitude toward religion by retrieving concepts of the United Front policy which enunciated that all social elements are to work for the good of the state. This did not necessarily mean a lessening of control over Christian groups, nor in the case of Catholics, an approval of the so-called underground Church. Nevertheless, it led to the reopening of many church buildings and the reorganization of communities of believers so that in recent years a better picture of the status of Christianity in China has emerged. Although not a completely clear black and white photograph, it has gray hues and perhaps even streaks that are quite noticeable.

The second half of the theme of this conference is "Hopeful Future," and indeed that phrase contains many issues that the Christian Church in China faces in the long term. Traditionalists and modernists within the Catholic Church after Vatican II still have their differences on several key issues such as the role of the Church in modern society. The Council that ended one year before the Cultural Revolution began in 1966 is now the focus of study by more and more leaders of both parts of the Catholic Church in China, though the Patriotic Association was somewhat slower in accepting them. Now that seminarians and priests from the Patriotic Association are studying in a fairly wide variety of ecclesiastical institutions throughout the world, a new cohort of leaders is emerging. The effect of their training in the parishes and seminaries in China, as well as the more recent trend of the reconciliation of a number of priests of the Patriotic Association with the Vatican, warrants research. The dichotomy of Patriotic Association and underground Church of two decades ago is not always operative in reality in China itself. To the Western-oriented legalistic mind this may be unsettling, but all Christians would support such a reconciliation since it is emerging on Chinese terms.

This leads to another element that Christians outside of China but interested in helping that country may want to ponder, i.e., the use of the word *missionary*. The nineteenth and early twentieth century meaning of being sent to an area of the world where the Christian message had never been heard before is no longer operative. In terms of organizational structures for the Catholic dioceses and archdioceses exist in China, and for other Christian denominations, various kinds of indigenous organizations have been formed, but not always with ties to an external group. Even if the political order in China were to change, the Christians outside of China would not enter Guangzhou or Beijing as the missionaries of yesteryear, but as auxiliaries to assist in the further expansion of the indigenous Church. How this could be achieved will depend on the training received before entry into China.

In his recent study entitled *China's Catholics: Tragedy and Hope in an Emerging Civil Society*, Richard Madsen has called attention to the need for the Chinese Catholic Church to contribute to civil society. He observed that for another generation, rural society or seventy percent of the population, will need leadership from the urban middle class that can be expected to emerge gradually.[30] Such civic culture in China will necessitate additional commitment to social responsibility that will depend on the vitality of moral education. This attractive perspective could be widened further by including all Christians in China today, from the "house churches" to the traditional forms of worship. To what extent the Chinese Christians can learn about contributing to China's welfare, and thus to its civic culture, is a topic that needs further exploration and analysis by a wide range of scholarship. To do so will require an ecumenical dialogue among all Christian bodies. That may not be possible within China, but can be achieved elsewhere by conferences. Some have already occurred, yet more needs to be done. Last, but not least, studying the role of Christianity in Taiwan as well as Christianity in Hong Kong and Macau during the past fifty-year period may offer insights into understanding Christianity in China's future.

This sketch of the five periods of Christianity in China has highlighted historical burdens and hope for the future. The message of Christianity remains constant as the Catholic Church in China, whether "open" or "clandestine," seeks communion with the universal Church outside China, according to Ren Yanli.[31] Recently the China Christian Council and the Chinese Christian Three-Self Patriotic Movement Committee reiterated the need to respect different beliefs and liturgies, rejected any claim to a restoration of denominationalism, and insisted that the church in China can have a future "only if it is united."[32] This position does not mitigate, but may add complexity to the role of the different denominations outside China assisting their fellow Christians in such a setting.

In "The Future of Christianity" John Taylor remarked, "Like a hot soufflé, prognostication should be served the moment it is cooked."[33] The universal teaching of Christianity, although originally from the West, is undergoing a process of inculturation in China that has taken and continues to take various forms. The path (*dao*) that this process will follow in the next millennium may be obscure, but there is no doubt that Christianity, despite its size relative to the population, has become an integral element in the history of China.

Chinese Perspective—
A Brief Review of the Historical Research
on Christianity in China

ZHANG KAIYUAN

One of my predecessors, Francis C. M. Wei, the former president of Huachung University, was invited in 1945 to be the Henry W. Luce Visiting Professor of World Christianity. The topic of his inaugural speech was "Rooting the Christian Church in Chinese Soil," in which he emphasized, "In interpreting the Christian teachings and institutions in terms of another culture the important thing is first of all to enter into the spirit of the culture."

I am of the opinion that the slogan Francis Wei put forward "Rooting the Christian Church in Chinese Soil," as well as the one Frank Joseph Rawlinson raised in 1937 "Christianity Settles Down in China," are much wiser than that unfortunate slogan, "The Christian Occupation of China," which was used in the 1920s, at least from the view of us, Chinese. The former two have a friendly spirit of communication on an equal basis and thus have weakened the arrogant colonialist gesture of past times.

Like any other great religion with a long history, Christianity does not belong to any particular nation or nationality. The process of Christianity's spread worldwide is also the process of its transplantation into one new culture after another. Meanwhile, for many centuries the dream of converting non-Christian areas actually involved the indigenization of Christianity in these areas. Of course, normal cultural communication is a two-way interactive process. From the perspective of us historians, the universality of Christianity lies in its theological core, and is formed through multilingual and multicultural interpretation, development, and gradual integration.

We may view the history of Chinese Christianity in this way.

Before 1949

It has been over 1,300 years since Christianity first spread into China, but research on the history of Chinese Christianity, in a strict sense, began no earlier than the 1930s and the 1940s. A few Chinese scholars who studied the history of Chinese-Western communication opened up this field. The famous historian Chen Yuan published *Yuan Yelikewen* early in 1918 and compiled a collection of sixteen relevant articles over the years which eventually became *Minyuanyilai Tianzhujiaoshi luncong* (Collection on the History of Catholicism in the Early Republic of China), edited by Ye Delu in 1943. As Chen Yuan's student, Fang Hao inherited and developed Chen's work. He published *Zhongwai wenhua jiaotongshi luncong* (Discussions on the History of Sino-Foreign Communication), *Zhongguo Tianzhujiaoshi luncong* (Collection on the History of Chinese Catholicism (Collection No. 1), and other such works since the 1940s and thus became the strongest pillar in this field. In addition, *Zhong Xi jiaotongshi ziliao huibian* (A Compilation of Source Materials on the History of Chinese-Western Communication), and *Ouhua dongjian shi* (The History of European Cultural Dissemination Into China), both written by Zhang Xinglang, and *Zhong Xi juaotongshi* (A History of Chinese-Western Communication), by Xiang Da, have also included expositions on Catholicism's spreading in China. Since the 1930s scholars in this area, such as Feng Chengjun, have translated a number of Western language books on the history of Chinese Catholicism and biographies of important Catholic missionaries which greatly promoted research on the history of Catholicism in China.

Comparatively, the research on the history of Chinese Protestantism, though started almost at the same time, is a bit weaker. Influential works include *Zhongguo wenhua yu Jidujiao* (Chinese Culture and Christianity), *Zhongguo Jidujiao shigang* (An Outline of History of Chinese Christianity), by Wang Zhixin; *Jidujiao yu Zhongguo wenhua* (Christianity and Chinese Culture), by Wu Leichuan. Unfortunately, later they ceased to place their main energy into this research, and did not become as outstanding and diligent successors as was Fang. Yet, it should be admitted that *Zhongguo Jidujiao shigang* (Outline of the History of Chinese Christianity) is a book of serious attitude, clear presentation, and objective narration, and is a pioneering work with a comprehensive history of China's Christianity written in Chinese. It has been republished time and again, and still holds the prestige of referential value.

Many of the problems that the researchers of Christianity's history in China attended to are connected with those that are discussed by Western missionaries. For example, the conflict and blending of Christian doctrines and Chinese traditional culture, especially of the intrinsic religious concepts and customs; the influence on Chinese society by the dissemination of Christianity; the relationship between the undertakings of Christianity in China and Chinese modernization; the self-adjustment of Christianity and how to be accepted by the Chinese society, and so on. The above questions still attract our attention even at present.

Owing to the participation of celebrated scholars in this area and their profound achievements, the objectivity and academic value of the early research on the history of Chinese Christianity, on the side of the history of Catholicism, has been greatly enhanced. Many important works appeared and spread. Regretfully, the limitations of the traditional research approach resulted in the shortcomings of being trivial and fragmentary. On the other hand, the history of Protestantism, which came to China later than Catholicism and had a shorter history, did not attract enough attention from the scholars of Chinese-Western communication history. So the writers were mostly people within the churches. They had a fairly distinct understanding of the Christian doctrine and evolution, but at the same time inevitably had an obvious church stand, and thus limited their field of vision and lacked high academic value.

Japan's large-scale invasion in 1937 brought chaos to society, deprived researchers of a comparatively settled surrounding, and prevented the further development of research.

From 1949 to 1976

Since 1949, due to the reason that everyone knows, research on Christianity and on the history of Christianity in mainland China found itself in a woeful predicament and could hardly be carried out. Even the research on the history of Chinese-Western cultural communication was politicized. The activities of Western churches and missionaries were considered in the framework of imperialistic cultural invasion and espionage. There were not many historical works related to Christianity and most of those were limited to "anti-foreign religion fighting" (including the Boxer Movement). At that time, the emphasis was that the study of history should serve politics. Hence, these works were inevitably forced to shoulder the responsibility of anti-imperialism and patriotic education, which resulted in severe drawbacks in choosing materials and research approaches, and there was scanty academic value. It is a pity that during this period there was only one pamphlet written directly related to the history of Christianity, that is, *Fanyangjiao yundong* (Anti-foreign Religion Movement), by Li Shiyue. Li was a prominent scholar who pushed forward the innovation of history after the Cultural Revolution, yet at that time he was not immune from "Leftist" influence.

Unexpectedly, the twenty-seventh chapter of "Tianzhujiao chuanru de shidai beijing he Yesuhuishi de zuoyong" ("The Background of Catholicism's Entering and the Function of the Jesuits"), written by He Zhaowu, which is in the fourth volume of *Zhongguo sixiang tongshi* (General History of Chinese Ideology), edited by Hou Wailu, is of considerable academic value. There were a few scholars such as Zhu Qianzhi carrying out research in this area. The book *Zhongguo Jingjiao* (Chinese Nestorianism) was finished in 1966, but could not be published until after the Cultural Revolution.

With the departure of a group of scholars such as Fang Hao from mainland China to Hong Kong and Taiwan and the successive relocation of the educational institutions founded by the churches, research on the history of Christianity in China made obvious progress in these two areas. Fang Hao was the forerunner in research at that time and published *Zhong Xi jiaotongshi* (History of Chinese-Western Communication), three volumes of *Zhongguo Tianzhujiaoshi renwuzhuan* (Biographies in the History of Chinese Christians/Catholics), and other important works. Luo Guang also published many works including his *Xu Guangqi zhuan* (Biography of Xu Guangqi), *Li Madou zhuan* (Biography of Matteo Ricci), *Jiaoting yu Zhongguo shijieshi* (Vatican and the History of Chinese Envoy), and *Tianzhujiao zai Hua chuanjiaoshiji* (Collection on the History of Catholicism Spreading in China). Zhang Fengzhen published *Fuyin Liuchuan Zhongguoshilue* (Brief History of Evangelism in China).

There is considerable improvement in the research on the history of Chinese Protestantism. The book *Zhongguo Jidujiaoshi* (History of Christianity in China), published by Yang Senfu, continued and developed the research compiled in Wang Zhixin's *Zhongguo Jidujiao Shigang* (Outline of the History of Chinese Christianity). It was better written with regard to the scope of its expounding and the quotation of documents, and in paying more attention to the use of historical viewpoint and method. This is opposed to Wang's emphasis on presenting his argument with a Christian viewpoint, so this book has a high academic prestige. The book *Jidujiao zai Zhongguo zhi chuanbo yu jindai Zhongguo* (The Dissemination of Christianity in China and Modern China), edited by Lin Zhiping, was published by the Taipei Commercial Press in 1970. Later he and his Universal Light played an important role in advocating and promoting research on the history of Chinese Christianity. They combined the dissemination of Christianity and Chinese modernization together, which has recently entered upon a new phase of this research.

Besides these, a great deal of work has been done by Taiwan scholars in the sorting out of the materials and publishing Chinese Christian historical documents over the years. For example, *Jiaowu jiao'an dang*, edited by the Modern History Research Institute at Academia Sinica, has made research in this field much more convenient.

After 1978

The reform and opening policy has brought new vitality to the development of the academy and culture in mainland China. What is more important is that the increasingly frequent exchange between China and foreign countries has enhanced research on the history of Chinese-foreign cultural communication. Christianity, as an important component of Western culture, has attracted more and more attention from Chinese scholars.

In the last two decades, besides the Religion Research Institute at China's Social Science Academy, some provincial and municipal social science academies and universities have established their own religion research institutes, departments or other corresponding research organizations. They have published *Shijie zongjiao yanjiu* (World Religions Study), *Shijie zongjiao wenhua* (World Religion Culture), and other publications. The church publications such as *Zhongguo Tianzhujiao* (Chinese Catholicism) and *Tianfeng* have restored their normal publication. All of these have provided a broader exchange space for research on the history of Chinese Christianity. According to incomplete statistics, over 1,000 papers and nearly 100 monographs, translations, and compilations were published over these twenty years, and both the quantity and quality of the above-mentioned works have surpassed those in the previous thirty years.

The development of the research can be viewed from the following three items:

Due to its inherent advantage, the history of Chinese Catholicism, especially the history of the Society of Jesus in the Ming and Qing Dynasties, is still the hot focal point . The published achievements amounted to almost half of those in this field. Besides a great amount of translated works, the published works written by Chinese scholars include *Xu Guangqi nianpu* (Chronology of Xu Guangqi), edited by Liang Jiamian; *Ming Qing jian zai Hua de Tianzhujiao Yesuhuishi* (Catholic Jesuits in China during Ming and Qing Dynasties), written by Jiang Wenhan; *Shizijia yu long* (Cross and Dragon), written by Sun Jiang; *Long yu Shangdi: Jidujiao yu Zhongguo chuantong wenhua* (Dragon and God: Christianity and Chinese Traditional Culture), written by Dong Conglin; *Yesuhuishi yu Zhongguo kexue* (Jesuits and Chinese Science), written by Fan Hongye; *Mingmo Tianzhujiao yu Ruxue de jiaoliu yu chongtu* (Exchange and Conflict of Catholicism and Confucianism in the late Ming dynasty), written by Sun Shangyang; *Li Madou yu jindai Zhongguo* (Matteo Ricci and China), written by Lin Jinshui; *Dao yu yan: Huaxia wenhua yu Jidujiao wenhua xiangyu* (Dao and Yan: Encounter of Chinese Culture and Christian Culture), edited by Liu Xiaofeng, and so on.

Most of these works had gotten rid of the simple framework of "anti-imperialistic cultural invasion" and were able to view the Western missionaries' religious, cultural, and academic activities under the different historical condition and human background of Chinese and Western societies at that time. Take the study of early Jesuits as an example. Besides pointing out their certain links with Portuguese colonialists, the researchers also affirmed their important contribution to Chinese-Western cultural exchange at the end of the Ming dynasty and the early Qing dynasty.[1] Though there are different opinions on the extent of Western missionaries' connection with colonialism and the level of the dissemination of Western knowledge,[2] most of the scholars are against the simple conclusion that all missionaries in China were "cultural aggressors" or the "advance party of colonialism" without making a specific analysis by different historical stages.[3]

There is a great change in the research after 1979 on anti-foreign religion fighting which in the past was brought into the framework of anti-imperialist and patriotic struggle. The first is that the study of the history of the Boxer Movement has gradually cast off the influence of the extreme "Leftist" ideological trend and, with the help of some foreign scholars, the approaches of sociology and theology have been introduced. More and more Chinese scholars are making an effort to study anti-foreign fighting from the aspects of national psychology, the origin and development of religion, social customs, and the conflict of Chinese-Western cultures, thus it has become an important part of research on the history of Chinese Christianity. The historical circle in Shandong and Sichuan Provinces has made great contributions. Several international symposia on the Boxer Movement have been held in Jinan, and the *Yihetuan yanjiu tongxun* (Boxer Movement Research Newsletter) was put out. While in Chengdu, symposia on anti-foreign religion fighting and the history of religious cases were held. From 1987 to 1990, academic meetings on the same subject were held in Anhui, Guizhou, and Hunan. Besides the publication of the correspondent works, translations, and collection of the symposium papers, much more has been done relating to the sorting out of materials and their publication. Some examples are: *Fanyangjiao shuwen jietie xuan* (Selection of Articles and

Notices on Anti-foreign Religion), edited by Wang Minglun; *Shangdong jiao'an shiliao* (Shandong Religious Cases Documents), edited by Tang Lisan; *Sichuan jiao'an yu Yihequan dang'an* (Sichuan Religious Cases and Documents on the Boxer Movement), edited by Sichuan Archives; and *Qingmo jiao'an* (Religious Cases at the End of Qing dynasty), coedited by China's First Historical Archives and the History Department at Fujian Normal University.

Mainly, there are three kinds of opinions toward the nature of religious cases. Some hold that the nature of religious cases is anti-imperialism fighting, some think that it is both anti-imperialism and anti-feudalism, others believe it is the peasants' revolution. There is another school who suggests that it is a conflict incited by the conservative gentry for their vested interest. Most of the works carried out an objective and penetrating study regarding the social and historical background of anti-foreign religions fighting, the blind opposition to everything foreign (xenophobia), and slogans such as "supporting Qing and annihilating Foreign," as well as the relations among religious cases, secret societies, gentry, and officials.[4]

There has been great improvement in research on the history of Chinese Protestantism since 1980s. Gu Changsheng took the lead with his publication of *Chuanjiaoshi yu jindai Zhongguo* (Missionaries and Modern China) and *Cong Malixun dao Situleideng: Laihua xinjiao chuanjiaoshi pingzhuan* (From Morrison to Stuart: Critical Biographies of Protestant Missionaries in China). Though the historical conditions cited contained a few biased or false points, they could still be regarded as works of initiating the current tendencies. Consequent publications of related works in the 1990s include *Jidujiao yu jindai wenhua* (Christianity and Modern Culture), edited by Zhu Weizheng, *Xixue dongjian yu wan Qing shehui* (Western Knowledge's Dissemination into China and Late Qing Society), written by Xiong Yuezhi, and others. These works have been released from the "Leftist" influence, thus their academic objectivity and scientific quality are increased.

Research regarding the history of Chinese Christian colleges, as an important part of the history of Chinese Protestantism, has made considerable progress since the 1980s. In previous years, affected by political elements, Chinese Christian Colleges used to be regarded as "the tool of imperialist cultural invasion," so there was no possibility of any earnest academic research. At the beginning of the 1980s, there appeared a few scholars who began to publish articles about Chinese Christian schools. In 1986, Xu Yihua published "Jidujiao zai Hua gaodeng jiaoyu chutan" ("Initial Inquiry into Christian Higher Education in China"), which comprehensively raised the question of whether Chinese Christian colleges should be re-studied and re-recognized. In 1987, Liu Zijian, from Princeton University, came to Wuhan and met the president of Central China Normal University, Zhang Kaiyuan, and discussed with them cooperation in research on the history of Chinese Christian colleges. Then in 1988, Arthur Waldron, from Princeton, went to Chengdu and further discussed the issue on how to push forward research in this field with twenty-one Chinese scholars from Central China Normal University, Sichuan University, Beijing University, Suzhou University, Fudan University, and Hangzhou University. The predecessors of the above-mentioned universities all have historical origins as Christian colleges, so they are very enthusiastic about the task at hand. Henceforth, the First International Symposium on the History of Chinese Christian Universities was held at Central China Normal University on June 1–3, 1989, and one of the consequences has been the publication of a collection of the symposium papers, *Zhong xiwenhua yu jiaohui daxue* (Chinese-Western Cultural Communications and Christian Colleges). This may be considered as a new start to research on the history of Chinese Christian colleges in mainland China.

From then on, focused on this subject, eight international symposia have been held in mainland China, Hong Kong, Taiwan, and the United States, and six collections of the symposium papers have been published. At the beginning of 1994, the Research Center for the History of Chinese Christian Colleges was founded at Central China Normal University. Supported by the Henry Luce Foundation, the United Board for Christian Higher Education in Asia, and other brotherly universities, the Center has made a painstaking effort to promote research on the history of Chinese Christian colleges at home and abroad. Up to this day, the Center has coedited with Chung Chi College of the Chinese University of Hong Kong and released ten issues of *Zhongguo jiaohui daxue shi yanjiu tongxun* (Newsletter for Historical Research on Chinese Christian Colleges). The Center is also editing a series of books on Christianity and Chinese culture, two of which, *Wenhua chuanbao yu jiaohui daxue* (Cultural Communication and Christian Colleges) and *Shehui zhuanxing yu jiaohui daxue* (Social Transformation and Christian Colleges), have been published. And the third one is in progress. The first set of research collections on Chinese Christian colleges edited by the Center include ten works and translations by Shi Jinghuan, Dong Li, Xu Yihua, and other scholars. These books will be published by Zhuhai Press before the end of this year. At the same time, with the collaboration of scholars from mainland China, Chung Chi College of the Chinese University of Hong Kong has published *Zhongguo jiaohui daxue wenxian mulu* (Catalogue of Documents on Chinese Christian Colleges), and established the Research Center for Christianity and Chinese Society.

In addition, the research of the Non-Christian Movement and the Indigenization Movement of Chinese Christianity has aroused some scholars' deep interest. Articles include: "Zhongguo Jidujiao de zili yundong" ("Self-Support Movement of Chinese Christianity"), in *Shanghai shehui kexue* (Shanghai Social Science), March 1982, by Shen Yifan; "Lun woguo 1922–1927 nianjian de fei Jidujiao yundong" ("On Non-Christian Movement in China 1922–1927"), in *Hangzhou daxue xuebao* (Journal of Hangzhou University), Februry 1988, by Xia Guiqi; "Zhongguo fei Jidujiao yundong (1922–1927)" ("Non-Christian Movement in China 1922–1927"), in *Lishi yanjiu* (Historical Research), August 1993, by Yang Tianhong; "Jidujiao de Zhongguohua jiqi nandian" ("The Indigenization of Christianity and its Difficulties"), in *Shijie zongjiao yanjiu* (World Religions Study), January 1996, by Wang Meixiu, and others. All these works deeply elaborated on these two parallel movements in terms of their social background, origin, influence, and their cultural connotation.

Research on Christianity's present situation in China has also begun. The main works are *Zhongguo Tianzhujiao de guoqu yu xianzai* (Chinese Catholicism in History and at Present), by Gu Yulu; "Zhongguo zongjiao shinian" ("Ten Years' Chinese Religion"), in *Shijie zongjiao yanjiu* (World Religions Study), February 1990, by Fang Litian; "Zhongguo Jidujiao sishinian" ("Four Decades of Chinese Christianity"), in *Shijie zongjiao yanjiu* (World Religious Study), April 1990, by Wang Weifan and others; *Zhongguo Tianzhujiao sishinian* ("Four Decades of Chinese Catholicism"), in *Shijie zongjiao yanjiu* (World Religious Study), March, 1993, by Zhu Shichang, and so on. These scholars have done some new exploration and broadened the vision to study the reason for the rapid increase of Christians in some regions since 1978 and how to adjust religion and socialism, and other problems. A few scholars even enlarged their research field to the study of popular religions and secret folk sects, such as Ma Xisha and Han Bingfang, *Zhongguo minjian zongjiaoshi* (A history of Chinese folk religions). See also Hou Jie and Fan Lizhu, *Zhongguo minzhong zongjiao yishi* (Concepts of Popular Chinese Religion). Although these religious sects are not necessarily connected with Christianity, their research orientation and methods certainly will benefit the study of the history of Christianity.

Retrospect and Prospect

Within twenty short years, research on the history of Chinese Christianity has developed from a child to a grownup. It started at a comparatively low level and there are still obstructions to progress, but an academic circle full of vitality has been formed which can hardly be ignored. In terms of personnel and achievements, the situation is very optimistic and prosperous. This, of course, has brought to our participants great relief.

Contemporary research on the history of Christianity in China has long ago cast off the simple political dichotomy, viewing it as either enemy or friend, reactionary or progressive. More and more scholars have endeavored to explain history as it really is, utilizing a great amount of rich materials and the approach of multi-disciplinary integration. Thus, many expositions are of considerable academic value.

With the increasing Chinese-Western cultural communication since the 1980s, research on the history of Christianity in China has had the distinct character of international collaboration from the very beginning. Scholars in mainland China, Hong Kong, and Taiwan have established fairly stable cooperative relations with their counterparts in Europe and North America. Scholars in the former three regions are in particularly close contact, as can be seen from their work together on holding international symposia, publishing collections and newsletters, and training young scholars. This kind of cooperation has promoted dialogue, links, and understanding between scholars at home and abroad. By breaking away from the state of estrangement and lack of mutual comprehension, rapid progress in research has been achieved.

There is no hiding the fact that, due to historical and realistic reasons, the research on the history of Christianity in China is still at the starting line and international cooperation is not yet satisfactory. Compared to the rich and complicated content of such a research project as well as its vast and scattered historical documents, what we have done is just a drop in the bucket. There is still a long way to go. As for our researchers, very few of them have professional training and concentrate their study in this area. Most of them are historians, philosophers, and sociologists who switched to this job which they were not trained for. This situation is helpful to trans-disciplinary integration, but it has brought some inherent shortcomings to some research products. We can take my late teacher, Searl Bates, as an example. Although he was a missionary, he always felt remiss in his lack of specialized theological training even in his old age, and considered it a significant weak point in his research on the history of churches. This said, according to strict academic standard, it is a pressing matter of the moment to cultivate a new generation of researchers on the history of churches in China.

The rapid progress of research on the history of Christianity in China, is not only due to its own colorful history, which has an everlasting academic charm, but also because the development of Christianity (including Catholicism and Protestantism) in mainland China has become the focus of attention. People need to know more about Christianity itself, as well as the history and current situation of its development, to absorb wisdom from past experiences. Then they will try to set up a sound interacting relationship between Christians and non-Christians, Christianity and other religions, and relations within the different sects in Christianity. Of particular importance are the relationships among Christianity, government, and society, and the need to build a harmonious, prosperous, and healthy society together.

With the forthcoming of the twenty-first century, people are predicting that the higher technology will bring the new century into an "information age" or the age of "knowledge-based economy." But will the swift development of high technology bring us human beings happiness or disaster? Might it even result in humanity's destruction by our killing each other and damaging the environment? The key to the question lies in the men who are creating and mastering high technology. Attaching more importance to the technology than to the humanities, more importance to the materials than to the spirit, became our common failing in the twentieth century, which is turning into an incurable persistent disease within the space of modernization. This is a very adverse signal. Is peace and development the keynote of the twenty-first century, or will hegemonism and war run wild in the world? The pursuit of power and interest has taken humanity away from many people. The ruin of morality finds its expression in the whitewashing of the evil reality under a beautiful lie. Under this critical situation, all those who have intuitive knowledge should rise to the occasion and unite to safeguard justice and defeat evil, explore all the beneficial ideological sources in history and in reality, and reestablish a harmonious spiritual homeland, so as to protect the globe and save ourselves.

II

China and Christianity
in the Traditional Past

China and the West:
The Image of Europe and Its Impact

ERIK ZÜRCHER

From the very beginning of their mission in China the Jesuits combined the preaching of the Christian message with what we nowadays would call "Europe promotion," as an integral part of their missionary strategy. They did so for several reasons. In the first place, it was a logical consequence of their persistent policy of associating themselves with the Chinese elite of scholar-officials and of stressing the congruity, or complementarity, of Confucianism and Christianity. If in China the Confucian doctrine was supposed to exert a "transforming" influence (*jiaohua*) upon state, society, and individual, resulting (ideally) in harmonious social relations, hierarchical order, high moral standards, correct ritual behavior, and benevolent government, it could be argued that something analogous had already been realized in the Far West, long ago, when Europe had been "transformed" by Christianity. Christianity was therefore not only presented as a system of religious beliefs and practices, but also as a great civilizing force. This theme occurs time and again in the Chinese writings of some prominent Jesuits, and from analogous passages in works written by converted *literati* it can be inferred that the image of the European utopia did not fail to impress Chinese believers.

There also were some other reasons for this glorification of European civilization. It had to be shown that the homeland of the doctrine of the Lord of Heaven, and of its propagators, was basically and totally different from the more or less "barbarian" states and tribes that lay within the traditional Chinese geographic horizon. It had to be set apart from that world of inferior (and in some cases aggressive) nations by presenting Europe as fully equivalent to China, and in some aspects, due to the beneficial influence of Christianity, even superior to it. This demonstration of "cultural equivalence," China and Europe being the only two islands of higher civilization in an ocean of barbarity, was not only pursued by means of the written word. As is well known, the Jesuits used any means to drive the message home, ranging from ingenious timepieces and scientific apparatus to religious paintings and musical instruments. Along with their written accounts they also impressed the Chinese with visual specimens of the wonders of Europe, notably copperplate prints and illustrated books showing "cities, towns, palaces, lofty towers, arches, bridges and majestic temples."[1] Western books, preferably large volumes with beautiful bindings and gilt work, were displayed and admired, not only as precious objects, but also as concrete proof that Europe was a region of books and scholarship. In this paper I shall confine myself to written accounts, but it must be kept in mind that these at all times were combined with more tangible evidence of European achievements in art, science, and technology.

Finally, there was the delicate problem of the presence of other Westerners in China's periphery; there were the "Red-haired" (*Hongmao*, i.e., the Dutch), notorious as pirates and marauders, and, above all, the *Folangji*, a name given to both the Portuguese and the Spanish. Educated Chinese were well aware of the Iberian colonial expansion in East Asia since the early sixteenth century, in regions that traditionally were considered tributary states, most of which also housed large groups of Chinese immigrants. Chinese sources, both official and private, contained extensive reports about the Portuguese conquest of Malacca (1511), followed by Portuguese piracy and illicit trade on the China coast, and about the Spanish conquest of Luzon, the founding of Manila (1571), and the repeated massacres of the Chinese; the first one took place in 1603, and is said to have made some 20,000 victims. Even more delicate was the close relation between the China mission and the Portuguese in Macau, who had been permitted to settle there (under circumstances that never have become quite clear) in 1557. Although the Portuguese presence there was accepted as a *fait accompli*, largely because of regional trade interests, many Chinese felt uneasy about it, the more so since no distinction was made by these "Frankish" traders in Macau and the *Folangji* of Luzon, both sharing the negative image of expansionism, aggressiveness, and cruelty.[2] There also were persistent rumors about their habit of buying or adopting children and eating them, and about the dangerous and fanatic nature of their African slaves in Macau, the "black sea devils," who were said to kill anybody at their master's command. Already before 1600 a well-known scholar and traveler expressed his concern about Macau as a potential center of rebellion.[3]

Obviously the Jesuit missionaries in China were in a difficult position: on the one hand, they could not deny their very close relation with Macau (the Portuguese emporium served, after all, as the bastion and training center of the China mission, the source of their income, the place from where they recruited their Macanese-Chinese coadjutors, and the haven of refuge in times of persecution), and the Chinese were no doubt well aware of that connection. On the other hand, in their presentation of "their" Europe they had to dissociate it—and themselves—as much as possible from the "Franks," their brutal habits and their expansionism. They could counteract the negative effect of their unavoidable connection with Macau by making clear that their real homeland, the "Great West" (*Taixi*), was a Europe of quite another nature, in which the "Franks" had no place: an eldorado of saintly rulers, justice, virtuous government, peaceful mores, and equally peaceful trade.

The Jesuit Sources: The Construction of the Image

As so often is the case, the story starts with the founding Father Matteo Ricci. A first step towards the glorification of Europe is to be found in the explication attached to his famous world map, in the version published in Beijing in 1602 (the only authentic version that has been preserved, and probably the first one bearing this inscription).[4] It differs markedly from the other comments on the map that generally are very factual and not laudatory. Here, however, when dealing with Europe (*Ouluoba*), quite a different note is struck. The more than thirty countries (a number that became stereotyped) of the continent "are all ruled according to the political laws of the ancient kings," in such a way that no heresy (*yiduan*) is admitted, and all are worshipping the Lord of Heaven.

> There are officials (*guan*) in three classes: the highest one is charged with furthering [religious] transformation-by-education (*jiaohua*); the next one settles and regulates the affairs of the common people; the lowest one exclusively deals with military affairs. . . . Their artisans' work is refined and ingenious, and they know all about astronomy as well as about the principles of human nature. Their morality is such that they sincerely value the Five Relations (*wulun*); their products are very abundant, and both rulers and subjects are happy and rich.

The image is evoked, in this first testimony, of a well-ordered, virtuous and prosperous society: polycentric, but held together by an orthodox doctrine, and governed by an elite of "officials" that includes, at the highest level, those who are responsible for the moral "transformation" of the people, that is, the clergy.

Here we find already *in nuce* some of the main constituents of the Europe image. Two more can be found in Ricci's own *Storia*, in a passage describing how he presented Europe in his conversations with scholars during his stay in Nanjing (1597–1600, the crucial phase that marked Ricci's real integration into the *literati* milieu). In this key passage[5] he mentions eight subjects to which he paid special attention. Four of these served to inform his audience about the practice and organization of religious life in Europe: the authority and virtue of the Pope (a subject also presented in his *Tianzhu shiyi*[6]); religious orders of men and women; the duties of bishops and priests, and holy days. It is hard to say to what extent his audience responded to this kind of topics, for which they could find no parallel in their own Confucian discourse. However, they may have been much impressed by the other themes listed by Ricci, the first of which concerns the practice of public charity: the management of hospitals and orphanages, the pious foundations and charitable societies caring for the poor, for destitute widows and prisoners, and the practice of almsgiving. Other subjects relating to the high standards of morality include the restitution of things found or stolen, the censoring of all books before publication, and marriage customs (notably monogamy and no child betrothal) that are binding for all, including the kings.

Thus a whole range of themes that continued to be standard ingredients of Europe promotion can be traced back to Matteo Ricci. Other *topoi*, that soon came to play a very important role, appear still to be lacking: as far as can be ascertained, the element of "law and order" does not loom large, nor does Ricci stress the aspect of education, exams, and scholarship that in later descriptions contributed so much to the image of Europe as a bookman's paradise.

Ricci may have left notes or a draft for a world geography to be presented to the court; we are told that after his death (1610) the Jesuits Diego de Pantoja (Pang Diwo) and Sabatino de Ursis (Xiong Sanba) used Ricci's and some other materials to compile a comprehensive world geography.[7] Since it remained unfinished and was never published, we do not know in what way Europe was presented in it.

However, the lacuna is to some extent filled up by a document that bears the names of the same two missionaries, although both external and internal evidence suggest that it may have been composed (or at least thoroughly edited) by their protector, the famous Xu Guangqi (1562–1633). The document, called *Jujie*, (Memorial of Defense),[8] contains an extensive apology written by De Pantoja and De Ursis in response to the accusations made against the missionaries by the vice-minister of Rites in Nanjing, Shen Que, the instigator of the first persecution of Christianity (1616). Almost simultaneously Xu Guangqi also wrote a lengthy memorial in defense of the missionaries and their doctrine.[9] Both documents constitute a further stage in the formation of the idealized Europe image, presented in very strong terms, as is to be expected in an apology written to counter Shen Que's accusations.

Since according to one of Shen's charges the missionaries actually were spies employed by the Portuguese in Macau, De Pantoja and De Ursis had to dissociate themselves as much as possible from these Franks and their commercial activities. In an almost pathetic way they plead ignorance: We have no idea how they got hold of Macau; they do their business to make profit, whereas we are a totally different kind of people. "We come from other places and belong to a different profession—it really is a situation in which 'in the mating season horses and oxen do not approach each other' (we belong to two different worlds)."[10] And, incidentally, the "black sea devils" do not constitute a danger: they are bought by Westerners in a very distant country to do menial work; they are very stupid, but docile and not malicious. The real danger comes from the feared Red-haired ones, ruthless pirates and killers who should be chased from the seas.[11]

The missionaries had every reason to remain aloof from the Franks of Macau. Only ten years earlier (1606), as reported by Ricci, the existence of the mission, and indeed of the Portuguese settlement itself, had been threatened by a rumor that had spread in the Guangzhou region and even had been reported to the court. According to the story, the priests in Macau, led by Lazzaro Cattaneo (who in 1606 happened to be in Macau, walking around "in disguise" as a Chinese scholar, and alleged to know all the roads and the situation in both capitals) were preparing to invade China; they were expecting fleets from India and Japan, and Cattaneo's companions, spread all over China, were ready to start the revolution. The rumor had led to a massive exodus of Chinese from Macau, and the mobilization of the armed forces by the governor at Guangzhou.[12] In due time the tension subsided, but the incident shows how imperative it was for the missionaries to dissociate themselves and their homeland from the Iberian colonizers.

In the same *Apology* a clear line is drawn between the civilized nations of Europe and the barbarian peoples that border upon China, and who have for centuries harassed and invaded the empire—peoples who rightly are considered "unreliable, of a wrong kind, and with a different mentality." Thanks to the doctrine of the Lord of Heaven, Europe has nothing in common with them: "What a pity that (great Chinese travelers like) Zhang Qian of the Han, Xuanzang of the Tang, Du Shi of the Yuan, and Zheng He of the beginning of the present dynasty, never have reached it!"[13]

The second theme related to Europe, already suggested by Ricci, but here presented with much greater force, is that of the civilizing influence of Christianity. The key passage, which occurs in the *Apology* and is summarized in Xu Guangqi's memorial, with partly verbatim correspondence, runs as follows:

> With the help of the Lord of Heaven, and by obeying his rules, there has been no disturbance within the territory of the more than thirty western states, for a period of 1,500 years—not even one that would make a watchdog bark. Larger states feel sympathy for the smaller ones; the strong support the weak. (Peoples) unite their forces and riches, and live together in unbroken harmony. . . .[14]

Or, in the words of Xu Guangqi, who describes Europe in terms reminiscent of the Confucian utopia of the *Liyun* chapter of the Book of Rites:

> Since the more than thirty countries of the Western Ocean [region] that border upon each other have respectfully received and practiced this doctrine, a thousand and several hundreds of years have passed, and even till the present the larger states feel sympathy for the smaller ones; superiors and inferiors live in peace with each other; objects lost on the road are not picked up, and at night the doors are not locked. Such is the way in which they have maintained lasting peace and order.[15]

The conclusion is obvious: only China and Europe can claim to be truly civilized, as is also demonstrated by the fact (reported by De Pantoja and De Ursis, although they must have known better) that only in China and in Europe large numbers of books can be found; elsewhere they are rare, and no more than scribbles on palm-leaves or knotted cords.[16] In fact, it is that partnership in civilization that makes China so well-suited to Christianity, much more than any other country.[17] According to Xu Guangqi, Ricci himself had greeted China as a unique revelation; he is reported to have said:

> Formerly, when I came from the West, I had sailed the seas over a distance of 80,000 *li*. During that long journey I had passed along several hundreds of countries, and [everywhere] it was as if I were walking on thorns and prickles. But once I had arrived in China, and I had the privilege of observing its humanity and righteousness, its rites and music, and the glory of its civilized institutions, it was as if all the clouds and mist cleared away, and I once more was seeing the blue sky![18]

In 1623 a decisive step was made in the elaboration of the European utopia, when Giulio Aleni (Ai Rulüe, 1582–1649), the future apostle of Fujian, published the two works that presented the subject in a more comprehensive and coherent way. Aleni, who in those years still was living in Hangzhou, collaborating with the prominent convert Yang Tingyun, had the opportunity to edit and expand the geographical texts left behind by Ricci, De Pantoja, and De Ursis. These he rearranged, adding other materials from various sources, and in this way compiled his very influential world geography, entitled *Zhifang waiji*, (A Record [of Countries] beyond the Imperial Geographer's [Vision]), a work in eight *juan*, provided with maps and lengthy descriptions of the five continents.[19] The section dealing with Europe is divided into a "general discussion" (*zongshuo*), and short paragraphs of a more factual nature devoted to the different states. The second major contribution made by Aleni in 1623 was the publication of his *Xixue fan*, (General Features of Studies in the West), an essay in which he presented a survey of the European (or rather Jesuit) system of higher education and its various branches of learning.[20] Somewhat later, in 1637, he summarized the contents of both works, with some additional topics, in his *Xifang dawen*, (Answers to Questions about the West), in dialogue form; as he states in his preface, it was intended to provide his audience of Fujian *literati* with written answers to the questions which they posed most frequently.[21]

Within the scope of this paper it is not possible to give even an outline of the contents of these works, for which the reader may be referred to the studies and translations of D'Elia, Mish, and Luk.[22] Here we may merely note the fact that Aleni's treatment of the subject, and especially his "general discussion," became the most authoritative source of information about Europe for those Chinese who were prepared to accept its message; at the same time, it was met with skepticism, or even total rejection, by Chinese scholars and bibliographers who were not predisposed to believe Aleni's "wild and unverifiable" stories.

After the publication of Aleni's accounts little has been added to the presentation of Europe. In 1674 Ferdinand Verbiest published his *Kunyu tushuo*, (Explanations of the World Map)[23] (that appeared in the same year), but the descriptive part of this treatise is little more than a slightly reedited version of the *Zhifang waiji*, even to such an extent that the text is preceded by Aleni's original preface. Around the same time, Verbiest, G. de Magalhães (An Wensi), and Lodovico Buglio (Li Leisi) compiled a brief survey of Western mores and institutions, entitled [*Yulan*] *Xifang yaoji*, (Concise Notes on the West),[24] which again was almost completely based on Aleni's geography, emphasizing the most positive aspects. The main interest of these later texts lies in the fact that they made Jesuit geography known in court circles, through the activity of those "foreign experts" in the service of the Kangxi Emperor. As a result, some (carefully selected) information from Verbiest's *Kunyu tushuo* found its way in official imperial compilations.

Likewise, the *Xifang yaoji* was expressly written "for imperial perusal" (*yulan*), probably at the request of Kangxi, whose interest in "Western exotics" is well-attested.

Apart from these primary sources of information, i.e., the works of the Jesuits themselves, in which the glorified Europe image figures as a consciously constructed missionary device, we have the many testimonies of Chinese Christian authors who were inspired by that vision of a perfect society—alien and distant, and yet somehow familiar, because in so many respects it seemed to embody their own Confucian ideals in a christianized version. When going through the analytical survey of that Europe image that follows, and that is based on a mixture of Jesuit and convert statements, we must constantly be aware of the fact that we are dealing with two very different levels of expression: if Chinese authors faithfully echo the statements found in their Jesuit texts or heard from their Western teachers, they were convinced of their veracity. This gives their words a ring of authenticity and sincerity—they are speaking as true believers, not as missionary strategists.

What then are the most outstanding features of this vision of Europe as presented by the "scholars from the West," and what can we know about their impact on the Chinese audience, on the basis of recorded reactions?

Political Stability, Peace and Order

Although Europe is a mosaic of "more than thirty states" (ten of which are large ones), the region as a whole enjoys lasting peace and social harmony. The internal peace is never disturbed by civil war or rebellion; the state of political stability is so absolute, and has lasted for so many centuries, that the people are no more aware of the possibility that such things could happen, or even ever have happened:

> As regards insurrection and rebellion, such acts and people who commit them do not exist, and, what is more: ever since people came to observe and practice the Holy Doctrine, they have never been heard of, nor are they recorded in (our) books.[25]

According to a somewhat later authority, there is not even a word for "rebellion" in European language(s).[26]

The internal stability is of course primarily the result of divine protection and royal devotion:

> If one has obtained the Lord of Heaven's support and help, the state will be protected and the people happy; clear evidence of this stands recorded in our

chronicles. . . . To cover it by one phrase: in the several tens of states in the western region rulers have succeeded one another for more than a thousand years, without a single change (of dynasty). In fact, the people even are no more aware of the surname of the ruling family.[27]

This concluding phrase seems to be a subtle allusion to traditional Chinese political lore; in any case, Chinese educated readers would immediately be reminded of the opening phrase of chapter 17 of the *Dao de jing*, stating that in highest antiquity there were rulers, but nobody knew they existed.

The Western concept of the king ruling *Dei gratia* is referred to, but in terms that sound more Confucian than Christian: "The officials receive their mandate from the king, and the king receives his mandate from Heaven."[28]

The states are ruled by kings (*wang*); in general, kingship is hereditary, but in some cases (Poland, Germany and Venice) a new ruler is elected from a number of worthy candidates. Conflicts between states are made impossible by various factors. In the first place, through intermarriage all European kings are connected by family ties, which has created strong bonds of solidarity, large states treating the smaller ones with sympathy and giving them their support. Secondly, this polycentric Europe is held together by the supreme moral authority of the Pope, who in cases of potential conflict acts as a supreme arbiter; in fact, if an important decision has to be made in an individual state about which there is no agreement, the matter is submitted to the Pope and his council of sages.[29] Also internally, on the level of national governments, policy is subjected to a kind of organized moral censorship (the text does not specify whether this committee of sages is clerical or secular in nature—could it refer to the Inquisition?): in every state there is a "Court of Heavenly Principles" (*tianli tang*), a council composed of the most virtuous and talented persons.[30] Whenever the government is planning to make an important decision, it has first to be submitted to this Areopagus, and the measure can only be implemented after they have ascertained that it agrees with the principles of Heaven.

And, finally, the task of maintaining stability, in the sense of law and order, is entrusted to the civil administrators, and especially to the courts of justice. Appointed and salaried officials, the class of people charged with "regulating the affairs of the people," play an important role, for the government of European states appear to be thoroughly bureaucratic, even to such an extent that the very existence of a hereditary aristocracy (of course, the mainstay of power in most seventeenth-century European states) is not mentioned. The illusion is created of centralized bureaucratic kingdoms with a high degree of government control. School and academies have all been established by the kings, and teachers on all levels are appointed by the government. Officials are selected from university graduates: occasionally the term *guan*, (official), is even applied to graduates in theology who are destined to become part of the clerical hierarchy.

For Chinese readers the congruity with the Chinese political order must have been obvious; the parallel is made very explicit in a remarkable passage in Aleni's *Xifang dawen*:

> Officials are selected from those who have passed examinations in the Six Disciplines *(liuke)*. Some are responsible for the exposition of the doctrine, and some for national security. Those who have passed the literary examinations are appointed professors similar to the Chinese Directors of Education (*xiangshi*) and national historiographers (*guoshi*). Outstanding professors of philosophy are employed by the kings for exhaustively expounding the principles (*qiongli*). Graduates in law are chosen to govern the people, exactly as prefects and magistrates, governors and commissioners, officials of the Six Boards and the Nine Ministers of State in China.[31]

Almost like China—but better, for the system functions in an exemplary way. After their "term of service" (no doubt understood by Chinese readers as referring to the regular three-year rotation system) all officials are thoroughly scrutinized by inspectors, at the king's order, as to their performance. Their verdict is also based on information gathered among the people. Their reports are decisive for the officials' career.[32] Corruption is rare, or does not even exist, for officials enjoy high salaries (according to Aleni even amounting to forty thousand taels a year, for a provincial governor).[33]

Needless to say that such a government does not oppress the people: taxes are light (no more than ten percent, paid without any coercion),[34] and there even is a welfare institution that any Chinese scholar would recognize, and that is here even called by its time-honored Chinese name, *changping cang*, (Normalizing Granary), the government buying and storing grain when it is cheap, and selling it in times of scarcity in order to regulate the price.[35]

Special attention is paid to the rule of law and the administration of justice. The rules of law, as laid down in the ancient normative texts (*gudian*), is considered the backbone of orderly governance and of public morality; law is "the voice of the Heavenly Mandate" and "the binding [element] in the Five Human Relations." A well-organized system of law education is therefore of the greatest importance. Future judges and lawyers are tutored in special law schools (*falü zhi xiang*); the courses are given by highly salaried administrators who have been trained in philosophy.[36] Naturally the judicial procedures are impeccable: the rights of the defendants are guaranteed (right of appeal to higher courts and of challenging an incompetent judge; beating and torture are not used to extort a confession); guilt must be proved by absolutely reliable evidence, and all court sessions are public.[37]

As a result of the rule of law, public morality is of the highest standards; the theme is presented in standard form, using conventional metaphors like "[lost] things are not picked up from the road" and "at night the doors are not locked."

Charity: The Caring Society

Much attention is paid to the aspect of "Christian morality in action." In Christian circles the ideal of charitable action undertaken by humanitarian societies (renhui) was well known, as was its source of inspiration, the Christian concept of the "seven bodily and seven spiritual works of compassion." The latter were explained at length in Giacomo Rho's (Luo Yagu) Aijin xingquan, (On the Practice of Compassion) (1633), a work that immediately inspired the well-known Christian scholar Wang Zheng to set up his humanitarian society in Xi'an in 1634. However, the program of social action as systematized into the "seven works of bodily compassion" (feeding the hungry, clothing the naked, etc.) was already known and practised before the publication of Rho's work; it was, among others, the source of inspiration for Yang Tingyun when he founded his Christian humanitarian society (or rather transformed a Buddhist charitable institution into a Christian one, under Aleni's influence) in Hangzhou around 1630. Several other similar initiatives are known; it was the Christian contribution to a larger movement of setting up "societies for the performance of good deeds," that was very popular in late Ming times.[38]

To Aleni we owe the most detailed description of charitable institutions in Europe; since he is known to have played an important role in the founding of Yang Tingyun's society, it is not amazing that he paid so much attention to that aspect. By evoking the image of Europe as a kind of Christian welfare state the Chinese could be encouraged to follow the Western model: there, it could be argued, these ideals were actually practiced on a grand scale, and it worked!

In a lengthy section of his Zhifang waiji, and again in his Xifang dawen, a survey of charitable activities is given, undertaken by the government, by private benefactors, and by foundations and societies. In Europe, no one is forced by poverty to sell one's children or to die of hunger. In every city there are houses for the poor that care for the destitute, especially for orphans, widows, and widowers; likewise there are institutions where the physically handicapped can engage in useful labor. Poor parents who cannot raise their babies can hand them over to an orphanage (for in the West "the killing of a baby is considered a mortal sin"—no doubt a veiled criticism of the Chinese custom of female infanticide); measures are taken to guarantee that the parents later can recover the child, if so desired.

In the same way, the organized care of the sick is exemplary. Thanks to the efforts and largesse of the ruler, rich families, and groups of citizens, there are many hospitals in three categories, with excellent doctors, attendants and medicines. The quality of the health care is guaranteed by the fact that in Europe physicians are required to have graduated in medical sciences; only then they are allowed to practice (again, no doubt a hint at the Chinese situation, where no such sanction existed).[39]

It is interesting that no attention is paid to charitable activities organized by the Church; the full emphasis is on public welfare and civil action, the kind of charity that would appeal to Confucian *literati*. The point is also clearly brought forward by Yang Tingyun:

> In the West all people abide by the doctrine of the Lord of Heaven. In accordance with that doctrine there are various societies (*hui*), each one with its own objectives. . . . " (There follows an enumeration of the bodily and spiritual works of compassion). "All those works can be performed by lay gentlemen who are living in the world (*zaijia jushi*); they do not have to abandon the family (*chujia*).[40]

Education, Examinations and Degrees

In the idealizing descriptions of Europe schooling, study and scholarship occupy an extraordinary amount of space; in fact, the system of academic study, examinations, and degrees is the only aspect of European culture that has been singled out for monographic treatment, in Aleni's *Xixue fan*.[41] The reason is not far to seek: the Jesuit self-image of being highly educated experts in both religious and secular sciences was an essential part of their missionary approach, as was their acceptance, not only among converts but also in a wider circle of sympathizing or interested *literati*, as *xiru*, (scholars from the West). The whole treatment of the subject by Jesuit authors testifies of that urge to demonstrate the "cultural equivalence" between the missionaries and the Chinese scholarly elite: years of intense and arduous study according to a well-defined program; a network of academies; competitive and extremely selective examinations, followed by a career in the service of the community, or the state, or, in the case of the spiritual elite of *sacerdotes*, of God and all mankind. The analogy is evident and must have appealed to Chinese degree-holders, from *xiucai* "bachelors" to *jinshi* "doctors," and it was reinforced by the occasional use of a terminology borrowed from the idiom of the Chinese examination system.

For the details of the presentation we may refer to the excellent study of Luk Hung-kay and the earlier article by Pasquale M. D'Elia;[42] here we must confine ourselves to a few essential features.

The treatment of the subject is extremely uniformizing and one-sided: it actually outlines the system of Jesuit higher education as laid down in the *ratio studiorum*, and does no justice to the immense variety of university education and institutions of learning in seventeenth-century Europe. The content of the curriculum is essentially medieval, and based on the authority of Aristotle for most sciences, Galen for medicine, and Thomas Aquinas for theology. The nucleus is formed by a description of the "six disciplines" (*liuke*): the two general sciences of "Letters" (*wenke, Rhetorica*) and "Principles (*like, Philosophia*), followed by the higher stage with its four fields of specialization: Medicine (*yike, Medicina*), Law (*fake, Leges*), Doctrine (*jiaoke, Canones*), and "The Way" (*daoke, Theologia*); some additional subjects, notably mathematics and its applications in astronomy and music are also included. In a wider context the whole system of education is described as consisting of three levels (primary schools or *xiaoxue*, middle schools or *zhongxue*, and universities or *daxue*—the first occurrence of these modern terms in a Chinese text); "all are established by the king."

Much attention is given to the system of written and oral examinations in the various faculties, the degree of specialization, and the hierarchy of disciplines, culminating in that of "The Way"—theology. In some respects an analogy is clearly drawn between the Western and Chinese systems; as we have seen, such a comparison is explicitly made by Aleni, and his description of the discipline of Letters (*wen ke*) contains elements that would easily fit in a Chinese context:

> This study of literary arts (*wenyi zhi xue*) consists of four parts: (1) famous teachings by the sages of Antiquity; (2) works about the history of various nations; (3) different kinds of poetry and prose, and (4) the writing of literary essays (*wenzhang*) and discussions (*yilun*).[43]

In addition Aleni also mentions some complementary subjects belonging to this discipline: etiquette, music, dancing, singing, writing, and arithmetic. The message to a Chinese scholar would be loud and clear: the Western *wenke* would more or less cover the content of his own literary formation that took him so many years of study and toil—but in Europe this *Rhetorica* was no more than a first stage, leading up to the higher levels of science!

Another point of contrast between the Chinese and the European system, apart from the supposed absence of nepotism and corruption in the latter, was the fact that in the West examinations are individual and (at least partly) oral, and not, as in China, collective and written. In a revealing passage Yang Tingyun does not hide his preference for the Western procedure:

> The way of examination in that country is very much different from the 'posting of names' (of successful candidates) in China and from (our way of) recommending and recruiting candidates. (In the West) the examination is always presided by a religious authority, the *episcopus*, and by virtuous and renowned scholars. Every participant in the examination is individually tested by many examiners; he is interrogated about various subjects with profound content, and only if he (can respond) without one single mistake he can be entered on the list of successful candidates. . . . The selection is very impartial and extremely efficacious. That is truly quite different from the way it takes place elsewhere (*viz.* in China), where one has to use one's relations and to fight for jobs![44]

On the other hand, the selection of graduates was believed to be extremely severe. When speaking about the most difficult exam, the one in theology, Yang states that only one or two out of a thousand candidates get through, thus highlighting the prestige of the Jesuits in China as members of an extremely select company.

Europe as Bookman's Paradise

A region where education and scholarship are held in such high esteem must also be filled with books. In all major cities the government has established learned academies (*shuyuan*), many of which have huge libraries for the convenience of scholars and students, some containing up to one hundred thousand *juan*. The texts belong to four categories: (1) sacred scripture; (2) the writings of saints and sages of all periods; (3) works dealing with 'the investigation of things and principles' (*gewu qiongli*, i.e., philosophy and science), and works of literature.[45] Some Western books are encyclopedic texts of enormous size and coverage; in the field of "heavenly studies" alone there is a single work (Thomas Aquinas' *Summa theologiae*), the table of contents of which covers some 3,600 topics.[46]

Needless to say that Chinese Christian scholars, people who were living in a world of books and literary studies, reacted with enthusiasm. Yang Tingyun is overwhelmed by the almost infinite number of books in Western libraries: if the Heavenly Studies alone boast works of such enormous size, the total number of texts available for all the different disciplines and branches of literature must truly be staggering.[47] Han Lin and Zhang Geng speculated about the immense richness of Western literature: so far only about a hundred texts have been translated into Chinese, and these already contain an infinite variety of subject matter, from Heavenly Studies to applied sciences.[48]

An ocean of books waiting to be revealed to the Chinese! It was this eager expectation that led to the formation of a persistent myth in the circle of Chinese converts since the early twenties of the seventeenth century: the missionary Nicolas Trigault (Jin Nige, 1577–1628) had arrived at Macau with a "tribute" of no less than seven thousand Western books; owing to some practical problems they had not yet been imported, but soon this vast store of knowledge would become available to Chinese scholarship. The theme is mentioned repeatedly in our texts, with interesting elaboration.

The origin of this scholar's pipe dream is quite clear. In 1613 Trigault had been sent to Europe as a "procurator" of the China mission. Beside other tasks he was charged with the acquisition—through donations and purchase—of a great number of books that were intended to become the nucleus of a large library in China, at the service of the missionaries. Trigault was very successful in this book-hunting. In 1619 he arrived in Macau with a sizable collection of texts, partly consisting of impressive folio volumes with splendid bindings. Its exact size is not known. It must at least have comprised of 757 works in 629 volumes—according to early seventeenth century standards a very large collection, but of course a far cry from the "seven thousand volumes" mentioned by Chinese authors. That number is quite impossible, and so far no satisfactory explanation has been given for it.[49]

In any case the theme, once established, became the subject of high expectations. According to Li Zhizao, master Jin Nige intended to present the books to the imperial library in Beijing, "in order thus to bring together the scholarship of East and West."[50] Yang Tingyun further elaborates the theme into a story about a fictitious tribute mission: Jin Nige had been sent by his king to the court in Beijing to express his gratitude for the imperial favors conferred upon Matteo Ricci; apart from "the usual tribute presents" he had provided Trigault with seven thousand volumes. On account of certain troubles (in fact, in 1619 the anti-Christian movement led by Shen Que still was in full swing), he had been unable to bring them to the capital.

> However, when one day he will get the opportunity to offer them to the enlightened court, His Majesty surely will forward them to the Board of Rites and the Hanlin Academy, to have them translated and edited in cooperation with the scholars from the West.[51]

Here we see the utopia in action: Trigault's mission had been an internal affair aimed at providing the Jesuits with a store of Western books, but the theme stimulated the imagination, and therefore could assume fantastic proportions, with a Jesuit procurator transformed into a tribute-bearer, and a non-existent king of Italy paying homage to the Son of Heaven.

With such an abundance of books there might be the chance that some of them would be used to spread dangerous or heretical ideas, and this required the constant vigilance of the authorities. Already in De Pantoja's *Apology* the efficacy of literary censorship is extolled:

> Therefore in the major cities of the western countries offices for the inspection of books (*jian shu yamen*) have been set up, so that not even one word or phrase that deviates from the orthodox way and true principles gets a chance to be spread with evil intentions,

and the same is stated with more detail by Aleni: no publisher is allowed to have a text printed without the censor's authorization; as a result even the largest libraries do not contain a single word that may poison the spirit and lead to moral corruption.[52]

A faint echo of Roman literary censorship, an institution that appealed to Confucian *literati* and officials brought up with the idea that literature should serve a moral purpose. In Christian circles familiar with religious texts the *nihil obstat imprimatur* approbation was well-known, for the Chinese version of that formula figured on every Jesuit publication, and it was appreciated as a guarantee of orthodoxy.

It is therefore not amazing that Yang Tingyun is full of praise; he even mentions some additional reasons why Europe is free from heretical texts. After having described the institution of official censorship, he gives three other reasons: printing Western-style books is so expensive that common people (apparently the obvious source of subversive ideas) cannot afford it; secondly, in Europe private printing is strictly prohibited by law and can even warrant the death penalty, and, finally, there are no clandestine publications simply because the people do not want to have them.[53] Here again a somewhat fantastic but very significant elaboration of half-understood information.

The Ecclesiastical Element and the Jesuit Order

In the descriptions of Europe little concrete information is given about the actual organization and functioning of the Church. For obvious reasons no attention at all is paid to competing forms of Christian belief like

Protestantism or the various orthodox churches. But even the picture presented of the Roman Catholic Church remains hazy and ill-defined. The Pope (*jiaohuang; jiaowang; jiaozong*) is described in stereotyped terms, as a supreme moral authority and arbiter, respected and obeyed by all secular rulers; his position as vicar of the Lord of Heaven and the fact that each Pope is elected by a body of sages are mentioned, as are the bishops who represent him. Since he is not married he can regard all people as his own family, and lead them to the Way.[54]

At a lower level there are the many priests who celebrate Holy Mass and instruct the people; they usually are referred to as *saze'erduode* (*sacerdote*; often abbreviated to *duode*). However, apart from being moral teachers and ritualists they also constitute the highest intellectual elite; as graduates in theology they have passed the most selective and formidable examination, and for that achievement they are honored by the whole population, "just as in China people honor the highest graduate of the state examination."[55]

The actual status and hierarchical position of the *sacerdotes* remains somewhat unclear. As we have seen, Ricci refers to the religious leaders as *guan*, "officials," and the confusion becomes complete in Aleni's Chinese biography by Li Sixuan, where it is said that Aleni at the age of twenty-six (*sui*)

> had already been appointed to the office of (*sacer*)*dote*. According to the system of official ranks in that country the ninth grade (*jiupin*) is considered the highest . . . ; (*sacer*)*dote* is grade seven, which in China would correspond to the third grade.[56]

Needless to say that the association of the Western system of holy orders with the "nine grades" of the Chinese official hierarchy is as confusing as it is significant. In fact, the bits of information supplied in Jesuit accounts could easily create the impression that Western priests were a special kind of scholar-officials "charged with the task of transforming the people," as Li Sixuan adds.

Aleni speaks about religious orders, but here the situation is even less clear: there are groups of devotees who form associations (*hui*) who abandon all worldly glory and observe the rules of chastity, poverty, and obedience. Some associations are aimed at moral self-perfection (*zixiu*), others, notably the members of the "Jesus-Association," go out to convert people everywhere, "regarding the whole world as one family, and all of humanity as one body."[57] From such a definition, Chinese *literati* could easily get the impression that the Jesuits constituted a special kind of scholarly humanitarian society working for the benefit of all people. The total silence in the sources about the internal organization of the Jesuit order, coupled with the strong emphasis on their achievements in study and examinations, must have added to the misunderstanding.

In any case the Jesuits themselves are singled out as the *fine fleur* of Europe, and that image was no doubt fully accepted, and even elaborated by their Chinese converts. In Europe parents will pray that one of their sons may one day be admitted to the Jesuit order, for that is the highest distinction one may obtain; "that is what ambitious men aspire to do, for everybody considers admission to the Association the beginning of a (glorious) career" (an interesting remark with a distinctly bureaucratic flavor!). But few people will reach that goal, for only young men of exceptional intellectual qualities will be admitted.[58]

Conclusion: Europe as a Utopia

The glorified image of Europe, of which we have presented some main aspects, shows a number of basic features that characterize a utopia, the vision of an ideal and perfect commonwealth. Like other utopias it is uniform (for variety does not exist in a state of perfection); timeless and static (for any change would detract from the ideal); extremely well organized and strongly guided according to fixed rules, by an elite of sages; the inhabitants' behavior is shaped and inspired by a single common ideology that allows for no deviations; and, finally, it functions as a model— it has a message for the world.

The European utopia struck a sympathetic note in Christian-Confucian circles, and more than that: because they had no reason to doubt that this perfect society really existed, it could become a target of living hope and expectation, a vision of what China could become. It is not without reason that Xu Guangqi proposes to "try it out" in one township or one prefecture, so that the golden age of highest antiquity may be restored, or that Han Lin after reading Vagnoni's *Tongyou jiaoyu* declares that by the application of these principles China would be able to realize Great Peace (*taiping*) within thirty years.[59]

However, for all its force as an inspiring example, the European utopia remained an isolated phenomenon encapsulated within a tiny religious minority. Its impact outside the Christian milieu appears to have been minimal; as has been demonstrated by Luk Hung-kay, in Chinese official texts dealing with Western countries or books, such eulogistic passages are either left out, or branded as false and fantastic.[60]

But within the Christian community the vision of Europe as a model to be emulated remained alive, and helped to define the converts' attitude towards the West. In order to show to what length of "Europhilia" at least one of them was prepared to go, let me conclude with a most remarkable statement made by the Christian scholar Zhu Zongyuan ("Cosmas Zhu") in his early work *Da kewen*, (Answers to a Guest's Questions) (c. 1633). In a way that is unique in early Chinese Christian literature, it proclaims the superiority of the West, not only in regards to science, technology, and material wealth, but also in the field of ethics and political order.

- Our Chinese morality is inferior to theirs, for (in the West) lost objects are not picked up from the roads; at night the doors are not locked, and sages and worthies are respected.
- We in China are inferior to them in maintaining peace and order, for [the rulers] of their more than thirty states, large and small, are bound together by intermarriage, so that there has been not a single change of dynasty for 1,600 years.
- Our Chinese learning is inferior to theirs, for they have exhaustively investigated all those things, like the meaning of heavenly and earthly phenomena, philosophical texts, the application of (mathematical) figures and numbers, and the explanation of musical modes and calendar systems; in this they are widely different from the scholars here who merely exhaust their minds in writing literary essays and classical poetry.
- Our Chinese signs of outward splendor are inferior to theirs, for their palaces and houses are made of fine stone, and rise to a thousand feet, decorated with gold and jewels; their costumes are brightly colored, and their food and drink are delicious.
- Our Chinese technical skills are inferior to theirs, for they show unsurpassed perfection in making self-sounding clocks; telescopes that make distant things visible; machines that raise heavy loads, and music that plays automatically.
- Our Chinese military defense is inferior to theirs, for each one of their armed fighters is a match for a thousand enemies; they are valiant when approaching the battlefield, and they have sworn not to care about dying. Strong city walls will instantly be smashed by the impact of their heavy cannon, and firm bastions have to surrender.
- Our Chinese prosperity is inferior to theirs, for their soil is rich and fertile, and produces all things in plenty; moreover they are trading with all the innumerable countries, so that (in their treasuries) the five metals are piled up like mountains.[61]

Words not written by some early twentieth-century nationalist leader but by a late Ming convert. One can only speculate about what would have happened with China if people like Zhu Zongyuan had had enough power and influence to start a reform movement, instead of remaining a lonely voice crying in the desert.

Does Heaven Speak? Revelation in the Confucian and Christian Traditions

PAUL A. RULE

My only misgiving about being invited to speak on Confucianism and Christianity is whether the topic might be regarded as exhausted. On reflection, however, I concluded that two areas had been neglected in the torrent of words of the last two decades. One was the Christian concept of revelation as the great stumbling block for many Confucians; and another was the neglect of the views of the indigenous "Confucian Christians" themselves on this issue and the evidence provided by their inner lives. Since my expertise lies in the early modern period, and time is limited, I will mainly restrict my comments to the seventeenth century, especially the early seventeenth century. This paper will focus on the question of revelation: does Heaven speak? and, if so, how? and on the understanding of these issues by educated seventeenth-century Christians, and to a lesser extent their indigenous critics.

Interpretative Models

Some may think that to even pose such questions in the last year (by popular reckoning) of the twentieth century is naive. Have not recent theoretical and philosophical advances made any such comparative study futile?[1] Cultural relativism, textual deconstruction, and post-colonial hermeneutics have persuaded us to eschew "matching concepts" (*geyi*) as practiced by the first apologists of Buddhism in China, and the seventeenth-century Jesuit missionaries. But concepts can be "matched" in a variety of ways. I think that it can be demonstrated that there are "elective affinities" and "disaffinities" between conceptual systems which help us to understand the history of their encounter. And I am not at all sure that it is, in the end, concepts that determine the outcome of such encounters.

Many argue that "the past is another country," irrecoverable, and the "other" necessarily miscomprehended because of a cultural imperative overriding biological commonality and apparent shared experience. I do not share these views for reasons philosophical, linguistic, and sociological far too complex to develop here, but simply note the contradiction between the theory and practice of many who claim to accept them. If true, silence is the only resort, a conclusion reached and breached by mystics of both the Christian and Chinese traditions and by postmodernist sinologists.

Two major recent attempts have been made to demonstrate the fundamental incommensurability of Confucianism and Christianity and I want to begin with some comments on each because, if they are correct, my whole enterprise is not only quixotic but hopelessly vitiated from its inception.

Manufacturing Confucianism

The most recent of these is Lionel Jensen's *Manufacturing Confucianism*, which purports to give a thoroughgoing deconstructionist reading of the early Jesuit interpretation of Confucius and Confucianism. In my view, Jensen fails in his attempt, mainly because he does not meet his own criterion of "accuracy" in his reading of texts.[2] Of course, in a certain and ultimately trivial sense, "Confucius" and "Confucianism" were "manufactured" by the Jesuit missionaries as the first Europeans to name and define, although not the first to describe, what was later called Confucianism. I think the term "invention" is a better label for the process than "manufacturing," since "invention" implies etymologically discovering something that is actually there prior to the investigation. Also, the Jesuits never spoke of "Confucianism," a convenient if misleading nineteenth-century reification,[3] but used the Chinese *ju kiao* (*rujiao*, the teaching of the scholars).

Nevertheless, Jensen is right to point to the early Jesuits' "invention" for purposes of apologetics of a monotheistic "orthodox" early Confucianism at odds with the predominant schools within the contemporary *rujiao*. What he does not seriously examine but dismisses *a priori* is the plausibility of this interpretation which he names a "hybrid theology."[4] All Christian theologies are, in a sense, "hybrid," since they involve the explication of a revelation in a specific philosophical language and a specific cultural context. But Jensen seems to be implying that Christian theology is a fixed, culturally determined product and that Jesuit theology in China borrowed illegitimately and indiscriminately from Confucianism. This is to ignore the complex history of Christian thought; that very conscious reflection, internal debate, and self-justification accompanied every stage in the development of the Jesuit presentation of Christianity to the Chinese; and that a vast literature of works by Chinese Christians attests their acceptance of an orthodox, if nuanced, Christianity.

Jensen's further claim that the early Jesuits misidentified Confucianism with Chinese culture as a whole is simply false. The very core of their argument in the Chinese Rites Controversy was that "ancestor veneration" and other "definitive cultural traits"[5] were cultural artifacts independent of religious beliefs. They certainly claimed a sociopolitical dominance for Confucianism, but this seems to me incontestable even today when we are so aware of the complexities of early modern Chinese culture with its folk religion elements and pervasive Buddhist and Daoist influences. And the Jesuits themselves, in the midst of this complex reality, whatever strategic alliances they formed, were well aware of the complexity and diversity of the Chinese world.

Jacques Gernet

The Western scholar who has most trenchantly argued for the incompatibility of the Jesuit "christianized Confucianism" and actual seventeenth-century Confucianism is, of course, Jacques Gernet.[6] Since I will discuss later some of the anti-Christian sources used by Gernet, I will focus here on the methodological issues. Gernet proclaims a thoroughgoing cultural relativism based on cultural linguistics, especially the theories of Emile Benveniste.[7] However, his main argument seems to be based on incompatibility of cosmologies.

It is undoubtedly true that cosmology looms large in early anti-Christian writings, but my reading of these texts suggests that it is not fundamental, merely the point of utmost divergence between Western and Chinese thinking, and hence an obvious point of attack by ideological rivals. Ricci, as Gernet rightly claims, misinterprets Neo-Confucian *li/qi* theory, but it is monism not "pantheism" that he objects to,[8] and in this respect, at least, I think he was right about the metaphysics of *Lixue*. Many "Confucian Christians" followed him, arguing, as he did, and correctly in the light of modern scholarship, that *li/qi* metaphysics were unknown to ancient Confucians.[9] The fundamental issue was a theistic vs. a naturalistic universe,[10] not that the former contradicts the latter,[11] but that it postulated something more, an act of faith not just in the physical universe but in something beyond it. Nevertheless, the opportunistic defense by the early

Jesuit missionaries of a postulated ancient or original Confucianism against those who believed themselves true Confucians was offensive and, I would argue, with hindsight, unnecessary.

There is also, as Paul Cohen has pointed out, an assumption on the part of Gernet that Chinese attacks on Christian morality—such as the Jesuits' espousal of celibacy and monogamy—were based on defense of some fixed Chinese moral essence, whereas such issues were matters of debate within the Chinese ecumene.[12] Many Confucians, on the other hand, including some of those cited by Gernet,[13] strongly approved Ricci's strictures on Buddhist ethics and cosmology. Ricci's extension of filial piety to respect for the fatherly God and the father Emperor[14] was certainly an unorthodox formulation, but hardly "bizarre and curious."[15] It provided a solution to the often tension-filled relationship between familial duty and loyalty to the emperor, and Kangxi's later approval of Christianity might owe something to this.

Gernet implies that the "Confucian Christians" could not have understood the fundamental contradictions of Confucian *tian* and Christian *tianzhu*, and were misconceiving the Christian God as a cosmological force.[16] Even if Gernet were correct over such a fundamental misunderstanding, and I do not think it can be supported from Christian writings,[17] I think this argument again overprivileges cosmology in late Ming *ru* debates which, as always, emphasized sociopolitical morality. Gernet also, in my view, misreads some of the most trenchant anti-Christian statements as opposition to "a creator God"[18] whereas the very texts he cites in support show a more fundamental objection, namely to the doctrines of the Incarnation and eternal punishment and reward, that is to Christian revelation.[19]

Gernet also underestimates the volatility of late Ming intellectual life. It was an age of heterodoxy,[20] polarization,[21] syncretism[22] and end-of-era uncertainty.[23] The posthumous reading of the late Ming by so-called "Ming loyalists" early in the following dynasty both overvalued and misinterpreted the role of the Donglin party as upholders of *Lixue* orthodoxy.[24] The Jesuits were well within the bounds of late Ming *ru* discourse, except in their exclusivist claims which, while overtly directed against Buddhism and Daoism[25] and "Three Religions in One" thinking,[26] were rightly suspected of ultimately eroding Confucianism, too.

Gernet, I believe, makes too much of alleged specific conceptual contradictions and not enough of institutional rivalries and personal commitment. As the Ningbo Christian Zhu Zongyuan wrote around 1630, the "Three Religions" all disagree with each other so in the end there can only be one religion, "There is only one religion and that's that!"[27] And writing in an autobiographical vein in a later work, he describes his search for salvation and spiritual satisfaction from "those who follow and love the revelations of the three religions and hundred schools (*yi ziyou suocong aiming zhe, sanjiao baijia*)," but to no avail because their scriptures are without truth (*jing wu zhenshi*). Finally, he finds satisfaction in Christian revelation as found in Christian books (*ji du tianxue zhushu*).[28]

The question of divided loyalties remains to the present day a problem for relations between China's Catholics and the Chinese government.[29] Until the crisis of the early eighteenth century, papal authority remained distant and theoretical for Chinese Christians, but their early seventeenth-century critics appreciated the potential for trouble. Zhang Guangtian was exaggerating when he envisaged a converted Chinese emperor being obliged to send tribute gifts to the "Religious Sovereign,"[30] (*jiaohua huangdi*), but Jesuit writings about the authority of the Pope (*jiaohuang*) easily gave credence to such claims.

In general, though, Gernet's arguments, as those of Jensen, rest on a misreading of the theology of the Jesuits which both construe in terms of Protestant biblicism, predestination, individual salvation, spiritual/temporal separation, body/soul dualism, and anti-immanentism.

To confine discussion to the last, Jesuit spirituality is very immanentist as is seen preeminently in the "Contemplation to Attain Love," the finale of the *Spiritual Exercises* of Ignatius Loyola:

> I will consider how God dwells in creatures; in the elements, giving them existence; in the plants, giving them life; in the animals, giving them sensation; in human beings, giving them intelligence; and finally, how in this way he dwells also in myself, giving me existence, life, sensation, and intelligence. . .[31]

This sounds very Chinese to me, apart from the references to the Christian God, which is followed by an allusion to the notion of the human being as a temple of God "created as a likeness and image" of Him. At the very least, it has functional and affective similitude to the famous "Western Inscription" (*Ximing*) of the Neo-Confucian sage Zhang Zai,[32] and, I would suggest, such factors were more significant in "conversion" than doctrinal considerations which were always secondary to the Jesuits.[33]

There are many elective affinities between what Max Weber called the "inner-worldly asceticism" of the Confucians and Jesuit spirituality. Wang Yangming's famous maxim, *zhi xing heyi*, (to unite knowledge and action) finds echoes in the Jesuit ideal of "contemplatives in action."[34] Jesuit practices such as daily self-examination and a careful recording of good and bad actions were common in late Ming gentry practice;[35] as was "quiet sitting" (*jing zuo*), which is much closer to Jesuit meditation with its emphasis on application to daily life[36] than the unitive practices of both other Christian and other Chinese schools.

Gernet, however, intellectualises Christian conversion and underplays the personal and experiential factors. His constant emphasis on Confucian naturalism vs. Christian theism is a point well made, and, as we shall see, it is the supernatural elements in Christianity which many Confucians rightly compared with Buddhism and rejected on the same grounds.[37] Moreover, both Jensen and Gernet, in my view, misconstrue the "light of natural reason" argument in early Jesuit apologetics in China. Jensen's location of the "light of reason" in God is simply nonsensical.[38] It is God given but operates, according to seventeenth century natural theology, in the natural realm.

Gernet assumes duplicity in Ricci's espousal of Confucian morality because:

> The Christian thesis is that the principle of morality lies in God, the Chinese that it is impossible to rise to comprehension of the universal order without first fulfilling one's duties to one's parents. The Chinese morality consists in a continuous process of perfecting the self, the starting-point being one's most immediate relationships. So the meaning of the Classics has certainly been distorted.[39]

This is to confuse two levels of understanding or, if you will, natural ethics and moral theology. For the Jesuits one could completely endorse natural morality, as true in itself, so far as it goes, while simultaneously attempting to create a larger theistic framework. Xu Guangqi's famous aphorism that Christianity "complements Confucianism" *bu ru*[40] came from his acceptance of this theory. This sharp dichotomy of natural and supernatural is, of course, largely rejected or heavily qualified in modern theology,[41] but Ricci was presenting the conventional theology of his age in this respect, and, as a humanist, he certainly did not depreciate "nature."

A further serious defect in Gernet's critique is his assumption that Ricci and his successors either unwittingly or illegitimately used concepts incompatible with their beliefs.[42] I find this notion of unwitting use of Neo-Confucian or Buddhist concepts peculiar given Ricci's deliberate intent to use Chinese ideas and turn them to his own purposes.[43] As to the legitimacy of the method, none of Gernet's examples strike me as being incompatible with Christian orthodoxy, however narrowly construed. What appears to underlie this is some sort of conceptual purism at odds with both the history of Christianity, and the development of Chinese Buddhism and Neo-Confucianism. Even further, Gernet seems to be proclaiming a sort of cultural solipsism: "The language itself (he says) deforms the Christian message, giving it alien, Chinese resonances that are quite incompatible with it."[44] But, if true, does this not apply equally to Marxism, science, and economic theory in Chinese, not to omit writing in French about Chinese Buddhism? And again we are confronted with the presumption that Christianity is in principle non-Chinese in "resonance," whatever that means.

Furthermore, Gernet's presentation of Ricci's views are often distortions of a quite subtle argument. His summary of passages in which he says "it cannot be denied that Ricci does attack both Confucianism as a whole and even its spirit"[45] is a travesty. He says that Ricci assaults Confucianism by claiming:

> that what defines man is his faculty of reasoning, while Confucius' virtues (*ren*, humanity; *li*, sense of rituals or propriety; *yi*, sense of duty; and *zhi*, wisdom) are secondary; when he dissociates moral good and natural good and, in opposition to the Chinese thesis of a natural science of morality and the superiority that this confers on spontaneity over reflection, maintains that there is no good without the intention of doing good and no good without effort; when he declares that perfecting oneself is not an aim in itself; when he says that, compared with the Master of Heaven, our parents are alien to us; when he denies the importance of maintaining lineages and perpetuity in the family cults; and when he subordinates filial piety to one's duties towards God.

I maintain that, apart significantly from the last point about duty to God, Ricci says nothing as blatant as this in the Seventh Book of the *Tianzhu shiyi* which Gernet cites. I can only refer you to the texts themselves and especially Ricci's shrewd and accurate opening gambit that there is no unanimity of opinion in the Confucian literature on "the moral nature" (*xingqing*).[46] He might well have added that there is a similar lack of unanimity in Western and Christian ethics.

What I am challenging are Gernet's overt theoretical positions and methodological procedures. He has certainly raised very important questions about the early Jesuit reading of some key Confucian concepts, and especially of Neo-Confucian metaphysics. The issue is how to resolve them. The mere fact of terminological borrowing does not vitiate their interpretations. What is needed is an emphasis on reader response, on the reception of the Jesuit interpretation of Confucianism. I do not claim to be able to read with any surety the minds of seventeenth-century Chinese *literati*, but I see no other way to approach the question than through a close and critical contextual reading of the writings of the followers and opponents of the Christian missionaries. Gernet's *China and the Christian Impact* gives us a masterly overview of the hostile *literati* reaction, but comparatively neglects those who accepted the message, partly because he wrongly claims there were no distinguished scholars in their ranks after 1620.[47]

Another important and neglected method of investigating the religion of the "Confucian Christians" is to examine their religious practice. Much has been written about ancestor rituals and the participation of Christians in official rituals, but comparatively little about the devotional and ritual life of Chinese Christians; this despite the fact that the majority of Jesuit works from the seventeenth century dealt with such matters. Historical ethnology, especially relating to a proscribed religion, is not easy, but there is a surprisingly extensive documentation in European archives that is just beginning to be explored.[48] As Zürcher and his Leiden colleagues have shown in their investigations of the early development of the Catholic Church in Fujian,[49] Christianity, in that region at least, had become by the mid-seventeenth century, "an indigenous marginal religion."[50] And Robert Entenmann's illuminating work on Sichuan Christian communities in the early Qing, especially his study of the role of the "virgins," shows us a vigorous, largely lay-directed, and distinctly Chinese Christian life.[51] My work in progress on the "Confucian Christians" of the seventeenth century will focus so far as the documentation allows on the interior life of these long neglected figures.

This paper, then, will proceed by examining the centrality of the problem of revelation in both anti- and pro-Christian Chinese polemical literature, and by exploiting the tantalizing occasional glimpses into the interior religious life of seventeenth-century Chinese Christians.

The Problems with Christianity

The objections to Christianity in the anti-Christian literature[52] may be summed up under a number of heads but, in the end, can mostly be reduced to a rejection of the Christian concept of revelation. I will leave aside the polemics about Jesuit astronomy and Western science, and the more specifically sectarian Buddhist points,[53] and concentrate on the Confucian and general cultural objections.

The question of the challenge of Western science cannot, of course, entirely be neglected. I think the Jesuits were well aware of the ambiguities of the label *Tianxue*,[54] which they and their converts applied generally and indiscriminately to their introduction of Western ideas, religious and scientific, in an attempt to mutually validate their respective truth claims. It is true that cosmologies do affect theologies in subtle ways.[55] It is interesting though to note that many of the remarks about Western scientific theories in the major late Ming anti-Christian publication, the *Shengchao poxie ji*

(Against Heterodoxy, 1639), accused the Jesuits not of scientific error but of *lèse majesté*. They invert the natural order by postulating that the stars are larger than the sun and moon since observation of the sun and moon is a royal prerogative: "Everybody can see that the three lights [sun, moon, stars] taken together make up only one sky. To diminish the sun is to diminish the king, while to magnify the sky is to aggrandize the ruler."[56] In their role as astronomical observers and calendar makers, the Jesuits were indeed attempting to "aggrandize the ruler" and hence secure toleration of their religious activities.

There were attempts to paint Christianity as contrary to Confucian morality.[57] Although specific aspects of Christian morality were attacked: the exaltation of celibacy and virginity contrary to filial piety,[58] views on male/female relationships,[59] monogamy,[60] the brotherhood of all Christians,[61] duty to God overriding that to parents and ruler;[62] most often Christianity was seen as a rival world-system and, as Douglas Lancashire pointed out, a rival "faith."[63]

Accusations that Christians affronted Confucian morality were often formulaic and ritualistic. For example, Xu Dashou accuses the missionaries of "downgrading" (*bian*) the key Confucian doctrines of *ren* and *yi* and Confucius, Yao and Shun.[64] Unless, as is unlikely given the date, he is referring to the Franciscan and Dominican friars, some of whom took a harder line against Confucian values and Confucian sages, this charge hardly squares with published Christian writings. But the famous *renyi er yiyi*, "*ren* and *yi*, that's all that matters!" (*Mencius* 1A.1) was proverbial as a summary of Confucianism. Feng Congwu, commenting on Ricci in his *Discussions in the Capital* (*Dumen yulu*) and echoing Zhang Zai, says: "Our way is by itself perfect; what business do we have to search elsewhere?"[65] To add anything was blasphemy and the Jesuits were certainly doing that.[66]

Furthermore, and perhaps even more significantly, Christian practice was not Confucian orthopraxis, which in many ways was more important than orthodoxy.[67] Christians may have observed *ren* and *yi* and filial piety but they also prayed together, had their own specific rituals not authorized by the Neo-Confucian ritual books (*Jiali*), and ceded moral authority to their foreign "spiritual fathers" (*shenfu*).

The Christian concept of sin is another notorious crux in Christian–Confucian dialogue,[68] but does not figure much in the early anti-Christian polemics, except for attacks on Christian notions of punishment for sin. This is, I think, mainly become because the full doctrine was reserved for the fuller instruction of converts and does not figure explicitly in works such as Ricci's *Tienzhu shiyi*,[69] which were the main target. In any case, the central issues here are the doctrines of sin as an offense against God, original sin, and redemption, which are, for Christians, revealed doctrines. But all are absent from, rather than contrary to, Confucian values.[70] Nevertheless, there was a penitential and fearful tone to some of the Jesuits' Chinese writings, echoing the "guilt culture" of Europe of the period,[71] which must have puzzled, if not repelled, Confucian optimists.

Related to this is the Christian doctrine of reward and punishment, heaven and hell. Ricci's extensive treatment of this issue in Book Six of the *Tianzhu shiyi* where he acknowledges that it is not found in the Confucian canon did not satisfy many of his critics who saw it as Buddhist superstition and unjust. It is the occasion for one of Ricci's most interesting excursions into text criticism but one which interestingly was not, to my recollection, taken up by his opponents:

> *The Western scholar says:* "The teaching handed down from the sages was geared to what people were capable of accepting; thus, there are many teachings which, though handed down for generations, are incomplete. Then there are teachings which were given directly to students and which were not recorded in books or, if recorded, were subsequently lost. There is also the possibility that later, perverse historians removed parts of these records because they did not believe in their historical veracity. Moreover, written records are frequently subject to alteration, and one cannot say that, because there is no written record, certain things did not happen."[72]

In the Qing this skeptical attitude towards the canonical texts was taken up, or independently invented by the school of empirical research (*kaozheng*).[73] Ricci, like most Europeans of his generation, seems to have exempted his own *sheng jing*, the Judaeo-Christian Bible, from these hermeneutical principles, but not to have perceived that most of his Confucian interlocutors held a similar attitude towards their *sheng jing*.

The Jesuit postulation of a primitive Chinese theism and their rejection of the role given by Neo-Confucians to *Taiji*,[74] "the Great Ultimate,"[75] were frequent targets.[76] Ricci correctly points out that *Taiji* was not worshipped in ancient times while *Shangdi* and *Tian* were,[77] but ingenuously classes it as an Aristotelean "accident," an attribute not a substantial being.[78] Nevertheless, apart from attributing the notion of *li* as "the source of all things" to Zhou Dunyi rather than to Cheng Yi,[79] the references to Neo-Confucian metaphysics are surprisingly accurate.[80] Ricci's crime was to displace *Taiji* from its central position and to replace it with a new concept, *Tianzhu*; a Lord (*zhu*) had been placed over Heaven (*Tian*).[81]

Gernet argues that popular Christian preaching gave a debased and theologically inaccurate account of the Christian doctrine of creation. He cites in support testimony of a street pedlar during the 1616 Nanjing investigation who claimed that "the convert from Macao," Zhong Mingren, whose "recollection of what he had been taught was not very good" had explained that "in the beginning, when the Master of Heaven produced the world by a magic transformation, there was only one man and one woman."[82] But what Zhong, actually an educated merchant's son from Xinhui near Guangzhou and a Jesuit Brother for twenty-one years,[83] at the time of the alleged incident (1612) said was: "In the very beginning the Lord of Heaven made by an act of transformation only one man and one woman" (*dangchu Tianzhu huasheng zhiyou yinan yinii*), a quite accurate account of the *Genesis* story of creation of the first man and woman.[84] What was offensive to Confucian ears, however, was Zhong's concluding claim that the same Lord of Heaven "had descended and been born in a Western country" some 1615 or 1616 years ago.[85]

I am not convinced that the central issue was "creationism;"[86] or even theism;[87] rather I would locate the difficulty in differing conceptions of the relationship of God (however conceived) to the world. Many Confucians went along with the identification of *Tianzhu* with *Tian* and *Shangdi*, but balked at the further equation with *Yesu* (Jesus), who had been born in an unknown, petty kingdom far to the West long after the sage kings.[88] The standard reply of missionaries and Chinese Christians that he came to save all men and that his birthplace was irrelevant was not likely to satisfy such critics.[89]

Matteo Ricci presented this (to many Chinese) outlandish claim in the very last section of his *Tianzhu shiyi* after his Chinese *alter ego* has asked why the Lord of Heaven has not come Himself to personally set men right.[90] The Western scholar, i.e., Ricci, says that in every generation. He has sent holy men (*sheng shen*), but they were increasingly ignored.[91] So finally, he "came in person to save the world" (*qinlai jiushi*)[92] in the *gengshen* year, the second year of the Yuanshou period of the Han dynasty Emperor Ai, 1603 years ago. He then reascended to Heaven after 33 Years.[93] Note that Ricci is evasive on exactly how he came to reascend. There is no mention here of the crucifixion which was even more offensive to Chinese ears than the descending and ascending God, however it was duly emphasized in later Jesuit writings.

As if to clinch the argument, Ricci then moves on to the question of proof. These, he says, are facts, "true traces of the Lord of Heaven."[94] He had earlier asserted that the *Tianzhu jiao* had its own "orthodox scriptures personally transmitted by the Lord of Heaven" (*Tianzhu qintai zhengjing*).[95] But how do we know these are true? They are attested by holy men, some of whom predicted the events of his life,[96] others wrote them down.[97] Above all, Jesus passed the strict tests applied in the West, by surpassing all others in his words and deeds. Ricci concludes by saying that he has not yet finished translating the *tianzhu jing* into Chinese, but has completed the essential passages (*qi yao yijing zhengzi*).[98]

It was these distinctively Christian claims, that were to prove the major obstacle to acceptance of Christianity and which, as we shall see, underlie most of the anti-Christian polemics of the seventeenth century. The great friend of Ricci and Aleni, Ye Xianggao, renowned scholar and holder of the highest offices, wrote poems in their honor and prefaces to Christian works praising their scholarship, integrity, and virtue; yet he never became a Christian. The reason, according to the mission historian Daniello Bartoli, being "a single but insuperable obstacle," namely that "it did not seem to him worthy of God to become man to redeem man."[99] But Ye's problem seems to be not incarnation as such, but a unique incarnation. The preface which he wrote for a now lost work on the ten commandments by Yang Tingyun suggests that he believed Yao, Shun, and Confucius were all "descended and born from Shangdi" (*Shangdi suo jiangsheng*) in the East, so that the same could happen in the West.[100]

Let us turn in conclusion to the question of revelation, and particularly the Incarnation of Jesus Christ as a problem in Confucian–Christian relations.

The Problem of Revelation

Revelation for Christians, at least in the seventeenth century, was conceived primarily as a *locutio Dei*, "God speaking out of the treasury of his own understanding, communicating to men truths which otherwise would be attainable by them only with difficulty or not at all."[101] This was the language of the Bible:

> You came down also upon Mount Sinai, and spoke with them from heaven, and gave them right ordinances and true laws, good statutes and commandments (*Nehemiah* 9:13).

The Christian God, then, speaks from Heaven. But does the Chinese Heaven speak?

Since this paper is confined to Confucianism, I leave aside completely, but reluctantly, the question of revelation, or better revelations, in Chinese Buddhism, Daoism, and popular religion where they abound. The superficial judgment that Christianity was always alien to Chinese culture has reference only to elite culture. In many respects, as Erik Zürcher has shown, Christianity fitted only too easily into the paradigms of Chinese popular religion—miraculous interventions, especially healing, apparitions, reinforcement of peasant puritan ethics, dramatic and emotional ritual expressions, sickness and death perceived as punishment for sin. It was always, and still is today, elite culture which puts up the strongest barriers.

That elite culture was based on the Confucian canon, the *jing*. We will not pursue the proliferation of *jing* in other Chinese traditions where the label is applied to anything from the contents of the Buddhist Tripitaka to treatises on sexology. But for Confucians, it meant the Five Classics (*Wujing*) and the Four Books (*Sishu*), and in a certain, but shifting, sense, the commentaries of the Confucian greats.[102] Ricci names the source of Christian teaching as the *jing zhuan*, "bible and commentaries (i.e., the Fathers of the Church?)."[103] However, in Christianity, the distance between the text, inspired by God, and the commentary was qualitative and much greater than in Confucianism.[104] The difference sprang from the notion of "revelation."

For Confucians, the authority of the *jing* rested on the person of the teacher and the model of behavior he presented. Once again Ricci's Chinese Scholar is true to the tradition:

> *The Chinese scholar says*: Confucians regard the sages as authoritative examples (*zong*) (for the rest of mankind), and the sages used the canonical writings and their authoritative commentaries (*jing zhuan*) as media of instruction (*shi jiao*).[105]

But whence did the Confucian sage draw his inspiration? From Heaven (*tian*) seems to be Confucius' answer in the *Lunyu*. But how? Heaven does not speak, its commands must be understood from the workings of the physical and moral universe (one not two distinct orders for Confucians):

> Confucius said: "I don't want to speak any longer." Zigong said: "If you don't speak, what could we, your disciples, pass on?" Confucius said: "Does Heaven speak? Yet the four seasons go their way, and everything flourishes. Does Heaven speak?" (*Lunyu* 7:19)

Even more emphatic that Heaven does not speak is Mencius:

> Wan Zhang said . . . "Since Shun got the Empire, who gave it to him?" (Mencius) said: "Heaven gave it to him." "If Heaven gave it to him, did Heaven give specific orders?" Mencius said: "No! Heaven does not speak but reveals its will through actions and deeds." (*Mencius* 5A:5)

Mencius is dealing here with political theology, the source of political authority, but the point is a general one all the same. It is the moral nature of humankind that "reveals" the will of Heaven, for Mencius a Heaven-given, innate sense. The typical Western response—but how precisely does this happen?—did not seem to disturb early Confucians although, in reaction to Buddhist and Daoist speculations, it received various answers in later Confucianism. We cannot penetrate the origins of sagely wisdom.[106] Even a skeptical naturalistic Confucian like Xunzi who rejects fear of spirits as a motive for correct ritual behavior concedes that the sage, and he alone, really understands why we should do these things.[107] But how the sage acquires this wisdom is never spelled out. Certainly it is not by direct communication, but through mystical intuition, introspection?

The developed Confucian understanding of these issues that leads from Mencius via the *Zhongyong* to Zhu Xi and Wang Yangming emphasises the moral nature of humanity as the prime source of contact with transcendence. As Tu Wei-ming puts it in his essay on the *Zhongyong*:

> (The *Zhongyong*) maintains that common human experience itself embodies the ultimate ground of morality, and thus provides the theoretical basis for actualizing the unity of Heaven and man in the lives of ordinary people. Even though only the sage, as the most genuine manifestation of humanity, can fully realize the unity, each human being is practicing it daily but without a profound awareness of its true meaning.[108]

In practice, such an approach emphasized the experience not its ultimate source in Heaven, more so in the case of Zhu Xi than Wang Yangming.

It is, in fact, surprising that the Jesuit apologists failed to make more use of the notion of the innate moral nature in their rapprochement with Confucianism. The convert Yang Tingyun, however, did not hesitate to relate Wang Yangming's "innate knowledge of the good" (*liang zhi*) to a source in the Lord of Heaven:

> The Lord of Heaven makes human beings and is the source of the goodness that is in them. . . . The Lord of Heaven granted human beings an intelligent nature which was originally a very clear and bright thing. In the clarity and brightness there exists the principle (*li*) of everything. That is what we mean when we speak of humaneness, justice, propriety and wisdom[109] as coming from nature (*xing*). That which the Lord of Heaven gives us we hang onto strongly. The Holy Scriptures call it "bright virtue" (*ming de*),[110] the Confucians call it "innate knowledge of the good." How could it be that something not good was bestowed on humans. After we got bodies there was evil but it was what each person did themselves through relying on their physical makeup not their true nature.[111]

This passage provides us with a glimpse of what might have been if Ricci had not misinterpreted and rejected Neo-Confucian "principle."

Confucians of the Zhu Xi school, however, would have been unhappy with the emphasis on the natural goodness of the mind[112] and both they and the Wang Yangming school would not accept the substitution of the foreign *Tianzhu* for the native *Tian*.

For those who did accept *Tianzhu*, however, most of the Neo-Confucian moral theory could be enlisted in the service of the new religion. For example, Mathias Xia,[113] in a manuscript commentary on some passages from the *Liji*,[114] comments on one passage:

> Sinful men reading this passage see only the original Chinese natural meaning of the ritual. But it is also fully in accord with the commands of revelation (*chaoxing zhi gui*). The first three commandments of God are to teach men to be at peace with God, and the following seven commandments are to teach men to be at peace with other men. Peace with other men is the beginning, then comes filial piety towards our parents and ancestors. The Chinese sage kings were also influenced by the Lord of Heaven who enlightened their minds *zhongguo shenwang, yimeng Tianzhu Kaiqi qixin*. They taught people to be peaceful and to exercise filial piety towards their parents and ancestors. The *Xiao Jing* says in Chapter one: "The former kings had the highest virtue and loved the way which they used to rule the empire. . . ."[115]

Thus were reconciled the natural and the supernatural, Chinese tradition and Christian revelation.

Another way of reconciling the two was to invoke a theory of stages of revelation. Christian theology, in addition to the historical revelation mainly found in the Bible, also embraced notions of "natural revelation" and "personal revelation."[116] In many seventeenth-century Chinese Christian works both by Jesuits and Chinese scholars there are references to such a scheme. Ricci's *Tianzhu shiyi*, insofar as it appeals to revelation, is mainly concerned with biblical revelation, *Tianzhu zhi jingdian*,[117] and makes no explicit reference to either natural revelation or personal revelation. But later Jesuit writings presented a sequence of *xingjiao*, (the revelation of nature); *shujiao*, (the revelation of the book); and *chongjiao*, (the revelation of love [or grace]); while others use for the last, the faith response to Jesus as the Christ, the terms *shenjiao*, (personal revelation), or *enjiao*, (the revelation of grace).[118]

A classic presentation of this sequence is found in the journal of the encounters between Giulio Aleni and various Fujian *literati*, Christian and non-Christian, the *Kouduo richao*.[119] One of Aleni's conversations (8 April 1631) is reported as follows:

> "In the teaching of the Lord of Heaven there are three stages. Do you know what they are?" We replied: "No." The teacher said: "The Lord of Heaven's love for

people is endless. He gave us the revelation of nature (*xingjiao*), the revelation of the book (*shujiao*), and the revelation of grace (*chongjiao*). What does that mean? At the beginning of mankind, the Lord of Heaven endowed us with intelligence (*lingxing*) so that we could understand and reason. At the same time an understanding of the ten commandments was engraved on our hearts. Every nation shared this understanding. This is what is called the revelation of nature. Eventually the desires of the flesh overran mankind, and thoroughly corrupted it, so, either directly inspired (*mingshi*) or on instructions (*ranqi*) certain holy men wrote down the scriptures (*jingdian*) to overcome the errors in the hearts of mankind. This is what is called the revelation of the book. And to come to the third way the enemy is overcome. Mankind had gone very bad. Through the scriptures alone they would have had difficulty in turning back, so the Lord of Heaven came down and became man. He himself began to teach and bring enlightenment everywhere. This is called the revelation of love (*chong*), the third revelation. It spread abroad the grace (*en*) of the Lord of Heaven. So he took on a body in order to teach us and to be present to us."[120]

The ambiguities of this passage are obvious. The first lies in the very terminology: *sanjiao*, usually applied to the "three religions" of China; *xing* with its overtones of Confucian *renxing* and ambiguity as to who or what was doing the revealing, *Tian*? *Tianzhu*? *Li*? And which book or books was referred to in *shujiao*? Even Aleni seems to leave open who were the "holy men" or "sages" (*shengxian*) who received the revelation, hence which scriptures were in question, especially since the Christian scriptures were not yet available in full translation. The last category, too, included some possibility of personal revelation, an experiential encounter as the basis of faith in Jesus Christ.[121] I would suggest that it is this that Yang Tingyun refers to in his conversations recorded in the *Shengshui Jiyan*, "Records of the Holy Water Society," when he speaks of "secret evidence" (*mi zheng*).[122] Certainly, it was the basis for the conversion of another early Christian, Li Sixuan, by his own account.[123]

One way of reconciling the earlier "revelations" and locating them in China as well as Judea, was to displace Fuxi as the first man, or rather to identify him and his successors with the biblical patriarchs. This dangerous move, to be repeated at the end of the seventeenth century by the so-called "Figurists," was first made in print by Li Zubai, and with fatal results. In his *Tianxue chuangai* (1664), Li denied that Fu Xi could have been the first man since mankind was created by *Tianzhu* in Judea. The Teaching of Heaven must therefore have been taken to China by men who had received the revelation on Mount Sinai:

The first Chinese really descended from the men of Judea who had come to the East from the West and the Teaching of Heaven (*tianxue*) is therefore what they recalled. When they produced and reared their children and grandchildren they taught their household the traditions of the family and at this time this teaching came to China.[124]

The Chinese sages (*shengxian*) of the Three Dynasties merely developed this teaching (which Li then illustrates by the usual tendentious citations from the Classics and Four Books) and he concludes:

> So you can see that they were not opposed to the commandments and laws of Teaching of Heaven. . . . And so there would not have been any Chinese teaching without the prior Teaching of Heaven, to be respected by the Three Dynasties, bequeathed to later generations and daily handed down.[125]

This view made Li a major target for Yang Guangxian who excoriated it in his anti-Christian polemic, *Budeyi*,[126] and Li was one of those executed in the subsequent purge of Western astronomy and Christian religion. Confucian and biblical traditions were not to be so easily reconciled.

In the end, what determined the reaction of those presented with the *Tianzhu jiao* was acceptance or rejection of a unique and definitive incarnation of God in Jesus. To the doubts of inquirers, the Jesuits could only appeal to testimony of eyewitnesses,[127] i.e., as represented by their reference to texts inaccessible to their hearers, or refer to no less incredible dogmas, such as redemption from sins.[128] From Celsus[129] to Ye Xianggao to Albert Einstein this has been the crucial question, and much of the case made by the critics of the Jesuits rested on its implausibility. Was it historical fact, and if so, why unknown to the Chinese until now?[130] Isn't it unseemly for *Tian/Shangdi/Tianzhu* to become man? Who looked after the universe while he was on earth?[131] And should we worship a crucified criminal?[132]

Today, again, the issue has arisen in the form of "Culture Christianity," with its admiration of the social and cultural utility of Christianity and the subtlety of its theology, but deep ambiguities about its truth claims. The late Edward Malatesta played an important and yet to be documented role in this twentieth-century reprise of the seventeenth century encounter, and it is as a monument to him that the Institute he founded continues the work on the two fronts, historical research and contemporary engagement.

Christianity in Late Ming and Early Qing China as a Case of Cultural Transmission

Nicolas Standaert, SJ

Introduction

Christianity in China can be studied from the point of view of different academic disciplines: missiology, church history, history of science, sinology, etc. For this conference which attempts "to reflect afresh upon Sino-Western cultural relationships, with particular regard to the experience of Christianity in China," I would like to undertake further reflection which is situated on the border of several of these disciplines. More precisely, I will consider the encounter between Christianity and China, mainly in the seventeenth and eighteenth centuries, as an example of contact between cultures. Without considering it as an alternative to the aforementioned disciplines, this analysis is very much influenced by studies of cultural anthropology.[1]

The principal idea of this paper is that what happened in the interaction between Christianity and China is a complex whole, the process of which could well be compared with the weaving of a textile. After bringing to light some general characteristics of this encounter in the first section, I will have to raise some methodological questions. The second section will indicate that the conclusions of this research are the result of a method that pays more attention to process and interaction than to impact, success, or effect. While in the third section the transmission between Christianity and China is situated within a broader framework of typologies of transmission, the fourth section looks at the particular characteristics of the encounter itself mainly by using different metaphors to understand the process of diffusion. By focusing on elements like social embedding, reproduction of knowledge, or the question of power, the fifth section analyzes the same process from the angle of long-term terminal aspects. The sixth and final section tries to explain the process of transmission by looking at conditions which favor or discourage diffusion.

I would like to take the various contributions to the *Handbook of Christianity in China: Volume One (635–1800)* which is to be published in Leiden, by E.J. Brill in 2000, as the main basis for reflection. In doing so, I acknowledge that my analysis is not necessarily the approach of the different contributors to this *Handbook* or of the *Handbook* as a whole. Yet, I am grateful to the different authors whose excellent research inspired these reflections and hope that other alternative views and analyses will come forward.

Christianity in China as a Case of Cultural Contact: The Study of Cultural Transmission or Diffusion

Cultural Contact

There are different ways of classifying contacts between cultures. Since it was the Europeans who went to China, one could take European expansion history as a starting point. The German scholar Urs Bitterli, who studied different types of European contacts with non-Western peoples,[2] distinguishes between the following general types: "cultural contact" (an initial, short-lived or intermittent encounter between a group of Europeans and members of an non-European culture); "collision" (in which the weaker partner, in military and political terms, was threatened with the loss of cultural identity, while even its physical existence was jeopardized and sometimes annihilated altogether); and "cultural relationship" (a prolonged series of reciprocal contacts on the basis of political equilibrium or stalemate). Bitterli places seventeenth-century China under the last category.

Seen from the perspective of China's relationship to foreigners, Chinese rulers sought to restrict foreign presence to border areas and to keep it under strict control even there. As far as official and formal relationships were concerned, the dominant form was that of a tribute relationship. Even if several European (Portuguese, Dutch, etc.) legations to China were treated as tribute legations, the infusion of Christianity in late Ming and early Qing cannot be placed under this system. Missionaries were not treated as tribute legations since their cases were considered individually, and once in China they were obliged to stay and could not leave without imperial permission (especially after the introduction of the "permit" (*piao*) in 1706–1708). The closest parallel experience was that of the arrival of Buddhism.

As such, the experience in the seventeenth century somehow evades prevalent categories. For some Western historians "it stands out as a memorable episode in mankind's efforts at cultural accommodation; it has been one of the few serious alternatives to the otherwise brutal ethnocentrism of the European expansion over the earth."[3] China experienced this episode differently from the Japanese pirates (*wokou*), the Mongol or Manchu invaders, or the Portuguese occupants of Macau. Therefore, this interaction can serve as an interesting case. One is tempted to call it a "laboratory" for the study of cultural diffusion, transfer of knowledge, and cultural change, leading to deeper insights for broader theories of cultural interaction.

A Laboratory

The European–Chinese contacts that came about through Christianity in the seventeenth and eighteenth centuries contain some specific characteristics that make them an interesting case as a field of observation, especially when one compares this with other intercultural contacts at that time.[4]

A first characteristic is that the observation sample is representative enough of cultural contacts, without being too large. The numbers of missionaries (maximum of ca. 140 in China in 1701–1705), of Chinese priests (maximum of ca. fifty in 1800, i.e., two-thirds of the total number of priests in China at that time) and of Chinese Christians (maximum of 200 thousand ca. 1700) were after all very small, especially compared with the overall population (150 to 200 million inhabitants).[5] The number of people directly affected by Western sciences also remained very limited: "the new technology from the West turned out to be, in most ways, a banquet to which never more than a few Chinese chose or could afford to come."[6] This, in fact, is not a surprise since science is always an elite activity. The interaction was clearly between groups of markedly different size. This limited and nevertheless significant segment of population, however, facilitates (laboratory) observation. Moreover, though Western primary sources informing us about this exchange are quite numerous, the Chinese primary sources (ca. 650) are very manageable.[7]

A second characteristic of the Sino-European encounter in the seventeenth century is that both cultures hardly knew each other before they met. In terms of methodology, this means that the period antecedent to the particular contact being investigated here can act as a base—line from which to deduce change, and thus provides the framework within which the resultant dynamic process can be analyzed.[8]

A third characteristic is that both cultures involved were relatively equal with regard to their cultural, economic, institutional, intellectual, and material complexity. Many studies on cultural transmission involve cultures with an unequal complexity. Here, it is an advantage that the means of reproduction of knowledge are more or less equal, and so facilitates the observation in a more refined way. This equality between Europe and China was the case in the seventeenth century, especially in two fields: printing and education. In China, as opposed to other countries, the missionaries did not introduce the printing press; there was already a widely available printing system.[9] In addition, missionary orders such as the Jesuits, known for having established schools in many countries, met in China a very good and well established educational system (which made it even impossible for them to establish schools). Due to such equality, Europeans and Chinese were able to communicate at a level that, at least from the European perspective, was very different from the encounters in other countries at that time.

A fourth and final characteristic to consider this period a suitable case for the study of intercultural contacts is that in the exchange the aspect of external power was relatively reduced. Though the missionaries themselves remained exponents of European culture and dependent on material support from ecclesiastical institutions and from the colonial administration,[10] it was the Ming and Qing administration that separated them from the trader and colonist and that ultimately decided whether or not they could enter and stay. Though several anti-Christian movements at times caused the expulsion of missionaries, the Chinese administration remained relatively open during the whole period, at least open enough to allow a constant influx and renewal of the corps. To a large extent, the Chinese side occupied the dominant position, since the Chinese received the foreigners in their own habitat and because of their strategy of "cultural imperative" which obliged the foreigner to accommodate to the native culture.[11] The clearest example is the predominance of the Chinese language in the exchange. Contrary to the interaction in Japan, where Japanese learned Portuguese or Latin, or to modern interactions, where many Chinese have to learn a foreign language to participate in cultural transfer, in the seventeenth and eighteenth centuries, except for a very small number of Chinese educated for the priesthood, no Chinese involved in the interaction learned a foreign language.[12] This aspect is important because "before these ideas could evoke response, they had to be communicated, and they could be communicated only by being filtered through Chinese language and thought patterns."[13]

These four characteristics are not unique to the Christian experience in China, since one can find similar situations in the cultural exchanges that took place with the arrival of Judaism, Islam, and especially Buddhism in China. Yet, what makes Christianity in the seventeenth and eighteenth centuries more particular is that it was an exponent, not only of a religious practice, but of a complete world view. That is why this historical encounter, more than the others, exerts influence on today. The question of "influence" will be dealt with in more detail below. At this stage it can be pointed out that the influence of Christianity in the seventeenth and eighteenth centuries should not be sought in the immediate influence it exerted on society, thought, or the sciences. Even if there was some influence in the fields of calendar and astronomy, it is fair to say that the effect of Christianity on the whole of Chinese culture was extremely limited and that the exchange was a case of minimal borrowing. The only aspect, however, which might perhaps be called an "effect," is that the case of Christianity in late Ming and early Qing contributed to raising some fundamental questions to Chinese culture which were fully developed in the nineteenth and early twentieth centuries, and which are not yet resolved today. The arrival of Europeans forced even the most opposing ones to accept that at least questions had been raised. As appears from many Chinese textbooks on Chinese history in which this encounter is clearly mentioned, the exchange in the seventeenth century is taken as the starting point from which China was radically confronted with itself. Taking Ricci's world map as an image, this map put China in another world, and China is still searching to find its place on it. Among the numerous questions related to this quest, are: Why did scientific and technological development stagnate in China and not in the West? Why was Jesus Christ born in Judea and not in China? What does modernization mean for China? In the twentieth century a wide variety of media, from the scholarly writings by Liang Qichao (1873–1929) to the TV-series *Heshang* (River Elegy; 1988), have raised these questions, and it is my impression that Chinese scholars will continue to treat them well into the twenty-first century.

Intermezzo: Why Christianity Did Not Take Root in China—Or Didn't It? Failure of Christianity in China as a Methodological Question[14]

Before proceeding to an analysis of the cultural transmission of Christianity in China, one must first raise the question of what one is going to study with regard to this transmission. Many studies are devoted to the success or, in most analyses, the failure of the transfer, whether religious or scientific. One can therefore start with the question of success or failure that is brought up most often in the evaluation of this period.

Reasons for Failure

Erik Zürcher has treated the question of failure of Christianity by relating it to the success of Buddhism in China.[15] The question can be reformulated as: How can one explain that Buddhism could become a permanent and creative force in Chinese culture, whereas Christianity never became more than a temporary and marginal phenomenon? He has presented and evaluated the following reasons.

One possible answer stresses that the mission always had to face the hostility of xenophobic and conservative elements: stubborn, narrow-minded mandarins, jealous Buddhist monks, and Western adversaries in the Rites Controversy. In other words, the (Jesuit) mission failed, because others made it fail, and suffocated it. This explanation is both one-sided and superficial. Persecution in China was, after all, not such a dramatic affair, and the Rites Controversy only hastened a process of decline that had started before.

A second explanation stresses the cultural isolation of late imperial China: "Sinocentrism," the traditional idea that China is the only center of true civilization. As a foreign doctrine, Christianity was in principle considered unacceptable. Still, while sinocentrism was a factor, it was not a decisive one.

A third explanation mainly lies in the sphere of intellectual history. The main argument is that the most basic religious and philosophical ideas and assumptions of traditional Chinese thought were totally incompatible with those of Christianity. The clearest example of this explanation is Jacques Gernet's *Chine et christianisme* (Paris, Gallimard, 1982). In spite of many similar contradictions, however, Buddhism did become fully incorporated into Chinese culture. The limited success of Christianity in seventeenth-century China, therefore, cannot wholly be ascribed to some kind of "intellectual incompatibility."

A final explanation, advanced by Zürcher himself, focuses on the institutional aspect of religion in China, more particularly the different ways in which the two religious systems have spread. It is the difference between the "spontaneous diffusion" of Buddhism and the "guided propagation" of Christianity. In the Chinese context, planning and guidance in the Jesuit mission were factors of weakness, whereas Buddhism was strengthened by the very absence of such planning and central guidance, by its spontaneous and entirely uncoordinated development.

The question of success is indeed an intriguing one, and the way in which Zürcher deals with it through a comparison with Buddhism has its fruitful aspects. There are, however, some methodological problems related to the general question of "success." The most important one is: 1) On the basis of which criteria does one academically define the "success" of a religion. The most common criterion is statistics. This method, although used by most authors in an explicit or implicit way, raises many questions: on what basis does one statistically determine success: the number of adherents (what percent of total population?), the degree of adherence (how does one define adherence?), their increase (how fast should the increase be in order to speak of success?), the social level (to what extent should the number of converts among the elite be taken into account?), etc. 2) Or, in more general terms: How to measure the influence of a religion on a culture (by the number of quotations in non-Christian writings?). 3) Related to success are also questions like: how to explain that Christianity seems to have been relatively successful in China in periods of political and economic disunity and weak in periods of political and economic unity? What is the relationship between China's "ultra-stability" and its reaction to Christianity?

Methodological Problems with the Idea of "Success" or "Failure"

Besides the practical problems involved in defining "success," there are some more fundamental problems related to this approach. The question of success or failure is raised in disciplines of both missiology and sinology. Some missiological works or works on the history of the church tried to find an answer to questions like: "What did the missionaries do to introduce and proclaim Christianity in China? How effective were the missionaries and what means did they use?" Church historians were interested in the overall success of the missionaries, the ways by which they led the Chinese to Christianity, and the extent of the influence of Western science and art. Putting Chinese culture as the first focus of research, sinologists study Chinese culture from the point of view of its reaction towards a foreign religion, *in casu* Christianity. Sinologists focus more on the reception "How did the Chinese accept Christianity or Western sciences? How did they react towards the missionaries?"

Both the missiological and sinological approaches are very valuable, and have significantly contributed to a better understanding of this encounter. The analysis attempted here, however, does not primarily fall under the disciplines of mission history or history of China. The main focus in this analysis is the transfer of ideas. Raising the question of success or failure within this approach implies two possible methodological pitfalls: the problems of the impact-response scheme and of essentialism.

Impact-Response; Action-Reaction; Means-Effect

The first pitfall is the paradigm of *impact and response* which has been pointed out by Paul Cohen. This conceptual framework rests on the assumption that the confrontation with Western Christianity had a very important *influence* on events in China. A further assumption is that it was Western Christianity that played the truly *active* role, a much more *passive* or *reactive* part being taken by China.[16] Instead, Cohen proposed a "China-centered approach" which begins with Chinese problems set in a Chinese context.

The most serious breakthrough in this regard, giving full credit to the Chinese side of the encounter, was the stimulating work of Jacques Gernet, *Chine et christianisme* (Paris, 1982). Yet, Gernet's work proves that even the shift towards sinology has in itself not resolved all problems. The aim of the book was not to study the history of Christianity in China, which has been the subject of many writings, but to study Chinese *reactions* to it. As is well known, Gernet considered the result of this transmission to be a failure, because Christianity and Chinese culture were fundamentally and irreconcilably opposed. It appears that this conclusion is partly induced by the fact that he focused on the reactive side, more particularly, the anti-Christian response. Gernet rightly presented the other side of the "success" story, but the question he took as his point of departure (namely, how these reactions could reveal the fundamental differences between Western and Chinese world-views) prevented him from sufficiently presenting the reactions in all their variants.

Closely linked to this paradigm of impact-response and action-reaction is the paradigm of "means and effect." Though means are important to study, the stress on them risks reducing transmission to a matter of instrumentality. Means are then evaluated on their effectiveness, implying that one means is more effective than the other in order to transmit, for example, Christian faith or Western science. Furthermore, one is tempted to speculate on the interchangeability of means. More significantly, in such a context "effectiveness" is conceived as resulting in the transfer of an idea in its purest form, that is, that in the new environment it corresponds as closely as possible to the idea in its original setting. As a result, if a certain theological concept was transmitted in an unaffected way, the means are considered effective, and the transmission evaluated as successful; if not, it would be a failure. Because of differences in the structure of language and thought—aspects stressed by Gernet—such a pure transmission rarely happens, and as a result the whole transmission itself is easily evaluated as a misunderstanding and thus as a failure. Such an approach, however, fails to see that pure transmission is impossible because communication of culture always takes place in a context.

The proposed alternative here is the paradigm of "*interaction.*"[17] We are interested in observing how Westerners and Chinese interacted with each other as human beings, with their ideas, institutions, or technology. Transfer of knowledge between cultures, indeed, happens through the meeting of persons who are the agents of culture. This paradigm does not reject the concepts of impact and response, action and reaction, or means and effect, but considers them to be more descriptive and less evaluative. The paradigm of interaction is interested in both the interaction itself and its result. The symbol of interactive communication is a network which contrasts with the image of the straight line between means and end. The method of interaction is interested in the means so as to observe what means produces what result, rather than to evaluate which is the most effective towards an implicit or explicit end. Instead, this is a descriptive and phenomenological approach.

Essentialism

The second pitfall is the so-called "*essentialist*" approach. It is based on a mostly implicit assumption that China or Europe have a quasi-invariable essence with which they are constantly identified. It concerns the myth of a "Confucian China," at the neglect of "marginal religions" such as Taoism, Buddhism, Judaism, Islam, Christianity, and many other popular religious movements. Essentialism is often linked to what is generally considered more important. When one considers "Christianity in China," for example, it is usually associated with keywords such as "Jesuit missionaries at the court, cannon, Rites Controversy," and rarely with "Chinese converts, popular rituals, local community leader."

Although one cannot completely avoid certain generalizations, the phenomenological approach proposed here uses a method of "differentiation." It tries to take into account at least four dimensions: time, space, social level, and classification of learned disciplines. In other words, opinions about astronomy at the end of the Ming were different from Qianlong's time and so was the European involvement; an anti-Christian movement in Shandong did not necessarily correlate to a similar movement in Fujian; the appropriation of clocks by the Kangxi Emperor was not exactly the same as the one by craftsmen in Canton or the elite in Jiangnan; transfer of knowledge in the field of medicine is not necessarily the same as in the field of music.[18] In discussions about Christianity in China, these aspects are all too often brought together under the same denomination of "China" which is fixed once and for all.[19]

The essentialist pitfall also applies to Europe. One often classifies the missionaries under the same denomination of Europeans, sometimes making the distinction between orders like "Jesuits" and "Dominicans." But even within the Jesuit order there were clear differences in educational background between, e.g., an Italian and a Portuguese.

By making all these types of differentiation one may end up stating nothing more than that any case of cultural diffusion is particular. We will attempt, however, to show that from the particularities one may still draw some general conclusions concerning the phenomenon of cultural transmission.

An Alternative: An Interactive and Differentiated Play

One could use the metaphor of a play in order to more explicitly present the approach of interaction and differentiation. In the traditional missiological approach, the play is mostly conducted in a European language, the protagonist is the missionary and the possible converts and opponents are the antagonists. The play usually ends with the successful conversion of a number of Chinese, despite the opposition by others. In the sinological play, the language is primarily Chinese, and the Chinese are the protagonists, the missionary being the antagonist. In the final scene, the theme is no longer necessarily Christianity but Chinese history, the missionary and the convert occupying a marginal place. In a play inspired by the history of cultural transmission, the setting is still China ("China-centered approach"), but there is a great variation in the themes of the different scenes, and the place the actors occupy in it: Chinese converts, sympathisers, opponents, missionaries, etc. One is less interested in the final scene, which resembles more an open end, but in the process, change and variation of interaction of the different scenes, trying to observe the different actors from their own point of view. One is less interested in whether one side understood the other, and vice versa, but in what type of interaction was established, and in the heterogeneity of the reactions.

Types of Transmission

The main focus here is the *transmission* or *diffusion* of certain cultural elements, both ideas and material elements, from seventeenth- and eighteenth-century Europe to China or, formulating it from the point of view of the receiver, the process of *borrowing* of these cultural elements by China. In this section we will first situate this transmission within a larger framework of types of transmission, using general characteristics of the process of diffusion. In general terms, the transmission between Europe and China can be called external, strategic, holistic, active, and cross-cultural.[20]

External (from Outside)

Cultural change can arise through origination, which means that the process of change comes from within the society, such as in cases of invention or discovery. These processes of origination were happening in late Ming or early Qing China as well as in Europe at that time. Here, however, we are interested in diffusion, which means borrowing *from outside* the society. The subject under investigation is a clear case of such *external* diffusion, i.e., the transfer of elements between two cultures which were geographically, and also in terms of communication (travel by sea took at least one or two years), clearly separated. In the late sixteenth and early seventeenth centuries, China and Europe were quasi-unknown to each other, even though they had communicated in the past. As a result, the missionaries who arrived can be considered to have been relatively unaffected by Chinese culture before their arrival.

As is often the case in external diffusion, foreigners tend to *reproduce* their original culture in the new culture. In other words, the behavior and ideas of the missionaries reflect to a large extent the state of their native culture at the moment when they left it. Methodologically, this means that in order to understand the actions of the missionaries, one has to study the religious, cultural, socioeconomic, as well as the political realities from which the missionary has come.[21] This background deeply affected the way in which he designed his missionary activities in China. For instance, the fact that Jesuits in China insisted so much on Aristotelian philosophy can be understood by its place in the *Ratio Studiorum*, the uniform study program for Jesuits. And the relatively reduced place of the Bible in their preaching activities can also be explained by the quasi-absence of the Bible in the Renaissance Catholic Church. The reproduction of knowledge was not merely reproductions of a general cultural background, but was also individually linked. When asked about mathematics, for instance, Matteo Ricci (1552–1610) based the Chinese translation of Euclid's *Elements of Geometry* on the textbook of the work made by Christophorus Clavius (1538–1612) at the *Collegium Romanum* where Ricci had studied. Reproduction of cultural elements, then, calls essentialism into question since reproduction is often particular. Though *Ratio Studiorum* was a common study program for all Jesuits, this program was applied in very different ways in the European formation centers and these differences were accordingly reflected in China. There is a clear difference, for instance, between the way in which Francisco Furtado, SJ (1589–1653) (from Portugal) or Alfonso Vagnoni, SJ (1568–1640) (from Italy) reproduced Aristotelian philosophy, which seems to find its reason in the different curricula they attended during their formation period. Moreover, production and reproduction take place in a specific cultural context, which implies that some elements are *not* being reproduced in a different context. For instance, one will search in vain for an obvious reproduction of the so-called reformation and counter-reformation activities of the Jesuits in China, because they were not in a context of predominant intra-church conflicts.[22]

As a result, the study of a transmission from without calls for a constant combination of both external and internal cultural developments and of a methodological interaction between the origin of an idea and the audience to which it is addressed.[23] For instance, an analysis of "Euclidean geometry" (1607, 1631, 1723), shows the evolution of the transfer of geometry. The authors' selection in these different texts was caused by the authors' proper education and the elements which they found most appropriate to their audience. Therefore, the interactions between the two civilizations cannot be epitomised as a static encounter between two immutable entities, but the changes both in China and in Europe have to be taken into account to understand their interactions.

Strategic

If in general terms, diffusion may be strategic or non-strategic, depending on whether or not the transmission calls for extensive preparation, the diffusion of European ideas in seventeenth-century China was to a large extent a *strategic* diffusion, because it was accompanied by a relatively clear plan of operation. The Jesuits were well prepared before leaving Europe, had a clear sense of mission, and once in China, established a conscious strategy to reach the emperor. As pointed out by Zürcher above, the "guided propagation" of Christianity differed considerably from the non-strategic "spontaneous diffusion" of Buddhism. Moreover, some elements which initially were considered accessory by the missionaries, later turned into a strategy. The Jesuits did not go to China with the clear intention to introduce sciences and the first Jesuits were not particularly prepared for it. But this became a clear strategy, when they requested their headquarters in Rome to send Jesuits trained in special domains, and towards that end even organized propaganda campaigns in Europe (e.g., Nicolas Trigault, 1613–1619;

another example are the so-called six French "King's Mathematicians") sent to the Manchu court by Louis XIV in 1685, and appointed correspondents of the Académie Royale des Sciences. In return for this patronage, they were to use their scientific capacities not only in the service of evangelization, but also for the advancement of science in France.[24] There were also changes in the Jesuits' strategy. In the first fifty years, access to the Throne was limited and Jesuits mainly tried to rely on the sympathy of *literati*. After ca. 1630, Jesuits made a double shift: in Beijing they mainly sought imperial protection and contacts with court officials who became more important than the *literati*, while at the local level (e.g., Fujian) they moved their attention to the lower levels of the *literati* and to commoners.[25]

The Chinese side initially engaged in a *non-strategic* borrowing, but at times it became *strategic*. The clearest examples are the proposals for calendar reform and the projects for translation by Xu Guangqi (1562–1633) His aim was to integrate (*huitong*) Chinese and Western astronomy, rather than to replace the former with the latter. Under his supervision, a special Calendar Office (*Liju*) was created. Twenty-two works, composed at this Office (besides a few written before 1629) and presented to the emperor between 1631 and 1634, formed the *Chongzhen lishu* (Chongzhen Calendar Compendium).[26] Other examples of strategic borrowing were the successive Qing emperors' employment of missionaries for very specific goals: Jesuit cartographers for the survey of the empire (which resulted in the famous *Huangyu quanlantu*, known in the West as the "Kangxi Atlas") and Jesuit architects and engineers for the construction of the "European palaces" at the Yuanmingyuan.[27]

Holistic

While transmission can be selective, when only a very limited number of cultural elements are diffused, the exchange that took place in the seventeenth and eighteenth centuries was a *holistic* and *comprehensive* type of exchange. It was not a diffusion of religious ideas or practices only, but also of sciences, technology, arts and crafts; not only ideas (sometimes called stimulus diffusion) but also material elements were transmitted. The holistic aspect appears clearly in the categories that are used to designate specific scientific fields. The categories we use today like "philosophy," "medicine," "astronomy," however, are primarily modern categories which were not all settled in the seventeenth and eighteenth centuries. For instance, only in seventeenth-century Europe did botany gradually established itself as a distinct science. During the same period in China, the concept of botany, as a science *per se*, did not yet exist. The Chinese approached the study of plants as a part of the general Neo-Confucian philosophy of "extending one's knowledge through the investigation of things" (*gewu zhizhi*). The only available literature, which became the main source of information for the missionaries, consisted of encyclopedias, horticultural treatises, and books, called *bencao* (*materia medica*), which were usually illustrated and introduced plants, as well as animal, mineral, and even human products considered medicinal.[28]

The present-day researcher is fully capable of analyzing these categorical differences, but at times fails to see that he or she applies modern categories which were not used at that time in the same way as they are now. A clear example is that of "religion." A major pitfall for researchers today is, while living in an academic context in which "science" and "religion" are strictly separated, to read this separation back into the seventeenth century both in China and in the West. Such clear separation, however, did not exist at that time; it only started to exist mostly in circles with which missionaries hardly had any relationship. Missionaries and Chinese scholars certainly interpreted each other on the basis of their own system, sometimes even of each other's system, but they both functioned in a world (Chinese *and* Western) in which fields like the sacred, mathematics, philosophy, sciences of heaven, sciences of human beings, etc., could be distinguished but were not strictly separated.[29] Therefore our present-day misunderstanding of their exchange might well be bigger than their own misunderstanding of each other's system in those days. We indeed tend to consider the exchange less comprehensive than it actually was.

Active

In general terms, diffusion is said to be active or passive, depending on whether the borrowing society participates in the diffused element or whether it is merely subjected to it or reduced to the role of observer. Because of the predominant impact-response paradigm, the Chinese partner has often been regarded as a passive or responsive element. It appears, however, that the Chinese played an *active* role in the exchange. The relative absence of power—religious or scientific ideas were not imposed by (military) force—and the small number of foreigners in China helps this active role of the borrower come to the fore. The fact that the transmission was not merely enforced, can be seen in the wide collection of anti-Christian writings.[30] They show that Chinese, especially *literati*, not only had the possibility and freedom to refuse Christianity but also to oppose it intellectually.

A good example of the Chinese sense of initiative was the diffusion of cannon: Chinese converts took the initiative to buy cannon in Macau, and the first treatises on Western military techniques and technology were not written by foreigners but by Chinese.[31] In addition, while the Jesuits themselves were initially not very interested in translation projects of works on mathematics, it was due to the insistence of converts like Xu Guangqi (1562–1633) that they engaged in such time consuming and lengthy activities. Later on, this insistence by Chinese (converts) on practical learning was one of the reasons which prevented Jesuits from engaging themselves in other translation projects like the translation of the Bible.[32]

Conversion stories by Chinese also confirm the active role played by the converts in their conversion.[33] The question of active participation also needs to be investigated with regard to Christian communities in China. It seems that community leaders and lay-catechists played a vital role in the continuity of the community and in the transmission of faith, since many communities were only visited once in a while by a priest. While it is a general tendency of scholarly studies to stress the role and responsibility of the missionary or transmitter, recent studies confirm that this role should not be overemphasized.[34] Such overestimation often stems from a greater methodological interest in the role of the transmitter than in the borrower.

Cross-Cultural

While the focus in this analysis is on the diffusion of cultural elements from Europe to China, one should not forget that there was also a transmission the other way, from China to Europe.[35] This *cross-cultural* interchange already took place in China. Europeans in China are sometimes discussed as if they themselves remained entirely unaffected by Chinese culture, but the life of the Europeans living in China, without the modern means of communication, was very different from European life. And the longer they stayed, the more they became removed from contemporary European lifestyle. The accommodation of missionaries to the Chinese lifestyle was not restricted to external influences, since their mental framework was also put into question. When the Jesuits arrived in China, they soon agreed that the practices of Buddhism and Taoism, considered as the "sects of the idolaters and sorcerers," should be considered "false religions," thus imposing their own categories. The first Jesuits, however, were so impressed by the Confucian moral teachings that they had difficulty in calling them "false," though they were unable to recognize them as fully "true." They called *ru* the "sect of *literati*," and considered their rituals "political" and "civil." This Confucian morality was then to be supplemented with revealed Christian doctrine.[36]

Another example of cultural interaction in China is "Figurism," an exegetical method based on the European typological exegesis, "ancient theology" and the Judaeo-Christian cabala. The figurists believed that one could find in the ancient Chinese texts "signs" (figurae) referring to Christian revelation. Figurist missionaries seem to have been considerably affected and sustained in their work by Chinese collaborators, an aspect that needs more exploration.[37]

The vectors of the transmission to Europe were mainly, but not exclusively, the missionaries who returned to Europe. They carried with them manuscripts, which became, due to the effective printing industry in Europe at that time, quickly and widely spread. This resulted in different types of cross-cultural transmission. Whereas in the seventeenth century the sciences introduced by missionaries had contributed to a renewal of Chinese astronomy, in the eighteenth century they contributed to the development of European astronomy, by providing data at the time European academies systematically collected them worldwide.[38]

A clear case of cross-fertilization was in the field of cartography. By means of world maps, on the one hand Jesuits introduced a new view of the world in China, while on the other hand they relied on the information of Chinese cartographers to introduce a better knowledge of Chinese geography to Europe.[39]

There was also a transfer of technology. Jesuits sent back to Europe models of Chinese agricultural devices such as a winnowing machine and a seed drill. These made an important contribution to the revolution in northern European agriculture from the seventeenth to the nineteenth centuries.[40] In certain cases, as in botany, the transfer from China to Europe was more significant than vice-versa. Chinese botany in the form of seeds, plants or illustrations aroused great interest among European botanists and the learned public.[41]

Cross-cultural transmission also occurred in the fields of literature and linguistics. The exchange brought Europe into contact with types of languages unknown until then, and obliged researchers to question their traditional schemes of interpretation. Interestingly enough, the European view of China in Western literature of that time, has been much better studied than the Chinese view of Europe at the same time.[42]

Result: Typology of Interaction

After having situated the exchange between China and Europe in the seventeenth century in a broad framework of types of transmission in the previous section, this section will look at some specific results of the exchange in China. As pointed out earlier, we will adopt a descriptive and phenomenological method which does not start from a normative or evaluative question (like failure or success), but which attempts to simply observe the interaction between Europeans and Chinese at that time. It is in this neutral sense that the term "result" is used.

Extent

A first way to describe the extent of this interaction is to classify the different types of exchange according to the categories in which the interaction took place. The *Handbook of Christianity in China*, for instance, is divided in some general categories, such as religion and ethics, science and technology, arts and crafts. These were further divided into disciplines such as philosophy, theology, ethics, mathematics, astronomy, botany, technology and mining, medicine, ballistics, geography, painting, music, architecture, linguistics, etc.[43] These lists show that the *extent* of the interaction was very wide. As mentioned before, there is an unavoidable difference between present categories and those at that time in Europe or China. An approach which divides the transmission according to scientific disciplines has the advantage of allowing a better analysis of which component parts are borrowed and which represent retention of older traits. The disadvantage, however, is that one risks to break up cultures involved and the transmission into small separate and independent components, while the categories are in fact interrelated and closely linked to each other. The way in which the scientific disciplines were transmitted can be quite different from what one would expect today.

A clear example is ballistics. In Europe, the art of calculating where a cannonball would arrive depending on its weight, the force used, and the length of the cannon, was a sophisticated seventeenth-century application of the section on "heavy and light" (*gravia et levia*) in Aristotle's treatise on *Physica*. Europeans were not only more advanced than the Chinese in making cannon, but also able to transform mathematical and physical knowledge of ballistics into mechanical calculating devices (such as squadra, sector, sight, etc.) by which gunners could promptly estimate the appropriate amount of gunpowder and the angle of elevation to be used for balls made of different materials and targets at various ranges. In China, Jesuits placed ballistics on almost the same level as astronomy, because both were a practical application of mathematical sciences. This method of transforming mathematical knowledge into calculating devices was an essential part of the scientific developments in Europe. By contrast, the Chinese at that time, while operating cannon, could rely on nothing but experience.[44]

There was also an intrinsic link between mathematics and music, since the latter, considered as mixed mathematics in the seventeenth century, aimed at transposing sounds into mathematical formulae. In the compendium *(Yuzhi) Lüli yuanyuan* (Imperially Commissioned Source of Pitch-pipes and Calendar), completed in the beginning of the Yongzheng reign (1723–1735), one finds Western and Chinese works on mathematics, astronomy, and music. According to some researchers, the association of these three fields points to the influence of the *quadrivium* (i.e., the four disciplines of arithmetic, geometry, music, and astronomy) of the Jesuit *Ratio Studiorum*. The link between calendar and the pitchpipes was a traditional one: both were about measuring and setting norms for the cosmos. Since numbers, that is, mathematics, were used in both, putting the three disciplines together would not seem strange to Chinese readers. The rationale put forward to justify it was borrowed from the Classics, the origin of all this learning being mainly located in *Yijing*.[45]

The extent of transmission did not only concern the link between different disciplines, but also subdivisions within a certain discipline. An interesting case is the transmission of medicine. In the interaction between China and Europe in the seventeenth century, there was only an exchange at the level of practical medicine, such as treatment by herbs or pulse diagnosis. The exchange on the level of anatomy, however, was very limited. In the European classification of sciences, medicine was considered a "theoretical science" which had as its aim "the sole knowledge of truth." At that time, anatomy was not in the first place oriented towards healing— the absence of good anesthesia made it difficult to apply detailed anatomical knowledge to the treatment of suffering people—but towards pure knowledge. As a result, what Jesuit translators of anatomical works aimed at was not the transfer of a practical art such as surgery, but the transmission of the whole complex of Aristotelian thought that was the foundation of Christian thought, in which anatomy had its place. Though some Chinese scholars were interested in this theoretical approach, most were interested in practical medicine.[46]

Level of Appropriation

A second way to analyze the transmission is to categorize the results according to the level of appropriation. One can construe a spectrum with two extremes. One extreme is the case of *total absorption*, that is, the appropriation of a foreign element in its total purity; the other extreme is *total rejection*. This spectrum can be used for the borrowing of foreign cultural elements by the native (or foreign) culture, that is, elements that are either accepted or rejected, but also for the agents of both cultures involved. In Chinese culture: from converts to opponents; on the foreign side: from the accommodationalists to those who plead for the destruction of native religious practices.

While the cases of total appropriation or total rejection are rather exceptional, most types of transmission can be classified between these two extremes, since in the end what is borrowed inevitably contains elements of both cultures. Anthropologists and historians of religion use a wide variety of terms to describe this result: mixture (*mélange*), syncretism, hybridization, *métissage*, fusion, amalgamation, etc.[47] While these terms often attempt to describe the same phenomenon of cultural exchange in a rather neutral way, they also often incite emotional reactions among scholars. This is linked to an a-priori expectation that a "successful" transmission is a transmission which keeps the cultural element in its "pure" form. While it is possible to investigate this success rate (cf. remarks in aforementioned intermezzo), the phenomenological approach that we apply here is interested in understanding the process of interaction itself. Therefore, we will use a whole range of metaphors and analogies to describe the process.

Translation

One of the most important means of cultural transmission is translation. In this process, the transmitter tries on the one hand to represent accurately the original culture, and on the other hand to make it understandable to the new culture. In order to do so, the transmitter has different options: to translate a term (and/or thereby to create a new term), to transliterate it, or to use the two options more or less at the same time. All these options have been used in the exchange between Europe and China in the seventeenth and eighteenth centuries. Characteristic for this exchange is also that translation was mostly done in close cooperation between foreign missionaries and

Chinese of whom only the former knew both the original and Chinese languages.

Translation is a good indicator of the differences that exist between cultures at a given point in history, but also of the way they bridged these differences. Most attention is usually paid to problems in the translation of theological and philosophical terms, but similar problems arise in other fields. Translation in the field of anatomy, at first sight, appears to be easy since, in principle, the human body in the East and in the West is the same. Translation here, however, reveals the different ways in which the two cultures view the functioning of the body. While in the field of technology, astronomy or mathematics, the relatively high number of Chinese terms equivalent to the Western notions seem to indicate the high level of correspondence, new terminology clearly indicates the transfer of new knowledge.[48] The case of music is particularly interesting since it reveals the translation of one type of notation to another type of notation.[49]

In these translations one finds a whole variety and complexity that can be found in translations that occurred between other cultures. Each group read into the other's language and behavior possibilities that the original speakers had not intended or foreseen.[50] Sometimes the missionaries consciously adopted the key concepts of the native culture. Giulio Aleni and Alfonso Vagnoni, for instance, described the major aspects of Western ethics in terms directly borrowed from the canonical *Daxue*: *xiushen*, self-cultivation (*ethica*), *qijia*, regulating the family (*oeconomica*), *zhiguo*, ordering the state (*politica*) and *ping tianxia*, bringing peace to the world.[51]

A literal translation could end up in the creation of a new notion: for example, *jihe* was originally a translation of the Aristotelian notion of quantity, also used to render the term magnitude. However, most readers of *Jihe yuanben* were unfamiliar with the ten categories, so that eventually the term came to refer to the content of the work, that is, geometry.[52]

The translation work entailed creating not merely new terminology, but also a new style. For instance, the new mathematical discourse aimed at showing "that through which things are the way they are" (*suoyiran*), providing not only methods (*fa*), but also explanations (*yi*).[53]

Object: What is Affected

When one raises the question of what is affected, then cultural transmission may occur in a wide variety of aspects of the object that is transmitted: the content, structure, or configuration; the form, meaning, use, or function, etc.[54] There are many examples of this variety of changes in the object of transmission during the exchange in seventeenth- and eighteenth-century

China. Visual arts are a good example. In some cases of transmission by painting, the *form* of representation has changed, as for instance the sinicization of the Madonna in the form of Guanyin. In other cases, the *scenes* have been completely transformed according to Chinese pictorial conventions. The European "narrative" pictures in which several successive scenes are combined in a single composition have been reduced to straightforward renderings of the main scene, eliminating all the secondary ones. Elements of the original have also been rearranged; shadowing has been left out, and the Western linear perspective has been changed into the traditional Chinese "isometric" perspective.[55] In several cases, the European artists had to adopt the *instruments* like brush, ink, Chinese pigments, paper, and silk. They had to give up painting religious and historical subjects and devote their time to Chinese landscape painting, portraits, animal, and flower painting.[56] The rendering of the form could clearly affect the transmission of the *usage*. Limitations of technological illustration in China, for instance, was one of the reasons why practical Western agricultural instruments became useless in China.[57] The form could also affect the *meaning*. For many Chinese, Western paintings were clever but had no inspiration.[58] Finally, the *function* could change as well. A religious painting which was primarily an object of worship for the missionary, often became a sign of prestige for the emperor.[59]

One should also point out some *structural* and *institutional* changes. It is significant that the organization of the church in China took very much the shape of a Chinese social organization. Christianity in China was not constructed around parishes as its basic structure, but around associations with important lay leadership. As such, the borrower shaped the transmitted institution.[60] Yet, the transmitter brought about new institutions and functions as well. By their choice to accommodate to the lifestyle of the Confucian elite, the Jesuits in the end played two different roles that typologically belonged to two different spheres: on the one hand the ideal of the Confucian teacher or moral guide, on the other hand the priest involved in ritual practices like mass, baptism, expulsion of devils, confessions of sins, etc., which resembled more the activities of a Taoist priest or Buddhist monk. This double role was experienced as incompatible by many Confucians.[61]

The statistics made by the missionaries point out another institutional concept of being a Christian. Traditional Chinese statistics about religions record the professionals, since they clearly identified themselves as belonging to a religious group and from them the explicit commitment to the state orthodoxy was expected. But statistics rarely record the "believers." Indeed, the ordinary believers rarely identified themselves as belonging to a religious faith; they rather tended to identify with certain rituals. In the Christian concept of religion, the aspect of faith is more determining, and from Western statistics appear the growing consciousness of belonging to an exclusive group within Chinese society.[62] Finally, an interesting institutional change was the geographical and institutional division of China into dioceses, headed by a bishop or vicar who was appointed by the Pope in Rome. There were hardly any comparable precedents in Chinese tradition. And these divisions, though they were based on the Chinese administrative divisions, functioned autonomously.

Manner

Another way to look at the result of the interaction is to focus on the manners of change. These are very diverse and different authors analyzing this process use different terms for them.[63] Since I have developed some of these with regard to changes in content or configuration in theological or moral issues in the thought of Yang Tingyun,[64] I will limit myself here to enumerate briefly some of these categories.

Substitution happens in the case when one existing cultural element is replaced by another with the same function, use, or meaning.

Loss consists of dislodging an existing pattern without at the same time providing a substitute.

Incrementation takes place by introducing additional elements into the culture without a corresponding displacement.

Retention arises when elements of the existing culture are retained and combined with the borrowed elements.

Selection occurs when certain elements of the borrowed ensemble are selected for borrowing while others are not.

Counter-accommodation is the rejection of an accommodated form of the foreign culture, but the acceptance of its (so-called) most authentic and original form.

Reinterpretation is the process by which notions, terms, concepts, and symbols, acquire a new meaning because they function in a different context.

Restructuring happens when the same information is restructured in a different way in the borrowing culture or leads to a new structure in which frames of both the transmitting and borrowing culture are involved.

A Complex Whole: The Metaphor of Textile

The above typologies tend to present the interaction of cultures as something static and clearly distinguishable. Nothing is less true. Such interaction is complex and dynamic. Instead of a using conceptual categories, I would like to use several metaphors to render this complexity.

A first metaphor is the one which considers the transfer of culture as a *transplantation of organs* (a metaphor which we will further develop in a section below entitled "Theory of Danger"). It has the advantage of considering the diffusion as a dynamic and living process, which also includes the risk of rejection. The disadvantage, however, is that in the case of transplantation an organ can only replace another organ with the same usage and function, while as already appeared from examples above, cultural diffusion is much more complex.

A second metaphor is that of a *graft*.[65] This metaphor has the advantage of exposing how a small element (scion) is grafted on a preexisting and stable element (stock), which if successful, bears fruit. It shows that the borrowing is not necessarily a negative experience, but can contribute to the flourishing of cultural element. The adoption of European mathematical and astronomical knowledge was experienced by certain Chinese in this way. The disadvantage of this metaphor is that a successful graft often requires the cutting off of a considerable part of the living tree.

A third metaphor is the one of *mingling chemical products*. The advantage of this metaphor is that it clearly shows that the interaction between cultures often results in a fusion, mixture, or synthesis of different cultural elements. In the experience of Christianity in China in the seventeenth and eighteenth centuries examples of such fusion abound. Within this metaphor one can sometimes compare the role of the missionary or transmitter with that of a catalyst: it activates a reaction but does not take part in the final result, as is the case with local Christian communities or the transfer of scientific knowledge.

The fourth metaphor is *hydrographic*: the conflux of two rivers, which finally end up in a large sea. It is close to the chemical metaphor but adds some elements, while losing others: the contact between cultures is conceived as a natural inclination, like rivers which follow their own bed for a long time, but finally all end up in a fusion, of which the confluence can never be entirely located since it is an ongoing and even natural process. It is the metaphor used by Joseph Needham to explain the fusion of different scientific traditions, as for instance the fusion between Western and Chinese mathematics and astronomy in seventeenth-century China.[66]

A last metaphor is the one of *texturing a textile*. It is less alive than the former metaphors, but, by the image of weaving, it has the advantage of insisting on the complexity of the diffusion, on how borrowing is often like the interweaving of many different threads and fibres. Moreover, "text" is based on the same etymology as "texture," *texere*: to weave, join, fit together, fabricate, construct, build, etc. Within the Chinese (Christian) texts, which are the primary sources for our study, one often finds the same cultural mixture as in textile.

The metaphor of textile allows us to look at what happens to specific fibers, but also to look at the usage, function, form, and meaning of the textile as a whole. The metaphor of textile helps us understand how at the same time, within the same person, or within the same geographical setting, or the same social group, there can be very different reactions. One person can accept certain religious ideas, while rejecting or discarding some scientific ideas and vice versa. Similarly in the same place some people can oppose diffusion while others support it. These can all coexist within the same textile.

An existing fiber (concept of *shangdi, tian*), is disrobed of its different layers of interpretations (e.g., *li* or *Taiji*) and reestablished in its (so-called) original state (personal God), while it is also linked with a new thread partly constructed on fragments of the existing textile (concept of *Tianzhu*, constructed on *tian*).

An existing fiber (concubinage) is taken away without replacement, while another fiber (monogamous marriage) is reinforced.

An existing fiber is reinforced: Confucianism is valued while Buddhism and Taoism are rejected.

A new thread is integrated, only after some parts have been removed: some Chinese Christians accept the moral but not the eschatological dimension of the Christian notions of heaven and hell.

The new thread is restored to its so-called original state: this happens when Chinese converts prefer transliterations (*ya-ni-ma* for *anima*) to translations (*linghun*), because transliterations would represent the "original" idea more closely.

The new thread fuses with the existing textile, which adds or reinterprets some elements of the new thread (god as *dafumu* and *dajun*).

A new thread replaces an old thread with a similar meaning or function: Christian heaven and hell, practice of fasting, and associative life replace Buddhist practices and institutions.

An existing thread receives a new color: for example, burial practices which are christianized.

By being woven into the existing textile, the new thread receives a different context: Jesus Christ is put into the genealogy of Yao, Shun, Yu, and Confucius.

An existing and new thread are juxtaposed: morality books in which Confucian and Christian stories are juxtaposed to illustrate Confucian-Christian virtues.

A new thread reactivates an older thread: in the field of painting, the example of Western paintings reactivated to some extent a taste for a certain realism in portrait painting and an interest in descriptive detail, perspective and new visual angles in landscape painting.

These examples should sufficiently illustrate the complexity, dynamism, and variety of the cultural transmission at that time.

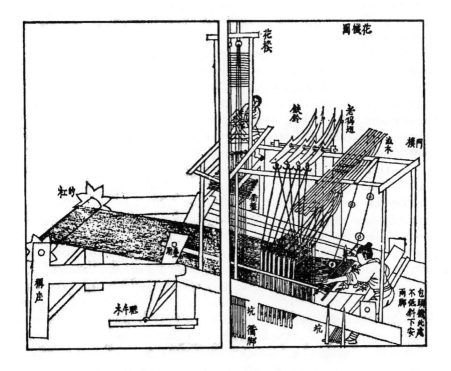

From Song Yingxing's *Tiangong kaiwu* (1637).

Terminal Aspects of Transmission

While the former section observed particular results, this section focuses on the terminal aspects of the transmission. This term designates the overall results of the constant change through diffusion and the constant multi-directional shifting from adoption to rejection.

Growth and Decline

A first way of bringing to light the terminal aspects of transmission is to take into account the long-term growth and decline pattern of transmission. This pattern can be numerically and statistically determined.[67] An important aspect influencing the growth is whether the contact is continued on a regular basis. Some Christian communities disappeared because they lacked such continuity, for instance during the expulsion of missionaries to Canton in 1665–1671. More importantly, however, is the capacity of a community to organize and perpetuate itself. In this regard, a study of the second half of the eighteenth century still deserves more attention, because, though the number of clergy was very low at that time, there seems to have been an increase in membership in many local communities. The fact that the large majority of the clergy was Chinese priests, who became agents of cultural reproduction, is significant. Moreover, in the final decades of the eighteenth century, there are cases where Christianity is transmitted as a kind of family cult without any intervention of a missionary or priest.[68]

The growth and decline pattern also pertains to the diffusion of scientific or artistic knowledge. This pattern can be studied from the point of view of the rationale used by Chinese scholars with regard to the acceptance of Western sciences. In the early seventeenth century up to and including the calendar reform, the initiative was in the hands of influential converts who promoted "Western learning" as a type of concrete studies (*shixue*). In the late seventeenth century, however, the atmosphere had changed. The emperor and scholars advanced the influential theory that Western science "originated in China" (*xixue zhongyuan*), which enhanced self-confidence, since Chinese traditional sciences had still some strong points in comparison to Western sciences.[69] In the late eighteenth century, "the Chinese were still extremely interested in technological advances and in what the West had to offer. The evidence was readily available to Europeans who chose to grasp it. Yet when in public the Chinese denied such an interest, primarily for reasons of domestic politics, Europeans, similarly influenced by developments at home, took that denial as evidence of an entire mental attitude: ingrained xenophobia and a concomitant resistance to progress."[70]

Social Embedding

A second terminal aspect, closely linked with the former, is how knowledge becomes socially embedded, or in other words, how ideas or cultural elements introduced from one culture into another lead to the constitution or reorganization of social groups. The most obvious examples of this are the communities of Chinese Christians. As is clear from the entire seventeenth and eighteenth centuries, Christian communities were not established as parishes, i.e., geographical units around a church building, but in Christian communities (*hui*), often according to age, sex, and social background, with lay people as responsibles (*huizhang*). In the late Ming period, several of these communities were patterned on Confucian or Buddhist models. In early Qing they were a mixture of European-inspired congregations and a Chinese way of social organization.[71] One of the major characteristics of these associations is that they were "communities of effective rituals." One of the characteristics of religion in China, and not only in China, is that a religion proves its worth by the immediate efficacy of its rituals. In most cases, the proven efficacy of these rituals, the happy discovery that "they work," appears to be a primary motive for conversion.[72] In this way a *christianitas* was constituted.[73] It was a community of mutual support, in the general fight against all kinds of fear (disease, death, demons, natural disasters). The regular intervention of the supernatural, by way of miraculous healing, rescue from disaster, appearance of auspicious objects, revival from temporary death, etc., in such a community was the way in which the efficacy of the faith was sustained. There are not many indications that the elite was less susceptible to these interventions. The difference in appropriation[74] between literary elite and the lower levels of society of these supernatural interventions, however, is that they were constitutive of the formation of the communities among common people, while the elite had looser and more individualized relationships with the priests, partly because they had higher mobility potential.

There are several other types of social embedding caused by the introduction of knowledge. There were loose networks of people who wrote prefaces to books about Western learning. Other examples of loose communities are the networks established by officials opposing Christianity.[75]

Reproduction of Knowledge

Another terminal aspect is the reproduction of knowledge by the native culture. Historically, it is not always easy to measure this reproduction since many sources have been lost. One type of reproduction is the ability to reproduce a technique, like in the case of painting or clock making. The most obvious way of measuring reproduction, however, concerns the reproduction by means of the printed word. It refers not only to the number of quotations adopted or reproduced, but also to the prints and reprints of books.[76] The reproduction of books expands the terminal aspect, since a certain aspect of knowledge that is not accepted at one time can become more acceptable at another. In this regard, the link between late nineteenth–early twentieth- century and seventeenth–eighteenth-century Christianity in China deserves to be studied in greater depth. Not only did missionaries and Chinese from the early twentieth century reprint many earlier writings, but some texts like *Mingli tan* that were hardly used in the seventeenth century, were appropriated on a larger scale only in modern times.[77]

Related to this reproduction of books, is reproduction of language. Some scientific words that are used in Chinese today date from the seventeenth century.[78] Probably more influential, however, was religious language and especially liturgical language. Christian communities in the middle of the twentieth century have recited some prayers in exactly the same way as in the seventeenth century.

Imperial Prestige and Power

One of the particular aspects of Christianity in China is the diffusion of European knowledge at the Chinese court. Here the terminal aspects are also of specific nature. For instance, the diffusion became a means of legitimation. By offering their services to the Kangxi Emperor, the Jesuits provided him with an accurate calendar which was an important means of legitimizing power. In addition they contributed to settling the dynasty's rule over China through their survey of the empire (1708–1818) which resulted in the famous atlas *Huangyu quanlantu* (1718).[79] Such a map, produced under imperial sponsorship, was viewed by the Manchu ruler as a necessary contribution to the successful policing of scattered local governments, to the maintenance of imperial control, but above all, to the understanding of the geographical situation and extent of the empire.[80]

In general, Kangxi's study of Western science was motivated by curiosity, but also by the way he chose to construct his imperial character: having realized that his officials were unable to judge astronomical matters, he strove to be in a position to control all issues and arbitrate all controversies, and to display his ability to all his subjects. In line with the late Ming trend of "real learning," he regarded most of the skills which the Jesuits put in his service as tools for statecraft. Western learning was thus integrated into the body of Confucian learning that the emperor—who emulated the Sages of antiquity—mastered.[81]

There were other manifestations of prestige. For instance, the sovereign drew a dual benefit from clocks: private enjoyment and public display of his prestige and power. Other instruments of imperial prestige were portraits, both official and private, recording the glorious events of his reign: military victories, political banquets, tours of inspection in the south, and also the celebration of anniversaries or festivals, as well as the great ritual ceremonies. The missionaries, clockmakers, or painters were at this service.[82]

Reinterpretation of Culture

A final terminal aspect that can be observed is the reinterpretation of one's own and the other culture as a result of the cultural exchange. Such an exchange, indeed, often leads to a certain imbalance and uneasiness with the new cultural elements, while members of the native culture usually search to restore a certain balance and consistency. Cultures employ several strategies to attain this aim.

One method is the *renaming* of cultural elements in order to make them acceptable. A clear example of this is the changes in naming Western learning, especially astronomy. At the beginning of the seventeenth century it was called "Western" method (*xifa*), but by the middle of the seventeenth century, when there was more opposition to the fact that something from abroad would take the place of the native culture, it was renamed "new" learning (*xinfa*) by scholars who still wanted it to be introduced.[83]

Another method is the use of the *historical* argument or the quest for historical precedent. The above-mentioned theory that Western science "originated in China" (*xixue zhongyuan*) is such a case. As a reaction against the overemphasis on Western theories and methods, many Chinese scholars turned to the history of Chinese mathematics and astronomy. (Native) history was also used by missionaries to make their ideas acceptable. A well-known example is Ricci's theory of original Confucianism combined with the story that during the Han dynasty China sent a mission to the West to adopt Christianity, but that it was misled on the way and brought back Buddhism.

Missionaries used other strategies to restore the imbalance, Chinese converts and non-converts, such as the emphasis on the congruity and complete compatibility between the minority religion and Confucianism, the notion of complementarity, etc.[84]

The problem of imbalance also occurred on a very limited scale in Europe. A clear example of this is the question of world chronology. The Chinese chronological tradition, with its continuous line of rulers from the beginning of the third millennium B.C., challenged the Biblical pattern, especially the universal flood which no Chinese could have survived. As a result, some European theories identified the biblical disaster with a flood occurring during the reign of Emperor Yao, and proceeded to associate Chinese rulers with persons of the Old Testament.[85] This reinterpretation integrates elements of foreign culture in its own historical framework which is itself reshaped.

Explaining the Transmission: Conditions Favoring or Discouraging Diffusion

After this overview of types of diffusion, with the results and terminal aspects of transmission, one can consider some conditions which favor or oppose diffusion.

Dynamism of the Culture Itself

One of the most important principles of interaction between cultures is that, in a first phase, a culture only accepts those elements of the other culture which, in one way or another, fit into its own pattern or framework.[86] In the case of religion this means that if there is no convergence at all between the transmitting culture and borrowing culture, between the new religion and existing religions, then conversion or the passage from one to another would anthropologically speaking be impossible.[87] In other words, the first aspect to be observed is the inner dynamism or movement of a culture, and how the diffused elements of the foreign culture follow this movement.

The transmission of science in late Ming times is a clear example of this principle. If Chinese scholars were interested in the science brought by the Jesuits, it was because prior to their arrival Chinese *literati* had developed an interest in practical learning. The search for "solid learning" or "concrete studies" (*shixue*) was a reaction against some intuitionist movements originating from the Wang Yangming school in the late sixteenth century. According to Wang Yangming (1472–1528), the principles for moral action were to be found entirely within the mind-and-heart (*xin*) and not outside. In the early seventeenth century, the influential intellectual and political movement of the Donglin thinkers reestablished the importance of "things in the world." Officials and scholars searched for concrete ways in which to save the country from decay.[88] It is this preceding quest that fostered the unique interaction between them and the Jesuits.[89]

A similar movement encouraged the reception of Christian moral teachings. The Christian view of objective and external ethical principles fit in well with the heteronomous approach of morality proposed by Donglin scholars as a reaction against the subjectivist and intuitionist tendencies of the Wang Yangming school. Moreover, late Ming *literati* responded to the crisis and moral decadence of the society by writing and circulating morality books (*shanshu*) which taught people to do good and avoid evil. Christian moral tracts that aimed at the same purpose were readily diffused by such *literati* in Shanxi-Shaanxi at that time.[90]

Prior Knowledge

An element that is linked to the former but more focused on the individual, is provided by educational sciences: the concept of prior knowledge.[91] It refers to an analysis of the learning process which considers that the most important single factor influencing learning is what the learner already knows. In fact it can be connected with an ancient adage of Thomas Aquinas who took it from Boethius, namely that "everything that is received in something else, is received in it by the way of the receiver" (*omne quod recipitur in aliquo recipitur in eo per modum recipientis*).[92]

The influences of prior knowledge on the learning process are very broad. For instance, prior knowledge increases the availability of information during the learning process and leads to a higher level of retention. More importantly for this subject is that prior knowledge implies the presence of relevant schemes into which the new information will be fit. Typical examples are the categories of sciences used in the seventeenth century in China and in Europe. Chinese translations of Western books were classified according to preexisting Chinese bibliographical categories, but at the same time put these categories into question. For instance, in the bibliographical chapters of *Mingshi* (Ming History), completed in 1739, mathematics came at the very end of *xiaoxue* ("lesser learning"). All other works included in *Tianxue chuhan* were mentioned in the astronomy section (*Tianwen*). *Chongzhen lishu*, attributed to Xu Guangqi, was in the following section, devoted to calendar (*Lizhi*).[93]

Prior knowledge sometimes explains why there is little transmission. For instance, one explanation for the relatively little diffusion of technology is that by the time the Jesuits were active in China, the Chinese had already developed a sophisticated technology that compared very favorably with what had been available in Europe until then.[94] Related to prior knowledge are cognitive strategies or heuristic methods which are also reflected in visual devices. The clearest example of this is that of the different notion of perspective, which strongly influenced the transmission of technology and anatomy by illustrations.

The inner dynamism and prior knowledge can be illustrated with the textile metaphor. The fact that culture can be transmitted is because there is already a textile present. The complexity of this textile determines how the knowledge will fit into the existing pattern or how new knowledge will be woven on the already existing threads.

Emotional-Affective Characteristics

Transmission of knowledge is always mediated, and in most cases it is a personal mediation. As a result, the transmission is influenced by the emotions which the transmitter and borrower have towards the transmitted object and to each other.

A clear example of this affective or aesthetic side of communication was music. To the ears of missionaries, Chinese music sounded decidedly off-key (*disconsonantia*) and as a result mutual transmission was rather limited.[95] Such emotions are often associated with a value judgment which concerns questions as to whether the other is good or bad, whether or not one likes the other, whether or not the other is an equal.[96] Clear examples of negative value judgment include the attitude of missionaries towards Buddhism and Taoism. Because both sides resembled each other too much, they often engaged in a process of inflated difference (see below).

There were, however, also very clear examples of positive value judgment. It is not always easy to deduce aspects such as enthusiasm, curiosity or admiration (as in the case of Ricci's memory) from written texts, though the authors certainly must have had such emotions. One emotion, however, that has been thematised is the one of friendship. Both Western and Chinese sources indicate that Ricci's natural gift of easily establishing interpersonal relationships must have greatly influenced the way in which he was accepted. There are other examples in which the reduced distance between teacher and disciple favored transmission.

Patterns of Transmission of Knowledge

One should also take into account the traditional patterns of diffusion of knowledge in a certain society. An important aspect of the Chinese society is network-building (*guanxi*). The relatively rapid and wide radiation of the spread of Christianity in very different Chinese provinces during the first fifty years was due to the importance of personal relationships and network-building in Chinese society and the high mobility potential of the elite (officials changed position every three years). Because of these factors, elite members and converts often invited the Jesuits to certain places the latter had not originally planned to settle in. The Jesuits were thus guided in their decisions of where to go.[97]

But the traditional patterns of transmission of knowledge could also make it difficult to diffuse new knowledge. For instance, it was difficult to break through the traditional organization of crafts in China in which techniques were transmitted from father to son(s) generation after generation.[98]

An aspect both encouraging and discouraging transmission of knowledge were the relationships between men and women. The missionaries had difficulty entering into contact with women who were confined to the *nei* sphere of the family. But once these women became Christians they became very active agents of transmission. At home they played an important role in the education of children. Outside they organized themselves in active Christian associations of women.[99]

Theory of Danger

A basic question in transmission is why in certain cases the diffusion of a cultural element is rejected. One of the often advanced explanations is that it is primarily due to a xenophobic reaction: the proposed element is foreign, therefore, inferior and unacceptable. The incompatibility of thought patterns, however, albeit important, seldom appears as a decisive reason, since one finds sufficient examples of compatibility. It is here that one can take up the analogy of transplantation of organs and new developments in the field of immunology. For many years immunologists have been well served by the viewpoint that the immune system's primary goal is to discriminate between self and non-self. The general view was that the immune system reacts against anything foreign and is tolerant of anything that is self. It appears, however, that the system does not really discriminate self from non-self, but *some* self from *some* non-self. Another explanatory viewpoint, therefore, proposes as an alternative that the driving force of the immune system is the need to detect and protect against danger and prevent destruction, and that it does not do the job alone, but receives positive and negative communication from an extended network of other bodily tissues.[100] It is not the purpose to discuss or further analyze this paradigm shift in immunology, but the analogy can shed a new light on opposing Christianity movements in China.[101]

Analogically speaking, one could hold that the primary reason for an opposing movement is not a xenophobic reaction, which distinguishes between self and non-self, but a reaction against something that is experienced as dangerous. Christianity and the Christian doctrine were often perceived as threatening the existing order in China. The question is less whether they formed a material threat, for example, in the case of a military presence, but that they were "perceived" as a threat, that is, challenging the existing order and hierarchy of Confucian ethics.[102] Interestingly enough, the danger theory is confirmed in the attitude of opponents towards the Chinese (self) who converted (become involved with the non-self). They are considered particularly dangerous and there are several cases of anti-Christian incidents in which they were punished much more severely than the foreigners (e.g., Nanjing, 1616–1617; Yang Guangxian's case: five Chinese executed). Unlike the metaphor of immunology, tolerance is often more limited towards "infected" elements of one's own culture than those of other cultures.[103]

The analogy can also be extended to the actors involved in these reactions. Reactions do not only originate from the cells of the receiving body. When an organ is transplanted, certain cells of this organ become activated because they have left their original environment. They send out certain signals which activate and interact with particular cells in the receiving body. Similarly, opponents to Christianity do not only react to "neutral" Christian actors. The missionaries, having left their natural milieu, may well overact towards certain aspects and pronounce more explicitly and more sharply their ideas in the new environment than they would in their original setting. This in turn asks for a reaction by members of the new culture. An example is monogamy, which as the marriage system hardly needed to be stated in Europe but which became accentuated in China.[104]

Related to these reactions is also the phenomenon of "inflated difference": that is the phenomenon in which the average (minority) group, pressed to consolidate its own identity, is prone to dis-identify with others and to play up otherwise negligible differences between those inside and those outside its boundaries.[105] This is very typical for the relationship between Christianity and Buddhism in China. Christianity shared with Buddhism elements such as belief in afterlife, the idea of heaven and hell, the practice of celibacy, etc., which were very un-Confucian. This similarity with the Other (Buddhists) forced the missionaries to differentiate themselves from the Other and emphasize their differences.

Conclusion

Despite its many limitations in scope, Christianity in China in the seventeenth and eighteenth centuries appears to be an interesting "laboratory" for the study of cultural transmission. Without considering it as a model, it is a "typical" case for one major reason, namely that the process of transmission was a complex whole. We have compared this complexity with the complexity of weaving a textile. This conclusion of complexity is largely induced by the method used by many scholars, among them contributors to the *Handbook of Christianity in China*, and that can be described by the following characteristics:

- the importance paid to texts, together with the terminology used in them, and the different layers of text history;
- the confrontation of both Chinese and European sources, which do not always correspond to each other;
- the attempt to understand the historical context, by integrating the differentiation of time, place, and social level; this context concerns both the Chinese and European context, since missionaries tended to reproduce their past in all its differentiation;
- the differentiation according to scientific disciplines, and the place they occupy in the mental categorization of their time;
- the fact that present-day research starts from certain concepts (mathematics, Christian, etc.), the definitions of which only seem to be very clear; through confrontation with Christianity in China they are put into question;
- the fact that more attention was paid to the process rather than the result, to the interaction rather than the paradigms of means-effect or understanding-misunderstanding.

Ilya Prigogine, Nobel prize winner of chemistry in 1977, quotes Karl Popper, who spoke about "clocks and clouds." Classical physics was primarily interested in clocks, while present-day physics is rather interested in clouds. He explains that the precision of clocks continues to pursue our thinking by making us believe that we can attain the perfection of particular and even unique models which are studied by classical physics. But what predominates in nature and in our environment are clouds, which have a complex, vague, changing, fluctuating, always moving form. The model of clouds supposes that all reality contains a part of incomprehensibility and that it always hides a degree of uncertainty and inconstancy.[106]

Though the missionaries of the seventeenth and eighteenth centuries introduced clocks into China, the complexity of their transmission of cultural elements resembles more the clouds in Chinese paintings.

Chinese Renaissance:
The Role of Early Jesuits in China

LI TIANGANG

Renaissance as a Chinese Question

The European Renaissance was one of the most important movements in modern history; it has formed the foundation for much of modern life. Did the Chinese experience their own renaissance, just as Europe and America and other nations did in their pre-modern history? According to Liang Qichao, one of the most influential thinkers of twentieth-century China, the answer is yes.

In October 1920, Liang Qichao wrote a preface for Jiang Fangzhen's book, *The History of the European Renaissance* (*Ouzhou wenyi fuxing shi*). Liang's preface turned out to be even longer than the book itself, a fact that embarrassed both himself and Jiang. Consequently, Liang decided to publish his preface separately, under the title of *An Outline of Scholarship of the Qing Era* (*Qingdai xueshu gailun*). At this time, Jiang Fangzhen agreed to write a preface for Liang Qichao's book,[1] but limited it to a relatively short introduction.

What specific idea or concept compelled Liang Qichao to write so much that he could not limit himself to a terse preface? Liang's answer was simple: the Chinese Renaissance itself. He realized that Chinese culture had also experienced a renaissance during the late Ming and the early Qing period. Furthermore, he believed that the Chinese Renaissance was strongly influenced by Jesuit missionaries, and Chinese translations of Western works, very much as the Italian Renaissance was influenced by the works of Asian cultures.

Chinese scholars of the late Qing loved to use "big words" borrowed from Western languages to express themselves. Kang Youwei called himself "a Chinese Martin Luther," and his establishment of a Church of Confucians (*Kongjiao hui*) was carried out under the label of "Chinese Reformation." The Hundred Days Reform (*Wuxu bianfa*) has been called an imitation of the "Glorious Revolution" in England, and both Zhang Taiyan and Sun Zhongshan regarded themselves as having undertaken a Chinese "French Revolution" to overthrow the rule of the Qing dynasty. And later, Hu Shi and Chen Duxiu initiated a movement called the "Chinese Enlightenment." Clearly, the one remaining, and perhaps the most important term that was yet to be used was the "renaissance."

"Discover the value of old learning" (*huifu guxue*) and "scientific induction" (*keguan guina*) were two important concepts that convinced Liang Qichao and Jiang Fangzhen that the Han School of Learning between the Ming and Qing was indeed a Chinese Renaissance. "The liberation of rediscovering ancient learning, and by the objective sciences replacing subjective thinking were the essence of the Qing academic spirit, and have the same resonance as the European Renaissance."[2] Liang Qichao was academically correct in pointing out that the Chinese Renaissance brought about the rebirth of the scientific spirit of the ancients.

An evaluation of the Han School of Learning during the Qing dynasty within the perspective of modernization is beyond the scope of a single paper. The question that most attracted me was mentioned by Liang Qichao: the influence of Western learning introduced by the Jesuits during the Ming and Qing dynasties. Whether the role of Jesuit missionaries had a positive or negative effect, the point is that Chinese scholars met with foreign knowledge, just as the European Renaissance imported foreign knowledge from the East. In another (very important) point of view, it was the Jesuits who helped Qing scholars find a new Chinese way to redefine the Confucian tradition. According to recent studies of the Jesuits contribution to Qing dynasty learning, Western missionaries played a very important role in the late Ming and early Qing period. The purpose of this paper is not only to reevaluate (*pingfan*) the Jesuit contribution, but also to demonstrate that under the influence of Western culture, Chinese scholars came to a deeper understanding of their own traditions. How contemporary Chinese scholars of the Ming and Qing dynasties studied Western leaning and how Qing scholars adopted Western learning to rebuild ancient Confucian tradition are the most important questions here.

"During the Ming and the Qing, the Society of Jesus brought Western sciences to China. They paid much attention to emperors and the scholar/gentry. . . . "[3] It is unusual for late Qing Chinese scholars to acknowledge Western influences on Chinese culture. It is even more unusual for Chinese scholars to compare this history within the Chinese context with the Western experience.

That the Jesuits in China had contributed to the movement of the Chinese Renaissance was the central message conveyed by Liang Qichao and his students. I agree with Liang in that he did not attribute the Chinese Renaissance totally to the Jesuits. I believe that the Chinese Renaissance was rooted in its own soil. But without the influence of the Jesuits, the outlook of the Chinese Renaissance would have been much different.

Chinese Jesuits and Their Influence

This paper intends to focus on a few Jesuit missionaries in China, namely Matteo Ricci, Giulio Aleni, Johann Adam Schall von Bell, and Francesco Brancati, as "Chinese Jesuits." It is not only because these men had Chinese names and wrote in Chinese, but also because they understood Chinese culture even better than many contemporary Chinese.[4] Clearly, it was not that the Jesuits invented Confucianism,[5] but that the Jesuits gave Confucianism a modern definition. Confucianism had a long tradition of rational thinking. Compared to European Christian tradition at the end of the Middle Ages, Confucian classical studies (*jingxue*) was more a (kind of) knowledge as history, philosophy, morality, even to some degree of theology, than a religious teaching. After many debates surrounding the Chinese Rites Controversy, European intellectuals began to recognize the Confucian tradition in a modern way. Ricci began to define Confucianism as humanism.[6] I am not sure if the Jesuits actually made serious comparative studies between Confucian humanism and European humanism before their use of this term. But we do know that Ricci was convinced by some Chinese Confucian Christians like Qu Taisu and Xu Guangqi that Confucius should not be the enemy, but the friend of Christianity.[7] As Xu Guangqi wrote in his famous article *Bianxue Zhangshu*, Confucius mainly dealt with secular knowledge (*shengqian zhi xue*), but Christianity focused mainly on the knowledge of Heaven (*tianxue*; *shenghou zhi xue*). The study of Heaven or God is by definition theology. Xu Guangqi believed that Christian theology would not be antagonistic towards Confucian secular knowledge; rather they would complement each other. Chinese Confucian Christians did believe that Confucianism was limited to humanism, and so they used Christianity to teach them about God.

Chinese Confucian Christians understood Confucianism in a manner different from the Neo-Confucianism as practiced during the Song dynasty by denying the truth of Heaven (*tianli*) and manifestation of God's will (*tiandao*). They believed that Song Neo-Confucianism lost the original

Confucian truth about God by absorbing Buddhism and Daoism into its doctrine. Xu Guangqi made a judgment about three major doctrines (*sanjiao*) in China: "We believe that Confucius knew many things about the truth of God, but we laugh at the Daoist's stupid activities, making drugs for long life. And we also sigh with the Buddhism bell and drum uselessly from morning to night."[8] The Jesuits told Chinese Christians that they brought three kinds of knowledge: "The highest knowledge is theology. The lower knowledge is humanity, the third is astronomy and mathematics."[9] Xu Guangqi described the system of Western knowledge in terms of Confucianism, in which Christian theology took a higher position, but Confucianism dropped to secondary knowledge. I do not think that looking down upon Confucianism was the Jesuits' original purpose, but systematic knowledge of Western theology enabled late Ming Chinese Christians to feel they could rebuild the lost traditions of Confucianism by studying Christianity. They were told by the Jesuits that Confucius touched much more of the truth about *Shangdi*, or God, than Zhu Xi did. Actually, redefining Confucianism is itself a tradition in the history of Confucianism.

The deferential attitudes toward both early and Neo-Confucianism remained unchanged until early Qing scholars like Huang Zhongxi, Gu Yanwu, Qian Daxin, and Dai Zhen attempted to rediscover Confucianism via the means of the so-called Han School. They had learned much scientific knowledge from the Jesuits, and started to reestablish Confucian theology about heaven, natural law, ritual theory, and moral principles. We often refer to *Qingxue* as factual learning which implies that it is concerned only with scientific and textual subjects, not with speculative matters. But according to my research, Qing dynasty scholars did in fact study *tian*, *li*, *xing*, *dao*, and other topics of Chinese metaphysics. It is true that sometimes Qing dynasty Confucianism criticized Song School Neo-Confucians for "talking too much of *xinli*." Dai Zhen represented the Qing scholars in this aspect. But I believe Qing scholars had their ultimate concern on God and Heaven. It was Dai Zhen himself who tried very hard to rebuild Neo-Confucian theological tradition based on "*xinxue*," and "*shixue*." Dai Zhen's book, *Mengzi zhiyi shuzhen*, represents the highest achievement of philosophy in the Qing dynasty. Almost every Qing scholar talked about *Shengxue* and *Tianxue*. This was a generation of Confucian theology established to meet the Jesuit challenge and criticism. It was a revision of Chinese theology and philosophy in terms of scientific method, a global view, and traditional expression. In other words, it was a philosophical and a cultural renaissance.

Confucian knowledge made great progress during the late Ming and middle Qing period. All of the Chinese classics and their historical heritage were put on the desks of Ming and Qing scholars.' If Wang Yangming freed the Chinese mind in the way of morality, then surely we can say that the Han School of Learning of the late Ming initiated a renaissance in scholarship for Chinese academics. This renaissance involved a revival of ancient learning. A new form of rational thinking based on logical and empirical methods was established. Meanwhile, works on Western theology, philosophy, ethics, astronomy, geography, and mathematics were translated into Chinese, and the Chinese scientific tradition of the "men of science" was rediscovered,[10] or in reality, reestablished, on the basis of the Han School of Learning. The concepts and ideals from Christian theological theory were integrated into Confucian cosmology. As is well known, Qing dynasty scholars made great strides in the fields of philology, linguistics, editing, and proofreading. This was equally true of the European Renaissance masters in the fifteenth century. We cannot attribute all of this to Jesuit workings, but much evidence has shown us that the Jesuits' very much translations stimulated and influenced Han Learning. I believe that it is one of reasons that Liang Qichao called this movement a Chinese Renaissance.

As recognized first by Liang Qichao, and later by Hu Shi in the 1920s, the Han School was stimulated by the Jesuits' Western learning. The Han School was established by Xu Shen and Zheng Xuan during the Han dynasty. During the Qianlong period of the Qing dynasty, "Every school and every scholar followed the Han masters like Xu, Zheng, Jia, Ma" (*jiajia Xu Zheng, renren Jia Ma*.) On the surface we may find that it was the Han academic tradition reborn. But if we read them carefully, we can find many resources were contemporary. Among them, the Jesuits' influence was very evident. For example, the important Xi'an scholar Li Erqu, who studied Christian theology, made a Confucian saying, "Look into myself three times each day in a ritual ceremony" (*wu ri sanxing wushen*), which is very close to Christian confession.[11] Qian Daxin, the most important figure among the Han School scholars, adopted the *Jiutianshuo* which was apparently inspired by Jesuit astronomical techniques. The God (*Shangdi*) he believed in did not have the same meaning with the Christian creator, but he changed his students' mind that Li was not the source of the world. Huang Zhongxi disagreed with the Jesuits' theology, but his Confucian explanation for *tian*, *di*, *hun*, and *po* are very close to Ricci's *Tianzhu shiyi*, and Xu Guanqi's *Bianxue zhangshu* in many aspects. What Fang Yizhi learned from Jesuits in theology, philosophy, astronomy, linguistics, languages, and technology in the late Ming was discussed by Willard G. Peterson in his paper, "Fang Yizhi and Western Learning."[12]

Of course, the Jesuits used Confucianism as a tool for their own mission. But the reason for Chinese Christian emphasis on Confucian humanity was not only a strategy. We could not say that Christianity looked down upon Confucianism, putting it on a lower level and Christianity on a higher. They attempted to define the universal truth, of a Christian God within Confucianism. The Jesuits thought in a Confucian way by defining human beings in moral terms, proving the existence of God with secular knowledge, borrowing terms from the Chinese classics, and taking the enemies of Confucianism (Taoism and Buddhism) as their own. They defended Confucianism when the Chinese Rites Controversy took place in Rome and Paris. They did it in this way because they shared the humanistic attitudes of the Renaissance. That was why their influence on Chinese scholars was so great, and so efficient, during the Ming-Qing transition.

Early Modernity Promoted by Jesuits

The contribution of the Jesuits in China is still controversial among Chinese historians. How to evaluate the early Jesuits' activities in the late Ming and early Qing is still in process in recent years. But at least it is now safe and just to say that the Jesuits' activity was one of the most important factors for Chinese modernization.

The Chinese Renaissance was always rooted in its native soil. It is mainly a local movement rather than an international one. In this sense we would not say that the Chinese Renaissance of the late Ming and early Qing was started by Jesuits, or transplanted from Europe. There were many domestic factors contributing to the Chinese Renaissance, and Chinese modernization between the Ming and Qing. But we should acknowledge the fact that China in the late Ming dynasty was no longer an isolated society. Foreign influence on China, especially in the southeast coastal area, was so strong that we cannot neglect it as an important factor in this significant era of social transition. Chinese Marxist historian Hou Wailu refers to this period as the Early Chinese Enlightenment (*zaoqi sixiang qimeng*), and the Rising of Chinese Capitalism (*zibenzhuyi mengya*).[13] In our sense, they were also talking about the early modernity of China. They dealt with the Jesuits' activities and international trade carefully, though they intended to prove that domestic social relationships and productive forces decided Chinese modernity.

American and European historians also believe there was a renaissance or enlightenment during seventeenth-century China. The distinguished French historian Jacques Gernet believes the Chinese Renaissance started from the Song dynasty.[14] The outstanding American intellectual historian, William T. de Bary believes that the Chinese initiated their own enlightenment during the Ming-Qing transition.[15] In his textbook, *The Rise of Modern China*, Immanuel C. Y. Hsu disagrees with the common view that modern Chinese history starts from the Opium War. In his view, Chinese modernity appears in the Ming dynasty, with the arrival of Portuguese traders and the Jesuits.[16] Compared with the crisis of confidence in the late Qing, Chinese scholars were self-assured in making dialogues with other civilizations. The Jesuits, together with European monarchs and the popes, respected Chinese culture. This made communication between cultures much healthier and easier than it was in the nineteenth and twentieth centuries. That is why we mention Ricci and the Jesuits with appreciation so frequently. The Jesuits contributed much to modern Chinese culture.

In what ways did the Jesuits contribute to Chinese modernity? May I only suggest a few of them. First of all, the Jesuits raised the ideal of global culture through cooperation with Confucianism. Any "renaissance" is a local movement in every nation. But one of the most important features of any renaissance man is a global viewpoint. Ming and Qing Confucianism opened people's minds to the whole world, and was no longer limited to the Middle Kingdom. The Ming scholars' geographical view was much broadened from the reading of Jesuits' translations. Furthermore, we find that the old Confucian ideal of *datong* (grand unification) was revived through contact with Catholic theology. The most frequently quoted words by both Confucians and Confucian-Christians, and the Jesuits were: *Donghai Xihai, xintong litong* (The East and the West share the same natural law). These were words of the Neo-Confucian scholar Lu Jiuyuan. According to Ricci's explanation, God (*Shangdi*) was the same one for both Chinese and Westerners. Heaven (*Tian*) was the same to everyone living on the earth. People believe that they can share God regardless of the differences in language, custom, ritual, culture, or civilization. If Lu Jiuyuan in the Song dynasty attempted to incorporate some Buddhist features into Confucian tradition, the Ming-Confucian Christians adopted this ideal further into Christianity. Christianity was discussed within Chinese civilization for the first time.

Secondly, Jesuits participated actively in the transformation of Ming dynasty scholarship. The first was two major revolutions of thinking during the Ming dynasty. The first took place in the name of *xinxue* spearheaded by Wang Yangming in the mid-Ming dynasty. The *xinxue* movement freed the thought of Confucian students from political bondage. Many scholars, such as Hou Wailu and Feng Youlan, believed that *xinxue* liberalized the intellectual mind and made the Chinese Enlightenment comparable with the Enlightenment in Europe. When a second intellectual revolution took place in the late Ming, Jesuits met the dramatic change and influenced it in many aspects. As Liang Qichao and Hu Shi pointed out eighty years ago, this time *jingxue*, the Confucian theological theory, had changed into a scientific theory. Knowledge of mathematics, geometry, logic, geography, and astronomy was translated first from Latin, then developed into Chinese classics. They were practiced not only as sciences, but as methods of thinking. Benjamin Elman correctly described this revolution as "from philosophy to philology."[17] The core of the Qing learning was philology. But beyond philology, the essential spirit of Han learning was rational nationalism. Scholars looked for solid links between facts and logical links according to experience. Eventually they traced the links to God in Heaven. As Elman points out, Qing learning became the foundation for modern Chinese culture. The rebirth of rationalism, is a most important factor for every modern nation. Max Weber attributes rationalism to the Reformation, but most historians attribute it to the Renaissance. In China, the Jesuits inspired and helped Chinese scholars rediscover the Han learning tradition and reestablish the spirit of rationalism.

As the European Renaissance man escaped from the old doctrines of the Church, Ming-Qing scholars escaped from the political and moral bondage of *lixue* in (neo-Confucian doctrines). Many Confucians no longer wanted to be a traditional sage (*shengren*) and work for the bureaucracy; they wanted to be scholars. They studied the kinds of knowledge which traditional Confucianism neglected for so long. Late Ming scholars studied everything, from plants to machines, from cannon to anatomy. From their point of view, knowledge was the basis for morality. The method of thought became more important than thinking itself. These new values helped to produce a liberal and objective attitude toward the truth. Their scientific spirit came from these values.

Another traditional Confucian doctrine, "apply Confucian knowledge in social practice" (*jiangshi zhi yong*) was suggested in the Ming-Qing period. Scholars used new knowledge and methods to solve practical problems. Confucian students were eager to acquire knowledge of agriculture, transportation, taxation, industry, technology, cannon making, and so on. They referred to this phenomenon as the rebirth of the Confucian tradition of *liuyi* (the six arts).

The Meaning of Chinese Renaissance

A renaissance is a global cultural phenomenon in world history. Historians adopt the term to describe the development of modern culture. Besides the European Renaissance, we often hear of the Indian Renaissance, American Renaissance, and Latin American Renaissance. Historians use the term both in broad and narrow ways. Broadly speaking, it applies to any kind of cultural revival. In the summer of 1932, Hu Shi gave a lecture at the

University of Chicago called "the Chinese Renaissance." He believed that China experienced a renaissance four times: during the Tang dynasty, the Song dynasty, the thirteenth, and the seventeenth centuries.[18] Hu Shi spoke of the renaissance in a broad sense. But Liang Qichao treats the renaissance in a narrow sense. We combine renaissance with the emergence of modernity. I believe that during the Ming and Qing transition, Chinese culture experienced a renaissance which led Confucian learning into a modern era. A very important fact here is that the Jesuits participated in and contributed to the movement.

Jesuit learning was one of the most important factors that enabled Ming-Qing learning to achieve a degree of modernization. It would not be fair to say Ming-Qing scholars like Fang Yizhi, Qian Daxin, or Dai Zhen were the students of Italian Jesuit Matteo Ricci or French Jesuit Joachim Bouvet, since mostly they ordinarily considered themselves Confucians, and never thought of themselves as students of the Jesuits.[19] But without the works translated by the Jesuits, we cannot explain the sudden changes of thought during the Ming-Qing transition. There were, however, controversies on how to utilize Western knowledge during the Ming-Qing transition. What the Qing scholars followed was the principle of "Using the West, but not to be used by the West." The famous late Qing model, of "*Zhongxue weiti, Xixue weiyong*" (taking something necessary from Western learning into the frame of Confucianism) already existed in the late Ming.[20] With this model, Chinese modernity developed within Chinese culture.

If there was indeed a Chinese Renaissance during the Ming and Qing dynasties, it lasted little more than two centuries, starting from the Wanli era of the Ming dynasty and stopping at the Jiajing era of the Qing dynasty. It was longer than the "Kangxi-Qianlong Prosperity" (*Kan-Qian shengshi*), but shorter than the period we usually call the "Late Imperial." This period coincided with Jesuit missionaries active in China. Many factors led to the end of the Chinese Renaissance. One was the absence of the Jesuits in key intellectual fields after the Chinese Rites Controversy. At the beginning of the nineteenth century, Chinese culture entered a difficult period as the domestic social fabric began to unravel, and another civil crisis happened within the Empire. From then on, the problem was not how to discover tradition, deepen learning, reform old faith, or construct a new civilization. The problem turned rapidly into how to save the imperial government, political system, traditional values, and Chinese-style civilization. This was happening several decades before the Opium War, which traditionally marks the beginning of modern China.

Chinese revolutionaries, from the Taiping Rebellion to the May Fourth Movement, always thought that destroying the old civilization would open the way for progress in China. They believed that revolution was the foundation for a modern society, and it was totally beyond this understanding that it was the Renaissance that supplied a solid base for every modern culture.

Historians tend to treat Jesuits as foreigners and often forget that they lived in China for many years. Some of them (such as Ricci) knew Chinese better than the Chinese, and many of them respected Chinese culture more than their own (such as Louis Le Comte) in some way. Most of them were humanists. They were the sons of the Italian Renaissance. They were pro-Confucian both inside and outside of China. They were not the enemy of China, but friends of China. Even Pope Alexander VII himself said during the Chinese Rites Controversy in 1659: "Missionaries never should export Italy, France, or Spain into China; we just export Catholic belief to Chinese. China should keep its own rites, customs, and civilization."[21] Two hundred and thirty-six years later, the American Protestant missionary Young J. Allen and his colleagues in Shanghai spoke almost the same words. They said that "Christianity in China is not to destroy Confucianism, but rebuild it" (*Jidujiao youyi Zhongguo, jiushi jiao chengguan Rujiao*).[22] The Ming and Qing experience tells us that the development of Chinese culture needs the world, just as the European Renaissance opened Europe to other nations. That is a simple, but not an easy principle to grasp in world history.

The Problem of Chinese Rites in Eighteenth-Century Sichuan

ROBERT ENTENMANN

In the seventeenth and eighteenth centuries, the Catholic Church was bitterly divided over the extent to which Chinese Catholics could participate in Chinese ritual observances honoring their ancestors.[1] Such rituals demonstrated the fundamental virtue of filial piety. If they were ruled idolatrous, Chinese Christians would be torn between their faith and their heritage.

The Jesuit position, articulated first by Matteo Ricci, regarded such rites as not religious but civil, intended to further the ethical teachings of Confucius and the corporate solidarity of the family. Nevertheless, over the centuries these rites had been corrupted by superstition. If the rites could be purified of superstition, Chinese Christians could engage in ceremonies honoring Confucius and their ancestors.[2]

Opponents of this view, primarily Dominican and Franciscan friars and secular priests of the Société des Missions Étrangères de Paris, believed that such rituals were intrinsically idolatrous and incompatible with Christianity. The question, essentially, was whether the average Chinese was, "in his official cult of Confucius and the ritualistic reverence he pays his deceased forebears, so compulsively motivated by pagan instincts that these everyday social acts are actually no less than illicit spirit worship? Or do these aspects of a high ancient culture spring instinctively from some inborn virtue of the race and hence, in themselves, have only a civil and familial function, even though an individual might observe them for obviously superstitious reasons?"[3]

The Société des Missions Étrangères de Paris (hereafter MEP) contributed much to the Church's eventual decision to prohibit Chinese Catholic's from engaging in such rites. The 1693 mandate of Charles Maigrot, MEP, vicar apostolic of Fujian, addressed the problem. Maigrot prohibited Chinese Christians from displaying tablets with the inscription *jingtian*, which he translated as *coelum colito* (worship Heaven).[4] He ordered missionaries not to permit Christians to perform, participate in, or even attend ancestral rites or the sacrifices offered twice annually to Confucius. Moreover, Christians were not to display tablets honoring the dead in their houses if the tablets carried the characters *shenzu* (spirit ancestor), *shenwei* (seat of the spirit), or *lingwei* (seat of the soul). Only the name of the dead and the character *wei* could be permitted, and then only if accompanied by a declaration in large characters stating Christian beliefs about death and filial piety.[5] Maigrot's views ultimately shaped Rome's decision to prohibit Chinese rites, and contributed to the Kangxi Emperor's hostility toward missionaries.[6]

The Rites Controversy appears at first sight to have little direct relevance to the history of Christianity in China. It was largely an internal conflict within the Church, generally between the Jesuits on one hand and the mendicant orders and secular priests on the other. To some, the controversy was "a purely European affair which can easily be omitted when attempting to understand the history of Christianity in China from a Chinese perspective."[7] Indeed, the voluminous polemical literature on Chinese Rites was written almost entirely by Europeans. (The only important Chinese contribution was by a non-Christian, the Kangxi Emperor).[8] The collection of essays edited by Mungello, despite its value in furthering our understanding of the Rites Controversy, reveals little about how the controversy affected ordinary Chinese Catholics.[9]

Nevertheless, Chinese Catholic behavior was profoundly affected by the Rites Controversy. Rome eventually prohibited Chinese rites in the apostolic constitution *Ex ille die* of Clement XI in 1715, reaffirmed in 1742 by Benedict XIV's *Ex quo singulari*.[10] The decision not to allow the accommodationist practices of the Jesuits shaped the way Chinese Catholics were instructed and, hence, how they behaved.

In the decades that followed, Sichuan province was one of the most fruitful of all Catholic mission fields in China, and the rich documentation of that mission provides a means for examining the effect of the Rites Controversy on ordinary Chinese Catholics. In particular, the journals of the French missionary Joachim Enjobert de Martiliat and the Chinese priest Andreas Ly (Li Ande) show in great detail the nature of their pastoral work among Chinese Catholics, including their efforts to enforce the Church's rulings on ritual observances.[11]

Chinese Rites and the Early Mission in Sichuan

Jesuit missionaries introduced the Catholic faith into Sichuan in 1640, just as Ming rule was waning. Their mission collapsed during the rebellion of Zhang

Xianzhong and the Manchu invasion.[12] Sustained missionary work resumed in 1702, when four European missionaries returned to Sichuan: Luigi Antonio Appiani and Johannes Müllener, members of the Congrégation de la Mission (Lazarists), and Jean Basset and Jean-François de la Baluère, MEP. Appiani was arrested and expelled because of a local disturbance in 1707; the three remaining missionaries left the same year because of the conflict between Tournon and the emperor. Müllener returned to reestablish the mission in Sichuan four years later; he became vicar apostolic of the province in 1715. For many years he preserved the province as an exclusive mission field of the Lazarists, but in 1734 he was joined by Martiliat of the MEP.[13] Müllener died in 1742; his successor as vicar apostolic was an Italian Dominican, Luigi Maggi. Upon Maggi's death in 1744, Martiliat, now vicar apostolic of Yunnan (but based in Sichuan), became the superior of the mission in Sichuan. The MEP received exclusive mission jurisdiction over the province in 1753.[14]

As early as 1703, when the Chinese Rites Controversy was far from settled, the issue of Chinese rites posed practical problems for missionaries in Sichuan. One Chinese Christian funeral, for example, included a dramatic performance, accompanied by music. Even worse, reported de la Baluère, although there was a cross on the casket, "the devil also wished to carry his banner next to that of Jesus Christ." A paper banner with the characters *daoli* (principle or truth) was affixed to the casket. After the burial, friends and relatives prostrated themselves before the grave, each devoutly pouring a cup of wine onto it. De la Baluère asked about the custom, and was told that it was a sacrifice one makes "to the devil."[15]

By the time the missionary effort revived after 1715, the Church had strictly prohibited any ritual observance that could be considered "superstitious." The French priests of the MEP and the Chinese priests they had trained were bitterly hostile toward what they regarded as Jesuit laxity toward paganism, and they insisted upon strict adherence to Christian practice as defined by the apostolic constitutions prohibiting Chinese rites.

No occasion caused more tension between Catholic and indigenous customs than funerals, which brought Christian and non-Christian relatives and acquaintances together. Nearly all Christians had friends and relatives who were not Christian, and often one's conversion to Christianity created conflict, either within a family or between it and its neighbors. To many non-Christians, the Christian rejection of ancestor worship suggested contempt for family solidarity and the norms of filial piety. In response, Martiliat emphasized the Fourth Commandment. "We would be seen as barbarians by the Chinese without it," he wrote.[16] While officiating at a funeral where some non-Christians were present, Martiliat said some of the liturgy in Chinese rather than Latin to show that Christians respect the dead.[17]

Martiliat reported on a Christian funeral at which Andreas Ly presided in 1735. Ly refused to allow any non-Christian ritual, nor were non-Christian mourners allowed to prostrate themselves before the grave or bind their heads in white mourning cloth. More than eighty Christians participated in the funeral. "All this took place peacefully," Martiliat wrote, "despite a great multitude of infidels, drawn by curiosity."[18]

Another funeral showed that religious differences within a family need not lead to conflict. Antonius Tang (Dang Huairen), a Chinese priest, was renowned for his work to persuade Christians to forsake "abuses," particularly ancestral tablets.[19] In 1740 he presided at the funeral of a Christian woman. Her sons, one an apostate and the other a non-Christian, asked Tang to perform Christian rites. Tang had the sons affix a sign to the door of the house, explaining that the woman had been a Christian and that she had expressly ordered that no "vulgar" ceremonies be performed at her funeral, only rituals that conformed to the Christian faith. Thus the two sons, though not Christian, demonstrated filial obedience by following Christian practice. "All the pagans obeyed," reported Martiliat, and no "superstitious" tablets were posted.[20]

The Church prohibited the common Chinese practice of displaying tablets honoring one's ancestors. Nevertheless, some Chinese Christians refused to remove them. Maggi was dismayed to find many under his jurisdiction engaged in superstitious practices (or practices he considered superstitious, according to Martiliat). In two families he found tablets honoring ancestors, and set before each of them a table with an incense burner and a lighted lamp. When one family refused to remove the shrine, Maggi refused to say mass there. At the other house the shrine was removed so Maggi could say mass.[21]

Converts, of course, were instructed to destroy such tablets and any pagan images. Martiliat reported in 1743 that a family in Jiading had been fervent idolators who had taken vows of perpetual fasting and had been tied to the White Lotus sect. The wife was more superstitious than the husband, according to Martiliat. A catechist, Jovita Tching, persuaded the family to embrace Christianity. They burnt their old images and replaced them with a tablet inscribed "Almighty Lord, Creator of Heaven and Earth."[22]

Andreas Ly's Pastorate in Sichuan

After the proscription of Christianity in 1724, European missionaries could no longer work openly in the Chinese interior. The Catholic evangelization effort, in Sichuan as well as elsewhere, depended increasingly on Chinese clergy.[23] Unlike Europeans, they were not highly visible to non-Catholics and could carry out their clandestine work with relatively little likelihood of discovery. The most celebrated Chinese priest of the time was Andreas Ly.[24] Born into a

Chinese Catholic family in Shaanxi in 1692 or 1693 (not long before his family moved to Sichuan), he studied as a boy with Basset and de la Baluère, and left China with them in the aftermath of the Rites Controversy in 1707. He continued his studies at the Collège de St. Joseph, a seminary for training indigenous clergy in Ayudhyia, Siam.

After his ordination in 1725 he returned to China, serving in Fujian and Hubei. In 1734, after an absence of a quarter century, Ly returned to Sichuan. For many years he worked with Müllener and Martiliat. In addition, several other Chinese priests worked in the province at that time: Paulus Sou (Su Hongxiao), Joannes Baptista Kou (Gu Yaowen), Stephanus Siu (Xu), Lucas Ly (Li Shiyin), and Andreas Ly's seminary classmate, Antonius Tang.[25]

Ly, trained by the MEP, had a thoroughly European education. He not only spoke but also wrote Latin, and to a great extent he had become alienated from his own cultural heritage. He shared with the MEP a profound hostility toward indigenous Chinese religion, suspicion of any compromise with elements of Chinese culture which could be in conflict with Christianity, and what one Jesuit scholar calls "a rigid Augustinian theology of damnation."[26] On one occasion, Ly edited a book of meditations by an unknown Jesuit and expunged terms prohibited by the papal bulls *Ex ille die* and *Ex quo singulari*.[27] Ly had a deep suspicion of the Jesuits; he even recorded in his journal the opinion of the Dominican martyr Pedro Sanz that the Jesuits were anti-Christ.[28]

In 1746 a persecution drove all European missionaries from Sichuan, leaving Ly as the senior Catholic priest in the province.[29] He maintained contact with the MEP by sending his journal, written in Latin, by courier to Macau and thence to Paris. For a decade Ly worked without direct European supervision. In 1756 he was joined by François Pottier, later vicar apostolic of Sichuan.[30] Ly closed his journal in 1763 and died in 1774.

Ly had long been concerned with problems presented by funerals. In 1739 he had composed an essay in Chinese on funerals, setting forth the Church's beliefs and practices and attacking the "superstitions and errors of the infidels." Martiliat praised the essay and posted it in his mission house.[31] That essay has been lost, but Ly's journal reveals his opinions and practice regarding funerals. Although no cultural relativist, Ly recognized that different places have different practices and quoted a well-known aphorism of St. Augustine to that effect.[32] Ly himself occasionally followed Chinese practices permitted to Chinese Catholics. When his mother died in 1742, Ly posted a tablet with her name, wore white mourning garb for 100 days, and did not shave.[33] Nevertheless, in his advice to a new missionary, he reiterated the rulings of *Ex quo singulari*, including the prohibition of food offerings at the bier of the deceased (although a kowtow at the bier or grave was permitted). Quoting Pope

Stephan I (d. 257), he declared that any innovation in practice had to conform to the faith.[34]

Ly was concerned about Christian comportment at the funerals of non-Christians. In 1751, he reports approvingly, a Christian named Benedictus Tseng behaved correctly on such an occasion. He contributed to the costs of the funeral of a non-Christian neighbor and genuflected before the bier while taking care not to show reverence to the tablet. He accompanied the corpse to the grave, but did not join in the funeral banquet because it was a Christian fast day.[35]

Because Ly was for some time the only Catholic priest in a province the size of France, he was not able to supervise closely all five thousand or so Christians under his jurisdiction. In 1748 he was unable to officiate at the funeral of Simon Tching. Tching's friends and family, including two apostates, buried the body "according to gentile customs and with superstitious tablets and ceremonies." Paulus Tching, evidently a relative, did not attend the funeral for that reason, "lest quarrels and contentions arise between Christians and gentiles, who have long been very hostile toward each other."[36]

Christianity, of course, had been proscribed for over two decades at this time. As a rule Christians were tolerated by their neighbors and ignored by local officials. Nevertheless, during times of persecution or tension with non-Christians, Chinese Catholics often found it prudent to conform to traditional practices. The persecution of 1746 had led some Christians in Tongliang district to bury their dead according to ceremonies presided over by Buddhist clergy. "It is difficult to carry out Christian prayers and ceremonies in such bad circumstances," Ly admitted.[37] In contrast, at a funeral three months later there was no customary musical performance with tambourines and gongs, "much less other indecent ceremonies," Ly reported approvingly, "only speeches and tears." Almost thirty local Christians participated.[38]

Nevertheless, for several years Andreas Ly found it a constant struggle to keep funeral rites free from illicit practices, especially the use of ancestral tablets. After 1751, however, references to such incidents no longer appear in his journal. Perhaps by then Christian norms for funerals were well established among Sichuan's Catholic population.

Moreover, for nearly forty years, from 1746 to 1785, Sichuan's Catholic population suffered no serious persecution, allowing relatively free pastoral activity and Christian religious practice. Similarly, the practice of displaying tablets with forbidden inscriptions in Christian households also appears to have gradually disappeared after the 1740s, when references to the practice disappear from Ly's journal.

Generally Christians had displayed such tablets in order to avoid difficulty with their neighbors or local officials. In 1739 the magistrate of Qianwei district investigated fasters presumably affiliated with the White Lotus sect. The neighbors and relatives of Christians there used that pretext to intimidate and harass them, forcing them to replace Christian images with tablets with the inscription *tian di jun fu shi* (Heaven, Earth, Ruler, Father, Teacher).[39] During the persecution of 1746 many Catholic families warded off suspicion by displaying tablets with the characters *tian di jun qin shi* (Heaven, Earth, Ruler, Ancestor, Teacher).[40] In Huayang district, relatives of the widow Magdalena Hoang forced her from her land because of her faith and compelled her to display a "superstitious" tablet.[41] In Huayang and in the neighboring district of Jianzhou, magistrates coerced Christians into signing statements of apostasy. They took part, reluctantly according to Ly, in "superstitious" ceremonies and put up illicit tablets—for fear of being betrayed by their neighbors.[42] Occasionally, however, local magistrates found Christian inscriptions acceptable. Two Christians told the judicial commissioner that they had no images, only inscriptions on red paper that read *Li tiandi zhi zhuhzai* (Master who created Heaven and Earth).[43] They also explained how they fasted, which led the judicial commissioner to conclude that they were not members of the White Lotus sect.

In 1747 Ambrosius Yang, fearing persecution, put up a tablet with the inscription *tian di jun qin shi.* After a fire destroyed every house in the neighborhood except Yang's, Andreas Ly assured Yang that Divine providence had protected him, and persuaded him to destroy the tablets.[44] Another incident related by Ly demonstrates that he believed that the displaying of illicit tablets could have supernatural repercussions. During the 1746 persecution, Simon Tching removed Christian images from his house and burned them, along with other evidence of his faith. He put up a "superstitious" tablet and forbade his family to pray or fast. Eventually he fled to a distant region, changed his name, and stayed with his wife's non-Christian relatives. Before long he fell into a critical illness. His host consulted a medium about the disease. A demon replied through the medium, saying that Tching had once worshiped the highest *shen* (God), but afterwards cast aside that God and put up superstitious tablets in his house, a most serious sin. The medium said that Tching should go home as quickly as possible, remove his superstitious tablets, and return to worshiping his *shen,* lest he be too late to repent his deeds.[45] The demon further indicated, by a means of bamboo slips (or *qian*) used in divination, that "three arrows are prepared against him, of which the first two are the open, exposed *yang,* and one hidden behind *yin,* indicating that the sick person should return home as quickly as he can, lest he fail to evade peril because of his tardiness." Simon

Tching returned home, and there immediately ordered the destruction of the tablets, which his mother had already taken down at Ly's direction. After recovering from his illness, Tching related this story to Ly, who administered the sacrament of penance. Ly reports, however, that he did not know with what demon Tching was entangled, and Tching still was "diffident and incredulous." The devil continued to entice Tching into the hell of heresies, Ly reported, but the sacrament of penance denies power to the devil and absolves sins.[46] As we have seen, however, Tching was eventually buried with non-Christian ceremonies.

This curious incident is revealing for several reasons. Ly was certainly not a modern skeptic, and he assumed the reality of demons and magical practices. He believed as well that forsaking the faith and displaying "superstitious" tablets could lead to a critical illness. In this case, Simon Tching's apostasy brought about his illness, and ironically, a medium possessed by a demon urged him to return to the Catholic faith.

The display of non-Christian tablets generally required penance. In the village of Maoping, Christians put up tablets with the inscription *tian di jun qin shi*, probably during the persecution of 1746. Ly accepted their confession, ordered the immediate removal of the tablets, and barred them from communion for one year.[47] Another family, in Xindu district, did not renounce their faith but had displayed the *tian di jun qin shi* inscription at the order of the magistrate. Ly denied them sacraments until the inscription was removed.[48] On another occasion, Ly had four families remove illicit tablets, replacing them with tablets reading *tian di ren wu zhen shen* (True God of Heaven, Earth, Humanity, and Creation). Ly thought a preferable inscription would be *wushi wuzhong ziyou zhi Zhushen* (Lord God in and of Itself Without Beginning or End).[49]

On another occasion a Christian named Eustacius Gheou was unable to remove an illicit tablet from his house. He lived with his landlord and had paid his rent a year in advance. He could not leave without forfeiting his rent, nor could he destroy the inscription or his landlord would evict him. Because Gheou was ill, Ly administered the sacrament of penance on the condition that he destroy the tablet at the earliest opportunity and replace it with a tablet or picture with the appropriate Christian message.[50]

In 1748 Ly visited the house of Joannes Lieou to celebrate mass. Besides Christian images on Lieou's wall, however, Ly found a banner of red paper with the inscription *Hedongtang chang lidai zhaomu Zhushen* (Illustrious and Profound Eternal Lord God of the Eastern River Hall).[51] He declared that the inscription was superstitious and prohibited by papal decrees, and unless it were immediately removed, neither he nor any other Christian could offer prayers in the hall, much less say Mass. Ly celebrated mass in an adjoining room. Joannes Lieou, greatly shaken, told Ly that he had taken down holy images and replaced them with the illicit inscription during the 1746 persecution. Ly had Lieou tear up the banner; thereupon he gave Lieou penance and admitted him to confession.

In 1762 Ly composed an inscription to be posted by "timid Christians." The Chinese text is not preserved, but Ly translates it as "Reverence, Sacrifice, All Glory be to the Ever-Living, Eternally-Reigning, Only True God: This One Lord Between Heaven and Earth, Father and King of Majesty, Worshiped by Succeeding Generations."[52]

Conclusion

Although none of the lay Catholics in Sichuan had any familiarity with the European debate over Chinese rites, Ly certainly was well informed about it. Although he was not formally a member of MEP, he had been trained by that Society. He shared its deep suspicion of the Jesuit order and its previous accommodation to Chinese rites. Ly believed that Chinese indigenous religious practices were incompatible with Christianity, and he accepted without reservation Rome's rulings prohibiting such practices. In his pastorate he endeavored to instruct his charges and prevent them from engaging in what he regarded as idolatry. His greatest concern was that popular indigenous religion might corrupt Christian practice.

In the late 1740s Ly found that several Christian families displayed tablets with illicit inscriptions, most commonly *tian di jun qin shi*. Those who displayed them evidently did so, without exception, in order to avoid conflict with neighbors or local officials. Most had put up tablets during the persecution of 1746, and the inscriptions appeared to have little or no real religious meaning for the families who displayed them. Nevertheless, Ly regarded such tablets as evidence of apostasy, and Christians who displayed them were required to do penance before being readmitted to communion. References to such tablets disappear from Ly's journal by 1749 and rarely appear in the reports of European missionaries in the decades that followed.[53] It appears that Ly and other clergy had succeeded in suppressing the practice. In any case, the decades that followed were relatively peaceful ones for Christians in Sichuan, who had, therefore, little reason to conform to the customs of their non-Christian neighbors.

Funerals, too, often brought Christian and non-Christian practices into conflict. Nearly every Christian in eighteenth-century Sichuan had non-Christian as well as Christian relatives and neighbors, and funerals would bring them together for a short time. During times of persecution or conflict between Christians and non-Christians, funerals could be fraught with tension. On occasion Christians were buried with non-Christian rituals. Nevertheless, by the 1750s these incidents disappear from Ly's journal. By the second half of the eighteenth century, Ly and his colleagues appear to have established orthodox Catholic practice among the Christians of Sichuan.

Sino-French Scientific Relations Through the French Jesuits and the Académie Royale des Sciences in the Seventeenth and Eighteenth Centuries

HAN QI

The French Académie Royale des Sciences (ARDS), founded in 1666, made important contributions to the development of science.[1] From the middle of the seventeenth century, the scientists of ARDS kept close contact with China through the Jesuits.[2] In 1688, a group of Jesuits known as the "King's Mathematicians," led by Jean de Fontaney (1643–1710) and sent by King Louis XIV (r. 1643–1715), arrived in Beijing. They brought with them plans for investigating China and making astronomical observations, as they had discussed earlier with French astronomers. In addition to promoting Christianity, the Jesuits also sought to advance science and glorify the French King.[3] In this paper, I will analyze the scientific correspondence between the French Jesuits and ARDS in the seventeenth and eighteenth centuries, discussing the scientific reports and articles published in ARDS journals.[4] Finally, I will talk about the introduction of Western science into China through the French Jesuits and explain the relationship between ARDS and the *Suanxue guan* (Academy of Mathematics) at *Mengyang zhai* (Studio for the Cultivation of the Youth) during the Kangxi reign (r.1662–1722) in a broader historical context.

French Jesuits and Their Scientific Correspondence with ARDS

In the 1660s, an anti-Christianity movement launched by Yang Guangxian was a key political, cultural, and scientific event in the early Qing period, and had great influence on the development of Western science and religion in China.[5] It led to the arrest of German Jesuit Johann Adam Schall von Bell (1592–1666) and his confrères, and the sentencing of many Chinese Christian astronomers to death. Because of his youth at the time, these events impressed Kangxi greatly. Then a dispute about the calendar directly led Kangxi to study Western science. The Belgian Jesuit Ferdinand Verbiest (1623–1688) began as his scientific teacher. At that time Verbiest was worried about the lack of Jesuit scientists, which he felt might lead to a decline in the future of evangelization efforts in China. In 1678, he made an urgent appeal in a letter to Jesuits all over Europe, and this letter had great influence on the French Jesuits' coming to China. In order to fulfill the task of ARDS, Jesuits were summoned to ARDS in late 1684 and early 1685.[6] A meeting was arranged between them and Gian Domenico Cassini (1625–1712), and Philippe de la Hire (1640–1718). Cassini, then director of Observatoire de Paris, handed a plan to the Jesuits that suggested making astronomical observations in various areas in the Far East, including China, in order to obtain more accurate data. In a history of ARDS, du Hamel also writes:

> A peu près dans la même période, le Père Jean de Fontaney et trois autres pères de la même Société (de Jésus), qui avaient l'intention de faire le voyage vers l'Empire chinois, discutaient sur les contacts mutuels à faire avec l'Académie, tant dans les matières d'Astronomie que de physique. Ils convenèrent avec les Messieurs Cassini et de la Hire sur quelles observations ils avaient à faire dans l'Empire chinois quand ils arrivèrent là-bas, et dans les endroits où ils firent passage pendant le voyage, particulièrement en rapport avec les éclipses des satellites de Jupiter, et ils s'accordèrent sur la correspondance réciproque avec l'Académie. Combien de profit ces (Jésuites) ont procuré pour l'amplification de la science de l'astronomie & de la géographie apparaitra clairement des choses que nous allons expliquer ici après.[7]

Cassini was one of the founders of ARDS. This shows that the French Jesuits' coming to China was closely related to the development of ARDS. Cassini was also very interested in Chinese astronomy. As early as 1689, he had studied Oriental (Chinese) astronomy after receiving manuscripts from the Duke du Maine (Louis-Auguste de Bourbon, 1670–1736).[8] He was interested in these matters because of the relationship between astronomical calculation and the reliability of Chinese chronology. This issue was important because of the varied opinions of Europe on the antiquity of China, often based on false or absurd evidence. One important means to determine China's antiquity was to compare Chinese chronology with accurate astronomical observations. Before leaving for China, Fontaney had already been a respected astronomer. When Fontaney led the "King's Mathematicians" to China, they took many scientific instruments with them. They were charged with making astronomical observations, investigating native Chinese flora and fauna, and learning other technical arts. They arrived in Beijing in 1688, after their journey was delayed for several months in Ningbo.

Regular correspondence between the Jesuits and French scientists of ARDS contributed to the promotion of science. In 1684, Fontaney and three of his fellow Jesuits had been appointed as corresponding members of ARDS. On November 8, 1687, Fontaney wrote a letter to Cassini, asking ARDS to guide them in scientific affairs. He writes,

> C'est donc à vous, Messrs, à prendre vos mesures là dessus pour achever l'ouvrage que vous avez commencé, à nous procurer des aides qui continuent ce que nous allons entreprendre et qui suivent les mêmes idées-à nous communiquer vos lumières, à nous expliquer en détail ce que vous désirez particulièrement, à nous envoyer des modèles c'est à dire ce que vous aurez fait sur les mêmes sujets, c'est à dire enfin à donner à chacun de nous un correspondant particulier dans l'Académie qui nous instruise de votre part sur nos matières et que nous puissions consulter aussy sur nos difficultés et nos doutes. De cette manière j'espère que vous verrez l'Académie de la Chine se perfectionner peu à peu et devenir capable de vous donner bien de la satisfaction.[9]

In 1699, Fontaney and four other Jesuits were designated as correspondents with Thomas Gouye (1650–1725). As suggested by the above passage, Fontaney was most likely the one to request that ARDS designate some of its members as correspondents with the Jesuits.[10]

The regular contact between the Jesuits and the academicians of ARDS allowed many science books, journals, and instruments—particularly astronomical and mathematical instruments used for heavenly observations and map surveying—to pass to Beijing; and helped to spread French science to China, especially in the Kangxi period. The Jesuits also translated into Chinese selections from scientific works sent by ARDS and other groups. At the same time, some French scientists were responsible for informing the Jesuits of scientific activities in China. The Jesuits, for their part, sent scientific reports back to France and answered various China-related questions raised by the French scientists. The correspondence and frequent exchanges enabled the Jesuits in China to keep up with the latest European scientific achievements and to have timely access to academic works by French scientists.

After their arrival in China, the French Jesuits made a great number of observations according to the instructions they received from ARDS. These observations, entitled *Observations physiques et mathématiques . . . envoyées des Indes et de la Chine*, were sent to Thomas Gouye and published in 1692. Based on the astronomical tables of Cassini, Gouye calculated the longitudes of some cities in China using observations of immersions and emersions of Jupiter's satellites. The *Observations* made significant contributions to the development of astronomy and geography. In the *Mémoires de l'Académie Royale des Sciences (MARS)*, some of Gouye's results were published,[11] including the longitudes and latitudes of twelve cities in China. This information helped to rectify the map of China.[12] Abbé Galloys also described Gouye's *Observations physiques* very briefly, believing that it would shed light on the perfection of essential aspects of physics and mathematics.[13]

ARDS was expected to keep in constant communication with the scientific community in France and abroad, to stay abreast of all scientific news, to read and discuss important publications, to repeat significant experiments carried on elsewhere, and to criticize the works written by its own members.[14] The secretaries of ARDS were an important conduit between France and China. Bernard le Bovier de Fontenelle (1657–1757), and Dortous de Mairan (1678–1771) were the most important among them. They served ARDS for many years, arranging the letters and papers they received from the Jesuits and publishing them in ARDS journals.

Although some French Jesuits in China were not appointed as corresponding members of ARDS, they also kept close contact with French scientists, as shown in the exchange between Dominique Parrenin (1665–1741) and Dortous de Mairan.[15] Parrenin arrived in China in 1698. During the Kangxi period, he was ordered to translate European books on anatomy into Manchu. After the Yongzheng Emperor came to power, he began to keep close contact with ARDS. In 1723, he sent a copy of one such anatomical text, translated into Manchu, to ARDS. On February 13, 1726, after having received it, Fontenell reported at a meeting of ARDS:

> J'ay (Fontenelle) porté à la compagnie plusieurs choses que le P. Dominique Parrenin missionnaire de la Société de Jésus luy a envoyées de la Chine, un livre d'anatomie qu'il a fait en Tartare, des racines de la rhubarbe & c. On a commencé à lire des mémoires instructifs qu'il a faits sur ces matières.[16]

Some academicians of ARDS were very interested in scientific findings from other countries, but no other academician in the history of ARDS surpassed the decisive action of de Mairan after he became its secretary. He kept close contact with the Jesuits in China. From 1728 to 1740, de Mairan wrote a number of letters to Parrenin including many questions on Chinese astronomy, traditional Chinese medicine, and Chinese civilization. He also posed an important question on the causes of the stagnation of Chinese science. On August 13, 1730, Parrenin wrote a letter to him, in which he explained in detail the reasons why Chinese science did not develop rapidly for many centuries. Having stayed in China for more than twenty years and having good command of Chinese history, Parrenin's reply attracted the attention of European scholars and influenced French Enlightenment thinkers.[17] This question resurfaced some 200 years later, when the English historian of science Joseph Needham wondered why modern science did not develop in China in a work that led to a reassessment of Chinese science and great interest among historians of science.[18]

In 1750, Antoine Gaubil (1689–1759) and Pierre Nöel Le Chéron d'Incarville (1706–1757), two distinguished French Jesuits, were invited to be correspondents of ARDS. Gaubil was a historian of Chinese astronomy.[19] D'Incarville was a botanist who learned botany from Jean Hellot (1685–1766) and Claude Joseph Geoffroy (1685–1752) before he left for China. He also had close contact with Bernard de Jussieu (1699–1777), a royal botanist of King's Garden.[20] As a corresponding member, d'Incarville was very active in sending letters and papers to ARDS in the 1750s.[21]

In addition to their correspondence with those designated academicians, the French Jesuits also kept close contact with other scientists in London (the Royal Society), St. Petersburg (the Russian Academy of Sciences), and Berlin (the Prussian Academy of Sciences).[22]

Scientific Reports and Articles in ARDS' Journals

Scientific contacts between the Jesuits in China and scientists in France in the eighteenth century markedly increased over those in the seventeenth century. This was because more French Jesuits were sent to China for the spread of Catholic doctrines from the late seventeenth century on. Before leaving for China, they frequently received guidance from French scientists, especially from those in ARDS and astronomers at the Observatoire de Paris.

From its inception, ARDS had often received many communications on the subject of the observations made in different countries. It provided competent observers who were willing to make observations with necessary instruments. To some extent, the Jesuits in China had been of great importance in sending astronomical observations back to France. Their Jesuit colleagues, many of whom were excellent astronomers, published many of these astronomical observations, conveying them to ARDS astronomers.

In the seventeenth and eighteenth centuries, many of the astronomical observations made in China were published in ARDS journals. Even a cursory inspection of these journals shows that the French scientists were interested in astronomy. Jesuits' observations were quoted, and their opinions accepted or refuted in numerous articles. ARDS could work successfully with the Jesuits together to promote its interests.

Before the "King's Mathematicians" arrived in China, there were already some materials about China published in the ARDS journal. After 1690, the number of observations and reports from the "King's Mathematicians" and other Jesuits in China increased, and became available to French scientists. These reports, published in *MARS, Mémoires de Mathématiques et de Physiques (MMP),* and other journals, included reports on astronomical observations, magnetic declination, meteorological observations, porcelain making, and other techniques, as well as reports on flora, fauna and Chinese medicine.

Some of the most important contributions of the Jesuits in China to science were in the field of astronomy. In addition to the "King's Mathematicians," the French Jesuits Gaubil, Jean-Baptiste Jacques (1688–1728), and those of other countries, such as Antoine Thomas (1644–1709), François Noël (1651–1729), Ignaz Kögler (1680–1746), André Pereira (1689–1743), and August von Hallerstein (1703–1774) made the most important contributions. The astronomical observations made in China of solar and lunar eclipses, eclipses of Jupiter's satellites, comets, and the passage of Mercury through the solar disk were all used to determine longitudes and latitudes in China, and to calculate the route of the comet that appeared in Beijing in 1699 and 1742.[23] Observing magnetic declination was very helpful to correct Halley's tables, which were often used by scientists. The Jesuit observations also contributed to determining the shape of the earth.

With Cassini's tables, the observations of the immersions and emersions of Jupiter's satellites helped to determine longitude in China. The calculation of longitudes and latitudes for all of China was completed between 1708 and 1718 by the Jesuits, a feat unprecedented in scope. Working with Jesuits' reports and ancient Chinese astronomical records, the French astronomer Alexandre-Gui Pingré (1711–1796) analyzed and systematically calculated the longitude and latitude of Beijing. His results, published in a 1764 *MARS* article entitled "Sur la longitude et la latitude de Pékin" became standard. Devoted to a description of Pingré's research, it began: "Quand la ville de Pékin ne seroit pas la capitale d'un grand Empire, le grand nombre d'observations utiles qui s'y sont faites, en rendroit la position intéressante pour les Astronomes & les Géographes."[24]

Measurements of the longitude and latitude of the Qing dynastic capital, Beijing, were important for comparing with similar measurements in other parts of the world. This is probably why Pingré's article received commentaries in the *MARS*. This article explained in detail the methods to determine the longitude and latitude of Beijing.

Many French astronomers were interested in the observations made by the Jesuits in China. In addition to the Cassini family, Giacomo Filippo Maraldi (1665–1729) also commented on the observations made in Beijing by the Jesuits, especially the observations of eclipses of Jupiter's satellites and the comet of 1723.[25] Joseph-Nicolas de Lisle (1688–1768) was also a very diligent astronomer who kept close contact with the Jesuits in China when he worked in Russia. He collected many astronomical observations that are still extant at the Observatoire de Paris.

Another important focus of research was the Jesuits' research into traditional Chinese astronomy. French astronomers used their results extensively. Gaubil, a very famous Jesuit scholar, made the history of ancient Chinese astronomy better known in Europe during the eighteenth and nineteenth centuries. His opinion on the changing obliquity of the ecliptic according to early Chinese histories of astronomy is a good example. Through the correspondence between Dominique Parrenin and ARDS, Gaubil's research on the changing obliquity of the ecliptic was passed on to the hands of Dortous de Mairan and published in *MARS*.[26] In the early nineteenth century, the famous French astronomer Pierre Simon de Laplace (1749–1827) used Gaubil's result in his article published in the *Connaissance des Temps*.[27]

In addition to using the astronomical observations in China made by the Jesuits, the French astronomers were also very interested in ancient Chinese records of astronomical observations. French astronomers used these to analyze Chinese chronology. At that time, the history of many ancient countries such as India, Egypt, and China were studied more and more thoroughly, not only by historians but also by astronomers, largely because of the deep interest in the origin of world history. In this context, ancient Chinese astronomical records were particularly useful and thus carefully studied. For example, the Belgian Jesuit Philippe Couplet's (1623–1693) *Traité de la chronologie chinoise* was cited frequently by French scientists. In 1730 Cassini's discussion of Chinese chronology was published in an ARDS journal.[28] He used Chinese records of the conjunctions of the five planets to determine the precision of chronological measurement in Chinese history. This method can be regarded as the beginning of Chinese historical astronomy. The results of this research by French scientists and Jesuits contradicted statements found in the Bible, and were sometimes used by French thinkers and historians in writing new world histories.

In addition to astronomy, the Jesuits' investigations of Chinese plants,[29] Chinese medicine, and Chinese porcelain making techniques contributed to the development of the European sciences. In the seventeenth and eighteenth centuries, French scientists gathered reports from all over the world through missionaries. Much material published in *MARS* was written by the Jesuits in China.[30] Following *MARS*, one more printing enterprise, begun in 1750, firmly fixed the practice of permitting the Academy to endorse the scientific productions of nonmembers. In that year, the *Mémoires de Mathématiques et de Physiques*, commonly known as the 'Mémoires des savants étrangers', was initiated. In effect, ARDS had created a new scientific journal, setting itself up as an editorial board.[31] In 1755–1763, three long papers written by d'Incarville on the manufacture of lanterns, varnishes, and fireworks in China were published.[32] This indicates that d'Incarville was not only interested in botany, but also in a variety of Chinese technologies.

The Introduction of Western Science into China by the French Jesuits: ARDS and the Academy of Mathematics

Another aspect of Sino-French scientific relations in the seventeenth and eighteenth centuries was the introduction of Western science into China by the French Jesuits. The Jesuits were primarily Christian missionaries, and from the beginning used science to interest Chinese scholars in Christianity. However, their influence in China was to prove more effective in transmitting science than it was in making converts to Christianity.

From a historical point of view, the Kangxi reign was a crucial period for the integration of Western and Chinese sciences. From 1689, the Jesuits began teaching mathematics to the emperor. According to Joachim Bouvet's diary in 1689–1691, he suggested the emperor use the French Jesuit Ignace Gaston Pardies' (1636–1673) *Eléments de Géométrie* as a textbook.[33] He and his Jesuit colleagues Antoine Thomas, Jean-François Gerbillon and Tomé Pereira translated it into Chinese and Manchu.[34] The Chinese translation was later incorporated into the *Shuli jingyun* (a mathematical encyclopedia). They also translated other mathematical books into Chinese. They went to the court frequently to teach the emperor, playing a major role in his mathematical education. They brought with them many mathematical instruments (e.g., Pascal's calculating machine, Napier's rods, and compasses) to the imperial court. A special mathematical table and models for the teaching of solid geometry were designed for the emperor to study European mathematics. Many of these instruments and the emperor's mathematical table are still conserved in the Palace Museum of Beijing. Because of the Jesuits' role in the treaty with Russia, cannon making and the dissemination of science, an edict of toleration was issued with the support of the emperor in 1692. Though this edict was very important for the spread of Christianity in China, from 1692 to 1702 there nonetheless seems to have been no systematic teaching of science in the imperial court.

From the beginning of the eighteenth century, the Kangxi Emperor launched a large project seeking to assemble mathematical and astronomical writings using Western knowledge. An imperial academy was created for that purpose in 1713. Many scholars who were versed in sciences were summoned to the court in Beijing, where the Jesuits taught them. The French Jesuits played an important role in the whole process. Among the books introduced and translated by the Jesuits were Henry Briggs' *Arithmetica Logarithmetica* (1624) and one of the James Gregory's formulas for the calculation of infinite series. The translation of Briggs' book, for example, comprised a very important part of the *Shuli jingyun*, which was compiled under the patronage of the Kangxi Emperor. The influence of Western mathematics was quite remarkable, in part responsible for a revival of Chinese mathematics in the late eighteenth and early nineteenth centuries.[35]

In the eighteenth century, the astronomers of the Observatoire de Paris had kept close contact with the Jesuits in China. Many of the astronomical translations were from the works of French astronomers. The applications of the results of the British scientists valued for their precision, were often used for astrological purposes at the court.

As mentioned above, Jean de Fontaney and his mathematicians regarded themselves as representatives of the "Académie de la Chine."[36] It is very interesting that in 1713 an Academy of Mathematics was created at the Changchunyuan, an imperial villa. This brings up the following questions: Did the Kangxi Emperor or his sons know of ARDS? Did the scientific activities of ARDS influence those at Mengyangzhai? Based on some Western and Chinese sources found in Europe and China, I will try to provide some clues to explain the parallel development of scientific activities in China and France.

In fact, Kangxi knew of ARDS as early as the 1690s, since Bouvet had written a booklet on the subject for him. In his biography of Kangxi, Bouvet reports how he advised Kangxi to create an academy that was associated with ARDS.[37] Due to the lack of Jesuit scientists in China at that time, the great map-surveying and compilation of scientific works could not be carried out before 1700. In the conflict between the French and Portuguese Jesuits in 1713–1714, Bouvet presented a memorial to Kangxi that says: "Before our departure, our King entrusted us with three tasks."

(Our King told us that) various academies of *Tianwen* (Astronomy) and *Gewu* (Investigation of Things) in our country have been extensively collecting knowledge from every country. The Middle Kingdom (China) has a long history with a large measure of principles (*daoli*). We have also heard that the mighty Emperor of the Middle Kingdom is wise by nature and supersedes all former emperors. After you arrive in the Middle Kingdom and get the very finest [products of Chinese arts and sciences], send them directly to our country and put them in (our) academies so we can retain them in perpetuity.[38]

Jean-François Foucquet (1665–1741) was a very important figure in the history of Christianity in China.[39] In about 1712 he was under orders by the Kangxi Emperor to translate many new European astronomical and mathematical theories into Chinese. Among these theories were the Keplerian Laws, the heliocentric theory of Copernicus, the theory of Jupiter's satellites, the observations made by the famous English astronomer Edmond Halley, as well as the theory of comets. Because his translations remained in manuscript and were not published, they had no influence on Chinese scholars. In his *Lifa wenda* (Dialogue on Astronomy), Foucquet mentioned two French academic institutions: the *Gewu qiongli yuan* (Academy of the Investigations of Things, i.e., the Chinese translation of ARDS), and *Tianwen xuegong* (Academic Palace of Astronomy, i.e., the Observatoire de Paris) and depicts the astronomical activities performed by the astronomers of ARDS. He says:

> In former days, the astronomers at the *Gewu qiongli yuan* in the country of *Fu-lang-ji-ya* (France) all worked on it [i.e., the obliquity of the ecliptic], because the theories about it differed from each other. It is hard to determine among various opinions. However, this is a key point of astronomy and it is impossible not to make a decision about it. Therefore in the tenth year of the Kangxi reign, the astronomers petitioned to the King. As a result several astronomers were sent separately to the old places where ancient astronomers made observations in order to test if there were any changes between the ancient and contemporary celestial movements. Also a famous astronomer at the Academy named Ri-shi-er (Richer) was sent to an island named Ga-ye-na (Cayenne) below the equator by a distance of more than ten thousand *li*.[40]

Since Foucquet's Chinese translation of *Lifa wenda* was presented to the emperor and the third prince Yinzhi (1677–1732), it is likely that they were familiar with ARDS. It is interesting to note, however, that Chinese astronomers also spent much time trying to determine the obliquity of the ecliptic at Changchunyuan. This shows that the activities of ARDS in Paris influenced scientific activities at Changchunyuan, and suggests that the Chinese tried to imitate the model of the French academy.

The French Jesuits played an important role in introducing ARDS. As mentioned above, one of their original plans was to create an academy that was a branch of ARDS in China. In order to meet the needs of ARDS, they sent many astronomical observations made in China to the French astronomers. This can explain why they willingly supervised the making of a great map of China.

While the Jesuits were in China they played an important role in the development of French science. Their success at promoting European science in China was of limited effectiveness. For example, the Kangxi Emperor did not understand the value of Western science, as shown in his views on Foucquet's translation of algebra.[41] On the other hand, the Jesuits themselves sometimes abridged the books they translated, as shown in the Chinese translation of Pardies' *Elémens de Géométrie*.[42] Moreover, some Jesuits (e.g., Pierre Jartoux) did not want to do scientific work for the Chinese since this would take them away from their primary mission of spreading Christianity. Although they were not primarily devoted to spreading science in China, their influence in China was quite considerable. By coming to China, French Jesuits helped to promote both French and Chinese science. The scientific exchanges between France and China formed a very important part of East-West relations during that time.

China in the German "Geistesgeschichte" in the Seventeenth and Eighteenth Centuries

Claudia von Collani

Introduction

From the first meeting between China and the West in 1583 by the Italian Jesuit pioneer missionaries Michele Ruggieri (1543–1607), Matteo Ricci (1552–1610), initiated by the Jesuit visitor Alessandro Valignano (1539–1606), China proved to be one of the few countries with whom the West had an exchange of culture instead of only a one-way religious and cultural mission. China offered a better and highly developed civilization with education, a state philosophy, a high agricultural technology, and an examination system which, in principle, democratically gave way every man the possibility to reach a high office in the state. Europe offered Christianity leading to eternal happiness, but also the new theoretical disciplines, natural sciences, technology (military, astronomy, surveying), and mathematics. With these qualifications, an exchange should be possible, as the German philosopher and scientist Gottfried Wilhelm Leibniz (1646–1716) suggested.[1]

The Jesuit Mission from the Sixteenth to the Eighteenth Centuries

The old Chinese mission started under the guidance of the Portuguese Padroado with the method of accommodation used by the Jesuits. Noticing the great need for good scientists, especially mathematicians and astronomers in China, the Jesuits succeeded in obtaining such a good standing in China, that they nearly became indispensable for the Ministry of Astronomy. The Jesuits had received a good scientific education at the Collegio Romano in Rome or at the University of Ingolstadt.[2] In 1685, Louis XIV sent the first French learned Jesuits to China, who were trained in Paris and members of the "Académie des Sciences." They had a scientific and missionary "mission" at the same time, and they started an exchange of science and art between China and Europe.[3]

Besides Portuguese, Italian, Belgian, and French, there were especially German missionaries sent to China from the seventeenth to the nineteenth centuries. Important German-speaking Jesuits were Johann Schreck (Terrenz, 1576–1630), Johann Adam Schall von Bell (1592–1666), Andreas Koffler (1612–1652), Martino Martini (1614–1661), Christian Herdtrich (1625–1684), Kilian Stumpf (1655–1720), Gaspar Castner (1665–1709), Karl Slavicek (1678–1735), Ignaz Kögler (1680–1746), Anton Gogeisl (1701–1771), Augustin von Hallerstein (1703–1774), and Gottfried von Laimbeckhoven (1707–1787).[4] Most of them were well trained in mathematics and sciences, and thus some of them became directors of the Astronomical Ministry and brought modern European sciences to China.[5] Whereas the Jesuits brought to China curiosities, Christianity, and European science, China gave to Europe philosophy, which led to the Enlightenment, Chinoiserie, Chinese language, and Chinese chronology. China's influence on Europe was accomplished primarily with the help of books about China, but also by the direct Jesuit correspondence with European scholars.[6] Direct contacts between China and Germany were also established with the help of Jesuits. The first was Nicolas Trigault (1577–1628), who had been sent to Europe as procurator from 1613–1618 and made a propaganda tour through Germany, including a visit to the Bavarian duke in Munich and the Franconcian duchy, Würzburg. He collected gifts, money, and missionaries for China.[7] The most famous of his recruits was Johann Adam Schall von Bell (1592–1666) from Cologne, who became the first European director of the Ministry of Astronomy.[8] In 1694, the Würzburg Jesuit Kilian Stumpf arrived in China, where he was summoned to the Imperial court because of his abilities in technics and science. He also became director of the Ministry of Astronomy in 1711 and left many manuscripts on the Rites Controversy.[9] His successor in the ministry became Ignaz Kögler, also an eminent astronomer, who was born in Landsberg/Lech.[10]

The Political Situation in Germany: The Holy Roman Empire of German Nation

Germany showed special features other countries did not have. Germany at that time was the "Heilige Römische Reich Deutscher Nation," the Holy Roman Empire of German Nation. Since the Middle Ages and Charlemagne, its emperors declared themselves successors of the old Roman Empire. But the long lasting struggles with the popes about supremacy, the expeditions to

Italy, the Crusades, the Reformation, and finally the War of Thirty Years (1618–1648) had significantly weakened the German Empire. The south of the German-speaking empire was more or less Catholic, the north Protestant. Under the weak emperors, the mass of local princes, counts, kings, and so on tried to get as much power as possible. There was no cultural center like Paris, where all kinds of science and art could grow. However, philosophy, enlightenment, and science flourished in the many little towns with universities and in the little courts, ruled partly by bishops (Münster, Würzburg).

One could perhaps expect that it was in the Catholic south of Germany, where, because of the Catholic missions in China, sinology and sinophilie would start. But this was not the case, as the south only became directly involved with the China mission. The beginnings of sinophilie in Germany started in the northern, Protestant countries, Brandenburg, Hannover, etc., or in the milieu of the academies and universities of Berlin and Halle. So we have the interesting fact that China influenced German sinology, philosophy, and enlightenment via the Catholic mission of Jesuits to Protestant theologians and philosophers. In fact, most of the German Protestant scholars, interested in China, were not only trained in philosophy, in the "worldly wisdom," but also in theology and the "wisdom of God." Whereas in France, this influence went directly from China to Catholic philosophers. Ideas about China and sinology were spread by the network of universities, newly founded academies, and their connections to the many courts.

The man in the center of that "network" was the German philosopher Gottfried Wilhelm Leibniz, the greatest admirer of China at the time. He exchanged letters with more than a thousand correspondents, among them nearly all the important scholars and princes and even learned ladies in Beijing, Paris, London, the Royal Court of Berlin, Rome, and Amsterdam. Among his correspondents in China were the Jesuits Ferdinand Verbiest (1623–1688),[11] and Joachim Bouvet (1656–1730).[12] His Jesuit correspondents in Europe on the subject of China were Carlo Maurizio Vota (1629–1715), confessor of the Elector of Saxonia and the King of Poland August II (1697–1704, 1709–1733), and Athanasius Kircher (1602–1680). He later corresponded with the early Protestant Sinologists Gottlieb (Theophil) Spizel (1639–1691), Andreas Müller (1630–1694), and Christian Mentzel (1622–1701); and then with the Pietist August Hermann Francke (1663–1727). Last, but not least, Leibniz influenced Christian Wolff.[13]

The learned German public was more or less influenced by the same books as the rest of Europe, but there are, of course, some special features. Most books were, of course, first published in Latin, the language of the European scholars since antiquity. In the eighteenth century, this language changed to French; Leibniz for example wrote many of his letters in French. But soon publishers started to translate the popular books into the different European languages to address a greater audience. The first bestseller on China was Juan Gonzalez de Mendoza's *Historia de las cosas mas notables, ritos, y costumbres del gran Reyno de la China* (Rome 1585), which was soon translated into the most important European languages, and in 1589 and 1597 it appeared in German.[14] Based on the reports of Martín de Rada, OSA and Gaspar da Cruz, OP, Gonzalez de Mendoza (1545–1618), OSA, wrote on Chinese history, manners and customs, but also edited a missionary report.[15] The second important book, Matteo Ricci's "diary," in Latin translation by Nicolas Trigault: *De christiana expeditione apud Sincas suscepta . . .* (Augustae Vindelicorum 1615), became a European best-seller. It was later translated into German translation.[16]

China in the History of Philosophy in Germany

In Germany, like in the other Western countries, sinophilie spread widely in the seventeenth and eighteenth centuries, but changed into sinophobia after the abolition of the Society of Jesus.[17] The most eminent of the sinophiles was the German philosopher Gottfried Wilhelm Leibniz, followed by his student, the philosopher Christian Wolff, the German "proto-sinologists" Andreas Müller and Christian Mentzel, and later Georg Bülffinger and Theophil Siegfried Bayer.[18]

Universal Language

Starting with the age of discovery, there has been substantial to find the primitive language spoken by Adam and Eve and destroyed by the building of the Tower of Babel (Genesis 11, 5–8), which aroused God's anger so that he scattered mankind. People believed that God had given a fully developed language to Adam and Eve, the first man and woman, of mankind, and that this language was without any change or evolution. There were many speculations as to which language had been the primitive one, but Athanasius Kircher and most of his contemporaries believed it was Hebrew.[19] The Englishman John Webb (1611–1672) started a new attempt with his *An Historical Essay Endeavoring a Probability that the Language of the Empire of China is the Primitive Language* (London, 1669). This thesis, combined with China's long history, led him to believe (like most people then) that China had been populated by the descendents of Noah, and he identified emperor Yao with Noah, as Martini had before him.[20] The strange Chinese scripture was compared with the Egyptian hieroglyphs, which, until the beginning of the 19th century, were not yet deciphered. Athanasius Kircher thought that the Egyptian script could be deciphered with the help of the Chinese one.[21] The Chinese language also seemed to be suitable for the role of a universal, philosophical language, which could be understood by everybody. The criteria were unity and simplicity. Its characters or symbols should be built up in such a way that it was possible to follow the line of ideas. For these demands, the Chinese language seemed to be perfect because its characters consisted of radicals and could be understood in many East Asian countries.[22] In Germany, such attempts were made by Gottfried Wilhelm Leibniz and by Christoph Theophil von Murr.[23]

The Pioneers of Sinology in Germany

At the beginning of the China mission, the Chinese language seemed to be a book with seven seals for Europeans; there existed no bilingual books, no dictionaires, and no vocabularies. Therefore the successful attempts made by the pioneers of China mission, Michele Ruggieri and Matteo Ricci, were quite a courageous enterprise. Later, the missionaries of different orders started to collect their own vocabularies which were often kept secret and only used within the order.[24] Most vocabularies and dictionaries never were printed, but existed only in manual written copies. The first printed list of Chinese words in Europe seems to have been published in the French translation of Athanasius Kircher's *China . . . illustrata: La Chine illustrée.* (Amsterdam, 1670).[25] Other printed vocabularies were Francesco Varo, OP, *Arte de la lengva mandarina* (1703), which, however, did not contain Chinese characters. The first three Chinese characters ever printed in Europe appeared in Juan Gonzalez de Mendoza's *Historia de las cosas mas notables, ritos y costvmbres del gran reyno de la China*, in 1585.[26]

Later, characters were shown in Álvaro de Semedo's (1586–1658) *Relação da propagação da fé no reynho da China e outros adjacentes* (Lisboa, 1642), or *Relatione della grande monarchia della Cina* (Roma, 1643), and the most prominent French translation *Histoire universelle dv grand royavme de la Chine* (Paris, 1645 and 1677).[27] Semedo started with the stroke, which is one, then the cross, meaning ten, then all together, meaning earth. Another stroke added is *wang*, king; with a point, it is pearl.[28] Some more characters are shown in Athanasius Kircher's *Oedipus Aegyptiacus* III (Rome, 1654).[29] Martino Martini, in his *Sinicae Historiae Decas Prima* (1658), also, displayed some characters.[30]

Gabriel de Magalhães (1610–1677), born from the family of the famous navigator, worked in China since 1640. In 1668, he wrote his *Doze excellências da China*, a general description on China, which was brought to

Europe by Philippe Couplet and published in French in 1688: *Nouvelle relation de la Chine*. One chapter dealt with the Chinese script and language. In this chapter, Magalhães illustrated by example how the Chinese script was built: one character is mo (*mu*), tree. A small forest is given by two trees, *lin*, or if it is greater, *sen*, with three trees. Another example is the character for house, family kia (*jia*), together with the character niu (*nü*), woman. The whole kia (*jia*) means that a woman marries and follows her husband to his house and family. At the end of his little essay, Magalhães quoted the beginning of the *Daxue*, and mentioned the comments of Zhu Xi and "Cham Kiu Chim" (Zhang Juzheng, 1525–1582). Magalhães' remark was astonishing; that it was easy to learn, to speak, and to write Chinese.[31]

The Jesuit polyhistorian and Egyptologist Athanasius Kircher played a special role among the other authors with his *China . . . illustrata* (Amsterdam, 1667), because he had never been to China. Living in Rome, he tried to decipher the Egyptian hieroglyphs by comparing them with the Chinese characters. He had contacts with the China missionaries Michał Boym (1612–1659), Martino Martini, and others, who supplied him with material about China. In his book on China, he published the inscription with translation of the famous Nestorian Stele of Xi'an, then he showed some Chinese characters and wrote about Chinese culture and Christianity.[32]

In Germany, sinological studies started in the relatively small, poor, and therefore unimportant duchy of Brandenburg-Preußen under Friedrich Wilhelm von Brandenburg (1620, reg. 1640–1688), "the Great Elector" ("Der Große Kurfürst").[33] He built a library in his castle for scientists and researchers. Since his country was too poor, he could not collect different curiosities, but concentrated on Chinese and Japanese books, which were extremely rare in Europe at that time. The Protestant Friedrich Wilhelm had good connections to Holland—he had studied in Leiden—to Nikolaas Witsen, the Mayor of Amsterdam, and to the Dutch East India Company (Vereenigde Ostindische Compagnie), where the German scientist and physician Andreas Cleyer (1634–1698?), born in Kassel, was the first physician. Cleyer had stayed in Batavia and Nagasaki-Deshima, where he bought Chinese and Japanese books and sent them, together with his scientific observations, to the Great Elector. In 1682, he published the famous *Specimen Medicinae Sinicae . . .* (Francofurti, 1682), containing different pieces about Chinese medicine translated by Jesuits in China and collected by Philippe Couplet.[34] We do not know the exact date when the Chinese library of Friedrich Wilhelm in Berlin was started, but perhaps it was between 1660 and 1680. The first catalogue was made in 1683 by Andreas Müller.[35] Christian Mentzel (1622–1701) was also responsible for the library. At that time, the court of Brandenburg had developed a good reputation for Chinese studies, which is also reflected by the rumor that Philippe Couplet had visited the Great Elector.[36]

Andreas Müller

Andreas Müller, born in Greifenhagen/Pomerania, had studied Lutheran theology and oriental languages (he had knowledge of Turkish, Persian, Syrian, a deeper knowledge of Arabic, and some knowledge of Aramaic, Samaritan, Armenian, Coptic, Russian, Hungarian, and modern Greek) in Greifswald and Rostock, then in Leiden, where he was first exposed to the Chinese language. The Great Elector called him to Berlin as provost of the Nikolaikirche in 1667 and charged him to take care of the Oriental books of his library.[37] In 1685, he left Berlin because of a theological controversy. Like Mentzel, he was more or less an autodidact of the Chinese language, but he obtained, comparably, a proficiency in reading Chinese. His most important publications were the *Basilicon Sinense* (Berlin, 1674), a collection of names of Chinese emperors, his *Hebdomas Observationum de rebus Sinicis* (Coloniae Brandeburgicae, 1674), as well as articles on China and some translations. He had invented the so-called "Clavis Sinica" (November 1667), a method to very easily learn to read Chinese, and wrote a pamphlet of four pages entitled, *Propositio de clave sua sinica*, praising the advantages of his "key" (1674). This "key" made him famous, but also gave him the bad reputation of being a fraud, because he looked in vain for a Maecenas to pay for the publication of this key. Because he found none, he burnt all his papers about this key a short time before his death.[38]

Christian Mentzel

Christian Mentzel had studied medicine in Padua, and in 1660, became Court physician of Friedrich Wilhelm. In 1685 he was given the task to manage the Chinese books and to be the chief advisor on East Asia of the Great Elector, when Andreas Müller had departed from Berlin.[39] His Chinese studies only started in the 1680s, when he was about sixty years old. With the help of the Chinese books and perhaps helped by his correspondents, Philippe Couplet and Thomas Hyde (1636–1703) for example, he started to learn Chinese. Mentzel also initiated the publication of the above mentioned *Specimen medicinae Sinicae* (1682). In 1685, he published his first booklet, *Sylloge Minutiarum Lexici Latino-Sinico-Characteristici observatione sedula* (Norimbergae, 1685), as part of the *Miscellanea curiosa*, with 24 pages and a short Latin-Chinese lexicon with romanization. The Chinese content is probably taken from Boym's paraphrase of the Nestorian Monument in *China illustrata*; other sources are still unknown. The second book on China that Mentzel published was a Chinese chronology, *Kurtze chinesische Chronologia oder Zeit-Register aller chinesischen Kayser* (Berlin, 1696), in the German language. Mentzel used Martini's *Sinicae Historiae Decas prima* (1658) and Couplet's *Tabula Chronologica* (1686) as souces. He began with the earliest periods and continued until his contemporary, the Kangxi Emperor (1662–1722). In contrast to Couplet and Martini, Mentzel added the Chinese characters to each emperor, which he had taken from a children's booklet, *the Xiao er lun*,[40] which had probably been a gift from Philippe Couplet. Mentzel was so proud of this booklet that he wanted to give it to the Kangxi Emperor, via Leibniz and Bouvet.[41] When the Jesuit procurator Philippe Couplet stayed in Europe (1684–1692), he exhanged letters with Mentzel and helped him with translations and Chinese books to publish a Chinese dictionary, the *Clavis Sinica* (Chinese key). Couplet advised him to use the characters from the Chinese *Zihui*. Mentzel's other sources were the "Vocabvulario de letra China con la explicacion castellana . . . " by Francisco Diaz, OP (1606–1646), and a grammar made by Martino Martini.[42]

Theophil Siegfried Bayer

Theophil (or Gottlieb) Siegfried Bayer (1694–1738) was a real pioneer sinologist in Europe.[43] He was a contemporary of the two French sinologues at the Académie des inscriptions et belles-lettres, Nicolas Fréret (1668–1749) and Étienne Fourmont (1683–1745). Bayer studied Greek, Latin, and Hebrew at the University of Königsberg. Because he wanted to study Chinese at the age of nineteen, he went to the "Königlichen Bibliothek" in Berlin, where he copied the grammars of Martini and Francisco Diaz. The librarian was Mathurin Veyssière de Lacroze (1661–1739), an Orientalist and former Benedictine, who became Bayer's mentor.[44]

In 1727, Bayer was appointed founding member of the Academy of Sciences in St. Petersburg (1726). In 1730, Bayer published his *Museum Sinicum in quo Sinicae linguae et litteraturae ratio explicatur* (St. Petersburg), the first manual of the Chinese language in Europe. In the 145 page preface, Bayer tells the whole history of sinology.[45] Only a short time after this edition, Count Savva Vladislavic-Ragnzinskii returned from China, where he had signed the Treaty of Kiakhta between Russia and China. The French Jesuit Dominique Parrenin (1665–1741), who had served as an interpreter, had given his Chinese-Latin dictionary to Count Ragnzinskii, who passed it to Bayer. At the same time, Bayer received two Chinese dictionaries, the *Zi Hai* and the *Hai Pian*. Another source for Bayer's sinology was his correspondence with French Jesuits in Beijing, namely Fathers Parrenin, Antoine Gaubil (1689–1759), Karl Slavicek (1678–1735), and Ignaz Kögler (1680–1746).

By these means, Bayer published his *De Horis Sinicis et Cyclo horario* (St. Petersburg, 1735), and some essays and began to write a big Chinese-Latin dictionary in twenty-three volumes with 60,000 characters. Bayer looked for the real "Clavis Sinica," forgotten by the Chinese themselves. Seven years after the *Museum Sinicae*, Fourmont's *Meditationes Sinicae* (Paris, 1737), and later his *Linguae sinarum mandarinicae hieroglyphicae grammatica duplex* (Paris, 1742), appeared. Both Bayer and Fourmont became prominent for their sinological studies and both worked for academies; Fourmont in Paris, Bayer in St. Petersburg. However, Fourmont had much better working conditions; he had the young Chinese Arcade Houang, the comparably large collection of Chinese books in the Royal Library of Paris, and he received information from China. When Fourmont publicly disqualified Bayer and his *Museum Sinicum*, Bayer was so devastated that his premature death in 1738 was perhaps caused by this unfortunate affair.[46]

China in German Philosophy

Whereas Ricci/Trigault, Semedo, and others had made only small remarks on Chinese philosophy, the first "translation" of the *Sishu* appeared at the end of the seventeenth century in Europe, namely Philippe Couplet's *Confucius Sinarum Philosophus* (Paris, 1687), followed in 1711 by François Noël's *Sinensis Imperii libri classici sex* (Prague, 1711). The translation project had been accomplished during the entire seventeenth century by Jesuit missionaries. Comparable to the dictionaries, these translations helped the missionaries get acquainted with Chinese vocabulary and with Chinese philosophical thought, which was vital in communicating with the leading Chinese scholars.[47] When Philippe Couplet came to Europe in 1682, he realized the publication of the translations of his brethren, the Latin paraphrase of *Zhongyong*, *Lunyu*, and *Daxue*, to which he added a "Proëmialis Declaratio" with more than 100 pages about the accommodation policy of the Jesuits and the philosophy of the Song dynasty.[48] François Noël, SJ (1651–1729), another Belgian, published several books in Prague about rites in China (*Historica notitia rituum et ceremoniarum Sinicarum*, 1711), and on Chinese philosophy (*Philosophia sinica*, 1711). His translation of the Chinese Classics also contained Mencius and two other booklets.[49] Noël's book was an abridged translation of Chinese texts, selected from the Confucian Classics and from Zhu Xi (1130–1200),[50] and was also published in French as *Les livres classiques de l'Empire de la Chine* (Paris, 1783).[51] In contrast to Noël, Couplet and Company refused Neo-Confucianism and based their translation on the three books by Zhang Juzheng, which had been intended for the education of the Wanli Emperor (1572–1620).[52]

Gottfried Wilhelm Leibniz

The universal genius and philosopher Gottfried Wilhelm Leibniz was one of the greatest admirers of all things Chinese and of the Jesuits' method of accommodation in China, which seemed to correspond with all his ideas about an ideal nation living in enlightenment and harmony. China's philosophy, scripture, culture, and political power aroused Leibniz' admiration. East and West, China and Europe seemed to be two poles that belonged together and were complementary to each other. They were connected via Russia which, under the rule of Tsar Peter the Great, expanded to the East and tried to become a more modern state under Western influence.

Leibniz' interest in China started in 1668 with some books on China, such as, *Artificia hominum miranda in Sina et Europa* (1655), *De re literaria Sinensium commentarium* by Theophil Spizel (1660), and Athanasius Kircher's *China . . . illustrata* (1667).[53] In 1689, Leibniz met the Jesuit procurator Claudio Filippo Grimaldi in Rome,[54] who initiated Leibniz' correspondence with French Jesuits in China.[55] Another source of information about China was the Jesuit Bartholomé des Bosses in Hildesheim, who informed Leibniz about the controversy of the Chinese Rites.[56] In 1697, Leibniz published his *Novissima Sinica*, a collection of documents on China, including a report about the Treaty of Nerchinsk between China and Russia of 1689, which had been gained with the help of two Jesuits.[57] In the preface, Leibniz proved to be an adherent of the tolerant policy of accommodation of the Jesuits in China, and closes with the prophetic warning not to destroy the China mission by fanatism or internal quarrels among the missionaries.[58] Leibniz had his most interesting correspondence with the French Jesuit Joachim Bouvet, who in 1697 had published his *Portrait historique de l'Empereur de la Chine*, which Bouvet sent to Leibniz and which was added to the 1699 edition of *Novissima Sinica*.[59]

The correspondence between Leibniz and Bouvet consisted of 14 letters between 1697 and 1707, the most famous letter being the one dated November 4, 1701, written by Bouvet.[60] In 1679, Leibniz had developed the system of binary arithmetic, that is, to write numbers only by means of 1 and

0. Leibniz' article on this subject was refused by the Académie des Sciences in Paris as being "not applicable."[61] Leibniz sent his idea on the dyadic to several of his correspondents, among them Bouvet, and proposed that he use this arithmetic as "imago creationis," to demonstrate the dogma of creation out of nothing and teach the Kangxi Emperor (1662–1722).[62] Bouvet, who had started to work with the *Yijing*, "found" Leibniz' binary arithmetic in the so-called *Fuxi* (2952 B.C.) order (*xiantian*) of the hexagrams.[63] The interpretation became possible by changing the material and assuming a new interpretation. The Wen Wang order (*houtian*), which Leibniz already knew, was not suitable for the purpose of identification.[64] This letter proved the "utilité palpable," and Leibniz was able to satisfy the Académie des Sciences in Paris.[65]

In many respects, China represented for Leibniz a model of how things could be ameliorated in Europe. The social organization, the system of independent examinations, the practical philosophy in China, and other things showed him a nation whose politics were based on reason. Leibniz also found in China the "natural theology" which should surrender the high morals to Europe.[66] Leibniz' program of exchange between China and Europe was the following:

1. to improve the ways of life and to develop the practice of natural religion.
2. to abolish the differences between the confessions (i.e., between Catholics and Protestants) in the China mission, which would perhaps help to do the same in Europe (reunion).
3. to use science as a primary means for missionary work, "Propagatio fidei per scientias." Leibniz thought that the Protestants had better preconditions in this respect.
4. to erect scientific academies and societies in Europe and in China, which should enable scientific exchange.[67]

Concerning the Chinese Rites Controversy, Leibniz was entirely on the side of the Jesuits and their policy of accommodation in China, thinking that the rites for Confucius and the ancestors were purely political.[68]

Christian Wolff

The story of Christian Wolff and his connection to Chinese philosophy demonstrates something of the climate at German universities of the time. Christian Wolff (1679–1754) had studied mathematics, philosophy, and law, but also acquired a good background in Protestant theology as well as Aristotelian scholasticism. His professors were René Descartes, Malebranche, Hugo Grotius, and Samuel Pufendorff, and he also corresponded with Leibniz, who helped him to become a professor of mathematics at the University of Halle in 1706.[69] Wolff, who was not an original, but more a deductive thinker, is now considered the first and main representative of German enlightenment, even before Voltaire. He had been inspired by Leibniz and his *Novissima Sinica*, from which Wolff borrowed the term "practical philosophy."[70] Wolff's philosophy dominated all philosophy at German universities in the eighteenth century until Kant.

The University of Halle, founded in 1694 by the Calvinist, Soldier King Friedrich Wilhelm I, was perhaps the most famous university with the largest number of students in Germany. In Halle, enlightenment and pietism were connected. Halle was the center of pietism, the place where August Hermann Francke (1663–1727) had founded the "Franckesche Stiftungen" (foundations) with an orphanage and several schools, seminary for teachers, etc.[71] At the end of his office as prorector, i.e., the leading officer of the university,[72] Wolff had to give a solemn speech (July 12, 1721) for his successor, the pietist Joachim Lange (1670–1744). Wolff chose Chinese philosophy as his subject, which he knew from François Noël's translation of the Chinese Classics. The title of this controversial speech was "Oratio de Sinarum Philosophia practica" ("Discourse on the Practical Philosophy of the Chinese"). For Wolff, there were three reasons for virtue: revelation, natural religion, or just nature. The Chinese had in his eyes neither revelation nor natural religion and therefore proved that high morals and ethics were possible without religion. According to Wolff, mankind by nature was able to distinguish good and bad, and high morality was not dependent on religion, as the example in China showed. There was no need for Christian missions in China, and the Chinese were not poor heathens. They were to be admired, and an example for Europe. Missions only improved their already extant virtue.[73]

Such a speech was, of course, a high scandal for the pietists in Halle. They considered Wolff's system subversive for the foundations of Christian theology and the belief in God, and he was considered an atheist (he himself claimed to be a Deist). For if the heathens and atheists could do so well, why then should anyone persevere in his faith in God, Christ, and the Church?[74] The scandal was even greater because Wolff's successor as prorector, Joachim Lange, was one of the most eminent pietists of Halle, and he was no friend to Wolff. Wolff's adversaries the pietists,, to whom Wolff was suspect for a long time because of his enlightened philosophy, used the occasion to get rid of Wolff. The good contacts of Francke to Calvinist King Friedrich Wilhelm I were the reason that a royal edict, dated November 8, 1723, mandated that Wolff had to leave Prussia within forty-eight hours under penalty of death. Of course, Wolff's life was not really in danger, but the scandal became known in all academic circles in Germany. The royal edict was looked upon as a terrible interference in the freedom of academic teaching and research. Wolff immediately got another position at the University of Marburg. But with his exodus from Halle, Wolff became the chief witness of the Enlightenment in Germany ("Kronzeuge der Aufklärung"). Finally in 1739, Friedrich I, in a generous act, prescribed all students of theology to listen to Wolff's philosophy for two years and to read his books. In 1740, Wolff returned to Halle, which was a great triumph for Prussia.[75] After Wolff's speech had appeared in several "Raubdrucken" (Rome, 1722) and another one seemed to appear in the *Journal de Trévoux* (1725), which was evidently wrong,[76] and yet another edition as *Oratio de Sapientia Sinarum Confuciana* (Frankfurt, Leipzig 1726), Wolff himself prepared his own edition in 1726 with more than 200 annotations, partly taken from *Confucius Sinarum Philosophus*, with the title *Oratio de Sinarum philosophia practica in solemni panegyri* (1726).[77]

Resume

The positive image of China in Germany changed gradually, by means of the more realistic picture of the China mission that the so-called *Welt-Bott* presented, partly a translation of the *Lettres édifiantes et curieuses* in 34 vols. (1702–1776),[78] but also containing new letters, which only appeared in the German language. But the pieces of the *Welt-Bott* were practically just nearly only "édifiantes" and not "curieuses." After the highlights of the China mission at the end of the Ming dynasty with Matteo Ricci and Johann Adam Schall von Bell, or the beginning of the Qing dynasty with the glorious arrival of the French mathematicians at the Imperial Court, they mostly describe the miserable but pious life of the missionaries and Christians in China after 1725, after the prohibition of the Chinese Rites in 1715. There is nothing more about theology or science, which played such an important role for the Chinese mission. At the end of the eighteenth century, China's role changed from a model of an enlighted culture to a model of horrible superstition and menace which had its climax in the famous "Hunnenrede" of Emperor Wilhelm II against the "yellow peril" during the Boxer Rebellion.[79]

The Russian Orthodox Church in China

Dina V. Doubrovskaia

A Few Preliminary Notes

Among the number of more or less successful enterprises of Christian churches in the East, and, particularly, in China, the attempt of the Russian Orthodox Church to establish and maintain its outpost in Beijing occupies a noteworthy position. Soon after the Christenizing of Russia due to the zealous missionary works of Orthodox preachers and particularly monks of ancient monasteries, many peoples formed in the cradle of the Russian state were enlightened by means of the Gospel.

Quite like the brilliant Jesuit mission in China, the Ecclesiastics, acting as their mother culture's scouts, established rather stable outposts in the Middle Kingdom, emulating ambassadors in the farthest Orient. Both Europe and Russia were discovering the lands of China, which were not even precisely defined as "Chinese" at the time of first contacts between China and the outer world.

Christianity was brought from Russia to China for the first time as far back as in the thirteenth century by several thousand Russian captives, whose descendants subsequently completely disappeared in the huge Chinese Empire. From those times to the end of the sixteenth century, Russia had too many domestic problems to settle before it was ready to start its political and ideological expansion to the East and get to know its great eastern neighbor, China.

It was in the eighteenth and nineteenth centuries that the Russian Church started to carry out its salvation mission in the vast spaces of Europe and Asia, reaching to the Baltic Sea and Carpathian mountains in the West, the Black sea and Pamir mountains in the south, and the Amur River and Pacific Ocean in the east.

The Jesuit mission, presenting a perfect experience of outstanding, long-lasting, and successful enterprise in Ming and Qing China, gives us a unique sample by which we can measure the achievements of the Orthodox mission. The Jesuits at the end of Ming dynasty, like all the Europeans, had many more obstacles to overcome in order to reach China even physically; their effort in comparison with the Russian advance to Qing China by Siberian routes was much more difficult. This disadvantage remained during most of the time that both missions stayed in China. It was a matter of wit, zeal, hard labor, and outstanding learning and skills for the Jesuits to maintain their rather troubled stay at the Ming and Qing court.

On the contrary, the Russian mission, self-concerned in a religious sense, was not interested in active proselytization among the Chinese and Manchu populations of the city.

The Society of Jesus, being the most flexible and advanced religious enterprise of the time, presents a dramatic contrast to the highly traditional approaches of the Russian Orthodox Church, reformed in the eighteenth century under Peter the Great. Activities at the court of Chinese emperors proved this difference, when the Russian Orthodox mission showed itself highly dependent on the provisions of the diplomatic regulations of the Russian government, concerning the *Qing lifan yuan* (the Qing agency for the administration of the barbarians or outer regions, sometimes interpreted as the "Mongolian Superintendancy") on tolerance, and on Jesuit assistance for translation work.

Though things changed noticeably in the nineteenth century, when the Orthodox mission achieved maximum stability in its more than 200-year history, it still remained a small alien body. The Jesuits, who made their advance to the celestial empire at the end of the sixteenth century, had tough competition propagating Christianity alongside the Catholic Franciscans and Dominicans. Unlike the Roman Catholics, Russian Ecclesiastics did not have any rivals in their activities and were the sole representatives of the Russian Orthodox Church. The deviant movement of *Starovery* (the worshippers of the old rites in the Orthodox Church) were outlawed by Peter the Great and his supreme religious organ, the Holy Synod ("*Священный Синод*" in Russian).

The Origins of the Russian Mission in China

The whole logic of the relations between China and Russia differed dramatically from that of Chinese-Western relations. In spite of the fact that during more than three hundred years of interaction between Russia and China, the two powerful world civilizations were in contact in the great territory from the Pacific Ocean to the Pamirs, they had already been developing, practically independent of each other, for centuries. Their historical coexistence commenced only at the turn of the sixteenth and seventeenth centuries. The meeting of the Russian Orthodox mission with China occurred quite geographically. It was a historical coincidence that Russia and China had become great Asian empires in the course of the seventeenth century. Both countries had reached a point in their historical development where territorial expansion became possible due to political and economic reasons within their own borders.

The first appearance of the Russian Orthodox representatives in China was the most important one. It provided the base for the future development of the missionary activities and without understanding the roots of this long-lasting phenomenon, its origins and circumstances under which it was born, we will not be able to appreciate the reasons for its long, two-century existence.

We can trace the beginning of Russian Orthodox activities in Manchu China back to the eighties of the seventeenth century, which is practically a century later than the first Jesuit missionaries appeared in Macau. In the summer of 1683, Russian frontiersman Grigorii Mylnikov, with seventy men and a priest, Maksim Leont'ev, set out from the outermost Siberian garrison of Albazin, which played a very important role in the relations between Kangxi China and Russia. Albazin was fortified in 1651, but in the next year its inhabitants met with a new force of "*bogdoiskii* people," that is, the Manchu conquerors of China. This concern was among the main purposes of Nikolai Spafarii's embassy to Beijing in 1676. Travelling through Manchuria, Spafarii identified the "*bogdoiskii* people" with the Chinese (or in Russian *kitaiskii*) rulers of China.

In the middle of the woods, Mylnikov's party came face to face with a contingent of Manchus. After a friendly feast, the Russians were not allowed to leave, and were escorted deeper into the forest. Later they reached Beijing, finding themselves the guests of the Kangxi Emperor himself.

Kangxi ordered to provide for those who remained in Beijing "in order to show Our intention of taking good care of them."[1] Those people, taken hostage in Beijing, symbolized the beginning of the Albazinian wars.

That is how the first Orthodox priest started his activities in the middle of Beijing, serving the group of compatriots who were suffering the hardships of captivity. The Kangxi Emperor's edict granted the captives some land in the northeastern sector of the city. Given to them was an old Buddhist prayer house and a graveyard in the outskirts of the city. The sanctuary was transformed into an Orthodox chapel and consecrated in the name of the favorite Russian Saint, Nicholas the Miracle-Worker. Dubbed the Nikolskii chapel, Father Maxim started to conduct religious service there. Thus, by late September 1683, while both Manchus and Russians were mobilizing along the Amur river, Kangxi and Maksim Leont'ev had together brought to life a precedent, that later became the Russian Orthodox mission in Beijing.

There is no doubt that the Nikolskii chapel was a step forward after the situation of which Spafarii had reported, when those few Russians who lived in Beijing would frequent the Jesuit church. Spafarii even had given Verbiest an icon of the archangel Michael, for the Orthodox needs. But Russians were dreaming about a church not only worthy of its merchants and diplomats, but also one that could change the situation with the Jesuits' religious monopoly on Beijing. Spafarii had written in 1676, "Now the Jesuits think that soon all the Chinese will be Catholic because in America and in the New World similar signs foreshadowed the coming of the Catholics; so too in Japan. We, however, believe that, with God's help and the Tsar's happy fortune, the Chinese will before long adopt the Orthodox Greek faith."[2] It is easy to see that those bright expectations have never come true, but the very hope for such a miracle was absolutely common for both Russian clerics and the Jesuits. Both were eager to convert not only the Chinese, but hoped that they would be able to achieve that goal starting with the emperor, Kangxi, himself.

Peter the Great and the Orthodox Mission

It should not be forgotten that at the end of sixteenth and the beginning of the seventeenth centuries, Russia was headed by Peter the Great, whose policy, though European oriented, was far from being passive in the vast lands of Siberia and bordering territories.

In 1700, Peter first published an edict (*ukase* of June18th), in which he ordered the Kiev metropolitan to find a decent and educated man to take the position of the metropolitan chair in Tobol'sk. He was to select two to three young people to study the Chinese and Mongol languages, so that they subsequently could spread Christianity in China. This edict defined the tasks for the mission: 1) to become a mediator between Russia and China; 2) to support Christianity among Russian colonizers, and, as far as possible, call Chinese to Christianity; and 3) to deliver interpreters, whose duties were performed previously by the members of the Beijing mission.[3]

In 1710, two Albazinians in Beijing, Aleksei Staritsyn and Dmitri Nestorovich, wrote to Filofei Leshchinskii that they had been left without a priest because Leont'ev had died. Leshchinskii advised them to write a letter to the Tsar, and in 1712, when Peter Khudiakov was in Beijing with his caravan, the two turned to him with their appeal. They asked him to transmit their request for a new priest to the Russian government, but Khudiakov, properly considering the Albazinians to be subjects of China, advised them to address the *Lifan yuan* first. The Manchus thought that the new priest for "their Russians" could be obtained nowhere else but from Russia. Khudiakov remained in Beijing until June 1712, when he received a letter from the *Lifan yuan* to Prince Matvei Gagarin, governor of Siberia. He then left for the frontier with the message that several priests would be welcome in China.

The first official Russian Orthodox mission was approved in 1712 and included Archimandrite Ilarion Lezhaiskii, Hieromonk Lavrentii, Hierodeacon Filipp, and seven junior monks. Little information is available on the first mission's activity.

Not a great deal can be said about the life of this first Russian mission, for many of the documents relating to it were subsequently destroyed by fire in Tobolsk. Its life was very short, hardly more than two years. But its tenure in Beijing began amid favorable conditions. Of the Russian missions to China in the eighteenth century, it was perhaps one of the more advanced in its own level of preparation for what awaited it there. Besides, it arrived at a time when foreign life in Beijing was not as difficult as it became later, after the Treaty of Kiakhta, when Russian missionaries retreated behind new walls that the Manchu regime built for them. The Qing government made very liberal provisions for its maintenance.

In 1718, Peter promised the Jesuits unrestricted Siberian mail routes and their own freedom of passage through Siberia to China in exchange for their assistance there. But instead, in 1719 Peter added to the problems of the Society by expelling them from Russia. Envious of these highly placed rivals, Russia was nevertheless helpless without them. In Russian historiography, the Society of Jesus has very often been blamed for whatever went wrong in early Sino-Russian relations.

In the larger view, the first Orthodox mission to Beijing remained part of the interest in "opening" China which originated in Russia after the first Treaty of Nerchinsk in 1689. In this sense, the very existence of the institutions of that relationship were more important then the extent of their success. Trade was of course on every mind, and religious representation in Beijing went along with it. According to Leibniz, international contact was needed more than something else.[4]

The Second Russian Mission to China and the Kiakhta Treaty

The history of the second mission is connected with the idea of sending a bishop to Beijing, which would help test the extent of the Roman Catholic grip on that city. Ilarion Lezhaiskii had failed to do that.

In 1719, Leshchinskii had added his own letter to the *Lifan yuan's* announcement of Ilarion Lezhaiskii's death. The letter said that, "we thank God that the Christian faith is spreading, that the name of God is reputable among the heathens, and that hope advances for the glorification of the name of God among the Chinese."[5] He suggested to choose a good and wise man for the China mission and said that, "You might consider [someone] of the rank of a bishop, because the Chinese will understand that the Tsar is sending such people for the strengthening of eternal peace."[6] His suggestion was considered a good idea in St. Petersburg. But because of the previous difficulties, the Senate decided in its introduction of the chosen person, Innokentii Kul'chitskii, to the *Qing* officials, to keep the fact that he was a bishop secret. In the accrediting letter he was therefore introduced only as "the religious person, *gospodin* (Mr.) Innokentii Kul'chitskii."[7]

By February 1721 arrangements for the appointment were complete. The Holy Synod and the Senate reported the matter to Peter the Great, suggesting to make Innokentii bishop of Beijing with administration over the Siberian cities of Irkutsk and Nerchinsk. Peter's reply went as follows: "Ordain him as a bishop, but better without the designation of cities, at least not those bordering on China, lest the Jesuits take it otherwise and bring calamity upon us."[8]

The Synod sent this letter to Kul'chitskii along with his final instructions, adding that: " . . . some sort of opposition should arise among the enemies of our Orthodox Russian faith, and even more among the main enemies, the Jesuits, who for a long time have been accustomed to stand in the way of our good intentions."[9]

Kul'chitskii described his situation in a number of reports to the Synod. On March 8, 1723, he wrote:

> . . . I stand at the frontier neither on this side nor on that. In China they will not accept me, and not only that, neither will they allow letters from me to them or from them to me. And I am hardly able to go back without orders from you, although it is not without want that I am staying here.[10]

But it was not for these preparations to be put into practice, as well as it was not for Kul'chitskii to become a bishop in Beijing, because the whole process had to wait until the signing of the Kiakhta Treaty which regulated the terms of the Orthodox mission's existence in China.

The final copies of the Kiakhta Treaty's articles arrived at the frontier on June 14, 1728, where they were signed and exchanged. The fifth article of the treaty of Kiakhta covers the status of the Russian Orthodox mission, heavily burdened by the Sino-Russian relationship. The regulation reads as follows:

> The *kuan* or hostel which is now used for Russians staying in Beijing will henceforth also be for Russians who arrive there. Only they shall live in this hostel. And what the Russian envoy, the Illirion Count Sava Vladislavich proposed on the construction of a church, has been completed in that hostel with the assistance of the ministers who supervise Russian affairs. In that hostel there will live one lama, now residing in Beijing, and there will be added three more lamas, who will arrive, as decided. When they arrive, provisions will be given them, . . . and they will be settled at the church. The Russians will not be prevented from praying and worshipping their god in their own way. In addition, four young students and two of more advanced age who know Russian and Latin, whom the Russian envoy, the Illirion Count Sava Vladislavich, wants to leave in Beijing for the study of languages, will also live in that hostel. Provisions will be given to them from the stores of the Tsar; and when they have completed their studies, they shall return, as they like.[11]

Thus, according to the Kiakhta agreement, it was allowed for one Russian priest to live in the so-called ambassadorial courtyard. The church building was consecrated in the embassy with the name Meeting of God, or *Sretenia Gospodnia* in Russian. Starting from the first mission henceforth within the determined time of each ten years, there would be sent to Beijing an archimandrite, two hieromonks, a hierodeacon, two junior monks, and four students from the spiritual-scholastic schools.

Thus, the second mission at last settled in ambassadorial quarters in 1729 (where it resided until 1863, when it returned to its former place), due to the long course of intrigues headed by Antonii Platkovskii. During the mission of Amvrosii Yumatov (1755–1771) the church and other buildings were repaired.

One of the major advantages of the Russian mission's position in comparison with the Jesuit one was that its existence and terms of living were practically, from the very beginning regulated by the country agreements, which necessarily included relevant articles. The members of the mission did not have to make their way to Beijing, using their wit, skills in numerous crafts and knowledge of different subjects, as well as confront its own church authority and compete with other orders like the Jesuits had to do. The only real rival among Christians in the Qing capital were the

Jesuits themselves, but they were too smart as politicians and courtiers to skip the opportunity of using the ignorance of Russian missionaries to their and their countries' advantage.

Father Hyacinth (Bichurin)

Speaking about the Russian Orthodox mission in the nineteenth century, one cannot help mentioning the life and works of a legendary mission leader and the founder of Russian sinology, the brightest personality in the history of the Orthodox mission, Father Nikita Yakovlevich Bichurin (Pichurinskii). Known as the monk Iakinf (Hyacinth), he was born in 1777 and died in 1853. Being a son of the lower Church priest in the village Bichurino of Cheboksarski region in Kazan diocese, he was educated in Kazan spiritual seminary, where he stayed as a tutor even after it had been reorganized into an academy. In 1800, he became a monk and in two years was appointed rector of Irkutsk seminary and abbot of the Ascension monastery, being promoted to the church position of archimandrite. But due to some of his activities he aroused displeasure and was transferred to the Tobolsk seminary as a teacher of rhetoric with a prohibition to preach. In 1805, he was nominated the chief of the Russian mission in China, where he lived more than fourteen years.

When Bichurin left Beijing in 1821, fifteen camels were required to transport all the books he had collected there. Fathers of the Russian Church did not like either his character or his activities. For "undesirable activities, introduced by him into the mission life" he was judged, his church san (position) was taken away, and he was exiled to the Valaam priory. In 1826, he was freed from imprisonment, lived for some time in the Alexander-Nevsky men's monastery (Lavra), and worked as a translator-interpreter in the Ministry of Foreign Affairs. In 1828, the Academy of Sciences elected him an associate member and his works were rewarded bonuses. He was a member of the Parisian Asiatic Society. In 1829–1830, on behalf of the Asiatic department, he traveled to Baikal with Baron Shilling. In 1830, he wanted to abandon his monastic san, but could not get permission from the Tsar. In 1835, he went to Kiakhta to open and organize the Chinese language school.

The development of trade and political relations between Russia and China created major prerequisites for better understanding of two great peoples' interest in each other's cultures. However, total absence of communicative skills posed one of the main difficulties in this aspect. There were no textbooks and, first of all, no Sino-Russian dictionaries. The basis of the dictionary, according to Bichurin's idea, was to be living and vivid colloquial language. So, clad in Chinese costume, he wandered around the marketplaces, fairs, commissaries, pointed at something, asked to write this thing's name by characters, and wrote down the pronunciation. He then checked the information, acquired in such a manner, with his Chinese language teacher. As a result of this preliminary enterprise, in a four year period they composed a small Chinese-Russian dictionary. It is easy to assume that this was the first handwritten Chinese-Russian dictionary, composed by our compatriots in China. Not being satisfied by the short Chinese-Russian dictionary, Bichurin decided to work on a big dictionary, which required diligent, prolonged labor for many years.

Bichurin is the author of multiple writings devoted to the description of the disposition, customs, and occupations of the inhabitants of China, Tibet, Mongolia, Turkistan, and other peoples of Central Asia. He left many manuscripts—Chinese dictionaries, geographical descriptions of China in eighteen volumes, and many others.[12]

Language Teaching and Dictionaries.

We have already seen how pitifully deficient Russia was in its capacity either to handle the languages of China or to do anything about learning them in the seventeenth and eighteenth centuries. Russians were forced to depend on Jesuits in Beijing, Mongols on the frontier, or treacherous Albazinians who were the least trustworthy of all. In such a position, Hyacinth Bichurin took the mission, and in 1818 he in turn left it to his successor Archimandrite Peter Kamenskii after fourteen years in office. Kamenskii introduced a school for Albazinians there. Students of St. Petersburg spiritual academy were invited to the mission, organized in 1839 by the Asiatic department, to study China. Thus Archimandrite Gurii Carpov translated the Gospel into Chinese. According to the Tianjin Treaty of 1858, there was allowed propaganda in internal areas of China, and missionaries were allowed to leave Beijing for other provinces of the country whenever they wished and could go anywhere. This new opportunity had a positive impact on the activity of the Beijing mission, especially since it included such outstanding members as Archimandrite Palladii Cafarov (d. 1878) and Hieromonk Isaiya Peshkin (Polikin: d. 1871).

Archimandrite Palladii was occupied in compiling the "Chinese-Russian dictionary" for quite sometime, which was finally published in 1889, while Father Isaiya worked on the accommodation of the mission in the new place and was a very active preacher. He initiated translation of the mass books into Chinese and promoted the spreading of Orthodox Christianity among Chinese outside Beijing. In 1868, he baptized several Chinese families in the

Dunding'an village, where afterwards the church was later built in the name of Innokentii Yakutskii.

The Orthodox Mission at the Turn of the Nineteenth and Twentieth Centuries

In 1866, it was allowed to conduct religious service in Chinese. The following mission, headed by the Archimandrite Flavian (Gorodetskii), was mainly occupied by scholastic and publishing activity. Its members, Hieromonks Alexei Vinogradov and Nikolai Adoratskii, engaged in collecting, checking former translations, and took part in the translation of other mass books which were published in 1884 in twenty volumes. In Archimandrite Amphilochii Lutivinov's office (1884–1895), the Orthodox Mass, aside from Beijing sites and Dunding'an village, was performed also in Hankou, Tianjin, Kalgan, and Urga.

In the time of the Boxer Movement in 1900, the Russian mission was rescued in the building of the English embassy, but the church buildings were incinerated, and the staff did not manage to rescue any church utensils. The loss of the printing house was particularly serious. Nearly 30,000 Chinese signs, engraved on wood boards and other boards with the texts of mass books, as well as the mission archive, were all destroyed. The Orthodox Church's fold in China lost 1,000 to 3,000 followers, who were either murdered or had simply abandoned Christ. On May 25, 1902, the former chief of the mission, Archimandrite Innokentii (Figurovskii), was nominated bishop in China under the name "Pereyaslavskii." Within three weeks the new staff was approved and according to the new regulations, the mission had to be headed by a bishop. His subordinates consisted of two hieromonks or priests, one hierodeacon, and two junior monks. Besides those three hieromonks, one priest, one catechism reader, and three teachers of Chinese language had to assist the main mission staff.

After the mission's return from Shanghai, where it stayed for some time after liberation by the international troops, it restored the first-class Uspenskii Priory in the place of the ruined church courtyard. In the beginning of the twentieth century in 1902, a feminine commune with a girls' school was founded. Besides that, the mission also had Sretenskaya church attached to the diplomatic mission, churches in Urga (since the 1860s), in Hankou (since 1884), P'ei-t'a-he (since 1901), on the Manchuria railway station (since 1902), and in Harbin (since 1903). I can not also help mentioning missionary branches: T'a-in (1904), the Haila-er branch, the Tianjin branch with the wagon church (since 1904), the Young-ping-fu branch with the church and school for boys, not to mention Beijing prayer house and male school for thirty to forty boys attached to the brick plant, as well as Beijing courtyard with the Sunday school. In 1904, "the Brotherhood of the Orthodox Church in China" was founded in Harbin at the initiative of Bishop Innokentii.[13]

The Brotherhood had its branches at the stations Handaohe-wuzi, Manchuria, Pogranichnaya, and Tsitsikar. Since March 1904, the Brotherhood started to publish its paper, "*Izvestiia Bratstva Pravoslavnoi Tserkvi v Kitae.*" Along with the building of the Siberian Railway, there were the so-called church schools built in many stations. During the war the church buildings in the cities of Dal'nii (*Daliang*), Liaoyang, and the chapel in the village Youngjikou were abolished.

Returning to the situation in Beijing, we can easily understand the jealousy that the Russian mission's exclusive position excited among other Western powers before the end of the nineteenth century, when they at last won an equivalent privilege. The opportunity to get to Beijing, to stay there for a decade, and then to return was a unique practice, which only the clerics and students of the Russian mission could enjoy. Roman Catholics in the eighteenth century had gained their entree into China at the expense of giving up any expectation of leaving again. By the nineteenth century, this was too high a price for most Europeans to pay. Russia somehow found a loophole, and that was a source of irritation; even worse was the fact that the Orthodox mission in Beijing had minimum use in traditional church activities. I cannot help citing the remark of one Englishman in the nineteenth century:

> ... by the treaty of 1728, the Russian government has had, for more than a century, a regularly established religious and scientific mission at Beijing; and to their disgrace it must be told that, with the exception of a geographical description of China in 1820, by Father Hyacinth (Bichurin), not a single advantage has either science or literature derived, after enjoying an opportunity that no other Christian nation has possessed, notwithstanding the example set them by the Jesuits. It is needless to say, how different the result would have been, had the natives of England and France been allowed to remain ten years in the capital. ... As Russia possesses a college and mission, at Beijing, the English, French, and other nations are equally entitled to hold a similar position.[14]

After a rather short period of active development, the missionary activities were terminated because of the 1917 October Revolution in Russia, and especially the 1949 Liberation of China. Some Orthodox services were still served in Harbin, which was one of the centers of Russian emigration after the revolution, but no active missionizing was in sight.

Evaluation of the Russian Mission

I have to admit that traditionally Western colleagues have basically underestimated the role and achievements of the Russian Orthodox mission. The unique place that the Russian mission occupied was often regarded as a curiosity, because the mission never boldly acted on the Chinese scene and presented none of those well-known nineteenth century "missionary cases." Another reason is that it left little behind when it disappeared from the scene in 1949. Eric Widmer said that "it has rarely achieved more than a senti-mental significance in the historiography of modern China."[15] Kenneth Scott Latourette, in his monumental *History of Christian Missions in China*, gives the Russian mission only seven pages and a few smaller references.[16]

Russian historiography was always proud of the fact that the mission survived from the time of Kangxi under the most oppressive, xenophobic conditions. Nikolai Adoratskii, whose history of the Russian mission in Beijing was published in 1887,[17] is content with its existence in the "spiritual wasteland of China," noting that it served the fatherland by "bringing together the two neighboring monarchies." Soviet authors used to put it in terms of playing a great role in the cultural exchange "between the two peoples," and "promoting the strengthening of the cultural ties of the Chinese and Russian peoples." Clifford Foust remarks in his study of Sino-Russian trade relations in the eighteenth century that "not all of the Russians in Beijing were dissolute, licentious, lazy, rude, perverted, dishonest, or deceitful, only most of them."[18]

It seems quite fair to say that by the mere fact of continuing its existence through the nineteenth and twentieth centuries and outlasting everything else the Kiakhta Treaty had provided for, requiring official attention to the replacement of personnel at scheduled intervals, the Russian mission contributed greatly to the regularity of contact between Russia and China. In a sense, the Orthodox mission was an equivalent of a Russian diplomatic outpost in China. The mission made Russia's relations with China appear closer to normal than they were before the second part of the nineteenth century. For the Manchus, the Russian mission became a lamasery of Russian monks, which, situated next to the Mongol camping grounds in the city, proved the fact that Beijing was the booming metropolis of an Inner Asian empire. Thus the Russian mission answered the opposite needs of two contending empires, and two international systems. And of course the fact that is known to practically everyone and noted in the *Guinness Book of World Records* is that the old Russian Orthodox mission in Beijing is the site of the largest embassy in the world.[19]

I presume that the reason for the crucial difference in the positions and achievements of the Russian Orthodox and Jesuit missions in China can be explained by political factors and not only by the personal qualities of the members of these two organizations. The Orthodox mission always represented for the Manchus the neighboring state, which should be handled with appropriate caution, because the relations with Russia sometimes balanced on the verge of war. The caravan trade, the question of fugitives to Russia, and Central Asian and Amur controversies, only added to these difficulties. Though the Orthodox mission took no part in all these calamities, it always served as a disputable point over which the relations of the two countries could promptly stumble. For the Russian empire, the mission served as a means to reach the Qing capital and as an outpost of Russian interests there. For the Qing rulers, the Orthodox mission was a good pretext to pursue its cautious policy towards Russia, using the mission status question as a lever to push Russian interests back a little.

As for the Jesuits, the rulers of Ming and Qing China had a much more vague impression of the countries they represented, and did not jump to any quick conclusions regarding the dangers and opportunities of further development of trade, political pressure, and so on.

Unfortunately, scientific research concerning Russian Orthodox missiology in Russia cannot be considered sufficient. Strange as it may seem, the last monograph published on the Orthodox mission and Church in China was written by the Hieromonk Nikolai Adoratskii in 1887, in which he estimated the results of the 200 years of mission activities in China. Since then, the only book that was devoted solely to the Russian Ecclesiastical mission was that of Eric Widmer, who limited his subject to just the eighteenth century. This painted an unfinished picture because the most productive century of Russian Orthodox activity remained practically unknown to Western readers.

Nevertheless, research on the outstanding phenomenon of the Orthodox mission existing in Beijing is very popular now in Russia, especially after the *perestroika*, when the Church could at last initiate and host the numerous conferences on Russian Orthodox activities in China and Orthodox sinologists. Among the scientists who are famous for their work with the Russian Orthodox materials in China are Alexander Chochlov, Peter Ivanov,[20] Dionisii Pozdniaiev,[21] and Alexander Efimov.[22]

One of the conferences on Orthodox missiology was held in Moscow June 11–13, 1997. The Conference was called, "Gospel in the Context of World Culture," and devoted to the commemoration of the outstanding Russian missionary—Moscow Metropolitan Innokentii Veniaminov.[23] This outstanding cleric led exclusively successful missionary activities in Siberia and Alaska and was subsequently canonized by the Church.

The ultimate spirit of missionizing is truly reflected in the words of St. Matthew:

> And Jesus came near and spoke to them, and told them, "All power in heaven and earth has been given to me, and where my father sent me, I too send you. Go therefore teach all the nations, and baptize them in the name of the Father and the Son and the Holy Spirit, And teach them to observe everything I commanded you, and behold I am with you all the days, until the end of the universe, amen.[24]

It is true that only the best pages of the Russian mission's history in China answered these high commandments.

III

China and Christianity in Modern and Contemporary History and Beyond

II

China and Protestantism:
Historical Perspectives, 1807–1949

Jessie G. Lutz

Christianity has worn many faces in China.[1] Not only was there Roman Catholic and Protestant Christianity with separable terms for the Supreme deity and the religion, but Protestantism itself found differing expressions. There were institutionalized "mainline" denominations and loosely organized evangelical communities, autonomous Chinese churches, and pentecostal or millenarian sects. During the early twentieth century, Christian movements such as the Young Men's Christian Association (YMCA), Young Women's Christian Association (YWCA), and Student Christian Movement were prominent. On the fringes were Chinese Christians whose orthodoxy was questionable, the Taipings, for example. Variety continues today. The number of Chinese who attend "meeting points" in rural China undoubtedly exceeds the membership of the government-sanctioned Three-Self Movement, strongest in urban China. Syncretic and faith sects like the Eastern Lightning group are a source of concern lest they harm church and society.[2]

Scholars have been slow to recognize the growth of an indigenous Chinese Christianity. Until recently, Chinese generally neglected the history of Christianity in China or viewed Christian missions as the cultural arm of Western Imperialism. Early Western studies by missionaries concentrated on China missions; though these works remain valuable for their data and the expression of Western attitudes, they tell little about the work of the Chinese.[3] With the establishment of the People's Republic of China in 1949 and the end of Western missions in China, it appeared that attempts to establish viable Christian communities in China had largely failed. Scholars turned to demonstrating the incompatibility of Confucian and Christian values and concepts.[4] Or, they traced sources of Chinese hostility to Christianity.[5] Cultural exchange via education, medicine, social services, and secular publications seemed the principal legacy of a century of Protestant missionary effort.[6]

As China moved toward a more open society in the 1980s and 1990s, however, came the revelation that many more Christians than previously thought had retained their faith. Christian communities were revitalized, while new converts and sects joined the ranks. An indigenous Chinese Christianity existed and its origins must be investigated.[7] The history of Protestant Christianity in China was more than the story of heroic efforts by Western missionaries and resistance by Chinese, for Chinese Christians themselves had played a crucial role in propagating and interpreting Christianity. The endeavors of Chinese called for study.[8] Chinese scholars sought to assess the role of missions as a cultural bridge between east and West and to study the history of the Christian colleges and regional Christianity. They began to search for Chinese sources, discovering that much had survived the political turmoil of twentieth-century China.[9] The history of Protestant Christianity in China is being rewritten from a new perspective, this time with greater attention to the Chinese side of the story.

Pioneering and Preparation, 1807–1860

Even so, the narrative begins with the early catalysts, the pioneer Protestant missionaries. This advance guard was generally enterprising, dedicated, and confident of the unique truth of Christianity, and the superiority of Western civilization. Products of the Great Awakening, they brought a confessional, salvationist Christianity centered on the transformative powers of faith. Individual acknowledgement of sin, repentance, an emotional experience of rebirth, and a determination to lead a new life were essential to conversion. Most missionaries taught a minimalist theology: God as the transcendent Creator and Ruler of the universe, Jesus Christ as the source of salvation for humankind through his sacrifice on the cross, and the Holy Spirit as the source of comfort and guidance. Not the church, but the Bible was the final authority. As the revealed word of God, it should be made accessible to all.

Since Christianity and its propagation were illegal in China and Westerners were permitted to reside only in Canton and Macau until the mid-1840s, the missionaries operated on China's fringes. There, they lived in a symbiotic relationship with Western merchants. Toleration of Christian evangelism, opening of treaty ports, and extraterritoriality were all won as a consequence of the Opium War of 1839–1842. Christian missions functioned within a political context and, in the minds of most Chinese, were associated with Western imperialism and opium.

The missionaries studied Chinese, translated the Bible, and published religious tracts. In the process they composed grammars and dictionaries to aid their successors and began to work out a Christian terminology. They itinerated in the Hong Kong-Canton region and Southeast Asia, preaching and distributing Christian publications. A few intrepid individuals, like the German missionary Karl Gützlaff (1801–1853) and Walter Medhurst (1796–1857) of London Missionary Society (LMS), made illegal forays into coastal villages. They popularized China missions in the homeland while painting for their supporters images of the Chinese: heathen and superstitious, industrious and family oriented, devious and patriarchal.

Above all, they made a few vital converts, the majority from among their employees. The Westerners, after all, were dependent on Chinese as language teachers, translators, colporteurs for interior China, and even preachers on their itinerations. Some of the first Chinese converts might be considered converts of convenience or "rice Christians," acting in accord with traditional Chinese patron–client relationships. The attrition rate was high. A small corps, however, internalized their Christian faith and became deeply committed to converting their fellow countrymen. During the next few decades most of the initial conversions were accomplished by Chinese, not Western missionaries. For example, Theodor Hamberg (1819–1854) of the Basel Mission reported in 1853: "I had the honor of baptizing forty-one persons. Most of them are from Lilong and belong to the Kong lineage . . . . Such a baptism in the interior of China is a rarity. . . . Rather than praise myself, I shall gladly credit Kong Jin (Jiang Jiaoren, 1818–1853) with these forty-one as the fruit of his labor."[10] Che Jinguang (Ch'ëa Kam-kwong, c1800–1861) converted some 150 inhabitants in Buluo and presented them to LMS ministers for baptism in 1860–61.[11] Westerners offered further instruction and, as ordained ministers, performed baptism, indicator of church membership.

The Chinese not only had the advantage of language facility and acquaintance with Chinese mores, but they could travel freely in the interior. Most importantly, they had family and lineage as avenues of approach. Whereas Westerners concentrated on conversion of individual souls, the Chinese operated through their kinsmen, fellow villagers, and guild members. Even amidst lineage feuds, community closure, and widespread banditry, they had access to these groups. For example, Zhang Fuxing (Tschong Hin, 1811–1890), founder of the Basel mission to the Hakka of Meizhou, had little success in the Lilang region opposite Hong Kong, but soon after returning to his homeland in Wuhua district in 1852, he reported over a 100 converts.[12] A Christian isolate in Chinese society faced inescapable pressures for conformity from family and village. Converts needed the support of Christian communities and so they began their evangelistic work with spouse, parents, children, and siblings, then branched out to in-laws and other relatives. By providing church centers and cemeteries, offering moral support and fiscal aid at funerals and weddings, creating funds for the poor and for schools, and holding joint festivities at Christmas and Easter, the Christian congregation became in some ways a surrogate lineage. The Protestant missionary's concept of the centrality of the individual gave way before the primacy of family and social harmony. Listings of the second and third generations of converts with their common surnames and village locales confirm the vital role of the Chinese associates and their methodology.[13]

Adaptation had begun, as Chinese conveyed their interpretations of Christianity and devised their own evangelistic style. Though they did employ the Western technique of public preaching, they relied heavily on conversations with small groups in informal settings. Frequently they visited tea houses or engaged in discussion on a one-to-one basis. An approach employed by Liang Fa (1789–1855), first ordained Chinese Protestant minister, was praying together or reading the Bible with an inquirer. Worship services could be held in the home and be quite informal; hymn singing, repetition of the Creed and the Lord's prayer, and Bible reading with explication of the text might be accompanied by drinking tea, smoking tobacco, and feeding babies. As congregations acquired their own chapels, however, the trend was toward more formal ritual and emphasis on religious decorum, including segregated entrances and seating for the sexes.

In their evangelism, the Chinese often appealed to the desire for the protection and intervention of a more powerful God, one who could offer supernatural help in times of illness and hardship. The Basel associate Xu Fuguang (Tshi Fuk-kong), in conversation with a bandit-soldier, argued for example: "You heathens are ruled by the devil, but we Christians rule the devil." The outlaw, to free himself from the devil's influence, decided to join the ranks of the believers.[14] Strict monotheism *vis à vis* Buddhist, Daoist, and folk deities was often combined with continued admiration of Confucian ethics.

Many Chinese converts found the concept of a loving and forgiving Jesus attractive in the light of personal troubles and social disorder. Perhaps, as the missionaries contended, they resisted the idea of original sin and continued to subscribe to the Confucian-Mencian concept of the essential goodness of human nature. But they readily acknowledged personal failings and they craved reassurance and hope. How could they explain the current harsh conditions except by their guilt? Even if they were not greatly interested in complex theology or specific denominational teachings and practices, they derived comfort and relief from the doctrines of grace and forgiveness.

Others were distressed not simply by their own inadequacies, but also by the widespread social and political breakdown surrounding them. Before turning to Christianity, Liang Fa, Huang Yungan (Wong Nyun-on), and Li Zhenggao (Li Tschin-kau, 1823–1885) had sought guidance from Buddhist monks and even tried Buddhist regimens such as meditation, repetition of mantras, or good works. All to no avail. The concept of the transformative power of the Holy Spirit seemed promising. Perhaps adherence to the Ten Commandments through the help of the Holy Spirit was the means to redemption of both the individual and Chinese society.[15]

Contributing to variant interpretations and strategies were divisions among Western missionaries. The majority of those answerable to home mission societies adopted the confessional approach, that is, conversion was followed by a period of catechismal training and probation before baptism was granted; such a methodology depended on hierarchical control. Other missionaries, especially independent ones like Karl Gützlaff, August Hanspach, Issachar Roberts (1802–1867), and William Burns (1815–1868), gave priority to spreading the Gospel message, confident in the persuasive powers of the Holy Writ and the regenerative powers of the Holy Ghost.[16] They offered baptism after confessional conversion and brief instruction in basic teachings; further training would follow. Chinese evangelists were allowed to baptize converts and found Christian communities. Despairing of the conversion of China's 350 million by the small band of Protestant missionaries and convinced that Chinese Christians communicated more effectively with their countrymen, Gützlaff in 1844 founded the Chinese Union (*Hanhui*) to recruit and train Chinese evangelists for all China. Union membership expanded rapidly and dramatically as did the reported number of converts. As was soon revealed, the majority were charlatans interested only in employment and the Chinese Union disintegrated upon Gützlaff's death in 1851. A small number, however, remained true to their call; they were instrumental in founding viable Hakka Christian communities in Meizhou and southeast Guangdong and small Cantonese congregations in the Pearl delta region.[17] The nondenominational, evangelistic orientation of Gützlaff, Burns, Hanspach, and others would be adopted by many Chinese as well as by J. Hudson Taylor (1832–1905), founder of the China Inland Mission (CIM).[18] Emphasis on itineration and heavy reliance on local Chinese workers also characterized the work of the American Presbyterian John L. Nevius (1829–1873), whose methodology shaped the Korean Protestant church.[19]

Foundation Building and Expansion, 1860–1900

By 1860, guns had opened China to the Western presence while missionary publicity had popularized China missions among home congregations. An era of foundation building and expansion ensued. Volunteers, mission societies, and funds all increased. The number of Protestant missionaries in China grew from approximately 189 in 1860 to approximately 3,445 in 1905[20]; single women, working primarily in education and social services, comprised a significant component. Chinese Protestants totaled about a quarter of a million. There were perhaps 300 ordained Chinese ministers, but many, many more Chinese evangelists and Bible women, who remained largely invisible in mission records and generally absent from nationwide mission conferences.

Both missionaries and Chinese preachers experienced a decline in autonomy. Additional missionaries and residence in the interior meant closer supervision of Chinese workers. Zhang Fuxing, who had presided over the Wuhua Christian community for fourteen years before the first Basel missionary was stationed there in 1866, lost both his leadership position and his lodging in the church center. Establishment of administrative structures in China and mission enclaves in the treaty ports, plus more rapid communication with home boards reduced the operating space of pioneering, experimental missionaries.

The few thousand Protestant missionaries touched interior China only lightly, however. In 1905 about 630 central stations with mission residences, chapel, school, and perhaps a medical dispensary were located in treaty ports or cities and under the guidance of a Western minister.[21] Some 4,500 substations, usually manned by Chinese, were the actual arena for much of the evangelistic work. Jiang Falin (b. 1845) and Chen Minxiu (Tschin Min-syu, b. 1844), both Basel ordained ministers and sons of Christians, founded numerous new congregations in northeast Guangdong, and in 1885 Jiang even became head of a central station. Wang Yuanshen (1817–1914) of the Rhenish Mission was primarily responsible for establishing a Christian community in the pirate lair of Fuyong on the Pearl River estuary.[22] Westerners, of course, went on preaching tours and tried to visit the substations regularly, but administrative responsibilities and a high turnover rate often limited the time devoted to direct evangelism and/or its effectiveness. Though CIM missionaries concentrated on itineration in order to spread the word as broadly and rapidly as possible, Chinese conducted much of the follow-up work and nurtured converts between visitations.

The active evangelistic career for a large proportion of the Westerners was cut short by illness, death, or resignation. In the interim, Chinese often filled the gap. Acquiring language facility, particularly in spoken dialects, was a formidable and time-consuming challenge so that even after years of study, a missionary ordinarily had a Chinese associate accompany him to help establish contacts and communicate with the local populace. George Hood quotes J. Campbell Gibson (1849–1919) of the English Presbyterian mission on the importance of having Chinese assistants present to share in the preaching. "(T)he native speaker supporting and enforcing Christian teaching with a wealth of local knowledge and native experience which no missionary can possess, carries more weight with a native audience."[23] Despite the virtual absence of individualized Chinese associates in mission correspondence, the Protestant mission was in reality a Sino-foreign enterprise.

Even so, Westerners monopolized the roles of guardian of the faith and dispenser of funds so that some Chinese chafed under the restrictions on their authority. Wang Yuanshen's son, Wang Yuchu (1843–1902) of LMS became pastor of the independent Chinese church of Hong Kong *Zhongshi shehui* (Hop Yap church) and an articulate advocate of autonomy. Wang, along with He Jinshan (817–1871) of LMS, wrote on filial piety with the goal of transmuting it into a more encompassing virtue that focused on God the Father. Rather than rejecting family loyalty, they cited as its sanction the Fourth Commandment exhorting believers to honor their parents. Ancestors should be remembered and respected, but only God was to be worshipped.[24] Zhang Falin was said to "rule over his congregation like a little mandarin" and he dared to write directly to the Basel home board protesting against the mission's insistence on using romanized Chinese to the neglect of Chinese characters and literature.[25] Xi Shengmo (Pastor Hsi, 1835–1896), a former opium smoker who had overcome his addiction upon conversion to Christianity, founded more than a score of opium refuges, where a combination of medicine and joint prayer enabled addicts to rid themselves of the habit. He acquired considerable influence among Christians in Shanxi and, though nominally associated with CIM, he worked independently and was quite critical of Western missionaries.[26]

Converts came slowly, while attrition statistics remained worrisome. Missionaries looked for other means to attract and retain converts. Some sought to appeal to Chinese scholars through translations of Western secular works, science demonstrations, Chinese language periodicals, and philanthropic projects.[27] They hoped to persuade Chinese that Christianity was an essential component of a civilization with a long and respectable heritage. Though their converts were few, they did provide technological and scientific information that was useful to the Self-Strengthening Movement of the 1860s and 1870s, along with alternative world views and political institutions that influenced the 1898 reformers and 1911 revolutionaries.

Other missionaries turned to education, social service, and medicine to supplement evangelism. Westerners wanted the children of converts to receive training in a Christian environment, while Chinese began to perceive parochial schools as a means of mobility, not into bureaucratic ranks, but to lower middle class status as artisans, merchants, clerks in foreign firms, teachers in parochial schools, and even ministers. Particularly innovative were schools for girls, many of whom became the wives of Christians who had risen to the middle class while others became teachers and Bible women themselves. Courses to prepare Chinese associates for teaching, medical work, and evangelism were organized. By 1906 there were over 2,500 Protestant schools with about 57,000 students. The institutionalization of Protestant missions in China had begun as Christianity and Western civilization were becoming conflated. Though most converts were from families of modest means, the percentage of literacy among Christians rose well above that of the total population.

The increase in converts, educational and social service activities, and above all, foreign privilege provoked opposition. Village, family, and lineage members viewed with alarm the conversion of fellow members. Harm might be visited upon them by neglected ancestors or angry deities. When Christians refused to contribute to festivities for lineage founders or village deities, funds were reduced and the cultural unity of village or lineage was undermined. Kinsmen and fellow villagers were initially the principal source of attacks on converts and they continued to vent their opposition throughout the century.[28]

After 1860, the gentry began to take the initiative by producing anti-Christian literature and instigating attacks on Christians and their property.[29] They perceived parochial education and philanthropy as infringing on their spheres of responsibility and threatening the traditional social order. The extraterritoriality of foreigners, combined with legal protection for converts and the Westerners' interference in law suits, undercut the authority of local officials. Mission cases, which fill several volumes of Qing records, were a continuing source of humiliation and anguish, for settlement often meant formal apologies, indemnities, and new concessions. The culmination of the anti-Christian movements of the nineteenth century was, of course, the Boxer Uprising of 1900 when some 30,000 Chinese Christians and 200 foreign missionaries lost their lives, and an international expeditionary force occupied Beijing.

Good Times; Popularity and Growth, 1900–1925

The opening of the twentieth century ushered in what has been called Christianity's golden age in China. In reality, it was a period of transition for both church and nation. China moved from Qing dynastic rule to a warlord-dominated republic to a United Front of the Guomindang and Chinese Communist Party in league against warlords and imperialism. Christianity enjoyed unprecedented popularity for two decades only to be targeted by anti-imperialist nationalists in anti-Christian movements during the 1920s. Variety within the Protestant community increased; conservative, evangelical societies strengthened their presence; the Social Gospel approach gained momentum, and Chinese formed their own faith sects and autonomous churches.

Reaction to the failures of nineteenth-century reform movements and to international humiliation subsequent to the Boxer Uprising helped create a readiness for change in China. Many Chinese assumed that to modernize, China would have to import and adapt from the West. Since missionaries contended that Western progress derived from its Christian heritage, Christianity gained new favor. The missionaries, their writings, and Christian schools were accessible sources of information. Church membership expanded; parochial schools filled to overflowing, and Christian movements like the YMCA and YWCA became popular. The number of Protestant missionaries had surpassed 8,000 by 1925 and in the process, the nature of the community had altered. Estimates for the Chinese Protestant community ranged around 500,000.

The majority of Protestant missionaries continued to come from small towns, mainline denominations, and church-related colleges, but the Student Volunteer Movement, the YMCA and YWCA attracted hundreds of college youth, many from elite institutions. They were eager to demonstrate the Christian ideal of service by working in education and philanthropy. In accord with Social Gospel theory, they believed that dedicated Christian individuals were the key to reform and they hoped to contribute to the reconstruction of China while also attracting Chinese to Christianity. Many expected to serve primarily as professional educators or social workers rather than as evangelists. As a nondenominational organization with Christian leadership and funding, but with both Christian and non-Christian participants, the Y became one of the fastest growing youth organizations in China. Many prominent Chinese Christians preferred to work within such Christian movements rather than through the church. Deng Yuzhi (Cora Deng, 1900–1996), advocate of women's liberation and head of the YWCA Labor Bureau, and Yan Yangchu (James Yen, 1894–1990), founder of the

Mass Education Movement, come to mind. Even individuals like Qu Qiubai (1899–1935) who eventually joined the CCP were awakened to social activism through participation in Y-sponsored social programs.

With quite a different orientation were the growing numbers of conservative evangelicals. Some came from traditional denominations, but others worked independently with minimal support, and many were sponsored by fundamentalist and faith groups like the Seventh Day Adventists (SDA), the Christian and Missionary Alliance, and the Assemblies of God. Pentecostal, charismatic, and millenarian preachers brought a new zeal to the drive to evangelize the world. Never unitary, the Protestant missionary enterprise had lost its consensus. Tensions mounted as the Fundamentalist-Modernist controversy grew acrimonious in the U.S. and spilled over into China.

Variety among Chinese Christians also increased. After the abolition in 1905 of civil service examinations based on the Chinese classics, parochial schools attracted both youth who wished to learn English before going abroad and those who wished to acquire Western learning but could not afford education in the West or Japan. They joined the offspring of Christians in studying mathematics and science, world history and geography, politics, and English, along with the required religion courses. By 1925 there were thirteen colleges with approximately 3,500 students and about 250,000 pupils in Protestant primary and middle schools.[30] The agenda of numerous students, however, differed from that of the staff members, whose goal was to serve the Christian cause; many of the former never became Christians, for they quickly decided that Western learning as a means to power and wealth was separable from Christianity and they found other avenues for information about the West.

The parochial schools, though few and small in comparison with government institutions, did make distinctive contributions to women's education and to formal training in such fields as medicine and nursing, agriculture, journalism, law, and library science. They also nurtured a corps of Christian leaders who acquired influential positions in education, diplomatic service and other government bureaus, medicine, business, the Christian church and Christian movements. In the Christian community, individuals like Yu Rizhang (David Yui, 1882–1936), Zhao Zichen (1888–1989), Xu Baoqian (1892–1944), and Liu Tingfang (Timothy Lew, 1890–1947) stand out. Most were characterized by liberal theology, commitment to social reform, deep Chinese patriotism, and acquaintance with Western learning and mores. Many held positions either in the Christian colleges or with the YMCA, but there was also Ding Limei (1875?–1936), who as secretary of the Chinese Students Volunteer Movement for the Ministry, held popular revival meetings in Christian schools throughout China. These leaders, along with conservative churchmen like Cheng Jingyi (1881–1939) sparked the drive for greater Chinese autonomy and leadership in the church. They became Chinese spokesmen in the National Christian Council, a liaison committee for Protestant churches, and the Church of Christ in China (CCC), established in 1927 to work toward independence and a post-denominational union of all Protestants in China. Even so, progress toward autonomy proved frustratingly slow, for Western mission boards and many missionaries were reluctant to relinquish the power of the pocket book, which gave them a decisive voice in most matters of importance.[31]

Adding to the diversity and also to the conservative trend was the proliferation of completely autonomous Chinese Christian churches and communities, a new phenomenon in Chinese Protestantism.[32] Noteworthy was the China Christian Independent Church (*Zhongguo Yesujiao zilihui*), a federation which by 1920 had over 100 member churches, drawn mostly from the urban middle class. In contrast was the True Jesus Church (*Zhen Yesu jiaohui*), founded in 1917; pentecostal, millenarian, exclusivist, and often anti-foreign, it was concentrated in the central interior provinces.[33] Sometimes independence derived not so much from a desire to indigenize Christianity as from the nature of leadership. Wang Mingdao (1900–1991) and Song Shangji (John Sung, 1901–1944) were zealous, confident of possessing the truth, and critical of what they perceived as lukewarm formalism in the Protestant establishment.[34] They drew on the revivalism and mysticism of Western "faith sects" and the pentecostalism of the True Jesus Church. During the 1920s and 1930s both Wang and Song worked as independent itinerant preachers, holding highly successful and emotional meetings in established churches and other venues. Their message was simple: today's evil world demands repentance; otherwise, hell is our destiny. To this doomsday prophecy, Song added faith healing. Their premillenial eschatology attracted tens of thousands of followers set adrift in an environment of political chaos, civil war, and personal hardship. Their rejection of the missionary hierarchy elicited admiration even among some nationalistic youth.

Hard Times; An Era of National and Social Challenges, 1925–1949

Popularity often begets criticism. The May Fourth Movement of 1919 had spawned anti-Christian movements among urban intellectuals, who criticized religion as anti-scientific and outdated.[35] Then, the May 30, 1925 Movement combined anti-imperialist nationalism with the GMD-CCP drive for political power, while Marxism provided a new framework for interpreting world history.[36] Christian missions and schools were condemned for cultural imperialism. Christian college students were accused of being denationalized even though some joined in the anti-imperialist demonstrations. Chinese Christians experienced a crisis of identity and credibility. Were they, as critics contended, serving as "running dogs" of Western missionaries, who were, in turn, the vanguard of imperialist capitalists?

In the aftermath of World War I, many Westerners experienced a crisis of confidence. How could Western nations, which had just emerged from the most destructive war of modern times, justify preaching morality to others? Volunteers, financial, and intellectual support for missions began a steady decline. The 1929 depression soon compounded the economic troubles, making the extensive institutional structure of schools, hospitals, and other service facilities a burden difficult to maintain.

Yet the difficulties accelerated indigenization. Though numerous Chinese Christians ceased affiliation with the church, others undertook to demonstrate the social and ethical relevancy of the Christian message, thereby proving that they were both loyal patriots and believers.[37] The CCC and Y, already under Chinese leadership, procured greater control over allocation of funds; denominational churches ordained more Chinese ministers and granted them greater authority. A Christianity stripped of many Western accretions and emphasizing the humanity of Christ was offered by theologians like Zhao Zichen. Parochial schools were required to register with the government, increase the number of Chinese administrators, and make all religion courses and activities voluntary. Of equal importance was the temporary exodus of most Protestant missionaries from the interior when violence against foreigners attended the Northern Expedition of 1926–27. Chinese were left to keep churches, schools, and other institutions operating. On returning, Westerners found an altered environment and relationship with their Chinese colleagues. Such movement toward indigenization, however, came too little and too late in the view of many Chinese.

Protestantism faced other problems as well. The theology presented by Western-educated Chinese intellectuals in the collegiate churches diverged widely from the more simplistic, emotional faith attractive to the masses. Graduates returning to their community churches often felt uncomfortable and ceased attendance, depriving congregations of lay leadership. The gap between urban and rural churches was further broadened by a shortage of ministers which meant that rural parishes usually received pastors with minimal training. Even though three-fourths of the population lived in rural

China, Protestant missions and social service programs were oriented toward urban China.

During the Northern Expedition young propagandists and organizers came into actual contact with village life. For those who had idealized the peasants from afar, this was an eye-opening experience. Communist party organization of the peasantry also presented a challenge to Christianity. Belatedly, the Y, several Christian colleges, and Yen's Mass Education Movement began rural reconstruction projects, only to discover that reform was a long-term process requiring multiple changes in landlord–tenant relations, marketing, agricultural techniques and materials, education, medical care, and so forth. The small, promising projects were soon undermined by the political needs of the GMD struggling to consolidate its rule in opposition to the communist party and local power holders. However, much was learned and the information and personnel proved useful later in rural reconstruction on Taiwan.

Since many Chinese Christian leaders were internationalists and pacifists, Japanese invasion of Manchuria in 1931 presented a dilemma. Most abandoned their pacifism, and many joined the National Salvation Movement, which came increasingly under left-wing influence as Chiang Kai-shek temporized. The Japanese invasion of 1937 brought short-lived unity, but also a halt to reform efforts. Evacuation to interior China and relief for refugees absorbed the attention and funds of Protestant missions and their supporters. Actually, of course, most Chinese had no choice but try to survive under Japanese occupation. Several Christian colleges, invoking extraterritorial status, remained in the east to serve a burgeoning student body; missionaries, especially those at central stations in the cities, offered Chinese what protection they could. Rural congregations frequently resorted to lay leadership, often women.

In December 1941 Pearl Harbor occurred, with the evacuation or internment of most Westerners. Once again Chinese were left to carry on and once again the Chinese Protestant church moved toward independence, union, and Chinese control.[38] Social service and educational activities contracted and self-support became necessary so that many ministers had to rely on secular employment. Though freed of the taint of Western Imperialism, church leaders soon discovered that Japan hoped to mobilize Christian support for its regime. Cooperating in the nondenominational Sino-Japanese organizations, albeit reluctantly, they worked to employ the union structures to protect their congregations. Upon allied victory in 1945, church and mission turned to rehabilitation of Christian institutions. All too soon, civil war between the GMD and the CCP engulfed the nation.

The chaos that was China during the 1930s and 1940s spawned religious movements that emphasized direct spiritual experience and an eschatology offering hope and comfort beyond this cruel world. In opposition to the Y and the Student Christian Movement, conservatives organized the Intervarsity Christian Fellowship in 1945; for them, Social Gospel theology was not simply impotent; it had lost sight of the centrality of a personal relationship with the divine. The Jesus Family (*Yesu jiating*), founded about 1927, expanded in rural north and central China. Communitarian, pentecostal, and millenarian, its family communities lived, worked, and held property jointly; worship often included speaking in tongues and revelations from the Holy Spirit. The salvationist promise of Wang Mingdao, John Sung, and Ji Zhiwen (Andrew Gih, 1901–1985) continued to attract throngs of followers, many of them already Christians. Ni Tuosheng (Watchman Nee, 1903–1972), founder of the Assembly Hall (*Jidutuhui*, Little Flock), drew adherents with his assurances of a glorious New Jerusalem in the next life for those who experienced rebirth and adhered to a strict morality. By 1945, Ni's hierarchically-controlled and sectarian movement claimed a membership of over 70,000, organized into some 700 assemblies.[39] The independent churches altogether probably accounted for well over 200,000 Protestants.

Liberals, particularly those working with Christian movements rather than the church, remained committed to the implementation of Jesus's social teachings, but could not ignore the growing evidence that social reconstruction necessitated political and military might. For many Chinese by 1947, the political disarray and corruption of the GMD made it no longer acceptable as an instrument of reform or rule. Christians like Wu Yaozong (1893–1979) and Jiang Wenhan turned toward the CCP. Wary of its espousal of atheism and intolerance of competitors, they endorsed its socialism and hoped that it would implement the social reform and equity that had eluded Social Gospel gradualists. Communist victory in 1949 hardly presaged bright prospects for Christians, but many Chinese and even some missionaries hoped a modus vivendi could be effected.

The Chinese Protestant church entered the communist era having made significant progress toward self-support and self-government. Though Chinese rulers had traditionally sought to regulate organized religion and the CCP would continue the practice, Chinese Christians had gained experience in the art of accommodation in order to protect their members. Independent churches and a variety of evangelical sects broadened the appeal of Protestantism, especially in rural China. They also redefined Chinese Christianity as they incorporated elements from folk religion and Buddhism. More than was realized at the time, Christianity in all its variety had taken root in China and possessed the strength and techniques to survive decades of hostility and/or persecution.

Protestant Christianity in China Today: Fragile, Fragmented, Flourishing

Ryan Dunch

"China: God is Back" was the dramatic cover heading on the influential *Far Eastern Economic Review* one week in 1996.[1] The resurgence of religion in the People's Republic of China was by no means a new story then, but it has continued to generate headlines in the mainstream media on a regular basis for the last twenty years, in China and overseas. If one were to scan those headlines, the message gleaned from them concerning the Protestant church in China would, I suspect, be confusing. One might gather, for example, that Protestant Christianity is growing faster in China than perhaps anywhere else in the world; that the Chinese government is among the world's worst persecutors of Christians; that the Amity Press in China recently printed its twenty-millionth Chinese Bible; and that the open churches to which the Amity Foundation is linked are no more than cynical control mechanisms of an atheistic government.[2] Delving beyond those mainstream media into more obscure sources, such as the newsletters and websites of Protestant organizations, the many books on the Chinese church published in English by various religious publishers, the press releases and reports of international human rights agencies, and the internal-circulation laws and policy statements of Chinese government organs, would yield even more confusion.

The reason that the messages we find in reportage and popular writing on Protestant Christianity in China are so mixed is that there are indeed deep complexities and contradictions within the Protestant experience in China. In this chapter I argue that while on the one hand the Protestant church is flourishing in China, it is at the same time both fragmented and fragile; fragmented due to the great diversity of theological, practical, and regional streams that make up the contemporary Protestant church, and fragile due to the limited role which the church, despite its growth, plays and can play in Chinese social and cultural life. In making this case the chapter will first identify the main strands within the Protestant church in China, then treat several broader interpretive issues: whether we can discern a "Chinese Protestantism" amidst the variety of Protestant expressions in China, the implications of the Protestant presence for Chinese society, and the place of Chinese Protestantism in world Christianity.

Preliminary Considerations

Before proceeding further we must decide what we mean by Protestantism. This is more difficult than one might expect, since the boundaries of Protestantism in China are drawn differently by different interested parties. Most restrictive in their definition are those elements within the state and Communist Party bureaucracies which, from a desire to strengthen the state's management of religious affairs, define it in so narrow a way as to exclude all corporate manifestations of Protestant religious belief outside of registered religious premises. By enshrining the administrative mechanism of registration in the spate of religious laws passed since the late 1980s, the Chinese state has provided itself the legal means to suppress unregistered Protestant activities while simultaneously insisting to the world that "no-one in China is punished because of his or her religious belief"—only for breaking the law.[3]

The leaders of the officially recognized Protestant bodies in China, the China Christian Council and Three-Self Patriotic Movement (hereafter abbreviated as TSPM/CCC) have adopted a less narrow definition, at times acknowledging Protestants who dissent from their leadership as orthodox, though mistaken, believers.[4] However, beginning with the suppression of the "Shouters" in 1983, they have also at times sided with the state in defining certain sectarian Protestant groups as heretical, and thus, in the awkward religious/legal/political amalgam of the Chinese government's religious policy, outside of the scope of the "legitimate" religious activity entitled to legal protection.[5] With the upsurge of sectarian activity in China in the 1990s, some publications of the TSPM/CCC have defined heresy according to criteria which are essentially political rather than doctrinal (rejection of Three-Self, secrecy), potentially putting any Protestant activity autonomous from the open churches into the category of heretical sects.[6]

Other Protestant groups in China can be just as narrow in their definitions as the state. Many of the groups commonly classified in English under the misleading term "house churches" spurn the religious credentials of the China Christian Council, or at least its leaders, regarding them either as Christians hopelessly compromised by the world, or as not Christians at all. Few if any of these groups would recognize China's Roman Catholics as fellow Christians. Some of them also reject each other, insisting that their own particular beliefs about certain matters of doctrine or practice are the only valid ones. Having nearly five hundred years of schism in Western Protestantism to draw upon, plus disputes wholly Chinese in origin, the potential for bitter divisions is very great, whether over forms of baptism and communion, the manifestations of the Holy Spirit, the marks of true conversion, how to hold Bibles, or in what posture to pray, to list only a few.

Divisions within China over whom the label Protestant encompasses have been reduplicated abroad in the literature in English on the church in China. Some commentators have denied the existence of any significant number of Protestants outside of the auspices of the TSPM/CCC.[7] Others have gone to the other extreme, dismissing the officially recognized Protestant bodies as "atheistic government-controlled churches" and portraying the "house churches" as the sole repositories of authentic Christianity, and even as exemplars to complacent Western Protestants, a "voice to the Church in the West," as the title of one popular book put it.[8]

A further complication of definition is posed by the many Christian offshoots, Chinese and foreign in origin, which have operated in China and consider themselves Christian, such as the "local church" or "Shouters" of Witness Lee, the Jehovah's Witnesses, the Latter-Day Saints, the Children of God sect thrown out of China in 1986, or Chinese quasi-Christian groups like the "Established King" sect suppressed in 1995.[9]

Fortunately it is not the role of the historian to judge which groups are in fact Protestant; for scholarly purposes we have no alternative but to take their self-representation as Protestant Christian as the chief criterion for inclusion.

Main Strands of Protestantism in China

The Protestant church in contemporary China is comprised of a bewildering diversity of streams. Many ways of classifying them are possible, but the simplest is to group them in terms of three historical points of origin: the mission-founded churches, the indigenous Chinese Protestant movements of the early twentieth century, and the new Protestant movements that have emerged in the PRC since the 1970s.

Earliest are the churches founded by the Western denominational and inter-denominational missions going back to the nineteenth century. While the majority of Protestant missionaries were from the large denominational churches of Great Britain and America—Anglican, Methodist, Presbyterian, Baptist—there were also many smaller groups and traditions represented among the missionary body, which at its peak in the mid-1920s numbered around 8,300 persons, the majority women.[10] Over 170 different missionary bodies operated in China at some time between 1867 and 1941, from every major and minor branch of Protestantism, with missionaries speaking most major European languages.[11]

If the story of Protestant Christianity in China stemmed only from these missions, it would be reasonable to cast that story as a history of convergence, as many works have portrayed it. Beginning in the last decades of the nineteenth century, the mission societies began cooperating along lines of regional proximity in the running of universities and seminaries, combining along lines of denominational commonality into Chinese denominations independent of the mother churches, and ultimately joining in the two major ecumenical initiatives of the 1920s, the National Christian Council (formed in 1922), and the Church of Christ in China (formed in 1927).[12]

The mission-derived Protestant churches in China shared certain defining features. First, they were characterized by a relative richness of resources, in which the churches were part of an interlocking network of Protestant religious, educational, medical, publishing, and philanthropic institutions. This fact shaped the identity of the Chinese Protestant community in several ways. It meant that by the early twentieth century Protestants were on the whole a well-educated population with a large representation among the modern professions, and particularly among professional women, relative to the wider society. Since these institutions represented a large investment by overseas mission boards, it also contributed to disagreements among their missionary colleagues and mentors over the control of mission institutions, a widely shared experience among Chinese Protestants in the Republican period.[13] The visibly Western character of the institutions contributed to making the question of identity—how to be both Chinese and Christian—another widely shared aspect of mission-derived Protestantism before 1949.

In religious culture, the mission-founded churches generally had a professionalized, educated clergy leading worship services which took place in church buildings on Sundays, stressed preaching from Biblical texts, and featured some form of liturgy, vestments, and hymns consisting of Western tunes and translated Western lyrics, played on pianos or organs. Many of these features are still evident today in the open churches, especially in urban centers, where most congregations are descended from the pre-1949 mission-founded churches.

In the historiography of Christianity in China, the theme of convergence has sometimes been presented as a story of failure or at best limited success, which was only brought to successful completion under the political conditions of the People's Republic, in which divisions were eliminated and a "post-denominational" church established.[14] Arguably it could easily support the opposite reading, given the diversity of missions at work in China and the concrete obstacles to working together. Regardless, however, of whether we read it as a tale of the dramatic transcending of differences or the failure to do so, it is increasingly clear that a simultaneous centrifugal trend, less noticed at the time, has shaped Protestantism in Chinese society in the twentieth century at least as much as the trend towards institutional convergence. That trend was the emergence in the twentieth century of independent and indigenous Protestant sects apart from or in reaction against the mission-founded churches. These ranged from single congregations formed around individual Chinese preachers (the best-known example, Wang Mingdao's church in Beijing, was but one of eleven such congregations in the city in 1949[15]) to large nationally-led movements such as the "Little Flock" of Watchman Nee, the True Jesus Church, the Jesus Family.[16] Daniel Bays, who has made the most extensive study to date of these developments, believes that the Little Flock, True Jesus Church, and Jesus Family between them may have amounted to twenty to twenty-five percent of all Protestants in China by the 1940s.[17]

While they differed from one another in important ways, these new Protestant movements shared some features in common. They were all reactions against the institutional and hierarchical character of the mission-founded churches, and sought to purify the church of its worldly entanglements. They were all theologically conservative, and often aggressively in reaction against what they regarded as the liberal and progressive theology emerging within the mission-founded churches. All placed a strong emphasis on direct spiritual experience, either through the Holiness teaching and mysticism which shaped Watchman Nee's work, or through Pentecostal manifestations, or both.[18] All of them accorded a high degree of autonomy to individual congregations, and most required no institutional authorization beyond the congregation for preachers and leaders.

Could these groups have come into existence without the prior establishment of the missionary churches? That seems to me unlikely, for a number of reasons. Firstly, the initial leaders of them were for the most part raised in the milieu of missionary Protestantism. Nee was the grandson of the first ABCFM pastor in Fuzhou, and his father was a YMCA leader and active layman; the revivalist John Sung was the son of a Methodist pastor; Paul Wei of the True Jesus Church was raised in a church of the London Missionary Society. Secondly, one feature of these movements was a stress on the direct access of the believer to God's word in the Bible, which without necessarily acknowledging it, built upon the struggle of missionaries and Chinese over the previous century to decide on terms for key Christian concepts and to translate the Bible into Chinese. This culminated in the Union version of 1919, which became and remains the generally accepted Chinese text of the Bible among Protestants. Thirdly, for all the anti-missionary and anti-institutional sentiment of these groups and their leaders, their separateness from the mission churches was not as complete as we might suppose. On the contrary, in the 1930s and 1940s there seems to have been considerable interpenetration of membership between the indigenous movements and the older missionary churches, and it is likely that many of the members of the Assembly Hall congregations, and possibly also of the True Jesus Church, were products of the missionary establishment, either from Protestant families or through the schools and student groups.[19]

The last stream is the most difficult to pin down, due to the paucity of reliable documentary sources on it. However, there are many indications that some of the most energetic Protestant movements in China today were begun by Chinese Protestants with no institutional links to the older churches, under the conditions of suppression of all open religious activity in the latter stages of the Cultural Revolution (1966–1976). It was once common to regard China during the Cultural Revolution as the ultimate controlled society, but it is clear in hindsight that the power of the state to oversee the day-to-day lives of the population was weakened by the dismantling of the bureaucracy in many respects.[20] In Protestantism, one result of the suppression of clerical and institutional structures during this period was a remarkable unleashing of lay initiative.[21] In locations all over China, particularly in rural areas but also in some cities, Protestants began meeting together in small and sometimes large groups by the early 1970s.[22] There are good reasons for thinking that the persistence of Protestant and other religious activities in the 1970s was recognized by the Chinese Communist Party, and that the desire to bring those activities into the open and under control was a major reason for the reinstitution of the policy of "freedom of religious belief" in 1979.[23]

Some of these informal Protestant groups were made up of people who had been part of the pre-1949 churches, mission-founded and independent, often combined in new ways under the exigencies of the time. Some of these reintegrated into the open churches as those reopened, while others chose to remain independent. Other groups emerged in the 1970s that seem to have been wholly new in origin, or perhaps to have sprouted from earlier seeds but grown into distinctly new movements.[24] One of the best documented of these groups was founded by Peter Xu Zongze, an independent evangelist who began preaching in Henan in 1968. His organization, variously called the *Chongsheng pai* (New Birth sect), the *Quanfanwei jiaohui* (Full Scope Church), or the Criers, is accused by some of being heretical. It is distinguished by a strong emphasis on a definitive experience of conversion, usually during an intensive three-day "life meeting," and by an emphasis (some say a requirement) on the confession of sins with tears. Xu has claimed that his organization consists of over 3,500 congregations and has sent evangelists to more than twenty of China's provinces.[25] These numbers cannot be independently verified, but it is evident that there are several other organized networks claiming a similarly large number of adherents, and many other groups of smaller scope.[26]

Again, the lack of field studies and other detailed sources limits our knowledge of the religious culture of these groups, but in general it seems clear that they are heavily experiential and revivalist in emphasis, stressing direct personal experience of God, centered on literal reading of the Bible, spread by itinerant preachers with little in the way of formal education (theological or otherwise), but a great deal of dedication and enthusiasm. Suspicion of the state, and of the TSPM/CCC for its ties to the state, are characteristic, as is an otherworldly and often eschatological orientation.[27]

In a long-term perspective, these movements represent a continuation of the impulse towards self-started churches independent of existing structures and external validation systems seen in the earlier part of the twentieth century. As Hunter and Chan argue, in organization these groups reflect the community-based structure of Chinese popular religion.[28] They are also reminiscent of the sectarian history of Protestantism in America during the nineteenth century.[29]

It is also worth noting that the creation of independent congregations and movements has been a characteristic trend in Chinese Protestant circles generally since World War II. According to sociologist Yang Fenggang, about half of the Chinese churches in the U.S.—and a decisive majority of the ones founded since 1950—are nondenominational; moreover, many of the denominational ones belong to denominations that give a high degree of independence to each congregation, such as the Southern Baptist Convention.[30] Yang ties this trend to the decline of denominations and proliferation of small groups and special agencies in American Protestantism over the same period, drawing on the work of Robert Wuthnow.[31] A similar shift away from the denominations towards independent congregations, often with Pentecostal roots and based around charismatic individual pastors, has been evident among Chinese Protestants in Malaysia since the 1970s, according to Judith Nagata. She links the shift to the social mobility of the Chinese middle class (business people and professionals) in Malaysia, noting in particular the importance of the Full Gospel Businessmen's

Fellowship and the Christian entertainment industry among such churches, many of which rent space in luxury hotels for their services.[32]

Overall, institutional fragmentation has been a major trend in the history of Protestantism in China since the 1920s. The proliferation of new movements and independent churches in Chinese Protestantism since then can be attributed to the relatively weak historical attachment to the Western denominations, to changes in Protestantism globally in the twentieth century, and to broader social changes such as social mobility and the growing ease of travel and access to education and information.

Not unrelated to these social changes is the fact that since the opening of China in 1979, a great number of Western Protestant groups (as well as Chinese groups based outside the People's Republic) have attempted to conduct missionary work of some nature in China. The proliferation of special agencies analyzed by Wuthnow, coupled with the secrecy exercised by many such groups and their lack of ties to larger structures, makes it very difficult to get a clear handle on this sector, but it clearly includes a wide array of parachurch agencies, single congregations, and individual religious entrepreneurs. Some operate relatively openly and in a genuine service role, such as the groups which supply English teachers and other "foreign experts" to Chinese educational institutions. Others try to work directly with the autonomous churches, and not always on very sound missiological principles. One agency collects money in the United States to supply Chinese house church leaders with laptop computers equipped with cellular modems, and with $1,500 scholarships for them to study English "because home church networks often work with Western ministries!"[33] The number of Protestants associated with these Western-based efforts and their relationship to the wider church in China are not clear, but we are on safe ground in assuming that at least the more scattershot efforts like the one just cited are not of central importance to the overall Protestant presence in China.

One of the many questions about Protestantism in China for which we lack good data is the extent to which the different strands of Protestant life are regionally defined. Where in China are Protestants more numerous, and can we discern regional variations in the Chinese church? Amid all the conflicting claims about the total number of Protestants, estimates of which range from the 10 to 12 million currently acknowledged by the national TSPM/CCC to ten times that figure, there is general agreement that Protestants are most numerous in three distinct areas: the coastal provinces of Fujian, Zhejiang, Jiangsu, and Shandong, which were centers of missionary work before 1949; the provinces of the central China plain, particularly Henan and Anhui; and among the minority peoples of southwest

China (Yunnan and Guizhou).[34] There are indications that the adherents to the post-1949 new church movements are more numerous in central China, while in the coastal provinces most Protestants have roots in the mission churches or the pre-1949 indigenous churches, but this can only be a tentative conclusion.[35]

Although the churches have been growing in the cities as well, the majority of Chinese Protestants are in rural China, where the composition of Protestant congregations has been summed up as the "four manys": many old people, many women, many sick, and many illiterate.[36] Other studies emphasize similar characteristics for the urban churches, such as a recent Chinese study of five churches in Shanghai which surveyed the educational level and gender by age cohort of 12,000 Protestants baptized between 1980 and 1990, finding that sixty-three percent were over sixty, fifty-eight percent of primary school or lower educational level, and eighty percent women.[37] Other reports indicate a significant number of young people, people with higher education, and professionals joining the urban churches, however, and the rapid spread of the market economy and consequent social mobility may well tend to reinforce this trend.[38]

Chinese Protestantism?

Having considered the diversity in Protestantism in China today, we turn to discerning commonalities; is there such a thing as Chinese Protestantism, and if so, what characteristics does it have? Broadly speaking, we can trace two common orientations that characterize most manifestations of Protestant belief in China today: an experiential emphasis and Biblicism. On the first score, Hunter and Chan, whose 1993 book *Protestantism in Contemporary China* is the most comprehensive treatment of the topic to date, argue that many Chinese Protestants, particularly in rural areas, understand their Christian faith in terms drawn from Chinese popular religion. Jesus functions much like a Chinese deity, and is a source from which to seek healing for illness and other supernatural help.[39] Many other sources also testify to the importance of faith healing, exorcism, and other supernatural manifestations in the Chinese Protestant churches, open and otherwise.[40] In this respect the contemporary Protestant scene continues the emphasis on the experiential immediacy of the supernatural that has characterized much of Chinese Protestantism throughout its history. As we have noted, that experiential emphasis was characteristic of the revivalist movements in the Republican period.[41] In addition, I am convinced from my study of early Protestants in the Fuzhou area that immediacy of spiritual experience was also an important part of the Protestant appeal in the late Qing period, and that the primary frame of reference for most first-generation Protestant converts before 1900 was the vivid unseen pantheon of "gods, ghosts, and ancestors" which marked Chinese popular religion.[42]

In doctrine, most Chinese Protestants have a literal belief in the Bible as the inspired word of God, and the Bible plays a central role in preaching, which in turn is the core of the worship service in most Chinese Protestant churches. How Biblical texts are *employed* in preaching and devotional writing in Protestant circles is at least as important to understand, however, and on this there is good evidence that often a particular Biblical text will be given an allegorical or "spiritual" interpretation. This predisposition towards allegorical modes of understanding Biblical texts, which is evident both in contemporary preaching in Chinese churches and in the writings of many Chinese Protestant leaders of the early twentieth century, including Watchman Nee, John Sung, and Jia Yuming, is one of the more fascinating characteristics of Chinese Protestantism.[43] In some interesting articles on this topic, Ji Tai of Nanjing Seminary suggests that the prevalence of allegory may reflect a special affinity for allegory in Chinese culture, perhaps connected to the nature of the Chinese writing system, as well as the lack of higher textual training among Chinese evangelists.[44] One can interpret this use of allegory as another manifestation of experiential immediacy in Chinese Protestantism, since allegorical interpretation serves to bring the Biblical text within the sphere of immediate relevance to the hearer, which is to say, the sphere of experience. One might also speculate that it is related to the absence of culturally-embedded Christian referents in China, which may make it easier to interpret the Biblical text allegorically, without regard for context or commentarial tradition. However, cultural referents are only fixed points to those who acknowledge them, and in the late twentieth century it is just as easy, and probably just as common, for Western Protestants to interpret Biblical passages without regard to the context or traditional interpretations. This could also be the case in Chinese interpretation of Confucian texts in isolation from the rich corpus of commentary which informed and channelled the interpretations of those texts while Confucianism remained a living tradition of the Chinese elite.[45]

Indigenization and the Problem of Chinese Culture

In attempting to delineate the shared features of Chinese Protestantism, we must confront the much discussed issue of "indigenization;" what does it mean for Protestant Christianity to become "indigenous" in Chinese society? This has been a major topic of debate within Chinese Protestant circles since the 1920s, and even earlier if we see it as linked to missionary concerns with self-support. However, much of that debate has been marred by a lack of clarity stemming from the different assumptions about the nature of Chinese culture which have been adopted by different writers on the subject.

Chinese theologians have tended to approach the issue from the vantage point of the Chinese elite tradition, combing the ancient texts for echoes of or parallels to Christian ideas.[46] Some of this work parallels and addresses the attempts of Chinese thinkers in Hong Kong and abroad to resurrect a modernized version of Confucianism as a new basis for Chinese culture.[47] Interestingly, the most ambitious and thorough effort I know of to find Christian analogues in the Chinese intellectual heritage was written not in recent years but in 1903, when that heritage still constituted the vital core of Chinese education, high culture, and political life, by the Fuzhou Protestant scholar Huang Zhiji (Uong De-gi). In a magisterial work in 12 *juan*, Huang tracked down textual support in the Chinese classical canon—from the pre-Qin philosophers to the major intellectuals of the early Qing—for Protestant moral teachings and Protestant critiques of Chinese social practices.[48] He later anticipated the great Republican period historian Gu Jiegang in locating an alternative Chinese tradition in the pre-Qin thinker Mozi, whose work Huang analyzed for its compatibility with Christianity in a book published in 1912.[49] Ironically, by the time Huang published these works the intellectual heritage which he combed with such care was already ruptured and would soon pass from the forefront of the concerns of Chinese thinkers with the coming of revolution, nationalism, and the rejection of tradition in the May Fourth Movement.

Other scholars have approached indigenization more in terms of popular culture. For instance, Chen Zemin, Vice-President of Nanjing Seminary, has in recent years been collecting and writing about the new hymnody generated in the rural Chinese church, welcoming it as an indigenous alternative to the many missionary-era translations of Western hymns which fill the Chinese hymnal.[50] Hunter and Chan's analysis of the similarities of Protestant practice in China to popular religion also takes popular culture as the benchmark for indigenization.[51]

In some definitions, originating under Chinese leadership independently of the Western missionary effort is sufficient to qualify a Protestant group as "indigenous," as in the now commonplace labelling of the Little Flock or the True Jesus Church as "indigenous."[52] In his important work on Protestants in Taiwan, Murray Rubinstein makes indigenization central to his analysis, but defines it, partly at least, in terms of distance from the Western missionary heritage, such that the most "indigenous" of the Protestant movements in Taiwan are those which arose most independently, the True Jesus Church and the New Testament Church. (He also argues that their authoritarian structures and ecstatic styles of worship—both are Pentecostal movements—

are indigenous in that they parallel the Chinese sectarian tradition, and that their appeal as measured by their rapid growth in Taiwan is due to their successful indigenization.)[53] From one point of view this is a reasonable conclusion, but it raises several problems. First, it leaves little possibility for the missionary-founded denominational churches to become "indigenous." It also raises the question of the equally dramatic growth of Pentecostal churches elsewhere, especially in the United States and in Latin America: might the appeal of these churches in Taiwan have more to do with the shared context of capitalist modernization than the unique one of Chinese culture? Last, having non-missionary origins seems an inadequate definition of indigenization, especially considering that the New Testament Church is considered heretical by most other Protestant groups; by that definition the contemporary sects in China most removed from the historical Protestant tradition, like the Established King, the Eastern Lightning, or historically the Taipings, would be the most "indigenous."

Chinese Communist Party policy also contains an implicit definition of indigenization in its insistence that religion must be made compatible with socialism. This definition of indigenization, which makes a particular political economy, socialism, central to the definition of "Chineseness," is echoed in policy pronouncements and in the writings of some Chinese scholars about the contemporary Protestant situation.[54]

The difficulty of defining indigenization can be traced, I believe, to the difficulty of defining Chinese culture, which is both a historical and distinctly modern problem. Historically, thanks to path-breaking work since the 1970s on late imperial popular culture and religion, we are more aware than ever before of the diversity that existed within Chinese culture in the late imperial period, between regions, between rural and urban settings, between social classes, and over time.[55] Even in so-called "traditional" China, being Chinese meant very different things to different groups and individuals.

Nevertheless, while it meant different things to different people, taken as a whole Chinese culture also provided an integrated system of meaning and identity, with a coherence that was taken for granted in late imperial times. This system of meaning and identity disintegrated in the twentieth century, on many levels. The high culture of officialdom was thrown into crisis with the defeat of China by Japan in 1895, and the abolition of the old examination system in 1905 altered it forever.[56] The vertical integration between elite and popular culture was ruptured by the new modernizing spirit of elite nationalism, which redefined popular culture as ignorance and popular religion as superstition, and thus a barrier to modernization.[57] As recent work by Chinese and non-Chinese scholars has highlighted, the result has been an ongoing crisis of Chinese identity, uncertainty about what Chinese culture is and how Chinese identity may be understood (apart from nationalism, which has been the default mode of identification in the absence of agreed cultural content of Chineseness in the twentieth century).[58]

Given these uncertainties about what Chinese culture is, it is not surprising that the attempts to identify an indigenous Protestant Christianity would vary so widely. Perhaps the best approach is to treat the different manifestations of Protestant life in China as plural indigeniza*tions*, recognizing each as a blend of Chinese and foreign elements which makes sense to its adherents on some level. Making sense to its adherents is surely the main issue, after all, as we are reminded by the story told by Richard Zhang of a woman in a rural church who was surprised to learn that there were also Protestants *outside* China.[59] Ever since it became a major topic of debate in the 1920s, much of the discussion of indigenization has been given its urgency by the sense of a need among Chinese Protestants to overcome the perception of Christianity as a foreign religion. Such a perception was no doubt "there" in Chinese society from the time of anti-Christian movements in the 1920s, but it gained its sting from being internalized in the subjective self-understanding of Chinese Protestants. In other words, the problem of indigenization is ultimately a matter of perception rather than "reality," since it flows from the subjectively experienced tension between Chinese and foreign identities among some sectors of the Protestant church in China; where no such tension is experienced, the question of indigenization is answered.[60]

Protestants in Chinese Society

Discussion of indigenization leads to one sense in which Protestantism in China is fragile; it lacks a well-developed awareness of its own history. In one way this is a problem of growth; small, localized communities are more likely to preserve an institutional memory of their history than the large, diverse, and dispersed movements that comprise Chinese Protestantism today. Also, however, it results from the political disruptions and institutional limitations imposed on the church under the People's Republic, and from the generational change which has taken place over the same period.

Before 1949, the major Protestant denominations and independent Protestant sects all fostered a sense of their history and corporate identity through regular synod or conference meetings; through visible historical markers such as wall plaques, inscriptions, and even stele; and, crucially, through publishing, both of periodicals and of commemorative volumes and institutional histories, some of them very extensive.[61] By contrast, very little such activity is or can be undertaken by the Protestant churches in China today. The number of current Protestant periodicals in China is a tiny fraction of the dozens that circulated nationally and regionally in the Republican period. In Fujian most of the books and primary records of the pre-1949 churches either no longer exist or are not accessible. Attempts commissioned by the United Front Department to write a public history (*zhi*) of the Protestant and other religious communities in the province have been bogged down in questions of the political standpoint of historical interpretation. While the local church authorities in some areas have begun publishing useful volumes of historical reminiscences (*wenshi ziliao*), these are limited in scope, restricted for the most part to pre-1949 history, and cannot replace primary documentation.[62] Meanwhile, the number of old pastors and lay people who have some direct knowledge of the past is dwindling, and many of those are reluctant or unable to write down a frank account of their lives.

If the print vehicles for the formation of Protestant identity and the conveying of community history are now limited in number and nature compared to the period before 1949, so too are the other physical markers of that history and identity. Most obviously, the church buildings themselves are fewer in number and diminished in grandeur. Overall in China, only some of the former church or mission property has been returned to the churches, despite the official central government policy since 1979 that such property should be returned. In 1993 there were about ten churches open in Fuzhou City, which is less than half the number before 1949. Physically, those churches are quite bare. The pipe organs and bells of the past, which announced the existence of those churches to their neighborhoods, are gone, as are any commemorative plaques or stained glass windows that once existed. Furthermore, the other institutions that were so much a part of the Protestant presence in Chinese society before 1949—schools, hospitals, YMCA and YWCA buildings, and the like—are no longer connected to the churches, even where the institutions or their buildings survive.

The problem that results is twofold; not only do Protestants in China today lack a sense of their own history, but when they do it is a separate history, not as one embedded in the history of modern China. This is one of the problems with the *wenshi ziliao* approach, and is also reflected in the historiography in English on Protestantism in China. Having a greater consciousness of history would strengthen awareness that Protestantism is indeed firmly rooted in Chinese society and culture and need not be continually justifying its existence.[63]

So far in this paper I have skirted the difficult question of the relationship between Protestantism and the state in China. It is clear enough that, along with other religious believers, Protestants of all types experience state pressure and intervention in their activities. As is well known, a series of laws passed during the 1990s attempted to formalize the institutional oversight of the state over all religious practice by requiring all places of religious activity to apply for registration from the government.[64] Pastors and church leaders in the open church structure are obliged to attend lengthy political study meetings (like everyone else employed in public-sector work units in China), cutting into the little time available for pastoral visitation and other church work. Government officials interfere in the routine work of the Protestant bodies, or intervene in the election of officeholders. Young church workers who are too outspoken can have their ordinations blocked or delayed by the Religious Affairs Bureau.[65]

Protestants who eschew registration or affiliation with the TSPM/CCC lay themselves open to police harassment and penalties running the gamut from short-term detention and hefty fines, to reeducation through labor sentences (which can be up to four years in length), to a full-scale criminal trial and prison sentences of up to fifteen years, most often for violation of one or more of the articles on "counterrevolutionary crimes" (redesignated crimes against national security in 1997) in China's Criminal Code.[66]

Despite the obvious political weakness of Chinese Protestantism under the present Chinese regime, however, the question of the relationship to the state concerns not only the impact of the state on Protestants, but also its converse, the impact or potential impact of Chinese Protestants on state and society. This is a significant preoccupation of Chinese Communist leaders, who fear that "hostile international forces" will use Christianity as a "breakthrough point" to "Westernize China."[67]

What then are the implications of the growth of Protestantism for Chinese society? Or, to turn the question around, how would China be different if there were no Protestant presence? Here again the comparison with history is instructive. For the generation of Chinese Protestants active between 1900 and 1920, the political and social implications of Protestant belief were self-evident: the reform of Chinese social practices held to be immoral (e.g. gambling, opium smoking, concubinage, child brides, prostitution), unnatural (footbinding) or unhealthy (poor hygiene practices), and the establishment of a republican system of government modeled on that of the United States. Their perception of the world was deeply shaped by a vision of making China a modern, Protestant nation, a vision that was both powerfully coherent and deeply flawed, not least because they were unaware of the extent to which their view of the United States reflected a residual

Protestant hegemony in U. S. public culture that was never likely to be reproduced in China. Moreover, Protestant institutions and individuals acted as crucial intermediaries for the dissemination of this model of modernity in local society.[68]

By contrast, in China today, the social and political implications of the Protestant presence are much less clear. Most basically, Protestantism variously understood is clearly providing millions of Chinese with a frame of reference for their lives that is unconnected to or at least distinct from the state and its ideology. In those areas where Protestants are more numerous, like Wenzhou in Zhejiang Province, we know that Protestantism is deeply enmeshed in local society, but we can only speculate how (if at all) that fact affects the social fabric—business practices, divorce rates, child rearing, entertainment, conflict, and so on. In other places Protestants are a small minority with little social visibility. Institutionally, the Protestant churches are carefully prevented from playing the sorts of roles that made the Protestant community influential beyond its numbers in Republican China. Now, although there have been some experiments in social service, in general the range of relevance of the church is much narrower than it was then: personal religious belief and religious meetings within registered religious premises at certain times. Neither the TSPM/CCC structure nor the autonomous churches act as a public voice providing a distinctly Protestant perspective on issues of pressing national concern—materialism and official corruption, say, or the social dislocations brought about by economic reform.[69] More importantly, even if they could exercise such a role, it is by no means as clear today what the political implications of Protestantism are.

There are two principle comparative frames of reference within which the place of Protestantism in contemporary China must be discussed. The first of these is the voluminous literature on the role played by religion (and *qua* Weber Protestantism) in modernization. On this score, I have little to add to the observations made by Hunter and Chan in 1993. They concluded that while Protestantism in some social/historical settings has been directly connected to the emergence of both capitalism and democracy, there is no necessary causal relationship between Protestantism and these economic and political systems, nor is there any particular evidence to connect the rapid spread of Protestantism in China today to increased support for either.[70]

The second is the less voluminous but still substantial literature around the question of "civil society," which has been a preoccupation of scholars of modern China in the last decade. The debate stems from two sources, theories about the social changes in early modern Western Europe that led to modern politics based on the notions of popular sovereignty, representation, and citizenship, and analyses of the process which triggered the collapse of the East European Communist regimes in 1989. Central to both questions has been the work of German social thinker Jürgen Habermas.[71]

The effort to apply the concept of civil society to China has been hampered by a lack of agreement on what the term means. While most writers would agree with on the general definition of "the realm of organized social life that is voluntary, self-generating, (largely) self-supporting, [and] autonomous from the state," differences have emerged in the literature over how to define autonomy from the state, how to identify forms of corporate life in China which exemplify such autonomy, and whether the presence of autonomy is sufficient to qualify an association as a manifestation of "civil society."[72]

Almost none of this literature has discussed the implications for "civil society" of the resurgence of religion in China. This omission is striking given the important roles played by religious bodies in many of the East European countries in 1989, and more recently the intense alarm among China's leaders over the growth of a new religious movement, *Falun gong*. The major exceptions are Richard Madsen, who makes "civil society" central to his book on China's Catholic church but defines the term rather differently than most who have applied it to China, connecting it more to civility as a moral quality than to associational attributes; and Kenneth Dean, who, in an article on the revival of popular religion, rejects the term entirely as a "nostalgic myth that Westerners live by and still seek to impose on others," instead analyzing popular religious practice as the disruptive assertion of local identities against the totalizing pretensions of the state.[73]

Most broadly, the civil society debate represents one effort by scholars to conceptualize the structural changes in Chinese social life that have taken place with the retreat from the Maoist revolutionary vision—which was explicitly antipluralistic in the sense that in it society, culture, the party, the people, the revolution were all coterminous—and the return to a market economy and limited recognition of plural interests in society. The gradual downplaying of overtly political themes in literature, art, and popular culture, the broadening of intellectual discourse, the appearance of private enterprises, and the resurgence of communally-based popular religion are all dimensions of the trend towards reclaiming space for culture and society as autonomous from the state. "Civil society" is only a conceptual tool with which to study these changes, and perhaps not the best one possible, but since it has been in such common use it is worth reflecting on whether the Protestant situation has any bearing on the question.[74]

Concerning the officially recognized Protestant bodies, the first fact to be noted is the anomalous position of these and other "patriotic religious organizations" in the political structure of the People's Republic of China.

Like all other social associations representing distinct functional and identity constituencies (e.g., non-Communist political parties, ethnic minorities, women's associations, labor unions), the religious organizations fall under the supervision of the Party's United Front Work Department. Unlike those bodies, however, the supervision exercised by the United Front Department over the religious organizations cannot be direct without compromising the credibility of the organizations with their constituencies, a credibility which is essential if they are to play their intended role of uniting religious believers to be patriotic and support the Communist Party. Thus, the religious associations are unique among organizations under the United Front in not having their leadership positions included on the list of positions for which the candidates for "election" must be approved in advance by the Communist Party.[75]

In formal terms, the Three-Self Movement and the China Christian Council exemplify many of the qualities normally associated with manifestations of "civil society." They operate on a constitutional basis, with a rational bureaucratic structure, regular meetings, and a leadership chosen through elections. Membership in them is voluntary and cuts across regional and social lines, and they are self-supporting. In at least some locations, they have been able to arrive at an effective *modus vivendi* between different Protestant traditions, suggesting that the qualities of civility which Madsen finds wanting for the Catholic church in Hebei may be more in evidence among the Protestants, at least in some areas.[76] Like other social associations under the United Front, their stance vis-à-vis the state has changed gradually over the post-Mao period, from the role of a "transmission belt," disseminating party policies to their members and uniting their members behind those policies, to one of advocacy, seeking to assert and defend the autonomy to run the church which Chinese law and Communist Party policy grant them on paper but which is too often denied or infringed in practice.[77] Thus, since the late 1980s TSPM/CCC leaders have begun to use the channels at their disposal—the national church magazine *Tianfeng*, their seats in the National People's Congress and Chinese People's Political Consultative Committee, and their contacts with the Protestant churches abroad—to express their dissatisfaction with aspects of the state's religious policy and its implementation.[78]

While a few individual Protestants have been active in labor organization and political protests in the 1990s, the organized Protestant bodies have not directly challenged the political supremacy of the Communist Party.[79] What they have sought is summed up in the phrase, "(CCP) leadership in politics, self-government in religion"—the freedom for Protestant religious activities to be governed by Protestants themselves, without political interference.[80] On the local level, many pastors and church workers seek to exercise autonomy from the political in day-to-day practice, by avoiding study classes and giving their energy to pastoral work.

Turning to the Protestant groups that are not affiliated with the TSPM/CCC, the situation is similar in that we find large numbers of people organized on a voluntary basis in self-supporting associations of varying degrees of sophistication, from single, small congregations to large transprovincial networks. Even more than the open churches, the autonomous networks are mostly quite explicitly apolitical, since the most characteristic reason for resisting affiliation with the TSPM/CCC is the perception that these bodies are political and the church must remain totally separate from the political sphere.[81] In refusing to register or to affiliate with the TSPM/CCC, these groups are also demanding autonomy for Protestant religious activities from the political sphere; paradoxically, they are doing so by the political act of resisting state control, and exposing themselves to punishment for what the state considers political crimes.

What does all this mean for civil society in China? Firstly, it is clear that there is no direct correlation between Protestant demands for autonomy and political opposition to the government. That should not surprise us. As Brook and Frolic have pointed out, in looking too much for signs of opposition to the state in civil society, the literature on civil society in China has failed to recognize that civil society in the West developed "in close relationship to the state, working with it more consistently than opposing it."[82]

Secondly, the Protestant situation raises the question of the political implications of the choice to be apolitical in a society like China: To what degree is the seeking out of autonomous space in which to be apolitical a political act? What implications does it have? Here the work of David Martin on Latin American Pentecostals provides some helpful points of comparison. Martin argues against those who would dismiss Pentecostalism as a politically irrelevant force since, unlike the base communities or liberation theologians, Pentecostals do not articulate a political theology or seek to bring political change. He argues on the contrary that the choice to convert to Pentecostalism represents a choice to withdraw from a political sphere held to be corrupt, and to "alter what is in their capacity to alter, beginning with themselves, their families and congregations. They bind themselves together on rafts of discipline, and hope, so far as is possible, to cut themselves off from the corruption and violence all around them, most evidently in the political sphere."[83] This is, he argues, a political choice, and tends to "erode all-embracing systems" and "accelerate the shift to pluralism," both in Latin America and in the case of other apparently apolitical religious movements elsewhere, such as in Eastern Europe before 1989.[84]

In the Chinese case, in believing in Christianity, Protestants implicitly reject or at the least modify key planks of the ideology of the Chinese Communist Party, even in its greatly attenuated post-Mao form. Moreover, the inherent conflict between the formal autonomy of the churches contained in the Chinese constitution and policies and the routine experience of political interference creates an ongoing pressure point between the churches and the state, as is reflected in the pages of *Tianfeng* on a regular basis. Lastly, the increasing importance of a new generation of church workers with no personal experience of either the missionary era or the suffering of pastors during the political campaigns of the Maoist decades will continue to be a catalyst for change.[85]

To sum up this section, the Protestant churches in China do indeed constitute part of an emerging "civil society" in China in the sense that the ongoing struggle to claim an autonomous space for religious activity is at the core of the Protestant experience, both in the open and in the autonomous churches. This has not resulted in political opposition to the Communist Party, nor should we expect it to; indeed, the Protestant demands for autonomy are made precisely on the basis of the state's formal granting of that autonomy on paper, at least in the case of the open churches. On the other hand, the growth of Protestantism in China probably does represent a massive withdrawal from the political, which in time may have political implications, in undermining the claims of the Communist Party to ultimate ideological allegiance and forcing recognition of a *de facto* pluralism. The political implications are potentially more dramatic, also; examining the role played by religious institutions in the uprisings that brought down the Communist governments of Eastern Europe in 1989, Martin argues that churches which exist on the margins of a politicized culture have a latent power which can burst out, even if briefly, into the public square, with decisive influence.[86] He also argues, however, that their influence on public life in the Eastern European cases was rather transitory, and that the period since has created new and unforeseen struggles for the post-Communist governments and for the churches.[87] To refer back to Madsen's alternative definition of "civil society," the political influence of religion may emerge suddenly and perhaps decisively in particular historical moments, as in Eastern Europe in 1989, but that does not go far to building a sustainable social order based on civility. If that can happen at all it will require a more arduous transition; after all, Habermas, whose theory undergirds the whole debate, identified the emergence of civil society in the eighteenth century only to lament its decline in the nineteenth and twentieth centuries.[88]

Chinese Protestantism in World Christianity

To sum up the features of Chinese Protestantism as we have identified them: a warm, experiential piety, centered on a concern for salvation and for tangible blessings in this life; literal faith in the Bible; rapid growth accompanied by increasing institutional diversity and fragmentation, expanding with China's market economy, despite efforts to restrict and control it; detachment from institutions giving continuity to the Protestant experience, including history and local or kin solidarities. All these elements, we should note, tend towards making Chinese Protestantism an increasingly individualized faith.[89]

When we seek to fit this picture into the mosaic of world Christianity at the end of the twentieth century, it is striking how little is unique about Chinese Protestantism, despite its very specific history and circumstances. Institutionally, the erosion of denominational structures, the breakdown of the correlation of ethnic or communal with religious identities, and the proliferation of new sects, movements, and congregations are all recognizably part of the modern Protestant trajectory elsewhere. So is the tendency to place individual experience at the center of Protestant spirituality, at least since the evangelical revivals of the eighteenth century. While scholars of modern religion have been moving away from assuming that modernization leads to secularization, it remains widely accepted that industrial market economies, of which China is one, tend to erode cultural consensus, traditions, and community solidarity, and to create the more or less autonomous self. Rather than producing a straightforward decline in religion, such changes have instead changed its nature, from one that is part of an ascriptive identity acquired at birth to one that is voluntary, individualized, experiential, forcing religious institutions to change accordingly, from structures of religious authority to commodities in a religious marketplace, oriented towards satisfying the needs of the religious consumer-self.[90] Pentecostal movements, once routinely presented as reactions against modernity, are now being reevaluated as especially reflective of these forces, in their emphasis on the self, and in equipping their adherents, especially in the developing capitalist societies of Latin America and South Korea, with the "values of ascetic Protestantism . . . so essential for social mobility in a capitalist economy."[91]

Putting these things together, we can suppose that the forces at work in changing the social forms and expressions of Protestantism in other industrializing and post-industrial societies in the late twentieth century will continue to work in China in the twenty-first century. Among other things, that will tend to make it more difficult for the church authorities to generate unity in the Chinese church.

The other key point that must be made about the Protestant church in China is that it is part of the long-term shift in the center of gravity of world Protestantism, away from the old Protestant world of Western Europe and its derivatives, and towards Africa, Asia, and Latin America, where most world Protestants now reside. What will this mean for the development of Protestantism in the century now dawning? Just as the forces of modernity do on a micro scale, this macro shift clearly raises the question of how to maintain an agreed core in the absence of an overarching authority structure—which is of course a new variation on a problem that has been implicit in Protestantism from its beginnings. On the other hand, there is also a great potential for creative dynamism and theological and practical cross-fertilization in the new situation.

In conclusion, it is clear that Protestant Christianity has an established place in the People's Republic of China at the dawn of the twenty-first century. It also has an established place in the transnational reality of Chinese culture, in the middle-class churches of Hong Kong and the overseas Chinese communities, and as a focus of interest and cultural inquiry among Chinese intellectuals. Whether in the villages of Henan or the plush hotels of Penang, Chinese Protestantism is a hybrid, or in fact many hybrids, as all are cultural products. But in the fluid mutations and recurring patterns which make up Chinese culture today, there is an undeniable Protestant element which will continue to develop in tense and dynamic interaction with that culture. To borrow Nicolas Standaert's expressive phrase, there is a "Christian fragment in the Chinese fractal"—or fragments, and fragile ones, yet flourishing nevertheless.[92]

Hungarian Missionaries in China

Péter Vámos

Hungarians—Nation from the East?

In the year 2000, when the world celebrates the coming of a new millenium, Hungarians commemorate the millenium of the state established by their first Christian king, Saint Stephen. Hungarian tribes conquested the area of present day Hungary with the final wave of the great migration from the East in 896.[1] One hundred years after the Hungarian conquest of the land within the Carpathians, Hungary became part of Europe by adopting Christianity. The European state ideology of modernity which existed a thousand years ago took shape in the ideal of the Christian kingdom. Hungary was established on the border of Roman and Byzanthean Christianity, under the religious and political influence of both powers.

Nevertheless, the notion of the "nation from the East" was part of the Hungarians' consciousness throughout the centuries. The first Hungarian to go to the East was a Dominican friar named Iulianus in the thirteenth century. His aim was to visit the Hungarians who were supposed to live in the land of the Bolgars near the confluence of the rivers Volga and Kama. By the Volga he found the way to *Magna Hungaria*, the area where Hungarians were said to live. Indeed, Iulianus found Hungarians who remained in the original homeland of the Hungarian people.

In the eighteenth century the debate over the Asian origin of the Hungarians took on a new element. A French sinologist Deguignes, in his work entitled *Histoire Générale de Huns, des Turcs, des Mogols, et des autres Tartares occidentaux, avant et depuis J. C. jusqu'á présent* (Paris, 1756–1758) identified the European Huns with the Asian Xiongnus, based on Chinese sources. Not long after its publication, a Hungarian Jesuit historian, Georgius Pray, introduced the new theory to Hungary, accepting every statement of the French author. Pray had several followers in Hungary, due to the fact that national pride swelled at the mention of any connection with the glorious past of the Huns. Those who supported Pray's ideas, on the basis of gut emotion and reaction, rejected all criticism. The assumption of identity took root in common understanding without actual scientific proof. For scholars trying to substantiate this assumption, it would have been imperative to know not only the Chinese language, but also the history of China and Central Asia. Thus, by the second half of the eighteenth century, a clear awareness of Hun kinship and Asian origins was formed in Hungary. While for the Western world Attila and his Huns were the symbols of barbarism and destruction, in Hungary he was the Scourge of God, the model of braveness and greatness.

The tradition of the Hungarians' Oriental origin is alive not only among Hungarians. Several Chinese intellectuals believe even today that Hungarians are the only representatives of the yellow people to reach Europe. The origins of this tradition also go back to the past century. Liang Qichao, a reformer politician-ideologist devoted a long essay to the Hungarian politician and leader of the 1848–1849 revolution, Lajos Kossuth. The title of the treatise, written in 1902, is "A Hungarian patriot: Kossuth." The reason why a monarchist-reformist Chinese thinker devoted a long treatise to the republican revolutionary Kossuth is that Liang believed that his hero is Asian. The author briefly introduced the history of Hungary, and also mentioned the relationship between the Xiongnu and Hungarians: "Hungarians are Asian, yellow people, descendants of the ancient Xiongnu. . . ."[2]

Nationalism and the Mission Movement

At the beginning of the twentieth century the Hungarian search for origins gained new impetus. The Eastern origins of the nation, and the location of the country between East and West made it possible for philosopher-politicians, amateur historians and linguists to initiate a new debate about whether Hungary should belong to the East, whether it should renew and continue its Asian traditions, or whether it should belong to the West, to the circle of European culture.

Following World War I, Hungary found itself in an entirely new predicament. The Great Powers decided upon the fate of the country and its people without actual Hungarian participation. The Austro-Hungarian Monarchy, which used to be one of the biggest states in Europe in terms of both territory and population, fell apart. According to the Peace Treaty of Trianon after World War I, the thousand-year-old Hungary was deprived of two-thirds of its territory and one-third of its Hungarian-speaking population. The new states of Czechoslovakia, Romania and Yugoslavia were formed around Hungary. Therefore, it is not accidental that after the failure of the civil revolution in the autumn of 1918 and the Hungarian Soviet Republic in 1919, the two pillars of ruling ideology became Christianity and nationalism. The minority question became part of foreign policy and in the country torn into pieces, the question of revisionism was high on the national agenda. One of the main aims of the political elite in Hungary was to regain possession over the lost territories, and the reunification of the mutilated country under the Holy Crown.

Following the trauma at the beginning of the twentieth century, opposition to Western tendencies was revived. It was under these circumstances that Turanism, the ideology of Orientalism took shape in Hungary and served as a basis for a nationalistic ideology which grew into a racist-fascist movement in the first decades of the twentieth century.

Among the members of the Turan Society established in 1910 we find the most prominent scholars of that time. In the scientific circles of the society, emphasis was first of all laid not upon the kinship between Hungarians and Eastern peoples, but they used the term Turan rather in a geographical sense. Followers of political Turanism, however, emphasized the theory of kinship, thus winning the sympathy of the public very quickly. The most radical members of the movement simply identified the term Turan with the East, thus they considered the Chinese, Japanese, Koreans, etc., as peoples of Turan, kindred to Hungarians. At that time it was in fashion to speak about Hungarian-Japanese, Hungarian-Korean, and even Hungarian-Chinese relationships.

In the confusion caused by World War I, the revolutions and the peace treaty, Turanism received a new stimulus. Disappointment towards Europe caused by "the betrayal of the West in Trianon," and the pessimistic feeling of loneliness, led different strata in society towards Turanism. They tried to look for friends, kindred peoples and allies in the East so that Hungary could break out of its isolation and regain its well deserved position among the nations. A more radical group of conservative, rightist people, sometimes even with an anti-Semitic hint propagated sharply anti-Western views and the superiority of Eastern culture, the necessity of a pro-Eastern policy, and development of the awareness of Turanic racialism among Hungarian people. In the 1920s the impact of the theory about the Hungarians' Eastern kinship was stronger than ever.[3]

This theory was well received by the Church, for its aim corresponded to the churches' missionary vocation. After the shock caused by the measures of the Peace Treaty which had so much influenced Hungary's national self-identity, Hungarian religious orders and mission societies felt that they were facing new challenges. After Trianon, the Hungarian nationalistic context of the foreign mission sometimes gained more emphasis than the biblical background of missionary work. It was especially so in the case of the Hungarian Reformed Church, which had always had a strong nationalistic character and, in a way, has been a symbol of Hungarian national identity and national power throughout its history. Members of mission organizations constructed an ideology out of this tragic situation. As they said: "Maybe He made a mutilated Hungary of Greater Hungary so that the small Hungarian mission enterprise, which still lived in its early days, could grow into a great Hungarian mission and the power and appreciation of the great Hungarian mission could rebuild Greater Hungary again."[4] The Hungarian Evangelical Christian Missionary Society reaffirmed its task of going eastwards. In 1921, the report of the Society's annual meeting declared: "If we want to be valuable for Western Christianity, we should radiate Christian culture to the South and the East, which could only be accomplished by Hungarian foreign missions."[5] The new Constitution of the Mission Society of the Reformed Church in 1932 stated as its purpose "to spread the Gospel to all the nations on the Earth, especially to the non-Christian members of the kindred peoples of the Hungarians."[6] Both Reformed and Lutheran mission societies felt responsibility towards peoples kindred to Hungarians. They referred, first of all, to those ethnic Hungarians who found themselves out of their home country after 1920, but also kindred groups in Russia and in the Far East. They referred to these missions as "Russian Mission" or "Turan Mission."[7] It was also at that time that the provincial of the Hungarian Jesuits made a proposal to the *Praepositus Generalis* of the Society of Jesus to go to the Chinese mission.

Hungarian Jesuits in China

The first independent Hungarian mission in China was established by the Jesuits.[8] The Hungarian Jesuit Province had become independent from the Austrian Province in 1909. In 1919, during the 133 days of the Hungarian Soviet Republic, the Hungarian provincial made an oath: if the Jesuits did not suffer any harm during the dictatorship of the proletariat, he would be willing to take a foreign mission somewhere in the world. Father Jenő Somogyi submitted the proposal to the *Praepositus Generalis* in 1920. The idea of taking a foreign mission first appeared in the correspondence between the Hungarian Province and the Jesuit Curia in Rome in a letter of February 21, 1920. Provincial Somogyi wrote to the general as follows: "P. Johannes Hemm asks for permission to be sent to a foreign mission, which I in no way wish to obstruct. . . . He himself would be happy to go to China. . . ."[9]

Father Somogyi also asked the general about the possibility of forming an independent Hungarian mission in China. General Ledochowsky in his answer suggested Africa, where the Hungarians could have not only a mission station, but a whole mission immediately. The *Praepositus Generalis* did not suggest the Chinese mission because of the problems to be faced.[10] In 1920 the possibility of an Estonian or Finnish mission also arose, but the Hungarian provincial did not accept the North European mission.[11]

In 1921 the news arrived in Hungary about the division of the French Jesuits' Xianxian mission.[12] In his letter of October 30, 1921, Somogyi asked for the approval of the general to send a Hungarian Father to the French mission in the following year. Father General forwarded the Hungarian request to the French provincial, Father Devillers.[13] The superiors of the Hungarian Province got in contact with the Jesuit Champagne Province and agreed that the Hungarians would join their French fellow Jesuits in the Xianxian mission. Missionaries working at that time in the Xianxian mission were mostly elderly people, who had already arrived in China in the previous century. There were no young missionaries coming from France, therefore Henri Lécroart, bishop of the mission in 1921, made a decision in accordance with the Jesuit general to divide the vast territories of the mission into smaller missions.

Territories south of the Yellow River with Dongming as their center were handed over to SVD Fathers. It was at that moment that an opportunity arose to give a section of the mission to the Hungarians. It was a shared view among Hungarian Jesuits that Hungarians were people from the East, so they accepted the Chinese mission with the awareness that they would go back to China, the place where the Huns, ancestors of the Hungarians, might have started their migration towards the West.[14]

According to the original plan, Hungarians would have gotten the mission in Xuzhou, Jiangsu Province, and Daming was planned to be given to Canadian Jesuits. However, Hungarians thought that the Xuzhou mission was too big for the small Hungarian Province, and they could not send enough people there. In accordance with the Canadian Province, they exchanged the two mission fields, so Daming became "Hungarian." In January 1922 the first two Hungarian Jesuit missionaries to China were chosen, Miklós Szarvas, who spent his third year of probation, and a scholastic, István Gábor.[15]

The first Hungarian Jesuit, Miklós Szarvas, went to China on September 22, 1922. He spent the first year studying the Chinese language, in the second year he worked with an experienced French missionary in Anhui Province, and arrived in Daming in June 1924.

Bishop Lécroart visited Budapest in January 1926. The aim of his visit was to coordinate the necessary steps needed for the division of the Xianxian mission. He agreed with the Hungarian provincial that still in that year more missionaries would be sent to the Chinese mission. One of them, Gáspár Lischerong, went to China from the United States in the summer of that year, after his successor had been found for the job in the U. S.[16] Also, in 1926 ten Sisters from Kalocsa joined the Daming Mission. They worked together with the Jesuits right until the destruction of the mission in the 1940s.

Missionaries went to China with the aim of establishing an independent Hungarian mission as soon as there were sufficient personnel and financial means. Miklós Szarvas urged the separation of the mission and asked the superiors of the Hungarian Province to send as many people to the mission as they could, possibly every year, otherwise Hungarians might miss the chance to have their own mission.[17] In 1926 Szarvas complained that the Hungarians did not get enough financial help from France. His opinion was that the Hungarians could collect much more alms if the Hungarian people donated the money for their own mission.[18]

The question of an independent Hungarian mission was on the agenda in the official correspondence between the Curia and the Hungarian Province since 1927. In the 1920s, the Hungarian opinion was that the province was not ready for taking a foreign mission.[19]

The first step towards an independent mission was the appointment of Miklós Szarvas as vice-superior of the Daming district. In his letter of February 3, 1931, General Ledochowsky wrote to the Hungarian provincial that although the conditions for the independent Hungarian mission were still missing, in accordance with Bishop Lécroart, he had already made the decision relating to the appointment.[20]

On March 14, 1932, Father General wrote a letter to Visitator Willekens to Hungary and informed him that Father Bornet, superior of the Xianxian mission, proposed Daming's handover to the Hungarians. On April 7 the visitator consulted with the superiors of the Hungarian Province on the question, but the Hungarians still did not support the idea. They referred to financial problems, and said that it would be possible within four to five years. Provincial Bíró, in his letter dated April 8, 1932, opposed the plan of an independent Hungarian mission because the Hungarian Province could not bear the expenses.[21] Father General, in his answer, reassured the Hungarians regarding the status quo in the mission, but on the other hand he asked the provincial to send as many scholastics to the mission as he could.[22]

It took more than a decade after the arrival of the first Hungarian Jesuit to Daming until independence could become reality. The first step was made by Pope Pius XI on March 11, 1935 when, upon the proposition of Bishop Lécroart and Apostolic Delegate Zanin, he promoted Daming to the rank of Apostolic Prefecture. The text of the papal edict ran as follows:

> Parts of the territory of the Xianxian Apostolic Vicariate which include Daming, Nanle, Qingfeng and Puyang governmental subprefectures as well as the Changyuan subprefecture's parts lying west of the Yellow River are being separated. On the above mentioned territories we establish a new Apostolic Prefecture under the name Daming and in the name of the Holy See we entrust the members of the Society of Jesus to take care of that region.[23]

The Jesuit general appointed Miklós Szarvas *Superior Regularis* on March 26, 1936, and at the same time declared the Chinese Jesuits born on the territory of the Daming Mission members of the Hungarian Jesuit Province.

Finally, the Papal edict dated July 10, 1947 changed the status of the Daming Apostolic Prefecture to that of a diocese. The *Administrator Apostolicus* of the new diocese became Gáspár Lischerong, who kept his rank after his expulsion from mainland China in Taiwan, until his death in 1972.[24]

Other Catholic Missionaries

The Jesuits' was the first independent Hungarian mission in China. Nevertheless, there were many other Hungarian missionaries in China in the interwar period. According to the data in the Yearbook of *Unio Cleri* in 1939, there were altogether 102 Hungarian Catholic missionaries (including nuns) in China. Hungarian Salesians worked in southern China, SVD missionaries worked in Qinghai and Gansu Provinces, three Hungarian missionaries worked in a leper colony in Tibet, and Marist Fathers taught English for Russian and Chinese students in Shanghai. There were Hungarian nuns in Baoding and Qiqiha'er.[25] But apart from the Jesuits, only Franciscans had their own independent Hungarian mission.

Hungarian Franciscans worked in Hunan Province, where Tirolean Franciscans set up a mission and had tried to convert the local people to Christianity since 1830, but without much success. In 1907 there was only one Christian family in Baoqing, the future center of the Hungarian mission. The first church was built in 1913. Yongzhou became independent from the Changsha Apostolic Prefecture in 1925. The Austrian Franciscans invited the Hungarians to the mission after their work had been destroyed during the civil war in 1927–1928.[26] When the call for the mission was announced by the provincial, more than forty friars applied.[27] The first group of Hungarian Franciscan missionaries, three priests and four Brothers left Hungary for China on September 29, 1929.[28] They studied the language in the Franciscan College in Hankou before they were sent to the Yongzhou mission in Hunan. They were offered a mission with Baoqing as center, where American Franciscans worked at that time. To set up an independent mission, Hungarian Franciscans needed to find financial means. They raised money by collecting alms throughout the whole country, and even in America among Hungarian expatriates.[29]

The circumstances existing in Baoqing, a town with 60,000 inhabitants, made it difficult to start a new mission at the beginning of the 1930s. Communist groups had destroyed the mission, and the faithful had been dismissed. American missionaries arrived in Baoqing in 1930, but they could hardly gather thirty to forty Catholics. Their work did not yield any results in the growth of the number of the faithful, despite the fact that they had a large hospital in the city. Hungarians took over the Baoqing mission in November 1931. As the number of missionaries grew in the 1930s, they opened new mission stations one after another, sometimes several tens of kilometers away from the mission center. Sometimes the differences between the local dialect spoken in the mission stations were so big, that even the catechists had difficulties in understanding.

In the autumn of 1933, the Saint Elizabeth Orphanage was built under the supervision of the Hungarian Franciscans. The orphanage was run by Hungarian Sisters from Szatmár. The first four Sisters went to China in October 1933. In December 1933, Rome made the first step towards making an independent Hungarian mission, when the Baoqing mission was declared *missio sui iuris*. Baoqing became an independent diocese in 1938. The territory of the mission was 45,000 square kilometers (almost as big as the Transdanubian part of present-day Hungary), and a population of 6 million people lived in those nine districts which were left for the care of the Hungarian missionaries under the Yongzhou Apostolic Prefecture. The fifteen Hungarians had four permanent mission stations and regularly visited eighteen Christian communities. Within five years, the number of Christians had grown from 340 to 2,000.

During the wartime period, the connection between the missions and Hungary was cut off and missionaries worked in almost total isolation. They could hardly send any news from China to Hungary.

There were three Catholic mission magazines in Hungary in the first half of the twentieth century. The first one, entitled *Katolikus Hitterjesztés Lapjai* (Journal of Catholic Propagation of the Faith), was published between 1881 and 1918 in Nagyvárad. Jesuits published their own mission periodical, the *Katolikus Missziók* (Catholic Missions) between 1925 and 1948 with a four-year break during World War II. The monthly journal of the Franciscan Mission Association, *Isten Dalosai* (Singers of God) was published between 1931 and 1944.

Protestant Missionaries

Although it is often stated that the Hungarian Protestant mission movement was entirely foreign in its origins, it is more accurate to say that Hungary was part of an international (first of all Central European) network of mission societies.[30] Hungarian mission organizations at the time of their formation were in close contact with several organizations from German-speaking countries, such as the Liebenzell Mission, the German Mission Prayer League for Women or the Frankfurt Mission (the former *Deutsche Orient Mission*), as well as with Anglo-Saxon organizations, such as, in the case of China, the China Inland Mission (CIM) or the United Free Reformed Church of Scotland. Most members of the Hungarian Foreign Missionary Society, founded in 1903 and later named Hungarian Evangelical Christian Missionary Society, studied in mission schools in Basel and Liebenzell. The Hungarian Lutheran Mission Association was founded in 1909, and had close connections with the German Leipzig Mission. Hungarian Lutherans described their main task as to "closely join the Lutheran mission associations, and among them primarily the Leipzig Evangelical-Lutheran Mission. . . ."[31] They also built contacts with the Finnish Lutheran Church, for "our brothers in the North" had a mission field in Hunan Province.

While most Hungarian Catholic missionaries worked in groups, Protestant missionaries were much less in number (we know of only four) and they worked individually, mostly in the framework of foreign mission organizations, but with the support of Hungarian mission societies. Hungarian Protestant missionaries joined the mission societies abroad, and most of them took their families with them to the mission, this being the reason why the last two Hungarians left China together with their families in 1947, well before foreigners were expelled from China.

Born in Hungary, Adolf Hermann (1880–1967) joined the CIM in 1905, after having finished his studies at the Mission School of CIM in Glasgow. After a year of Chinese language studies, he worked in Shundefu from 1906. In 1909 he married an American missionary, Erna A. Hieks. They visited Hungary in 1914 and gave lectures about their missionary work in China. Not long after his return to China in 1915, Hermann was granted the Senior Missionary Certificate and became manager of the Presbyterian Mission Hospital in Baoding. Not long after taking his new job, however, he confessed to his mission superiors that he had more than once been on the point of resigning from missionary work because of his sense of lack of suitability for the task. He made his final decision and retired from CIM in 1917.[32]

Some of the missionaries themselves were not "genuine" Hungarians, for they were of German origin by birth. Among them, the first and most influential Protestant missionary supported by the Hungarian missionary organizations, was Irene Kunst (1869–1934), who was born in East Prussia as the daughter of a German Father and a Swedish mother. She moved to Hungary with her mother at the age of eleven. Inspired by Graham Brown, missionary of the CIM who visited Hungary in 1903, she applied to the mission school in Liebenzell, and half a year later in 1904, at the age of 35, she was allowed to go to China. She worked as an independent missionary in Changsha, Hunan Province, and received support not only from Hungarians, but also from the *Deutscher Frauen-Missions-Gebetsbund* (German Women Prayer League for Missions). Between 1904 and 1914 she was director of a school for blind children, an institution established by CIM. In 1907, a German missionary, Matild Vasel (1875–1939) joined her, and both were financially supported by Hungarian organizations. Matild Vasel also worked in the school for the blind, and was responsible for the pastoral care for women in Changsha and in the surrounding hamlets. We know of only seven Christians in their mission district in 1907, but the number of faithful grew to about 500 by 1921.[33]

Sándor Babos (1903–1996)[34] was offered the opportunity in 1930 both by French Protestant churches to go to Africa and by the Scottish Reformed Church to go to Manchuria under their partial support. His bishop accepted the latter, for he felt that Hungarians had a special responsibility towards their blood relatives in Asia. As he wrote in a circular in 1933: "Our church decided for the Manchurian mission, feeling that if we, Hungarians have some mission duties, those must be sought in Manchuria, among our kinfolks."[35]

Babos arrived in Manchuria in 1933 as a missionary of the Hungarian Reformed Church of Transylvania. He was involved in a Sunday school, and also served in the hospital and participated in evangelistic work. In 1935 the Reformed Church of Manchuria offered an independent mission field for him, which was accepted by the Transylvanian Reformed Church, but before he was to move to his new station he took a period of leave in 1936.[36] In 1942 he was invited to the Theological Seminary in Mukden to teach history, Greek, and German. In September 1943 he wrote that he was the only one in the whole of Manchuria who still had permission to be involved in mission work.[37] The Babos family left China for the United States in October 1947.[38]

In 1936, a Hungarian missionary, Jenő Kunos (1914–1994), went to Finland to study the mission work of the Finnish Church, with the aim to join the Finnish Lutheran Mission in China. His interest in the Chinese mission was further encouraged by the visit of Irene Kunst to his hometown, Győr, in 1932. Kunos was supported by the Hungarian Lutheran Mission Association, as they said, "in a moral sense completely, and financially as far as our possibilities and abilities enable us."[39] Kunos arrived in China in March 1939. After one and a half years of language study in Beijing, he wanted to go to his original mission, but because of the war, he had to stay in Beijing. He also planned to establish an independent Hungarian mission with Babos in Northern China, but it could not become a reality. He went to Hubei in August 1941, to teach Church history at a Lutheran Theological Seminary. Hungarian Lutherans were able to support him financially until the end of 1943. After the Japanese occupation of the city, the Kunos family (his wife joined him in the mission in 1940) lived with Swedish missionaries until the end of the war. It was not until 1946 that the Kunos family could move to the mission station where he was originally assigned. Jenő Kunos spent eight years in China with wife and four children, and left the war-torn country for the United States in 1947.

Starting from as early as 1896, Hungarian Lutherans published their mission periodical, *Külmisszió* (Foreign Mission), later named *Missziói Lapok* (Mission Pages), as a counterpart for the Reformed *Hajnal* (Dawn), the most influential mission periodical, published since 1909.

Being Hungarian in China

Did Hungarian missionaries enjoy the advantage of being Hungarian in China? Were there any differences between them and the other missionaries either in the eyes of the Chinese, or in the behavior of the Japanese occupants towards Hungarians and other foreigners? In order to answer this question, we shall recall some moments from the life in the mission.

In order to secure good conditions for everyday missionary work, the missionaries tried to be on friendly terms with the local officials. The mandarin attended the school examinations, paid courtesy visits to the mission, and sometimes visited the church as well. In 1933, the newly assigned local mandarin visited the Hungarian Jesuits as soon as he had taken his new post. He liked the church so much that he attended mass regularly: "On every holy day when we celebrate mass, the organ swells and the chorus sings, the mandarin announces his arrival and politely listens to the holy mass. Normally he is accompanied by his wives, children and fellow officials" wrote the Hungarian missionary, József Szajkó in his letter.[40] The local mandarin and the military commander of Baoqing also paid a courtesy visit to the mission immediately after the arrival of Hungarian Franciscans. They referred to Sino-Hungarian kinship as a reason for their visit. During the Sino-Japanese war, a Hungarian Franciscan missionary-doctor was requested by the town's Chinese leadership to organize medical care in Baoqing in the event of bombardments, and at the same time he was promoted to the rank of colonel.

During the Japanese occupation of Daming, the Japanese did not do any harm to the missionary works nor to the missionaries anywhere in the territory of the mission. For the Chinese women, a cross or a picture of a saint on their neck could guarantee safety against the Japanese. The Japanese did not hurt the men who asked for asylum in the mission either, they even donated rice to the mission.[41] There was a political reason behind this friendly relationship. The Japanese government signed the Anti-Comintern Pact with Germany on November 25, 1936—just a month after the Berlin-Rome Axis treaty was signed—and since Hungary maintained good relations with both European powers, the Japanese did not consider the Hungarian missionaries as enemies. The other reason for the good relations between the Japanese occupiers and the Hungarian mission could be that the Japanese military commander used to be the military attaché in Berlin and had also visited Hungary.[42]

There were approximately 40,000 Catholics living in the Hungarian mission at the end of the 1930s. In the cities the number of the faithful grew, while in the villages there was a decrease in the number of the Chinese Christians. There are several reasons for this difference. First of all, the missionaries could not pay the catechist in every village, and in many places financial means were not sufficient to run a school. The increase in the number of Christians in the towns had political reasons too, namely that after the Japanese occupation, the American Protestant missionaries left their mission in Daming and several Protestant Chinese converted to Catholicism. Many people asked to be baptized because they saw that the Japanese and Hungarians were on friendly terms and felt that the missionaries could give them shelter from the Japanese. The people living along the railways occupied by the Japanese were especially scared of Japanese aggression. On several occasions they offered their houses to the mission in the hope that in the event of an emergency they would be safe in the mission's buildings. In the 1940s, during the time of high inflation and food shortages, the Christians donated a part of their own harvest to the mission. The people had so much respect for the missionaries that in Puyang, the southern center of the Daming Mission, they asked Gáspár Lischerong to accept the post of the local mandarin.

Hungarian Protestants were also treated better by the Japanese than their fellow missionaries. The fact that in 1942 all missionaries of the Scottish Mission were taken to Japanese camps and soon after expelled from the country and only a Hungarian could continue his service in Manchuria shows that the friendly approach of the Japanese towards Hungarians was a general phenomenon. For the Hungarian missionary, Sándor Babos, it was of considerable advantage that his ancestors once lived in Asia, so he was considered as a fellow Asian. In one village, his arrival was announced with the words: "Come and hear a Chinese from Europe!"[43]

Conclusions

Hungarian missionary activity corresponded with the Christian churches' missionary vocation, but on the other hand, in the first decades of the twentieth century and especially after the Peace Treaty of Trianon, the missionary vocation took on a nationalistic dimension. As Christian-nationalistic ideas served as the foundations for the ideology of the ruling classes, for the propagators of such ideology the presence of Hungarian missionaries in foreign missions was useful, and especially the presence of those who worked in the Far East among kindred peoples, using the terminology of that time. In the Hungary of the 1920s and 1930s, missionaries were widely known and numerous mission magazines published articles about their work time and again. It would not be an exaggeration to say that the presence of those few dozen missionaries in China was more important for Hungarians than for the Chinese. In China, missionaries had direct contact with some thousands, probably tens of thousands of people, and indirectly some hundreds of thousands knew about their presence, while in Hungary alms were collected for them in nationwide campaigns, and official propaganda saw and presented them as a pillar for the belief in Greater Hungary.

The presence and activity of Hungarian missionaries in China was the most important part of Sino-Hungarian relations during the interwar period. According to a list of Hungarian citizens (in all probability drawn up in the Consular Department of the Hungarian Ministry of Foreign Affairs at the beginning of the 1950s on the basis of the applications for a new passport to the Hungarian Embassy in Beijing), there were seventy-four Hungarians in China in 1950, out of whom forty-four were missionaries; twenty-two Jesuits, ten Sisters from Kalocsa, six Franciscans, three Sisters from Szatmár, two Marist Fathers, and one Salesian.

The activity of Hungarian missionaries in China did not differ significantly from the practice followed by missionaries of other nations. They learned the methods used in the mission from experienced foreign missionaries, so their activity can be described as a continuation of a long tradition. As for their social situation, they adapted themselves to the new conditions, as far as it was possible for a European to do so. Nevertheless, their situation in China was a little peculiar. Chinese intellectuals, political and military leaders, and under their influence, peasants, craftsmen, and merchants, believed in common origin and felt that Hungarians were a little closer to them than other Western missionaries. Hungarians also felt that there were more similarities between them and the Chinese than between Chinese and other Westerners.

Their job had always been free of any political background. However, their Hungarian origin proved useful during the Japanese occupation. One of the main reasons for the continued operation of the Hungarian missions in areas occupied by the Japanese during the War of Resistance was that Hungary was perceived to be an ally of Germany and thus part of the axis with Tokyo. Consequently, whereas the Japanese interned the missionaries of enemy states, German, Italian, French, and Hungarian nationals were able to continue their work in the occupied areas, albeit with certain restrictions.

After the establishment of the People's Republic of China, the authorities watched their missionary activity with suspicion, but since their motherland was a friendly country (Hungary was among the first countries to establish diplomatic relations with the People's Republic of China) they were treated slightly differently from the citizens of "imperialist enemies." The reason behind this distinction was made first of all because they were needed for employment as teachers or doctors. As such, some of them could stay in China until 1954 and 1955.

Most of the Hungarians expelled from mainland China could not return to their homeland, therefore they either remained in the Far East to work among Chinese, or took on the responsibility for spiritual care of Hungarians living all over the world, particularly in the United States.

In Hungary it was, until recently, impossible to conduct research into the life and work of Hungarian missionaries. One of the reasons for the lack of study is that there was no interest in this topic, and the other is that documents were inaccessible and that chances of research abroad were very slim. In the past decade or so, however, it has been possible for scholars to study this area of history and publish their results in books and articles. Unfortunately, Chinese sources have not been accessible so far. My Chinese experience shows that the impact of the missionaries' activities can be felt even today, in the bigger cities as well as in small villages in the countryside, where priests and faithful often recall their former priests, teachers, doctors, and benefactors.

Missionaries only wanted to fulfill their spiritual vocation, but during the revolutionary changes and the trials of the war years in China, they witnessed and documented events that we cannot know about from other sources, and which greatly contribute to our knowledge of Chinese history.

Beyond Orthodoxy:
Catholicism as Chinese Folk Religion

RICHARD P. MADSEN

From both Western and Chinese sides, the history of Catholicism in China has commonly been told from the perspective of those who would be orthodox. The main issue in most accounts of the Rites Controversy is whether or not the Jesuits were correct in their claim that participation in orthodox Confucian rites was compatible with orthodox Catholic doctrine. In accounts of the Catholic Church after the Opium Wars, the issue is the degree to which the missionaries' connection with imperialism undermined the legitimacy of China's orthodox (*zhengchang*) political system. Histories of the early twentieth century are focused on controversies about whether Chinese priests could be entrusted with episcopal authority. During the Mao years, the main controversies were about the degree to which Catholic Church leaders could submit to the authority of the Communist government while still remaining in communion with the Holy See. During the Reform era, from 1979 down to the present day, the issue is whether the "underground" or the "official Church" represents the precepts of Catholic orthodoxy.

There is usually a difference between Chinese and Western sides in these controversies. But representatives of either side usually see the issue from the perspective of the top of ecclesiastical or governmental hierarchies. The main actors in the controversies are emperors and popes, mandarins and bishops, cadres and nuncios. What is at stake is the ability of parties on either side to define doctrinal orthodoxy or political orthopraxis. Were the Kangxi Emperor's requirements for accepting Catholicism as an officially approved Chinese religion compatible with papal teaching about correct Catholic doctrine? Should Church leaders have accepted the benefits of political extraterritoriality in the nineteenth century or should they have respected the authority of the imperial government? If Chinese priests became bishops, could they be relied upon to properly understand and teach orthodox doctrine and to follow official Church discipline? And so on.

It is hard to discern the faith of ordinary Catholic laypeople from this point of view. The focus on orthodoxy, whether Catholic or Confucian, leads to a neglect of the heterodox, or "superstitious" magic and myth that—to the consternation of Chinese Church and government leaders down to the present day—are intertwined with precepts from the catechism in the living culture of many Chinese Catholics, especially in rural communities. The concern with the exercise of proper authority—whether ecclesiastical or political—or with challenges to that authority leads to a neglect of the ways in which ordinary Chinese people organize their own associations and their own communities.

Catholicism in China, especially in the rural areas where the vast majority of Chinese Catholics live, is as much folk religion as world religion. I would not advocate abandoning a top-down view of Chinese Catholicism as part of a world religion and a universal Church. I will argue, however, that this view should be complemented by one that sees Chinese Catholicism as a localized folk religion. Such folk-Catholicism should not simply be seen as an impure form of the genuine Catholic faith, but an authentic form of belief and practice to be understood on its own terms. There are important scholarly benefits from viewing Chinese Catholicism in this way. First of all, some of the best Chinese historians, sociologists, and anthropologists who are studying Chinese Catholicism view it mainly as a folk religion. If Western scholars study Catholicism from this perspective, they will have a basis for fruitful dialogue and cooperation with Chinese colleagues. Secondly, one of the most vibrant fields of scholarship among the younger generation of Western social scientists is the study of popular culture, and a focus on Chinese Catholicism as folk religion can make good use of the innovative theoretical and methodological tools being developed by such scholars. Thirdly, viewing Chinese Catholicism as a folk religion calls attention to many important aspects of Chinese Catholic belief and practice that have been ignored. Finally, such a view may shed important light on current conflicts within the Catholic Church and between the Catholic Church and the Chinese government.

Although this way of viewing Chinese Catholicism will be, I believe, of great benefit to social scientists, it may be more problematic for theologians and Church leaders who, after all, usually want to define the orthodox, not revel in the heterodox. But the problems may turn out to be a constructive challenge to theologians. Viewing Chinese Catholicism as a folk religion may help us understand the Church more fully, in the spirit of Vatican II, as the People of God rather than an ecclesiastical structure; and it may sensitize us more fully to the variety of ways in which God can be revealed within the world's cultures.

In this essay, I can do no more than suggest an agenda for viewing Chinese Catholicism from the bottom up as part of China's heritage of folk religions. Fulfillment of such an agenda would require the collection of more information, more data, than is now available. It would also require the development and application of new theoretical perspectives. This essay is not completely speculative, however. Anthropologists like Eriberto Lozada[1] and Wu Fei[2] have recently been gathering important ethnographic data about everyday life in contemporary rural Catholic communities, and resourceful historians like Robert Entenmann,[3] Alan Richard Sweeten,[4] and Charles Litzinger[5] have been mining the historical record for similar information about the Chinese Catholic past. Such work gives us a tantalizing glimpse of the insights that can be had by studying the bottom rather than the top of religious and political hierarchies and by viewing Chinese Catholicism as a folk religion.

Folk-Catholicism as Heterodox Sect

From Ricci on, all Catholic missionaries—indeed, those on both sides of the rites controversy—were firmly opposed to every kind of Chinese folk religion. As Kristofer Schipper writes,

> When, in the sixteenth century, the Jesuit missionaries in China were faced with the historic choice to ally themselves either with religion against the state or with the state against religion, they chose the second alternative. Christianity entered the sphere of the imperial court and placed itself under the protection of the government. Back home, in Europe, the missionaries glorified the official imperial ideology and the image of Confucius as *Sinarum Philosophus* ("the only one"), while minimizing the religious role of the state cult. Thus China had no religion for the missionaries, and it was they who introduced into Chinese the term *mi-sin*, literally "deviant belief" (and now usually translated as "superstition"), to describe Taoism. Matteo Ricci, the most influential among the early missionaries, sought to confer on Confucianism the image of an agnostic doctrine or moral wisdom, a philosophy that had already recognized the existence of the Supreme Being and that lacked only the revelation of the Gospel.[6]

While the missionaries thought that all of the popular belief in gods, ghosts, and ancestors and all of the rituals practiced to venerate or placate them or use their power were superstitious and ought to be eradicated, Confucian scholar-officials were more discriminating. To varying degrees they looked down on folk religion. (One issue in the rites controversy was to what degree they truly rejected all folk religion and to what degree they had contaminated their worldly philosophy with pagan religion.) But they distinguished between the heterodox religion of certain folk-Buddhist sects and the relatively harmless worship of ancestors and village gods that constituted the diffuse religion of Chinese rural communities. I will argue that, despite the intentions of the missionaries, Chinese Catholicism eventually assimilated elements of both kinds of this folk religiosity. But the first kind to be assimilated was that of folk-Buddhist heterodoxy.

Chinese Heterodoxy

The traditional Chinese distinction between "orthodoxy" and "heterodoxy" has been a key focus of attention for China scholars in the past generation. *Zheng* or *zhengdao* (straight or straight path) are the Chinese terms which we translate as "orthodoxy" and *yiduan*, *zoudao*, or *xie* are the terms rendered as "heterodoxy." The terms for "orthodoxy" go back at least until the time of Confucius (551–479 B.C.); the terms for heterodoxy "share a common meaning which may be roughly (if somewhat ambiguously) rendered 'different from the way of the sages.' The words for heterodoxy

> were used by the upholder of one philosophical or cultural norm to stigmatize the beliefs and practices of those who professed allegiance to other and divergent norms. Presumably they could be used by Buddhists against Confucians or by Taoists against Buddhists. But in actual practice they seem to have been employed most frequently by Confucians, either to attack an existing social order with which they were dissatisfied . . . . or to subvert the status quo against all teachings which threatened to subvert it. . . . [7]

An older tradition of Western sinology—one, it might be argued, that originated with Matteo Ricci and his fellow Jesuits—tended to define Chinese culture in terms of Confucian orthodoxy. What China's scholar officials saw as the "straight path" was true Chinese culture. (And for Ricci it was this culture that Catholic doctrine could and should accommodate.) Anyone with a minimal familiarity with China could see that there were many Chinese beliefs and practices that were seen as heterodox by the scholar officials—but for an older generation of sinologists these were often seen as impure deviations from genuine Chinese culture. Contemporary scholars of Chinese culture will not make this distinction. Chinese culture, like all cultures, encompasses contrasting elements, which gain their meaning from their relationship with one another. Like yin and yang, both orthodox and heterodox beliefs and practices are interdependent parts of a single cultural reality.

Present day scholars of Chinese culture also emphasize the fluidity of the distinctions between orthodox and heterodox in the Chinese tradition. What was considered orthodox by one group in one time and place might be considered heterodox in different contexts. Modern scholars are also sensitive to the ways in which the invidious distinctions implicit in the orthodox-heterodox dichotomy were sustained by inequalities of power between scholar officials and common people. Indeed, influenced by democratic sensibilities, many modern Western scholars tend to take the side of the poor and powerless and to have more sympathy for their beliefs and practices than for those of the elites.

Despite the efforts of Ricci and his colleagues to get the Catholic faith accepted as part of Confucian orthodoxy, within decades after the introduction of Christianity into China, some Confucian *literati* were denouncing the foreign faith as heterodox. In the words of Paul Cohen, "Like Buddhism earlier, (Christianity's) foreign origin, its fundamental nonadherence to Confucianism (particularly in its Song and post-Song guise), the miraculous content of some of its doctrines, and its suspected motives of political subversion all combined to cast it in this undesirable role."[8] In 1692, the missionaries managed to get the Kangxi Emperor to issue an edict of toleration towards Christianity, which in effect declared Christianity to be an orthodox part of Chinese culture. But after the papal decisions in the early 1700s against the Jesuit policy of accommodation with Confucianism, the Yongzheng Emperor in his Sacred Edict of 1724 decisively stamped Catholicism as heterodox.[9]

To many scholar-officials, indeed, Christianity was ominously similar to the most subversive of the folk-Buddhist sects, the White Lotus. Let us briefly describe the content of White Lotus teaching, and show how Catholicism was considered to be similar to it. Like other folk-Buddhist sects that became popular during the Ming and Qing dynasties (and in some places in China remain popular to this day), the White Lotus was a salvation religion. Unlike Confucians, who thought that this world was basically good and could be improved by human effort as long as people underwent proper moral cultivation, folk-Buddhist sects believed that the world was hopelessly corrupt and could be saved only by supernatural intervention.

There were a great variety of sects that preached this, but most of them were offshoots of popular Buddhism. Although Buddhism had been considered a heterodox religion by Confucians when it was first introduced into China, by the Song dynasty monastic Buddhism had become well enough integrated into Chinese culture and subordinated enough to a Confucian state that it was not generally considered heterodox by Confucian scholars. However, by the Yuan dynasty there had developed a number of lay Buddhist religious organizations that were considered heterodox by both monastic Buddhists and Confucian elites.

A major preoccupation of these new offshoots of Buddhism was salvation. They believed that salvation did not require a monk's total renunciation of family and worldly occupation. From the point of view of monastic Buddhists, this was heterodox. These folk-Buddhist sects were also heterodox because they introduced new myths and practices from outside of the Buddhist tradition. Some of them continually gained new revelation through trances and "spirit writing."[10]

The most important myth for many of these new groups was the myth of the Eternal Mother (*wusheng laomu*). The Eternal Mother existed before all other things. She gave birth to a man and a woman, whose union then produced the whole human race. The Eternal Mother had sent her children to live in the "Eastern World," but they unfortunately become fallen and confused. "The Eternal Mother in the Native Land weeps as she thinks of her children. She has sent messages and letters [urging them] to return home, and to stop devoting themselves purely to avarice in this sea of bitterness. [She calls them] to return to the Pure Land, to come back to Mount Ling [the Vulture Peak, so that] the mother and her children can meet again and sit on the golden lotus."[11]

To call her children home, the Holy Mother had sent Buddhas to teach people the way to salvation. She had already sent two Buddhas, the Lamp-Lighting Buddha and the Sakyamuni Buddha. Each of these Buddhas had presided over a long *kalpa* (eon) of human time. However, most people remained lost. So the Eternal Mother was going to send a third Buddha, the Maitreya Buddha, who would open a new *kalpa*, which would bring salvation to all. The end of the old *kalpa* would bring vast cataclysms, but these would be but the necessary prelude to a wonderful new world.[12]

From the point of view of Confucian scholars, such hopes for millenarian salvation were dangerously heterodox. The White Lotus insistence on the need for a radical salvation was not only intellectually wrong to Confucian scholar officials; it was politically dangerous, because it might inspire people to rise up against the established social order if they believed the turning of the *kalpa* was imminent.

Although the White Lotus was the most extensive of the folk-religious traditions in the Ming and Qing dynasties (and White Lotus traditions continue today in such organizations as the Unity Way, or *Yiguan dao*),[13] there were a number of other such traditions, like the Lo sect, and the White Cloud sect. Moreover, within the White Lotus, as within each of the other traditions, there were many different religious organizations, led by teachers with different ways of expounding the traditions.[14] From the point of view of the bottom of Chinese society, the world was populated by a great variety of sects promising different versions of salvation.

The salvation was immediate and physical as well as long term and spiritual. The sects usually attracted followers by healing illnesses, through *qigong* exercises as well as through exorcisms and bathing in magical water—magical healing practices that derived more from the Daoist than the Buddhist tradition. Other sects promised the ability to perform superhuman feats through martial arts. In the folk-Buddhist sects, however, the quest for religious salvation usually took precedence over material benefits. In this respect, the religious sects were different from secret societies like the triads, which utilized religious rituals, but were primarily devoted to earthly aims.[15]

One important feature which the religious sects did share with the secret societies, however, was that they were voluntary associations rather than communities based on kinship. They preached a universal salvation, irrespective of family or lineage or village. Anyone, therefore, could join a folk-Buddhist sect and be on an equal standing with all other members, as long as one properly believed. One became a member of a folk-Buddhist sect, as well as of a secret society, by choosing to join. It was much easier to enter or exit a folk-Buddhist sect than a secret society, however. Often one could join the former simply by expressing interest and undergoing a simple initiation process. And one could just stop participating if one lost interest. The secret societies, which were often involved in dangerous and illegal activities, required careful scrutiny of members, a complicated initiation ritual, and they imposed severe penalties on defectors.[16]

As voluntary associations that extended well beyond the boundaries of villages and lineages, the folk-Buddhist sects were considered politically dangerous by Imperial authorities. The Imperial government's system of political control was predicated on having people remain settled in villages and families, while scholar-officials provided the main means of communication across the empire. The religious sects preached a universal salvation that encouraged people to move beyond the confines of their families, and go beyond the standard family roles. Thus, although few women were sect leaders, women often played an important role as educators and organizers in the folk-Buddhist sects—something which the guardians of Confucian orthodoxy condemned as violating proper gender distinctions. The folk-Buddhist sects also built extensive networks of communication across long distances, a resource which the government rightly feared could be used under certain circumstances to organize rebellious activity.

The folk-Buddhist sects drew members from almost all social strata, rich and poor, with the exception of Confucian scholar-officials, who defined their identity and their life's work in terms of defending Confucian orthodoxy against sectarian heterodoxy. One consequence of this was that the sects lacked a systematically educated leadership. As Daniel Overmyer says,

> This relative absence of lay leadership had incalculable significance for Chinese religious and cultural history. It meant that popular movements lacked thorough-going intellectual formulation and that dissenting religious ideas rarely had the chance to find legitimate social expression. The Chinese state was never strong enough at the village level to prevent sectarian religious activity, but to the end it tenaciously kept them in a state of semisubjection and intellectual decapitation.[17]

The lack of a professional priesthood led to great diversity in local understandings of the traditions and to widespread syncretism.

Most of the time such folk-Buddhist sects were peaceful and their members were devoted to purely religious rather than political pursuits. Sometimes, however, they did indeed provide the impetus for massive peasant rebellions, which severely tested the state and sometimes toppled dynasties, even though these rebellions did not succeed in fundamentally changing the structure of Chinese society. Even when they did not make a lot of commotion, they provided a tremendous reservoir of cultural creativity within Chinese civilization. Recent scholarship on Chinese folk religions realizes that understanding Chinese history through the lens of Confucian orthodoxy gives a very one-sided story. As Kristofer Schipper puts it,

> The uncritical approval of official China—at the expense of its popular culture— by Western minds ready to acknowledge Christian or pseudo-Christian virtues in China continues to be expressed by a sinophilia whose excessive nature betrays the existence of deep misunderstandings. . . . This opinion held by the missionaries, revised and simplified by our intellectuals, and still current today, shows how poorly we know China.[18]

A comprehensive understanding of Chinese culture requires a positive appreciation of its folk religious traditions. Objective scholarship, moreover, requires that we reject the Confucian claims that these heterodox religions are a deviant, inferior form of belief. We have to accept them as just as authentic a form of religious experience and moral practice as Confucianism.

Catholicism as Heterodoxy

It is a maxim in sociology that people often become what they are socially labeled. Despite being taught to avoid "paganism," Catholics in China took on many of the characteristics of heterodox folk religions, once they had been labeled as heterodox by the Yongzheng Emperor. The causes of this were multiplex. First of all, Catholics lost almost all opportunities for dialogue with the Confucian scholar-officials. With no more chance to gain converts from this class, they focused their missionary efforts on uneducated rural people, whose religious imaginations were imbued with the mentality of the folk religion. Secondly, many foreign missionaries were expelled and new ones forbidden to enter. There were no opportunities to train native priests through advanced seminary training. Most of the organization and catechesis of local Catholic communities were carried out by laypeople with a minimum of formal education. Following its common strategy for dealing with heterodox religions, the Chinese government kept Catholicism in a state of "intellectual decapitation." This increased the possibilities for developments in doctrine and spirituality which would fit more closely with the characteristics of traditional rural mentalities than the foreign missionaries would have wanted. Furthermore, Catholics were now vulnerable to waves of state-sponsored persecution. Even if they had no wish to be a political threat to the government, they were sometimes forced to act in a secretive way and encouraged to think of themselves as in opposition to official authorities.

Finally, the Catholics fit into the heterodox part of the cultural classification system. From the point of view of modern theories of culture, this might be the most important reason of all. According to both "structuralist" and "post-structuralist" theories of culture, the meaning of religious symbols, or for that matter, of any of the kinds of symbols that make up a culture, comes not from the internal characteristics of the symbols but from the way they are contrasted with other symbols. Thus, there is nothing about the color red in itself that makes it signify "stop." But it gains such a meaning by being contrasted with the color green in a stoplight system. The major ideas of any culture gain their meaning through contrast: for example the notion of "good" has meaning only by virtue of its contrast with a notion of "evil." A culture is a vast web of such contrasting pairs, and to interpret the meaning of a culture's religious beliefs and rituals is to locate them within that web.[19]

Even though Catholics may not have wanted to think of themselves as heterodox, their location within the heterodox part of Chinese culture put pressure on them to shape their lives in similar ways to other religious groups that were so classified. One can see this influence in folk-Catholic beliefs, institutional structures, and in a general attitude of Catholics toward the rest of the society.

Although Catholics rejected the specific content of folk-Buddhist heterodox beliefs—they certainly could not believe in the Eternal Mother or in the Maitreya Buddha or in magical charms, for instance—they naturally tended to find analogous beliefs among their own doctrines. Chinese Catholic thinking seemed to be more dominated by the search for salvation than the quest for ethical perfection. They were fascinated by the role of the Virgin Mary in bringing about this salvation. Marian devotion, of course, was prevalent throughout Counter Reformation Catholicism. But down to the present day, Chinese Catholics have an exceptionally strong devotion to Mary, who is often depicted in robes like those of a Chinese goddess. As time went on, Marian devotion in China was also connected with miraculous events. There have been many reports of apparitions of the Virgin in China, and some of these apparition sites have become major pilgrimage centers, such as the Marian shrine at Donglu in Hebei Province. In the late nineteenth and twentieth centuries, shrines to Our Lady of Lourdes became extremely popular in China. The shrines depict the Virgin Mary appearing in the famous grotto in France to Saint Bernadette and pointing out the sacred spring, whose waters miraculously heal the desperately sick. Catholics thus have their own magical waters and supernatural powers of healing, similar to those of the folk-Buddhist sects. They also have apocalyptic visions associated especially with the Virgin Mary. When the Boxers, who were an offshoot of folk-Buddhism and who believed they possessed magical powers, attacked Catholics in north China in 1899–1900, the Catholics responded with their own magic visions of the Virgin Mary, Our Lady Queen of Victories, driving back the pagan enemy.[20]

The folk Catholic belief in visions and miracles continues down to the present day. It is reported that underground priests in China's interior practice exorcisms and healing rituals that seem of dubious orthodoxy to educated Western Catholics.[21] There continues to be an apocalyptic dimension to such beliefs. Some Catholics in Tianjin believed that the world was going to come to an end on the Feast of the Assumption in 1992, and they stayed indoors waiting for the sky to darken and a wrathful Virgin to descend and punish the world's evils.[22] The Feast of the Assumption of Mary, one of the four great Catholic festivals in China (and a more prominent festival than almost anywhere else within the Catholic Church) takes place on August 15. Many folk-Buddhists believed that the fifteenth day of the eighth month was the date on which the *kalpa* was to turn and the Maitreya Buddha to arrive.[23]

Chinese Catholics naturally see their beliefs as fundamentally different from that of "superstitious" Chinese folk religion. But an observer trained in anthropology cannot fail to notice the way in which Catholic beliefs in miraculous salvation (mediated through a heavenly woman) bear a relationship to rational, amelioristic Confucian orthodoxy that is structurally similar to the relationship borne by heterodox folk-religions. Almost all of these Chinese Catholics' beliefs, of course, could be found somewhere in the rich Western Catholic tradition. But in different cultural contexts, Catholics will emphasize different elements of that tradition. If Chinese Catholics had been able to define themselves as belonging to the orthodox part of the Chinese cultural classification system, they would probably have emphasized the more rational parts of the Catholic tradition, for instance Thomistic teachings about how virtues can be cultivated with the aid of grace within the principles of natural law. Chinese Catholics picked and chose parts of their tradition that made their beliefs similar in structure to those of heterodox folk-Buddhism.

Catholic historians of the Church in China, however, tend to downplay the fascination with the miraculous and apocalyptic that links Chinese Catholicism with its other heterodox counterparts. Like members of Church hierarchies everywhere, Chinese bishops also tend to regard reports of apparitions and miracles with suspicion. Such events are usually deemed to be peripheral to "real" Catholicism, and since Mary appears where she will, without getting permission from the ecclesiastical hierarchy, such events are potentially threatening to proper Church discipline. Church elites still want to be orthodox. If they want to indigenize their faith, they want to see it reconciled with the elite culture of the Chinese tradition. They thus fail to give proper account to the tremendous influence the folk culture has had on the practical, day to day religious beliefs and practices of Chinese Catholics.

The institutional structures of Chinese Catholic communities also bear marks of the influence of the heterodox tradition. For instance, lay leadership was a predominant feature of the folk-Buddhist sects. The same has been true for Chinese rural Catholic communities—long before the Second Vatican Council's renewed emphasis on the laity. Research by Robert Entenmann on Catholics in eighteenth-century Sichuan, by Alan Richard Sweeten on nineteenth-century Jiangxi, and Charles Litzinger on nineteenth century Zhili demonstrates the strong influence of lay leadership. As Sweeten puts it,

> missionaries and priests were few in number and their actual presence in the scattered Catholic congregations was restricted to periodic visits. Consequently, the priests had to rely heavily on *jiaotou*—the local lay leaders. These lay leaders played a crucial role in sustaining and preserving the Catholic congregations. Lay leaders conducted religious services and in general tended to the religious needs of the converts. Most significantly, lay leaders frequently initiated contact with non-Catholics, who converted mostly as individuals and occasionally as families. Lay leaders were the catalyst for conversions and their importance cannot be overstressed.[24]

When missionaries again returned in large numbers after the Treaty of Tianjin in 1858, they sometimes came into conflict with local lay leaders, who had gotten used to running their communities and carrying on the faith for over a century, but who sometimes were lacking in proper Catholic orthodoxy, from the point of view of the missionaries.[25] Similar problems persisted into the twentieth century, sometimes in the form of conflict between foreign missionaries and the local catechists upon whom they heavily relied in preaching the doctrine and maintaining the Catholic communities.

Another distinctive feature of the institutional structure of Chinese Catholic communities was the role of women. As early as 1640, missionaries established communities of "virgins," Catholic women devoted to a life of celibacy but without taking the formal vows of religious nuns (because the Chinese women were not seen as ready for such a step). Although these organizations of Catholic virgins went into decline in the twentieth century, a remnant continues down to the present—I encountered some such women during my fieldwork around Tianjin in 1993. According to Robert Entenmann, in the eighteenth century, "these women undertook the duty of teaching girls, training catechumens for baptism, and baptizing dying infants. They also engaged in famine relief and medical care. They actively sought converts as well. Their most lasting contribution was undoubtedly as teachers in schools for girls."[26] This represented a different set of public roles than the domestic roles to which women were confined in the orthodox Confucian tradition. It was, however, a role similar to those of folk-Buddhist sectarians. Qing dynasty officials noted this. Interrogating Catholics during the eighteenth century, a Sichuan magistrate asked questions similar to what would have been asked of suspected White Lotus sectarians. "They say that every day, morning and night, you pray to God, and men and women gather together; that at night, you keep in good order as long as the prayer lasts, then as soon as it is over, you extinguish all lights and engage in shameful and abominable crimes. Is that true?"[27] Neither White Lotus nor Catholic women were usually guilty of the licentious behavior suggested by these questions. But the suspicions arose from the confrontation of orthodox Confucians with ways of life that gave to women roles of public education and leadership that were supposed to be reserved for men.

The establishment of institutes of Catholic virgins was perhaps born as much out of necessity as out of any European precedent. But the idea of employing women in this way might have been suggested by the role of women in the folk-Buddhist sects. In any case, this vital feature of the Chinese Catholic Church never met the wholehearted approval of orthodox

Catholic missionaries. One French missionary bishop in the eighteenth century objected, for instance, that the virgins "preside over communal prayer in assemblies including men; they read meditations in a loud voice and preach sometimes like a missionary. . . . "[28] However, the institutes of Catholic virgins have carried on for several centuries, despite such criticisms from clerical authority.

In this we discern an attitude among rural Chinese Catholics which, in addition to their beliefs and institutions, also manifests the influence of the heterodox parts of Chinese culture. It is an attitude of independence from both political and religious elites. Although the folk-Buddhists were usually law abiding in practice, they saw no need in principle to follow the direction of Confucian scholar officials, because the world dominated by such officials was coming to an end. Nor did they see any need to follow the religious guidance of Buddhist monks, because the folk-Buddhists believed that they could receive revelation directly. Similarly, folk-Catholics felt free to act independently from government officials, because Catholics were loyal to a higher authority. And sometimes they also felt free to act independently from their own priests and bishops because they felt that they could directly discern the will of God, whether by seeing visions or simply by using their own common sense.

Like the folk-Buddhist sects, however, Chinese Catholics did not constantly stand in opposition to the government and to the elite monks and priests of their own religious traditions. Instead of a sharp split, there was a continuum between orthodoxy and heterodoxy. As Susan Naquin writes, some folk-Buddhists "took monks and nuns as their models, and suspicious officials were convinced that there was nothing heterodox about them."[29] After missionaries returned in the second half of the nineteenth century, Chinese Catholics, too, were often very loyal to them. And rural Catholics followed their priests and bishops when, during the 1930s and 1940s, the Catholic Church hierarchy won favor with the Nationalist government of Chiang Kai-shek.

Catholics and Communal Folk Religion

One should not make too sharp a distinction, however, between the heterodox traditions and the religious beliefs and practices that formed the basis for the particularistic bonds of family and village. Under many circumstances, the folk-Buddhist traditions blended closely with village and family rituals. Sometimes, for example, whole villages belonged to a White Lotus sect, and villagers blended their ancestor worship and their worship of local patron gods into the worship of the Eternal Mother. Such village-centered religion was not regarded by government officials as heterodox, because it supported good family order and community stability. But the principles governing family and community worship, on the one hand, and the folk-Buddhist salvation religions on the other, were sufficiently different that under some circumstances the two forms of religion could diverge.[30]

Up until the twentieth century, on the other hand, Catholics had a more difficult time blending into the diffuse folk religiosity of village and community. For Catholics, ancestor tablets, household gods, and village deities were all forbidden superstition. Thus, Catholics, from the point of view of the Qing government, were more dangerously heterodox than the folk-Buddhist sects, because, in the words of an official writing in 1811, the Catholics "do not respect heaven and earth, do not worship ancestors, do not show filial piety toward father and mother, . . . do not seek to make money, and do not urge people to do good deeds. . . ."[31]

However, by the early twentieth century, Catholicism seemed to blend more fully into the fabric of village and family culture. Religious differences between Catholics and their non-Christian neighbors, which had been endemic throughout the late nineteenth century, now seemed to diminish, although Catholics still refused to take part in ancestor worship and in worship of the gods ensconced in local temples. Part of the reason was that the religious rituals of the local folk religion began to lose their importance. As Roger Thompson puts it, there was a "twilight of the gods in the Chinese countryside."[32] This was caused by the actions of modernizing governments, which now accepted the old Jesuit idea that all folk religion was superstition, unworthy of modernity, and which accordingly expropriated much land belonging to temples and slowly tried to discredit folk religious beliefs through modern education. The old rituals at the local temples were still practiced, but they did not seem to have the great force that they had once had. The moral part of village and family folk religion then came to the fore—what religion was really about, more people thought, was loyalty to family and kin and community.

Catholics, however, were as loyal as anyone. In many areas, missionaries had converted whole lineages or whole villages, or sometimes regrouped scattered Catholics into totally Catholic villages. (The missionaries feared that if only individuals were converted, they might be tempted to backslide by their non-Christian neighbors—and this was a surer route to hell than if they had never been converted at all.) In these villages, Catholics maintained strong family lives, with the same rules for patrilineal marriage as practiced in non-Christian society. They honored their ancestors, not by offering sacrifices of food on the ancestors' graves, but by praying fervently to them on the Feasts of All Souls and All Saints, by having priests say Masses for the Dead, and by offering Catholic prayers in front of their graves at the Qing Ming festival. They celebrated all of the main festivals of the agricultural calendar, from the New Year to the mid-Autumn festival, and engaged in many of the same customs, although they gave them a somewhat different interpretation than non-Christians. The church or chapel at the center of each village was as much a symbol of village community as were non-Christian temples to the local Earth God. In my fieldwork in northern China in the early 1990s, I found that non-Christian farmers considered Catholics to have the same moral values as they did, although the Catholics followed different rituals, especially for funerals. Indeed, since Catholics tended to be concentrated in poorer areas of the country, which had not been so affected by the modern market economy, they actually adhered more closely to traditional values and customs than did many other rural Chinese. Therefore, like traditional heterodox folk-Buddhism, Catholicism has been at least partially domesticated into the traditional lifeworld of family and village.[33]

Multidimensionality of Folk-Catholicism

Thus, like folk-Buddhism, folk-Catholicism is multidimensional. One dimension of folk-Buddhism placed it in opposition to the present world and thus in opposition both to government orthodoxy and to family and village-based religion. Another dimension embraced the world of family and village. Still another dimension connected it to the elite tradition of orthodox Buddhism. Which dimension predominated was dependent on fluid circumstances of time and place. Different members of the sects might be attracted to one dimension or another. At different times, one dimension might so predominate that the others faded completely into the background. Sometimes, indeed usually, folk-Buddhist sects blended smoothly and peacefully into ordinary village folk piety. Sometimes, they approximated the teachings of elite monastic Buddhism. But under other circumstances, they might rise up in massive rebellion. This fluid changeability affected the attitude of imperial governments toward the folk-Buddhist sects. Even when the sects seemed completely peaceful—and even when most members sincerely thought of themselves that way—the government mistrusted them and tried to restrict them. The restrictions, however, made it even more likely that someday the apocalyptic dimension might someday come to the fore. This tension between the Chinese government and a mercurial folk-Buddhism continues today, as seen by the harsh political campaign in 1999–2000 to suppress the *Falun gong* (Wheel of Dharma Practice).

In China today, folk-Catholicism manifests similar characteristics. For most rural Catholics most of the time, the faith is completely melded with the structures of family and village life. One becomes a Catholic by being born into a Catholic family in a Catholic village, not by making any faith commitment to a doctrine of universal salvation. Such Catholics seem indistinguishable in terms of mentality, morality, and lifestyle from non-Christian villagers, the only major difference being the performance of different rituals to mark important events in the life cycle. For many, there is a sincere willingness, or at least a pragmatic commitment, to accept the regulations of the government-controlled Catholic Patriotic Association. However, at other times, perhaps because they have been outraged by government persecution or perhaps inspired by rumors of visions and miracles, Catholics will rise up in opposition to established authorities, and sometimes these uprisings are coordinated over wide regions by the networks of the "underground Church." Therefore, even when Catholics are sincerely peaceful and law abiding, the government mistrusts them and tries to inhibit them. But this makes it even more likely that the Catholics will react negatively.

The Future of Chinese Folk-Catholicism

If Chinese Catholicism has indeed become part of the Chinese folk religious tradition, at least in the countryside, and if, consciously or not, Catholics have modeled their beliefs and practices around some of the elements of the heterodox folk-Buddhist tradition, then there is cause for both hope and concern about the future of the Church in China. Connection with the folk religious tradition would give the Church enormous vitality, at least until that distant time when China becomes thoroughly urbanized and industrialized. This seems indeed to have been the case. Few people expected the Church to survive the persecutions of the Maoist era—not even many foreign missionaries, who thought that the Chinese Catholics on the eve of the Communists' accession to power were deficient in knowledge of and commitment to the doctrine. But the Church did indeed survive the persecution, and despite continuing government restrictions, is flourishing with remarkable vigor. Its survivability and creativity is, I would suggest, precisely the result of its resonance with traditional folk culture—just that resonance that made many Chinese Catholics seem poorly indoctrinated and even vaguely heterodox to many of their foreign missionaries.

At the same time, if Chinese Catholicism has many of the features of a folk religion in the heterodox tradition, the current conflicts between the Church and the government will not be ended by successful diplomacy between the Vatican and China. This official dialogue is a dialogue between the orthodox. Even if the Vatican normalizes relations with China, many rural folk Catholics will probably not listen to official instruction extending downward from a Papal Nuncio toward the grassroots. Folk-Catholicism will continue to develop as it has over the past centuries, through the creative imagination of the ordinary people. (This will continue to be likely because of the shortage of orthodoxly trained priests.) And from time to time, folk Catholics will come into conflict with the Chinese government as well as the official Church hierarchy. The Spirit will blow in strange ways in China, but it may be hard for Catholics around the world to discern what is truly from the Spirit and what is from human culture.

From Past Contributions to Present Opportunities: The Catholic Church and Education in Chinese Mainland during the Last 150 Years

JEAN-PAUL WIEST

No history of China's past 150 years would be complete without mentioning the role played by Christian schools in the modernization of the country and the reform of its educational system. Protestant and Catholic missionaries alike opened the way to new disciplines of study in sciences and technology as well as in medicine. They were the first to make music and athletics an integral part of curriculum. They popularized the study of foreign languages. Academically, they run outstanding private schools that ranked among the leading institutions of the country. Socially, they opened education to all strata of the Chinese society, including women. Morally, they were deeply concerned with character building before government schools began grappling with problems of probity and discipline. Spiritually, they nurtured the faith of millions of followers and trained a Christian leadership for their Church as well as the Chinese society at large.

After 1949, subsequent to the departure of Western missionaries, the arrest of many Church leaders, the confiscation of Church properties, and the government monopolization of all schools and social services, the contribution of Christian Churches to the education of a modern Chinese society came crashing down. The policies of "reform and opening" launched by Deng Xiaoping in 1978 led the regime to relax its restrictions on religious practice and to implement a new religious policy that allows religion to flourish within carefully controlled conditions. As a result, step by step churches have reopened places of worship, seminaries, convents, and training centers for their leaders and followers. Although they are still forbidden to open schools, they have resumed several of their former activities and are engaged in very creative new ways of educating society.

This essay focuses on the Roman Catholic Church, which I know best, and refers occasionally to the Protestant Church for the purpose of comparison.[1] The first part reviews and assesses the educational work of the Catholic Church prior to 1949. The second looks at how the Church today attempts to fulfill an educational role and to remain relevant to contemporary society.

Catholic Education in China Prior to 1949

From its inception, the Catholic Church has understood teaching to be its most important tools of evangelization: "Go to the whole world and preach the Good News to all mankind" (Mark 16.15). It refers to itself as the *Magistra* to whom Jesus entrusted its *Magisterium*, that is the authority and power to teach and interpret the good news. Its calling is to proclaim the salvific love of God in Jesus Christ and to urge all human beings to love one another as God loves them. Religious and secular education have therefore been traditionally, inseparably linked to the evangelizing mission of the Church. In 1622, the Holy See established the Sacred Congregatio de Propaganda Fide for the specific purpose of centralizing the evangelization of non-Christian countries. This office has since periodically issued instructions reiterating the importance of Catholic schools in missions.

In pre-1949 China, the educational work of the Catholic Church served two purposes, each representing a different current in the understanding of what it meant to preach the good news of Jesus Christ. The first trend, especially noticeable at the lowest levels of the missionary educational enterprise, stressed the preservation and nurture of faith among Catholic believers. The second characteristic, more prevalent at the higher echelons of education from the 1920s on, reflected a commitment to train China's elite and provide modern Chinese society with a profound and lasting Christian influence.

From Nurturing the Faith to Evangelizing

The new wave of Catholic missionaries who began to arrive in the 1840s brought along a typical Counter Reformation Church whose model was further reinforced by the difficulties of preaching openly in China. While these missionaries' ultimate goal was to save from eternal damnation as many Chinese as possible through baptism, their immediate concern was to preserve existing Catholics and new converts from the "contamination of paganism." For the most part, they favored a Church that regrouped the faithful into Catholic villages. The strategy was to nurture a strong faith among rural Catholics whose deeds and words would, in time, convince their relatives and friends in neighboring villages to believe. These communities, it was thought, would become, in the long run, the foundation of a future, vibrant, native Church.

In many Catholic villages, therefore, missionaries established schools that gradually grew from places strictly for religious instruction—the so-called prayer schools (*jingtang*)—to establishments offering the basic primary school curriculum in separate buildings for girls and boys. This was in sharp contrast to the traditionally male-oriented Chinese system of education.

Propaganda Fide endorsed this procedure in its *Instructions* of October 18, 1883 and urged the heads of Mission in China to expand even further by establishing institutions of primary and higher education. The text of the document shows without ambages, however, that the Roman office did not view Catholic schools as an important avenue of conversion but rather as the proper religious environment to protect children of Catholics and catechumens from adverse influence.[2]

By 1900, the Catholic Church in China reported some 50,000 students in more than 2,000 schools. These schools catered mainly to Catholic children because schools for non-Christians were disparaged as a waste of time. Indeed until then, the few attempts at running such schools in the hope of converting "pagan" parents through their children had proven largely unsuccessful.[3]

The turn of the century also coincided with the arrival of orders of Sisters and Brothers whose purpose was the education of youth. The Sisters played an especially important role in making education available to the female population. In 1905, the government's abolition of the traditional civil service examinations and the adoption of a more Western educational structure and curriculum further enhanced the attraction of Catholic schools.

Meanwhile, as more and more non-Christian children enrolled in Catholic institutions, the notion of schools as a tool of evangelization gained momentum. By the 1920s, Catholic schools had lost their previously narrowly defined purpose as exemplified in this 1922 letter of a Maryknoll missionary:

> Our Catholic schools in China are not only safeguards (for our Catholic boys and girls) against pagan corruption, but positive nurseries of manly virtues and refined habits. So much so that pagan parents are anxious to send their children to our schools and conversions of both parents and pupils result.[4]

A more diversified understanding of the role of Catholic schools was taking shape. To the original goal of safeguarding the faith among Catholics were added as equally important those of converting non-Christians and cultivating civil virtues. In subsequent years, the first objective remained a given and the second failed to produce significant results. But the third one, as will be shown later, gained increasing support in the missionary community and, in time, became the cornerstone of the educational strategy of the Catholic Church at the secondary and tertiary levels.

All Catholic missions in China followed the same basic hierarchical educational system: a lower primary school in each station with a priest in residence, a higher school in each mission district, and a secondary and a normal school in each vicariate. This model remained flexible enough to adjust to changing circumstances. The first test came in the mid-1920s when the governments of North and South China stipulated that private schools would not be recognized unless they registered and followed a curriculum banning the teaching of religion as a required subject. Many small village schools located in rural areas did not seek governmental approval and continued nonetheless to teach the basic "three Rs" as well as the catechism. But in large villages, towns, and cities, missionaries opted to convert their schools from elementary grades onward into "registered schools" when they realized that without officially recognized diplomas, Catholic students would be denied admission into higher educational institutions. From 1929 on, these Catholic schools offered religious instruction in separate buildings after school hours. At its peak, in 1936, the Catholic Church ran 4,283 registered primary schools and 11,827 unregistered prayer schools with an enrollment of 413,479 students.

The ensuing years of Sino-Japanese conflict and civil war put these Catholic lower schools again to the test by forcing many to close or to consolidate. By 1946, their combined number had been cut by half and then tumbled to about 4,250 in 1948. Yet the enrollment of students in elementary education still stood at more than 267,000, demonstrating a trend toward larger Catholic schools.[5]

These schools provided the Catholic Church with an abundant reservoir of candidates who would be trained further as teachers and catechists, or even as priests and Sisters. In the beginning, teachers often doubled as catechists and vice versa. Separate male and female normal schools prepared the teaching personnel until the need for a more specific training for catechists led, in the 1920s, to the creation of separate catechist schools. In 1935, the number of catechists peaked at 13,817 and declined slightly thereafter due to the Sino-Japanese war. The conflict, however, did not seem to hamper much the formation of future priests and Sisters. The number of Chinese priests grew from about 400 in 1900 to 1,835 in 1936 and reached 2,700 in 1948. As for the Chinese Sisters who did not exist in 1900, they were already 3,626 by 1936 and had passed the 5,100 mark in 1948.[6]

The communist victory brought all private religious and non-religious education to a rapid end. By the fall of 1950, en masse departures of missionaries, restrictions on teaching religion, and the introduction of textbooks of materialistic orientation resulted in the disappearance of most prayer schools. Meanwhile only 1,800 registered Catholic primary schools remained in operation. Within two years, like all remaining private schools, they had all been taken over by the government or pushed out of existence for lack of funds. Only a few seminaries and novitiates managed to remain open until 1955.[7]

With the Bible as the centerpiece of their faith, Protestant missionaries also made educational enterprises an essential component of their work. Like Catholic missionaries, they at first emphasized the Christian education of children of converts and the formation of native ministers and evangelists. But they differed by choosing to establish their schools mostly in cities and large market towns. In 1842, the Anglo-Chinese College (*Ying-Hua Shuyuan*), which had originally been set up in Malacca by Robert Morrison, moved to Hong Kong to become one of the first Protestant schools in China. Moreover, under the influence of advocates of the Social Gospel, Protestants developed an extensive system of secondary schools and universities much faster than Catholics. The hope was that, by serving the Chinese society at large, these institutions would create a Christian environment and nurture China's future Christian elite.

From Converting to Improving Modern Chinese Society

For the most part, the Catholic missionaries who were in China at the turn of the twentieth century preached the Gospel with great zeal, loved their converts, and contributed to their welfare without much thought of self. Yet their psychological attitude toward the Chinese was radically different from the one displayed by Jesuits a few centuries earlier. Matteo Ricci and his companions had carefully avoided the pitfalls of cultural confrontation and instead followed a policy of cultural accommodation, hoping to reconcile two disparate systems of faith and thought. Their approach, in fact, much resembled that of the Greek Fathers who, like Clement of Alexandria, brought the heritage of Homer and Plato to the service of Christian thought.[8] By contrast, the new wave of missionaries unconsciously carried along the sense of superiority and the arrogance that the industrial age had given

Europe. They also were the products of an Ultramontane education of particular inflexibility and dogmatism that triumphed at the First Vatican Council (1869–1870). Consequently, they viewed the Chinese civilization and its people as inferior, odious, and full of corruption; they treated Christians as children and kept the Chinese clergy in subordinate positions; and they relied on the protection and interventions of the Western powers, France in particular, to preach their Christian faith. Whereas the early Jesuits had come as humble emissaries eager to foster cultural exchanges between the West and China and in the process bring Christ's message, the latter missionaries prized themselves as bearers of civilization and Christianity to a hostile and decadent culture.[9]

This attitude eventually led to the idea that the more Catholic schools would espouse a Western style of education and expose the good of Western civilization, the more likely students would understand Catholicism and eventually embrace it. Ruth Hayhoe, in an excellent study of the French educational interaction with China, noted that the French Jesuits in Shanghai "saw their role as providing models or exemplars for missionary work throughout China and in some ways they were both ahead and emulated by other Catholic mission groups."[10]

As early as 1853, according to the superior of the Kiangnan Mission—that is, the Shanghai area—the French Jesuits had already laid down the foundation of a multi-level Catholic education:

> To bring about a healthy Chinese society, we have to begin with its youth. Without schools, we will never succeed in regenerating the pagan population. . . . If we count all the places where children are receiving some instruction we have 144 schools for boys and 33 for girls. In the more narrow sense of the word, we have 78 primary schools all financially supported by our benefactors and us. Among these, three function somewhat between the level of a village (primary) school and a junior high school.[11]

The Jesuits certainly did not reject any of the ideas that Catholic schools should serve as a bulwark for Catholic youth, a seedbed for the recruitment of an ordained and lay leadership, and a locus for the conversion of non-Christians. But above all, they believed that schools should serve as a springboard for the transformation of China into a modern society inspired by Christian principles. Beyond the elementary level, Jesuit-run schools rapidly displayed a mixed enrollment of Catholic and non-Catholic students that reflected the Fathers' commitment to remove boundaries between the closely-knit Catholic world and the non-Christian world.

After the turn of the century, the Jesuit idea continued gaining support among Catholic missionaries. By the 1920s, Catholic education beyond the primary level aimed by and large at training graduates—Catholics as well as non-Catholics—who by their professional excellence and moral qualities would greatly benefit Chinese society. Yet a split had by then occurred among missionaries regarding the form that training should take and what it meant for the Catholic Church to be at the forefront of China's modernization. One group of educators, at best represented by the French Jesuits at Aurora University, believed that the evangelization of China and its modernization would be best achieved by the infusion of Western— meaning mostly French—culture and values. This would be possible thanks to a Western educated elite, appreciative of the Old World civilization, and respectful of the present religious and political authorities.

The trio of Father Vincent Lebbe and learned Chinese Catholic laymen, Ma Xiangbo and Ying Lianzhi, were perhaps the most prominent persons in the other group. They called for the Catholic Church to be more sensitive to Chinese culture and to become really Chinese, including its leadership. They believed that the evangelization of China depended on the Church being at the forefront of the movement of modernization, not only through the teaching of academic disciplines but by promoting social responsibility and discussing contemporary social and moral issues in the light of the Gospel. Ying, therefore, founded in Tianjin the daily newspaper *Da Gong Bao,* soon noted for its firm commitment to democratic ideals and its service of the public interest. When, in 1911, Lebbe began using public lecture halls as a venue for getting into the life of the city and bringing the Church before the educated people, Ying became one of the regular speakers. They also teamed up in pioneering a Chinese Catholic press. In 1912, they launched the first Catholic weekly and, three years later, the first daily, entitled *Yi Shi Bao* (The Social Welfare), which became an instant success among Christians and non-Christians alike because of the accuracy of its news and its independent outlook. By 1936, Catholic periodicals, published wholly or partly in Chinese, numbered seventy-two and ranged from daily newspapers to religious magazines and even scientific journals. The three Catholic presses of Nazareth in Hong Kong, Tousewei near Shanghai, and the Lazarists in Beijing printed the bulk of these publications[12]

Meanwhile, in 1903, Ma Xiangbo and the Shanghai Jesuits got together to open the first Catholic university by the name of L'Université l'Aurore (Zhendan Daxue, Aurora University). It took another twenty years before the Jesuits would open another similar institution in Tianjin, which they called L'Institut des Hautes Etudes Industrielles et Commerciales (Tianjin Gongshang Xueyuan). In 1925, the trio of Lebbe, Ma, and Ying saw their hope of a Catholic university in Beijing come to fruition with the opening of Fujen Catholic University under the direction of American Benedictine monks. In time, each one of these three institutions developed a Women's division. In 1938, the Dames du Sacré-Cœur opened Aurora College for Women and Fujen College for Women was started by the Sisters Servants of the Holy Ghost. The Jesuits of Tianjin followed suit in 1943 with the addition of a Women's Division to Gongshan Xueyuan. Altogether with a combined student population of 3,400, these institutions constituted 5.5 percent of the total enrollment in China's tertiary level. By comparison, the Protestants already maintained thirteen universities and colleges. Prior to 1920, because of the shortage of government-run modern schools, these Protestant institutions had accounted for up to eighty percent of the higher education in the country. By 1943, they still represented twelve to fifteen percent of China's student population at the tertiary level.[13]

Whereas, in rural areas, the disruption brought about by the Sino-Japanese conflict and World War II sharply reduced the number of Catholic primary schools and their enrollment, it had almost an opposite impact on Catholic secondary schools and colleges, located in large town and cities. In striking contrast to the Nationalist Government and most of the Protestant denominations which closed their schools and moved them out of east China, the Catholic Church kept its institutions running. As a result, Catholic secondary and tertiary schools—mostly staffed by French, German, Italian and Chinese priests—remained, together with the lone Protestant university of St. John's in Shanghai, the only institutions in occupied territories with a semblance of neutrality and some degree of independence. Catholic schools experienced the largest ever increase in their non-Christian population.[14]

After Japan's defeat, the reopening of other schools at their original locations failed to slow down enrollment in Catholic secondary and tertiary schools, which by then enjoyed a good reputation of discipline and high academic standards. Between 1936 and 1948, the number of such schools for male students grew from fifty-eight to one 108 and those for female students went from forty-five to eighty-five. Statistics also show that for the same period the number of non-Catholic male students swelled from 7,868 to 26,809, while Catholics inched up only from 3,671 to 4,942. The same proportion is reflected in the female population's figures. Whereas Catholic students grew only from 2,538 to 3,174, Non-Catholic students more than tripled from 4,729 to 16,224. If the percentage of Catholics during that period dropped from some forty-eight to nineteen percent of the student body, this still constituted a higher percentage than the one found in typical Protestant schools.[15]

The gap between the increase in non-Catholics students versus Catholics stems from the fact that the pool of Catholic applicants was much smaller to begin with. The other aspect not to overlook, however, is that since the mid-twenties, the number of Catholic students attending secular institutions also increased. Reasons varied from a deliberate choice to the absence of a Catholic school in the area, to the impossibility of affording tuition. In response to this situation, some missionaries, especially in south China, created hostels that provided Catholic students attending government schools an atmosphere of quiet study and enhanced the development of their "natural and supernatural virtues."[16]

In any event, the large numbers of student conversions missionaries had hoped for never materialized. At Aurora University, for instance, the first baptism was not administered until 1919 and thereafter there was never more than three per year until 1933 when eleven students became Catholics. The number of baptisms remained around that mark until 1939 when it climbed to twenty-four for a total student population of about 500. Over the next ten years, enrollment gradually climbed to 1,000 but baptisms did not increase further.[17]

Although missionaries failed to register large numbers of converts among the educated, their educational system had a significant impact on the development and improvement of Chinese society. The best students were channeled from the lowest to the highest schools and eventually became highly qualified persons ready to assume roles of leadership in all sectors of Chinese society, including the government. In 1936 and 1937, the Jesuits of Aurora proudly reported that some 100 of their graduates filled significant posts in the administration of the Nationalist government, including the Ministry of Education and the Vice-Ministry of Justice. They also boasted that their Chinese medical doctors staffed more than forty institutions, starting with the university's own teaching hospital, L'Hôpital Sainte Marie.[18]

Catholic universities were successful to instill in their students a deep sense of service and dedication to the society. This was best demonstrated during the trying period of 1936 to 1937 that transformed Shanghai alternatively from a war zone to a refugee zone. The Jesuits at Aurora responded in ways that would involve their students. On campus, some students helped to provide basic medical attention in a temporary Red Cross hospital installed in one of the buildings; others attended to the relief of refugees in a camp set up on the soccer field. Outside campus, third- and fourth-year medical students served in the neighboring hospitals or accompanied their professors to more distant locations as volunteers for a couple of months at a time. Others helped another professor, Father Jacquinot, to dispense relief in a special security zone for refugees he had set up on the outskirts of Shanghai.[19]

Discipline and order were major characteristics of Catholic secondary and tertiary education. Contrary to many secular academic and Protestant institutions where large numbers of students took part in the nationalistic movements that periodically shook China, Catholic schools discouraged student activism on campus as well as in the streets. As time went by, the Catholic Church became closely allied with the Nationalist government. Catholic educators "sustained a vision of China in which an intelligent elite of good character who worked hard within the established political system would make China into a better place, for the greater glory of God."[20] Unfortunately for the Church, it had channeled most of its prominent alumni into the service of a regime soon to be overthrown by the Communists.

Would things have turned out differently for the Catholic Church had it nurtured graduates more critical of the Guomindang government and of inequalities in Chinese society? Probably not, because the Church also paid dearly for having remained so much under foreign missionaries' control and for maintaining close ties with Western powers. But in the end, it is the fundamental ideological difference between Marxism and all religious beliefs that explains most of the pain the Catholic Church and other religions have endured in Communist China.

Once the Communists took over the country, the growth of Catholic higher education was short lived. In September 1950, the Ministry of Education issued "The Provisional Regulations for the Management of Private Educational Institutions." The document gave the new regime the right to assume the control of private schools that ran out of funds or failed to abide by the country's atheistic educational policy. Many religious schools, among them Fujen University in Beijing, were taken over by government on one account or the other. The regulations also strictly forbade religious institutions to open new schools, thus preventing any future resurgence of Church-sponsored educational activities. The final blow came on August 5, 1952, with the promulgation of the "University Reorganization Program" that decreed the closure of all remaining private universities. Private secondary schools did not fare better nor did the Catholic press. By 1955, all had been either forced out of existence or confiscated by the new regime.[21]

Catholic Church and Education in Present Day China

The situation began to change in the 1980s. Under the impetus of Deng Xiaoping's guiding principle that "education should be geared to the needs of modernization, of the world and of the future," private schools were again allowed.[22] Another effect of Deng's new approach was a greater freedom to practice religion. Yet these two changes did not mean that religions could freely reactivate their former involvement in private education. The government makes a clear distinction between private schools as houses of religious formation and training, and private schools as alternative options within the public education system. While the five recognized religions of Taoism, Buddhism, Islam, Protestantism, and Catholicism are permitted to open the first kind under certain conditions, they are barred from any involvement in public education.

In the Catholic Church, the situation is further complicated because its unity has been threatened by a division between one group who chooses to function with the approval of the government—the so-called Open (or Official) Church—and another who refuses to have anything to do with the regime—the so-called Underground Church. After years of distrust and vicious accusations, both sides seem on the mend, but the government still follows a carrot and stick tactic in trying to eradicate the underground group. Under the present regulations of the Chinese State, the Open Church is allowed to run places of worship as well as houses of formation, but the activities of the Underground Church remain illegal.

Religious Education Within the Chinese Society at Large

In July 1997, the State Council of the People's Republic of China issued a long decree that gave private schools official recognition by integrating them into the overall socialist educational enterprise. It encouraged social organizations to engage in all domains of educational activities, higher education, compulsory nine years of primary and middle schools, preschools, and even vocational and adult training. But among the long list of regulations, first and foremost stood the stern reminder that "no social organization is allowed to operate open or covert religious schools."[23] This provision came as a big disappointment for the Open Catholic Church because, despite the greater freedom it has enjoyed in recent years, it found itself still barred from entering the field of education. Neither can it "interfere with the State's education" nor can the State "use religion in its own service."[24]

Yet, as the case of the Open Church in Shanghai demonstrates, the doors are not as shut as they seem. In 1949, the citywide educational operation of the Catholic Church included a university, four middle and high schools, and several primary schools all registered with the government. But soon, it lost everything with the departure of foreign missionaries and the suspension of all private education. Today private schools are again thriving. In November 1999, the *Shanghai Daily* proudly reported that the city had twenty-nine private universities and colleges as well as 170 private middle and primary schools.[25] Yet the Church has not been part of this expansion because the civil authorities have routinely rejected Bishop Aloysius Jin Luxian's proposals, including the one to revive Aurora University.

But Jin, being a person who does not easily accept no for an answer, did not give up. Shortly after he became a bishop in 1985, he began to direct the action of his Church toward pressing but still not well addressed problems of the Shanghai society. When the bishop, for instance, applied for opening a Home for the Elderly, he got quick approval from the local government because, with an overall population getting increasingly older, the city of Shanghai is in great need of such facilities. Out of a total of 13 million city dwellers, 2.5 million are over sixty years old and 200,000 over eighty. Moreover, young city couples are less and less able to care for their old parents, and the one child policy will only make things worse within a few years.

Since his Church was denied access to the "regular" field of education, Jin followed the same approach as for the welfare of the elderly. In 1987, he applied for the opening of an evening school to teach the common people a minimum of computer literacy and foreign language proficiency, skills much needed to succeed in a place like Shanghai. Again, the local authorities welcomed this proposal that would alleviate one of their pressing concerns.

The school, by the name of Guangqi Xuexiao, is presently under the direction of a Catholic laywoman trained in the U.S. Professors from major universities who come to teach during their spare time assist her. This private institution offers six-month courses and shorter summer sessions of beginner, intermediate, and advanced day and evening classes held Monday through Saturday. Foreign language courses are mostly for children between the age of seven and twelve. Computer classes are open to all age groups, with a priority given to people with physical disablities. Adults have a choice of classes in internet technology, secretarial work, and accounting and learn their trade on recent computers loaded with the latest software. Upon completion of 100 to 120 hours of classes, they take the regular exam in their field of study at one of the local universities and receive a diploma if successful. Total registration averages 3,000 students per year.

To stay within the law, Guangqi Xuexiao's official owner is not the Catholic Church but the Shanghai Association of Catholic Intellectuals. The school is not allowed and does not intend to openly proselytize, but that it is a Catholic school is an open secret. After all, it is housed on the ground of one of the city's parishes and its Chinese name is taken after the famous late-Ming, Shanghai-born Catholic scholar, Xu Guangqi. Unlike most other private schools that are moneymaking enterprises and thus charge a heavy tuition, Guangqi Xuexiao's aim is to witness Christian compassion by offering the less fortunate an opportunity to succeed in the modern world. It even offers full scholarship to people out of work and reduced tuition to the handicapped and the very poor.[26]

Asked why he was more successful than most bishops in his dealings with the civil authorities, Jin offered the following insightful comment:

> In China, one has to ask; one must not confront, but persuade. So with the government authorities, I insist, I ask, I persuade, I parley. I do not remain passive, and as a result I am given more freedom to do things. If we stay passive, they will never be willing to grant us anything.[27]

It is well known that Chinese local civil authorities often accommodate Beijing's orders to their specific situation, and regulations on education have been no exception. In 1996, upon hearing that the city authorities of Nanchang in Jiangxi province were favorable to the Catholic Church providing the funds for the construction of a primary school in a neighboring poor village, Bishop Jin joined the bishop of Nanchang in raising the sum of RMB 300,000. The city authorities in a public ceremony acknowledged the receipt of that money for the education of poor children and named the future school, Guangqi Xuexiao. When it opened the following year with some 600 pupils in attendance, the facility became the second school in the country by that name and the first school funded by the Chinese Catholic Church to be integrated into the national compulsory education. Since then, as will be explained later, several primary schools have been funded or restored thanks to the donations of mainland China Catholics.[28]

The examples above show that religion as an institution can still influence modern education, even though it is not on the same scale as before and every new initiative will be watched and somewhat controlled by the Chinese government.[29] It may well be that the Catholic Church will never again be allowed to participate in a big way in state controlled education, but other possibilities await to be explored, especially at the personal level. One such area would be for the Church to encourage more committed Catholic individuals to work in public education. If exploited more fully, albeit carefully, this presence could create a ripple effect throughout the broad educational sector.

In recent years, a significant segment of the Chinese educated class has shown a genuine interest and appreciation for the Christian Churches. Several current historical studies, for instance, point to biases in previous research and present instead a more balanced and generally more appreciative assessment of Christianity. This trend toward a great intellectual probity is symptomatic of a widespread yearning for spiritual values among the intellectuals and the youth. Many look toward religion for answers, but the Chinese Catholic Church is not well prepared to respond to their queries. Since the early 1980s, the Church has mostly trained priests and Sisters to satisfy the religious needs of the bulk of Chinese Catholics who are simple people without much education. But ignoring the spiritual quest of non-Christian intellectuals much longer would be missing an opportunity to influence the movers and shakers of Chinese society, if not the future of education as a whole. On the part of the Catholic Church, interlocutors within China are too few: a handful of Chinese professors, some foreign experts and guest professors, and some occasional visiting Chinese scholars from Macau, Hong Kong, and Taiwan. What are urgently needed are well-trained Chinese Catholic intellectuals and educators able to dialog with their non-Christian counterparts.

It is therefore imperative that the Chinese Church provides those Catholics who choose a teaching career with a solid religious training. Educators have a great influence on their students. In elementary schools, Catholic teachers, without departing from the curriculum, can give the proper religious connotation of many topics of general culture, such as the true meaning of Christmas. In high schools and universities, Catholic professors have even more leeway in disciplines such as history, Western literature, and foreign languages and cultures, which often touch upon the topic of religion. Many foreign teachers of English and French languages at Chinese universities have reported that literary topics dealing with religion always occasion lively and profound discussions. The Chinese Church should also look at the recent multiplication of religious studies centers and the increasing number of courses on religion in philosophy departments as an opportunity to provide the academia with a solid Christian presence. The titles of the following three recent lectures will suffice to give an idea of the broad range of interests: "What is Mystical Experience? History and Interpretation." "Religious Life and Theology in the Time of European Renaissance." "Giulio Aleni and the Gospel in China." Christian foreign professors regularly appear at these institutions as guest lecturers, but Chinese Christian scholars are so few in this discipline that they are still mostly absent from faculty rosters.

Religious Education Within the Catholic Church

With the restoration of religious freedom in the early 1980s, the Chinese Catholic Church reemerged, but long years of imprisonment and labor camps combined with the closing of seminaries and novitiates had left it with a very old and sparse leadership. The remaining fifty or so bishops made the rebuilding of clergy their top priority. In October 1982, Sheshan regional seminary became the first major Catholic training school allowed to reopen, and others quickly followed suit. At present, the Open Church forms about 950 young men in seven major seminaries and 700 boys in seventeen minor seminaries. Bishops began to pay attention to the training of women religious in the early 1990s only, but the number of congregations and Sisters has grown rapidly. In late 1999, the Open Church had forty diocesan congregations of Sisters with some 1,000 novices and postulants. Over the past ten years, priest and Sister theologians and formation-teachers from Hong Kong and other countries have regularly been invited to several of these places to strengthen the religious formation of the future priests and Sisters. Meanwhile the Underground Church survives on its own and maintains another ten seminaries with some 800 major seminarians and twenty houses of religious formation for women.[30]

Since the early 1990's the Open Church has been allowed to send some of its brighter prospects to seminaries and universities abroad to further their studies and prepare to assume important positions upon their return. Of the fifty-three sent to the United States since 1993, thirty already went back to China, and eighteen—eight priests, two Sisters, six seminarians, and two laywomen—are still enrolled in universities and seminaries. In 1994, the Open Church also began to send priests and seminarians to Europe. Twenty of them have returned and fifty-eight continue their studies—twenty-five in France, fifteen in Italy, thirteen in Germany, and three in Belgium. Each year, the Underground Church also manages to send a few people to study abroad, but it is difficult to even approximate how many there are at present.

Thanks in part to the help of sister Churches like that of Hong Kong, the Catholic Church of mainland China has in recent years put more emphasis on continuous education for its clergy, religious, and lay leaders. These seminars and courses at first held mostly in Hong Kong are now increasingly conducted in mainland China itself where they can benefit a larger number of people. In 1998, for instance, the continuous education and specialization of the clergy included a spring course held in Hong Kong for eight young priests teaching dogmatic theology at major seminaries in China. By the fall of the same year, these same people gathered in Beijing for an advanced seminar in counseling and spiritual direction while some thirty-two other faculty members gathered in Wuhan for a refresher course.

The year 1999 was undoubtedly marked by the preoccupation to enhance the formation of Sisters. In April, the nine diocesan congregations of Hebei province set up the first association of women religious superiors. On their agenda for forthcoming meetings figured administration classes for superiors, exchange visits between congregations, and the improvement of formation in novitiates. Two months later, leaders of women religious superiors from about half of the nearly fifty congregations in mainland China gathered in Beijing for their first experience in exchanging ideas on convent management and formation.[31]

The rebuilding of a lay leadership has not received as much attention and needs to be included in the process of ongoing education. Two Hong Kong-based Catholic organizations have worked for several years with mainland China dioceses and seminaries to provide training sessions inclusive of priests, Sisters, and laypersons. The Catholic Institute for Religion and Society specializes in weeklong intensive seminars that teach participants how to integrate Christian faith and morality into the daily familial and social life as well as into the broader Chinese cultural context. The Hong Kong Diocesan Catechetical Centre has over the past three years led sixteen seminars on child, youth, and adult catechetics which have drawn a combined attendance of two bishops, twenty priests, 377 Sisters, 488 seminarians, fifty novices, and seventy laypersons.

As a result, several dioceses are able to conduct short programs of continuous education on their own. Shanghai has taken the lead with the inauguration in April 1998 of the Guangqi Formation Center, a three-story retreat house to facilitate ongoing formation and spiritual training of priests, Sisters, and laypersons. But even dioceses with fewer resources in finance and personnel are laying down the foundations for programs in continuous education. In June 1999, for instance, the diocese of Nanchong followed up on a course offered the previous December by the Hong Kong Catechetical Centre to all the dioceses of Sichuan with its own first one-day seminar for some seventy lay catechists. One of the most promising programs seems to be the one launched in Beijing in 1997 at the request of a group of laypersons eager to enrich their theological knowledge. The seventy-five or so students spend their Saturdays over a three-year period completing eighteen courses in theology, biblical knowledge, philosophy, Church music, and Church history.

A better-trained leadership results in more imaginative and bold ways to encourage Christians to confess their faith publicly. There is no better example than those Beijing lay theology students who, in 1998, organized the first Beijing Catholic Cultural Festival on the grounds of the cathedral to bring cultural aspects of the Catholic faith closer to the ordinary believers. The festival featured essay writing, poetry, singing, Chinese calligraphy, drawing, photography, and sculpting competitions as well as spiritual sharing among lay Catholics.

In spring 1997, after a flood ravaged Fuping county, one of the poorest areas of Shaanxi province, the Catholic church of Shijiazhuang diocese in Hebei launched a campaign to raise funds to support the education of children in that place. The cathedral parishioners alone donated some U.S. $1,500 and their representatives visited the schools in Fuping to get a better understanding of the children's need. This was the first time since the founding of the People's Republic of China that a local Catholic Church had raised money for charity.[32]

The success of the drive encouraged the Hebei Catholic newspaper *Xinde* (Faith), to publicize other charitable causes such as rehabilitating school dropouts, helping families in need, and assisting victims of tragic accidents or natural disasters. Responses to these calls for help come from all over China and have been so enthusiastic that a Catholic social service center called *Beifang Jinde* was established to handle the donations. This phenomenon might signal a new breakthrough in the Catholic Church's efforts to educate both Christians and non-Christians through the print media.

The Catholic Church operates nationwide three publication houses recognized by the government. Xinde Press is the newest one; established in 1991, it is jointly owned by the eight bishops of Hebei. Catholic Church in China Press was founded in 1980, and is run both by the Chinese Catholic Patriotic Association and the Bishops' Conference of the Open Church. The third outfit is Guangqi Press, established in 1984 and operated by the Shanghai diocese. Besides the publication of bibles, Church documents, and liturgical missals, these three houses combined also put out about 160 titles a year of religious books and pamphlets. Some are originals; many are works that are already published in Taiwan and Hong Kong but converted to simplified characters. So far the outreach of these printed materials to non-Christians has been rather limited because they cannot be publicly advertised or sold. They are only available on Church premises or through direct orders.

Three magazines, available by subscription only, cater to a more diversified audience, including non-Christian academics and intellectuals. The oldest and only one circulated both within China and overseas to some 10,000 subscribers is published by the Beijing Press. Called, *Catholic Church in China (Zhongguo Tianzhujiao)*, this quarterly speaks for the Chinese Catholic Patriotic Association and the Bishops' Conference of the Open Church, and for this reason presents a favorable viewpoint on religious policies in China. The two other journals are the product of the Shanghai diocese and have a more modest subscription list of 2,000 each. Materials on the activities of the *Overseas Catholic Church (Tianzhujiao haiwai dongtai ziliao*) is a biweekly providing information on the Catholic religion worldwide. The other magazine is a bimonthly compilation of research materials by the name of, *Collection of Research Materials on the Catholic Church* (*Tianzhujiao yanjiu ziliao huibian*).

But the Catholic publication that reaches the largest audience in China, and has the most far-reaching informational and educational outreach to Catholics as well as non-Catholics, is with no doubt, *Xinde*. Launched in September 1991 as a monthly, it is the only Catholic newspaper published in mainland China. From a local newspaper of barely 7,000 copies, it has grown into a nationwide publication fed by the contributions of voluntary local contributors from every province in the country. Its success has been such that in June 1996, it doubled its size to eight pages and recently, on its eighth anniversary, it became a biweekly and topped the 45,000 copies mark. This is quite an achievement for a paper that cannot be sold at newsstands and is available only by subscription. One understands even better the esteem and the popularity it enjoys among Catholics when one realizes that, in rural communities, ten to fifty persons often share the same copy, bringing the total readership to at least 450,000 people, if not well over 2 million. [33]

Xinde seems to be on the right track to achieve what no other Catholic magazine has yet accomplished, that is to become a publication that fulfills the expectations of Catholics of both sides. *Xinde* not only provides a great variety of news about the Catholic Church at home and abroad, but also has become a means of communication and a place of exchange that transcend divisions between Catholics. Writers can express their feelings and desires, discuss Church and social issues, address challenges, and talk about their faith. The newspaper is also a source of spiritual enrichment as each issue provides articles and book excerpts by Chinese and foreign spiritual writers. But, as mentioned earlier, the greatest achievement of *Xinde* might well be to have awakened Catholics all over the country to a sense of a corporate social responsibility towards those in direst need, thus creating among nonbelievers a favorable new image of the Church in China.

Conclusion

Obviously the field of education is much broader than the topics of schools and press developed in this presentation, but these two were and, in a sense, still form the two key pieces of the Catholic educational enterprise. Among other aspects of this enterprise figure scientific contributions that have been the subject of previous studies, in particular the Jesuit observatories of Xujiahui, Sheshan, and Lujiabang, with their valuable research and information on weather, seismology, astrophysics, terrestrial magnetism, and geophysics. The educational role of missionaries in the rise of a Christian art form, especially in architecture and painting, cannot be ignored either. Even on the subject of schools, I had to leave out areas of relative importance—such as trade schools and orphanages—in order to keep the essay within a reasonable length.

Over the past 150 years, the involvement of the Catholic Church in Chinese education underwent several changes. Three dates, 1905, 1950, and 1980, stand as major turning points in that history. Prior to the abolition of the Chinese traditional civil service examination system in 1905, the Catholic Church emphasized the revitalization and the development of strong Catholic communities. Missionaries were mostly concerned with protecting the faith, livelihood, and lives of their Christians from outside threats. Catholic schools taught Catholic families' youngsters the tenets of the Church as well as the basic three "Rs." Despite mounting pressure from within the Church as well as from non-Christian Chinese parents on the outside, Catholic schools rarely opened their doors to non-Christians.

With the educational reform of 1905, Catholic education began to move into two directions. One trend, especially noticeable in the rural areas at the primary school level, continued to emphasize the religious instruction of Catholic children. Meanwhile, more and more Catholic missionaries viewed schools and the press as a means to reach the great mass of non-Catholics. They were also increasingly wary of the growth and success of the Protestant press and the Protestant secondary and tertiary schools offering an education based on Western educational principles. A second trend therefore emerged advocating a Catholic press and schools that would provide a Western type but Catholic-inspired education for all Chinese. From then on, in the estimation of Roman Catholic and Protestant Churches, schools and publications were not only a very visible sign of their presence, they were also their most pervasive tools for building a new Chinese society on Christian principles.

Further reforms of the Chinese educational system in the 1920s accentuated the dichotomy within the Catholic Church. On the one hand, the Church maintained low-level schools in which religious classes were part of the curriculum. These establishments were mostly attended by Catholic children. On the other hand, the Church ran government-recognized schools from which religion courses had been banned. Both Catholics and non-Catholics attended these institutions, but the majority was definitively non-Catholic. This second type of schools opened new dimensions to the understanding of the name "Catholic school." On a superficial level, such schools would remain Catholic as long as they were run and financially supported by the Catholic Church. But at a deeper level, one came to realize that schools did not need to teach religious courses or boast large numbers of converts to be called Catholic. They earned that name because of a Christian atmosphere, a Christian spirit, a Christian example, and way of life displayed by their Catholic faculty and students.

For the Catholic Church and all religions in general, the advent of the People's Republic of China signaled a thirty-year disappearance from the field of education and a loss of all its schools and press services. In any case, the educational structure the foreign missionaries had put in place was very much dependent on outside funding. So one wonders how many of these schools and publications the Chinese Catholic Church could have maintained after the departure of missionaries, had the Chinese government not suppressed them first?

The greater religious freedom of the past twenty years has allowed the Church to again make some modest forays in the educational field. Its most significant progress has been in the religious education of its leadership. Still officially barred from playing a part in the regular academic teaching of the Chinese people, the Chinese Church has begun to rethink its role in education. Rather than being nostalgic about its past educational grandeur, some Church leaders have realized that the confiscation of their schools in the secular domain was a blessing in disguise. They have begun to explore new avenues, some by responding to problems created by the rapid changes in Chinese society, others by urging people to come to the rescue of those in need, others again by providing news of the Catholic Church on a nationwide scale. These efforts offer a compassionate and caring image of the Church that goes a long way toward educating Catholics and non-Catholics alike about the true meaning of the Christian faith.

Ruth Hayhoe and Lewis Pyenson have pointed out that changes in the Catholic and secular education systems of France during the first half of the twentieth century influenced the development of Catholic education in China.[34] A more systematic study from the mid-nineteenth century to the present day is needed. A comparison of the past fifty years will be particularly interesting as the Catholic Church in some Western countries has begun also, but without any government pressure, to disengage itself from many of its formal educational enterprises.

Christianity and China's Minority Nationalities—Faith and Unbelief

RALPH R. COVELL

Introduction

When the People's Republic of China drew up its first constitution in 1954, it defined the country as a "unitary multinational state in which all the nationalities are equal." After many years, during which ethnographers, sociologists, and historians sorted out the evidence presented by more than 400 groups who wished to be considered a nationality, fifty-six were identified. The principal nationality was the Han people.[1] This dominant group numbers more than 1 billion people. The other fifty-five nationalities, ranging in number from 15 million to several hundred, live within the geographical boundaries of China, are loyal, for the most part, to its government, and are considered citizens of the country. Politically they are Chinese, but culturally, usually having their own language, culture, history, and land, they have another identity.

Even though the fifty-five nationalities number nearly 100 million, this represents only eight percent of China's total population. But the minorities weigh far more than they count. For example, they live in 60 percent of China's huge territory, an area larger than that of the United States, supply most of China's livestock, and have in their territories most of China's mineral resources. Their music, poetry, and customs have greatly influenced national life. The fifty-five minority nationalities may be classified by location, language, or religion.[2]

For the purposes of this paper, the religious classification of China's minority nationalities is the most relevant. Some are Muslims, some are Buddhists, some are largely Christian, and some adhere to traditional or folk religions, often called animism in the past. This may be too simple an analysis, for there are different combinations of religious belief in many groups. In general, however, we may say that all groups in northern China are Muslims, with the exception of the Mongols. The Mongols and Tibetans follow Lamaism, a form of Buddhism. Nearly every group in southwest China and in Taiwan has been dominated by a belief in spirits, a traditional religion. One exception is the Dai who historically have adhered to Hinayana Buddhism. Even for groups that are Islamic or Buddhist, the principal reality is the spirit world. With the Korean people and many groups in southwest China and Taiwan, the Christian faith has gained a strong hold. Some of these people, such as the Lisu and many of the Yuanzhu Min in Taiwan, consider Christianity to be their major faith.

Christian missionaries have sought for more than 1,200 years to bring the Gospel of Jesus Christ to the minority nationalities of China. Beginning with the Tang dynasty (618–907) and continuing at least until the advent of the People's Republic of China (PRC), emissaries of the cross have tried to penetrate Mongolia, Tibet, and areas in what is now Xinjiang in northwest China. Only within the modern era of Christian missions to China, in the late nineteenth century, was missionary work commenced among the many minority groups in southwest China. Dutch missionaries established churches among minorities (they referred to them as "Indians") in Taiwan early in the seventeenth century, but no concentrated efforts were made to reach these people until about 1870.

Despite acknowledging that China was a pluralistic state, the Guomindang government over the years emphasized *zhongzu*, the Chinese race or nation, and not *minzu*, people groups. Its policy was one of assimilation. It was expected that all minority groups, since they were Chinese politically, should become Chinese culturally. When the PRC came to power, it did not follow the nonassimilative model used by the USSR wherein its minorities were given political status in various republics, particularly in Central Asia. Mao's policy, formulated in 1938 even before gaining power, provided that minority nationalities would be encouraged to live in autonomous regions, prefectures, and counties, would have equal rights with the Chinese and freedom to use their own language and cultures, but would not have separate states. The non-Han people would live in the same unified country with the Han Chinese.

Traditionally Resistant Peoples

Buddhists

Muslims and Buddhists, whether in China or elsewhere, have traditionally not received the Christian faith easily. Therefore, it is no surprise, for example, that there would be few converts from missionary work among llamaistic Buddhism in either Tibet or Mongolia. Roman Catholics commenced their work among the Tibetans much earlier than did the Protestants. Comparatively, then, the number of their converts far exceeded those of the Protestants. Dajianlu, the entry point into Tibet from Sichuan, was recorded as having 5,301 converts in 1948, but it is not certain how many of these were Tibetans.[3] Likewise, it is impossible to analyze general statistics for Yunnan and determine how many of the 1,000 converts reported in northwest Yunnan were Tibetan. Nor are there any statistics for Yanjing (Yerkalo) and Mangkang in Tibet.[4] No comparable Protestant statistics are available. One of the largest Protestant efforts was by the Christian and Missionary Alliance (CMA). When it closed down its work in 1949, there were very few converts and no purely Tibetan churches.

As Protestant missionaries agonized over the paltry nature of their results, they had a variety of conclusions. Some felt that they were so busy in evangelizing that they failed to take the time to understand the Tibetan or Mongolian culture. One speculated that Protestant missionaries in the early 1900s knew far less than their Roman Catholic colleagues seventy-five years earlier. Often, some missionaries were so anxious to get into Tibet proper and go to Lhasa that they neglected the more accessible opportunities in the "lama-controlled areas of West China."[5] Religious sensitivity was usually lacking, and few attempts made to empathize with the people in their religious striving.

Results were no better in Mongolia than in Tibet. When the Scheut missionaries began work in Mongolia in the late 1800s, the order's aim to have "Missions in Mongolia" quickly became "Missions amongst the Chinese in Mongolia."[6] By 1940 Catholic converts in the southern and central sections of Mongolia numbered 200,000, but these were almost entirely Han Chinese. Several Protestant mission agencies worked in Mongolia, but attained less results than the Catholics.

Muslims

Chinese Central Asia is a vast territory inhabited by a confusing mixture of peoples whose appearance, languages, and lifestyles would seem to fit them for the Middle East. The minority nationalities to whom missionaries sought to bring the Christian faith lived in several areas: Qinghai, Gansu, and Xinjiang. Apart from the non-Hui Chinese, Russians, Xibo, Uighur, and Mongols, all the people of central Asia are Muslims. Most of them are Sunni and belong to the Hanifi school of Islamic law.

During the Mongol dynasty (1260–1368), Franciscan and Dominican missionaries went through Central Asia and gave their witness to the regional rulers. Many churches were established in the area. The two Protestant groups exerting the most effort were the China Inland Mission (CIM) and the Swedish Missionary Union. The CIM missionaries engaged in extensive itineration, translated portions of the Bible into local languages, and distributed tracts and Scripture portions. As time allowed, these activities were accompanied by preaching and teaching. The results were few among Muslim peoples, and the churches formed were made up almost exclusively of Chinese members. The Swedish Missionary Union work began in 1894, and it eventually included medical work, schools, a printing press, literature, and evangelism. Missionaries took up residence in Kashgar and Yarkand and carried out their ministries on an ongoing basis in these cities. They did not use itineration nearly as much as the missionaries with the CIM. By 1933, the total number of baptized Christian was 163, mostly Uighurs and Kirghiz, but some Chinese. After a protracted period of persecution when Christians were imprisoned and tortured, the number dwindled, only to reach a new high of 200 after the missionaries were forced to leave in 1938 because of violent antiforeign feelings by the people and by the new government of the Turkish-Islamic Republic of Eastern Turkestan.[7]

In addition to the ethnic Muslims found in Qinghai, Gansu, Ningxia, and Xinjiang, are the Islamic Hui peoples who are concentrated in southwest China, with significant groups in Hebei and Manchuria. A large number live in Beijing and in Nanjing. Speaking Chinese and having lifestyles very similar to non-Hui Han Chinese, these Muslims have frequently been referred to as "hidden Muslims." From the missionary viewpoint they faded into the dominant Chinese Confucian and Buddhist background. When missionaries proclaimed the Christian message to them, their presentations were no different from those given to the non-Hui Han Chinese. As a result of failing to contextualize the message to the Hui, a positive response to Christianity was very little.

Traditionally Receptive Peoples

Compared with the resistance to the Christian faith among the Islamic and Buddhist minority nationalities in China, the response among many of the groups adhering to folk religions has been high. This has been so, particularly among the Miao, Lisu, Lahu, Wa, the Black Yi of Yunnan, Jingpo, Hani, and the several nationalities among the original inhabitants of Taiwan. Among many other minorities in southwest China, the results have not been nearly as good. Among these more resistant adherents of folk religion are the Zhuang, Naxi, Tujia, Yao, Dong, Bouyei, Yi of southern Sichuan, and Li of Hainan Island. Often even within a generally responsive minority there are pockets of resistance which set them against the majority within their group. One of the most puzzling of these is the differences among the responsive Black Yi of Yunnan and the independent Nosu or Yi of south Sichuan. Researchers have proposed many theories to isolate causal factors leading to either response or resistance. We may divide these factors into political, personal, strategic, practical, sociological and cultural, and religious and theological ones. Obviously, these several factors often overlap and cannot be rigidly separated from one another.

Political Factors

In analyzing the massive positive response by the Lisu in Yunnan to the Christian faith, Qin Heping, in an article in *Study of World Religions*, published by the Institute of World Religions of the Chinese Academy of Social Sciences, concludes that among four reasons the most dominant one is that Western imperialism manipulated and took advantage of the people as it preached a foreign religion. Religious imperialism, he contends, was carried out much more easily along the indefinite border between China and Burma, an area controlled very imperfectly by the Chinese government.[8] Several consideration might support his argument. Mission groups, whose administrative offices were usually in Shanghai, found that they could enter China more easily from its back door in Yunnan. This was made easier for British missionaries when Burma was annexed by Great Britain in 1898 and also from certain treaty provisions of the Chefoo Convention in 1876. This treaty resulted from the death of Augustus Margary, an English vice-consul killed near the Burma-China border in 1875 by a Kachin tribesperson as he was facilitating a British trade mission into China.

Personal Factors

In every situation where there has been a substantive response to the Christian faith, the charisma of the proclaimer, not necessarily a foreign missionary, cannot be neglected. Among the Sediq in Taiwan, the key person was a middle-aged woman by the name of Jiwang. Relatively uneducated, she had many qualities which prepared her for being the initiator of a people movement to the Christian faith, which in turn was a catalyst to faith among several other Taiwan minorities. She was open to the outside world beyond her tribal roots, she was an astute business woman, she was chosen by the Japanese government to be the reconciler between the officials and her people, and when she became a Christian, she knew how to instruct her compatriots in the basics of the Christian faith. She was not daunted by the persecution that came to her as a result of her commitment.[9]

Among the Lisu the principle missionary proclaimer was James O. Fraser. Unlike other missionaries of that period, he did not often appeal to officials on behalf of the Lisu. But, in every other respect, he was a strong and yet compassionate director of the work. Committed to an indigenous policy, he immediately delegated to developing leaders the responsibility of carrying on many aspects of the work.

Samuel Pollard was a champion of the oppressed Miao. Undoubtedly heavy handed in the ways in which he fought political, religious, and cultural oppression against the Miao, whether by the Chinese government, Nosu landlords, or the wizards in their own society, Pollard was the protector of the Miao. One of his colleagues commented, "It was to him these long suffering, sinning and sinned against thousands made their first appeal in hope of a deliverer."[10] James R. Adam, a missionary among the Miao with the CIM in the Anshun area of Guizhou is not as well known as Pollard, but his unusual sensitivity was a major factor in the first conversions among the flowery and black Miao. His simple invitation for a number of these people, despised by the Chinese, to eat with him in a small roadside inn opened the door of faith to believe in an impartial God who treated all people alike. It is impossible to weigh the personal factor, but it is also impossible to neglect it.

Strategic Factors

The time when the Christian faith came to a group of people, the particular emphasis made, and the methods employed can all be considered strategic factors. Obviously, these factors relate intimately to the personal factors. As contrasted with missionary work among the Han Chinese, those who worked with the minority nationalities advocated that conversions to Christ were best if they came by families, and not merely by individuals. Fraser preached in many different contexts—in open-air meetings, in tea shops, in Chinese inns, in small chapels—but increasingly his focus was not on individuals, but on the bridge they might give to their families. The clan system among the Lisu was strong, and unless the village elders approved, it was difficult for even the father in one home to do away with the family altar and sacrifices so crucial in demon worship. A people movement, the term now popular in missiology, did not mean that every family member would make a full commitment to Christ. It did mean that all responsible family members would publicly disavow and leave all aspects of demon worship in an initial step of repentance. This kept the door open for further decisions and meant that everyone was moving along the path toward conversion, rather than turning against one another.[11]

Many efforts had been made, beginning in the early seventeenth century, to establish Christian churches among the original inhabitants of Taiwan. In each effort, the response had been minimal, probably as the result of many factors. Somehow the time did not seem ripe. This changed during the 1935–1946 period before and during World War II. Because of Japanese oppression of the Sediq people that had deprived them of headhunting, they had lost a sense of tribal identity. Now, as contrasted with earlier periods when their identity was strong, an ideological vacuum existed in which the Gospel message was welcomed.

When the Gospel was preached as a liberating force, it appealed strongly to people who felt that they were oppressed not only physically and economically, but spiritually by the manipulation of wizards with their seeming control of the world of evil spirits. Forgiveness of sin and new life in Christ has traditionally been the center of the Christian faith. This focus was not immediately appealing to many of the nationalities who lived much more by a system of taboos rather than by a sense of morality and sin.

Practical Factors

It is common to note in many articles and books that the reasons advanced for faith are very practical. Heading this list is the economic. The people will save money by not following the old paths of sacrificing to the evil spirits. By no longer having expensive ceremonies to celebrate births, marriage, and funerals, they will also save much money. The Christian faith will deliver them from the use of wine and drugs and give them more motivation and energy for work. To these reasons Li Tseng Hsiu adds "cultural entertainment." Life in a mountain village is boring. Government organs and educational institutions do nothing much to allay this situation. The church, in addition to being a religious institution, is a social and educational center for the village. It puts on entertaining programs of singing, dancing, storytelling, and the playing of musical instruments. People are introduced to an entirely new dimension of life.[12]

These practical factors are often discussed under the rubric of the Chinese phrase *duanque* (or shortcoming). Zhang Tan, in his excellent book on the Miao turning to the Christian faith, mentions five of these: poverty of the people, poor livelihood in general, lack of privileges in society, lack of a moral sense, and a psychological lack.[13] These various factors undoubtedly are important, but not so much because they are causal as that they represent the influence upon the life of the people after they are committed to the Christian faith. It is difficult to know to what degree they were motivating factors to faith.[14]

Sociological and Cultural Factors

The factors that we have discussed to this point have to relate more to the source of the message than to the nature of the receptor societies to which the message has come. The specific situations of receptor groups are a part of the bigger picture of cross-cultural religious diffusion. The study of diffusion has concentrated on technological innovations and social and cultural practices; how a religion passes from one culture to another has not been given equal attention. Robert Montgomery suggests that a fruitful area for investigation is what he calls a "sociology of missions—the sociological study of the spread of religions." To do this he proposes that scholars pay attention to "corporate self-identity—that part of an individual's self-concept which derives from his knowledge of his membership of a social group (or groups) together with the value and emotional significance attached to that membership."[15]

Religion is a valued aspect of social identity, and, unlike race or gender, is changeable. Whether or not it will change depends on several complex inter-group relations that involve domination and subordination. A dominant group will probably see no need to change its religion; a subordinate group may feel that an outside religion cannot help it. It then would resist a new religious faith, certainly one associated with the dominant group. It responds either by strengthening its traditional religion or by mixing it with some outside elements.

A group that is dominant politically, economically, or culturally may feel that its social identity can be enhanced by taking the religion from a culture it perceives as superior in this respect to its own. Does this, along with other factors, explain the success of Buddhism, a foreign religion in China? Likewise, a subordinate group threatened by a dominant group may find great help and new strength in the religion of some nonthreatening group. To determine the dynamics of change, a careful analysis must be made of all of the internal groups within a given receptor society.

Psychological, social, and cultural factors may also aid or hinder transcultural communication. Charles Kraft has identified some of the basic relationships between two societies that influence the diffusion of ideas.

Factors Influencing Acceptance/Rejection of New Ideas[16]

Factors	Hinder Acceptance	Help Acceptance
Basic premises of source and receptor cultures	Very different	Very similar
Attitude of receptors toward own culture	Very positive	Very negative
Attitude of receptors toward source culture	Despised	Respected
Openness to new ideas	Closed	Open
Pace of change	Slow	Rapid
Borrowing tradition	None	Strong
Morale	Proud	Demoralized
Self-sufficiency	Strong	Weak
Security	Threatened	Stabilized
Flexibility	Resistant	Adaptive
Advocate	Nonprestigious	Prestigious
How ideas relate to felt needs	Unrelated	Related
Fit of new ideas to present beliefs	Incompatible	Compatible

This table shows well the characteristics of an oppressed people. For example, with the Sediq in Taiwan and the Lahu, Wa, Miao, Yi (Yunnan), and Lisu, they were dominated and weak. They were threatened, but not by the people from whom they were receiving the Christian faith. They were negative toward their own cultures, and because of what they had suffered, they were relatively open to new ideas, adaptive, and even willing to undergo rapid change. These people respected the source culture and perceived its messengers as prestigious. When the gospel was presented with some degree of cultural sensitivity, the people saw it as related to their felt needs and compatible with their spirit-filled lives. The peoples of Yunnan and Guizhou, with many of their villages often intersecting with one another, often borrowed social, cultural, and religious ideas, as well as implements related to their work and living. Groups that have resisted the Christian faith do not have as many factors compatible with receiving new ideas.

In much the same vein, Zhang Tan affirms that the Christian faith helped the Miao to have a new sense of their corporate identity. Their old culture was not able to deal with their financial, physical, moral, and ideological "short comings." In each instance of need, however, the Christian faith brought a type of revitalization.[17]

An important consideration in analyzing how a society is open to change is revitalization. Anthony Wallace paints a broad picture of the types of crises into which a society may fall. The crisis need not come from a dominant group oppressing a subordinate one; it may derive from strife among equal groups or it may be stimulated by internal social and economic problems. These provoke disequilibrium within society, leading to a decline and collapse. Then new leaders, new ideas, new goals, and new values may lead to revitalization, putting the society back again on a steady state.[18]

T'ien Ju-k'ang, a scholar from mainland China, has made an extensive analysis of Miao, Lisu, and Lahu societies to find reasons for their large-scale conversions to Christianity. He finds the key in the relationships between dominant and subordinate groups. Each of these three minority nationalities was oppressed, either by the Chinese or by other minorities, such as the Yi, Bai, and Naxi. They responded by rebellions, migrations to other areas, and seeking out the top of the mountains for their villages and farmlands. Some were easily assimilated and became those called "tame" (*shu*). Those who resisted were considered "wild" (*sheng*) Between these two extremes were variations on a long continuum. Those groups that responded best to the Christian faith were decentralized in their political and religious structures. Thus, they were unable to resist cohesively, either in their overall internal tribal structure or on the village and temple level, the invasion of a new religion.[19]

Paul Cohen has made similar observations that relate not only to minority nationalities but to resistant peoples in general:

> When resistant peoples were oppressed by the Chinese, they had close-knit communities and systematic religious beliefs, and they focused on these and resisted even more vigorously.
>
> The past was a path for the future. Only a few on the margins dared to think of change, and these were the ones who encouraged the missionaries, but their power was limited for the most part to small enclaves.
>
> With the responsive groups there was not such a close-knit community cohesiveness, and nothing in their overall framework that could resist, except maybe a clan leader. As the people went through persecution or oppression, they found the Christian faith and its emissaries to be their protectors, and, in one way or another, the faith became the focal point of a new identity for a large number of people.[20]

Religious and Theological Factors

Closely related to the sociological and cultural factors are religious views that are related in part to the religious backgrounds of a specific national minority. One scholar, Cheung Siu-woo, makes a strong case that over the centuries as the Miao resisted oppression, they developed the concept of a Miao King who would lead the people into a new order and act as a savior to deliver them from domination and oppression by the Han and Yi. When Pollard came proclaiming the Christian message, the people saw in Jesus, and perhaps also in Pollard, "the friend of the oppressed," the fulfillment of this long held millenial hope.[21] If this hope was indeed vitally held by the people and was partially a beginning point for their belief in Jesus, would it have been any different from the messianic expectations held by the early Christian church? We have no clear record that Pollard preached a millenial doctrine that connected directly or indirectly with the people's expectations.

He did, however, clearly present the meaning of the suffering of Jesus as it related to the past and current oppression of the people. One Miao Christian expressed it well: "I did not use to understand the meaning of the suffering endured by Jesus on the cross. But now we Miao have suffered all forms of cruelty that have punished us. This has caused us to know something of the Lord's teaching. . . . "[22]

In analyzing the differences between the Methodist work at Shihmenkan in northwest Guizhou, where Pollard had worked, with its relative slow growth in the 1970s and the very rapid growth in the CIM work farther south in Guizhou, Zhang Tan uses theological categories. In his view, the current Miao leaders in the CIM were much more charismatic and inspirational. They used spiritual songs and dancing, prayed in tongues, trusted in visions and dreams, and utilized spiritual power to heal the sick. They emphasized evangelism as their principal ministry. The more reformed work in the Shihmenkan area was characterized by holiness with many rigid requirements for Christian living. While they did evangelistic work, they seemed to put much more emphasis on what Zhang Tan called the "social gospel." His conclusion is that the charismatic emphasis fit much better with the traditional culture of the Miao and its heavy emphasis upon the spirit world.[23]

Do these many factors in the receptor cultures seem to relegate God to a spectator and not an active participant in the culture? A popular proverb notes that "man's extremity is God's opportunity." Whenever an individual or society has particular needs, a readiness is created to receive new information and values and to adopt new goals that will remedy the "short-comings."

Tentative Conclusions

In one way or another each of the factors which we have listed—political, personal, practical, strategic, sociological, cultural, and religious or theological—has played a part at different times and in different ways in producing an openness to the Christian faith among China's minority nationalities. We may or may not agree with the theories generated by sociologists, anthropologists, and historians or the tactics followed by some missionaries. Be this as it may, the relationships among dominant and subordinate groups have played a major part in the resistance or receptivity to the Christian faith. A simple, tentative paradigm is this:

Receptive

Oppressed by dominant group, submits, and is partly sinicized. Finds a new social identity through Christian faith (Black Yi, Sediq, Lahu, Wa, Miao, and Lisu.

Resistant

a. Oppressed by dominant group, but does not submit; essentially independent. Retains its own identity and resists any new religion (Sichuan Yi).
b. Oppressed by dominant group. Submits partially, and/or sinicized totally or in part. Adopts a new social identity that has elements of Chinese social identity or reinforces features of traditional religious beliefs and values (Mongols, Tibetans, Islamic peoples in Xinjiang; traditional religious groups like Zhuang).

Discussion on "Cultural Christians" in China

ZHUO XINPING

The expression "Cultural Christians" was first raised by Bishop Ding Guangxun (K. H. Ting) after the opening of China to the outside world in the 1980s. At that time, many Chinese intellectuals outside of Christian churches had already translated and written many books on Christian history, culture, and theology. Through their highly qualified publications, they showed sympathy for Christian existence in China and also tried to understand the Christian faith and its claim of truth. By contrast, people in Chinese churches for theological studies, mission, and preaching were relatively backward and conservative. Partly because of this, most such intellectuals did not want to contact the Chinese church, let alone enter the church. In this situation Bishop Ting used the term "Cultural Christians" to express his welcome to such intellectual research on Christianity and his active attitude toward a mutual dialogue and understanding. Of course, this attempt immediately aroused different reactions and commentaries. Since then, people in the Chinese mainland are very sensitive and cautious in using the term "Cultural Christians."

In the 1990s, Liu Xiaofeng once again took up the issue of "Cultural Christians" in Hong Kong. He wrote some articles dealing with the phenomenon of "Cultural Christianity" or "Cultural Christians," such as "The Sociological Comments on the Phenomenon of 'Cultural' Christians" (1991), and "Chinese Christian Theology in the Modern Context of Languages" (1995). In 1995, Ping-cheung Lo published an article entitled "Christian Apollos and Crisis of 1997 in Theological Circles of Hong Kong." This article evoked a heated discussion and controversy among the Chinese scholars. But most publications for the debate dealing with this phenomenon in the Chinese mainland were in Hong Kong or abroad, though some mainland scholars already took part in it. In the analysis of this phenomenon of contemporary "Cultural Christians" in China there were also two articles published in *Regent Chinese Journal* in 1996. One is "The Formation of 'SMSC' from a Historical Perspective Cultural Background" by Chen Cunfu, who analyzed and described the similarity and difference between SMSC (Scholars in mainland China studying Christianity) and "Cultural Christians." The other is "The Phenomenon of 'Cultural Christians'—An Overview and Evaluation," by Edwin Hui. As a result of this discussion, the Institute of Sino-Christian Studies in Hong Kong edited and published the articles concerning the issue in the collection *Cultural Christian: Phenomenon and Argument* in 1997. Now this topic has attracted wide interest in the contemporary studies of the development and future of Christianity in China. The phenomenon or the understanding of "Cultural Christians" is also unique in Chinese history. As a scholar of Christian studies in the Chinese mainland, I would like to give my evaluation and commentary on this phenomenon.

The Background for the Appearance of the Term "Cultural Christians"

The term "Cultural Christians" has its context. After the opening of China to the outside world, Christianity has developed rapidly in the Chinese mainland. People talk about a revival or "renaissance" of Christianity in China. The number of Christians is increasing, which would be estimated from 5 to 10 million Catholic Christians and from 11 to 20 million Protestant Christians now in the Chinese mainland. But this development has pluralistic characters. There are already many Christians in the Chinese mainland in comparison with the past, yet the interests and intentions of those Christians are quite different. This phenomenon gives a complicated and mixed picture of Chinese society. Although there are still some problems and misunderstandings concerning the knowledge of Christianity in contemporary China, many people outside of the church already have more tolerant attitudes toward Christianity and a more objective observation of Christians in China. In this process, some of them suspect the "quality" of contemporary Christians in the Chinese mainland through their observation and evaluation of the characteristics and the social functions of those Christians. In comparison with church development abroad and social development at home, the Chinese church is temporarily in a relatively conservative situation in its theoretical construction, and to a certain extent is also self-isolated from the thought and activities of the social transition in China today. The Chinese church leaders have worries about this situation, but up to now they have not found an ideal way out of this difficult position. As a result many people, especially many intellectuals in China, talk about three kinds of Christians in contemporary Chinese churches. The first kind are the so-called elite Christians, who have a high level of education and theological knowledge. They are namely Christian intellectuals in China. But they consist only of a very small proportion in both Chinese Christian and Chinese intellectual circles. The Chinese church still lacks these "elite Christians" for Christian reconstruction and development in China today. The second kind are the so-called church Christians, who have a correct understanding of traditional Christian faith and enjoy a normal religious life through church activities. But most of them have no academic concern for the destiny and significance of Christianity in China. The third kind are the so-called folk Christians, who constitute the majority of the Chinese churches. Normally the folk Christians have a "charismatic" enthusiasm for religious life, which explains the rapid development of Christianity in some areas, especially in the countryside. They pray to God for personal salvation from trouble, illness, and death, and also for a harmonious relationship in family and in community. But most of them have a relatively low level of education, theological knowledge, and even in Christian faith itself. Some of them only combined their traditional folk religions or local beliefs with the outer form of Christianity. So the identity of Christianity by some "folk Christians" is not clear. In this situation some Chinese intellectuals keep their distance from the churches and Christians in China, though they are quite interested in Christianity for different reasons. Through the great change of attitude toward Christianity by these intellectuals, and through their meaningful achievements in Christian studies, people began to talk about the emergence of "Cultural Christians" in the Chinese mainland. On the one hand, this phenomenon explains the attempt by some Christians, especially the so-called elite Christians, to understand those intellectuals in the paradigm of the Christian faith. On the other hand, it also shows the self-consciousness of some Chinese intellectuals in their coincidence with the Christian ideals and values, but at the same time their distance from the existing Church and its practice now in China. The possibility of this appearance has been given by the contemporary social background and theological background in China and in the whole world.

Contemporary Social Background

In the twentieth century, the study of religions entered a new stage. A new research field "science of religion," (or "religious studies") developed rapidly, and already became an important part in the domain of the social sciences and humanities. Many new subjects in this field such as philosophy of religion, sociology of religion, psychology of religion, anthropology of religion, and historiography of religion have attracted wide interest and special attention in the academic world. One of the characteristics of these new studies of religion is that they do not take any religious faith as a prerequisite for the research. This neutrality in faith by religious studies is quite different from the theological studies in Christian churches. With the appearance and development of this kind of religious study, it is possible for a non-theological research on Christianity. So in the contemporary time, theological study and cultural study of Christianity develop in parallel. Besides seminaries and theological faculties, there are also departments of religious studies, or institutes for research on religions. Since this new subject or new method for religious studies was introduced into China during the period of the May Fourth Movement, the scholars outside of Christian churches but in charge of Christian studies gradually increased. They were not Christians, but they had made great efforts in their serious studies and achieved exciting results, which deeply influenced the academic development in Chinese modern times. These scholars might be called the very beginning of "Scholars in mainland China studying Christianity," whom Chen Cunfu mentioned as SMSC in his article.[1] According to his opinion, SMSC is the basis and soil for the growth and development of "Cultural Christians" in China.

With the rise and development of religious studies in modern China, academic and humanistic studies of Christianity outside of the Christian church are also in full swing. Strictly speaking, these scholars are not trained in Christian theology or dogmatics, but are more or less influenced by Christian cultural context. Some of them were once graduates of Christian universities, a few studied Christian theology abroad after the "Cultural Revolution," and many of them studied philosophy, history, sociology, and literature at home and abroad. Most of them do not have a systematic training in Christian theology, so they show a wide-ranging interest in Christianity and emphasize the historical, cultural, and philosophical studies of Christianity in the fields of humanities, social sciences, and even natural sciences. In this way, the purpose of their research is also not for self-salvation, which is stressed especially by some Chinese Christians, but for the consideration of cultural value and significance of Christianity towards human beings, and of its historic and social function in the development of human society.

In the process of this academic study of Christianity, many Chinese intellectuals show a paradoxical attitude about the present existence of Christianity in China and in the world. On the one hand, they highly praise the Christian value system and its cultural achievements, they idealize the Christian pursuit and want to find this Christian identity in real life. But on the other hand, they are disappointed with the actual existence of Christianity in the form of church structure, denominational differences, and social activities. As a result they sharply criticize the stagnant situation of the Christian church in Chinese society and the conservative attitude to church reform and theological reconstruction.

In contemporary Chinese society, the problem of correct understanding of religion is not yet solved. The study and evaluation of Christianity in the Chinese mainland is still sensitive and suspicious. For the Chinese acceptance, many biblical and theological studies have been done in the name of "cultural studies." Religion in general and Christianity in particular are considered as "culture." The positive analysis of Christianity begins with the cultural evaluation of the Christian contribution to human civilization. Instead of the study of Christianity or Christian theology, Chinese scholars in the mainland obviously emphasized their study of "Christian culture." For example, the international symposium, "Christianity and Modernization" held in Beijing in 1994, was translated or intentionally expressed in Chinese as "Christian Culture and Modernization." The significance of culture is easy to understand and is also acceptable by most Chinese. Cultural interest in religion has already gotten resonance from the Chinese public. So Christian studies in the name of "cultural studies" can avoid misunderstanding and sensibility in the contemporary Chinese context. The emphasis of "culture" created a better atmosphere for religious studies in China and also afforded the possibility for those activities which became the origin of "Cultural Christians" in China.

After the opening of China to the outside world, the tendency of pluralism and individualism in Chinese society and the Chinese church gradually became visible. With the deepening of knowledge of Christianity, people in China also have different understandings of Christianity. The intellectuals in Chinese society try to find some important or at least some useful elements in Christianity for China's cultural reconstruction in the present process of social transformation. So their interest is mainly in value creation and spiritual sublimation through the Christian world outlook and value system. They work for the progress of Chinese mentality and to help in the striving for spiritual civilization of the Chinese nation. This is, of course, very typical and self-evident in the long tradition of Chinese intellectuals. So there is a group of Chinese intellectuals outside of the Chinese church who are making serious studies of Christian philosophy and theology, and standing for the affirmation and acceptance of Christian values and basic ideas, but without their personal conversion. They pursue an ideal state of Christian identity in the pluralistic concepts of value and life. By this kind of emphasis they do not care much about their personal salvation, which would be considered as the most important thing in the life of faith by many Chinese Christians. In comparison with their Christian ideal, they are not satisfied with the present status of church existence and have no intention for a dialogue with those Christians whose concern is only their personal redemption in daily life. This attitude toward Christianity has also been criticized by Christians, as a narrow interpretation of Christianity from "intellectual aristocrats," completely lacking real religious or mystical experience.

In Chinese society, "culture" and "cultural value" are usually understood positively. The analysis and evaluation of religion is also often on the level of human culture. So the cultural study and cultural understanding of Christianity is most fruitful in contemporary China. In contrast to Paul Tillich, many Chinese intellectuals interpret religion from human culture. They believe that culture is the nature of religion, and religion is only a manifestation of culture, namely, a form of its expression. They put stress on the essence and the core of religion. As to Christianity, they want to explore its cultural spirit. Its outer form and its ritual are not essential or important to them. This coincides with the basic concepts of Chinese intellectuals in the process of modernization, which respect and stress the spiritual value of self-confidence, personality, and inner experience and enlightenment, at the same time shunning all superficial forms or formalities.

Contemporary Theological Background

The way of cultural study and understanding of Christianity by Chinese is also inspired by the intellectual study of contemporary theology in the West. Traditionally, the study of theology should be done mainly by Christian churches, especially by theological departments of universities and seminaries. But in contemporary China the situation is quite different. There have been no theological departments or Christian universities in the Chinese mainland since the 1950s. Seminaries in the mainland remained only at a low level. After the "Cultural Revolution," there is a new upsurge for church reconstruction in China. In this period, numerous tasks have yet to be undertaken. The Chinese church leaders are very busy with their church affairs and have relatively little time for research on the new development of contemporary theology in the world, and for their own theological contemplation and reconstruction. For historical reasons, there is a "generation gap" in the Chinese church. The young seminarians are still in the process of studying and training. Some of them go abroad for theological studies, but few have returned to China up to now. In this situation, a group of scholars in the fields of social sciences and humanities in research institutes and universities began their own academic studies of Christianity, and opened up a new prospect for the understanding of theology in China. They take the study of Christian thought and culture as a prerequisite for their thorough studies of history, philosophy, literature, and so on. For this purpose they have their own perspectives in viewing Christian theology, and would not be limited by the denominational or dogmatic demands of Christian churches. So, in comparison with the weakness of theological studies within the churches in China, an academic study of theology in Chinese intellectual circles is thriving. For the reason and justification of their study, they find some inspirations and acknowledgements in the contemporary theological development.

First, in the Protestant tradition, justification by faith is a basic principle. Contemporary theology provides many discussions about the forms and contents of "faith." Nowadays people understand Christian faith with a comprehensive sense. Conversion or church participation is only one form or a part of Christian faith. This faith can also include a kind of spiritual or cultural profession. It can also combine itself with other spiritual elements in human culture. Faith is no more a narrow expression of church existence or a pure form of religious life.

Second, Christian theology has departed from its traditional, sacred forum controlled by priests or theologians in the past. Contemporary theology is generally considered a product of its cooperation or reunification with human knowledge, especially in social sciences and humanities. Theology is one subject in these fields. Other subjects are no longer "maidservants" of theology. Theology must find its value and significance through dialogue and confluence with other subjects. So the study of theology is an interdisciplinary research. People enrich theological knowledge from this interdisciplinary study and vice versa. Many scholars in the Chinese mainland begin their Christian studies with humanistic studies in history, philosophy, and literature. For example, Liu Xiaofeng, a typical "Cultural Christian" in China, experienced his progressive academic and spiritual development from literature to aesthetics, and to theology.

Third, contemporary theology puts stress on cultural life and the cultural significance of human beings. So there is now no distinct difference between theological and humanistic interests. Theologians talk about "non-religious interpretation" of Christianity and "demythologization" of biblical beliefs. We can observe a tendency of secularization or inculturation of contemporary theology. In close connection with contemporary society politically, economically, and culturally, there appears a "contextualization" of Christianity or a "contextual theology." At the same time, contemporary philosophy, sociology, and other studies find resonance in theology, too. Academic circles take an active part in theological discussions today. Especially in the Chinese mainland, theological research and publications by academic circles may be even more influential than those by the Chinese church itself.

Fourth, the theology of "universal grace" in the contemporary Catholic church has partly avoided the confrontation between the church and the outside world. The theory of "outside of the church no salvation" (*extra ecclesiam nulla salus*) is already revised or abandoned to a certain extent. People also try to find the Christian spirit in secular society and see the function of Christian values in social progress. Many contemporary theologians show a tolerant attitude toward the theological studies of laymen or non-Christians.

Fifth, there is a heated discussion of Karl Rahner's term "anonymous Christians." This is a way for Christian theologians to understand non-Christians who have made a contribution to human society in the spirit which Christianity strongly advocates. The point of view by Rahner also reflects an opinion by many Catholic Christians since the Second Vatican Council, which described those people as "Christians already in essence but not yet self realized."

Finally, through the philosophical defense of Christianity in the twentieth century, there is already a new interpretation and understanding of the relationship between faith and reason, between "*credo ut intelligam*" and "*intelligo ut credam*." With the existential experience of contemporary people, the concept of "*intellectus fidei*" or "*fides informis*" is deepened. The intellectual understanding of Christian faith is perhaps a kind of reinforcement of Christian identity today.

These developments in contemporary society and theology created an ideal atmosphere for the new intellectual interest in Christianity in the Chinese mainland. With the orientation of a cultural understanding of Christianity comes the phenomenon of "Cultural Christians" or SMSC, who play a leading role in the introduction and evaluation of Christian knowledge for contemporary Chinese through their unique orientation and method.

The Understanding of "Cultural Christians" in China

There is no exact definition or common understanding of "Cultural Christians" in China. The focus of the debate is on the meaning of "Christians" today. And for some people it is still doubtful whether "Cultural Christians" are Christians at all. About the connotation and extension of "Cultural Christians," there are two basic opinions among Chinese scholars.

"Cultural Christians" Are Those Intellectually Cultured Persons Who Already Have a Personal Conversion to Christianity

According to Liu Xiaofeng, "'Cultural Christians'" doesn't mean those people who are engaged in research on the history and culture of Christianity in universities and academic institutions of the Chinese mainland, but mean those intellectually cultured persons who have professed faith personally. One can be called Christian only by professing the belief in Christ, while those, who just engaged in the research of Christian culture, cannot be called Christian."[2] Here, the expression of "Cultural Christians" has a very concrete connotation but a limited extension. According to this understanding, "Cultural Christians" have no fundamental difference with ordinary Christians, in essence. So the prerequisite of "Cultural Christians" is that they must first be Christians, namely, they must have professed faith themselves.

With this understanding the difference between "Cultural" and ordinary Christians shows itself in the following two aspects:

First, these "Cultural" Christians are engaged in either ideological research or in literary and artistic creation. The way to express their profession is not only in their life and behavior, but also philosophically or artistically. They are normally baptized Christians, but their participation in church activities is rare or not as obvious ordinary Christians. The interest and orientation of their religious profession are mainly decided by their social status, cultural breeding, and ethical responsibility.

Second, the way of their Christian profession is culturally oriented. "Cultural Christians" are those Chinese intellectuals who reached their conversion to Christianity directly from cultural and ideological interests and research, namely, from a kind of cultural acknowledgement. At the beginning of their spiritual development, maybe they were not baptized Christians and only had an intention to become Christian through their cultural initiative. This process of conversion is from a spontaneity to a necessity. By the first stage they are only "implicit Christians" or "pre-Christians," who would be called "Cultural Christians" by some church leaders or by themselves. In the second stage of their spiritual development they are already "baptized Christians," who would then be understood as "explicit Christians." Here we can see a subtle difference in the position to the importance or necessity of Christian baptism. For the understanding of the first stage of their spiritual feeling, "Cultural Christian" means an intellectually cultured person who believes in Jesus Christ, but doesn't want or is not yet prepared to be baptized or to join any church. For understanding their second stage, "Cultural Christian" means a "church Christian," a Christian intellectual. Of course this process should be observed as a whole. Otherwise the first stage as a Christian profession would be meaningless or misleading.

Generally speaking, both aspects of "Cultural Christians" still emphasize the conversion or profession to Christian faith. Obviously, "Cultural Christians" in the above understanding cannot be identified with the SMSC.

"Cultural Christians" Are Chinese Intellectuals Who Agree with the Christian Truth but Do Not Belong to the Christian Church

In this understanding, the identity of "Christian" is indistinct. If it means profession through "baptism" or a kind of church identity, these intellectuals are not at all "Christians," let alone "Cultural Christians." Maybe they constitute a part of SMSC, but not the whole SMSC. The question is what the "faith" means in Christianity after all.

On the one hand, the profession is understood differently. Some people insist that "baptism" or "conversion" is only one form, but not the only form of profession. Profession is from the heart and the real behavior of a person. "Baptism" or "church identity" doesn't play the decisive role in Christian profession. It is only a kind of formality. Combination and coincidence between outer form and inner identity are of course good, but even after "baptism" some "Christians" still lack consistency. They have professed their faith through a certain form, but their behavior doesn't reflect the spirit of this faith. Many Chinese intellectuals feel disappointed for this reason. They look down upon the idea: "if you are baptized, you mean all and get salvation; if you refuse baptism, you mean nothing and would be condemned." So they pursue a spiritual profession and do not consider baptism or church identity necessary. For them, Christian profession is only a private, inner, spiritual existence of themselves or their cultural intention and interest. Its outer expression should be a "universal love," just as the biblical belief shows: "If you have love for one another, then everyone will know that you are my disciples."[3]

If baptism or church identity is not necessarily the prerequisite of "being a Christian," some of these Chinese intellectuals can then be called "Cultural Christians" through their cultural profession. For them, the form of "church" is only a historical and social product, and the schism of the churches and the development of denominations are, in nature, the result of social and political controversies and struggles in human history, especially in Western history. So the "church" doesn't represent the unique form of Christianity. The truth of Christian faith should be a development which transcends its denominational and church history. In contrast, some people point out the "nominalist" tendency of "church Christians" who put stress on "name" and on the formality of "baptism," and the "realist" tendency of "Cultural Christians" who emphasize the testimony through their cultural spirit and practical experience, and do not care about the "name" of "being a Christian."

On the other hand, so-called Cultural Christians acknowledge or agree with the Christian truth, but do not profess Christianity. They are unconscious of any identity of "being a Christian," and maximally feel themselves dialogue-partners or friends of Christianity. They do not belong to Christianity, let alone to a Christian church. Their cultural orientation and academic activities do not have the characteristics of Christian faith. So they belong to the majority of SMSC. Their attitude to Christianity is "seeking common ground while reserving differences." Some of them agree not only with Christian values and morality, but also with the values and morality of other religions and other ideological systems. Cultural interest and academic study of Christianity serve as their pursuit of the goal of "Great Harmony" in the world.

In fact, "Cultural Christians" in its exact meaning are only a few, but SMSC are many in the Chinese mainland. Although SMSC may afford the soil in which "Cultural Christians" are grown and nurtured, the majority of SMSC still remain non-Christian scholars. SMSC show themselves by and large as a cultural or academic phenomenon, and try to avoid any misunderstanding in being called "Cultural Christians."

Social Response to the Term "Cultural Christians" in China

There was once a heated debate on the phenomenon of "Cultural Christians" in Hong Kong and there were also some discussions about it overseas. But there is seldom a theoretical response to it in the Chinese mainland. We have heard some critics' voices recently, for example, an article entitled "Theology and Culture" by An Ximeng in 1999.[4] Of course, the social and academic response to the term "Cultural Christians" shows a multiplicity of understandings. This response reflects the reality of Christian understanding by Chinese and the situation of Christian existence and development in contemporary China.

Acquiescence and Approval of This Term by Some "SMSC"

The number of real "Cultural Christians" is very small. And these few "Cultural Christians" are still in charge of cultural, artistic, and academic activities. But their influence as "Cultural Christians" on Chinese society, especially on Chinese academic circles, is not as strong as the influence of most SMSC. They are usually reluctant to go public. Some SMSC feel sympathy for Christianity and evaluate Christian truth highly. In their comprehension they take the term "Cultural Christians" as the way of Christian understanding of these intellectuals studying Christianity, namely, as the interpretation or the hope of Chinese Christians for their cultural study, objective knowledge, and positive evaluation of Christianity. They acquiesce to and approve of this expression directed towards them, and in this way they try to adjust their relationship to Christianity. They are willing to explore the possibility of an interaction and a combination between Chinese culture and Christianity in the process of social transformation in contemporary China, and to seek the significance and possible contribution of Christianity for the modernization and progress of China. But by this acquiescence and approval they do not think it is a kind of cultural profession to Christian faith. They take it as an attitude for a mutual dialogue and understanding.

Boycott of This Term by Some Church Christians

Many Chinese Christians do not agree with this expression because they see in it a division of Christian groups and a possibility for misunderstanding. According to their opinion, Christians are equal and have the unity of communion. In the division of "Cultural Christians" and "church Christians" or ordinary Christians, it might be misunderstood as following an interpretation that only "Cultural Christians" possess "culture," whereas "church Christians" have no "culture." As a consequence, people would think that Chinese Christians include Christians with cultural education and those who do not have cultural knowledge, namely "Cultural Christians" and "Non-cultural Christians."

These church Christians emphasize that people without church identity cannot be called "Christians" at all. They oppose abusing the name of "Christians" and do not agree with the expression of "anonymous Christians" or "implicit Christians." For them the church is a "*Sanctorium Communio*" (Sacred Community). To enter the church means to go through "the straight gate" which leads to salvation and eternal life. Not everyone is qualified to do so. The Christians are only a "small flock" in society. They have special quality and responsibility. If man can easily use the term "Christians" to identify any people outside of the church, then the sacredness of church and Christianity would be more or less blasphemed.

By exaggerating the term and the function of "Cultural Christians," there is a tendency to abandon church organization and tradition in the name of "Cultural Christianity." So the church in China would have worries about the possibility of the development of a so-called "non-church movement." In the description of "Cultural Christians" outside of the Chinese church, church Christians may have an uncomfortable feeling that they might be misunderstood as "Non-cultural Christians."

Negation of This Term by Most Chinese Academicians Studying Christianity

In the universities and research institutes of Chinese mainland, most scholars (namely SMSC) do not agree with the intention to treat them as "Cultural Christians." Christian scholars or Christian intellectuals are real "Cultural Christians" who profess their faith openly in their research on Christianity. But SMSC normally have no prerequisite of such a Christian claim in their research or cultural activities. Usually they take an objective, neutral position in their research on Christianity, and also stand outside of the church. In this sense they can only be called researchers and observers of Christianity. Their intention is to do the sober-minded, authentic description and analysis of the cultural phenomenon of Christianity, which are urgently needed in contemporary Chinese society. If they were labeled as "Cultural Christians," there would also be misunderstanding as to their research in the present context. In China there is still little understanding or misunderstanding regarding Christianity. People need a neutral, objective attitude or explanation of Christianity from SMSC. With the label of "Cultural Christians," the research work of SMSC would then be misunderstood as a "limited" research with "subjective intention and personal feeling" in it, which couldn't be acknowledged as an "objective and scientific" research by most Chinese today.

If one uses this term to call SMSC, there might also be political and social misunderstanding in China. After the opening of China to the outside world, the situation of Christian understanding by Chinese is much better than ever before. But the problem of correct understanding of religion in general, and of Christianity in particular, is up to now not yet solved. Many people in China still have the traditional misunderstanding of religion as a backward, conservative, and ignorant ideology and social existence. The Chinese church has its own problem to solve. If one identifies research of

SMSC with belief in Christianity, their sympathy and affirmation or favorable impression of Christianity with Christian profession itself, and their introduction or research of Christian culture with "Cultural Christianity," the position of SMSC would be isolated in this context, and their influence and significance in Chinese society would also be limited. As a result, they might lose their function as a mediator between government departments having jurisdiction over religion and Chinese churches, and between Chinese intellectuals and the Christian system of values and truth.

According to Chinese academicians, there are "Cultural Christians" indeed, as for example in Europe in the nineteenth century. H. Richard Niebuhr once explained that "Cultural Christians" were those Christians who thought that Christianity should belong to culture and conform with culture. These people with such a profession are, of course, "Cultural Christians" in the real sense of this term. They are Christians first, and also place themselves in the midst of the culture. They explain culture through Christianity and at the same time understand Christianity by the insight of culture. They advocate a kind of "cultural faith" and try to establish a "cultural theology." They respect Jesus Christ as "savior of culture" and want to erect a bridge between Christianity and culture. With this interpretation, it is already clear that "Cultural Christians" are the Christians in the church who are bent on social reform and stress cultural research. Opposite to these "Cultural Christians" in the church, it is supposed that there would also be "Non-cultural Christians."

In contrast with these "Cultural Christians" in church history, most SMSC can only be called "Cultural Non-Christians." Maybe they are good partners and friends for dialogue and mutual exchange with Christian intellectuals, but they are not, or some of them might not yet be within the church or within Christianity. The SMSC have created a good atmosphere for a correct and objective understanding of Christianity in Chinese society. They have also promoted dialogue between Christianity and Chinese culture. The SMSC make systematic study of Christian theology and philosophy. Through their introduction and analysis of theological development in history and its present tendency, they can perhaps help the reconstruction of Christian theology in China with contemporary Chinese characteristics. But they are not theologians, they cannot and will not create a theology through their research. They will only prepare the social foundation and create the cultural condition and atmosphere for the growth and development of Chinese theology. The construction and the real success of a Chinese theology depend on the Chinese theologians themselves in the church. Here we can see a clear distinction in the intentions and tasks between SMSC and Christian theologians or scholars in China. In this sense, "Cultural

Christians" (if they really exist in Chinese churches) and "Cultural Non-Christians" (SMSC) should be good friends and allies. Their research and cultural activities have indeed some similarities, but they have different orientations and destinations, use different methods or standards, and have to face different people in contemporary China.

The "Marginal" Position of "Cultural Christians" as Christian Intellectuals in China

If we define "Cultural Christians" as Chinese intellectuals in the church, they are namely the "elite Christians" in China. Their research and cultural activities are closely connected with church activities. Most of them belong to the leading group of Chinese churches. But their function and significance are not the focus for our discussion here. If we define "Cultural Christians" as baptized SMSC in contrast to the church scholars, there might be only a few, who work individually in isolation and do not have a noticeable influence in Chinese society and Chinese academic circles. In fact, they do not constitute a group of "Cultural Christians" and their activities are not yet observed as a "phenomenon" in China. If we define "Cultural Christians" as SMSC without baptism and open profession, then it is an ambiguous and controversial definition because the explanation of it is already a paradox. The circumstance of SMSC is very complicated and allows no simple interpretation. In many cases, when we mention the phenomenon of "Cultural Christians," we point in fact to the phenomenon of "SMSC." By some Christian observations and analyses, many SMSC should be anonymous, implicit, potential, and unconscious "Christians." If this were true, it would mean a decisive turning point in the Christian development in China. But this might be perhaps only a wish or a too optimistic expectation. Many SMSC have called their equation with "Cultural Christians" in overseas discussions as an "epistemic violence." Instead of "Cultural Christians," they would like to profess themselves as "Cultural Non-Christians." Even their identity with the Christian profession has also been denied by many Christians.

So the real "Cultural Christians" are a few scholars who once worked to spread Christian knowledge and later on entered Christianity through the way of cultural interest and academic study in Christianity. Now they are already baptized Christians but are still without a clear church or denominational identity. It is clear that they belong to Christianity from their profession and baptism, but because of their reluctance and distance from a church they do not belong to any church or denomination. These few "Cultural Christians" have only a "marginal" position in China. For example, one of the important initiators of the discussion about the phenomenon of "Cultural Christians" in the Chinese mainland is Liu Xiaofeng who is considered as the typical representative of "Cultural Christians" in China. But now he already lives in Hong Kong as a long time resident and works in a Christian institution there. With the policy of "one country, two systems," the scholars in Hong Kong face many similarities between Hong Kong society and Western societies. The context in Hong Kong and in the mainland is not the same. Although they travel a lot in the mainland and keep connections with mainland scholars, their "experience of existence" is totally different from mainland scholars. Namely, they stand outside of the mainland and in fact play the role of an "onlooker." This is a so-called marginal position of a few "Cultural Christians." There is a great difference between outside and inside experiences. If Christian intellectuals already left the political, ideological, and cultural context of the Chinese mainland, can they still be considered as "Cultural Christians" in the Chinese mainland?

Maybe there are still a few "Cultural Christians" in the Chinese mainland who do not belong to any university or research institute in the Chinese organizational system, but work privately or in a folk organization, and simultaneously engage in cultural and academic activities for promoting Christian knowledge. But their influence in Chinese cultural and intellectual circles is very little. Since they cannot make a significant impact on the public and on the whole structure of Chinese society, their existence cannot be described as a "phenomenon of Cultural Christians," either.

Evaluation of the Phenomenon of "Cultural Christians"

In spite of whether the term "Cultural Christians" is a misunderstanding or a goodwill understanding by Christians, and also in spite of whether, or not there is a strict distinction between SMSC and "Cultural Christians," this phenomenon in China, according to its original impression or explanation, is very significant.

First, the phenomenon shows a positive and an optimistic atmosphere for understanding and accepting Christianity in the Chinese mainland. After the opening of China to the outside world, the policy regarding religion in general and Christianity in particular, is constantly being revised to a better situation and development. The Chinese scholars studying Christianity have not only observed this process of revision and improvement of religious policies in China, but have also made great contributions to it. Their research results and suggestions have been accepted to a great extent by the government for the improvement of Christian existence and development in contemporary China. They helped to build a bridge between government and religious circles for mutual understanding and exchange. So their academic activities have been influential in the formulation of new policies toward religions and in the improvement of the existing context of Christianity in China. With their academic studies, they also work as a mediator between government departments in charge of religious affairs and the Christian church, so as to help to bring about their mutual correspondence and adaptation.

Second, the phenomenon promotes political and cultural understanding of Christianity in the Chinese mainland. After the "Cultural Revolution," the reevaluation of Christianity was possible. But at the very beginning, a positive evaluation of Christianity was still a taboo. Many Chinese had a negative picture from Christianity according to the past ideological and conceptual evaluation. But through the academic studies of Chinese scholars, the situation has gradually changed. Their objective study with scientific methods is, to a certain extent, a rehabilitation of Christian values and social function. By reading their publications it is now quite common to see many Chinese talk openly about the Christian contribution to the development of education, medicine, publication, charities, and the welfare of other social institutions both in China and in the whole world. With this reevaluation, it is already possible for Chinese to get a positive picture of Christianity.

Third, the phenomenon contributes a great deal to academic progress in religious, and especially Christian, studies. The research and translation activities of Chinese academicians have promoted the introduction and better understanding of theological and cultural achievements of Christianity in history and at present, and have popularized Christian knowledge among the Chinese people. These scholars have introduced classical and contemporary Christian literature into China, and are responsible for disseminating information on research of Christian thought and culture in the Chinese mainland. Their own research also constitutes an important part of theological and historical studies on Christianity.

Fourth, the phenomenon helps the inculturation and contextualization of Christianity in Chinese culture. In their reflection and historical analysis of the role of Christianity in China, Chinese scholars have also explored ways and experiences in which Christianity and Chinese culture may interact. Their academic studies and cultural introspection have given impetus to the transformation and indigenization of Christianity in China, namely, from a Christianity in China to a real Chinese Christianity. With this effort as a solid foundation, we can already discern signs of articulation of a Christian theology with Chinese characteristics in the present social, political, and cultural context of China.

Finally, the phenomenon awakens the Chinese consciousness to the role of Christianity in the process of Chinese modernization and its cultural reconstruction. The study of Christianity by Chinese scholars is a kind of "borrowing stones from other hills" for the reform and reconstruction in China. It means a reexamination of the position and function of Christianity in world civilization, especially in Western development, and also a reevaluation of Christian value and truth for Chinese society and its development. In this direction, Chinese scholars can afford an ideal setting for Christian existence and its positive function in Chinese society. If most Chinese could consider the Christian values system and social teaching as a powerful spiritual strength for their social modernization and cultural reconstruction, there would be a real hope for Christian revival and prosperity in the Chinese context.

In conclusion, the phenomenon of "Cultural Christians" in the Chinese mainland is, to a certain extent, overestimated. The figure of "Cultural Christians" is still obscure or imaginary. Chinese intellectuals have not yet discovered an ideal example of "Cultural Christians" to follow. We are facing the best time for dialogue and mutual understanding between Christianity and Chinese culture since the Ming-Qing periods in Chinese history. But there are still many difficulties and obstacles to correct understanding and a positive evaluation of Christianity, especially for its role and significance in Chinese cultural reconstruction. For Christianity in China still lacks as an example of guidance and orientation for Chinese spiritual development. Most SMSC are not Cultural Christians. Their action and position may be a positive and significant challenge to so-called Cultural Christians or to Christians in China overall. Christians at home and abroad should grasp and make good use of the opportunity of this spiritual encounter. It is not the time for them to immerse themselves in an optimistic myth of "Cultural Christians" in the Chinese mainland. For the future of Christianity in China, there still needs to be a "prophet voice," a "servant spirit," a sincere dialogue, and a tolerant sympathy.

The Catholic Church
in Post-1997 Hong Kong:
Dilemma in Church-State Relations

BEATRICE LEUNG

Introduction: The Catholic Church and the Colonial Government

Britain, with its Christian heritage, might not normally be expected to have any conflict with the Roman Catholic Church, although it would not normally enjoy the close relationship with it that it has with the Anglican Church. During the British colonial period in Hong Kong, the government enjoyed a smooth working relationship with Christian churches including the Catholic Church. In the whole period of colonial rule (1841–1997), for the sake of convenience, the government entrusted the Church to be a provider of education, medical, and welfare services, especially during the 1950s to 1970s when hundreds of thousands of mainland refugees flooded into Hong Kong. Thus a working relationship was forged between these two parties which was based on the common values of their Christian heritage. However, this working relationship could not be defined as a "partnership" because the Church was not given the opportunity to be involved as an equal partner as it had no say on policymaking. It could be defined as a "contractual relationship" in which the Church operated under governmental policy while obtaining financial subsidy. Later, in the last phase of colonial rule, the Church indirectly assisted the British in its attempts to advocate the democratization of Hong Kong through elections to the Legislative Council in 1991 and 1995.[1] Since 1980, in responding to the call of John Paul II, Hong Kong was involved in bilateral church-state relations by actively participating in the bridge-building effort to reactivate the Catholic church in mainland China.[2]

On July 1, 1997, Hong Kong reverted to mainland Chinese rule, becoming a Special Administrative Region (HKSAR). With the socio-political environment in Hong Kong undergoing subtle changes, the Catholic Church is now a dilemma as it attempts to readjust conflicting roles it has been playing in order to redefine its new relationship with the HKSAR government. Therefore, its major concern is how to continue its educational and welfare services and political participation in Hong Kong, while at the same time continuing its bridge-building effort between China and the Vatican.

This article discusses the Catholic relationship with the HKSAR government after the Chinese takeover, through an analysis of the development and changes of the church-state relationship since the colonial period. Three important issues are covered—Catholic educational and social welfare services; the political participation of Catholics; and the bridge-building effort of Hong Kong Catholics between China and the Vatican in order to manifest the dilemma of the Catholic church after the handover. Finally, I examine how the Catholic Church tried to make a breakthrough from the dilemma after two years of struggling to chart its path.

There are symbols and images in Catholic theology to illustrate and define the term "church," which is an amalgamation of believers who follow the teachings of Jesus Christ, the founder and head of the church.[3] Theologically, when Christians gather together in the name of Christ, Christ is with them and they can be called the "church." Organizationally, the church is a community of Christ's believers in various hierarchical order, empowered with functions of teaching, sanctifying, and governing.[4] In the Catholic tradition, the Pope is the sovereign head of the Vatican State as well as the supreme leader of the whole Catholic population, and has the highest teaching authority to Catholics all over the world who constitute the universal church. The local bishops are assigned by the Pope to form a smaller branch of the church or a diocese which is called the local church. Thus, institutionally, a diocese is an ecclesiastical bureaucracy headed by the bishop assisted by priests, nuns, and Catholic laity to facilitate the governance and teaching roles of the universal church. The Catholic laity has collaborated in this church structure in various endeavors. In recent decades, due to a shortage of priests and nuns, more laity have begun to participate in the administration and work of the church.[5]

Contractual Relationship versus Christian Social Teaching

After the victory of the 1949 Communist revolution in China, Britain, being the traditional ally of the U.S., adopted a policy to contain the Communist

Bloc. Thus, London decided it would not allow the population of Hong Kong, which is 95 percent ethnic Chinese, to be the recipient of Mao Zedong's revolutionary ideology. Thus, a strategic plan was implemented by the Hong Kong government to block the spread of Communism at the most elementary level.[6]

The Hong Kong government realized that the mass influx of Chinese refugees from the mainland provided the best opportunity for the infiltration of unwanted Communist ideology. The Christian churches were given exclusive control of the education of refugee children because Church schools were insulated from the penetration of Communism. Subsidies were offered by the colonial government to Church schools to teach refugees because Christianity is fundamentally opposed to atheism as promoted by the People's Republic of China, which is Marxist-Leninist oriented. This monopoly continued until the 1970s, when a shortage of Church personnel made it impossible to cope with the increasing demand for new schools.[7] Sharing a common aim in blocking the spread of Communism in Hong Kong, the Christian churches and the British government cooperated in the education field. Hong Kong's more traditional Chinese associations were not provided with government subsidies to run their educational institutions during the 1950s and 1960s because the government feared that Chinese leaders of these traditional associations might sympathize with Chinese Communist ideology. With education in the hands of the Christian churches, infiltration of Communism into the education sector was almost impossible.

The Hong Kong government, as the supreme policymaker, chose the Church as a sponsor of education without allowing it any opportunity to be involved in formulating educational policies. Thus, financial aids were used as an incentive to attract Christian churches to run secondary and primary education while incurring no financial burdens through expenditure for education. Since that time, Christian churches, including the Catholic Church, have been faithfully working for the government in offering education and social service. On the operational level, churches implement government education polices. They work during different stages of the colonial period. In this sense, the Christian churches were not working partners with the government because they were not afforded a share in policymaking. On the other hand, they fulfilled the important role of "contractors" in educational and social services, thereby indirectly channeling government policies.[8] The 80 percent of current expenditure subvented by governmental subsidy can be a means of regulating the activities of these churches whose organizations provide education and social medical services. Such activities would be difficult to operate if government subsidies were suspended. The adherence to the government subsidies had a deep impact on the perpetuation of the contractual relationship. In relying upon governmental subsidy, the Church runs the risk of losing its independence and the relationship becomes more one-sided and more unequal. The contractual relationship has made it possible for the government to influence the internal affairs of the Church and its policymaking role.

The Catholic Church, in the late 1960s after the Second Vatican Council (1963–1965), declared that it should become more involved in society and that Christians should integrate their personal faith more closely into their daily lives. "*Gaudium et Spes*" (The Pastoral Constitution on the Church in the Modern World), one of the four major Vatican Council documents, put special emphasis on this point.[9] The document contains a clear and strong affirmation of the transcendence and freedom of the Church to pursue its ministry in the world. The ministry emphasized the protection of human dignity, promotion of human rights, fostering of social unity, and provision of a sense of meaning to all areas of social life.[10]

The Hong Kong Catholic Church could not cogently pursue the implementation of these Christian social teachings in the 1970s for fear that the translation of these teachings into action might embarrass the colonial rulers and jeopardize the contractual relationship. The Vatican had itself set up a Pontifical Justice and Peace Commission, and wished to promote justice and peace at the grassroots level around the world. Only one aspect, the Justice and Peace Commission, was established in the Hong Kong Catholic diocese as the only gesture in compliance with the Vatican Council. In a Diocesan Convention in 1970–1971, an effort was made to include human rights, social justice, and the Church's relationship with the People's Republic of China in the discussions, but it caused great misunderstandings and controversy because it was interpreted as a pro-Communist gesture. At that time public opinion in Hong Kong was, after the pro-Communist riot in 1966–67, dominated by anti-Communist sentiment. And so, the Hong Kong Catholic diocese yielded to public criticism and put an end to any discussion on such sensitive issues.[11]

The final document of the Convention did not reflect the call for discussion on human rights and social justice issues and the Church's relationship with the PRC.[12] This issue had long-term implications for church-state relations in Hong Kong. The failure to establish a dialogue with Communism as suggested by some participants in the Diocesan Convention, perpetuated the distance between the Hong Kong Catholic Church and the PRC. The pro-British and anti-Communist stance adopted during this period by the Hong Kong Catholic Church set a basic tone in the next decade on Catholic-government relations.

Catholic Political Participation

The signing of the 1984 Sino-British Agreement on the future of Hong Kong initiated the transitional period of this British colony for reversion to Chinese rule on July 1, 1997. The turnover to Chinese rule prompted London to launch a policy of democratization through the introduction of representative government.[13] The democratization in the last phase of British rule was met with suspicion by the Chinese, but, in effect, it was caused by British concern about how history would judge them if they failed to make an extra effort to prepare their last colony, one of the world's major cosmopolitan cities, for self-rule.

The Parliamentary Foreign Affairs Committee Report (FAC Report, 1994) reflects White Hall's intention by recommending that "Hong Kong people must be allowed to decide on their own system of government before 1997 and after 1997."[14] The British policy of democratization in the transitional period (1984–1997) before the handover of sovereignty was supported by the middle class and professionals in Hong Kong, as well as Christian churches including the Catholic Church. The support of Catholics in democratization was based on several reasons: First, because democratization was promoted by the British, the Catholic Church had no reason to fear that its support would embarrass the Hong Kong government and subsequently jeopardize their financial contractual relationship. Second, Hong Kong's new middle and professional class, whose interests would be most threatened by Chinese Communist rule, threw their weight behind democratization.[15] Many of this class had converted to Catholicism while being educated in Catholic schools, which generally are of high repute, and as young Catholic laity they pressured the Church authorities to support the democratic movement. Third, many Catholics had no confidence in the practice of "one country, two systems," which promised to preserve religious freedom. The democratic movement itself could be a means whereby Hong Kong could acquire greater autonomy after the handover to secure religious freedom.

During the transitional period Hong Kong Catholic groups, following the social teachings of the Church, were active in the local democratic movement. Thus, the Catholic Church actively supported the campaign in the 1991 and 1995 Hong Kong Legislative Council elections, so much so that the turnout rate of Catholic voters was much higher than the general public (1991: 86.6 percent vs. 39.1 percent; 1995: 81.5 percent vs. 35.8 percent). The majority of Catholic voters were pro-democracy.[16]

The political participation of Catholics was extended to the democratic movement in China, with the belief that a democratic China would eventually lead to a democratic HKSAR. In the crackdown on the pro-democratic movement marked by the massacre at Tiananmen Square on 4 June 1989, the Justice and Peace Commission of the Catholic diocese led other Catholic associations to set up the Union of Hong Kong Catholic Organizations in Support of the Patriotic and Democratic Movement in China (Union). Many Hong Kong Catholics under Catholic banners and chanting religious songs were among 1 million citizens at rallies in support of the democratic movement in China. It was argued that the Catholic Union offered more moral support than material support. Father Louis Ha, a diocesan priest deeply involved in the Alliance of Hong Kong Citizens in Support of the Patriotic and Democratic Movement in China (Alliance)—headed by leading democrats such as Szeto Wah and Martin Lee—was the key liaison between the Catholic Union and the Alliance after the Tiananmen Square crackdown.

Generally speaking however, Catholic political involvement in the territory had already been on the increase since the start of Sino-British negotiations over the future of Hong Kong in 1982.

The Bridge-Building Effort of Hong Kong Catholics

Church-state relations in Hong Kong are further complicated by the mission given by Pope John Paul II in 1981 to be a bridge to narrow the gap between China and the Vatican, and draw the Chinese Catholic Church closer to the universal Church.[17] Although the mission was given to overseas Chinese Catholics, Hong Kong's geopolitical affinity, and its being under British rule, provided the best political environment for the bridge building endeavor. The revival of the Chinese Catholic Church in Deng Xiaoping's modernization era, with its open door policy, was mainly the result of the effort of bridge building. However, the revival and growth of the Chinese Catholic Church was not in line with the interests of the Chinese Communist Party which aimed at the elimination of religion.[18] The bridge-building endeavor is a two-edged sword to the Catholic Church in Hong Kong. With its experience of dealing with the Chinese government and the Church in China over the last two decades, the Hong Kong Catholic Church has learned the tactics of church-state relations. Thus there is a better opportunity to prepare for a new direction in church-state relations after 1997 when Hong Kong reverted to Chinese rule. However, the bridge effort, frowned upon by Beijing, inevitably would serve to dampen the Catholic-state relationship in the HKSAR.

The bridge-building endeavor has included helping in the training of mainland clergy, women, religious and other church personnel, the distribution of religious literature, and financial aid for the running of parishes and church-related social service projects.

The assistance, which was extended both to the government sponsored and non-government sponsored sector of the Church, played a crucial role in the revival of Catholicism in the mainland during the 1980s and 1990s.[19] Even after the Tiananmen Square crackdown, when many international non-governmental organizations withdrew from China, Catholic aid continued. Most of the aid funded by foreign Catholic organizations with the blessing of the Vatican, was kept low-key. Every year, annual meetings for the co-ordination of such organizations have been held in Hong Kong for planning as well as evaluating previous projects, but the exact cost of the assistance has not been released.[20]

Chinese government officials, however, hold the view that religion is employed by international subversive forces to "Westernize" and "divide" China. The CCP believe that through the pluralization of religious questions, "dark forces" could be trying to politically pluralize China as a means of subversion.[21] Chen Yun, the second most important figure in China after Deng Xiaoping in 1990, had this view. He expressed his concern about the flourishing of religion to Jiang Zemin and asked him "to do something about that."[22] Despite the Chinese government's concern and efforts, statistics have shown a revival of the Catholic Church in China. In 1983 there were 300 Catholic churches in China, by 1987 the number had increased to 2,100, while in 1992 this had risen to 3,900. The number of Catholics rose from 3.3 million in 1986 to more than 10 million in 1992[23] (This figure represents the members of both the government sponsored and non-government sponsored sector of the Church[24]). The revival of the Catholic Church in China was impossible without the aid of the bridge-building endeavor among overseas Catholics.

The Catholic Church in Hong Kong has played an effective role in bridge building during the past nearly two decades, largely due to the territory's geopolitical proximity. During the colonial period, Hong Kong was beyond China's jurisdiction and its Catholics were relatively free at the time to promote a revival of religion on the mainland, while the territory's closeness to China enabled Hong Kong to obtain firsthand information on the situation in the mainland. Since the return of Hong Kong to Chinese rule, the local Church's future role as a bridge between China and the universal Church has been put in question. By definition a bridge is relevant only when there are two separate entities, but when two entities become one, a bridge is no longer necessary.

The Catholic Church in Hong Kong, under the leadership of Cardinal John Baptist Wu Cheng-Chung, has been helping the revival of the Catholic

Church on the mainland and at the same time helping to bring the latter into the orbit of the universal Church under the leadership of the Pope. Moreover, since 1987 the Vatican has been attempting to normalize relations with Beijing. The Catholic Church's activities, however, have been at odds with the policies of the CCP, which aim to eliminate the influence of religion in society as explicitly spelled out by the director of the Religious Affairs Bureau of the State Council.[25] The CCP has also been concerned about the growth of religious followers, particularly in the face of a hollowing of morality and crisis of belief in the ideology of Communism among the population. Prior to 1997, Hong Kong was viewed by the Vatican as an asset in Sino-Vatican negotiations because of its role as a bridge between the Chinese Catholic Church and the Vatican. Since the handover, however, Hong Kong has become a liability because it becomes an issue on the agenda of the Sino-Vatican negotiations. Thus, the handover has changed the nature of the triangular relationship among China, the Vatican, and Hong Kong.

China Sets an Orbit for HKSAR Catholics

During the transitional period, the political participation of the Christian churches drew the attention of Beijing. Therefore, in the process of writing the Basic Law of the HKSAR some members suggested that it should be written explicitly that religion should not interfere with politics.[26] However, due to the politicized environment of Hong Kong in the transitional period, it was felt that it was too sensitive to have this clause in the Basic Law as it might frighten foreign investors. Although the intended clause on the "separation of religion and politics" was not able to be included into the Basic law, Beijing was not satisfied with Hong Kong Christians' political participation.

Eventually in 1987, Beijing's view on church political participation was revealed through its mouthpiece, the *Wen Wei Po*.[27] Xinhua (New China News Agency), the quasi-Chinese embassy in Hong Kong, began a discussion in the *Wen Wei Po* on the inclusion of religious freedom in the Basic Law of the future HKSAR and openly denounced senior clergymen from both the Catholic and Protestant churches who participated in political assembly or spoke openly on political issues, and further advocated a separation of religion and politics. The newspaper openly criticized Father J.B. Tsang, the vicar-general of the Catholic Diocese, who had spoken at the Assembly on Constitutional Reform and who had openly opposed the building of the Daya Bay Nuclear Plant in 1986.[28] The newspaper argued that speeches made by religious leaders could stir up anti-China sentiment and was critical of clergy who supported political reform in Hong Kong. Furthermore, it argued that clergy should not become involved in politics but restrict their attention to religious affairs.[29] Beijing embraced this view because it feared the ability of religious organizations to promote, in the name of religion, a particular political view.[30] The CCP, being familiar with the organizational weapon as a tactic developed by the Bolsheviks in Russia, sought to curb any civil organization including religious organizations as a means to secure state control of the society.[31] The political leaders in Beijing were well aware that the Catholic Church in Hong Kong, as an organization with its structural hierarchy and high mobilizing capacity, is opposed to the spread of Communism. Therefore, the CCP was determined to prevent the Church from becoming involved in politics and sought to limit the Church to purely religious affairs.

Secondly, China was not immediately concerned about the Catholic Church's involvement in education and social services, or its cooperation with the colonial government in helping to preserve stability and its attempts to narrow the social gap by serving the poor and educating the elite. Basic Law Article 141 states that "a religious organization may, according to their previous practice, continue to run seminaries and other schools, hospitals and welfare institutions and to provide other social services."[32] On informal occasions, Beijing officials verbally promised that Basic Law Article 141 would be honored after the handover.[33]

Thirdly, Ye Xiaowen, the director of the State Council's Religious Affairs Bureau, spelled out the limits of Hong Kong's religious activities after the handover on a visit to Hong Kong in 1996. In particular, he set a limit to the "bridge-building effort" of Hong Kong Christians. Ye stressed Article 148 of the Basic Law, which spelled out the future relationship between Hong Kong Catholics and their counterparts in the mainland after the handover. ". . . Religious organizations in the Hong Kong Special Administrative Region and their counterparts on the mainland shall be based on the principles of non-subordination, non-interference and mutual respect."[34] Ye reminded Christians in Hong Kong that after July 1, 1997 they should not attempt to interfere in the internal affairs of the mainland, while he promised that China would not attempt to impose its own religious policy on Hong Kong. He strongly suggested that Hong Kong Christians should not, through material aid, try to change the religious system in China.[35] In other words, the church's bridge-building efforts should be curbed after Hong Kong's reversion to Chinese rule.[36]

Beijing and Hong Kong Catholics in the Transitional Period (1984–1997)

The anti-Communist undertone of the Hong Kong Catholic Church in the 1950s set its political orientation. The yielding to public criticism and the failure to initiate a dialogue with Communism in the Hong Kong Diocesan Convention in 1970 perpetuated Catholic alienation from the PRC. Because of this historical series of events, Catholics in Hong Kong did not gain the trust of Beijing.

Moreover, Cardinal Wu's pastoral exhortation "March into the Bright Decade," launched in 1989, gave the green light on sociopolitical participation activities. The pastoral letter proposed a multifaceted strategy in response to political change in Hong Kong beyond the handover in 1997. The letter encouraged Catholic groups to follow Christian principles when active in sociopolitical affairs.[37]

In the transitional period, a cool relationship developed between Beijing and the Hong Kong Catholic Diocese. This is obvious in comparing Beijing's treatment of the Bishop of Macau with the treatment of the Bishop of Hong Kong. Hong Kong is one of the world's major international cities and financial centers with a cosmopolitan nature while it next-door neighbor, Macau, is a small parochial enclave at the estuary of the Pearl River Delta. In church hierarchy, the Bishop of Macau enjoys a much lower position than the Bishop of Hong Kong, John Cardinal Wu. By definition, a cardinal is a prince of the Church, and automatically a consultant to the Pope in important matters of the universal Church. Beijing appointed the Bishop of Macau as the only religious representative of the Drafting Committee of Macau's Basic Law, while neither Cardinal Wu nor any Hong Kong Catholic clergy were included in the Drafting Committee of the HKSAR.

In the political sphere, Sino-British relations did not go smoothly in the transitional period. The Chinese leaders had long suspected the British of seeking ways to drain away the surplus capital of Hong Kong and leave the territory in disarray and in the hands of an influential pro-British group. The distrust between London and Beijing during the pre-handover period made negotiations difficult.[38] Following the Tiananmen Square crackdown in 1989 and the collapse of Communism in Eastern Europe, the Communist leaders in Beijing believed that the British were in alliance with the United States in seeking to subvert Communist rule in China. This added fuel to the fire of the distrust between Beijing and London. This explains why the Chinese refused to accept the efforts of the last colonial governor, Christopher Patten, to introduce democracy in 1992—a last ditch attempt by the British to regain the confidence of the people of Hong Kong. It was perceived by China that

Patten's attempt to introduce democracy was aimed at subverting the rule of HKSAR.[39]

Since all religious beliefs are seen as incompatible with the ideology of Marxism-Leninism, the CCP does not endorse any religious belief whatsoever. According to Beijing's "patriotic" political leaders, Christianity is a form of cultural imperialism. As nationalists, CCP leaders refuse to support Christianity because it is also considered to be a foreign religion. The alliance between the Catholic Church in Hong Kong and the British in the democratization of the territory during the transitional period, as well as troubled Sino-Vatican relations, increased the alienation between Beijing and Hong Kong Catholics and the possibility of strained relations between China and the Catholic Church in Hong Kong beyond July 1, 1997. The change of sovereignty left the Catholic Church in Hong Kong in a dilemma over how to adjust itself to the new status quo in the HKSAR, where the new government's policy towards religion would not be the same as the British.

Catholic and HKSAR Government: Downgrading Relationship

Immediately after World War II, the Hong Kong government developed a close relationship with the Christian churches. Three Christian leaders (two Catholics and one Protestant) were among seventeen appointed members who advised the government on its education policy in the colony.[40] Since the 1980s there were no Christian leaders advising government policy. As stated previously, the Christian churches were given financial aid to run extensive primary and secondary education institutions because fear of Communist infiltration ran deep within the Hong Kong government. This situation saw a gradual shift when the Communist underground network in Hong Kong was crushed by the British after the 1966–1967 pro-China riots which shocked the colony.[41] Thus, Hong Kong government began to grant subsidies to non-Christian schools and to schools sponsored by non-Communist Chinese associations such as the Tung Wah Group of Hospitals and Po Leung Kuk in order to eliminate criticism that it was showing favoritism towards Christian schools.[42]

Christian bishops (the Anglican and Catholic bishops of Hong Kong) since the establishment of the Hong Kong colonial government have enjoyed a very high position, ranking fifth on the government's Precedence List.[43] After the establishment of the HKSAR, the Anglican and Catholic bishops, along with Buddhist, Taoist, and Islamic religious leaders, were downgraded to the eleventh position on the Precedence List. The creation of a Buddhist holiday on the birthday of Buddha was seen as an attempt by the HKSAR government to stress the importance of oriental as well as Western religions.

Its elevation of the position of Buddhism indirectly downgraded the high position which Christianity had enjoyed during the colonial period. The downgrading of the Christian churches, and the Catholic Church in particular, has forced Christian churches to redefine their relationship with the HKSAR.

The Hong Kong Catholic Church in a Dilemma

Hong Kong Catholic authorities read the messages disseminated from Beijing at different stages of the political development of Hong Kong. Subsequently, its response to China's demands was manifested in its behavior which spearheaded Catholic policy in the church-state relationship in the HKSAR. The response to these sociopolitical issues reflect the dilemma which the Catholic Church had faced.

Issue I: Catholic Political Participation

The Catholic Church, due to Beijing's pressure, put a brake on its political involvement in 1990, especially in mainland affairs, which Beijing described as "water in the well interfering with water in the river." The Catholic Union was disbanded by the order of the bishop. Father Louis Ha was transferred from the Diocesan Social Communications Office to the Diocesan Archives. The Church remained unchanged in its political involvement in the local scene, especially in the 1991 election campaign. Thus, it continued its usual political role by supporting the British colonial government's promotion of the 1991 Legislative Council (Legco) elections.[44] However, signs of the Diocese's gradual withdrawal from the political arena were seen before the 1995 Legco elections. The Catholic voting rate dropped slightly from 86.5 percent in 1991 to 81.5 percent in 1995 due to its lessening involvement in the electoral campaign.

At the eleventh hour of the transition, a Provisional Legislative Council was set up by Beijing to replace the existing Legco, which had been elected according to a political reform launched by Hong Kong's governor Christopher Patten. Beijing rejected Patten's Legco election system and was quick to have its largely pro-democracy legislators ousted. The Provisional Legislative Council was seen as illegal because it was not mentioned in the Basic Law or in the Sino-British Agreement. The Catholic Diocese was asked to send four representatives to sit on the Selection Committee, from which the Provisional Legislature members were to be elected. The Selection Committee was made up of 800 members, although the business sector occupied more than half of the total seats while some other groups were heavily underrepresented. Hong Kong Catholics were divided over whether to send representatives to sit on the undemocratic Selection Committee. By deciding to send representatives, the Catholic Diocese broke with its practice of siding with the pro-democracy camp. The Diocese compromised and agreed to endorse candidates who wished to take part rather than directly appoint representatives. But the candidates were to participate on an individual basis, not as representatives of the Church. Moreover, the Diocese stipulated that any Catholic candidate should only be involved in the vote for the future chief executive of the HKSAR. The decision to "passively cooperate" disappointed many, both inside and outside the Church, and critics condemned the Diocese for failing to take a strong moral stance. Its compromise demonstrated the Church's weakness and lack of courage to voice the truth at such a critical moment in Hong Kong.

Throughout the process, the Catholic Diocese expressed its unease at having to cooperate "passively" and its unwillingness to participate further in future Legco elections in the new HKSAR. For the Legco elections in 1998, an unelected 800-member Election Committee, made up of largely pro-China supporters, businessmen, former Provisional Legco members, and NPC delegates was given the responsibility of choosing ten seats in the Legislative Council of the HKSAR. At the beginning of 1999, however, Bishop Joseph Zen, the coadjutor or the second-in-charge in the Catholic Diocese, began to publicly express a desire to withdraw the Diocese from involvement in the Legco elections in 2000.[45] A withdrawal from political involvement and the Diocese's lack of support for the HKSAR electoral system, sparked discussion within Catholic circles. The recent decision by the Diocese not to participate in the election system was a sign that the Catholic Church in Hong Kong was in a dilemma. Its decision went against its own policy to become more active in sociopolitical affairs, as outlined in Cardinal Wu's 1989 pastoral exhortation "March into The Bright Decade."[46]

Issue II: Bridge Building Effort with China

The second issue facing the HKSAR's Catholic Church is its future role as a "bridge" between Catholics in China and the universal church. The Hong Kong Church has been proud of its "bridge-building role," which began soon after Deng Xiaoping launched his policy of modernization in 1979 and China began opening up to the world. It seems that the Hong Kong Church has been reluctant to give up its bridge role despite receiving clear signals from Beijing that it would not tolerate such activity after the handover.

At the Synod of Asian Bishops at the Vatican in May 1998, Hong Kong's two auxiliary bishops, Joseph Zen and John Tong, were invited to address the synod. Their talks focused largely on the state of the Catholic Church in China rather than in the HKSAR. This was despite a vast array of topics that could have been discussed on the Catholic Church's position following the handover of Hong Kong on July 1, 1997. The bishops' talks could have been interpreted by Beijing as a violation of Basic Law Article 148, which stipulates "non-interference" in the affairs of the mainland, including Chinese church affairs.[47] But, China openly decided to stick to its policy of keeping out of Hong Kong's internal affairs and did not, therefore, openly reprimand the Hong Kong Catholic Church. Later, however, during a private meeting in Shenzhen between Bishop Joseph Zen and Ye Xiaowen, the director of the Religious Affairs Bureau, in November 1998, Ye outlined Beijing's objection to the Hong Kong Catholic Church's role as a "bridge" with the universal church.[48]

Issue III: Catholic Education Policy

The third issue placing the Hong Kong Catholic Diocese in a dilemma was its involvement in education. During his maiden policy speech at the Provisional Legislative Council meeting, on October 8, 1997, the new HKSAR Chief Executive Tung Chee-hwa launched an education reform strategy that included promoting "mother-tongue teaching" in Hong Kong's schools.[49] From a rational policy analyst's perspective, the promotion of "mother-tongue teaching" is a mediocre policy that could reduce Hong Kong's ability to maintain its strategic position in China and the world.[50] However, the Catholic Episcopal Delegate for Education, Lo Kong-kai, without sufficient consultation with veteran Catholic mission school staff, supported the government's reform policy. Some of Hong Kong's most prestigious schools are run by international Catholic religious congregations specializing in education, such as the Jesuits and La Salle Brothers. Many of the religious congregations expressed their opposition to "mother-tongue teaching" but their opinions were ignored by the Diocesan delegate for education. Research proves that the religious congregations were right and also shows that the government's policy will not enhance Hong Kong's economic vitality or promote economic growth.[51]

The Catholic Diocese in Hong Kong has also expressed concern that future changes in the government's education policy could affect its role in the sector. On the other hand, there is no unity of strategy in the Catholic Diocese over future education policies, as was shown in the division over the introduction of "mother-tongue teaching." It is true that the Catholic Church is in a dilemma as far as education is concerned, and it is now debating how to resolve the dilemma by developing a unified Catholic policy on education.

End of Dilemma: The Turn of Catholic Stance, in the Right of Abode (June 1999)

Hong Kong's Court of Final Appeal on January 29, 1999 ruled that under the Basic Law, all Mainland children born of Hong Kong permanent residents are entitled to live in the HKSAR. Before this verdict, only legitimate children, born after at least one parent had become a Hong Kong permanent resident, were admitted. However, the HKSAR government did not like the Final Appeal Court's verdict and tried to circumvent it. The result was a battle between the administration and the rule of law striking at the heart of the autonomy of Hong Kong and the independence of its judiciary. The government tried to create a climate of fear by whipping up public opinion against newcomers and forecasting extreme pressure on housing, employment, and public health.[52] Secretary for Security Regina Yip alarmingly announced in the Legislative Council on April 28, 1999, that "the number of people to be absorbed by Hong Kong as a result of the judgement, that is, some 1.6 million people, is likely to pose a very heavy and even unbearable burden on Hong Kong."[53] The Hong Kong Policy Research Institute was asked to conduct a survey and found that 83.8 percent of respondents were opposed to the ruling of the Final Appeal Court. This survey was one of many actions taken to inflame public opinion and demonstrate its unwillingness to accept the ruling of the Final Appeal Court. Scholars and some human rights groups accused the government of manipulating figures to instill fear in the public and to give the impression that the only possible solution would be to have the judgment effectively overturned.[54]

Catholics' Dissenting Voice

Cardinal Wu backed up by his successor Bishop Joseph Zen, in his pastoral letter titled "God is Love," which challenged the government's stance on "the Right of Abode" with his argument based on humanitarian reasons and Christian love, including assertions that "blood is thicker than water" and "all within the four seas are one family." The following was his main argument:

A large number of adult Hong Kong residents came from the Mainland to settle here in the 1950s and 1960s. Hong Kong at that time was not blessed with a strong economy or firm social structure. Nevertheless, when faced with a continuous flood of refugees, there was no hesitation and doors were opened to welcome them. At present, the economic outlook is not so bright. Yet, compared with the rest of the world, Hong Kong is still regarded as the envy of many. Based on the belief that "blood is thicker than water" and that "all within the four seas are one family," the Chinese people have always shown kindness to others and taken delight in sharing. Faced then today with the question of children born to Hong Kong parents in the Motherland, how can we harden our hearts, look on with indifference and a lack of humanity, and use "interpretation" to deny them hope?[55]

Arguing from a humanitarian angle, the Cardinal's comments put the government's stance to shame: "Now that you are getting rich, how can you refuse others who seek the abode in Hong Kong like you did some few decades ago?" He offered his option by suggesting that "Hong Kong's zealous people, philanthropists, voluntary bodies and church communities can deal with the present question of right of abode. United in hand and in heart, they could respond to the challenge, meet the difficulties, and grasp the opportunity to develop a spirit of love and create a new miracle."[56] That means the Catholic Church, together with people of good heart, could take care of the newcomers.

The Cardinal was exceptionally candid is criticizing the government about asking the NPC to reinterpret the Basic Law.

... It (the government) seeks the long term prosperity of Hong Kong by requesting the Standing Committee of the NPC to reinterpret the Basic Law in order to limit the right of abode of children born in the Mainland to Hong Kong parents, then it engenders a certain resistance on the part of Hong Kong residents to Mainland people, with lamentable consequences. ... It is extremely important that the Basic Law and a government be maintained in all their integrity. Solving the question of the right of abode is a Hong Kong matter. The SAR should itself give its own interpretation, but it has not done this. Asking for a reinterpretation from the Standing Committee of the NPC cannot help but damage the foundation of the autonomy of the SAR, shake the foundations of the Hong Kong family, raise doubts in people's minds about the Central Government's promise of "one country, two systems with a high degree of autonomy," and undermine the confidence of the international community towards Hong Kong. Who can be sure how far-reaching the effects will be?"[57]

Political critics and the general public were surprised by the pastoral letter which was perceived as voicing the conscience of Hong Kong society. The Catholic Church was the first organization to denounce the government's policy on the right of abode.[58] The archbishop of the Hong Kong Sheng

Kung Hui (The Hong Kong Anglican Church), Archbishop Kong Kwong Kit, who is also a member of the NPC and the CCPCC, openly supported the Cardinal's statement based on the fundamental Christian social teaching that: God is love, and all human beings are Brothers and Sisters.[59] The public was quick to follow the Catholic Church to condemn the HKSAR government and Beijing.[60] Christians and progressive Catholic groups such as the Commission of Justice and Peace, and the Commission on Labor also allied themselves with Protestant groups to carry out a signature campaign, issue announcements, and held public conferences and seminars to manifest their support of the views of the Cardinal.[61] Inspired by the official stance of the Catholic Church, hundreds of individual Christians and twenty-three Protestant groups signed a full page notice in the *Ming Bao* newspaper on June 17, 1999, outlining the reasons why they opposed the government's handling of the right of abode issue.[62] Unprecedently, the Secretary of Security, Regina Yip, on June 17, 1999, wrote a long letter to the Cardinal defending the government's position. However, the Justice and Peace Commission published a statement in the newspaper repudiating Yip's claim.[63]

The Church risks offending the HKSAR government and Beijing by openly opposing the controversial policy on the Right of Abode. This is the first prominent case in which the Catholic Church has expressed its concern, knowing very well that its stance would set the Church against the state.[64] Cardinal Wu's landmark pastoral letter began a new era for the Catholic Church in Hong Kong and ended a dilemma in its relationship with the government.

Then the Catholic Church in Hong Kong demonstrated another sign of involvement in sociopolitical issues by reactivating the parish social concern groups. A very detailed strategy was launched with a supporting team from the Diocese and guidelines to ensure a success.[65] The Catholic Diocese emphasizes that the social teaching of the Church is part of Catholic doctrine and should be taught and practiced among the Catholic population.[66] The actual launching at the parish level is to be held in 2000 after church personnel are trained in this area.

Twilight in the Distance: Bishop Coadjutor on Front Stage and Diocesan Synod

The gradual emergence of Bishop Joseph Zen to the front stage of the Catholic drama turned a new page in the Hong Kong Catholic Church. Zen was consecrated in 1996 to be the successor of Wu who will retire in 2000 at the age of seventy-five. It is believed that Zen was the chief architect of the controversial pastoral letter of Cardinal Wu to challenge the Right of Abode, and it ended two years of dilemma after the reversion to Chinese rule. It was his design that parish social concern activities were reactivated, which put emphasis on the social teachings of the Church.[67] This indicated that the Catholic Church has charted its future path which is diverting from its past. The first Diocesan Convention was held in 1970 to implement the Vatican II doctrine in Hong Kong which was experiencing a great change when Hong Kong began to develop socially and economically. The Diocesan Synod that was called by the Cardinal in November 1999 aimed at coping with the changing society in the HKSAR, and promised a glimpse of hope in seeing a twilight in the distance after two years of dilemma following Hong Kong's reversion to Chinese rule. Its Preparatory Committee is working and the theme of the synod and areas of study will be issued soon. It is expected that this synod will be a policymaking body of the Catholic Church on its internal affairs, as well as on its relationship with society and with the government. This diocese synod that will redefine church-state relations deserves our close observation and study.

Conclusion

It was natural and convenient for the British colonial government to ally itself with the Christian churches, and in particular the Catholic Church in Hong Kong to work for the people. It was natural because of a shared ideological outlook and because of Britain's Christian cultural traditions. It suited the purpose of both bodies to offer each other mutual support, in particular in the area of education and social service especially when government desperately needed cooperation in order to cope with the needs of Chinese refugees flowing into the colony in the 1950s from the mainland. The anti-Communist undertone of the British and Catholic Church led the Hong Kong government to entrust refugee services to the Church without the danger of allowing the infiltration of Communism into the colony.

But, as Sino-British relations soured during the pre-handover period, the alliance between the Hong Kong Catholic Church and the British colonial government enlarged the stumbling block which prevented the Church from formulating a smooth relationship with Beijing and, to a certain extent, with the future HKSAR government. This situation was aggravated by the Catholic Diocese's reluctance to abandon its bridging endeavour with the Catholic Church in mainland China.

Before the handover on July 1, 1997, Beijing had set the orbit for future church-state relations in the HKSAR by insisting that the Hong Kong Catholic Church should refrain from political participation and from sharing resources with its counterpart on the mainland, but allowing the Church to continue its involvement in the education and social service to enhance prosperity and stability of the HKSAR. Facing Beijing's demand, the Catholic Church in Hong Kong at the beginning of the political handover was in a dilemma over how to respond to the orbit set by Beijing while still not losing its identity as a church. However, with the emergence of a new Church leader who is going to take the lead in 2000, some initial plans and actions have been taken to end the dilemma and to inspire a new beginning of church-state relations. This deserves close observation in days to come.

Christianity in Modern Taiwan—Struggling Over the Path of Contextualization

PETER CHEN-MAIN WANG

Introduction

While the history of Christianity in China has become a topic in more and more publications, the church history of Taiwan has remained obscure both in church circles and in the academic world. This small island which has been richly invested by foreign missionaries and has been diligently cultivated by local Christians did not produce a "Taiwan miracle" in the churches as it did in economics. During the past half century in Taiwan, the Christian population, though sometimes varying, has never passed the level of 5 percent of the total population. One cannot but question the strategies and efforts of Christian adherents in their spread of Christianity to others.

A lack of contextualization of Christianity is a widely accepted explanation for the slow development of the Christianity in China.[1] When the Christian churches in China were forced to adopt a three-self method in the 1950s, Christianity was still viewed in many Chinese eyes as a "foreign religion" with various connections with foreign governments. Thus, the foreign flavor of the Christian churches and the difference between Christianity and Chinese culture have often been blamed for the "slow" development of Christianity in China. However, the slow growth of Christianity in Taiwan cannot be blamed on lack of contextualization. That is because one striking similarity of Christian churches in Taiwan is their promotion of contextualization. In Taiwan, both Catholics and Protestants, both independent churches and denominational churches, all adopted a strategy of contextualization in one way or another. Yet, these efforts did not seem to help them much.

This paper, based primarily on Chinese Christian publications and documents as well as academic works in English, attempts to give a general overview of the phenomenon of the contextualization of Christianity in Taiwan in the past half century. The first part of this paper will be a general survey of the development of Christianity in Taiwan since 1949. The following two parts of the paper will examine and discuss the phenomenon of contextualization in two Christian groups—Presbyterians and Catholics. Through a comparative and analytical examination of the theories and practices of contextualization in these two organizations, we will not only be able to better understand the Christian churches in modern Taiwan, but we can also reevaluate the strategies and direction of the contextualization for the future missions in Taiwan as well as in other parts of the world.

Survey of the History of Christianity in Taiwan Since 1949

Christian churches came back to life in Taiwan at the time Japanese colonial government ended in 1945. All Japanese controls and restrictions which had been imposed on the churches were removed.[2] Not only did the four existing Christian bodies—the Presbyterian Church, the True Jesus Church, the Taiwanese Holiness Church, and the Catholic Church—become free to expand, but more and more missionaries from other denominations also entered the island.[3]

The year of 1949 brought, in many ways, important changes to Taiwan and also to the churches. The Nationalist government retreated to Taiwan in December, but no one knew how long it could last against the Chinese Communists. Not until the outbreak of the Korean War in June 1950 and the arrival of the U.S. Seventh Fleet in the Taiwan Strait, did Taiwan become stabilized. The U.S. government resumed its economic and military aid to the Nationalist government the next year. Especially helpful to the stability of Taiwan was the establishment of the U.S.-ROC Mutual Defense Treaty in 1954. This treaty not only assured the security of Taiwan, but also gave the people on Taiwan needed time and resources to initiate internal reforms.[4]

The Mutual Defense Treaty also had tremendous influence on the Christian churches. Foreign missionaries poured into Taiwan and by 1954 the number of denominations reached thirty-three. There were about 300 foreign missionaries in 1955. Five years later, "there were close to 600 Protestant missionaries and an equal number of Catholic priests and nuns."[5]

The arrival of a great number of missionaries in Taiwan in the 1950s is quite understandable. First, when the door of evangelism was shut in China, mission boards and missionaries who were committed to preach the Gospel to the Chinese found an island where thousands of Chinese people needed their service.[6] Most of the missionaries who came to Taiwan in the 1950s had had experience serving in China.[7]

The second reason for the influx of missionaries was that Taiwan at that time was an extremely understaffed mission field. In the year 1948, there were only 51,000 Protestant believers in a total population of 6,500,000.[8] Appeals for more missionaries were transmitted to the mission boards. Furthermore, more than a million mainlanders who had retreated with the Nationalist government to Taiwan badly needed Mandarin-speaking missionaries. Requests to serve the mainlanders were especially appealing to those experienced missionaries who had a calling to serve the Chinese.

The third reason was the relatively harmonious relationship between the church and the state in Taiwan. In contrast to the religious persecution on the other side of the Taiwan Strait, Taiwan in the 1950s appeared to be a missionary heaven. In addition to Generalissimo and Madame Chiang Kai-shek who professed their faith in Christianity, quite a few high-ranking government officials were Christians. Moreover, the Nationalist government adopted a favorable attitude toward missionaries in order to cultivate the friendship and sympathy of the international community.[9]

The civil war in China (1945–1949) and the numerous upheavals in Taiwan, such as the tragic February 28, 1947 Incident, gave people on Taiwan a feeling of uncertainty.[10] Not only did the more than a million mainlanders suffer from dislocation and uncertainty, but the people of Taiwan also faced disorienting changes. Thus, they became "fertile soil" for the Gospel because they needed help and guidance both materially and spiritually.

Under these favorable conditions, Christianity expanded quickly. In terms of both numbers of churches and numbers of believers, growth in the 1950s was faster than at any other time. This phenomenon was true both for Protestants and Catholics. As pointed out by Allen J. Swanson, "Roman Catholics soared from 13,000 after World War II to 180,000 by 1960. The Protestant community shot up from about 37,000 after the war to over 200,000 in the same time period."[11] This church growth naturally included many Protestant denominations. For example, the Presbyterians, who will be discussed in the next part of the paper, jumped from 56,591 in 1952 to 86,064 in 1954 and to 179,916 in 1964.[12] As for the Southern Baptists, in 1949, there was but one Baptist church and the total Chinese Baptist population stood at forty-six. In 1961, thirteen years later, church membership had increased many times over and the total Baptist community was over 8,000, jumping from 2,195 in 1953, to 4,586 in 1956, to 8,165 in 1961.[13] The growth of the Taiwan Lutheran Church expanded from 791 members in 1953 to 1,884 in 1955, to 4,264 in 1959, and 4,952 in 1961.[14]

An important trend which is closely related to the church growth of this period was the natural division of the Taiwanese-speaking churches and the

Mandarin-speaking churches. Because they had learned Mandarin, most missionaries who used to serve in China, both Catholics and Protestants, spent their time and efforts with mainlanders.[15] Like the missionaries that transferred from China, the Catholic Church basically focused its attention on mainlanders and aboriginal peoples. The Presbyterians and the True Jesus Church, in contrast, focused on Taiwanese and aboriginal peoples.[16]

Sociological studies have confirmed Swanson's study: most of the receptivity was found among two groups—the mainlanders and the aboriginal peoples. While the churches did attract many Taiwanese in this period, the most spectacular phenomenon was the number of mainlanders and aboriginal peoples joining the churches. This growth occurred even though the mainlanders only represented 10 to 13 percent of the population and the aboriginal peoples only 2 percent. This phenomenon is true of both the Catholic Church and the Protestant churches. According to a leading sociologist, Qu Haiyuan, the average growth rate for the Protestant churches from 1949 to 1964 was 26 percent for the plains people (both Taiwanese and mainlanders) and 32 percent for the aboriginal peoples.[17] The rapid church growth primarily happened in Taidong, Taizhong, and Hualian; other areas of high growth include Xinzhu, Taoyuan, Pingdong, Taipei, Taizhong Hsien, and Nantou. There are two possible reasons for rapid church growth in those areas. First, most of these areas were the homelands of aboriginal peoples and they were converted in great numbers. Ninety percent of the church growth in Hualian and Taidong happened among aboriginal peoples.[18] Sixty to 80 percent of the church growth in Nantou and Pingdong and 50 percent in Taoyuan and Xinzhu also happened among aboriginal peoples. The second reason is that the mainlanders were the majority of the city population in Taipei and Taizhong. And this indirectly proves that the majority of the people who joined the churches were mainlanders.[19]

Qu Haiyuan also shows the similar development of the Catholic Church. Hualian and Taipei were the two fastest areas of Catholic growth between 1952 and 1964. The growth rate in Hualian reached 49.83 percent and Taipei 18.78 percent; all other areas were below 7 percent.[20] Hualian was an area of aboriginal peoples and Taipei was crowded with mainlanders. During the years 1955 to 1958, over 70 percent of total Catholic gains came from the mainlanders and the aboriginal peoples. The figures show mainlanders 34,834, Taiwanese 19,193 and aboriginal peoples approxi-mately 15,000.[21]

Many scholars try to explain this fast growth of Christian churches. As stated before, church growth among the mainlanders came from the influx of many experienced missionaries and resources to this specific group of people who were dislocated in a foreign land and needed both spiritual and material consolation. In her study, Dorothy A. Raber also points out that within the immigrating groups came experienced pastors and some 50,000 Christians.[22] Finally, the church and the state relations were rather friendly at that time, and the Nationalist government and its officials often gave advantages and privileges to missionaries and their institutions.[23]

Qu Haiyuan suggests several sociological reasons for the wide receptivity among aboriginal peoples. First, their traditional religions could not perform their functions in the new environment. Second, the traditional religions were often simple and without theoretical basis and therefore could not compete with Christianity. Third, the traditional religions began their decline under strict Japanese control. Fourth and the most important, Christian missionaries adopted a sympathetic attitude toward aboriginal peoples and won their friendship and trust.[24] Later, Qu Haiyuan adds one more reason: Christian churches seem to play some social functions among aboriginal peoples. When Christianity became a common activity among a certain group of aboriginal people, it caused a kind of social pressure on individuals to join the churches.[25]

According to church scholars and other sociological researchers, the church growth reached a plateau in the mid-1960s. A review of the overall picture from 1945 to 1964 shows that the total Christian community (Protestants and Catholics) jumped from 60,000 to over 540,000. This means the percentage of Christians on the island rose from 1 percent in 1945 to 5 percent in 1965. The number of Protestants reached approximately 283,255 and the number of Catholics 265,555.[26]

The Catholic development reached its plateau in the 1960s. The number of Catholics went beyond 300,000 in 1968 and reached its highest point in 1969 with 305,793.[27] However, the number of Catholic members began to decline after 1969. The number dropped below 300,000 in 1973, and has not been able to jump above that level. The lowest figure is 276,591 in 1979 and the latest statistical figure available is 299,548 in 1995.[28]

The Protestants also encountered many difficulties in the second half of the 1960s and the first half of the 1970s. The exact figures for the Protestant community are difficult to attain, but one way to look at the growth of the Protestant community is to look at the number of church buildings. According to Qu Haiyuan, the growth rate of church buildings between 1964 and 1979 is close to zero.[29] The estimated number of Protestants in 1964 is between 278,768 to 303,380, and in 1979 is between 306,700 to 360,000.[30] No matter what figure we adopt, the Protestant churches entered a period of slow development. As Raber points out, the church growth rate during the period from 1964 to 1974 had fallen far behind Taiwan's population growth. In 1964 there were 540,000 Christians in a total population of 12,257,000 and by 1973 there were 650,000 Christians in a population of 15,565,000.[31]

Of course, it is not fair to assume there was stagnation in all Protestant denominations. In Raber's survey of twelve major Protestant denominations, two of them show good growth, four show slow growth, two show no growth, and four show decline.[32]

The reasons for this stagnation and decrease are many-faceted. One reason is that the missionaries who came to Taiwan did not have a thorough and thoughtful plan for the evangelization of local people. Many of the missionaries simply followed the old patterns they had established in China. They did not encourage the laity, a truly indigenous leadership, or a self-supporting spirit.[33] Qu Haiyuan believes that the Catholic Church suffered severely because the foreign priests often adopted authoritative ways in church affairs and cultivated passivity among church members.[34] Further, some problems arose from the missionary measures that had been adopted to deal with the rapid church growth of the 1950s. For example, in order to take care of the great number of new believers, missionaries established 10 seminaries in the 1950s. These seminaries accepted many low-quality students without strong faith and character who later were not good pastors.[35] Gradually, as local Christians participated more in church affairs, church-mission relationships became tense.[36] Furthermore, even missionaries of the same denomination could not cooperate with each other because they belonged to different mission boards or came from different countries.[37]

Scholars often connect the church problems with the rapid social change in Taiwan. Taiwan was in a process of moving from an agricultural society to an industrial society. Urbanization enticed people, including Christians, to move from rural areas to the cities. The church leaders, however, did not foresee or prepare for this change. Therefore, while the rural churches were losing many members, many of these Christians were not being integrated into the urban churches.[38] This phenomenon is especially true among the aboriginal peoples. Another reason for the decline in church growth is the anti-Christian atmosphere which became strong again in the intellectual community. During the time of the national and social disturbance the intellectual community was silent, but the anti-Christian atmosphere reemerged when Taiwan became more stable.[39] Some people have argued that when the society became affluent, people began to pursue material gains and no longer pursued spiritual satisfaction.[40] At the same time, the traditional Chinese religions which lay strong emphasis on *Bao* (retribution) became popular as people became wealthy or established.[41]

The Protestant community was alarmed by the slow development and began to think about church growth and to adopt various methods to spur church growth. From 1971 on, a number of church growth lectures, seminars and conferences have been held in Taiwan. Many distinguished international pastors, theologians, and church leaders have been invited to share their successful strategies.[42] Further, thousands of Taiwanese church leaders and lay members have visited the Full Gospel Central Church of Seoul under Paul Yung-chi Cho since 1979. Cho has also been invited to give lectures in Taiwan a couple of times. The newest and currently most popular strategy of church growth in Taiwan is the "Cell Group Church" model which was developed in Singapore by Ralph W. Neighbour Jr. Because of the success of this church growth model in Singapore, about 400 to one 1,000 church leaders have visited Singapore annually from 1993 to 1998 hoping to study the "cell group" model and apply it to Taiwan.[43]

The number of Protestants painfully struggles upward. The number moved to over 400,000 in 1987, and once passed 500,000 in 1993 (501,662), but shrunk back to 493,577 in 1995. The membership of the Presbyterian Church in Taiwan has fluctuated between 200,000 and 230,000 in the decade of 1985–1995. The total Christian population (both Catholics and Protestants) reached 844,067 and constituted 3.99 percent of total population in Taiwan in 1995.[44]

The Contextualization of Christianity of the Presbyterian Church

World War II played an extremely important role in the history of Presbyterian contextualization of Christianity in Taiwan. When all English and Canadian missionaries withdrew from Taiwan in 1940, the churches were left in the hands of local Christians. Although Taiwanese Christians suffered severe persecution under the Japanese rule, they persisted in their religion and they supported their own churches. The experience turned out to be a blessing and also a valuable experience in pursuing an indigenous church after the war.

The first step toward the indigenization of Christianity was to develop a new structure for all the Taiwanese Presbyterians. After the end of the war, the Northern Synod and the Southern Synod were soon restored and they took over the church property and church affairs. Although there had been some discussion of the union of the two synods, the ideal of a unified Presbyterian Church could not yet be put into practice. In spite of this, the younger generation exerted an effective push at this time. About 1,200 young Presbyterians published an open letter appealing for a union of the two synods while attending a summer camp in July 1948. The next year, the youth, coming from both south and north Taiwan, formed the Taiwan Church Young Adult Group (TKC).[45] The leaders of the two synods began to seriously discuss this issue when they met on the occasion of a meeting concerning the future of missions and church strategy in June 1949. After a series of discussions and negotiations, the General Assembly of the Presbyterian Church in Taiwan was formed in 1951.[46] Six years later, the powers and functions of the General Assembly were strengthened in a resolution of the fourth General Assembly meeting. The Southern Synod was dissolved and gave all its institutes to the General Assembly and the Northern Synod did the same, except that they retained the structure of the board of directors of the synod and kept the management of synod property.[47]

Mission-Church Relationship

When many of the old missionaries returned to the mission field they were joined by some newcomers, such as missionaries of the Reformed Church in America. It was apparent that to build up a new church structure it would be necessary to define the status of the foreign missionaries. The newcomers were from a different background and therefore there was no consistency in dealing with the local churches.[48] Basically, up to the early 1950s, the English and Canadian Presbyterian missionaries were organized in their own mission councils which were not directly related to the new General Assembly. Nonetheless, the mission councils "exercised considerable control over the church. They sent delegates with greetings to presbytery meetings and ensured missionary representation on important committees."[49]

Both missionaries and local church leaders began to reexamine the mission-church relationship and reached a breakthrough in the third General Assembly meeting in 1955. An ad hoc committee was formed and reached some basic agreements that were drawn up in a document entitled "The Relationship between the General Assembly and the Mother Churches (i.e., the Presbyterian Church of England and the Presbyterian Church in Canada)." It runs as follows:

> We hope that now and in the future the Mother Churches will, in accordance with their own principles, assist the General Assembly of the Presbyterian Church in Taiwan with spreading the Gospel in Taiwan.
>
> 1. The General Assembly will request needed personnel (including numbers and professional qualifications) from the Mother Churches in accordance with the requirements for evangelism in Taiwan.
> 2. When a worker (missionary) takes office his name shall be entered on the appropriate Church roll, depending on whether he is a minister, elder or layman.
> 3. The General Assembly appoints him to his work.

4. He has the same responsibilities and rights as other ministers and elders who have membership in the General Assembly of the Presbyterian Church in Taiwan.

5. The requesting of financial support from the two Mother Churches shall be done by the General Assembly in accordance with its budget. The General Assembly shall be directly responsible for paying out money and taking care of money.

6. The General Assembly shall make year-end reports to the two Mother Churches about General Assembly enterprises, the situation of the work and its results, including a financial statement.[50]

These agreements were ratified as a formal resolution in the next General Assembly meeting in 1957. The whole process was an epoch-making step in the Taiwanese Presbyterians' effort in indigenization. Based on this resolution, the General Assembly was able to put all important Mission-Church issues under its own control, including the invitation and deployment of missionary personnel, all financial matters in Taiwan, and communications with the Mother Churches. In fact, those principles paved the way for a further contextualization of Christianity in Taiwan.

In response to the above resolution, the English and Canadian Mission Councils held three meetings in 1958 and 1959 and decided to form a new mission council which would become a committee of the General Assembly. In February 1959, at the sixth General Assembly meeting, this new Mission Council was inaugurated. According to the constitution of this Council, its functions fell under two main headings—advisory functions and those functions concerning the "domestic" business of the missionary community. The new Mission Council surrendered the power to assign missionaries to the General Assembly with the words: "To request the Assembly's Personnel Committee to arrange for the membership of ordained missionaries in presbyteries."[51] Elizabeth J. Brown, a senior English missionary, highly praised this change by commenting, "This is a very significant change, since a missionary who is a member of a presbytery has obligations to that presbytery which a visitor to a meeting certainly does not have. At the same time, he has the opportunity to be part of the working fellowship of the presbytery, to be a colleague sharing actively in the strategy for mission in that area."[52]

As individual members or as a small minority in a certain presbytery, missionaries are inclined to become followers, instead of sharing or influencing the direction of the Presbyterian Church. The Mission Council was destined to decline and then, in 1977, "after its functions had progressively decreased, it became a fellowship group under the guidance of the General Assembly's Missionary Personnel Committee."[53] The current

Presbyterian missionaries have been categorized as "providers of expertise," according to Mark C. Thelin, "a role in which a missionary in a non-administrative, non-supervisory position fills a need which cannot be met with locally trained or appointed people."[54] In this situation, the missionary performs "staff" functions only, rather than "line," "executive" or "leadership" functions.

Political Contextualization

The Presbyterian Church in Taiwan maintained an intimate identity with the language, people, and culture of Taiwan. This trend dramatically increased and strengthened in accordance with the development of domestic and international circumstances. As time went on, this identity was transformed into political advocacy and activities. The role of the church in the state has become a special concern of the Church, and the Church has also made an effort at the political contextualization of Christianity in Taiwan.

The "Double the Church Movement" was the first large-scale movement which was initiated by the Presbyterian leaders; it demonstrated their sense of responsibility for the propagation of the Gospel in Taiwan. As early as 1954, when Reverend Huang Wudong, General Secretary of the Southern Synod, prepared a report for the conference of the World Council of Churches (hereafter WCC), he found out that, after ninety years in Taiwan, only 0.72 percent of Taiwan's population was Christian and there were 161 villages without a Christian church. The Presbyterian Church, at this time, also faced another crisis. They found they faced competition from the many newly arrived denominations and also many of the mainlanders who had earlier attended the Presbyterian congregations now preferred to attend Mandarin-speaking churches.[55] Rev. Huang, therefore, presented an overture at the annual meeting of the Southern Synod with the aim to double the Presbyterian members and churches in ten years—the centenary of the founding of the Presbyterian Church in Taiwan. This proposal was well received and adopted in 1954. Five years later, the Movement won support at the meeting of the General Assembly.[56]

The results of this Movement were very impressive. Within the ten years, the Presbyterian population increased from 86,064 in 1954 to 176,255 in 1964, and churches and chapels increased from 410 to 839.[57] This phenomenal growth on the one hand demonstrated the hard work of the Presbyterians, and on the other hand it encouraged significantly their faith in God. While Presbyterians have generally credited the Movement for the impressive growth, sociologists have proposed quite different explanations for the growth of the Presbyterian Church. Few Presbyterian leaders or scholars, however, have reviewed or dealt with the academic findings.[58] Regardless, the Presbyterian Church has remained the largest Protestant denomination in Taiwan and its members and strength have gone far beyond other denominations.

While the Presbyterian Church became established in its structure and continued to develop its membership, domestic and international stimuli forced the Church to examine its relations with the Nationalist government. First, it is necessary to understand the church and the state relationship before the year 1965. During these early years, both the Presbyterian Church and the Nationalist government maintained an attitude of self-restraint toward each other. No direct conflict broke out in this period. It is quite clear, however, that since a number of Presbyterian elite were killed in the February 28, 1947 Incident and Taiwan was under martial law after that, the Church dared not to be involved in politics during the 1950s.[59] At the same time the Nationalist government needed the sympathy and friendship of the international community and therefore they tried to maintain a friendly relationship with all the churches. As Sheldon Sawatzky correctly spelled out: "Missions and churches in Taiwan are given relative freedom to pursue their ministry as long as their activities and public preaching do not counter or criticize government policies."[60]

A series of domestic and international issues brought about tension and later open conflicts between the government and the Church. The first pressure the government put on the Church concerned the membership of the Presbyterian Church in Taiwan in the WCC. The WCC recommended in 1966 that the People's Republic of China should be allowed to enter the United Nations. The Church decided to inform the government in 1969 about the issue and asked for advice. The government expressed its regret at the political standpoint of the WCC and suggested that religion should not interfere in politics. Then, the Church, under strong pressure from the government, withdrew from the WCC in 1970.

The early 1970s were a difficult period for the Nationalist government in the international community. First, it was replaced by the PRC in the United Nations in 1971. Then U.S. President Richard Nixon visited Beijing and co-released the Shanghai Communiqué with the PRC. Further, Japan also betrayed the friendship of the ROC and formally recognized the PRC. The entire population of Taiwan was in a state of uncertainty. The General Assembly of the Presbyterian Church in Taiwan, based on its identity with the land and people of Taiwan, felt obliged to express their concern through a series of three statements that were issued in 1972, 1975, and 1976. The first statement, "Public Statement on our National Fate by the Presbyterian Church on Taiwan," contains two parts. The first part, addressed to the international community, makes clear that they [the Presbyterians] identify with their homeland—the island Taiwan—and it declares that the fate of Taiwan is not to be decided by outsiders. The second part, addressed to the domestic audience, urges political reform to open up the political process and pushes the government to hold elections for the National Assembly. After that statement was issued, church-state relations became very tense and the government kept the Church under close surveillance.

In January 1975, another conflict occurred. Government officials confiscated Bibles in tribal languages and the new Taiwanese translation of the New Testament. In the eyes of the Presbyterians, the government's policy in only honoring Mandarin Chinese as the official language did not show respect to the language and people in Taiwan. The second statement, "Our Appeal," was released on September 18, 1975. It first reaffirms the first statement and then proclaims the universal human right to worship God in one's mother language. It also urges the promotion of trust between government and the Church, the seeking of reconciliation of all peoples living in Taiwan, the preservation of human rights, and permission for the Church to participate in world organizations (such as the WCC)."[61]

Events in the international community continued to put pressure on Taiwan. Chairman Mao died in September 1976 and the Gang of Four was arrested the next month. U.S. President Jimmy Carter decided to establish diplomatic relations with the PRC. In harmony with its efforts to promote human rights, the Presbyterian Church sent an open letter to the President of the United States. The title of this letter is "Statement on Human Rights" and it championed the idea that "human rights and homeland are God given, and that the future of Taiwan should be determined by the 17 million residents on Taiwan." In its most crucial statement it urges the "Taiwan government to face reality by making Taiwan a new and independent country."

The last statement was in direct contradiction with the unification policy of the Nationalist government and hence immediately drew sharp criticism from various sources. However, to the Presbyterian Church in Taiwan, this statement demonstrated their will to participate in the democratic movement to build up a new nation. Quite a few church leaders led their church members to join various anti-government activities. From this time on, the Presbyterian pastors and members appeared at all major political activities, such as the Gaoxiong Incident, the establishment of the Democratic Progressive Party (hereafter DPP), and later the Jianguodang (Taiwan Independence Party), concern for the victims of the February 28, 1947 Incident and their descendants, and the abolishment of the martial law, etc.[62] "Making Taiwan a new and independent country" has become the highest standard and goal of the Presbyterian Church. Because of this goal, the

Church has given both spiritual and material support to the DPP, especially in election times. Ironically, the DPP recently has downplayed the idea of building a new nation (i.e., to create a new name for Taiwan instead of using the Republic of China) because it recognizes that realistically they might not receive much support from the international community. Therefore, the General Assembly of the Presbyterian Church published an article on April 29, 1999 to criticize the DPP for its detour in building a new country.[63] Another interesting development is that the General Assembly has softened its attitude toward the Nationalist Party and released an article to affirm and support President Lee Teng-hui's statement of "a special state-to-state relationship."[64]

While it is accurate to interpret the political activities of the Presbyterian Church in Taiwan as an interaction with the domestic and international context, it is also important to note that those political activities are in harmony with the general development of Asian/Taiwanese theology. Xue Bozan (David Po-Tsan Hsueh), a teacher at Taiwan Theological College, points out that the Presbyterian Church's evangelism is deeply influenced by several new theologians, such as Choan-Seng Song, Shoki Coe, and Wang Xianzhi.[65] C.S. Song, in his book *Third-Eye Theology*, suggests that Christian concern about justice and freedom is expressed by participating in God's politics of construction.[66] Gao Junming held that the reason that the Church is concerned about society and politics is to help laborers understand the total reality of Jesus' life.[67] Through Presbyterian statements, activities, and bearing witness, contemporary people can understand God's political structure.[68] Out of these theological convictions, the Presbyterians began to articulate the relevance of the Christian Gospel to the daily life in this society. Many of the leaders place emphasis on the social-oriented church which not only preaches the Gospel but also puts the Gospel into practice.[69]

However, because of an overemphasis on Taiwan locality and Taiwan consciousness by the Presbyterian Church in Taiwan, the Presbyterian pastors and members seem to adopt a narrow-minded "Taiwan first" or "Taiwan only" mentality. It should be pointed out that the Presbyterian Church has championed its mission of propagating the Gospel to the Taiwanese-speaking community and aboriginal peoples in Taiwan. This narrow vision might be evidence to demonstrate their identity and loyalty to the language and people in Taiwan, but the fact remains that even during the period of the influx of a million mainlanders and the "Double the Church Movement" there has been little mention in the General Assembly meetings of the propagation of the Gospel to the mainlanders.

There is ample evidence that supports the narrow mentality of the Presbyterian Church members. For example, the "official" language of the two main theological colleges (Tainan Theological College and Taiwan Theological College) is Taiwanese. In the theological colleges, students are reluctant to study English or other modern instruments (like the computer) to reach other peoples. There are scholarships and free Training in Mission programs for students to study cross-culture missions, but "the applicants from Taiwan have always been few. . . . There is almost a total lack of interest."[70] The Presbyterian Church in Taiwan did establish an Overseas Missions Committee in 1959. However, it seems that the priority is given to work among Taiwanese-speaking communities in Malaya, Singapore, Thailand, Mauritius, and Japan.[71]

In fact, as the tide of Taiwan self-consciousness rose higher and higher (see next section), the relationship between mission and church seems to have deteriorated. At the same time that many Taiwanese Christians were proclaiming that "the day of the foreign missionary is over," Taiwanese church historians also began to find fault with the missionaries. For example, historians pointed to the Barclay controversy. When the conquering Japanese armies began to attack Tainan, Thomas Barclay, the founder of Tainan Theological College, was asked by local people to serve as a peacemaker. According to his latter-day critics, however, with his efforts "he thwarted the legitimate aspirations for nationhood of millions of Taiwanese opposing the Japanese colonization of the Island."[72] Another Taiwanese church scholar, while reviewing church history in Taiwan, also blamed missionaries for only paying attention to the issue of conversion to Jesus Christ and therefore they could not dig deeply into the various levels of society and culture. He states that the missionaries were not able to effectively fight against political threats, unjust social systems, exploitation of labor, and unequal distribution of wealth among the people. Further, the missionaries could not level sharp criticism against contemporary rulers.[73]

The Presbyterian Church in Taiwan has, in many ways, been indigenized. The Taiwanese Presbyterians, for instance, do not have to rely on missionaries and missionary resources and they hold the leadership in the General Assembly, local churches, and church-related institutes. More importantly, they have their own distinct theological points of view. They have transformed their understanding of their identity with the context into political action. However, the Presbyterian Church has been rarely associated with other denominations or non-denominational churches. In fact, people who do not share their identity are not even the subject for Presbyterian evangelization. Perhaps partially because of this, the Presbyterian Church in Taiwan has not experienced any significant growth for the past fifteen years.

The Contextualization of the Catholic Church

The Catholic Church in Taiwan had a rather different experience during the war. Although from 1941 the foreign Catholic Dominican priests were restrained in their apostolic work and had no freedom of travel, the native Taiwanese Catholics did not have an opportunity to take over the church affairs. The Holy See, fearing the Japanese authority might reject a Chinese candidate, appointed a Japanese Catholic Father, Jose Satowaki, to become the new Apostolic Administrator of Formosa.[74] When Father Satowaki left for Japan after the war, a Taiwanese priest, Father Tu Minzheng (Raimundo Tho Hieng-chia) became pro-administrator until Father Jose Ma Arregui, OP, was named apostolic prefect in 1948. The Dominicans at this time targeted the Taiwanese, and therefore established a seminary in 1949 to cultivate native priests.[75]

Back to the Old Strategy of Evangelism

However, after the large flocks of Catholic priests and believers came with the Nationalist government to Taiwan before and after 1949, Taiwanese were no longer the main target of Catholic evangelism in Taiwan. When other Catholic orders and congregations, mostly moving from mainland China, began to share the apostolic work, Taiwan was gradually divided into several Catholic Prefectures (dioceses or special ecclesiastical regions). Northern Taiwan was assigned to the Disciples of the Lord, the Prefecture of Taizhong in central Taiwan to the Maryknoll Fathers, the Prefecture of Hualian to French missionaries, etc.[76] In 1952 Taiwan became the twenty-first Chinese Ecclesiastical Province. The newly-arrived priests were able to speak Mandarin, and they quite naturally focused their service on the over a million mainlanders and the aboriginal peoples who needed help both spiritually and materially.

These two groups of peoples were in a miserable situation and the Catholic Church began to offer various kinds of necessities of life, such as butter, flour, milk, second-hand clothes, and free kindergarten education. It was for this reason that many people at that time called Catholicism "powdered milkism" (*naifenjiao*) or "flourism" (*mianfenjiao*).[77] And the Church was known as the "flour church."[78] Many people attended the Church in order to get relief goods while Catholic Fathers used relief goods to attract people. As a Maryknoll Father confessed later:

> Some priests were careful not to use relief goods directly as a means of
> evangelizing. Others were not so scrupulous. All of us used relief as an indirect

means. Though no doubt there were exceptions, it is time this general truth was openly acknowledged. And it was a most efficacious means. It succeeded in putting the Church on the map. And it is just possible that the growth rate on the graphs is in exact proportion to the amount of flour and milk powder and old clothes and medicines distributed. The Church gave unstintingly, and while it gave it grew.[79]

This strategy was adopted from the nineteenth-century missionaries who did the same things in China in order to attract people to the church. "Rice Christians," the old term for those who sought handouts in the churches, appeared and would, sooner or later, drop their memberships once those handouts were not available or became unnecessary. Maybe for this reason, the Catholic Church has often cultivated a mentality of reliance among its church members. This reliance makes it difficult for the churches to develop self-support. The Catholic Church seldom releases information about their budget, but one Church scholar revealed in 1977 that 80 percent of expenditures for the Church in Taiwan came from "foreign aid."[80]

Catholic charity and apostolic service did attract many people into the church. The Catholic Church enjoyed quick growth during the first twenty years after the war. In 1945, there were about twelve to twenty clergy and 8,000 to 10,900 Catholics.[81] In 1949, the number of priests went up to forty while the number of believers rose to 12,000–13,000.[82] The membership went up every year and reached a record 305,793 in 1969.[83] However, as stated before, "the Catholic Church obtained most of its converts from the two most receptive groups—the Mountain and Mandarin communities. During the years of 1955–1958, for example, these two groups produced over 70 percent of the total baptisms, even though they constituted only 15 percent of the total population."[84]

Several problems later emerged that had their roots in the early period. Although the Catholic Church had been well received in Taiwan, the Church itself did not identify with this region. The Church preferred to use the term "China"—a gesture in tune with the Nationalist government (Republic of China).[85] For example, when the bishops decided to establish their own organization, they used the name the "Chinese Catholic Bishops' Conference" for their meeting, rather than the "Catholic Bishops' Conference in Taiwan." They chose the term "Chinese" because ten out of the sixteen bishops still maintained Apostolic Prefectures in China in 1967, although they had been assigned new prefectures in Taiwan.[86] A priest also pointed out that the "hierarchy is made up of bishops who were born on the mainland or in foreign countries; one semi-bishop, whose 'see' is the Pescadores, was born in Taiwan."[87]

Swanson also points out another similar problem. Because of the over-emphasis on the two peoples, the Church did not try to cultivate native priests. "As late as 1969 the Catholic Church still had produced only seven or eight native born Taiwanese priests out of a total of 809 priests on the island."[88] According to a Maryknoll source, the non-native priests, "were evenly divided into two groups—from mainland China and from Europe and America. Most priests from mainland China did not pay attention to the Taiwanese language while most foreign priests also used Mandarin. The Catholic Church in Taiwan was generally recognized as a foreigners' society."[89] There are reports that the Maryknoll priests' study of Taiwanese even incurred criticisms from Catholic Church circles.[90] According to a Catholic publication in 1974, "Of the Chinese Church personnel, about one in four was born in Taiwan; three out of four have come to Taiwan from the other thirty-four provinces of the Chinese Mainland."[91] These statistics may well illustrate a lack of contextualization of the Catholic Church in the first two decades after the war.

Cultural Contextualization

Although the early Jesuits, especially Matteo Ricci, enjoyed a high reputation for their efforts in the contextualization of Christianity in China, the Catholic leaders and scholars in Taiwan had not given much attention to the contextualization issue before 1970. Even though Vatican II (1962) encouraged the Church toward contextualization, few articles provided profound reflection in this field. Before 1970, only a few Chinese authors in church publications mentioned the relationship between Christianity and Chinese culture. The common tone in those articles was: 1) The Chinese people have been a religious people, or there was a religious element in Chinese culture; and 2) there was no conflict between the original religion of China and Christianity.[92] All of these authors felt that the Catholic Church had done little in the propagation of the Gospel through cultural accommodation, and they all urged Catholics to explore the points of contact between Christianity and Chinese culture.[93]

The term *benweihua* (inculturation) has become a catchword for Catholic contextualization in Taiwan since 1970. This development was directly influenced by a Hong Kong meeting in 1970 that was attended by representatives of the bishops in Taiwan, Japan, Korea, Vietnam, Hong Kong, and Macau. The reason these representative bishops were invited was that the peoples from the selected regions all shared Confucianism and the use of Chinese characters.[94] In their discussion, they concluded that the inculturation of theology was a necessary step in the propagation of the

Gospel. Therefore the bishops' conferences in each country should encourage studies and publications on this topic.[95] From that time on, the Chinese Bishops' Conference promoted discussion and research of inculturation.[96] This trend came to high tide when the Chinese Bishops' Conference published the "Draft Plan for the Establishment of the Chinese Local Church" in 1976, which states, "There are two stages for the propagation of the Christian religion: imitation and adaptation. The process from imitation to adaptation shows the sign of gradual maturity of the local churches. This so-called adaptation is the same issue as inculturation that has been often mentioned recently. The issue is the most basic and the most important link in the establishment of the local churches."[97] The definition of "inculturation," according to Father Zhang Chunshen (Aloysius B. Chang), is "to adopt modern Chinese thought and to carry forward the revelation of the Lord; and at the same time create a new Chinese culture by the contents of that revelation."[98]

"Inculturation" and "local churches" have become two major topics in Catholic publications since 1970 as well as in many seminars, lectures, and workshops. Basically, the various Catholic opinions concerning inculturation can be divided into two major categories: theory and practice. The theoretical approach involves working to create a Chinese theology. Most authors start by making comparisons between some common or similar concepts in both Christianity and Chinese culture. Some concepts discussed include "*xiao*" (filial piety), Confucian "*ren*" (benevolence) and Christian love, the relationship between "*tian*" (heaven) and "*ren*" (human being), "*tiandao*" (the way of heaven) and "*rendao*" (the way of human beings), meditation and *zen*, "*fuxing*" (restoration of nature) and devotion.[99]

Concerning practice, although the Vatican declared in 1939 that the veneration of Confucius, ceremonies in honor of deceased ancestors and other national customs, were purely civil in character and therefore permissible for Catholics, the Catholic Church, in fact, did not actively encourage these kinds of ceremonies. There had been no fixed pattern or regulations for the Catholic Fathers, Sisters, and Church members to follow. The breakthrough did not come until Cardinal Paul Yu Bin (Yu Pin) formally promoted honoring of Heaven and the ancestors in the Chinese Spring Festival in 1971.[100] The Liturgy Commission of the Chinese Bishops' Conference has also now translated all of the Roman Mass liturgies into Chinese. Some examples of cultural adaptation in the liturgy includes:

> There is a special Mass for the Chinese New Year. This is followed by a ceremony honoring the ancestors during which flowers, incense, wine and fruit may be offered. Chinese customs may be incorporated in Christian celebrations,

especially in the Funeral Rite. At Mass, mention of our Ancestors is included in the intercession for the Dead. A ceremony for visiting the graves on the Ching-Ming (Qing Ming) Festival, a Mass to be used on popular feasts of the local people and a special Mass for the country have been composed. There is a special Mass for old people to be celebrated on Chung-Yang (the ninth of the ninth month of the Lunar Calendar). A common festival of the Chinese Blessed and Martyrs is celebrated each year on Teachers' Day, September 28th.[101]

Father Zhang Chunshen further explains the Catholic position concerning the adoption of "*jizu*" (worshipping the ancestors) by highlighting these three points: 1) the Catholic Church has three kinds of rites: Latria for the Lord, Hyperdulia for the Virgin Mary, and Dulia for angels and saints. Catholic theology only requires the use of Latria for the Lord; the two other rites are relative and are used for creatures; 2) The Catholic Church has only one worship rite—the Mass—that is for the Lord. "*Jizu*" is held after the Mass and only expresses profound respect; 3) The purpose for *jizu* in the Catholic Church is to show the relationship between the Gospel and culture and it does not let this issue become an obstacle in the acceptance of the Gospel.[102] In a further adaptation, modern church buildings in Taiwan now adopt the Chinese style, not like earlier ones which sometimes used Spanish style (one in Tainan), or Gothic style (one in Gaoxiong).[103] Some authors also made suggestions for adapting a Catholic funeral to the Taiwanese context.[104]

The promotion of cultural contextualization did not have any positive effect on the church growth. On the contrary, the Church began to lose members in 1970, from the highest figure of 305,793 in 1969, to the lowest figure of 276,591 in 1979. The Church was alarmed by the decline and began self-examination. The Church, on the one hand, blamed external factors: "The migration of the population to industrial centers and the shift from rural to city life results in a consequent process of deep cultural change, secularization, and autonomy from traditional customs and former social controls." On the other hand, they also blamed a lack of cultural contextualization: "The approach in evangelization is not adapted to the new situation, and the process of re-adaptation through concerted action in the Church is too slow. The witness of Christian values is weak and blurred by the image of a western world known through mass media. . . . (T)here is widespread feeling that adaptations were always halfway and progressed too slowly. Some minor ceremonies have given only a superficial touch of Chinese flavor."[105]

In order to explore the problem of evangelism in Taiwan, the Chinese Bishops' Conference financed a three-year project to conduct an island-wide survey and published its report in 1987. The issue of inculturation received conflicting responses. Most Fathers, Sisters, and church leaders were in favor of inculturation which, in their opinions, will not only transform Chinese customs into Church liturgies, but will also bring about the integration of Christ's spirit and Chinese culture. But there were also various negative opinions toward inculturation. These criticisms were based on the belief that local customs and culture contain superstitious elements and inculturation will cause Christianity to lose its tradition and characteristics.[106]

One interesting point is reflected in the survey. Some Catholic Fathers pointed out there are differences between Chinese culture and Taiwanese culture and, therefore, inculturation might cause problems in racial relations between mainlanders and Taiwanese. Additionally, inculturation with Chinese culture would have no appeal to the Taiwanese.[107] However, the survey also suggested that the Catholic Church has not yet preached the Gospel to the Taiwanese people who constitute the majority of the population, and many Church leaders are not able to speak Taiwanese.[108] Although the survey faithfully reflected the tension existing in Taiwanese society, this tension did not receive much attention in the survey.[109] At that time most Catholic publications in Taiwan carried news, reports and articles on the Pope's messages to the Chinese Bishops' Conference in the 1970s and 1980s. Pope John Paul II, on several occasions, expressed his hope that the Catholic churches in Taiwan could serve as a bridge to help Catholic members in mainland China.[110]

A Realistic Turn in the 1990s?

The decade of the 1990s, especially the past several years, have been troubling times for Taiwan. On the domestic side, Taiwanese consciousness has been on the rise and has caused great tension and disputes concerning the question of whether Taiwan should move towards independence or towards unification with China. The people's sense of national identity have soured ethnic relations, have spurred factional power struggles in the political parties, and have become problematic at every election time. Taiwan also faces challenges from the international community, particularly constant pressure and coercion from the People's Republic of China. Taiwan not only struggles for survival, but must also deal with the serious problem of gradual economic dependence on the trade with China. This turbulent context has also influenced the Catholic Church in Taiwan.

The Catholic Church in Taiwan, in fact, has again begun to reexamine itself, its direction, and the issue of inculturation. More and more articles appearing recently in Church publications criticize the Catholic Church's failure to identify with Taiwanese society. For example, Liu Jinchang states frankly that the Catholic Church in Taiwan has adopted a mentality of "Greater China" instead of using a more realistic point of view, that is, identifying itself with Taiwanese society.[111] Liang Jinwen states that the Catholic Church in Taiwan, in order to keep in tune with the needs of the Nationalist government and mainland believers, has attempted to represent the whole of China and has neglected the Taiwanese and aboriginal peoples.[112] Several articles call on the Church to show more concern for the aboriginal peoples. Aboriginal peoples have suffered because of disadvantages in wealth, education, and social status. The articles point out that although the aboriginal believers constitute about one-third of the total Catholic population in Taiwan, the first aboriginal bishop was not consecrated until August 1998. These articles also complained that the Church has not shown sufficient concern for the life, culture, social status, and employment disadvantages of aboriginal peoples.[113]

A major transition for the Catholic Church in Taiwan began in 1998. In that year the Chinese Catholic Bishops' Conference (*zhongguo zhujiaotuan*), under the recommendation of the Vatican, changed its name to the Chinese Regional Bishops' Conference in Taiwan (*Taiwan zhujiaotuan*). Additionally, in 1998 the Pope decided to let Taiwan have a cardinal. These measures seem to suggest a move in a realistic direction; the Vatican will now downplay the role of the Catholic Church in Taiwan as a bridge to mainland China, and it will also allow the Church in Taiwan to pay more attention to the Taiwanese people and domestic affairs.[114] The new Bishops' Conference in Taiwan released a statement in which it explains why it changed the name. In the last paragraph, the statement urges people not to politicize the name issue, or the Church will not be able to "correct the mind of the people of our nation, [teaching them to] use a true heart and sincerity to love our own country, to love Taiwan, and to maintain a way of life which is considerate of the [local] people. We need realistically to work hard for this land—Taiwan. Based on the Gospel, the Catholic Church has always expressed its love for Taiwan's society and offered service. The reason we changed our name is to express our willingness to offer more services and have deeper roots in Taiwan's society."[115] The message clearly indicates that the Catholic Church in Taiwan desires to adopt a new direction in which it will identify with Taiwan, transforming itself from identifying with Chinese culture to identifying with Taiwanese culture.

Today, there are only occasional articles in Church publications that encourage the study of contact points between Christianity and Chinese culture—a dramatic contrast with the numerous articles before 1990. This contrast demonstrates that the old generation of Church leaders is gradually fading away.[116] And the old watchwords, such as "inculturation" and "local churches," are now applied to the establishment of a Taiwanese Church.[117]

Conclusion

When we study the issue of the contextualization of Christianity, we can find different aspects of the contextualization, or, so to say, various kinds of contextualization. Whenever Christianity has been introduced into a non-native place, Christian churches will adopt different strategies to cope with the new contexts. Based on the above examination, we can conclude that the contextualization is not necessarily related to church growth. The contextualization strategy of a certain church, in fact, only reflects the degree of that church's understanding of its context. Contextualization also reflects the church's understanding of how the Gospel must be preached and defended in that particular culture as well as its justification of their efforts of evangelism.

The examples from the Presbyterian Church and the Catholic Church in Taiwan show two different ways that contextualization developed. This paper uses the term "political contextualization" to describe the contextualization strategies of the Presbyterian Church in Taiwan. The Church transforms its identity with the local language, people, and culture into political thought and action. The Church, in fact, saw itself as a political spokesperson for the Taiwanese. Their protest against the Nationalist government and their statements in seeking a better political environment have become their Christian "witness." This radical development of the Presbyterian Church in this aspect has also influenced their relationship with the foreign missionaries. The Church has become so Taiwanese-centered that the foreign missionaries do not have much of a role to play in the direction of the Church.

The Catholic Church provides a different picture. Like the Presbyterian Church, the Catholic Church also emphasizes the importance of contextualization. But in the Catholic version, contextualization is not political, but rather contextualization means the church attempts to identify and highlight points of contact between Christianity and Chinese culture. It approaches the issue of contextualization through cultural contacts. The first Church leaders after the war were mostly composed of mainlanders and China-related missionaries. Thus they were naturally inclined to favor the use of Mandarin language and to honor Chinese culture. Further, Vatican II, and its following instructions with its call on Church leaders to emphasize "inculturation" and "local churches," encouraged Catholic leaders to give strong support and promotion to search for points of contact between

Christianity and Chinese culture. Now, after twenty years of efforts in this respect, the Church recognizes the change of the context, and has begun to pay attention to the Taiwanese context. In this context Chinese elements are gradually decreasing. During these years, even though the Church does not object to its members worshipping the ancestors, and has reformed the liturgy, these efforts at contextualization have not helped in the expansion of the Church.

The context in Taiwan has been in a rapidly changing state during the past five decades. Taiwan society has changed dramatically. The churches within have done their best to cope accordingly with these changes. These efforts in contextualization, in fact, are a major characteristic of the churches. Looking into the future, it seems that Taiwan will continue to evolve, pushed by both international and domestic aspects and pressures, and the churches will also continue to interact with the context. Whether these efforts at contextualization will result in church growth, however, is difficult to predict. The judgment as to what kind of contextualization is best for the Church and for society must be left for future historians to make.

Christianity and China:
Toward Further Dialogue

PHILIP L. WICKERI

A few years ago, the Church of Norway decided to host a conference to celebrate the entry of Christianity into that country. They invited churches from different parts of the world to share in their ceremonies, and they were particularly interested in having churches from the various countries to which Norway had sent Christian missionaries in the nineteenth and twentieth centuries. And so they invited the China Christian Council to send a delegation to celebrate with them 1,000 years of Christianity in Norway. The China Christian Council graciously accepted the invitation. In his return letter to the presiding bishop of the Norwegian church, the president of the China Christian Council noted in passing that that very same year, Chinese Christians were celebrating the 1,360th anniversary of the arrival of Christianity in their country.

The conference hosted by the University of San Francisco on which this volume is based attempted to survey those 1,000 and more years of history. Scholars from around the world spent two and a half days discussing selected aspects of Christianity in China and attempting to peer into the future. We looked at our subject from above and from below. We had an overview from the beginning. And now I have been asked to write a review from the end.

In broad strokes, John Witek opened our conference with a survey of the encounter between Christianity and China since the Tang dynasty. Following this, we discussed twenty-one papers on a wide array of subjects, eighteen of which are included in this volume, along with an additional paper by Jean-Paul Wiest. Taken together, the papers represent an interdisciplinary approach to the theme, with presentations not only by historians, theologians, and social scientists, but also by specialists in architecture, art, and education.

Some of these papers explain how Christian missionaries contributed to the development of sinology, not only in Western Europe and North

America, but in Russia and Hungary as well. Others show how an idealized image of China was appropriated in seventeenth- and eighteenth-century Europe, and also how the Jesuits presented an idealized image of Europe in roughly the same period in China. There was a review of recent research on Christianity in China, as well as a review of historical perspectives on China in American Protestantism. Meeting in a Jesuit institution, it is understandable that fully one third of our papers were concerned with the Jesuits, primarily in the Ming and Qing periods. Although only one paper dealt with the period before 1550, at least a third of the papers look toward the future. The title of the conference was "China and Christianity: Burdened Past, Hopeful Future." However, quite a number of papers reflect upon different aspects of the past that were hopeful; and as much as we would like to speak about a hopeful future, it appears from the papers collected here that the future of the encounter between Christianity and China will carry its own burdens.

In this summation, I want to suggest ways of bringing the subject of our inquiry together by reviewing some of the connections which can be made which indicate directions for future research. This is an attempt to look for commonalities in our cultures and in the papers which have been presented. It gets back to what Matteo Ricci intended, and as William T. de Bary suggested in his comments at the conference, this should be part of the purpose of our scholarship. I will also note some aspects of the encounter which have been remarkable for their absence.

Universal Teaching from the West?

John Witek's paper raises the question of whether a universal teaching from the West can ever become a Chinese religion. The expressions of Christianity which we reflect upon in the West today are seldom referred to as universal teachings. Rather, our focus is on contextualization and the particularity of all our reflections in the pluralistic situation in which we find ourselves. For Christians, the universal has to become particular if we take the Incarnation seriously. When Chinese scholars asked early Jesuit missionaries how Christianity could possibly be a universal teaching if they had never heard of it, they were raising a similar question.

The issue of the "foreignness" or "Westernness" of Christianity in China comes up again and again in this volume. It is a question which has also been raised about Christianity in China itself, as well as in other parts of Asia, Africa, and Latin America, a question which is involved in all the current debates over contextualization and inculturation, and the shift in the axis of Christian initiatives from the North to the South, and from the West to the East. Can a teaching originating in first century Palestine which claims to have a universal message for people everywhere become a faith or a way of understanding which is also Chinese? And if it becomes Chinese, will it still be acceptable and recognizable as a universal teaching, in China or in the West?

The answers to these questions depend upon what it means to be Chinese and to be Christian, and how one relates to the other culturally and intellectually, politically and socially, religiously and theologically. The papers presented at the conference offer very different responses to these questions.

One perspective is concerned with the intellectual and cultural dialogue between Christianity and China. Li Tiangang presents an excellent survey of the role of the Jesuits in promoting a "Chinese Renaissance" in the Ming and Qing periods. Through their cooperation with Confucianism, writes Li, the Jesuits promoted the ideal of a globalization of culture, and they contributed methodologically to Ming-Qing study and research, particularly in their analysis of texts. In so doing, they were able to overcome their own "foreignness." No wonder why Zhang Kaiyuan writes in his paper that the Jesuits are still a "focal point and hot point" in the study of Christianity in China.

According to Erik Zürcher, the Jesuits presented an idealized image of Europe in China. Theirs was a missionary construct, with an implicit criticism of Chinese culture, and this was part of their message. Europe, in this view, was a society enjoying "stability, peace and order;" one promoting charity and a sense of caring; a society which emphasized "examinations and degrees;" and a "bookman's paradise." Europe was presented as a utopia, "an ideal and perfect commonwealth." Although this view was never accepted at the Qing court, it did help to define the Christian convert's view of the West.

There are interesting parallels today in the attitudes of some Christian converts in China. I have heard my own country extolled as a Christian paradise, where everyone is free because our culture has been shaped by Christianity. Most American scholars would reject such a view outright. But I have also heard America dismissed in China as a land in which there is neither theology nor respect for intellectual achievement. This makes it necessary to go to Europe to drink from the wells of a culture that produced a Karl Barth or a Hans Uhr von Balthasar. There are some Chinese who believe that the universal teaching from the West can produce an ideal and perfect commonwealth, at least on the theological level, despite the fact that most European theologians have given up this idea.

This is why it is always necessary to pose questions not only about the nature of cultural exchanges, but also about what is actually exchanged in the encounter between different cultures. So much can be represented even in the giving of a horse, as Lauren Arnold reminded us in her conference presentation. Her paper is not included here, but she has published her findings in an attractive and well researched book.[1]

Actions and ideas convey different meanings in different cultures, and so the process of cultural transmission needs to be explored. Nicolas Standaert's paper is an outstanding survey of various forms of cultural transmission. He analyzes Christianity in Ming-Qing China as a laboratory of cultural exchange. The encounter cannot be judged simply according to its success or failure, but rather it must be viewed in the multifaceted and deeply textured nature of the exchange. Standaert's methodology is based on the importance of texts in cultural transmission; the different sources (Chinese and European) describing the encounter; and the different attempts to understand the historical context. It is a methodology, he concludes, which resembles the exploration of the "clouds" of Chinese paintings, more than the precise working of the European clocks and instruments which the Jesuits brought with them.

A very different method of cultural analysis, with a very different purpose, is employed by Ralph Covell, drawing on the work of the missionary anthropologist Charles Kraft. Covell is also interested in the transmission of religious ideas, but with a missiological purpose. In his careful study, he has focused on minority groups in southwest China, and the revitalization which Christianity brought to some of their communities, culturally and religiously. Covell is not interested in texts—most of the minorities he has studied were not literate cultures—but in contexts and experiences. And so his categories are receptivity and resistance to the Christian message, suggesting more of a one-way transmission process than that proposed by Standaert's work on Christianity in the Ming-Qing encounter.

The case of Christianity among China's minority Korean population and in Korea itself may provide yet a third example of cultural and religious transmission. This is one area in which further comparative study is needed. Unlike minority groups in China's southwest, Koreans in the northeast have a long literate culture. It would be instructive to compare the Korean encounter with Christianity (and with Confucianism) with that of China. Christianity came to Korea through China, long before the first Protestant missionaries arrived, and today northeast China remains an area of intense interest among Korean Christians. What is going on in terms of Christianity and cultural transmission among Koreans in China? The study of Chinese

Christianity in Korea itself is growing in importance, and we need more contact with scholars there.

Nationalism and Cosmopolitanism

In a conference paper not included in this volume, Shi Jinghuan discusses another aspect of the Christian encounter with China. She is interested in the theme of nationalism and cosmopolitanism as it was reflected in the Chinese Christian colleges in the years before 1949. She observes that "in some ways, the tension of nationalism and cosmopolitanism was displayed more clearly at Christian colleges than any place else," and her paper demonstrates the ways in which the two were related. My own work on Bishop Ding Guangxun (K. H. Ting) indicates how nationalism and cosmopolitanism were related during his years at St. John's. Many church leaders of his generation were both nationalists and cosmopolitans, fully committed to the national salvation movement in China, yet also at home in the ecumenical movement, and therefore able to move back and forth easily between both worlds. The question this raises for the future is whether a new generation of Chinese Christian intellectuals will be able to move between these two worlds as easily.

Peter Tze Ming Ng discusses the "cultural knot" of pre-1949 Christian higher education in China in another conference paper not included in this volume. His interest is in the religious studies and Chinese studies programs at the Christian colleges, and the "cultural knot" is his way of speaking about the contextualization of Christianity in China. In Ng's reconsideration of the mission legacy of the Christian colleges, he draws on the "fulfillment theory"—the Christ who comes to fulfill not destroy culture—as a way of untying the knot. Theologically and culturally, however, this theory has serious limitations in societies characterized by cultural and religious pluralism. It assumes the superiority of the Christian cultural expression. The question of what it means to be a Christian college in a pluralist society, and the related question of Christian identity formation in a multireligious setting, needs further study in the future.

In his extensive survey of research on Christianity in China, Zhang Kaiyuan observes that cultural exchanges should "have a friendly spirit of communication on an equal basis." He cites the example of the late James T. C. Liu, who was a graduate of one of the Christian colleges, and who, while at Princeton University, became very interested in the promotion of dialogue on Christianity in China. Liu studied at Yenching University in the years of Leighton Stuart. Shi Jinghuan wants us to see and judge Leighton Stuart according to the standards of his own times. But the evaluation of Stuart is a very complicated and sensitive issue in China, and by no means a clear-cut issue in North America, either. The issue in the late 1940s for many of Stuart's students, friends, and colleagues was whether he should have accepted the appointment of American Ambassador to China in the first place. Some argued then that this confused cultural, religious, and political categories and saw Stuart's decision as a mistake. When he left Yenching, Leighton Stuart was in a sense saying farewell to the approach to cultural exchange with China that he had spent all of his life promoting.

The late Ran Sailer spent thirty years teaching at Yenching and was one who disagreed with Stuart's choice. Sailer was one of the first Americans invited back to China after the visit of President Nixon. While there, he was asked if he was sorry that Yenching was no more. He replied that while he still believed in everything Yenching had stood for, he hoped that the "Yenching spirit" would be kept alive wherever its alumni/ae served. This is also the hope of Yenching graduates who have formed their own Alumni/ae Association.

The paper by Jean-Paul Wiest which is contained in this volume deepens our understanding of the Catholic contribution to education in China over the last 150 years. The contrast he makes between the role of Catholic educational institutions in China before 1949 and the new opportunities for Catholic education since the 1980s is especially important. Wiest shows that the role of Catholics from China and overseas in the area of education has been transformed, but that they continue to make contributions to society based upon the new opportunities presented to them. Like the "Yenching spirit," the Catholic spirit continues to inspire contributions to secularized education in China.

Christian Contributions to Sinology

One aspect of the encounter between Christianity and China which is discussed in a number of papers is the contribution it has made to Western sinology. In her paper, Claudia von Collani discusses the ecumenical appropriation of sinological information in seventeenth- and eighteenth-century Germany: "It is an interesting fact that China influenced German sinology, philosophy, and enlightenment via the Catholic mission of Jesuits to Protestant theologians and philosophers." Von Collani discusses the proposal for a program of scientific and cultural exchange made by Leibniz. It sounds very idealistic, but it is interesting that he hoped such an approach would lead to reconciliation between Protestants and Catholics in Europe. On the scientific level, Leibniz's approach resonates with the exchanges between the French Académie Royale des Sciences and the Chinese Imperial

Court described in Han Qi's paper. In both cases, science was to become a means of improving life, abolishing differences, and creating mutual understanding. Although there may still be support for this approach in our scientific communities—the recent American controversy over nuclear secrets notwithstanding—it seems an incredible idea in our post-Enlightenment and post-modern age.

Dinara Doubrovskaia's paper addresses a subject which has been neglected in the West, the encounter between Orthodox Christianity and China. This is a subject which is important in its own right, but also for comparison with Roman Catholic and Protestant missions. She provides a useful survey of early Orthodox mission work in China. Doubrovskaia's suggestion that the first representatives of Orthodoxy may have come to China as prisoners of war should give us pause in our evaluation of missionaries who were more often associated with conquerors. It is a difference which has been described by Kosuke Koyama as one between a "crusading mind" and a "crucified mind" in mission.[2] Since so much mission work has been of the former kind, it is no wonder that the Christian mission has sometimes been described as an extension of the crusades.

Péter Vámos has presented a fascinating view of Hungarian missionaries in China, another subject which has been neglected in research on Christianity in China thus far. The Hungarian interest was in part stimulated by the theory of the Asian origins of Hungarians, which Vámos discusses at some length. It would be instructive to compare Chinese and Hungarian accounts of this theory of origins as another perspective on the Christian encounter in China.

The Hungarian Jesuit best known to contemporary students of China is Father Laszlo Ladany (1914–1990), founder of the *China News Analysis*, who did a great deal to shape Western perceptions of China from the 1950s through the 1980s. There needs to be a reassessment and evaluation of the role of the so-called Christian China watchers including Ladany, who were active in the West from the 1950s to the early 1980s. They had widely different lenses through which to view China, from the strongly anti-Communist to the committed Christian Leftist, and everything in between. There has thus far not been a systematic study of this encounter, and it may still be too early for a reassessment.[3] However, it should be put on the agenda for future study for several reasons. First, it helped shape the outside world's view of China in the 1960s and 1970s, especially among Christians in Europe and North America. It also laid the foundation for the encounter between Chinese churches and churches overseas in the early 1980s. Finally, it was an ecumenical effort, something that Leibniz had hoped for, but which we do not see much of today. This period of Christian China study culminated in the conference held in Montreal in 1981, "God's Call to a New Beginning."

Popular Christianity

Research on the cultural importance of Christianity in China involves a great deal more than the study of texts, mission history, and Confucian-Christian encounters. In different ways, both Ryan Dunch and Richard Madsen have argued for greater attention to popular and indigenous Christianity in China.[4]

Both Dunch and Madsen argue that we need to address questions associated with popular culture and not only elite culture. Madsen's interest is in popular Christianity on its own terms, what Zhuo Xinping terms "folk" Christianity. This is Christianity as seen "from below" not "from above," an important area of research among Western scholars looking at Christianity in many parts of the world. In China, folk Christianity, whether Catholic or Protestant, is expressed in experiences of healing, personal salvation, and rural Christian communities. It tends to be led by the laity not the clergy, a phenomenon which is easier to understand in Protestantism than in Catholicism. Rural folk Catholic practice should not be regarded as "deviant" or "inferior," argues Madsen, because it is in itself an authentic form of religious experience. Madsen adds that any rapprochement between Beijing and the Vatican will not settle the problem of Catholic "heterodoxy" because folk-Catholicism has its own social base in rural communities.

Robert Entenmann puts this same subject in historical perspective. His paper is a fascinating study of how one Chinese priest was affected by the Rites Controversy in the eighteenth century, and how he responded in the practice of his ministry. The priest, Father Andreas Ly, was deeply suspicious of the Jesuits' approach to accommodation, but the Chinese Rites Controversy forced him into the impossible choice over whether he was to respond as a Chinese or as a Christian. Father Ly chose the latter, but the broader question was whether the choice should ever be necessary. Father Ly's concern, according to Entenmann, "was that popular indigenous religion might corrupt Christian practice." In other words, Ly was not particularly open to the folk Christianity which Madsen argues for.

For Chinese Protestants, the issue of popular Christianity is no less complex, and the choices have at times been no less difficult. In her paper, Jessie Lutz offers us a broad historical overview of Protestantism in China, which provides a creative new approach to the periodization of the Chinese Protestant experience. She speaks of the loss of consensus in the Protestant missionary enterprise in the early twentieth century due to the Fundamentalist-Modernist controversy. In fact, the origin of this dispute is related to the Protestant missionary experience in China. In 1920, a Canadian professor of the Old Testament visited China to survey the situation of missionaries there. When he returned, he published an article in the *Princeton Theological Review* which charged that most Western missionaries in China were "Modernists."[5] As a result, this controversy was imposed upon China by North American missionaries, and it continues to cast a long shadow over Chinese as well as North American Protestantism.

It also bears a major responsibility for the institutional fragmentation of Chinese Christianity today which is so well described by Dunch. His description of the Chinese Protestant community as "fragile, fragmented, and flourishing" could be used with minor variations to describe Christianity almost anywhere in the modern world. According to Dunch, "the proliferation of new movements and sects has been one of the major trends within Chinese Protestantism since the 1920s." It is part of what mission historian Andrew Walls has termed the "great transformation" of Christianity all over the world, the recession of Christianity from the North and the West, and the transplantation of Christianity, with varying degrees of success, to countries in the South.[6] And yet, the proliferation of new movements and sects is a problem for Protestants who are concerned about the unity of the church and ecumenical witness. "Institutional fragmentation" may be one trend, but there are also counter trends, represented by the ecumenical movement and interdenominational cooperation.

Terms are important here, although I am not speaking of what Confucians term the rectification of names (*zhengming*). Different disciplines often use the same terms in different ways, so it is important for them to learn to speak to one another. Orthodox and heterodox, denominational and indigenous Protestantism, elite and popular Christianity: the meanings of these terms must be decided contextually. In scholarly exchanges about Christianity in China, all of these terms are preferable to "official" and "patriotic" versus "unofficial" and "underground" churches, which are still in common usage in the Western media. Zhuo Xinping makes the helpful distinction among "elite Christians," "church Christians" and "folk Christians" in contemporary China. He also observes that the Christian identity of the latter is not at all clear, and this is a reason why we cannot all be so sanguine about what is happening to rural Christianity in the Chinese countryside, however attractive it may be as a subject of research. The question of the orthodoxy of Christian beliefs cannot be entirely put aside, even as we try to understand Christianity in the diversity of its ecclesiological, confessional, and theological expressions.

A distinction should also be drawn between "heterodox" and "heretical" (*xiejiao* and *yiduan*), for the terms are often conflated in Chinese, reflecting the cultural differences over church-state relations in Chinese and Western contexts. Not all political heterodoxies are heretical in Christian terms, and not all theological heresies are politically disruptive. It is important to recognize that in China, the church and the state sometimes have a common interest in opposing heterodox and heretical movements. It is important to stress this point, because theologians and scholars in the West tend to give the term "heresy" a very wide birth, if they think it still has any meaning at all.

Christianity and Chinese Cultures

I have already referred to Zhuo Xinping's excellent paper on "Cultural Christians," if we may still use that term. He has made important clarifications in our understanding of how the term is used. The phenomenon he describes has attracted a great deal of interest in Hong Kong and overseas, but relatively little interest in China. Zhuo argues that the phenomenon has been overestimated, and I cannot help thinking that this is at least partly due to the romantic notions that many people in the West still entertain about the prospects of "christianizing" China. Zhuo observes that it was K. H. Ting who coined the term, mainly as a way of affirming the interest in or sympathy for Christianity among Chinese intellectuals. Others in the Chinese Church have referred to these intellectuals as "Chinese Nicodemuses" or "Christians without a Church."

There are a number of Chinese intellectuals who are cultured non-Christians, yet interested in Christianity. This is certainly preferable to the "cultured despisers" of Christianity to whom F. W. Schliermacher addressed some of his essays. It is not only in China that non-Christians have developed a sympathetic interest in Christian theology and Christian ideas. A strong case can be made for the study and even the writing of Christian theology by non-Christians. The American theologian Schubert Ogden is one who has argued this point. In India, Japan, and other Asian countries, there are also many prominent non-Christians who have made contributions to the theological enterprise, developing insights from Christian teaching that church-related scholarship never would or never could.

Different faiths and worldviews can in this way become somewhat mixed-up, or to put it more positively, they can learn from one another. Reason and revelation, as Paul Rule observes in his paper, are not mutually exclusive categories. He argues that "all Christian theologies are in a sense "hybrid" since they involve the explication of a revelation in a specific philosophical language and a specific cultural context. . . . " No theology is fixed and determined. The danger of theological constructs in the period of Christendom was that they did not recognize their own borrowings, and thought that their "orthodoxies" were universal. The term "hybridity" is on a continuum with terms like contextualization and inculturation, but where the latter puts the accent on the acceptance of one cultural context and opposition to another, hybridity recognizes the interculturality of all ideas, and therefore suggests a form of cultural transmission which goes back and forth. This is precisely what Standaert argues for in his paper.

Wai-ching Wong, a theologian from another part of China (Hong Kong) has spoken of Asian theology as a form of "post-colonial theory."[7] By this she means that the idea of "Asianness" in theology is both a strategy of resistance to Western universalism—sometimes disguised as Christian universalism—and also an idea to be contested in the construction of theology. It means that theological ideas are open to negotiation or dialogue with respect to different questions, different cultures, different societies, and different ways of doing theology. In this way, "hybridization" becomes a new theological method, one which has implications for the future of Chinese theology.

Hybridity is also a way of speaking of eclecticism in the architecture of Christian colleges, which Dong Li discussed in his conference paper, which is not included in the present volume. We can see various kinds of eclecticism today in architecture all over the world. It would be interesting to study the eclectic architecture of the Tao Fong Shan Christian Centre in Hong Kong, and determine what this represents in terms of different forms of cultural transmission. This center is the base from which Liu Xiaofeng is now promoting "theology in Chinese" (*Hanyu shenxue*), another form of hybridity, through an ambitious program of translation, publication, and research. Tao Fong Shan is also a conference and retreat center, originally a mission to Chinese Buddhists, designed by a Scandinavian architect, in an eclectic combination of Buddhist, Christian, and imperial styles. We could also look at the Maryknoll buildings in New York and Stanley through similar lenses, or even the newly constructed churches in many parts of China.

Hong Kong and Taiwan are other centers for eclectic cultural transmission in the Chinese speaking world. We have heard provocative discussions of Christianity in these areas by Beatrice Leung and Peter Chenmain Wang. Leung's subject is church-state relations in post-1997 Hong Kong, and she provides a useful survey and overview. She argues that Christians in Hong Kong have serious concerns about the future. This is in part because the Church in colonial Hong Kong enjoyed a privileged status, in comparison to Buddhists or Taoists for example. In colonial Hong Kong, Christians were often "elites and middlemen" to use Rev. Carl Smith's phrase.[8] In this sense, the "downgrading" of status which Leung speaks of needs to be put in perspective. This is not to minimize potential difficulties, but to recognize the crucial need for church and state in Hong Kong to redefine their relationships for the future.

Peter Wang has done us all a great service in his lucid exploration of Christianity in modern Taiwan, viewed in terms of the process of contextualization. The term was actually coined by a Taiwanese in the 1950s, Shoki Coe, formerly associated with Tainan Theological Seminary.[9] Taiwan has been a neglected area of study at our China gatherings in the past. Tracing what he terms the "political contextualization" of the Presbyterian Church in Taiwan, and the shift in the "cultural contextualization" of the Catholic Church (from Chinese to Taiwanese emphases in inculturation), Wang raises important issues which have implications for Christianity in other parts of Asia as well. Korea can again be cited as an example, because there are similar theological issues involved for both Catholics and Presbyterians there. After several decades of phenomenal growth, the Presbyterians in Korea are now experiencing membership losses, although the numbers of both Catholics and Buddhists are on the rise. Such comparisons have implications for our understanding of inculturation as a strategy, and for the broader process of intercultural transmission.

Towards Further Dialogue

By way of conclusion, I want to suggest three aspects of the encounter between Christianity and China which are remarkable for their absence in the papers presented in this volume. I make these observations primarily to suggest future areas for research and reflection, and fully understand that that others could come up with equally valid lists of what I have been omitting in this very subjective listing.

(1) Women in the Experience of Christianity in China. Our conference was held at the Lone Mountain campus of the University of San Francisco, which was once a campus of the Sisters of the Sacred Heart. Sacred Heart Sisters, and other religious women, have been extremely important in missionary work in China. We need to do more work on women's missionary orders in China. (And as important as the Jesuits are, we need more work on other orders of religious men as well.) Women were also important in Protestant missions. There were, by the end of the nineteenth

century, more women missionaries than men, but they have not been adequately studied.[10]

In every church in the world, there are more women than men, and there are a whole host of questions which historians, social scientists, and theologians are asking about this phenomenon. For the most part, however, the role of women in Chinese Christian history is also an area which has not been well researched.[11] Questions about the voice of women in the Chinese Church, the leadership of women in popular or folk Christianity, and other questions involving gender and Christianity in China deserve much more attention.

(2) The Bible in the Study of Chinese Christianity. In order to study theology and Christian thought in China, we need to look more closely at the ways in which the Bible has been and is being interpreted. Biblical scholars tell us that the sixteenth-century Reformation put Christian scripture into a polemical context, because scriptural authority was used to counter ecclesiastical authority. Since then, in Christianity all over the world, there has been an uneasy tension between biblical authority and ecclesial authority, each defining and limiting the other. We have seen this tension in Protestant Christianity in China, and it may also be a factor in Chinese Catholic popular religion, as it is in other parts of the world.

A conference on the Bible in modern China was held in Jerusalem several years ago, but Biblical interpretation has not received serious attention in the study of Chinese Christianity.[12] There has been very little scholarly study of the Bible in mainland China, either by Chinese Christians or by intellectuals involved in religious studies. The Bible needs to be studied as part of the whole process of contextualization and cultural transmission in Chinese Christianity, and in order to clarify the questions which have been explored in theology both inside and outside of China. Rule has spoken of the value of reader response criticism in understanding the Qing *literati*. This is relevant to the contemporary scene as well. Other tools of Biblical interpretation which deal with the context, the text, and the Biblical reader will also be useful in understanding the variety of Christian communities which have developed in China historically.

Dunch observes that the "lack of culturally embedded Christian referents in China" make it easy for Christians to interpret the Bible allegorically. This is one aspect of the creative process of Biblical interpretation in China. For example, the works of the Protestant thinker Jia Yuming have now been republished in Zhejiang, and he has been a defining voice in allegorical interpretation, and has a strong influence among rural Chinese Protestants. But there is another side of the argument as well. Allegorical interpretation also makes it easier to interpret the Bible incorrectly, in ways far from that which the authors intended or which the church has traditionally accepted. This is why it has by and large been rejected as a method in serious Bible scholarship in the West. This brings us back to the question of orthodoxy, and the legitimate range of diversity within Christianity. But we must know something about the methodology of critical Biblical interpretation even to understand what such terms as "orthodoxy" and "diversity" imply in this discussion.

(3) Dialogue with Chinese Christians themselves. Imagine if a university in Japan were to organize a conference on "Buddhism in America: Universal Teaching from the East." They would invite Buddhist scholars from East and West, including Buddhists from Asia. But it would be very odd if there were no Buddhists from North America to present papers reflecting their side of the encounter.

There is a difficulty in establishing a dialogue between intellectuals in China and Chinese Christians. If the Christian's only concern is the question of salvation and redemption, then there can be no meaningful dialogue. If the intellectual has a condescending attitude towards a Chinese Christian for his/her lack of education, then there can be no meaningful dialogue, either. The obstacles to dialogue with and not only about Chinese Christians are very real, but the attempt is important nonetheless. At our conference, we had Christian scholars presenting papers from Hong Kong and Taiwan, and a few Christians from mainland China were with us for part of the time. We all hope that in future such gatherings, there can be greater involvement of Chinese Christians.

This is a creative time for the study of Christianity in China. At the conference from which the papers in this volume have been drawn, all participants made significant contributions to this dialogue. The papers which are collected here have tried to promote mutual understanding, contextualization, and a deepened interest in the social role of Christianity in China. I think we can all agree with Zhuo when he says: "For the future of Christianity in China, there is still a need for a " 'prophet voice,' a 'servant spirit,' a sincere dialogue, and a tolerant sympathy." This is also important for scholarship about Christianity everywhere in the new millennium.

Notes

Uhalley: Burdened Past, Hopeful Future

1. Sayers, *Creed or Chaos?* p. 25.
2. "China Condemns U.S. on Criticisms," *AOL* October 7, 1999.
3. Segal, "Does China Matter?" *Foreign Affairs* (September–October 1999): 24–36.

Witek: Universal Teaching from the West

1. Geffré and Spae, eds., *China as a Challenge to the Church*, p. viii.
2. Gal. 3:27–28. Similar texts of St. Paul are "It was in one Spirit that all of us, whether Jew or Greek, slave or free, were baptized into one body" (1 Cor. 12:13) and "Just as in Adam all men die, so in Christ all men will be brought to life" (1 Cor 15:21–22).
3. Poggi, "Cristologia e Chiesa Sirorientale," pp. 9–16.
4. Forte, "The Edict of 638 Allowing the Diffusion of Christianity in China," pp. 349–73.
5. See Roh, "Research into the First Christian Evangelization of China: The Theological Ideas Expressed in the "Stele of the Luminous Religion," pp. 169–84.
6. De Rachewiltz, *Papal Envoys to the Great Khans*, pp. 121–43. The Mongols took Friar William's mission as a political one, but his aims were ambiguous.
7. Dawson, *Mission to Asia*, p. ix.
8. Quoted in Dawson, p. xiv.
9. Ibid., 76.
10. Ibid., p. xxix; see also de Rachewiltz, op. cit., pp. 157–59.
11. For a fascinating study on this topic, see Arnold, *Princely Gifts and Papal Treasures*.
12. For example, Lo Kuang, ed., *Collected Essays of the International Symposium on Chinese-Western Cultural Interchange*, and Ronan and Oh, eds., *East Meets West: The Jesuits in China, 1582–1773*.
13. Ricci, *The True Meaning of the Lord of Heaven (T'ien-chu shih-i)*. In his letter of transmittal of this first edition to Claudio Acquaviva, the superior general in Rome, Ricci translated this first sentence: "Regna habent regem, universum hoc non habeat? Regnum continetur uno, Universum hoc duos habet dominos?" Biblioteca Casanatense, *Mss. 2136*, fol. 3v. Note that this section of the Latin text was not included in the edition, pp. 460–72.
14. Ibid., 61. Capitalization is in the original.
15. Ibid., 435.
16. Standaert, *Yang Tingyun Confucian and Christian in Late Ming China*, pp. 214–15.
17. Criveller, *Preaching Christ in Late Ming China*, p. 357.
18. Dudink, "The Religious Works Composed by Johann Adam Schall von Bell," p. 856.

19. Ibid., 864.

20. Ibid., 865.

21. See Zhang Dawei, "The 'Calendar Case' in the Early Qing dynasty Re-examined," pp. 478 and 494. This is similar to the position of Eugene Menegon, that Yang's opposition to Schall meant "attacking the whole church of China as well as the Company of Jesus." See his "Yang Guangxian's Opposition to Johann Adam Schall," ibid., p. 336.

22. Witek, "Principles of Scholasticism in China," p. 288.

23. Cronin, *The Wise Man from the West. Matteo Ricci and his Mission to China*, p. 270.

24. Widmer, *The Russian Ecclesiastical Mission in Beijing During the Eighteenth Century*, p. 116.

25. Lowenthal, *The Religious Periodical Press in China*, pp, 268–69.

26. See the recent, perceptive study by Jonathan Spence, *God's Chinese Son: The Taiping Heavenly Kingdom of Hong Xiuquan.*

27. D'Elia, *The Triple Demism of Sun Yat-sen*, p. 708.

28. Ibid., p. 716.

29. Ibid., p. 718.

30. Madsen, *China's Catholics: Tragedy and Hope in an Emerging Civil Society*, pp. 141–42.

31. Ren Yanli, "Repubblica Popolare Cinese e Santa Sede," p. 283.

32. Duan Qi, "Contextualization in the Contemporary Chinese Church," p. 46.

33. See John McManners, ed., *The Oxford Illustrated History of Christianity*, p. 663.

Zhang: Chinese Perspective

* During the writing of this article, the following books and papers were consulted: Zhuo Xinping, "Jidujiao yanjiu gaishuo" (Survey of Research on Christianity), pp. 279–83; Guo Xiwei, "Zhongguo Jidujiaoshi yanjiu" (History of Chinese Christianity Study); Tao Feiya, "Jindai guoneide Jidujiaoshi (Xinjiao) yanjiu jianping" (Review of Research on History of Chinese Christianity in Recent Years).

1. Chen Shenru and Zhu Zhengyi, "Shilun Mingmo Qingchu Yesuhuishi de lishizuoyong" (An Initial Discussion of the Historical Role of the Society of Jesuit in the Late Ming and Early Qing Period), *Zhonguo shi yanjiu* (Research on Chinese History) (February 1980).

2. Zhang Weihua and Sun Xi, "Shiliu shiji Yesuhuishi zai hua chuanjiao zehngce de yanbian" (The Evolution of Jesuits' Evangelistic Policy in the Sixteenth Century China), *Wen shi zhe* (Literature, History and Philosophy) (January 1985). Xu Shuming, "Guanyu Shun Kang Yong Qian shiqi de Yeshuhuishi pingjia wenti" (Concerning the Question of Evaluation of the Jesuits during the Shunzhi, Kangxi, Yongzheng and Qianlong Reigns), *Zhongguoshi yanjiu dongtai* (Development of the Study of Chinese History) (October 1985). He Guichun, "Guanyu Mingqing Yesuhuishi zai Hua huodong pingjia de jige wenti" (A Few Questions Concerning the Assessment of Jesuit Activities during the Ming-Qing Era), *Xueshu yuekan* (Academic Monthly Journal) (November 1992).

3. Lin Jinshui, *Li Madou yu Zhongguo* (Matteo Ricci and China).
4. Li Shiyue, "Fan yangjiao douzheng de xingzhi ji qita" (The Characteristics of the Anti-foreign Religion Struggle and Others), *Jindaishi yanjiu* (Modern History Study) (May 1986). Lu Zhongwei, "Xiangshen yu fan yangjiao douzheng" (The Rural Gentry and the Anti-foreign Religion Struggle), *Jindaishi yanjiu* (Modern History Study) (January 1986). Zhao Chunchen, "Wanqing yangwupai yu jiao'an (Late Qing Westernizers and Religious Cases), *Lishi yanjiu* (Historical Research) (April 1988). Lu Yao, "Lun jindai Zhongguo jiawu zhanzhengqian de jiao'an yu fanyangjiao douzheng" (About the Struggle Against Foreign Religions and Religious Cases Before the Sino-Japanese War of 1985), *Shandong daxue xuebao* (Journal of Shandong University) (January 1990). Ding Mingnan, "Guanyu Zhongguo jindaishishang jiao'an de kaocha" (An Investigation Concerning Religious Cases in Modern Chinese History), *Jindaishi yanjiu* (Modern History Study) (January 1990). Qi Qizhang, "Jindai jiao'an he Yihetuan yundong de xingqi" (Modern Religious Cases and the Rise of the Boxer Movement), *Guizhou shehui kexue* (Guizhou Social Sciences) (January 1991).

Zürcher: The Image of Europe and Its Impact

1. D'Elia, *Fonti Ricciane:* vol. II, No. 310, p. 259 (hereafter: FR II).
2. The use of the name "Folangji" for both Portuguese and Spanish conquerors is found in all early sources; e.g., Zhang Xie, *Dong Xi yang kao* (A Study about the Eastern and Western Oceans), *juan* 4, pp. 43 and 57–62 (hereafter: DXYK); Mao Ruizheng, *Huang Ming xiangxu lu* (Record of the Imperial Ming Court Interpreter), *juan* 5, pp. 263–283 (hereafter: HMXXL). Cf. Also Zhang Weihua, *Mingshi Folangji Lüsong Helan Yidaliya si zhuan zhushi* (A Commentary of the Four Chapters on Portugal, Spain, Holland and Italy in the History of the Ming Dynasty).
3. Wang Shixing, *Guang zhi yi* (Comprehensive Gazeteer Explained) (1597 ed.; reprint in *Yuan Ming shiliao biji congkan*. Beijing, 1981), pp. 100–101 (hereafter: GZY).
4. D'Elia, ed., *Il mappamondo cinese del P. Matteo Ricci S.J.*.
5. FR II, No. 570, pp. 95–96.
6. Ricci, *The True Meaning of the Lord of Heaven* (*T'ien-chu Shih-i*), pp. 409–10.
7. Cf. Li Zhizao's preface to *Zhifang waiji* (Record of [Countries] outside the Imperial Geographer's Vision), by Giulio Aleni (hereafter: ZFWJ), in *Tianxue chuhan* (First Correspondence on the Heavenly Religion) (hereafter: TXCH), vol. III, pp. 1273–76.
8. Presented around the middle of August, 1616; cf. Dudink, "Nangong shudu (1620), Poxie ji (1640) and Western reports," pp. 44–45 and 169.
9. Entitled *Bianxue shugao, var. Bianxue zhangshu*; in *Xu Guangqi ji* (Collected Works of Xu Guangqi) (hereafter: XGQJ), vol. II, pp. 431–37.
10. De Pantoja and de Ursis, *Jujie* (Memorial of Defence) (hereafter: JJ), Courant 7321, p. 94.
11. JJ, p. 101.
12. FR, II, No. 781–783, pp. 372–75.
13. JJ, pp. 89–90.
14. JJ, p. 98.

15. *Bianxue shugao* (cf. note 9), p. 432.
16. JJ, pp. 112–13.
17. Ibid., pp. 122–23.
18. Xu Guangqi's postscript to *Ershiwu yan* (Twenty-five Sayings) (hereafter: ESWY), by Matteo Ricci, vol. I, p. 328.
19. Hangzhou, preface by Aleni dated 1623 in TXCH, vol. II, pp. 1269–96.
20. Text with preface by Yang Tingyun dated 1623, in TXCH, vol. I, pp. 9–60.
21. The text of the first edition (Fuzhou, 1637) is reproduced in the article by John L. Mish mentioned in the next note, pp. 4–30.
22. D'Elia, "Le Generalità sulle Scienze Occidentale di Giulio Aleni," pp. 58–76; Mish, "Creating an Image of Europe for China: Aleni's *Hsi-fang ta-wen*," pp. 1–87; Luk, "And Thus the Twain Did Meet? The Two Worlds of Giulio Aleni"; see also Luk, "A Study of Giulio Aleni's *Chih-fang wai-chi*," pp. 58–84; and Luk, "Aleni Introduces the Western Academic Tradition into Seventeenth Century China," pp. 479–518.
23. Reproduced in *Congshu jicheng*, vol. 3266.
24. Undated version published in *Congshu jicheng*, vol. 3278; according to Courant there is a version in the Bibliothèque Nationale dated 1668.
25. JJ, p. 122.
26. Buglio, *Budeyi bian* (1665), of *Tianzhujiao dongchuan wenxian* (Documents Concerning the Spread of Christianity to the East) (hereafter: DCWX), vol 24, pp. 289–90.
27. JJ, pp. 120–21.
28. Giulio Aleni, *Xixue fan* (Survey of Studies in the West) (hereafter: XXF), vol. I, pp. 46–47.
29. Aleni, *Xifang dawen* (Answers to Questions About the West) (hereafter: XFDW), text reprinted in Mish, "Creating an Image of Europe for China," pp. 43–44; ZFWJ, p. 1386.
30. ZFWJ, p. 1368.
31. XFDW, Mish, pp. 46–47; translation by Mish with slight changes, as in other quotations from XFDW.
32. ZFWJ, p. 1362.
33. XFDW, Mish, p. 47. Aleni adds that such highly salaried administrators will receive especially severe punishment in case of corruption or abuse of power.
34. ZFWJ, p. 1370.
35. Ibid., p. 1367.
36. XXF, p. 45–47.
37. Ibid., pp. 1370–72; XFDW, Mish, pp. 49–50.
38. For Chinese Christian humanitarian societies and their context see Standaert, *Yang Tingyun, Confucian and Christian in Late Ming China*, pp. 62–66.
39. ZFWJ, pp. 1364–67; XFDW, Mish, pp. 53–55, and Yang Tingyun, *Tian Shi ming bian* (The Clear Distinction Between [the doctrine of] Heaven and Buddhism) (1628, hereafter: TSMB), p. 272.
40. TSMB, pp. 378–79.
41. In this section on "study in the West" (*xixue*) one would be tempted to include four works written by Alfonso Vagnoni (Gao Yizhi) which are dealing with Western moral and political philosophy: *Xiushen xixue* (Self-perfection according to Western Science, c. 1631); *Qijia xixue* (Regulating the Family

according to Western Science, 1631); *Zhiping xixue* (Governing [the Country] and Pacifying [the Realm] according to Western Science, manuscript, no printed edition before 1935); and *Tongyou jiaoyu* (On Child Education, c. 1620). However, these purely scholastic works (mostly extracts from the standard commentaries on Aristotle's *Ethica*) are not descriptive but purely prescriptive; they also appear to have circulated on a very limited scale (mainly among the Christians in Jiangzhou in southern Shanxi, where Vagnoni was active between 1624 and 1640). They have therefore not been used as source materials in writing this paper.

42. Cf. note 22.
43. XXF, p. 28.
44. TSMB, pp. 382–83.
45. Academies and libraries: ZFWJ, pp. 1362–63; categories of texts: XFDW, Mish, p. 4. According to Yang Tingyun, *Dai yi xubian* (Instead of Doubting, Further Essays) (hereafter: DYXB), Courant 7111, p. 30a, the volume of text would increase tenfold if translated into Chinese and printed in the standard format of Chinese books.
46. Cf. Aleni's description of the Summa in XXF, pp. 51–56 (translated by D'Elia in his *Generalità*, pp. 71–74), and Yang Tingyun's admiring comment in *Dai yi pian* (Instead of Doubting) (1621, hereafter: DYP), p. 542.
47. DYXP, p. 30a and DYP, pp. 543–44.
48. Han Lin and Zhang Geng, *Shengjiao xinzheng* (Reliable Evidence Regarding the Holy Doctrine) (hereafter: SJXZ), vol. 1 of *Tianzhujiao dongchuan wenxian sanbian* (Third Collection of Documents Concerning the Spread of Christianity to the East) (hereafter: WXSB), pp. 279–80.
49. For Trigault's mission see Lamalle, "La propagande du P. Nicolas Trigault en faveur des missions de Chine (1616)," pp. 49–120. The "fonds Ricci-Trigault" still constitutes the invaluable nucleus of the present Beitang Library, now housed in the Beijing National Library. For the stereotyped "7,000 volumes" mentioned by Chinese Christian authors like Yang Tingyun, Li Zhizao and Wang Zheng see Verhaeren, *Catalogue de la bibliothèque du Péi-t'ang*, pp. xi–xii; the tentative explanation given for that number is very implausible.
50. Li Zhizao's preface to ZFWJ (1623), pp. 1282–83.
51. DYP, p. 545.
52. JJ, p. 113; ZFWJ, pp. 1362–63.
53. DYP, p. 545.
54. TZSI, pp. 603–604; ZFWJ, pp. 1385–86; XXF, p. 48; TSMB, pp. 406–407.
55. DYP, p. 562.
56. Li Sixuan, *Siji Ai xiansheng xingji*, Courant 1017, p. 2a; cf. Erik Zürcher, "Giulio Aleni's Chinese Biography," *op. cit.*, pp. 85–127, especially p. 100.
57. ZFWJ, pp. 1368–70.
58. DYP, pp. 562–63.
59. Xu Guangqi, *Da xiangren shu*, in *Zengding Xu Wending Gong ji*, ed. Xu Mouxi, *juan* 1, p. 13 (not in Wang Zhongming, ed., *Xu Guangqi ji* [Collected Works of Xu Guanqi] [hereafter: XGQJ] on account of its supposed inauthenticity); Han Lin in his preface to *Ertong jiaoyu* (cf. note 41); manuscript copy from Xujiahui, Shanghai.

60. Luk, "A Study of Giulio Aleni's *Chih-fang wai-chi*," pp. 58–84, especially pp. 79–83; cf. also Masini, "L'Italia descritta nel *Qingchao wenxian tongkao*," pp. 285–98.

61. Zhu Zongyuan, *Da kewen* (Answers to a Guest's Questions), Courant 7036, pp. 50b–51b.

Rule: Revelation in the Confucian and Christian Traditions

1. Such would seem to be the logical conclusion of the views advanced by Hall and Ames, *Anticipating China: Thinking through the Narratives of Chinese and Western Culture.*

2. "The question of accuracy is a critical one in any discussion of representation. . . . " (Jensen, p. 140). See my review in the *Journal of Chinese Religions* (forthcoming) for substantiation of the charge of inaccuracy.

3. Jensen, correctly, in a quotation from Wilfred Cantwell Smith (on p. 136) notes the "invention" of the term "Confucianism" in the nineteenth century, yet persists in attributing it to the earlier Jesuits.

4. Jensen, *Manufacturing Confucianism,* p. 55.

5. Ibid., p. 142.

6. Especially in works by Jacques Gernet, *Chine et christianisme: action et réaction* (English translation *China and the Christian Impact: A Conflict of Cultures*).

7. Jacques Gernet, *China and the Christian Impact,* p. 240ff.

8. Jacques Gernet "Christian and Chinese Visions of the World in the Seventeenth Century," pp. 1–17. Cf. D'Elia, ed., *Fonti Ricciane,* Vol. I, No. 176, p. 116 where Ricci specifies "questa unità di sustantia" as the problem. He is presumably referring to statements such as that of Huang Zhen in his letter to Yan Maoyou in the *Shengchao poxie ji* (hereafter: PXJ), p. 150, that *wanwu yiti* (everything comprises one body [or substance]).

9. See, for example, Liu Ning, "Yuanben lun" (On the origin of things), in *Juesi lu*, JapSin I, fol. 165d. All translations are my own except where specifically acknowledged.

10. The Fujian Christian, Li Jiugong in a manuscript miscellany, "Wenda Huichao" (A Compilation of Questions and Answers) argues that the key issue is the priority of *Tianzhu* over *li*, which can only have an instrumental role. See JapSin I, 34/37, *juan* 1, No. 4, fol. 2b–4a.

11. Young, in his *Confucianism and Christianity: the First Encounter* (p. 58), finds it surprising and remarkable that Xu Guangqi could have retained a belief in "the unity of Man, Heaven and Earth" after accepting the Christian God which made such beliefs "meaningless." But Zhu Xi's commentaries on the Four Books reflect the same dilemma: an unavoidable acceptance of Kongzi's belief in "an anthropomorphic deity" combined with *Li/Qi* metaphysics. There is only a problem for the Christian if the role of that deity in shaping the universe is denied.

12. Review of *China and the Christian Impact,* in *Harvard Journal of Asiatic Studies* 47 (1987): 679.

13. For example, *China and the Christian Impact,* p. 39.

14. Ricci, *The True Meaning of the Lord of Heaven* (*T'ien-chu Shih-i*), No. 532, pp. 414–15. Later references are to TZSY and refer to this edition.

15. Ibid., p. 27. It was echoed by the Christian scholar, Han Lin in his *Duoshu* (Gong Book), JapSin I, 144, fol. 1a–b, which uses *Tian* and

Shangdi throughout rather than *Tianzhu* but like Ricci connects filial piety and obedience to the Emperor (*tianzi*) to obedience to Heaven, the "great father and mother" (*da fumu*). The Gong Book was so named as an echo of the practice of assembling the populace to hear imperial ethical precepts read aloud. This interpretation also had a solid basis in earlier usage. See Knapp, "The *Ru* Reinterpretation of *Xiao*."

16. See, especially Chapter 5 "Chinese Heaven, Christian God," in *China and the Christian Impact.*

17. See, for example, Li Jiugong, *Shensi Lu* (JapSin I, 34/37, *ji* I, p. 1b), where he argues that Confucians have forgotten that "high heaven has a lord" (*shangtian zhi you zhu*). A similar argument is found in Chapter 9 of Qiu Sheng, *Shuwen pian* (JapSin I, 40/4), a section entitled "Tianzhishang biyou zhuzhishu." Also see Xu Guangqi, *Zaowuzhu huaxiang lueshuo*, 2:549–550, distinguishes clearly between two "heavens", "the sky above which we can see" and "the other we know we cannot now see, the heaven after whom heaven the place is named. And this heaven is where the angels and all the saints see the Lord of Heaven."

18. *China and the Christian Impact*, p. 40.

19. Ibid., pp. 39–40, where Gernet quotes and comments on texts of Zhang Erqi (1670) and Zhang Chao (1697).

20. De Bary, ed., *Self and Society in Ming Thought*. The enigmatic Li Zhi (1527–1602) with his provocatively titled works *Fenshu* (A Book Which Should Be Burnt), and *Cangshu* (A Book Which Should be Hidden), was archetypal and, significantly, very attracted by Matteo Ricci's personality and ideas. See Brook, *Praying for Power: Buddhism and the Formation of Gentry Society in Late-Ming China*, Chapter 2, on the reasons for the attraction of Buddhism for Confucian scholars in the late Ming.

21. Bauer's nice title to a section of his chapter on the Ming (Book IV, Chapter 2) in his *China and the Search for Happiness: Recurring Themes in Four Thousand Years of Chinese Cultural History.*

22. Judith Berling, *The Syncretic Religion of Lin Chao-en.*

23. Wakeman, *The Great Enterprise: The Manchu Reconstruction of Imperial Order in Seventeenth-Century China*, especially Chapter 2.

24. Huang Zongxi in his *Ming Ruxue'an* both promoted the legend of the group and specified their contribution as opposition to the popularity of the misinterpreted ideas of Wang Yangming. See Huang Tsung-hsi, *The Records of Ming Scholars: a Selected Translation*, p. 223ff.

25. TZSY, No. 494, p. 393: "Further, there cannot be two truths which are both correct. If the religion of the Sovereign on High (Shangdi) is true, then all other religions are wrong. If any of the other religions is true, then the religion of the Sovereign on High is wrong. . . . Buddhism and Taoism are essentially different from one another; how much more, then, must they be different from the religion of the Lord of Heaven?"

26. TZSY, No. 598, pp. 400–401.

27. Zhu Zongyuan, *Da kewen*, JapSin II, 75, fol. 1b.

28. The author's preface to his *Zhengshi lueshuo*, JapSin I, 145, fol. 1b–2a.

29. Standaert, "Confucian-Christian Dual Citizenship in the Chinese Context."

30. PXJ, p. 276.

31. Translation by Ganss, ed. *Ignatius of Loyola: The Spiritual Exercises and Selected Works*, p. 177.

32. Wing-tsit Chan, *A Source Book in Chinese Philosophy*, pp. 497–500. Chan's commentary is particularly relevant here since he highlights the conflicting monist and dualist interpretations of the text.

33. O'Malley, in *The First Jesuits*, p. 19, states: "They sought to be mediators of an immediate experience of God that would lead to an inner change of heart or a deepening of religious sensibilities already present. . . . The religious and cultural framework in which the Jesuits lived meant that they believed that acceptance of the basic Christian dogmas was a necessary precondition for such an experience to be complete and fully genuine. They therefore studied that dogma and inculcated it, but not always in ways we might expect. Moreover, they hoped and intended to help others beyond an intellectual assent to orthodox truths to an acceptance of the lived reality of God's action in their lives."

34. "Simul in actione contemplativus" was Jerome Nadal's description of Ignatius Loyola. See *The Spiritual Exercises and Selected Works*, p. 44 and p. 231.

35. Wu Pei-yi, "Self-Examination and Confession of Sins in Traditional China."

36. J. Ching, *To Acquire Wisdom: the Way of Wang Yang-ming*, pp. 45–46. The Society of Jesus, early in its history, and before the China mission began, resolved the question of appropriate Jesuit prayer in favor of an orientation to action. See Cognet, "La crise spirituelle de la Compagnie de Jésus."

37. For example, Zhang Erqi, quoted by Gernet in *China and the Christian Impact*, p. 39, indicates: "Furthermore, what they say about paradise and hell appears to differ barely from what the Buddhists maintain and they go even further than the latter when it comes to extravagance and nonsense" (From the *Hao'an xianhua* [1670] not *Hao'an xinhua* as in both the English and French text). In another passage quoted by Gernet in *China and the Christian Impact*, p.107, he finds puzzling its comparison of Christianity to Buddhism and Daoism, but his oversimplified translation of the passage in question, from the late Ming *Pixie Ji* (p. 923), misses the point that it is worship that is objected to, not monotheism.

38. See *Manufacturing Confucianism*, p. 63: "the natural light of divine reason to which all natural phenomena could be reduced."

39. *China and the Christian Impact*, p. 56.

40. Curiously the phrase *buru yifo* seems to have first been used in a preface by Xu, dated 1612, to a Jesuit work on hydraulics, the *Taixi shuifa* of vol. III in *Tianxue chuhan*, p. 1506. The *yifo* is problematic. In what way is Buddhism to be "changed" (*yi*)? Jensen's "excise" (*Manufacturing Confucianism*, p. 102) seems too strong. I would prefer "correct" or "reform." Cf. the formula Xu used in his 1616 apology for Christianity, the *Bianxue zhangshu*: "to complement and assist the royal reforms, to assist the efforts of the *literati* and to correct the Buddhists" *(buyi wanghua, zouyou rushu, mizheng fofa)* (*The Chinese repository* 19 [1850], p. 129).

41. Leaving aside the twentieth-century contributions of such theologians as Henri de Lubac, Karl Rahner and Bernard Lonergan, since at least the First Vatican Council it has commonly been held that revelation encompasses natural religion. See Bulst, *Revelation*, p. 18.

42. *China and the Christian Impact*, p. 48. Jensen takes a similar position when he complains: "Jesuits, like Matteo Ricci and Michele Ruggieri, could become Chinese, yet never be aware of how much they had relinquished their

hold on the faith they came to China to propagate" (*Manufacturing Confucianism*, p. 283).

43. Cf. *Fonti Ricciane*, Vol. II, No. 709, p. 296: "I make every effort to turn our way the ideas of the leader of the *literati*, Confucius, by interpreting in our favour things which he left ambiguous in his writings. In this way our Fathers gain great favour with the *literati* who do not adore the idols." It may be objected that Ricci is here invoking Confucius against Buddhism, as elsewhere against Neo-Confucianism, but the principle seems the same.

44. *China and the Christian Impact*, p. 49.

45. Ibid., p. 55.

46. TZSY, No. 422, pp. 348–49. In the following No. 423 he alludes specifically to the Chinese debate about "human nature and its original goodness" (*renxing qi benshan*).

47. *China and the Christian Impact*, p. 43. I would concede that there was never in later times an equivalent to Xu Gungqi in rank or accomplishment, but there were many of second rank in both respects such as Han Lin, Qu Shisi, Shang Huqing, Wang Zheng, Zhang Xingyao, and Zhu Zongyuan.

48. These works, many in manuscript, include spiritual diaries, rules for fraternities devoted to good works, wrestling with problems of conscience, and pugnacious defenses of their newly acquired faith against Buddhist and Confucian critics. They give insights into the lives of *literati* Christians other than the "big three," Xu Guangqi, Li Zhizao and Yang Tingyun who have mainly been studied hitherto. The forthcoming catalogue raisonné of the Chinese works in the Jesuit Archives in Rome by Albert Chan, SJ should make them more accessible.

49. Zürcher, "The Jesuit Mission in Fukien in Late Ming Times: Levels of Response," "Aleni in Fujian, 1630–1640: The Medium and the Message," and "Confucian and Christian Religiosity in Late Ming China."

50. See the opening section of Zürcher, "Jesuit Accommodation and the Chinese Cultural Imperative."

51. Entenmann, "Chinese Catholic Clergy and Catechists in Eighteenth-Century Szechuan," pp. 389–410; "The Establishment of Chinese Catholic Communities in Early Ch'ing Szechwan," pp. 147–162; "Christian Virgins in Eighteenth-Century Sichuan," pp. 180–193.

52. The major seventeenth-century work in this genre is the *Shengjiao poxie ji*, fortunately now available in a new edition published by the Alliance Bible Seminary, Hong Kong, as well as the rare 1855 Japanese edition. I have drawn other items from the secondary literature, especially Gernet.

53. It should be noted, however, that the grounds invoked by Buddhist critics of Christianity were often Confucian rather than Buddhist. See Hung Ming-shui, "Yüan Hung-tao and the Late Ming Literary and Intellectual Movement," pp. 213–227.

54. *Tianxue* could be regarded as a abbreviation for *Tianzhu xue* (the study of Christianity) on the one hand, and *tianwen xue* (the study of astronomy) on the other. Good examples of this ambiguity are the title of Li Zhizao's compilation of Jesuit works, the *Tianxue Chuhan*, which indiscriminately, one might even say promiscuously, put back to back scientific and religious works; and the inscription that the Chongzhen Emperor bestowed on the Jesuit astronomer Adam Schall's church in Beijing in 1630, *Qinbao Tianxue* (Imperially Protected Study of Heaven). On the other hand, when a definition of *tianxue* was given it was always as an abbreviation of *Tianzhujiao xue*. See, for

example, the opening of Li Zubai, *Tianxue chuan'gai* in *Tianzhujiao dongchuan wenxian xubian*, Vol. II, p. 1055.

55. Wilders, *The Theologian and His Universe: Theology and Cosmology from the Middle Ages to the Present.*

56. Xu Dashou, in *juan* 4 of the PXJ, p.224.

57. Gernet, in Chapter 4 of *China and the Christian Impact*, amply documents this, but it is interesting to note that the authors cited, mostly from PXJ, often take a covert Buddhist rather than Confucian standpoint. If we must have superstitions let them at least be Chinese!

58. PXJ, p. 205. Cf. Ricci's attempt to demonstrate that Mencius (4A.26) had misinterpreted Confucius on this issue, or been himself misinterpreted, or (a very modern touch this) that times have changed and population control is now necessary (TZSY, Nos. 551–52, pp. 428–29).

59. PXJ, p. 206 where Xu Dashou argues that Christian morality reverses the natural priority of Yang over Yin.

60. See Xu Dashou in PXJ, p. 207. The response given by Li Jiugong in the *Wenda huichao, juan* 4, pp. 28b–29a that infertility may be due to the husband, in which case taking a concubine will not produce the desired son, while undoubtedly medically accurate, would hardly have placated Xu Dashou.

61. Xu Dashou in PXJ, p. 207.

62. See especially Chen Houguang, PXJ, p. 243.

63. Lancashire, "Anti-Christian Polemics in Seventeenth Century China," 38:222. One may quibble about definitions of "faith." When Jullien in *Procès ou création* denies the presence of "dogma" (p.15) and "faith" (p. 203) in Neo-Confucianism, I think he is construing both terms too narrowly. Of course, there was no Christian "faith" as a theological virtue, and no revealed "dogma" but the Confucian protagonists in the anti-Christian polemics defended their values in ways at least functionally analogous to these Western conceptions. Recent commentators on Neo-Confucianism such as De Bary, Taylor and Tu Wei-ming do not hesitate to use the term.

64. PXJ, pp. 205–206.

65. Quoted by Busch in "The Tung-lin Academy and Its Political and Philosophical Significance," pp. 160–61.

66. See, for example, Ricci's "translation" of *ren* as love of God and neighbor in TZSY, No. 468, pp. 374–75.

67. The sad fate of Li Zhi seems to have been as much due to his moral aberrations as his "perverse doctrines." See *Fonti Ricciane*, Vol. II, p 193, note 5.

68. J. Ching, "The problem of Evil and a Possible Dialogue Between Christianity and Neo-Confucianism," and *Confucianism and Christianity: A Comparative Study*, especially pp. 73–79.

69. There are allusions which to the initiated could be read in terms of "sin" e.g., No. 429 on the conflict of the passions and reason, No. 431 on the choice of good or evil, and No. 577 on man "turning his back on reason" (*beili*) and "transgressing the commands of the Lord of Heaven" (*fan tianzhu ming*).

70. Santangelo, *Il peccato in Cina: bene e male nel neoconfucianesimo dalla metà del XIV alla metà del XIX secolo.*

71. Delumeau, *Sin and Fear: The Emergence of a Western Guilt Culture 13th–18th Centuries.*

72. TZSY, Nos. 390 and 329.

73. The question of the Jesuit influence on critical textual studies in China is as yet unresolved. In my judgment they were an influence but a minor one.

74. TZSY, No. 77ff.

75. "Great Ultimate" or "Supreme Ultimate" are preferable translations to Gernet's "Cosmic Origin" which is entirely interpretative and certainly to Jensen's "Supernal Ridgepole" which reads into it western notions of the supernatural. James Legge's "Grand Terminus" (*The I Ching: The Book of Changes*, p. 373), while accurate, reminds one of traveling, and a literal "Big End" of motor mechanics.

76. The passage already referred to (note 31) from the *Pixie Ji*, translated by Gernet (*China and the Christian Impact*, p. 107) which contrasts the notion of *Taiji* pervading and ordering nature and society with the Christian sovereign God.

77. TZSY, No. 78, pp. 106–107.

78. TZSY, No. 84, pp. 110–11. A note in this edition points to this as "the root of Ricci's misunderstanding of Neo-Confucianism" (p. 110, note 26). What is not clear, however, is where it came from. I suspect the explanation lies in the kind of Thomism then taught in the Roman College. Although Francesco Suarez SJ did not begin teaching metaphysics there until just after Ricci's time, his predecessors, the Coimbra school of Jesuit philosophers, especially Pedro de Fonseca, had already begun to elaborate a systematic Aristotelian metaphysics which conceived God as self-subsistent substance. See Caraman, *University of the Nations*, pp. 24–25; Copleston, *A History of Philosophy*, Vol. 3, Chapters XXI and XXII.

79. TZSY, No. 86, pp. 112–13.

80. Gernet's claim (*China and the Christian Impact* p. 253, note 51) that Ricci misdates the advent of neo-Confucianism to fifty years before his time is due to his mistranslation of *quingentos*, "five hundred" as " fifty." Zhou Dunyi's dates (1017–1073) fit perfectly.

81. See Shen Que's 1616 deposition, *Nangong shudu*: "These barbarians cunningly misname Heaven as the Lord of Heaven in order to impose the latter above the former and confuse foolish people. How can that be right?" (p. 59).

82. *China and the Christian Impact*, pp. 97–98, almost a word for word translation of the original French where we find the misleading "produisit le monde par transformation magique."

83. Zhong Mingren, also known as Sebastian Fernandez, was the principal catechist for Matteo Ricci and later Alfonso Vagoni, and had studied some Latin as well as Chinese. See A. Pfister, *Notices biographiques et bibliographiques sur le Jésuites de l'ancienne mission de Chine, 1552–1773*, pp. 47–48; Dehergne, *Répertoire des Jésuites de Chine de 1552 à 1800*, p. 89.

84. *Huasheng* was a technical Buddhist term for the beginning of a new kalpa but even in this context hardly implied "magic" in the technical sense. It is clear, however, that it is not the creation of "the world" that is in question here, but that of the first humans which Genesis describes as Adam formed out of dust, and Eve out of Adam's rib (2:7, 2:22).

85. PXJ, p. 103.

86. Zürcher, " 'In the Beginning': 17th Century Chinese Reactions to Christian Creationism," pp. 132–66. When Zürcher comments that "the most fundamental notion in Chinese traditional cosmogony [was] the belief that Heaven and Earth had not been "created" at all but had "evolved" in the course of a natural process of polarization and diversification" (p. 134), he is assuming

an opposition between evolutionary schemes and "creation" which holds only for certain kinds of "creationism," i.e., fundamentalist and biblical literalist versions of creation. A similar dichotomy lies behind F. Jullien's *Procès ou création: une introduction à la pensée des lettrés chinois.* The fundamental issues are an eternal world vs. a finite beginning and the distinction between "creator" and "universe" and these were open questions within Chinese culture.

87. See my paper at the Fifteenth Congress of the International Association for the History of religions, "Neo-Confucianism: Theism, Atheism or Neither?"

88. See Jiang Dejing in PXJ: "They consider their Lord of Heaven to be the same as that Shangdi which we Chinese worship but how can that be since their Jesus became Lord of Heaven only in the time of Han Aidi" (p. 139).

89. Li Jiugong, *Wenda huicahao, juan* 2, fol. 7b, and cf. No. 34 of *juan* 2 where he gives an elaborate explanation for the late arrival of this important news in China.

90. TZSY, No. 574, pp. 444–45.

91. TZSY, No. 579, pp. 446–47.

92. TZSY, No. 580, pp. 448–49. The translators add an unjustified "descended" here, although it could be argued that the *fusheng guitian* at the end of the passage implies it.

93. Ibid.

94. Ibid., Lancashire and Hu render *Tianzhu shuji* as "concrete actions of the Lord of Heaven," which misses the implications of "evidence" or "proof" in the phrase.

95. TZSY, No. 473, pp.378–79.

96. TZSY, No. 588, pp.452–53.

97. TZSY, No. 590, pp.452–53.

98. TZSY, No. 594, pp.454–55. Nothing has survived of Ricci's biblical translation but Jesuit writings refute the myth that they did not translate the Bible. There were many versions, some magnificently illustrated, of the life of Jesus and of Old Testament stories. All the liturgical readings were translated by Luigi Buglio in the seventeenth century, and in the eighteenth century a complete though unpublished Bible by Louis Poirot. Nevertheless, it is true that the text of the Bible was much less important to the Jesuits than it was to later Protestant missionaries.

99. Quoted from *Fonti Ricciane*, vol. II, pp. 42–43, note 1.

100. Text, translation and comment in Standaert, *Yang Tingyun, Confucian and Christian in Late Ming China*, p. 187. Standaert is probably right in reading *jiangsheng* as an "incarnation" but the expression is vague and may mean no more than a divine mission.

101. Bulst, *Revelation*, p. 17.

102. Henderson, *Scripture, Canon and Commentary: A Comparison of Confucian and Western Exegesis.*

103. TZSY, No. 21, pp. 66–67.

104. Jensen confuses the issue greatly by referring to "something approaching a hybrid canon of revealed literature" (*Manufacturing Confucianism*, p. 60), which would include Augustine, Aquinas and Ignatius Loyola in addition to the Bible.

105. TZSY, No. 389, pp. 328–29.

106. J. Ching, *Mysticism and Kingship in China: The Heart of Chinese Wisdom.*

107. *Xuezi* 19. Also see Watson, trans. and ed., *The Basic Writings of Hsun-tzu*, p. 111.

108. Tu Wei-ming, *Centrality and Commonality: An Essay on the Chung-yung*, p.104.

109. The key Confucian virtues, *ren, yi, li* and *zhi*.

110. A phrase from the opening line of the Daxue. "The Holy Scriptures" *sheng jing* here must refer to the Confucian jing not the Bible, but note the contrast between the jing and the Confucians (*ru*).

111. Yang Tingyun, *Tian Shi mingbian*, Vol. 1, p. 366.

112. Standaert, *Yang Tingyun, Confucian and Christian in the Late Ming China*, pp. 145–52.

113. A Christian *literati* and Jesuit catechist/secretary (*xianggong*) originally from Jianzhou (modern Jian'ou) in Fujian, but at the time of writing (the 1680s?) residing in Ganzhou in Jiangxi. See Lin Jinshui, "Christian *Literati* and the Rites Controversy," p. 67.

114. *Jili paozhi* in JapSin I, 39/4.

115. Ibid., fol. 5b.

116. Bulst, *Revelation*, pp.72–81. Bulst is writing about contemporary theology. More work is needed on early seventeenth-century theology of revelation as taught in Portugal and Rome to the future missionaries.

117. TZSY, No. 485, pp. 388–89.

118. Standaert, *Yang Tingyun, Confucian and Christian in Late Ming China*, pp.129–31; Zürcher, "Jesuit Accommodation and the Chinese Cultural Imperative," pp. 48–49.

119. Copy in JapSin I, 81. For a summary of its contents, see Zürcher, "Aleni in Fujian, 1630–1640: The Medium and the Message." I am endebted to Zürcher's paper for locating some of the key passages in that textual jungle.

120. *Kouduo richao* (henceforth KDRC), *juan* 2, pp. 5b–6a.

121. See Dulles, *Models of Revelation*, Chapter V, Model 3.

122. JapSin I, 53/3, fol. 1b., Yang's conversations recorded by Sun Xueshi.

123. See Zürcher, "Giulio Aleni's Chinese Biography" (p.110), where Li attributes his conversion to a "silent instruction" (*moyou*). This document is important testimony to the psychological aspects as well as the reality of the conversion experiences of a group of Fujian "Confucian Christians." I have used the copy in JapSin III, 23/4, fol. 15–23, entitled *Xihai Ai xiansheng yulu* not the two Bibliothèque Nationale manuscripts used by Zürcher.

124. *Tianxue chuangai*, p. 1058.

125. Ibid., p. 1601.

126. *Tianzhujiao dongchuan wenxian xubian*, 3:1084–86.

127. For example, Matteo Ricci, TZSY, No. 473, pp. 378–79.

128. See an exchange between Aleni and Li Jiubiao, where Li's doubts re the Incarnation are answered by a discussion of redemption of sinners (*shuzui*), KDRC, *juan* 1, p. 14b.

129. Origen. *Contra Celsum*. Book 7, Chapter 27. Translated with an introduction and notes by Henry Chadwick.

130. KDRC, *juan* 7, fol. 19b–20a for an exchange on this topic between a certain *juren* called Zhou and Aleni.

131. Dai Qifeng in PXJ, p. 255.

132. Yan Wenhui in PXJ, p. 79, cf. Zhou's exchange with Aleni, KDRC, *juan* 7, fol. 15a ff.

Standaert: A Case of Cultural Transmission

The author would like to express his gratitude to C. Defoort, A. Dudink, C. Jami and V. Neckebrouck for their critical remarks on earlier versions of this text.

1. For an example of an earlier study explicitly focusing on the theme of cultural contact, see Harris, "The Mission of Matteo Ricci, S.J.: A Case Study of an Effort at Guided Culture Change in China in the Sixteenth Century," pp. 1–168.
2. Bitterli, *Cultures in Conflict: Encounters Between European and Non-European Cultures, 1492–1800*, pp. 20–51.
3. Ronan & Oh, eds., *East Meets West: The Jesuits in China, 1582–1773*, p. xxxiii; quoting Wolfgang Reinhard, "Akkulturationsprozesse und Missionsstrategien in Asien," pp. 184–195.
4. For an overview of theoretical studies and studies mainly concerning Latin America, see Gruzinski, "première partie"; for an overview of recent publications concerning Asia, see Wills, Jr., "Maritime Asia, 1500–1800: The Interactive Emergence of European Domination," pp. 83–105. Compare also with some characteristics brought forward by George L. Harris, op. cit., p. 156ff.
5. *Handbook*: Standaert, "2.1.1. General characteristics: Number of missionaries," and "2.5.1. General characteristics: Number of Christians."
6. *Handbook*: Golas, "4.2.6. Technology."
7. *Handbook*: Golvers, "1.2. Western primary sources," and Dudink, "1.1. Chinese primary sources."
8. Cf. Herskovits, *Man and His Works: The Science of Cultural Anthropology*, p. 528.
9. *Handbook*: Dudink & Standaert, "4.1.2. Apostolate through books."
10. *Handbook*: Golvers, "2.1.1. General characteristics: Finances of the mission."
11. Zürcher, "Jesuit Accommodation and the Chinese Cultural Imperative," pp. 40–41.
12. *Handbook*: Walle, "4.3.5. Linguistics."
13. P. Cohen, *Discovering History in China: American Historical Writing on the Recent Chinese Past*, p. 14.
14. Compare with the methodological questions raised by Sivin, "Why the Scientific Revolution Did Not Take Place in China—Or Did It?" pp. 89–106; and Graham. "China, Europe, and the Origins of Modern Science: Needham's *The Grand Titration*," pp. 45–69; Bray, "Some Problems Concerning the Transfer of Scientific and Technical Knowledge," pp. 203–217.
15. Zürcher, "Bouddhisme et christianisme," pp. 11–42; "The Spread of Buddhism and Christianity in Imperial China," pp. 9–18.
16. P. Cohen, op. cit., pp. 9 and 53. As a corrective to these distortions, Cohen proposed to think of Chinese history in the nineteenth century as being comprised of several distinct zones (pp. 53–55). Similar zones could be found for the seventeenth century. While raising these questions with regard to impact and effect, we do not want to deny that the actors involved saw themselves as oriented towards a clear aim, and that, therefore, one could study the impact and effect of the actions with reference to their aims.
17. For this term, compare also with the notion of "interactive emergence" applied to the study of history of Maritime Asia, see Wills, op. cit.

18. *Handbook*: Hashimoto/Halsberghe, "4.2.2. Astronomy," Dudink, "2.6.3. Opponents;" Jami, "4.3.3. Clocks," Holler, "4.2.7. Medicine," and Picard, "4.3.4. Music."

19. For the reception of religious ideas according to social level, see *Handbook*: Zürcher: "4.1.3. Key theological issues."

20. These categories are inspired by Luzbetak, *The Church and Cultures: An Applied Anthropology for the Religious Worker*; see also Herskovits, op. cit., Chapter 31: "Acculturation: Cultural Transmission in Process." The term "diffusion" is used in its neutral sense, and does not refer to "diffusionism."

21. For example, Dujardin, "Historiography and Christian Missions in China," pp. 92–93.

22. An exception is the Jesuits' reluctant attitude towards the Dutch (Protestant) legation in 1686.

23. Jami, "From Euclid to Pardies: The Geometry Transmitted to China by Jesuits (1607–1723)," pp. 175–199.

24. *Handbook*: von Collani, "2.2. Legations and travellers"; Jami, "4.4. Cultural transmission to Europe: Academies."

25. *Handbook*: Dudink, "2.6.1. Symphatising *literati* and officials."

26. *Handbook*: Jami, "4.2.1. General reception."

27. *Handbook*: Jami, ibid.; Foss, "4.2.4. Cartography," and Pirazzoli-t'Serstevens, "4.3.2. Artistic issues in the eighteenth century."

28. *Handbook*: Métailié, "4.2.8. Botany."

29. Standaert, "The Classification of Sciences and the Jesuit Mission in Late Ming China," pp. 287–317.

30. *Handbook*: Dudink, "2.6.3. Opponents."

31. *Handbook*: Stary, "4.2.5. Cannon."

32. *Handbook*: Dudink & Standaert, "4.1.2. Apostolate through books."

33. *Handbook*: Standaert, "2.5.2. Well-known individuals."

34. Compare Neckebrouck, *Paradoxes de l'inculturation: Les nouveaux habits des Yanomani*, p. 44.

35. *Handbook*: Sachsenmaier, "4.4. Cultural transmission to Europe."

36. *Handbook*: Standaert, "4.1.1. Theological background."

37. *Handbook*: von Collani, "4.1.5. Figurism."

38. *Handbook*: Hashimoto/Halsberghe, op. cit.

39. *Handbook*: Foss, op. cit.

40. *Handbook*: Golas, op. cit.

41. *Handbook*: Métailié, op. cit.

42. *Handbook*: Sachsenmaier, op. cit.

43. For a detailed contemporary classification, see also Golvers, *The Astronomia Europaea of Ferdinand Verbiest, S.J.*

44. *Handbook*: Stary, op. cit..

45. *Handbook*: Jami, "4.2.1. General reception."

46. *Handbook*: Holler, "4.2.7. Medicine."

47. For these words, Serge Gruzinski, op. cit., pp. 34–36, 40–42, and 56. For a discussion of "syncretism," see Stewart & Shaw, eds., *Syncretism/Anti-Syncretism: The Politics of Religious Synthesis*, especially "Introduction: Problematising Syncretism," and "Chapter 10: Syncretism, Multiculturalism and the Discourse of Tolerance."

48. Compare also with Needham, "The Roles of Europe and China in the Evolution of Oecumenical Science," p. 402ff.

49. *Handbook*: Picard, op. cit.

50. See e.g., the analysis by Rafael, *Contracting Colonialism: Translation and Christian Conversion in Tagalog Society Under Early Spanish Rule*, especially pp. 210ff.

51. *Handbook*: Zürcher, "4.1.3. Key theological issues," and Pan Fengchuan, "4.1.4. Moral ideas and practices."

52. *Handbook*: Jami, "4.2.3. Mathematics."

53. *Handbook*: ibid.

54. Cf. Louis J. Luzbetak, op. cit., p. 199.

55. *Handbook*: Zürcher, "4.3.1. Prints and painting in the seventeenth century."

56. *Handbook*: Pirazzoli-t'Serstevens, op. cit.

57. *Handbook*: Golas, op. cit.

58. *Handbook*: Zürcher, "4.3.1. Prints and painting in the seventeenth century."

59. *Handbook*: Pirazzoli-t'Serstevens, op. cit.

60. *Handbook*: Standaert, "3.1. The creation of Christian communities," and "2.5.6. Social organisation of the church: Associations for lay-people."

61. Cf. Zürcher, "Confucian and Christian Religiosity in Late Ming China," pp. 614–653.

62. Thoraval, "Pourquoi les 'religions chinoises' ne peuvent-elles apparaître dans les statistiques occidentales?" pp. 37–44.

63. Cf. e.g., Neckebrouck, op. cit., p. 95ff.

64. Standaert, *Yang Tingyun, Confucian and Christian in Late Ming China*, pp. 222ff.

65. See also Bray, op. cit., p. 217; and Tu Youguang, "Cultural Graft and Higher Education," pp. 43–50.

66. Cf. Needham, op. cit., p. 397.

67. *Handbook*: Standaert, "2.1.1. General characteristics: Number of missionaries," and "2.5.1. General characteristics: Number of Christians."

68. See e.g., studies on the emergence of popular Christianity in Northern China (eighteenth century) by Lars Peter Laamann.

69. Han Qi, "Joachim Bouvet's Study of the Yijing and the Theory of the Chinese Origin of Western Learning in the Kangxi Period."

70. Waley-Cohen, "China and Western Technology in the Late Eighteenth Century," pp. 1543–1544.

71. *Handbook*: Standaert, "2.5.6. Social organisation of the church: Associations for lay-people."

72. On this efficacy, see Zürcher, "The Lord of Heaven and the Demons: Strange Stories from a Late Ming Christian Manuscript," p. 371.

73. For this concept, see Van Engen, "The Christian Middle Ages as an Historiographical Problem," pp. 519–552.

74. Cf. Chartier, *The Cultural Uses of Print in Early Modern France*, pp. 6–7. With this term Chartier wants to avoid identifying various cultural levels merely on the basis of a description of the objects, beliefs, or acts presumed to have been proper to different social groups, since his approach concentrates on differentiated uses and plural appropriations of the same goods, the same ideas, and the same actions.

75. *Handbook*: Dudink, "2.6.1. Symphatising *literati* and officials."

76. *Handbook*: Dudink & Standaert, "4.1.2. Apostolate through books."

77. In the beginning of the twentieth century, this work became the foundation of the educational system designed by Ma Xiangbo (1840–1939) for

the Aurora Academy (1903). To Ma Xiangbo, logic was the chemistry of thought. His classification of sciences was one of the last attempts of integration of the Western and Chinese systems. See Hayhoe and Lu Yongling, *Ma Xiangbo and the Mind of Modern China (1840–1939)*, pp. 160 ff., and 253 ff.

78. See the writings of Masini, e.g., "Aleni's Contribution to the Chinese Language," pp. 539–554.

79. *Handbook*: Jami, "4.2.1. General reception."

80. *Handbook*: Foss, op. cit.

81. *Handbook*: Jami, ibid.

82. *Handbook*: Pirazzoli-t'Serstevens, op. cit.

83. Bernard, "L'encyclopédie astronomique du Père Schall," pp. 463–464.

84. See Zürcher, "Jesuit Accommodation and the Chinese Cultural Imperative," p. 36ff.

85. *Handbook*: Sachsenmaier, op. cit.

86. Cf. Josselin de Jong, *Contact der continenten*, p. 67ff.

87. Cf. Neckebrouck, op. cit., p. 102.

88. Übelhör, "Geistesströmungen der späten Ming-Zeit die das Werken der Jesuiten in China begünstigten," pp. 172–185; and "Hsü Kuang-ch'i und seine Einstellung zum Christentum," 15 (1968): 191–257 (I); 16 (1969): 41–74 (II).

89. *Handbook*: Jami, "4.2.1. General reception."

90. *Handbook*: Pan Feng-chuan, "4.1.4. Moral ideas and practices."

91. See Dochy, "Assessment of Prior Knowledge as a Determinant for Future Learning," especially Chapter 2.

92. Aquinas, *Summa Theologiae*, Ia, 75, 5.

93. *Handbook*: Catherine Jami, "4.2.1. General reception."

94. *Handbook*: Golas, op. cit.

95. *Handbook*: Picard, op. cit.

96. Tzvetan Todorov, *La conquête de l'Amérique: La question de l'autre*, especially p. 191.

97. *Handbook*: Foss, op. cit.

98. *Handbook*: Golas, op. cit.

99. *Handbook*: Standaert, "2.5.1. General characteristics: Women."

100. For this interpretation, see Matzinger, "Tolerance, Danger, and the Extended Family," pp. 991–1045.

101. Without wanting to fall into the pitfall of social Darwinism.

102. *Handbook*: Dudink, "2.6.3. Opponents."

103. *Handbook*: Dudink, ibid.

104. *Handbook*: Pan Feng-chuan, "4.1.4. Moral ideas and practices."

105. For the concept of "inflated difference," see Ruland, "The Inflated Catholic Difference," pp. 20–22.

106. Prigogine, *Les lois du chaos*, p. 26, referring to Popper, *Of Clouds and Clocks*. This reference is given by Gruzinski, op. cit., pp. 54–55.

Li: Chinese Renaissance

1. See Liang Qichao, *Qingdai xueshu gailun*. Earlier in the winter of 1918, when Liang Qichao was visiting Paris with other famous scholars Zhang Junmai, Ding Wenjiang, Xu Xinliu, and Jiang Fangzhen for the Conference of Versailles after World War I, a French expert from the Musée de Louvre gave them a lecture on the Renaissance. After the lecture, Liang Qichao believed that China had actually experienced its own Renaissance. It took place during the

seventeenth to the nineteenth centuries, in other words, from late Ming to his own time. The record of the lecture developed into a book by Jiang Fangzhen entitled *The History of European Renaissance.*

2. Jiang Fangzhen, Preface to *Qingdai xueshu gailun.*

3. Ibid.

4. François Brancati (1607–1671) lived in Shanghai for over thirty years. He was integrated into local community as if he were a native Shanghainess. He was the leader of the Shanghai Chinese Christian community during the ressistant movement against Manchu's invasion.

5. See Jensen's point of view in his *Manufacturing Confucianism.*

6. Li Tiangang, *Zhongguo liyi zhi zheng: lishi wenxian he yiyi.*

7. This happened in Shaozhou, Guangdong province, where Xu Guangqi and Qu Taisu from Jiangnan explained the principles to Ricci. After his conversation with them, Ricci abandoned the performance and outlook of Buddhism, and called himself *xiru* (Western Confucian), but not *Xiseng* (Western Buddhist). See *China in the Sixteen Century: The Journal of Mathew Ricci.*

8. Xu Guangqi, "Zhengdao tigang."

9. Xu Guangqi, "Ke jihe yuanben xu."

10. In Ruan Yuan's *Chouren zhuan,* Ricci's, and many other Jesuits' biographies were included. In his book, Ruan attempted to recover the practical tradition of Confucius' *Liuyi.* He regrets that Chinese had lost the scientific tradition after the Han dynasty, but was very satisfied with the revival of this kind of learning in his generation.

11. Li Erqu, Yu Tian Yue, Li Yong Ji. When Li Yong prayed to the God in front of the Confucius's portrait, he burned incense, called God's name in *tian, Shangdi,* and asked for grace or forgiveness. He devised the ceremony similar to that of a Catholic ritual.

12. De Bary, ed., *The Unfolding of Neo-Confucianism: The Conference on Seventeenth-Century Thought.*

13. See Hou Wailu, *Zhongguo sixiang tongshi.*

14. Gernet, *Le monde chinois.*

15. De Bary, "Neo-Confucian Cultivation and the Seventeenth-Century 'Enlightenment'," p. 141.

16. Hsu, *The Rise of Modern China.*

17. Elman, *From Philosophy to Philology: Intellectual and Social Aspects of Change in Late Imperial China.*

18. Hu Shih, *The Chinese Renaissance: The Haskell Lectures in Comparative Religion, 1933.*

19. Why were scholars, especially the Qing scholars, reluctant to acknowledge their learning resources from Jesuits? I made some explanation about this question in *Zhongguo liyi zhi zheng: lishi wenxian he yiyi.*

20. When Qian Daxin met Dai Zhen in Beijing the first time and had an academic discussion, Dai believed that his teacher Jiang Yong ranked the first in the field of astronomy. Qian totally disagreed. The reason he offered is that Jiang Yong simply followed the Jesuit learning, "He is used by Westerners" (*wei xiren suoyong*), but Mei Weiding can "use the West" (*yong xi*). Qian's attitude and expression resulted in the late Qing culture policy of *Zhongxue weiti, Xixue weiyong.*

21. See *100 Roman Documents Concerning the Chinese Rites Controversy.*

22. Li Tiangang, ed., *Wan'guo gongbao wenxuan,* pp. 129 and 142.

Entenmann: The Problem of Chinese Rites

1. Mungello, ed., *The Chinese Rites Controversy: Its History and Meaning.* I am grateful to Claudia von Collani, Péter Vámos, and my colleagues in the History Faculty Colloquium at St. Olaf College for comments on an earlier version of this essay. Any errors, of course, are entirely my own.

2. For Ricci's discussion of "superstition," see Gallagher, trans., *China in the Sixteenth Century: The Journals of Matthew Ricci*, especially Chapter 9, "Concerning Certain Rites, Superstitious and Otherwise." "Superstition," in this context, refers to non-Christian religious beliefs and practices.

3. Rouleau, "Chinese Rites Controversy," in *New Catholic Encyclopedia*, III:611.

4. *Jing* should be more accurately translated as "respect," "honor," or "venerate," which is significantly different from "worship." Ultimately the Church revised its rulings in 1939 to permit veneration of ancestors and certain rites that were determined to be civil rather than religious. See Minamiki, *The Chinese Rites Controversy: From Its Beginnings to Modern Times.*

5. The Mandate of Maigrot is reprinted in St. Sure and Malatesta, trans., *100 Roman Documents Concerning the Rites Controversy*, Document 6.

6. Von Collani, "Charles Maigrot's Role in the Chinese Rites Controversy," pp. 149–84.

7. Mungello, "An Introduction to the Chinese Rites Controversy," p. 4. Mungello is summarizing the views of "one extreme" of scholarship on the Rites Controversy; needless to say this does not represent his opinion.

8. As Mungello points out (op. cit., p. 8), there are manuscripts on issues concerning the rites written by Chinese Christian *literati* preserved in the Jesuit Archives in Rome. But they were not published and had no direct influence on the debate.

9. Two exceptions are the contributions by Zürcher, "Jesuit Accommodation and the Chinese Cultural Imperative," which examines Catholic *literati* converts, and Wills, "From Manila to Fuan: Asian Contexts of Dominican Mission Policy," which discusses the Dominican mission in late Ming Fujian.

10. See the full texts in *Collectanea S. Congregationis de Propaganda Fide: seu decreta, instructiones, rescripta pro apostolicis missionibus ex tabulario eiusdem Sacrae Congregationis deprompta*, no. 1762.

11. *Journal of Joachim Enjobert de Martiliat* (hereafter: MJ), *Archives des Missions Étrangères*, Paris (hereafter AME), Vol. 434; See Adrien Launay's introduction in Ly, *Journal d'André Ly, prêtre chinois, missionnaire et notaire apostolique, 1747–1763: Texte Latin* (hereafter JAL).

12. Entenmann, "Chinese Catholic Communities in Early Ch'ing Szechwan"; see also *Shengjiao ru Chuan ji.*

13. See the entry on Martiliat in Launay, *Mémorial de la Société des Missions-Étrangères*, II:433–35.

14. The jurisdictional disputes between the Lazarists and Missions Étrangères are discussed at length in Launay, *Histoire des Mission de Chine: Mission du Se-Tchouan.*

15. De la Baluère to de Lionne, 17 March 1703, AME 408.37.

16. MJ, January 9, 1735, AME 434.509.

17. MJ, March 27, 1735, AME 434.522.

18. MJ, December 1739, AME 434.580.

19. MJ, December 1739, AME 434.580.

20. MJ, March 1740, AME 434.681.

21. MJ, September 1740, AME 434.634.

22. MJ, June 1743, AME 434.721. Martiliat does not record the Chinese characters.

23. Entenmann, "Chinese Catholic Clergy and Catechists in Eighteenth-Century Szechwan."

24. Ly's life and his diary have been examined in Olichon, *Aux origins du clergé chinois: Le Prêtre André Ly, missionnaire au Set-chouan*; Borer, "Das Tagebuch André Ly's als Quelle der Missionspastoral," 1:194–203 (1945); Serruys, "Andrew Li, Chinese Priest, 1692 (1693?)–1774," 32.2:39–55 and 130–44 (1976); and Fang Hao, *Zhongguo Tianzhujiao shi renwuzhuan*, 3:122–33.

25. Gourdin, *Catalogus cleri indigenae in Provincia Se-Tchouan, 1702–1858*, pp. 1–4 and 10–11.

26. Rouleau, op. cit., p. 615. Maigrot, along with others in the MEP, was suspected by the Society's opponents of being a Jansenist. See Launay, op. cit., II:418.

27. JAL, December 11, 1747, p. 33.

28. JAL, June 13, 1760, p. 505. Pedro Sanz, vicar apostolic of Fujian, was executed in 1747. The best scholarly account of this incident is José Maria Gonzáles, *Historia de las misiones Dominicanas de China*, II: 347–361.

29. This persecution is examined in Entenmann, "Catholics and Chinese Society in Eighteenth-Century Sichuan."

30. For Pottier's career, see Guiot, *La Mission du Su-tchuen au XVIIIme siècle: Vie et apostolat de Mgr. Pottier son fondateur*.

31. MJ, December 1739, AME 434.580. Ly gives the essay a Latin title: *De exquiis christianorum*. JAL, December 11, 1747, p. 33. Two decades later Ly also wrote a prayer for use at funerals. JAL, March 10, 1758, p. 453.

32. "Dum Romae fueris, romano vivito more, et cum Africae fueris, africano more vivito," JAL, 1752, p. 212.

33. JAL, August 12, 1757, p. 418.

34. "Nihil innovetur nisi quod traditum est," JAL, 1752, p. 213.

35. JAL, July 24, 1751, p. 179. In 1778 the vicar apostolic, François Pottier, ruled that Christians could attend non-Christian funerals as long as they did not contribute to any rituals. Pottier to Jean Joseph Descourvrières, October 15, 1778, AME 437.824.

36. JAL, April 27, 1748, p. 60. Ly refers to non-Christians as "gentiles" (gens, gentis), sometimes "heathens" (ethnicus, ethnici).

37. JAL, February 25, 1748, p. 43.

38. JAL, July 8, 1748, p. 72.

39. MJ, July 1739, AME 434.582. This tablet is a variation of the more common *tian di jun qin* [ancestor] *shi*. The "teacher" is Confucius.

40. JAL, March 7, 1753, p. 233. The printed text does not include the characters which, however, appear in the manuscript (AME 500.288).

41. JAL, January 4, 1748, p. 37.

42. JAL, January 19, 1748, pp. 37–38.

43. JAL, February 25, 1748, p. 42. The printed text lacks the characters, romanization, and Latin translation of this inscription, which appear, however, in the manuscript (AME 500.56).

44. JAL, October 31, 1747, p. 28.

45. Maigrot's mandate of 1693, and later rulings, explicitly prohibited *shen* as the proper name for the Christian God. It could, however, be used as a generic word for god, even referring to the Christian God when properly modified, i.e., *zhen shen*, True God.

46. JAL, July 8, 1748, pp. 72–73.

47. JAL, July 3, 1747, p. 17.

48. JAL, November 1, 1747, p. 28.

49. JAL, January 4, 1748, p. 37. The printed text lacks the Chinese characters, which appear in the manuscript (AME 500.49). Ly incorrectly writes *zi you* (see Glossary).

50. JAL, January 19, 1748, p. 38.

51. JAL, June 16, 1748, p. 69. The printed text lacks the Chinese characters, which appear in the manuscript (AME 500.92). Ly writes both the characters and romanization in traditional right-to-left order. The printed text thus reverses the word order.

52. "Cultus, sacrificium, gloria sit supremo, semper viventi, aeternum regnanti soli vero Deo: intra coelum et terram solis hic Dominus, per saeculi generationes colendus majestatis Pater, Rex." JAL, June 16, 1762, p. 586.

53. See the correspondence preserved at AME, some of which has been published in the *Nouvelles lettres édifiantes des missions de la Chine et des Indes Orientales*.

Han: Sino-French Scientific Relations

I am grateful to Lowell Skar and Cynthia Brokaw for correcting the English.

1. The founding of ARDS marked a revolution in the organization of scientific research. Much recent research has focused on the many significant activities and contributions of its members. See Hahn, *The Anatomy of a Scientific Institution: The Paris Academy of Sciences, 1666–1803*; Hirschfield, *The Académie Royale des Sciences, 1666–1683*; Sturdy, *Science and Social Status; The Members of the Académie des Sciences, 1666–1750*; Brian and Demeulenaere-Douyère, ed., *Histoire et mémoire de l'Académie des sciences: Guide de recherche*; Stroup, *A Company of Scientists: Botany, Patronage and Community at the Seventeenth-Century Parisian Royal Academy of Sciences*.

2. The academicians' interest in China was part of the general French interest in China during this period. Many books on China were printed in French at this time.

3. See Du Shiran and Han Qi, "The Contribution of French Jesuits to Chinese Science in the Seventeenth and Eighteenth Centuries," pp. 265–275; Jami, "From Louis XIV's court to Kangxi's court: An Institutional Analysis of the French Jesuit Mission to China (1662–1722)," pp. 493–99; and Han Qi, "The Role of the French Jesuits in China and the Académie Royale des Sciences in the development of the 17th and 18th Century French and Chinese Sciences," pp. 489–92.

4. The following French seventeenth- and eighteenth-century journals and publications were used: *Mémoires de l'Académie Royale des Sciences* (hereafter: *MARS*), *Mémoires de Mathématiques et de Physiques*, *Mémoires de l'Académie Royale des Sciences de l'Institut de France Année 1817*, and *Lettres édifiantes et curieuses*. I have also used the *Procès Verbaux* (hereafter: *PV*) of ARDS, which is held at the Archives of the Académie des Sciences in Paris. I

have yet to explore the articles published in the *Journal des Savants* and *Journal de Trévoux*.

5. See Huang Yilong, "Court divination and Christianity in the Kang-hsi Era," pp. 1–20.

6. *PV* gives the exact date of Jesuits' activities in ARDS. On December 20, 1684, Jean de Fontaney and three other Jesuits visited ARDS. Gian Domenico Cassini and Philippe de la Hire met them and gave them *MARS*, especially those on astronomy and botany. On January 17, 1685, Fontaney and five Jesuits attended a meeting of ARDS. ARDS gave them *MARS* in the name of François-Michele le Tellier de Louvois.

7. Du Hamel, *Regiae scientiarum Academie historia*, p. 241. I am grateful to Noël Golvers for the translation of the Latin text.

8. *PV*, 23/02/1689, "Monsieur Cassini a fait voir à la compagnie une astronomie orientale qu'il a dechiffrée. Monsieur le duc du Maine l'a envoyée à Monsieur Cassini." 05/03/1689, "Monsieur Cassini a lu ce qu'il a ajouté à son traitté de l'Astronomie des Chinoix."

9. Archives Jésuites de la province de Paris (Vanves), A 2579, p.51.

10. On December 20, 1684, Fontaney, Joachim Bouvet (1656–1730), Claude de Visdelou (1656–1737), Jean-François Gerbillon (1654–1707), were designated as correspondents. On March 4, 1699, Fontaney, Bouvet, Visdelou, Gerbillon and Jean-Alexis de Gollet (1664–1747) were designated as correspondents of their fellow Jesuit scientist and an academician of ARDS, T. Gouye. See *Index biographique de l'Académie des sciences du 22 décembre 1666 au 1er octobre 1978.*

11. *MARS* (1699), pp. 82–85.

12. As the editor writes: "Les observations, d'où le P. Gouye a conclu ces latitudes & longitudes, qui serviront à rectifier la Carte de la Chine, sont dues aux P. P. de Fontaney, le Comte, Bouvet, Gerbillon, & Visdelou."

13. *MARS. Depuis 1666 jusqu'à 1699. Tome X (1730)*, pp. 130–138.

14. Roger Hahn, *The Anatomy of a Scientific Institution: The Paris Academy of Sciences, 1666–1803.* p. 59.

15. In addition to the scientists mentioned above, the following French scientists also had close contact with Jesuits in China or discussed scientific materials about China: Giacomo Filippo Maraldi (1665–1729), René-Antoine Ferchault de Réaumur (1683–1757), Alexandre-Gui Pingré (1711–1796), Charles-Joseph Messier (1730–1817), Jean-Baptiste Joseph Delambre (1749–1822), and Pierre Simon de Laplace (1749–1827). Besides the above French scientists, some Jesuits such as T. Gouye and E. Souciet were in charge of publishing the astronomical observations made in China.

16. On February 20 and 23, 1726, the academicians continued to read the "mémoire de la Chine." See *PV* of ARDS.

17. *Lettres de M. de Mairan, au R. P. Parrenin* (1759), *Lettres sur l'origine des sciences, et sur celle des peuples de l'Asie, addressées à M. de Voltaire par M. Bailly* (London, 1777). See Han Qi, "Europeans' Views on the Backwardness of Chinese Sciences in the 17th and 18th centuries," pp. 289–298. Parrenin's letters and reports are held in libraries and archives in Paris. Some of them were published in the *Lettres édifiantes et curieuses.*

18. This question was what motivated Joseph Needham to begin his monumental work, *Science and Civilization in China.*

19. See Gaubil, *Correspondance de Pékin (1722–1759)*. On August 22, 1750, Gaubil was designated as correspondent of Academician Joseph-Nicolas Delisle (1688–1768).

20. Le Cheron d'Incarville was designated as correspondent of Academician Claude Joseph Geoffroy. On D'Incarville, see Henri Bernard, "Un correspondant de Bernard de Jussieu en Chine: Le Père Le Cheron d'Incarville, missionnaire français de Pékin," *Archives Internationales d'Histoire des Sciences*, 6 (janvier 1949): 333–362; 7 (avril 1949): 692–717.

21. On March 3 and 10, 1751, Jean Hellot read letters of d'Incarville on different subjects. *PV*, T. 70 (1751), pp. 206 and 258. On March 17, 1751, Hellot presented a Plan of Beijing to ARDS, which was sent by d'Incarville. See *PV*, T. 70 (1751), p. 271. On June 28, 1752, Mr. Hellot read a letter of Father D'Incarville in which he asked the Academy not to engrave the plan of Beijing, because D'Incarville thought that it would be unfavorable (désagréable) to the missionaries. For details, see *PV*, T. 71 (1752), p. 347. On August 5 and 9, 1752, "Mr Hellot a lu pour le P. d'Incarville J. un Mémoire sur le Kin-t-cheou ou etoffe faite de soye des Vers à soye sauvages." *PV*, T. 71 (1752) pp. 407 and 413.

22. For example, Thomas Birch (1705–1766), the secretary of the Royal Society of London, was also in close contact with Jesuits in Beijing. See Han Qi, "Sino-British Scientific Relations through Jesuits in the Seventeenth and Eighteenth Centuries," pp. 43–59. Sometimes the scientific relations between the French Jesuits and ARDS were channeled through the Jesuits in Paris.

23. See Mairan, "Remarques sur une comète observée à Pékin," and "Extrait des observations sur la comète."

24. *MARS*, 1764, pp. 152–156. This was based on a paper on longitude and latitude of Beijing read by Alexandre Pingré on June 2, 1764, at ARDS. See *PV*, T. 83 (1764), pp. 206–216.

25. *MARS*, 1726, pp. 236–242.

26. "Anciennes observations de la Chine sur l'obliquité de l'Ecliptique," in *MARS*, 1743, pp. 151–152.

27. Joseph Needham has emphasized the influence of Antoine Gaubil on Laplace (*Science and Civilisation in China*, p. 183); Gaubil's result had also been used earlier by French astronomers. See Gaubil, *Correspondance de Pékin, (1722–1759)*.

28. Gian Domenico Cassini, "Réflexions sur la chronologie chinoise," in *MARS*. Depuis 1666 jusqu'à 1699, T. 8 (1730): 300–311.

29. For example, Pierre Jartoux's letter on ginseng (written in 1711), published in the *Lettres Edifiantes,* was of great importance because it led to the discovery of ginseng at Quebec.

30. There were also many papers written by the Jesuits and academicians of ARDS still held in libraries and archives in Paris.

31. Hahn, *The Anatomy of a Scientific Institution: The Paris Academy of Sciences, 1666–1803*. p. 62.

32. Pierre Noël le Chéron d'Incarville, "Mémoire sur la manière singulière dont les Chinois soudent la Corne à lanternes," in *Mémoires de Mathématiques et de Physiques* (hereafter: *MMP*), T.2 (1755): 350–368; "Mémoire sur le vernis de la Chine," T.3 (1760): 117–141; "Manière de faire les fleurs dans les Feux d'Artifice Chinois," T.4 (1763): 66–94.

33. Bibliothèque Nationale de Paris, Mss. fr.17240. See also Isabelle Landry-Deron, *Les leçons de sciences occidentales de l'empereur de Chine*

Kangxi (1662–1722): Texte des Journal des Pères Bouvet et Gerbillon (Paris, E.H.E.S.S. 1995).

34. The manuscripts of the Manchu and Chinese translation are still held at the Library of the Palace Museum in Beijing.

35. See Han Qi, "Shuli jingyun duishu zaobiaofa yu Dai Xu de erxiang zhankaishi yanjiu," 11.2:109–119.

36. It seems that the "Académie de la Chine" consisted of the "King's Mathematicians."

37. On the creation of the Academy in China, see von Collani, *Eine wissenschaftlische Akademie fuer China (Studia Leibnitiana)*.

38. Biblioteca Apostolica Vaticana, Borg. Cin. 439.

39. Witek, *Controversial Ideas in China and in Europe: A Biography of Jean-François Foucquet, S.J. (1665–1741)*.

40. Foucquet, "Richan" in *Lifa wenda*, p. 52. British Library. On Foucquet's *Lifa wenda*, see Martzloff, "A Glimpse of the Post-Verbiest Period," pp. 519–529. See also Hashimoto and Jami, "Kepler's laws in China: A missing link? J.-F. Foucquet's *Lifa wenda*," *Historia Scientiarum* 6.3:171–185.

41. Jami, *Jean-François Foucquet et la modernisation de la science en Chine: la "Nouvelle Méthode d'Algèbre."*

42. Han Qi, "Kangxi shidai chuanru de Xifang shuxue jiqi dui Zhongguo shuxue de yingxiang."

von Collani: China in the German "Geistesgeschichte"

1. Leibniz, *Novissima Sinica*, preface.

2. von Collani, "Johann Adam Schall von Bell und die Naturwissenschaften in China," pp. 25–29; *Die Jesuiten in Ingolstadt 1549–1773*, pp. 140–65.

3. Dehergne, *Répertoire des Jésuites de Chine de 1552 à 1800*, pp. 308f; Claudia von Collani, *Die Figuristen in der Chinamission*, pp. 4–7.

4. Huonder, *Deutsche Jesuitenmissionäre des 17. und 18. Jahrhunderts. Ein Beitrag zur Missionsgeschichte und zur deutschen Biographie*, pp. 183–97.

5. Dehergne, op. cit., pp. 307f.

6. See, for example, Gaubil, *Correspondance de Pékin 1722–1759*; Widmaier, ed., *Leibniz korrespondiert mit China. Der Briefwechsel mit den Jesuitenmissionaren 1689–1714*.

7. Lamalle, "La tour du propagande du P. Nicolas Trigault en faveur des missions de Chine, 1616," pp. 49–120.

8. Väth, *Johann Adam Schall von Bell SJ. Missionar in China*; Malek, ed., *Western Learning and Christianity in China*.

9. Reil, *Kilian Stumpf 1655–1720. Ein Würzburger Jesuit am Kaiserhof zu Peking*.

10. Stücken, "Der Astronom des Kaisers. Vom Leben des Chinamissionars Ignaz Kögler SJ (1680–1746)," pp, 439–69.

11. Mungello, *Leibniz and Confucianism. The Search for Accord*, p. 5.

12. See Widmaier, op. cit..

13. Bodemann, *Sämtliche Schriften und Briefe. Eyste Reihe, Der Briefwechsel des Gottfried Wilhelm Leibniz in der Königlichen öffentlichen Bibliothek zu Hannover*, and the edition of the Leibniz correspondence 1697 and 1698 in: *Sämtliche Schriften und Briefe. Erste Reihe, Allgemeiner politischer und historischer Briefwechsel*, I:14 and I:15. For the "Chinese" correspondence, see Widmaier, op. cit.

14. Streit and Dindinger, eds., *Bibliotheca Missionum* IV, No. 1972.
15. Walravens, *China illustrata. Das europäische Chinaverständnis im Spiegel des 16. bis 18. Jahrhunderts*, pp. 85–88.
16. Streit and Dindinger, eds., *Bibliotheca Missionum* V, Nos. 2095 and 2100.
17. Etiemble, *L'Europe Chinoise. II: De la sinophilie à la sinophobie.*
18. Mungello, *Curious Land: Jesuit Accommodation and the Origins of Sinology.*
19. Ibid., pp. 175–78.
20. von Collani, "Theology and Chronology," in *Sinicae Historiae Decas Prima*, p. 237.
21. Leibniz, letter, May 18th , 1703, in Widmaier, op. cit., p. 188.
22. Walravens, op. cit., p. 224f.
23. Widmaier, *Die Rolle der chinesischen Schrift in Leibniz' Zeichentheorie*, pp. 95–97.
24. E. Kraft, "Frühe chinesische Studien in Berlin," pp. 93f.
25. Kircher had obtained the Chinese characters for his book from Michal Boym S.J., who sent him copies from the *Shuowen jiezi*. See von Murr, *Litterae patentes Imperatoris Sinarvm Kang-Hi sinice et latine*, p. 41.
26. *Bibliotheca Missionum* IV, No. 1972f; German translation in 1589 and 1597.
27. Streit and Dindinger, eds., *Bibliotheca Missionum* V, Nos. 2176, 2187, 2336 and 2337; A. Pfister, *Notices biographiques et bibliographiques sur les Jésuites de l'ancienne mission de Chine, 1552–1773*, pp. 143–47; Mungello, *Curious Land: Jesuit Accommodation and the Origins of Sinology*, pp. 74–90.
28. Semedo, *Histoire universelle de la Chine*, pp. 51f; Mungello, *Curious Land: Jesuit Accommodation and the Origins of Sinology*, p. 154.
29. Kircher, *Oedipus Aegyptiacus* III, Chapter II, pp. 10–21; cf. Kircher, *La Chine illustrée. . . ,* plate 1; cf. Lundbæk, "Imaginary Ancient Chinese Characters," p. 5.
30. Martini, *Sinicæ historiæ decas prima: res à gentis origine ad Christum natum in extrema Asia, sive magno Sinarum imperio gestas complexa*, pp. 22f.
31. Magalhães, pp. 84–107; cf. A. Pfister, p.255; Mungello, pp. 96–105. For Zhang Juzheng, see Lundbæk, "Chief Grand Secretary Chang Chü-cheng & the Early China Jesuits," pp. 1–11; and Mungello, "The Jesuits' Use of Chang Chü-cheng's Commentary in Their Translation of the Confucian Four Books," pp. 12–22.
32. Mungello, *Curious Land*, pp. 134–73.
33. Brandenburg-Preußen had been founded in 1618, when Preußen (Prussia) was united with Brandenburg and when Friedrich Wilhelm liberated Prussia from Poland. In 1701, the duchy became a kingdom and Friedrich Wilhelm's son Friedrich I (1688–1713) became "King in Prussia" in 1701. He was followed by his son Friedrich Wilhelm I (reg. 1713–1749), called the "Soldatenkönig" (he only collected soldiers, but waged no wars), then followed by his son Friedrich II, "Der Große" (The Great, 1740–1786), a friend of Voltaire.
34. Walravens, op. cit., pp. 260f; E. Kraft, "Christian Mentzel, Philippe Couplet, Andreas Cleyer und die chinesische Medizin aus Handschriften des 17. Jahrhunderts," pp. 158–196.
35. E. Kraft, "Die chinesische Büchersammlung des Großen Kurfürsten und seines Nachfolgers," pp. 18–29.

36. E. Kraft, ibid., p. 20; E. Kraft, "Frühe chinesische Studien in Berlin," pp. 113–15; Mungello, *Curious Land: Jesuit Accommodation and the Origins of Sinology*, pp. 238f.

37. E. Kraft, "Die chinesische Büchersammlung. . . ," pp. 18–29.

38. E. Kraft, "Frühe chinesische Studien. . . ," pp. 97–107; Mungello, *Curious Land*, pp. 208–36; Walravens, pp. 216–18 and 266f.

39. Mungello, *Curious Land*, p. 237; Also see Artelt, *Christian Mentzel: Leibarzt des Großen Kurfürsten, Botaniker und Sinologe.*

40. Lundbæk, "Dr. Mentzel's kinesiske Börnbog."

41. Leibniz to Bouvet, January 1698, in Widmaier, *Leibniz korrespondiert mit China*, p. 68.

42. Streit and Dindinger, eds., *Bibliotheca Missionum* V, p. 966; E. Kraft, "Frühe chinesische Studien. . . ," pp. 115f; Mungello, *Curious Land*, pp. 236–44. The original manuscript of Mentzel's "Clavis Sinica" is kept in the Deutsche Staatsbibliothek, Berlin. It consists of 124 folio pages. Lundbæk, *T.S. Bayer (1694–1738). Pioneer Sinologist*, p. 110.

43. Ibid.

44. Ibid., pp. 12–15.

45. Ibid., pp. 39–97.

46. Ibid., pp. 204–10.

47. Lundbæk, "The First Translation from a Confucian Classic in Europe," pp. 2–11; Mungello, "The Seventeenth-Century Jesuit Translation Project of the Confucian Four Books," pp. 252–72.

48. Heyndrickx, ed., *Philippe Couplet S.J. (1623–1693). The Man Who Brought China to Europe.* Also see Lundbæk, "The Image of Neo-Confucianism in *Confucius Sinarum Philosophus*," pp. 39–53.

49. A. Pfister, op. cit., pp. 417f.

50. Ching and Oxtoby, *Moral Enlightenment. Leibniz and Wolff on China*, p. 49; cf. Mungello, "The Seventeenth-Century Jesuit Translation Project. . . ."

51. *Bibliotheca Missionum* V, pp. 887–80.

52. Lundbæk, "Chief Grand Secretary Chang Chü-cheng," and Mungello, "The Jesuits' Use of Chang Chü-cheng's Commentary."

53. Kühn, "Leibniz und China," p. 30–36.

54. Widmaier, pp. 1–10; Leibniz's letter, dated 1692, in J. Ching and Oxtoby, eds., *Moral Enlightenment. Leibniz and Wolff on China*, pp. 63–69.

55. Widmaier, ed., *Leibniz korrespondiert mit China. . . .* 70 letters.

56. von Collani, "Der deutsche Philosoph Gottfried Wilhelm Leibniz zum chinesischen Ritenstreit," p. 43.

57. Fuchs, "Der russisch-chinesische Vertrag von Nertschinsk aus dem Jahre 1689," pp. 546–96.

58. von Collani, "Der deutsche Philosoph Gottfried Wilhelm Leibniz zum chinesischen Ritenstreit," p. 37. In English, see Lach, *The Preface to Leibniz's Novissima Sinica*; cf. *Bibliotheca Missionum* V, No. 2734.

59. It was published in a Latin translation in Leibniz' second edition of the Novissima Sinica (1699); see *Bibliotheca Missionum* V, Nos. 2728 and 2779. The story of the correspondence Leibniz-Bouvet, also see von Collani, *P. Joachim Bouvet S.J.: Sein Leben und sein Werk*, pp. 31–44.

60. Zacher, *Die Hauptschriften zur Dyadik von G.W. Leibniz*, pp. 262–74; Widmaier, pp. 147–70.

61. Zacher, op. cit., pp. 66–68.

62. Widmaier, pp. 136–38.

63. von Collani, "Le Père Joachim Bouvet et le Mandement du Vicaire Apostolique Charles Maigrot," pp. 90–91.
64. Couplet, ed., "Proëmialis Declaratio," p. xliv; Zacher, op. cit., p. 112.
65. Zacher, op. cit., pp. 70, 129 and 55; von Collani, *Die Figuristen*, pp. 39f.
66. Kühn, p. 31; von Collani, "Leibniz."
67. Grimm, "China und das Chinabild von Leibniz," pp. 57f; also see von Collani, *Eine wissenschaftliche Akademie für China.*
68. von Collani, "Leibniz."
69. J. Ching and Oxtoby, op. cit., pp. 46f.
70. Mungello, "Confucianism and Enlightenment," p. 108.
71. *Lexikon für Theologie und Kirche* 4, cols. 250f; Wolff, *Oratio de Sinarum philosophia practica*, pp. XLVIf.
72. J. Ching and Oxtoby, op. cit., p. 51.
73. Wolff, *Rede über die praktische Vernunft der Chinesen*, pp. XXXVIII–XLVI.
74. J. Ching and Oxtoby, op. cit., p. 51.
75. *Lexikon für Theologie und Kirche* 4, col. 1332. Later on, Theology in Halle, based on pietism, but working with the scientific-critical method, started in the second half of the eighteenth century; See Wolff, pp. IL–LIII.
76. It appeared as *Pomvm eridis, hoc est de Sapientia Sinensivm Oratio. . . ,* and was printed in Germany. See Wolff, pp. XC–XCII.
77. See Wolff, pp. XC–CI.
78. Mungello, "Confucianism and Enlightenment," p. 113, and No. 45.
79. Laurentin, *Chine et Christianisme. Après les occasions manquées,* pp. 17–22.

Doubrovskaia: The Russian Orthodox Church in China

1. *Da Qing lichao shilu: Shenzu*, p. 37b.
2. Baddeley, *Russia, Mongolia, China*: . . . Vol. II, p. 430. *Dopolneniia k aktam istoricheskim.* Vol. VI, p. 43.
3. *Polnoe sobranie zakonov Rossiiskoi imperii s 1649 goda.* Vol. 4, No. 1800.
4. Lach, *The Preface to Leibniz's Novissima Sinica*, p. 277.
5. Adoratskii, *Pravoslavnaia missiia v Kitae za 200 let eia "sushchestvovaniia"* (February–November 1887), p. 478.
6. *Istoricheskii ocherk khristianskoi propovedi v Kitae.* Vol. 3, pp. 112–72 and 241–366.
7. "O nachale torgovych i gosudarstvennykh snoshenii Rossii s Kitaem i o dukhovnoi missii v Pekine," No. 18, pp. 99–164, and No. 19, pp. 165–96.
8. *Polnoe sobranie zakonov.* Vol. 6, No. 3734; Adoratskii, op. cit., p. 489.
9. *Polnoe sobranie postanovlenii*, Vol. 1, pp. 121–22.
10. Adoratskii, op. cit. (April), pp. 496–97.
11. Duman, ed. *Russko-kitaiskie otnosheniia, 1689–1916. Ofitsial'nyie dokumenty*, pp. 19–20.
12. Krivtsov, *Otets Iakinf: roman.*
13. Efimov, "Novyie materialy po istorii Pekinskoi Duchovnoi Missii."
14. R. M. Martin, *China: Political, Commercial and Social; in an Official Report to Her Majesty's Government*, Vol. I, pp. 395–96.
15. Widmer, *The Russian Ecclesiastical Mission in Peking During the Eighteenth Century*, p. 6.

16. Latourette. *A History of Christian Missions in China*.

17. Adoratskii, op. cit.

18. Foust. *Muscovite and Mandarin: Russia's Trade with China and Its Setting 1727–1805*, p. 51.

19. McWhirter and McWhirter, eds., *Guinness Book of World Records. 1976 Edition*, p. 248.

20. Ivanov, "K istorii vozniknoveniia Moskovskogo podvoria Pekinskoi duchovnoi missii."

21. Pozdniaiev, *Pravoslavie v Kitae (1900–1997 gg.)*.

22. Efimov, op. cit..

23. See http://www.russian-orthodox-church.org.ru/nr180772.htm.

24. Matthew, 28: 18–20.

Lutz: China and Protestantism

1. When I had largely completed the first draft of this essay, I turned to John K. Fairbank, ed., *The Missionary Enterprise in China and America* for a reference and discovered that Fairbank's Introduction was entitled "The Many Faces of Protestant Missions in China and the United States" (pp. 1–19). I am happy to acknowledge my indebtedness to Fairbank even if it was subliminal and my topic is broader. In composing this historical overview, I have benefited from Bays, "Missions and Christians in Modern China, 1850–1950," and from P. Cohen, "Christian Missions and Their Impact to 1900," pp. 543–90.

2. "The 'Eastern Lightning' Sect: A Recent Threat to the Church in China," *Amity News Service* 6.11/12 (1997):17–19; "Is the Church a Help or a Hindrance to China's Development?" ibid., 8.3/4(1999): 6; "Modern Sects and Cults in China," *China Church Quarterly*, 38 (Spring 1999): 1–2.

3. For example, Latourette, *A History of Christian Missions in China* remains an indispensable source of information as do the histories of the Christian colleges commissioned by the United Board for Christian Higher Education in Asia.

4. Gernet, *China and the Christian Impact*, was one of the most influential and controversial studies.

5. P. Cohen, *China and Christianity*; Lü Shiqiang, *Zhongguo guanshen fanjiao de yuanyin, 1860–1874*; Liao Guangsheng, *Antiforeignism and Modernization in China*.

6. Barnett and Fairbank, eds., *Christianity in China: Early Protestant Missionary Writings*; Lutz, *China and the Christian Colleges, 1850–1950*; Hayhoe and Bastid, eds., *China's Education and the Industrialized World: Studies in Cultural Transfer*; Borthwick, *Education and Social Change in China: The Beginnings of the Modern Era*; Bennett, *John Fryer: The Introduction of Western Science and Technology into Nineteenth-Century China*.

7. Bays, ed., *Christianity in China, From the Eighteenth Century to the Present*; Bays, "Indigenous Protestant Churches in China, 1900–1937: A Pentecostal Case Study," pp. 124–43; Covell, *The Liberating Gospel in China: The Christian Faith Among China's Minority Peoples*; Xi Lian, "No Earthly Salvation: Wang Mingdao, John Sung, Watchman Nee, and the Rise of Indigenous Christianity in China"; Li Zhigang, *Zaoqi Jidujiao zai Hua chuanjiaoshi*; Ren Zhongxiang, *Shanghai Jidutu juhuichu jianshi*.

8. Lutz and Lutz, *Hakka Chinese Confront Protestant Christianity, 1850–1900*; Lutz and Lutz, "The Invisible Missionaries: The Basel Mission's Chinese Evangelists, 1847–1866," 12.2 (October 1995): 204–27; Smith, *Chinese Christians: Elites, Middlemen and the Church in Hong Kong*; Zha Shijie, *Zhongguo Jidujiao renwu xiaozhuan*; Li Zhigang, *Jidujiao zaoqi zai Hua chuanjiao shi*; L. Pfister, "A Transmitter but Not a Creator: Ho Tsun-sheen (1817–1871), the First Modern Chinese Protestant Theologian," pp. 165–98; L. Pfister, "From the Golden Light Within: Reconsideration of James Legge's Account of Ch'ëa Kam Kwong, the Chinese 'Proto-Martyr'"; Kong Xiangtao, "Xinyang, renmin he zuguo: zaoqi Jidujiaohui de huaren budaoyuan qun," pp. 43–50.

9. For bibliographical essays, see *Xindai Zhongguo Jidujiao shiyenjiu jikan*, 1 (April 1998). Also, see Ying Fuzang, *Wenhua shiying yu Zhongguo Jidujiao (1860–1911)*; Tao Feiya and Liu Tianlu, *Jidujiaohui yu jindai shandong shehui*; Gu Weimin, *Jidujiao yu xindai Zhongguo shehui*; Li Zhigang, *Jidujiao yu jindai Zhongguo wenhua lunwenji*; Zhang Kaiyuan and Arthur Waldron, eds., *Zhong-Xi wenhua yu jiaohui daxue*; Zhang Kaiyuan, ed., *Shehui zhuanxing yu jiaohui daxue*.

10. Hamberg to Inspector, Pukak, 14 May 1853, in Evangelische in Basel. China: Berichte und Korrespondenz, 1846–1900, BMG, A–1.2, no 31.

11. L. Pfister, "From the Golden Light Within."

12. For a brief biography of Zhang Fuxing, see Bender, "Lebenskizze des verstorbenen Tschong Fuk-hin in Verbindung mit der Gründung der Tschonglok Gemeinden," *Tschongtshun*, 18 June 1880, BMG, A–1.14, no 70. A more detailed biography is available in Lutz and Lutz, *Hakka Chinese*, pp. 32–54.

13. Ibid., pp. 198–199; Smith, *Chinese Christians*, pp. 213–14.

14. Schaible, "A-Kwui, einer der Erstlinge von Nyenhangli, in seinem Leben und Sterben," Nyenhangli, 2 May 1893, BMG, A–1.27, no 95.

15. Bohr, "Liang Fa's Quest for Moral Power," pp. 40–44; Schlatter, *Geschichte der Basler Mission, 1815–1915*, vol. 2, *Die Geschichte der Basler Mission in Indien und China*, 2:337–340; Schultze, "Geschichte der Basler Missionsstation Tschongtshun," Tschongtshun, 27 October 1889, BMG, A–1.23, no. 120.

16. Hood, *Mission Accomplished? The English Presbyterian Mission in Lingtung, South China*, pp. 32–52. Nominally, Hanspach, Burns, and Roberts were associated with mission societies, but all three defined their own methodology and fields of operation.

17. Lutz and Lutz, "Karl Gützlaff's Approach to Indigenization: The Chinese Union," pp. 269–291.

18. Broomhall, *Hudson Taylor and China's Open Century*, Vols. 1–3.

19. Samuel H. Chao, *John Livingston Nevius (1829–1893): A Historical Study of His Life and Methods*.

20. Bays, "Missions and Christians."

21. Ibid.

22. Zha, *Zhongguo Jidujiao*, pp. 5–8; Lo Xianglin, "Zhongguo zupu suoji Jidujiao zhi chuanbo yu jindai Zhongguo zhi guanxi," 7 (1969): 1–22.

23. Hood, *Mission Accomplished*, p. 182.

24. Zha, *Zhongguo Jidujiao*, pp. 9–14 and 39–44; Pfister, "A Transmitter but Not a Creator."

25. Schlatter, *Geschichte der Basler Mission*, 2:316–21, 377–83, and 391–92.

26. Zha, *Zhongguo Jidujiao*, pp. 21–25; Mrs. Howard Taylor (M. Geraldine Guinness), *Pastor Hsi of North China: One of China's Christians*.

27. Notable among these were Gilbert Reid (1857–1927), Young J. Allen (1836–1907), Timothy Richard (1845–1919), W.A.P. Martin (1827–1916), and John Fryer (1839–1919).

28. Litzinger, "Rural Religion and Village Organization in North China: The Catholic Challenge in the Late Nineteenth Century," pp. 41–52; Thompson, "Twilight of the Gods in the Chinese Countryside: Christians, Confucians, and the Modernizing State, 1861–1911," pp. 53–72; Lutz and Lutz, *Hakka Chinese*, pp. 204–208.

29. P. Cohen, *China and Christianity*; Lu Shiqiang, *Zhongguo guanshen fanjiao*.

30. Lutz, *China and the Christian Colleges*, pp. 161–2.

31. A case study illustrating the problems is provided in Wang Chengmian (Peter Chen-main Wang), *Wenshe de shengshuai—erling niandai Jidujiao bensehua zhi ge'an yanjiu*.

32. Bays, "Indigenous Protestant Churches."

33. Bays, "Christian Revivalism in China, 1900–1937," pp. 161–79.

34. Xi Lian, "No Earthly Salvation."

35. Ka-che Yip, *Religion, Nationalism, and Chinese Students: The Anti-Christian Movement of 1922–1927*; Lutz, *Chinese Politics and Christian Missions: The Anti-Christian Movements of 1920–28*; Yang Tianhong, *Jidujiao yu jindai Zhongguo, A Study of the Anti-Christian Movement in China*.

36. Lutz, *Chinese Politics*; Waldron, *From War to Nationalism: China's Turning Point, 1924–1925*.

37. Jonathan T'ien-en Chao (Zhao Tian'en), "The Chinese Indigenous Church Movement, 1919–1927: A Protestant Response to the Anti-Christian Movement in Modern China"; Lam Wing-hung (Lin Ronghong), *Fengchao zhong fenqi de Zhongguo jiaohui*.

38. For detail's, see Brook, "Towards Independence: Christianity in China Under the Japanese Occupation, 1937–1945," pp. 317–37.

39. Zha, *Zhongguo Jidujiao*, pp. 305–40; Angus Kinnear, *Against the Tide*.

Dunch: Protestant Christianity in China Today

1. *Far Eastern Economic Review*, June 6, 1996.

2. For example, Rosenthal, "On My Mind: Persecuting Christians"; Amity News Service, "No Ordinary Day."

3. China State Council, *White Paper–Freedom of Religious Belief*, October 1997.

4. See e.g., Bishop K. H. Ting's 1988 letter to the Religious Affairs Bureau, in *Baixing* 187 (1 March 1989): 17–18.

5. K. H. Ting, "Discussion with Members of the Yeller Sect"; Tang Shuolin and Ren Zhongxiang, "Jianjue dizhi Li Changshou de yiduan xieshuo." Reports claiming TSPM involvement in suppressing alleged Shouters include "Detention of Christians in Shantou," *China News and Church Report* 205 (June 4, 1984); "Problems and Prayer in the House Churches," *China and the Church Today* 6:5 (1984): 13–16.

6. Cf. the signs of heresy listed in a CCC publication in 1997 in *China Study Journal* 12:2 (1997): 57–58.

7. For example, Stursberg, *The Golden Hope*, p. 229; Towery, *The Churches of China: Taking Root Downward, Bearing Fruit Upward*, pp. 46–47.

8. Glanzer, "International Persecution"; Wallis, *China Miracle: A Voice to the Church in the West*.

9. Lambert gives a useful survey in "Modern Sects and Cults." See also Lu Yunfeng, "Report on an Investigation into the Illegal Organisation, the 'Disciples Sect'"; Luo, "The Facts About the Activities of Heterodox Sect 'The Established King.'" On the "Children of God" in 1986, see "Teaching English in China," in *China and Ourselves* 48 (Winter 1986): 10–11; for sects generally in post-Mao China, see Munro, ed., "Syncretic Sects and Secret Societies: Revival in the 1980s."

10. Jerome Ch'en, *China and the West*, p. 95; Rabe, "Evangelical Logistics: Mission Support and Resources to 1920," p. 384.

11. Based on a rough count through Lodwick, *The Chinese Recorder Index: A Guide to Christian Missions in China*, Vol. 2, pp. 545–619.

12. Latourette, *A History of Christian Missions in China*, pp. 439–41 and 662–72; Worley, *Central Conference of the Methodist Episcopal Church*, pp. 304–305; Merwin, *Adventure in Unity: The Church of Christ in China*.

13. Cf. Brook, "Toward Independence: Christianity in China Under the Japanese Occupation."

14. Whyte, *Unfinished Encounter: China and Christianity*, pp. 155–59.

15. *Bridge* 83 (1997): 12.

16. Bays, "Growth of Independent Christianity in China, 1900–1937"; cf. special issues of *Bridge* devoted to these movements, e.g., 57 (1993) and 58 (1993) on the "Local Church," 62 (1993) and 63 (1994) on the "True Jesus Church."

17. Bays, "Growth of Independent Christianity," p. 310.

18. Hunter and Kim-Kwong Chan, *Protestantism in Contemporary China*, pp. 126–35.

19. Cf. Yao Mingquan, "Indigenization in China in the First Half of the Twentieth Century," pp. 36–38.

20. Shue, *The Reach of the State: Sketches of the Chinese Body Politic*, p. 6 and *passim*.

21. For the Catholic parallel, see Madsen, *China's Catholics: Tragedy and Hope in an Emerging Civil Society*, p. 58.

22. Zhao Tian'en and Zhuang Wanfang, *Dangdai Zhongguo Jidujiao fazhan shi*, pp. 228–48; Wickeri, *Seeking the Common Ground: Protestant Christianity, the Three-Self Movement, and China's United Front*, p. 177. For the continuation of religious practice more generally in the 1970s, see Parish and Whyte, *Village and Family in Contemporary China*, Chapters 13 and 14; Whyte and Parish, *Urban Life in Contemporary China*, Chapter 10.

23. See *Guangming Daily*, January 6, 1979; MacInnis, *Religion in China Today: Policy and Practice*, pp. 32–34. For more on the reasons behind the policy change see Dunch, "Protestants and the State in Post-Mao China," pp. 25–28.

24. For fascinating details on some autonomous Protestant groups, see Hunter and Chan, op. cit., Chapter 5.

25. *China News and Church Report* (May 23, 1997); Human Rights Watch/Asia, *China: State Control of Religion*, 32, No. 61; Lambert, *The Resurrection of the Chinese Church*, pp. 93 and 151; *China Study Journal* 12:2 (1997): 52–53.

26. The four leaders who drafted a joint confession of faith in November 1998 appear to represent such networks in Henan and Anhui; see *China News and Church Report* (December 21, 1998); Lambert, "Modern Sects and Cults," p. 8; cf. *China Study Journal* 13:2 (1998): 58–63. Hunter and Chan, however, see large networks as the exception rather than the rule among the autonomous churches; see op. cit., pp. 64–65.

27. Cf. Hunter, "Sociological Perspective on Chinese Christianity;" Tang Rongtao, "Refresher Courses in Guizhou."

28. Cf. Hunter and Chan, op. cit., Chapter 3.

29. Butler, *Awash in a Sea of Faith: Christianizing the American People*, Chapter 8 and *passim*; Hatch, *The Democratization of American Christianity*.

30. See Yang Fenggang, *Chinese Christians in America: Conversion, Assimilation, and Adhesive Identities*, Chapter 1.

31. Wuthnow, *The Restructuring of American Religion: Society and Faith Since World War II*.

32. Nagata, "Chinese Custom and Christian Culture: Implications for Chinese Identity in Malaysia."

33. *Religion Today* Feature Story for July 12, 1999; archived at http://www.ReligionToday.com; cf. the website of the agency in question, the "Persecuted Church Collection," at http://www.persecutedchurch.com.

34. *China Study Journal* 11:3 (1996): 68–69; Lambert, *The Resurrection of the Chinese Church*, Chapter 9, especially pp. 156–57; Lambert, "Counting Christians in China: Who's Right," p. 35.

35. Hunter and Chan, op. cit., p. 68; *Bridge* has reported extensively on the churches in Fujian, Zhejiang, and Shandong; see e.g., 42 (1990): 3–10.

36. Bao Zhimin, "Facing Reality and Responding to Challenges: On Ten Years of Chinese Church Reconstruction," p. 3; cf. Luo Zhufeng, ed., *Religion Under Socialism*, Appendix 9; Hunter and Chan, op. cit., p. 73.

37. In *China Study Journal* 12:3 (1997): 8–9.

38. Lambert, *Resurrection of the Chinese Church*, p. 136. By comparison, Protestants in China changed from a socially marginalized to a prosperous and upwardly mobile group over the late Qing; see Dunch, *Fuzhou Protestants and Making of a Modern China, 1857–1927*, Chapter 1.

39. Hunter and Chan, , op. cit., Chapter 4.

40. Hunter, "Sociological Perspective on Chinese Christianity"; Martinson, "The Protestant Church in Post-Mao China: Two Paradigms," pp. 14–15.

41. Bays, "Indigenous Protestant Churches in China, 1900–1937"; cf. Rubinstein, *The Protestant Community on Modern Taiwan: Mission, Seminary, Church*, pp. 129–40.

42. Dunch, *Fuzhou Protestants and Making of a Modern China, 1857–1927*, Chapter 1; cf. the biographies in Lutz and Lutz, *Hakka Chinese*.

43. For allegorical interpretation from two very different Chinese Protestants, see the selections from Ting and Nee in Chan and Hunter, *Prayers and Thoughts of Chinese Christians*, pp. 76–92. John Sung wrote a whole book of allegorical tales based on the books of the Bible; see Lyall, *John Sung: Flame for God in the Far East*, p. 186; cf. Hunter and Chan, *Protestantism in Contemporary China*, p. 132. On Jia Yuming, see Zhao Qiusheng, "The Old Testament Commentaries of Jia Yuming," pp. 47–59.

44. Ji Tai, "Hermeneutics in the Chinese Church"; and Ji Tai, "Preaching in the Church in China."

45. Cf. Standaert, "The Christian Fragment in the Chinese Fractal: Towards Chinese Culture in the 21st Century"; Elvin, "The Collapse of Scriptural Confucianism."

46. Covell, *Confucius, the Buddha, and Christ: A History of the Gospel in Chinese*, Chapter 9, especially pp. 189–92; Wang Weifan, "Chinese Theology and its Cultural Sources"; Kan Baoping, "Theology in the Contemporary Chinese Context."

47. Peter K. H. Lee, former editor of *Ching Feng*, has been energetic in encouraging Christian dialogue with new Confucianists like Tu Wei-ming; see Peter K.H. Lee, ed., *Confucian-Christian Encounters in Historical and Contemporary Perspectives*; cf. "Christianity and Chinese Culture," *China News Analysis* 1452 (January 15, 1992).

48. Huang Zhiji, *Jian dao ji*.

49. Huang Zhiji, *Ye Mo henglun*. On Gu Jiegang see Schneider, *Ku Chieh-kang and China's New History: Nationalism and the Quest for Alternative Traditions*.

50. Chen Zemin, "Inculturation of the Gospel and Hymn Singing in China."

51. Hunter and Chan, op. cit., Chapter 5.

52. Cf. Yao Minquan, "Indigenization in China in the First Half of the Twentieth Century."

53. Rubinstein, op. cit.

54. For example, Ye Xiaowen, "Speech to the Chinese Catholic Sixth National Representatives' Conference"; Luo Zhufeng, *Religion Under Socialism in China*, Chapter 5.

55. For example, Overmyer, "Alternatives: Popular Religious Sects in Chinese Society"; Johnson, Nathan, and Rawski, *Popular Culture in Late Imperial China*.

56. Elvin analyzes this as a process of secularization in "Collapse of Scriptural Confucianism."

57. M. L. Cohen, "Being Chinese: The Peripheralization of Traditional Identity"; Duara, "Knowledge and Power in the Discourse of Modernity: The Campaigns Against Popular Religion in Early Twentieth-Century China."

58. M. L. Cohen, ibid.; Schwartz, "Culture, Modernity, and Nationalism— Further Reflections"; and Standaert, "Christian Fragment."

59. Richard X.Y. Zhang, "Doing Theology in Chinese," p. 132, note 14.

60. Zhang, "Doing Theology in Chinese," p. 132; cf. Madsen's treatment of Catholicism as embedded in family and community self-identification in *China's Catholics: Tragedy and Hope in an Emerging Civil Society*, Chapter 2.

61. Examples from the Fuzhou area include *Fuzhou Meiyimei nianhui shi*; essays on local church history in the Anglican periodical *Fusheng*; 1910 stele commemorating the first Methodist church in the city, erected 1910, now in the municipal museum.

62. The Fuzhou TSPM has published several volumes of historical reminiscences since 1987, under the title *Fuzhou Jidujiao wenshi ziliao xuanji*. For an exception to the general lack of historical publications by the churches, see the *Gutian Jidujiao zhi* published by the Gutian County TSPM in 1989. With 16 pages of photographs and 90 pages of text, this work follows the gazetteer format of some of the Republican-era local church histories, combining narrative sections, accounts of each church institution, charts, and biographies.

63. The extent to which Chinese Protestants were embedded in Fuzhou society in the late 19th and early 20th centuries is one of the central themes in Dunch, *Fuzhou Protestants and Making of a Modern China, 1857–1927.*

64. Human Rights Watch, *China: State Control of Religion.*

65. Comments based on my conversations with church workers in Fuzhou in 1993–94.

66. Human Rights Watch, *Continuing Religious Repression.* The category "counterrevolutionary crimes" was removed from the Criminal Code in March 1997, but replaced with crimes against "national security," a term scarcely less sweeping than the one it replaced; see Amnesty International Press Release, *China 1997: No Cause for Complacency,* March 3, 1998.

67. UFWD director Wang Zhaoguo, quoted in Human Rights Watch, *China: State Control of Religion,* p. 11.

68. Dunch, *Fuzhou Protestants and Making of a Modern China, 1857–1927,* especially Chapter 5.

69. Cf. Tang Yi, "Chinese Christianity in Development," pp. 4–8.

70. Hunter and Chan, op. cit., pp. 271–80.

71. Habermas, *The Structural Transformation of the Public Sphere: An Inquiry into a Category of Bourgeois Society.*

72. The definition is from Diamond, "Toward Democratic Consolidation," *Journal of Democracy* 5 (1994): 5, quoted in Brook, "Auto-Organization in Chinese Society," p. 22. On the problem of definition, see Chamberlain, "Coming to Terms with Civil Society"; Madsen, "The Public Sphere, Civil Society, and Moral Community: A Research Agenda for Contemporary China Studies."

73. Madsen, *China's Catholics: Tragedy and Hope in an Emerging Civil Society,* pp. 11–15; Dean, "Ritual and Space: Civil Society or Popular Religion?" p. 192.

74. Brook and Frolic, "Ambiguous Challenge of Civil Society," p. 8.

75. Burns, "Strengthening Central CCP Control of Leadership Selection: The 1990 Nomenklatura." This has changed since 1984, when the posts were still centrally appointed; Burns, ed., *The Chinese Communist Party's Nomenklatura System,* pp. xxxi and 39.

76. *Bridge* 42 (1990): 3–10; cf. Madsen, *China's Catholics: Tragedy and Hope in an Emerging Civil Society,* pp. 14–15 and *passim.*

77. Cf. Zhang Yunqiu, "From State Corporatism to Social Representation: Local Trade Unions in the Reform Years."

78. This is discussed in detail in Dunch, "Protestants and the State in Post-Mao China," Chapter 3.

79. On individual political Protestants, see *Human Rights Watch,* "China: Religious Persecution Persists," pp. 18–21.

80. K. H. Ting and Wang Weifan, "Recent Developments in the Study of Religion," p. 82.

81. Cf. the statement adopted by house church leaders in Nov. 1998, which states: "The Three-Self churches practice the unity of politics and the church; . . . House churches believe in the separation of the church from the state. . ." *China News and Church Report,* December 21, 1998, p. 9.

82. Brook and Frolic, "Ambiguous Challenge of Civil Society," p. 12.

83. D. Martin, *Forbidden Revolutions: Pentecostalism in Latin America and Catholicism in Eastern Europe,* p. 12; cf. his *Tongues of Fire: The Explosion of Protestantism in Latin America.*

84. D. Martin, *Forbidden Revolutions*, pp. 37–38.

85. Some church leaders fear that the next generation will abandon the Three-Self policy; see Qin Shenglan, "Three-Self Education for Theological Students."

86. D. Martin, *Forbidden Revolutions*, Chapter 3.

87. Ibid., pp. 77–93.

88. Cf. Dean, "Ritual and Space: Civil Society or Popular Religion?"

89. Cf. Madsen on the breakdown of Catholic communities in today's fast-paced, market-driven Chinese cities, see *China's Catholics: Tragedy and Hope in an Emerging Civil Society*, pp. 114–18, and also his comments on the reasons for Protestantism's growth, pp. 137–38.

90. Cf. Bibby, *Unknown Gods: The Ongoing Story of Religion in Canada*; Wuthnow, *Christianity in the Twenty-first Century: Reflections on the Challenges Ahead*.

91. Walker, "Thoroughly Modern: Sociological Reflections on the Charismatic Movement from the End of the Twentieth Century," p. 36; cf. Percy, "City on a Beach: Future Prospects for Charismatic Movements at the End of the Twentieth Century;" D. Martin, *Tongues of Fire: The Explosion of Protestantism in Latin America*.

92. Standaert, "Christian Fragment in the Chinese Fractal: Towards Chinese Culture in the 21st Century."

Vámos: Hungarian Missionaries in China

1. The word Hungary (Hungaria) does not originate from the word Hun. It comes from the word *Onogur* meaning "Ten Arrows" or "Ten Tribes" which was conferred on Hungarians by neighbors in the steppes. Hungarian tribes comprised a blood federation that was known as *Onogur*. Likewise, there is no connection between the words *Xiongnu* (Hun) and *Xiongyali* (Hungary).

2. Liang Qichao, "Xiongjiali aiguozhe Gasushi zhuan," pp. 1–12; Vol. 6, pp. 1–27.

3. Farkas, "A turánizmus," pp. 860–69.

4. "Talán azért csinált Nagy-Magyarországból Csonka-Magyarországot, hogy a kis magyar misszióból nagy magyar misszió váljék, s a nagy magyar misszió ereje és becsülése építse fel újra Nagy-Magyarországot," *Hajnal*, VII/1:12 (1921).

5. "Ha a nyugati keresztyénség számára értékesek akarunk lenni, akkor keresztyén kultúrát kell sugározzunk dél és kelet felé," *Hajnal*, VII/1:12 (1921).

6. "Az evangélium terjesztése a Föld minden népeinek, főleg pedig a magyarral rokon népeknek nem keresztyén tagjai között," Archives of the Council of the Hungarian Reformed Church, 2f/15d.

7. Arthur Tompa devoted a series of articles to the Turan mission in the mission periodical *Hajnal* in 1923. See *Hajnal*, pp. 1–4 (1923).

8. About the history the Hungarian Jesuit mission, see Vámos, "The Hungarian Jesuit Mission in Daming, Hebei Province." See also Péter Vámos, *Két kultúra ölelésében, Magyar misszionáriusok a Távol-Keleten*.

9. "P. Johannes Hemm petit facultatem, ut in missiones exteras mittatur, quod ipse nullo modo volo impedire. . . Ipse P. Hemm in Miss. Sinensem libentius iret. . . ," February 21, 1920, Budapest. Hung. 1002–V in Archivum Romanum Societatis Iesu (hereafter ARSI).

10. "Epistolae Praepositi Generalis ad Prov. Hungar. a die 15. aug. 1909 ad diem 21 iulii 1926," March 10, 1920, Rome, ARSI.

11. December 18, 1920, Budapest. Hung. 1002–V in ARSI.

12. French Jesuits established a mission in Northern China in 1857. The center of the northern Jesuit mission was in Xianxian, about 200 kilometers from Beijing. The first French Jesuits arrived in Daming five years later, in 1862. The first Dean of the Daming Mission was Seraphin Couvreur (1835–1919), the famous sinologist, author of one of the first Chinese-French dictionaries and translator of the Confucian classics into French. See "Mission de Sienhsien. Etat de la Mission au 1er juillet 1929," Daming News folder, Archivum Provinciae Hungariae Societatis Iesu (hereafter: APHSI).

13. October 30, 1921, Budapest. Hung. 1002–V in ARSI; "Epistolae Praepositi Generalis ad Prov. Hungar. a die 15. aug. 1909 ad diem 21 iulii 1926," November 15, 1921, Rome, ARSI.

14. Interview with József Maron SJ in Vámos, Két kultúra ölelésében, Magyar misszionáriusok a Távol-Keleten, pp. 186–187. In their letters, missionaries often write about and refer to Hungarians' relations with Eastern peoples.

15. "Epistolae Provincialis," January 17, 1922, Budapest. Hung. 1002–X in ARSI.

16. "Epistolae Provincialis," March 9, 1926, Budapest. Hung. in ARSI.

17. Miklós Szarvas to the Provincial, 5. November, 1924. Published in Hírek a Provinciából, the Province News, No.4, p. 1 (March 1925).

18. Miklós Szarvas to the Hungarian Province, October 17, 1926, Daming. Budapest, APHSI.

19. Epistolae Provincialis, February 22, 1927, Budapest. Hung. in ARSI.

20. Epistolae Praepositi Generalis to the Hungarian Provincial, February 3, 1931, Rome. Hung. Epistolae Praepositi Generalis in ARSI.

21. Epistolae Provincialis to the Hungarian Provincial, April 8, 1932, Budapest. Hung. 1003 in ARSI.

22. Epistolae Praepositi Generalis to the Hungarian Provincial, April 17, 1932, Rome. Hung. Epistolae Praepositi Generalis in ARSI.

23. The Hungarian text of the document was published in Katolikus Missziók, 1935/8:161.

24. The original of the Papal edict can be found in the Archives of the Chinese Province, a photocopy of which can be found in APHSI.

25. Katolikus Missziók, 1939/8:120.

26. Miklósi, Magyar hősök öt világrészen, pp. 133–134.

27. Thun, A magyar misszió végnapjai Kínában, p. 7.

28. Katolikus Missziók, 1934/1:6–7. Szabin Scheidl, who was to be the first martyr of the Hungarian Franciscans in China, died on March 28, 1931.

29. Thun, op. cit., p. 8.

30. Kool, Az Úr csodásan működik I–II, Vol. II, pp. 273–274. (The English version of the book entitled God Moves in a Mysterious Way: The Hungarian Protestant Foreign Mission Movement was published in Zoetermeer, 1993.)

31. Scholtz, "Az evangélikus missziói egyesületek, s ezek között is elsősorban az egyetemes jellegű Lipcsei Evangélikus-Lutheránus Misszióegyesület áldásos munkakörébe kell szervesen belekapcsolódnia," p. 15.

32. Draskóczy, A magyar keresztyénség külmissziói szolgálata, p. 60.

33. Kool, op. cit., Vol. I, p. 247.

34. Babos was born in Budapest, but his parents were from Kolozsvár (Cluj), Transylvania. Babos entered the Reformed Theological Academy there in 1921. In 1926 he went to Basel, where he spent two years at the Basel University. He began preparing himself for the mission at the Mission Seminary of the Basler Mission. In 1928 Babos returned to Transylvania, where he worked among Hungarians.

35. "Egyházunk alaposan megfontolta a dolgot, a mandzsúriai misszió mellett döntött, érezvén, hogy amennyiben nekünk, magyaroknak is vannak missziói kötelességeink, azok Mandzsúriában, a rokon testvérnépek között keresendők." in Némethy, *Pagodák árnyékában*, p. 24.

36. During this time he married Rev. Mária Lőrincz, and they returned to Manchuria together in 1937. Their three children were all born in Manchuria, in 1938, 1939 and 1944.

37. *Hajnal*, 1944/1:5.

38. Kool, op. cit., Vol. II, p. 458.

39. Károly Németh to the Finnish Missionary Society, November 28, 1937, Budapest. Evangelical National Archive, 63f/3a.

40. Letters from the Chinese Mission, June 22, 1933, Daming. APHSI.

41. About the Japanese occupation, see "Tamingensis Missio," a report by Miklós Szarvas, February 13, 1938, Daming. Hung. in ARSI; Károly Németh to Father Elemér Reisz, August 20, 1938, Daming. Kínai misszionáriusok levelei in APHSI; Father Imre Kékessy to the Hungarian Provincial, March 3, 1938, Zikawei. Kínai misszionáriusok levelei in APHSI.

42. *Katolikus Missziók*, 1938/5:98.

43. *Hajnal*, 1944/1:b5.

Madsen: Catholicism as Chinese Folk Religion

1. Lozada, "God Aboveground: Catholicism and Transnationalism in a Chinese Village."

2. Wu Fei, "Maimangshangde shengyan: Yige xiangcun Tianzhujiaohui zhongde xinyang he shenghuo."

3. Entenmann, "Catholics and Society in Eighteenth-Century Sichuan," pp. 8–23.

4. Sweeten, "Catholic Converts in Jiangxi Province: Conflict and Accommodation, 1860–1900," pp. 24–40.

5. Litzinger, "Rural Religion and Village Organization in North China," pp. 41–52.

6. Schipper, *The Taoist Body*, p. 16.

7. P. Cohen, *China and Christianity: The Missionary Movement and the Growth of Chinese Antiforeignism, 1860–1870*, pp. 4–6.

8. Ibid., p. 21.

9. Ibid.

10. Overmyer, *Folk Buddhist Religion: Dissenting Sects in Late Traditional China*, pp. 1–6.

11. Naquin, *Millenarian Rebellion in China: The Eight Trigrams Uprising of 1813*, pp. 9–18. The quote is from a document cited by Overmyer, op. cit., p. 137.

12. Naquin, op. cit., pp. 9–18; and Overmyer, op. cit., pp. 73–108.

13. Jordan and Overmyer, *The Flying Phoenix: Aspects of Chinese Sectarianism in Taiwan*.

14. Overmyer, *Folk Buddhist Religion: Dissenting Sects in Late Traditional China*, pp. 109–29. See also Naquin, "The Transmission of White Lotus Sectarianism in Late Imperial China," pp. 255–91.

15. Naquin, op. cit., pp. 31–39 and 268–69.

16. Ibid. See also Overmyer, *Folk Buddhist Religion: Dissenting Sects in Late Traditional China*, pp. 62–69.

17. Overmyer, op. cit., p. 65.

18. Schipper, op. cit., pp. 16–17.

19. See Alexander, "Analytic Debates: Understanding the Relative Autonomy of Culture," pp. 1–27.

20. Madsen, *China's Catholics: Tragedy and Hope in an Emerging Civil Society*, pp. 87–95.

21. See Charbonnier, "The Underground Church," pp. 52–70.

22. Madsen, *China's Catholics: Tragedy and Hope in an Emerging Civil Society*, pp. 6–8.

23. Naquin, op. cit., p. 17.

24. Sweeten, op. cit., p. 39.

25. For conflicts in the nineteenth century between local Catholic lay leadership and clergy, see Hanson, *Catholic Politics in China and Korea*, pp. 17–18. For an account of roles of paid catechists in the early twentieth century, see Wiest, *Maryknoll in China*, pp. 77–130.

26. Entenmann, "Christian Virgins in Eighteenth-Century Sichuan," p. 181.

27. Ibid., p. 183.

28. Ibid., p. 190.

29. Naquin, "The Transmission of White Lotus Sectarianism in Late Imperial China," p. 289.

30. Ibid., pp. 289–91.

31. Ibid.

32. Thompson, "Twilight of the Gods in the Chinese Countryside: Christians, Confucians, and the Modernizing State, 1861–1911," pp. 53–72.

33. Madsen, *China's Catholics: Tragedy and Hope in an Emerging Civil Society*, pp. 50–75.

Wiest: From Past Contributions to Present Opportunities

1. Several papers in this volume have already amply developed the situation of the Protestant Church.

2. *Collectanea S. Congregationis de Propaganda Fide*, vol. II, p. 193.

3. Havret, *La Mission du Kiang-nan: Les trois dernières années, 1899–1901*, pp. 51–53. Statistics prior to 1900 are incomplete and difficult to come by. For the pre-1900 period, two good sources are *Lettres édifiantes et curieuses des missions étrangères* and Piolet, *La France en dehors: Les missions catholiques françaises au XIXe siècle*. From 1900 on, school data appear in the yearly *Annuaire des missions catholiques de Chine* first published by the Lazarist press in Beijing and then by the Sinological Bureau of Zikawei (Shanghai); complete detailed reports and statistics, however, do not become available in the *Annuaire* until 1922.

4. Letter from Father Francis X. Ford, August 7, 1922, Maryknoll Mission Archives.

5. *N.C.W.C. News Service (Fides)*, March 15, 1937, p.7. See also Dehergne, "L'Église de Chine au tournant." *Collectanea Commissionis Synodalis* is

another good source of information to follow the development of Catholic education in China: see in particular "Les écoles catholiques en Chine," 2:5–21 (1929), and Carroll "The Educational Work of the Catholic China Mission, 1929–1939," 14:129–53 and 528–30 (1941).

6. Compiled from statistical tables in *Annuaires des missions catholiques de Chine, 1928–1948* (1949).

7. *N.C.W.C. News Service (Fides)*, October 30, 1950, p. 3.

8. In the early post-apostolic era, Justin Martyr, Origen and Clement of Alexandria held the view that God's saving purpose was not confined to his covenant with the Hebrews and spoke of the Divine Word "seminally" present and active in the world before the birth of Christ. Clement went even further and refused to accept the opinion that paganism was an invention of the devil.

9. See Wiest, "Bringing Christ to the Nations: Shifting Models of Missions in China."

10. Hayhoe, "Catholics and Socialists: The Paradox of French Educational Interaction with China," p. 107.

11. Broullion, *Mémoire sur l'état actuel de la Mission du Kiang-Nan*, pp. 103 and 107.

12. Wiest, "The Legacy of Vincent Lebbe," 23/1:33–37 (January 1999). *N.C.W.C. News Service (Fides)*, ibid.

13. Carroll, op. cit.; Dehergne, "L'Église de Chine au tournant." See also the excellent study by Jessie G. Lutz, *China and the Christian Colleges, 1850–1950*.

14. For instance, Carroll on page 137 wrote: "This phenomenon (of greater increase among non-Catholic Chinese students) has been noticed throughout the entire field of Catholic education; not only among the universities but also, and especially, among the lower departments." Interestingly enough, he noted later on, on page 141, that the trend did not apply to the non-Chinese student minority among whom Catholics outnumbered non-Catholics.

15. Dehergne, "L'Église de Chine au tournant."

16. *N.C.W.C. News Service (Fides)*, September 10, 1924. *Revue d'Histoire des Missions* 2 (1925): 204. *The Field Afar*, March 1935, p. 71; September 1935, p. 235.

17. "Aurora, School Diary 1919–1948," especially December 23, 1947, and September 25, 1948, *Archives Françaises des Jésuites de Chine*, Vanves, France.

18. *Bulletin de l'Université l'Aurore* 33:8–11(1936). *Relations de Chine*, July 1937, p. 149. In 1946, a Jesuit report also mentioned that all important banks and enterprises of Tianjin were staffed by alumni from *Gongshang Xueyuan* and that, out of seven bureaus of Public Work, four were directed by former students: see "Archives des Hautes Etudes Industrielles et Commerciales de Tianjin, Rapport des Pères Charvet et Denys, le 10 décembre 1946" in *Archives Françaises des Jésuites de Chine*.

19. *Archives Françaises des Jésuites de Chine*, "Aurora, School Diary 1936–1937;" and *Bulletin de l'Université l'Aurore* 6:569–77 (1945).

20. Madsen, "Hierarchical Modernization: Tianjin's Gong Shang College as a Model for Catholic Community in North China," p. 29.

21. *N.C.W.C. News Service (Fides)*, October 30, 1950, pp. 2–3; *International Fides Service*, September 27, 1952, 328: 282–84; *Archives Françaises des Jésuites de France*, "Nouvelles des étudiants de l'Aurore, May-Août 1952," pp. 22–26.

22. Deng Xiaoping's message to Jingshan school on October 1, 1983 in *China*, p. 202.

23. The complete text of the Decree #226 can be found in *Tripod* 111:53–65 (May–June 1999). It should be noted that Chinese private schools are not "private" in exactly the same sense as their counterparts in Western countries. In Shanghai, for instance, only a few are individually owned and all headmasters and mistresses of private primary and junior high schools—which corresponds to the nine-year compulsory education—are appointees of district bureaus of the Municipal Education Commission.

24. *China*, pp. 53–54.

25. "Seeking College Diploma: Private University Is Seen as an Expensive Place for Second Best," p. 7. *Zhonglian* 85 (French edition): 3–5 (June 1999).

26. Based on an interview of the school director by the author on January 16, 2000. See also *Zhonglian* 85 (June 1999, French edition): 3–5.

27. "Dossiers et Documents," pp. 4–5 (1992) in *Eglises d'Asie/Supplément* 10, No. 10 B/92.

28. *China Study Journal* 12/1:38 (April 1997); 12/3:60 (December 1997). I refer here only to efforts from Catholics within China and do not account for "public schools" that have been funded by outside Catholic agencies such as Caritas Hong Kong, Caritas Taiwan and the Ferdinand Verbiest Foundation thanks to the contributions of Catholics from around the world.

29. Again the diocese of Shanghai provides a good illustration. Bishop Jin met with little difficulty in restoring the Shanghai Association of Catholic Intellectuals, which regroups mostly retired doctors and scholars. But he has not been successful in launching a student branch of the same association.

30. *Tripod* 114:42–43 (November–December 1999).

31. *Tripod* 108:51–52 (November–December 1998; 111:74 (May–June 1999); 112:54 (July–August 1999); 114:47 (November–December 1999). *Zhonglian* 86 (French edition):9 (August 1999). *China Study Journal* 13/2:48–50, 52 (August 1998); 14/1:38–41 (April 1999).

32. *Tripod* 108:52 (November–December 1998). *Zhonglian* 87 French edition): 9 (October 1999). *China Study Journal* 13/1:74–75 (April 1998); 14/1:42–43, 45 (April 1999). *China Church Quarterly* 31:5 (Summer 1997); 34:2 (Spring 1998).

33. John B. Zhang, "Catholic Press in Contemporary China," pp. 165–71.

34. Hayhoe, "Catholics and Socialists: The Paradox of French Educational Interaction with China," Pyenson, *Civilizing Mission: Exact Sciences and French Overseas Expansion, 1839–1940*. See also Hayhoe, "A Chinese Catholic Philosophy of Higher Education in Republican China."

Covell: Christianity and China's Minority Nationalities

1. Recent researchers believe that this number can be expanded to at least 500 that have mutually distinct languages and unique cultures. See *The Fifty Most Unreached People Groups of China and Tibet*. Chiang Mai, Thailand: Asian Minorities Outlook, 1996. Another book, in the process of publication by Asian Minorities Outreach, analyzes over 300 groups.

2. Nearly all of the languages of northwest, north-central, and northeast China are Altaic. The only exception is Tajik, which is Persian or, more broadly, Indo-European. The Altaic languages have three subdivisions in China: Turkic, which includes groups like Uighur, Kazakh, Kirghiz, and Uzbek; Mongolian,

3. which includes Mongolian proper and four other small groups; Tungus, which includes Manchu, Evenki, and three small groups. Korean may also be included under the Altaic family. The many groups of south and southwest China are divided into four subgroups: Tai, which has eight groups, including Zhuang, Dong, Bouyei, and Li; Tibeto-Burman, which has sixteen languages, including Tibetan, Yi, Lisu, Lahu, Naxi, Hani, Qiang, and Bai; Miao-Yao, which includes these two groups; Mon-Khmer, which has three groups, the most important being Wa. In Taiwan may be found the Gaoshan peoples (now referred to as Yuanzumin), which have at least eleven major and minor subdivisions.

4. One set of Catholic statistics for 1949 gives 1,200 Catholics in Tibet and 3,000 Tibetan Catholics in China. E.R. Hembeye, "Tibet," 14:151–52.

5. Charbonnier, *Guide to the Catholic Church in China 1989*, pp. 118–19, 120–21, 146–47, and 152–53.

6. Edgar, "The Exploration and Occupation of the Centres on the Tibetan Marches," *Chinese Recorder* 50 (September, 1919): 607–12.

7. Leyssen, *The Cross Over China's Wall*, p. 39.

8. Persson, "Christianity in the Tarim Basin," pp. 20–21.

9. Qin Heping, "Dianxi bufen shaoshu minzu diqu Jidujiao lishi wenti chutan," 3 (1987): 28–43.

10. For details on Jiwang and one of her most effective disciples, Weiran Takoh, see Covell, *Pentecost of the Hills in Taiwan: The Christian Faith Among the Original Inhabitants.*

11. *West China Missionary News*, p. 1 (November 1915).

12. For an elaboration of Fraser's views see Fraser, "Mass Movements Among the Aborigines," p. 205 (November 1937).

13. Li Tseng Hsiu (Carol), "The Sacred Mission: An American Missionary Family in the Lahu and Wa Districts of Yunnan."

14. Zhang Tan, *"Zhaimen" qiande shimenkan: Jidujiao wenhua yu Chuan Dian Qian Bian Miaozu shehui.*

15. The proper balance between causal and influence is seen in an article by Tetsunao Yamamori and Kim-Kwong Chan, "Missiological Ramifications of the Social Impact of Christianity on the Lisu of China."

16. These quotes and the following material on a sociology of missions come from Robert Montgomery, "Some Research Directions for the Sociology of Missions." He has worked among the Amis group of original inhabitants in Taiwan, and many of his reflections are based on observations made in Taiwan.

17. C. Kraft, "Ideological Factors in Intercultural Communication," *Missiology* 2 (July 3,1974): 300.

18. Zhang Tan, op. cit., pp. 217–18.

19. Wallace, *Religion: An Anthropological View*, pp. 30–37.

20. T'ien Ju-k'ang, "Cementations of Segregatory Tribes—The Protestant Church Among Minority Nationalities in Yunnan." See also his *Peaks of Faith.* In this publication, he elaborates these views much more fully. The same types of views are found in several Chinese articles written by Qian Ning of the University of Yunnan; Li Guangliang, "Lüetan Yunnan Miaozu diqu de Jidujiao," pp. 33–37; and Liu Dingyin, "Jidujiao xundao gonghui zai Zhaotong diqu de zaoqi chuanbo," pp. 35–41. Most of these articles analyzing the minority nationalities of Yunnan are found in the journal *Research on the Religions of Yunnan.*

21. P. Cohen, "Reflections on the Missionary Movement," pp. 543–90.

22. Cheung Siu-woo, "Millenarianism, Christian Movements, and Ethnic Change Among the Miao in Southwest China," pp. 236–40.

23. Zhang Tan, op. cit., quoting from "The Miao People's Savior," a small booklet published in Hankow in 1939.

24. Zhang Tan, op. cit., pp. 239–66.

Zhuo: Discussion on "Cultural Christians" in China

1. *Regent Chinese Journal*, No.1, 1996.

2. Liu Xiaofeng, "Xiandai yujingzhong de Hanyu Jidu shenxue," 2 (1995): 25.

3. John 13:35.

4. An Ximeng, "Shenxue yu wenhua," pp. 135–44.

Leung: The Catholic Church in Post-1997 Hong Kong

1. Leung, "The Catholic Voters," pp. 151–86. Chan and Leung. "The Voting Behaviour of Hong Kong Catholics in the 1995 Legislative Council Election," pp. 275–314.

2. Leung, "The Uneasy Balance: The Sino-Vatican-Hong Kong Relations after 1997," pp. 97–118.

3. Flannery, ed., "The Constitution of the Church," pp. 350–440.

4. Dulles, *Models of the Church*. pp. 31–41.

5. In this article, the term "church" alludes to the institutional church with hierarchical order.

6. Governor Sir Alexander Gantham of Hong Kong (1947–58), after a discussion with Secretary of State on Communist activities in 1949, reflected the British belief that legislation could be introduced in Hong Kong to prevent the spread of Communism and strengthen control over subversive elements in education and labor. See *Grantham to SofS.*, 311 *secret*, 1 April 1949, in 0537/4824 and *Grantham to SofS*, 384 *secret*, 30 April 1949, in 0371/5839, Hong Kong Public Records Office.

7. In a private letter from the Anglican Bishop Ronald O. Hall to the Director of Education Department Hong Kong, the bishop suggested that the British subsidies for primary school education should be given exclusively to the Christian churches in order to prevent the spread of Communism. Bishop Hall's letter is filed in Hong Kong Record Service 147 2/2 (No. 17 & 119), Hong Kong Public Records Office.

8. Discussion on contractors and institutional channeling of organizations by the state have recently received greater attention by scholars. See McCarthy, Britt and Wolfson "The Institutional Channelling of Social Movements by the State in the United States," 13:45–76 (1991).

9. Flannery, ed., "Pastoral Constitution on the Church in the Modern World," pp. 903–1014.

10. Yuen, "Hong Kong Catholics' Recent Participation In Social Movements," pp. 117–32.

11. The author was a delegate to the Diocesan convention and participated in the discussion. She followed closely how the discussion on social justice was misunderstood as the infiltration of Communism into the Catholic Church. On

the pro-Communist riot in 1966–67 and the anti-Communist sentiments derived from it, see Ian Scott, *Political Change and Crisis of Legitimacy in Hong Kong*, pp. 81–121.

12. *Xianggang jiaoqu huiyi wenxian,* pp. 345–80.

13. Sir Jeffrey Howe, the British Foreign Secretary, on a visit to Hong Kong in April 1984, announced the transfer of sovereignty of the territory and recommended a representative government for Hong Kong.

14. *Foreign Affairs Committee Report of the British Parliament 1994,* p. xxxvi.

15. So and Kwitko, "The New Middle Class and the Democratic Movement in Hong Kong," 3:364–98 (1990). For 1991 election, see Leung, "The Catholic Voter," pp. 151–86.

16. For 1995 election, see Chan and Leung, op. cit., pp. 275–314.

17. Wurth, ed., *Papal Documents Related to the New China 1937–1984.* pp. 177–79.

18. The religious policy of the CCP at this stage is to eliminate the influence of religion at the present stage of development of socialism as expressed by Ye Xiaowen, the director of religious affair Bureau, State Council. See Ye Xiaowen, "Dangqian woguo de zongjiao wenti," pp. 9–23.

19. Leung, "The Uneasy Balance: Sino-Vatican-Hong Kong Relations after 1997," pp. 97–118.

20. Since 1990, the papal representative in Hong Kong has been participating this coordination meeting every year. Participants vary from individuals interested in the Church in China to representatives of the religious associations engaged in helping China in various ways.

21. Luo Shugang, *Zongjiao gongzuo fangmian de yixie redian wenti,* pp. 11–13.

22. Documentation Center of the Party Central and Policy Section of the Religious Affairs Bureau. *Xinshiqi zongjiao gongzuo wenxian xuanbian.* p. 177.

23. The figure was taken from "A Chronology of the Catholic Church in China in the Context of Selected Dates in World and Chinese History," *Tripod* 76:19–76.

24. The term "official" sector refers to the open and government-established Chinese Catholic Church while the "unofficial" sector refers to the sector of the Catholic Church in China that refuses to be under the supervision of the government and the CCP. Therefore this sector of the church is out of the control of the government and is underground in nature.

25. Ye Xiaowen, op. cit., pp. 9–23.

26. It was revealed by a member of the Drafting Committee of HKSAR Basic Law.

27. Xin Weixi, *Xin Weixi zhenlunji.* pp. 121–31. The author used the pseudonym Xin Weixi, which alluded to Xinhua (New China News Agency), an official representative of the CCP and PRC in Hong Kong before 1997. Among intellectuals it was widely believed that Xin's view represented China's official view on Hong Kong's sociopolitical affairs.

28. The Daya Bay Nuclear Plant built by China is close to the Hong Kong-China border. Hong Kong citizens were afraid about the building of the nuclear facility and the possibility of a nuclear disaster similar to Chernobyl, the former Soviet Union nuclear plant that exploded in 1986.

29. Xin Weixi, op. cit., pp. 89–92.

30. Ibid., pp. 121–31.

31. As early as the 1960s Philip Selznick had conducted a study of how the Bolshevik had made use of organization as its strategy and tactics to treat civil organizations. See Selznick, *Organization Weapon: A Study of Bolshevik Strategy and Tactics*.

32. *The Basic Law of the Hong Kong Special Administrative Region of the People's Republic of China*, Article 141.

33. The delegates of the Precious Blood Sisters of Hong Kong, the largest Chinese Religious congregation, visited Beijing in December 1996 to meet officials from the Hong Kong and Macau Affairs Office of the State Council. The officials assured the delegation of Sisters that Catholic services would be allowed to continue after 1997.

34. *The Basic Law of the Hong Kong Special Administrative Region of the People's Republic of China*, Article 148.

35. On a number of informal occasions during the period of 1987–1997, this author heard the same opinion expressed by Beijing officials.

36. The delegates of the Precious Blood Sisters of Hong Kong heard this message during their visit to Beijing in December 1996.

37. Cardinal John B. Wu, "March into the Bright Decade: Pastoral Exhortation of Cardinal John Baptist Wu on the Pastoral Commitment of the Catholic Diocese of Hong Kong."

38. Yahuda, *Hong Kong: China Challenge*, pp. 61–82.

39. Ibid.

40. *Hong Kong Record Series* 147 2/2(2).

41. Xu Jiatun, *Xu Jiatun Xianggang huiyilu*, p.75.

42. In a history of the Tung Wah Hospital Group and Po Leung Kok, it is revealed that both began to run state subsidized schools in 1970s. See Pó, *Po Leung Kuk Hong Kong 110th Anniversary Report*. pp. 30–39. Li Donghai, ed., *Xianggang Donghua Sanyuan 125 nian shilue*, pp. 115–62.

43. The Precedence List of Hong Kong government is the protocol order on official gathering, the arrangement of which is according to the ranking of concerned people.

44. Leung, "The Catholic Voter," pp. 151–86. For 1995 election, see Chan and Leung, op. cit., pp. 275–314.

45. *Kung Kao Po*, 2 May 1999.

46. Cardinal John B. Wu, op. cit.

47. *The Basic Law of the Hong Kong Special Administrative Region of the People's Republic of China*, Article 148.

48. It was reported by someone who was near the Bishops Office in December 1998.

49. Tung Chee-hwa, "Preparing Hong Kong for a New Era."

50. Leung, "Strategic Development of the Hong Kong SAR: Social Policy, EIB Model and Implications," pp. 125–52.

51. Tung Chee-hwa's "Future of Excellence and Prosperity for All."

52. F. Ching, "Scare Tactics," May 1999, p. 18.

53. *Hong Kong Economic Journal*, 29 April 1999. *Ming Pao*, 29 April 1999.

54. F. Ching, op. cit..

55. Cardinal John B. Wu, "God is Love." The pastoral letter was issued on May 30, 1999, and was reprinted in *Kung Kao Po* and *Sunday Examiner* (Hong Kong), June 6, 1999.

56. Ibid.

57. Ibid.
58. *Xin Pao* (New Newspaper), June 7, 1999.
59. *Kung Kao Po*, June 13, 1999.
60. Callers on phone-in programs on various radio programs were very vocal in supporting the Catholic view in the Right of Abode.
61. *Kung Kao Po*, May 30, 1999; May 16 1999; June 13, 1999; and June 20, 1999.
62. *Ming Pao*, June 17, 1999.
63. *Ming Pao*, June 26, 1999.
64. *Sunday Examiner*, July 4, 1999.
65. *Kung Kao Po*, October 24, 1999, p. 1.
66. Ibid.
67. It was revealed by the one who was close to the Bishop's Office of the Hong Kong Catholic Diocese.

Wang: Christianity in Modern Taiwan

I am deeply grateful to John E. Geddes and Richard Cook, who carefully read through a previous version of this paper and offered many useful suggestions. I, however, am solely responsible for all errors of fact or interpretation.

1. There is a very balanced definition of "contextualization" in the *New Direction of Theology*, edited by Ferguson, Wright and Packer, "Contextualization is a dynamic process of the church's reflection, in obedience to Christ and his mission in the world, on the interaction of the text as the word of God and the context as a specific human situation" (p. 164).
2. For a general survey of the Christian churches under the Japanese colonial government, see Richardson, "Christianity in Taiwan Under Japanese Rule, 1895–1945." For a study of the Japanese attitudes and strategies toward Christian Churches in occupied China, see Brook, "Toward Independence: Christianity in China Under the Japanese Occupation, 1937–1945," pp. 317–37.
3. The Catholic Fathers first came to Taiwan in the early seventeenth century, but had to terminate their mission in the mid-seventeenth century. They resumed their mission in 1859. The Presbyterian Church was brought to southern Taiwan by the English Presbyterian missionary James Maxwell in 1865, and to the north by Canadian Presbyterian missionary George Leslie Mackay in 1872. The True Jesus Church was imported from China in 1926. Japanese missionaries brought in the Taiwanese Holiness Church in 1929.
4. For a survey of Taiwan in this period, see Peter Chen-main Wang, "A Bastion Created, A Regime Reformed, An Economy Reengineered, 1949–1970," pp. 320–38.
5. Tong, *Christianity in Taiwan: A History*, p. 84.
6. Murray A. Rubinstein pointed out that many of those who went to Taiwan at this time belonged to politically conservative and anticommunist denominations. See Rubinstein, *The Protestant Community on Modern Taiwan: Mission, Seminary, and Church*, p. 34.
7. At a missionary conference in Taiwan in July 1959, when "those who had previously labored in mainland China were asked to stand up, more than two-thirds of the 200 missionaries present rose." See Tong, op. cit., p. 84.
8. Zha Shijie, "Sishiniande Taiwan Jidujiaohui," pp. 880 and 890.

9. Although quite a few Presbyterian leaders suffered during the February 28, 1947, Incident, the General Secretary of the Presbyterian Church in Taiwan, Huang Wudong, admitted that the church and the state had a rather harmonious relationship in the 1950s. See Huang Wudong, *Huang Wudong huiyilu*, p. 298.

10. For the February 28 Incident, see Lai, Myers, and Wei, *A Tragic Beginning: The Taiwan Uprising of February 28, 1947.*

11. Swanson, *The Church in Taiwan: Profile 1980*, p. 25.

12. *Taiwan Jidu zhanglao jiaohui bainian shi* (hereafter: *Bainian shi*), pp. 352 and 491–92.

13. Rubinstein, "American Evangelicalism in the Chinese Environment: Southern Baptist Convention Missionaries in Taiwan, 1949–1981," II.3 (September 1983): 273–74.

14. Swanson, *Taiwan: Mainline Versus Independent Church Growth*, p. 124. The Assemblies of God did not have similarly good results because of its strategy to start work simultaneously with Taiwanese, mainlanders, and aboriginal peoples. Their resources and strength were divided and thus they did not have the harvest other denominations did. See Swanson, op. cit., pp. 115–21.

15. Ibid. It is said that in 1955 about two-thirds of all missionaries in Taiwan were working among the mainlanders, a group representing 13 percent of the population. Another source indicates that in 1954 thirty-three denominations were represented in Taiwan. Among their missionaries, 117 worked with the mainlanders, forty-six with the Taiwanese and ten with the aboriginal peoples. See Tong, op. cit., pp. 86–88.

16. Quite a few mainlanders did attend Presbyterian churches when they first came to Taiwan, but had difficulty understanding Taiwanese and therefore organized their own churches. This became the origin of some of the "local churches" in Taiwan. See Swanson, op. cit., p. 90.

17. Qu Haiyuan, "Taiwan diqu Jidujiao fazhan zhi chubu tantao," vol. II, p. 488.

18. There is a new book discussing the quick growth of the Christian churches among aboriginal peoples in Taiwan. See Covell, *Pentecost of the Hills in Taiwan.* For the postwar period, see Chapters 7–8. I thank John E. Geddes for calling my attention to this book.

19. Qu Haiyuan, "Taiwan diqu Jidujiao fazhan zhi chubu tantao," p. 498.

20. Qu Haiyuan, "Taiwan diqu Tianzhujiao fazhan qushi zhi yanjiu," 51 (Spring 1982):131.

21. Swanson, op. cit., p. 83.

22. Raber, *Protestantism in Changing Taiwan: A Call to Creative Response*, p. 77.

23. For example, the government was lenient in their educational policies when the missionaries and Chinese Christians applied to establish institutions of Christian higher education in the 1950s. See Peter Chen-main Wang, "Taiwan Jidujiao gaodeng jiaoyu de jiantao," 1 (1996): 79–96. A Catholic bishop also stated that he enjoyed special privileges when he administered church affairs in Hualian. Qu Haiyuan, "Taiwan diqu Tianzhujiao fazhan qushi zhi yanjiu," 51 (Spring 1982): 139–40.

24. Qu Haiyuan, op. cit., pp. 141–42.

25. Qu Haiyuan, "Woguo zongjiao bianqian de shehuixue fenxi," pp. 376–77.

26. Raber, op. cit., p. 79.

27. Qu Haiyuan, "Zongjiao pian," Vol. III, 1, p. 410.

28. Zhu Sancai, *1995 nian Taiwan Jidujiaohui jiaoshi baogao.*
29. Qu Haiyuan, "Taiwan diqu Jidujiao fazhan zhi chubu tantao," p. 488.
30. Ibid., pp. 488–91.
31. Raber, op. cit., p. 94.
32. Ibid., pp. 184–25.
33. Ibid., pp. 237–38.
34. Qu Haiyuan, "Taiwan diqu Tianzhujiao fazhan qushi zhi yanjiu," p. 145.
35. Swanson, *The Church in Taiwan: Profile 1980*, p. 26.
36. Ibid., p. 27.
37. For example, the Lutherans were divided into several different organizations. Li Jinpo, "Jidujiao Taiwan Xinyihui fazhan jianshi," pp. 117 and 119.
38. Zha Shijie, "Sishinian de Taiwan Jidujiaohui," pp. 884–85.
39. Qu Haiyuan, "Taiwan diqu Tianzhujiao fazhan qushi zhi yanjiu," p. 144.
40. Zha Shijie, op. cit., p. 884.
41. Qu Haiyuan, "Taiwan diqu Tianzhujiao fazhan qushi zhi yanjiu," p. 144.
42. Swanson, *The Church in Taiwan: Profile 1980*, pp. 27–33.
43. Chen Chuanzheng, "Zuzhi rentong celue yu fei yingli zuzhi de guanxi: dui Jidujiao jiaohui de xibao xiaozu moshi jiaohui zengzhang yundong zhi yenjiu."
44. Zhu Sancai, op. cit., p. 3.
45. *Bainian shi*, p. 301.
46. Ibid., pp. 301–307.
47. Ibid., pp. 311–12 and 315. The four institutes that the Northern Synod keeps are the board of directors of the synod, Taiwan Theological College, Mackay Memorial Hospital and Tamkang High School.
48. Elizabeth J. Brown, former Associate General Secretary of the General Assembly, has described several categories of missionaries in this period. See her thesis, "The Developing Maturity of the Presbyterian Church in Taiwan 1958–1985 as Reflected by Changes in Organization, Functions and Nationalities of Missionaries Serving with It in Taiwan," pp. 2–5.
49. Ibid., p. 17.
50. Ibid., pp. 5–6. For the text in Chinese, see *Bainian shi*, pp. 308–309.
51. Brown, op. cit., p. 8.
52. Ibid., p. 9.
53. Ibid., p. 17.
54. Thelin, "Propagation of the Gospel, Prophesy, and Prosperity," p. 7.
55. Song Guangyu, "Sishinian lai Taiwan de zongjiao fazhan qingkuang," p. 191.
56. *Bainian shi*, pp. 342–43.
57. Swanson, *Taiwan: Mainline Versus Independent Church Growth*, p. 97.
58. For example, Qu Haiyuan has painstakingly pinpointed all the problems in crediting the Movement for Presbyterian growth. First, the Presbyterian church had begun its rapid growth in the period from 1951 to 1954. That means church growth began before the Movement. Second, the Southern Synod started the Movement in 1954, but the Northern Synod did not follow until the General Assembly passed the resolution in 1959. Therefore, we can get an estimate of the impact of the Movement on church growth by making a comparison between the two synods from 1954 to 1959. The comparison shows the interesting finding that the Northern Synod had the better growth. In other words, the Movement was not necessarily the cause for the church growth. Third, although

the Movement lasted for ten years, the real church growth happened in 1954–1956. After the General Assembly passed the resolution initiating the Movement, the church growth rate actually slowed down—the annual growth rate fell below five percent. During the last year of the Movement, the church actually suffered a loss in membership. Fourth, all the Christian denominations, including the Catholic Church, enjoyed high church growth in this period. Qu Haiyuan, "Woguo zongjiao bianqian de shehuixue fenxi," p. 384; Qu Haiyuan, "Zongjiao pian," pp. 653–57. Song Guangyu also points out that the growth rate of the Presbyterian Church, since 1958, has been lower than that of the total population. In other words, the Protestant Church has been in a negative growth during the past thirty years. See Song Guangyu, op. cit., pp. 186–87. The only article I have seen that presents a self-examination of the Movement from the Presbyterians is a thesis from Tainan Theological College. The author states frankly that fourteen years later, eighteen out of the 212 churches which were established in the Movement had been closed while half of the remaining churches could not reach the stage of self-support, self-government, and self-propagation. Furthermore, Presbyterians often highlight the huge growth in church members between the 1955 and 1965. However, if a comparison is made by using the figure in 1956 and that in 1965, the growth in the churches is "poor." Cai Sanxiong, "Taiwan Jidu Zhanglao jiaohui beijia yundong de tantao jiqi shenxue yiyi," pp. 93–95.

59. As early as in April 1963, when Rev. Gao Junming, who later became the General Secretary of the General Assembly, reviewed the 300 years of church history, he sighed that "the Church has tended to become exclusive and self-centered, escaping from the reality of life in society. It has ceased to operate as society's conscience." See Gao Junming (Kao Chun-Ming), "Christianity and the Modernization of Formosa," 4 (September 1967): 79.

60. Sawatsky, "State-Church Conflict in Taiwan: Its Historical Roots and Contemporary Manifestations," IX.4 (October 1981): 458.

61. Ibid., p. 460.

62. Lin Benxuan, Taiwan de zhengjiao chongtu, pp. 102–109. For the concern and involvement of the Presbyterian Church in Taiwan in the protest against the government's suppression of the February 28, 1947, Incident, see Zhuang Tianci, "Zhanglao jiaohui yu 2.28 pingfan yundong (1987–1990)," 12 (November 1998): 25–44.

63. Jidujiao luntan 1728 (May 16–22, 1999): 2.

64. Ibid., 1738 (July 25–31, 1999): 2.

65. Xue Bozan (David Po-Tsun Hsueh), "Qishiniantai yihou Taiwan xuanjiao shigong zhi texing yu yiyi," 9 (March 1987): 37.

66. Ibid., p. 35.

67. Ibid.

68. Ibid.

69. Ibid., p. 41.

70. Brown, op. cit., pp. 107–108.

71. Swanson, Taiwan: Mainline Versus Independent Church Growth, p. 95.

72. Thelin, op. cit., p. 8.

73. Wu Wenxiong (Peter Wen-Hsiong Wu), "Taiwan Jidu Zhanglao jiaohui bentuhua zhi yenjiu," 9 (March 1987): 58–59. However, some missionaries did try, but were expelled by the government. The best known cases, for example, include Daniel Beeby and Rev. Michael Thornbury.

74. Fernandex, *One Hundred Years of Dominican Apostolate in Formosa (1859–1958)*, pp. 275–78 and 287.
75. It is said that there were 20 native students at the beginning. Ibid., pp. 288–91.
76. Tong, op. cit., p. 214.
77. Xie Sufen, "Serving a Changing Society: Catholicism in the Republic of China on Taiwan," 22.3 (March 1997): 4–7.
78. Collingnon, "The Catholic Church in Taiwan: An Interpretive Essay," p. 401.
79. Ibid.
80. 'Zhang Chunshen (Aloysius B. Chang), "Jiaohui benweihua de zhengjie," 33 (October 1977): 359.
81. Tong, op. cit., p. 221 and Qu Haiyuan, "Zongjiao pian," p. 398.
82. Qu Haiyuan, op. cit., p. 398.
83. Ibid.
84. Swanson, *The Church in Taiwan: Profile 1980*, p. 64.
85. Collingnon, op. cit., p. 404.
86. "Tianzhujiao Taiwan diqu zhujiaotuan shengmin," 2254 (May 3, 1998):1.
87. Collingnon, op. cit., p. 404.
88. Swanson, *The Church in Taiwan: Profile 1980*, p. 64.
89. "Taiwan Tianzhujiao de jianglai," 10.7 (July 1972): 28.
90. Chen Manhong, "Neidi Gang Tai sandi jiaohui de shehui jiaose," 114 (Winter 1977): 487.
91. Lo Guang, "The Present Situation of Evangelization in Taiwan," p. 7.
92. Zhao Binshi, "Zhongguo daotong yu chuanjiao," 16.10 (May 1967): 17–19; Fang Hao, "Tianzhujiao gen Zhongguo wenhua de guanxi," 18.2 (September 1968): 15–19.
93. In addition to the two articles in note 18, also see Liu Wenzhou, "Jiaoyou ruho yi wenhua chuanjiao," 17.1 (August 1967): 20–24.
94. Cheng Shiguang, "Youguan shenxue benweihua de jijuhua," 10.7 (July 1972): 25.
95. Zhang Chunshen (Aloysius B. Chang), "Zhongguo jiaohui de benweihua shenxue," 42 (January 1980): 414.
96. Cheng Shiguang, op. cit., p. 25.
97. Zhang Chunshen, op. cit., p. 431.
98. Ibid., p. 408.
99. There are, at least, several tens of articles on this topic. Zhang Chunshen provides a very good survey of these articles. Ibid., pp. 419–47. Also see Liu Jinchang, "Taiwan Tianzhujiao benweihua gaikuang," 111 (Spring 1997): 16–23.
100. Liu Jinchang, op. cit., p. 23; Song Guangyu, op. cit., p. 196.
101. Humphrey, *The Catholic Church in Taiwan*, p. 13.
102. Zhang Chunshen, "Tianzhujiao zai Taiwan weisheme jizu?" 20 (February 1994): 20–21.
103. Liu Jinchang, "Taiwan Tianzhujiao benweihua gaikuang," pp. 23–24.
104. Chen Suli, "Jiaohui dui Taiwan minjian sangli de shiying," 17.10 (July 1987): 56–67.
105. Lo Guang, op. cit., p. 5.
106. *Tianzhujiao zai Taiwan xiankuang zhi yenjiu*, pp. 50–63.
107. Ibid., p. 51.

108. Ibid., pp. 52, 57, 60, 63.

109. Father Zhang Chunshen did bring this issue out in an article. Zhang Chunshen, "Tianzhujiao zai Taiwan chuan fuyin de xiankuang yu weilai fangxiang," 74 (Winter 1987): 562.

110. Many articles mentioned about Pope's message. For example, Li Zhen [Gabrfiel Ly], "Fuyin *Zhongguohua* de jiqiexing," 14.7 (April 1984): 6; "Zhonghua minguo Taiwan diqu Tianzhujiao jiaowu jianbao," 35.5 (December 1985):1; "Jiaozong xiang Zhongguo zhujiaotuan zhici quanwen," 35.6 (January 1986), p. 4.

111. Liu Jinchang, op. cit., pp. 15–29.

112. Liang Jinwen, "Tai-Gang-Ao sandi jiaohui chutan, II" *Shenxue lunji* 114 (Winter 1997): 466–67.

113. Ding Liwei and Zhang Qifeng, "Taiwan yuanzhumin de shehui wenti," 111 (Spring 1997): 87–100 and 112 (Summer 1997): 265–76; Pingxintu (pseudonym), "Dui yuanzhumin zujiao zhusheng dadian de ruogan lianxiang," 2284 (October 4, 1998): 6.

114. Apparently the Catholic Church in Hong Kong has been in a better position to serve as a bridge church after 1997. For discussion on this issue, see Leung, "A Fragile Balance: Relations of the Vatican with China and Hong Kong," *Shenxue lunji* 113 (Fall 1997): 338–55, Zhang Chunshen, "Qiaoliang jiaohui yu jiemei jiaohui," 113 (Fall 1997): 355–57, and Mark Fang, "The Church in Post-'97 Hong Kong," *Shenxue lunji* 113 (Fall 1997): 358–66.

115. "Tianzhujiao Taiwan diqu zhujiaotuan shengmin," p. 1.

116. Liu Jinchang interprets this phenomenon as indicating that the Catholic Church in Taiwan no longer has enough capable people who have profound studies in church, theology, and Christianity, and are also equipped with a thorough understanding of culture, philosophy, and social change. See Liu Jinchang, "Taiwan Tianzhujiao benweihua gaikuang," p. 18.

117. Ibid., pp. 15–29; Wei Jiahua, "Fuchuan yu difang jiaohui zhi jianli," 2290 (November 11, 1998): 5.

Wickeri: Toward Further Dialogue

1. Arnold, *Princely Gifts and Papal Treasures.*

2. Koyama, "What Makes a Missionary: Toward a Crucified Mind Not a Crusading Mind," pp. 117–32.

3. Digan, *The Christian China Watchers: A Post-Mao Perspective.*

4. The subject is also of interest in China. See, for example, the history of popular religion in China by Ma Xisha and Han Bingfang, *Zhongguo minjian zongjiao shi.* On popular Christianity, see Liang Kalun, *Gaige kaifang yilai de Zhongguo nongcun jiaohui.*

5. Thomas, "Modernism in China," XIX (1921): 630–71. For a discussion, see Hutchinson, *Errand to the World: American Protestant Thought and Foreign Missions,* pp. 139ff.

6. See Walls, *The Missionary Movement in Christian History: Studies in the Transmission of Faith,* 1996.

7. Wai-ching Wong, "Asian Theology in a Changing Asia: Towards an Asian Theological Agenda for the 21st Century," p. 39.

8. See Smith, *Chinese Christians: Elites, Middlemen and the Church in Hong Kong.*

9. Coe, "Contextualization as the Way Toward Reform," p. 51 and *passim.*

10. For an excellent treatment of Protestant and Catholic American women in mission, see Robert, *American Women in Mission: A Social History of Their Thought and Practice*.

11. An outstanding exception is Kwok, *Chinese Women and Christianity, 1860–1927*.

12. Eber et al., eds., *The Bible in Modern China: The Literary and Intellectual Impact*; also see Yeo, *What Has Jerusalem to Do with Beijing: Biblical Interpretation from a Chinese Perspective*; and J. Wickeri, "Creating a Chinese Christian Idiom: Cultural Receptivity and Bible Translation."

Bibliography

Adoratskii (Nikolai, heiromonach). "Pravoslavnaia missiia v Kitaie za 200 let eia sushchchestvovaniia." *Pravoslavnyi sobesiednik.* Kazan: Tip. Imperatorskago universiteta, 1887.

Aleni, Giulio. *Xifang dawen* (Answers to Questions About the West), 1637. Reprinted in John L. Mish, "Creating an Image of Europe for China: Aleni's *Hsi-fang ta-wen.*" *Monumenta Serica* 23 (1964). Los Angeles: Monumenta Serica Institute, University of California at Los Angeles, 1964.

———. *Xixue fan* (Survey of Studies in the West). In *Tianxue chuhan,* vol. 1. Taibei: Taiwan xuesheng shuju, 1965. Modern reprint: Jinan: Qilu shushe, 1997.

———. *Zhifang waiji* (Record of [Countries] Outside of the Imperial Geographer's View). In *Tianxue chuhan* (First Correspondance on the Heavenly Religion). Reprinted *Congshu jicheng chubian* 3265. Shanghai: Shangwu yinshuguan, 1936.

Alexander, Jeffrey C. "Analytic Debates: Understanding the Relative Autonomy of Culture." In Jeffrey C. Alexander and Steven Seidman, eds., *Culture and Society: Contemporary Debates.*

Alexander, Jeffrey C., and Steven Seidman, eds. *Culture and Society: Contemporary Debates.* New York: Cambridge University Press, 1990.

"American Missionaries and Social Change in China: Collision and Confluences." Conference held at Linfield College, McMinnville, Oregon, 1994.

Amity News Service. "No Ordinary Day." Release dated March 16, 1999, at http://is7.pacific.net.hk/~amityhk/bible20mp1.htm.

An Ximeng. "Shenxue yu wenhua." In Zhuo Xinping and Edwin Hui, eds., *Jidu zongjiao yuanjiu* 1 (Study of Christianity, no. 1). Beijing: Shehui kexue wenxian chubanshe, 1999.

Anderson, Gerald H., and Thomas F. Stransky, eds. *Crucial Issues in Mission Today.* (Series: *Mission Trends,* no. 1) New York: Paulist Press, 1974.

Annuaire des missions catholiques de Chine. Shanghai: Imprimerie de T'ou-sè-wè (Zikawei), 1900–1931.

"Archives des Hautes Etudes Industrielles et Commerciales de Tianjin, Rapport des Pères Charvet et Denys." *Archives Françaises des Jésuites de Chine* (1946).

Archives Jésuites de la province de Paris. Vanves, France.

Archives internationales d'histoire des sciences. Weisbaden: Franz Steiner Verlag.

Archivum Proviniciae Hungariae Societatis Iesu. *Tamingi Hírek. Szarvas Miklós levelei. Kínai misszionáriusok levelei. P. Szajkó levelei. P. Kékessy levelei.*

Archivum Romanum Societatis Iesu (Jesu).

Archivum Romanum Societatis Iesu (Jesu). *Hung.* 1002–V. *Hung* 1002–X. *Epistolae Provincialis. Tamingensis Missio.*

Arnold, Lauren. *Princely Gifts and Papal Treasures: the Franciscan Mission to China and Its Influence on the Art of the West, 1250–1350.* San Francisco: Desiderata Press, 1999.

Artelt, Walter. *Christian Mentzel: Leibarzt des Großen Kurfürsten, Botaniker und Sinologie.* (Series: *Illustrierte Monographien zur Geschichte der Medizin* 1). Leipzig: Johann Ambrosius Barth, 1940.

Aurora (school diary). Shanghai: Zhendan daxue.

Baddeley, John F. *Russia, Mongolia, China: Being Some Record of the Relations Between Them from the Beginning of the XVIIth Century to the Death of the Tsar Alexei Mikhailovich, A.D. 1602–1676, Rendered Mainly in the Form of Narratives Dictated or Written by the Envoys Sent by the Russian Tsars, or Their Voevodas in Siberia to the Kalmuk and Mongol Khans & Princes; and to the Emperors of China . . . from Manuscripts in the Moscow Foreign Office Archives.* London: Macmillan and Company, 1919.

Bailly, Jean Sylvain. *Lettres sur l'origine des sciences, et sur celle des peuples de l'Asie, addressées à M. de Voltaire par M. Bailly.* London: Chez M. Elmesly, 1777.

Bao Zhimin. "Facing Reality and Responding to Challenges: On Ten Years of Chinese Church Reconstruction." *Chinese Theological Review* 5 (1989).

Barnett, Suzanne Wilson, and John King Fairbank, eds. *Christianity in China: Early Protestant Missionary Writings. Harvard Studies in American-East Asian Relations*; 9. Cambridge, MA: Committee on American-East Asian Relations, Dept. of History, and Council on East Asian Studies, Harvard University, 1985.

Bauer, Wolfgang. *China and the Search for Happiness: Recurring Themes in Four Thousand Years of Chinese Cultural History.* New York: Seabury Press, 1976.

Bayer, T.S. (Theophilus Siegfried). [*Theophili Sigefridi Bayeri*] *Museum Sinicum in quo sinicae linguae et litteratirae ratio explicatur.* Petropoli: ex typographia Academiae imperatoriae, 1730.

———. *Theophili Sigefridi Bayeri regiomontani De horis sinicis et cyclo horario commentationes accedit eiusdem auctoris Parergon sinicum de calendariis sinicis ubi etiam quaedam in doctrina temporum sinca emendantur.* Petropoli: Typis Academiae scientiarum, 1735.

Bays, Daniel H. "Christian Revivalism in China, 1900–1937." In Edith L. Blumhofer and Randall Balmer, eds., *Modern Christian Revivals*. Urbana: University of Illinois Press, 1993.

———. "The Growth of Independent Christianity in China, 1900–1937." In Daniel H. Bays, ed., *Christianity in China: From the Eighteenth Century to the Present*.

———. "Indigenous Protestant Churches in China, 1900–1937: A Pentecostal Case Study." In Steven Kaplan, ed., *Indigenous Responses to Western Christianity*.

———. "Missions and Christians in Modern China, 1850–1950." Paper presented at the Symposium on American Missionaries and Social Change in China: Collision and Confluences. Linfield College, Oregon, 1994.

Bays, Daniel H., ed. *Christianity in China: From the Eighteenth Century to the Present*. Stanford: Stanford University Press, 1996.

Bender, Heinrich. "Lebenskizze des verstorbenen Tschong Fuk-hin in Verbindung mit der Gründung der Tschonglok Gemeinden." Tschongtshun (18 June 1880). Evangelische Missionsgesellschaft in Basel. China: Berichte und Korrespondenz, 1846–1900. (BMG A–1.14:70).

Bennett, Adrian Arthur. *John Fryer: The Introduction of Western Science and Technology into Nineteenth-Century China*. (*Harvard East Asian Monographs* 24.) Cambridge, MA: East Asian Research Center, Harvard University Press, 1967.

Berling, Judith A. *The Syncretic Religion of Lin Chao-en*. New York: Columbia University Press, 1980.

Bernard, Henri. "Un correspondant de Bernard de Jussieu en Chine: le Père Le Cheron d'Incarville, missionaire français de Pékin." *Archives internationales d'histoire des sciences* 6 (janvier 1949); 7 (avril 1949).

———. "L'encyclopédie astronomique du Père Schall." *Monumenta Serica* 3 (1938).

Bibby, Reginald. *Unknown Gods: The Ongoing Story of Religion in Canada*. Toronto: Stoddart, 1993.

Bitterli, Urs. *Cultures in Conflict: Encounters Between European and Non-European Cultures, 1492–1800*. Oxford: Polity Press, 1989.

Bodemann, Eduard. *Der Briefwechsel des Gottfried Wilhelm Leibniz in der Königlichen öffentlichen Bibliothek zu Hannover*. Hildesheim: Olms Verlag, 1966.

Bohr, Paul Richard. "Liang Fa's Quest for Moral Power." In Suzanne Wilson Barnett and John King Fairbank, eds., *Christianity in China: Early Protestant Missionary Writings*.

Borer, Anton. "Das Tagebuch André Ly's als Quelle der Missionspastoral." *Neue Zeitschrift für Missionswissenschaft* 1 (1945).

Borthwick, Sally. *Education and Social Change in China: The Beginnings of the Modern Era*. (Series: *Education and Society*; *Hoover Press Publication*; 268). Stanford, CA: Hoover Institution Press Stanford University, 1983.

Bouvet, Joachim. *Histoire de l'empereur de la Chine.* Paris: chez Estienne Michallet, 1697.

Boym, Michał. *Specimen medicinae sinicae, sive, Opuscula medica ad mentem sinensium, continens I. De pulsibus libros quatuor è sinico translatos. II. Tractatus de pulsibus ab erudito europaeo collectos. III. Fragmentum operis medici ibidem ab erudito europaeo conscripti. IV. Excerpta literis eruditi europaei in China. V. Schemata ad meliorem praecedentium intelligentiam. VI. De indiciis morborum ex linguae coloribus & affectionibus: cum figuris aeneis & ligneis /* edidit Andreas Cleyer. Francofurti: Sumptibus Joannis Petri Zubrodt, 1682.

Bray, Francesca. "Some Problems Concerning the Transfer of Scientific and Technical Knowledge." In Thomas H.C. Lee, ed., *China and Europe: Images and Influences in Sixteenth to Eighteenth Centuries.*

Brian, Eric, and Christiane Demeulenaere-Douyère, eds. *Histoire et mémoire de l'Académie des sciences: Guide de recherche.* Paris: Tec & doc, 1996.

Bridge: Church Life in China Today. Hong Kong: Tao Fong Shan Ecumenical Centre.

Brook, Timothy. "Auto-Organization in Chinese Society." In Timothy Brook and B. Michael Frolic, eds., *Civil Society in China.*

———. *Praying for Power: Buddhism and the Formation of Gentry Society in Late-Ming China.* Cambridge, MA: Council on East Asian Studies, Harvard University and Harvard-Yenching Institute, 1993.

———. "Toward Independence: Christianity in China Under the Japanese Occupation, 1937–1945." In Daniel H. Bays, ed., *Christianity in China: From the Eighteenth Century to the Present.*

Brook, Timothy, and B. Michael Frolic. "The Ambiguous Challenge of Civil Society." In Timothy Brook and B. Michael Frolic, eds., *Civil Society in China.*

Brook, Timothy, and B. Michael Frolic, eds. *Civil Society in China.* Armonk, NY: M. E. Sharpe, 1997.

Broomhall, A. J. *Hudson Taylor and China's Open Century.* Sevenoaks, Kent: Hodder and Stoughton; Overseas Missionary Fellowship, 1981–1982.

Brouillon, R. P. [Nicolas]. *Mémoire sur l'état actuel de la Mission du Kiang-Nan, 1842–1855.* Paris: Julien, Lanier, 1855.

Brown, Elizabeth J. "The Developing Maturity of the Presbyterian Church in Taiwan 1958–1985 as Reflected by Changes in the Organization, Functions and Nationalities of Missionaries Serving with It in Taiwan." M.Div. thesis. Taipei: Taiwan Theological College and Seminary, 1987.

Buglio, Ludovico. *Budeyi bian.* 1665. Reprinted in *Tianzhujiao dongchuan wenxian* (Documents Concerning the Spread of Christianity to the East). (Series: *Zhonghua shixue congshu* 24). Taibei: Taiwan xuesheng shuji, 1965.

Bulletin de l'Université L'Aurore. Shanghai: Zhendan daxue.

Bulst, Werner. *Revelation.* New York: Sheed and Ward, 1965.

Burns, John P. "Strengthening Central CCP Control of Leadership Selection: The 1990 Nomenklatura." *China Quarterly* 138 (1994).

Burns, John P., ed. *The Chinese Communist Party's Nomenklatura System: A Documentary Study of Party Control of Leadership Selection, 1979–1984.* Armonk, NY: M. E. Sharpe, 1989.

Busch, H. "The Tung-lin Academy and its Political and Philosophical Significance." *Monumenta Serica* 14 (1949–55).

Butler, Jon. *Awash in a Sea of Faith: Christianizing the American People.* Cambridge: Harvard University Press, 1990.

Cai Sanxiong. "Taiwan Jidu Zhanglao jiaohui beijia yundong de tantao jiqi shenxue yiyi." Thesis. Tainan Theological College, 1979.

Cambridge History of China. [general editors, Denis Twitchett and John K. Fairbank]. Cambridge: Cambridge University Press, 1978.

Caraman, Philip. *University of the Nations: The Story of the Gregorian University with Its Associated Institutes, the Biblical and Oriental, 1551–1962.* New York: Paulist Press, 1981.

Carpenter, Joel. "Appendix: The Evangelical Missionary Force in the 1930's." In Joel Carpenter and Wilbert R. Shenk, eds., *Earthen Vessels: American Evangelicals and Foreign Missions, 1880–1980.*

Carpenter, Joel, and Wilbert R. Shenk, eds. *Earthen Vessels: American Evangelicals and Foreign Missions, 1880–1980.* Grand Rapids, MI: W. B. Eerdmans, 1990.

Carroll, Thomas D. "The Educational Work of the Catholic Church Mission, 1929–1939." *Collectanea Commissionis Synodalis* 14 (1941). Peking: Commission Synodalis in Sinas, 1928–1947.

Chamberlain, Heath B. "Coming to Terms with Civil Society." *Australian Journal of Chinese Affairs* 31 (1994).

Chan Che-po and Beatrice Leung. "The Voting Behaviour of Hong Kong Catholics in the 1995 Legislative Council Election." In Kuan Hsin-chi et al., eds., *The 1995 Legislative Council elections in Hong Kong.*

Chan, Kim-Kwong, and Alan Hunter. *Prayers and Thoughts of Chinese Christians.* Boston: Cowley, 1991.

Chan, Wing-tsit. *A Source Book in Chinese Philosophy.* Princeton: Princeton University Press, 1963.

Chao, Jonathan T'ien-en (Zhao Tian'en). "The Chinese Indigenous Church Movement, 1919–1927: A Protestant Response to the Anti-Christian Movement in Modern China." Ph.D. thesis. University of Pennsylvania, 1986.

Chao, Samuel H. *John Livingston Nevius (1829–1893): A Historical Study of His Life and Mission Methods.* Ph.D. thesis. Fuller Theological Seminary, 1991.

Charbonnier, Jean. *Guide to the Catholic Church in China.* Singapore: China Catholic Communication, 1990.

———. "The Underground Church." In Edmond Tang and Jean-Paul Wiest, eds., *The Catholic Church in Modern China.*

Charismatic Christianity: Sociological Perspectives. Stephen Hunt, Malcolm Hamilton, and Tony Walter, eds. London, Basingstoke: Macmillan, 1997.

Chartier, Roger. *The Cultural Uses of Print in Early Modern France.* Princeton: Princeton University Press, 1987.

Chen Chuanzheng. "Zuzhi rentong celue yu fei yingli zuzhi de guanxi: dui Jidujiao jiaohui de xibao xiaozu moshi jiaohui zengzhang yundong zhi yanjiu." Paper presented at the Conference on Management of Non-Profit Organizations, Jiayi, 1998.

Ch'en, Jerome. *China and the West: Society and Culture, 1815–1937.* London: Hutchinson, 1979.

Chen Manhong. "Neidi, Gang, Tai sandi jiaohui de shehui jiaose." *Furen daxue shenxue lunji* 114 (Winter 1977).

Chen Shenru and Zhu Zhengyi. "Shilun Ming mo Qing chu Yesuhuishi de lishi zuoyong" (An Initial Discussion of the Historical Role of the Society of Jesus in the Late Ming and Early Qing Period). *Zhongguo shi yanjiu* (February 1980).

Chen Suli. "Jiaohui dui Taiwan minjian sangli de shiying."*Jianzheng* 17 (July 1987).

Chen Yuan. *Yuan Yelikewen kao* (An Investigation of Yuan Dynasty Nestorianism). Beijing: Furen she, 1917.

Chen Zemin. "Inculturation of the Gospel and Hymn Singing in China." *Chinese Theological Review* 11:2 (1997).

Cheng Shiguang. "Youguan shenxue benweihua de jijuhua" (A Few Words Concerning Theological Inculturation). *Dousheng* 10.7 (July 1972).

Cheung, Siu-woo. "Millenarianism, Christian Movements, and Ethnic Change Among the Miao in Southwest China." In Stevan Harrell, ed., *Cultural Encounters on China's Frontier.* Seattle: University of Washington Press, 1995.

China. Beijing: New Star Publishers, 1999.

China and the Church Today. Hong Kong: Chinese Church Research Center.

China and the West. Proceedings of the International Colloquium held in the Koninklijke Academie voor Wetenschappen, Letteren en Schone Kunsten van België, Brussels, November 23–25, 1987. Brussels: Paleis der Academiën, 1993.

China Church Quarterly. South Orange, NJ: United States Catholic China Bureau.

China Mission Studies (1550–1800) Bulletin. Later *Sino-Western Cultural Relations Journal.* See Mungello, D. E., ed.

China News Analysis. Hong Kong: China News Analysis, 1953–1998.

China News and Church Report. Hong Kong: Chinese Church Research Center.

China State Council. *White Paper—Freedom of Religious Belief in China.* Beijing, October 1997. At http://www.china-embassy.org/Press/wpreligi.htm.

China Study Journal. London: Department for Chinese Relations, Council of Churches for Britain and Ireland, 1991–.

China Study Project Journal. London: China Study Project, 1986–1990.

China und Europa: Chinaverständnis und Chinamode im 17. und 18. Jahrhundert. Berlin: Verwaltung der Staatlichen Schlösser und Gärten, 1973.

La Chine entre amour et haine: Actes du VIIIe colloque de sinologie de Chantilly. Sous la direction de Michel Cartier. (*Variétés sinologiques*, no. 87.) Paris: Institut Ricci; Desclée de Brouwer, 1998.

Chinese Theological Review. Holland, MI: Foundation for Theological Education in Southeast Asia.

Ching, Frank. "Scare Tactics." *Far Eastern Economic Review* 18 (May 1999).

Ching, Julia. *Confucianism and Christianity: a Comparative Study.* Tokyo: Kodansha, 1977.

———. *Mysticism and Kingship in China: The Heart of Chinese Wisdom.* Cambridge, UK; New York: Cambridge University Press, 1997.

———. "The Problem of Evil and a Possible Dialogue Between Christianity and Neo-Confucianism." In *Contemporary Religions in Japan*, 9, 1968, and *Confucianism and Christianity: A Comparative Study.*

———. *To Acquire Wisdom: The Way of Wang Yang-ming.* New York: Columbia University Press, 1976.

Ching, Julia, and W. G. Oxtoby, eds. *Discovering China: European Interpretations in the Enlightenment.* (Series: *Library of the History of Ideas;* 7.) Rochester: University of Rochester Press, 1992.

———. *Moral Enlightenment: Leibniz and Wolff on China.* (*Monumenta Serica Monograph series* 26.) Nettetal: Steyler Verlag, 1992.

"Christianity and Chinese Culture." *China News Analysis* 1452 (January 15, 1992).

"A Chronology of the Catholic Church in China in the Context of Selected Dates in World and Chinese History." *Tripod* 76.

Coe, Shoki. "Contextualization as the Way Toward Reform." In Douglas J. Elwood, ed., *Asian Christian Theology: Emerging Themes.*

Cognet, Louis. *La spiritualité moderne.* Paris: Aubier, 1966.

Cohen, Myron L. "Being Chinese: The Peripheralization of Traditional Identity." In Tu Weiming, ed., *The Living Tree: The Changing Meaning of Being Chinese Today.* Berkeley: University of California Press, 1995.

Cohen, Paul A. *China and Christianity: The Missionary Movement and the Growth of Chinese Antiforeignism, 1860–1870.* Cambridge, MA: Harvard University Press, 1963.

———. "China and the Christian Impact (Review)." *Harvard Journal of Asian Studies* 47 (1987).

———. "Christian Missions and Their Impact to 1900." In *The Cambridge History of China*, vol. 10, *Late Ch'ing, 1800–1911.*

———. *Discovering History in China: American Historical Writing on the Recent Chinese Past.* New York: Columbia University Press, 1984.

———. "Reflections on the Missionary Movement." In *The Cambridge History of China*, vol. 10. *Late Ch'ing, 1800–1911*.

Collani, Claudia von. "Charles Maigrot's Role in the Chinese Rites Controversy." In D.E. Mungello, ed., *The Chinese Rites Controversy: Its History and Meaning.*

———. "Der deutsche Philosoph Gottfried Wilhelm Leibniz zum chinesischen Ritenstreit." *Sino-Western Cultural Relations Journal* 16 (1994).

———. *Eine wissenschaftliche Akademie für China: Briefe des Chinamissionars Joachim Bouvet S.J. an Gottfried Wilhelm Leibniz und Jean-Paul Bignon über die Erforschung de chinesischen Kultur, Sprache und Geschichte.* (*Studia Leibnitiana*, Sonderheft 18.) Stuttgart: Franz Steiner Verlag, 1989.

———. *Die Figuristen in der Chinamission.* Frankfurt am Main; Bern: Peter Lang, 1981.

———. *Die Jesuiten in Ingolstadt 1549–1773.* Ingolstadt: Stadarchive, 1992.

———. "Johann Adam Schall von Bell und die Naturwissenschaften in China." *Verbum SV* 33 (1992).

———. *P. Joachim Bouvet SJ: Sein Leben und sein Werk.* (*Monumenta Serica Monograph series* 17.) Nettetal: Steyler Verlag, 1985.

———. "Le Père Joachim Bouvet et le Mandement du Vicaire Apostolique Charles Maigrot." In *Actes du Ve Colloque international de Sinologie*, Chantilly, 1986. Paris; Taipei: Institut Ricci, 1993.

———. "Theology and Chronology in *Sinicae Historiae Decas Prima.*" In Franco Demarchi and Riccardo Scartezzini, eds., *Martino Martini: A Humanist and Scientist in Seventeenth-Century China.*

Collectanea Commissionis Synodalis. Dossiers de la Commission synodale. Digest of the Synodal Commission. Peking: Commission Synodalis in Sinas, 1928–1947.

Collectanea S. Congregationis de Propaganda Fide: seu decreta, instructiones, rescripta pro apostolicis missionibus ex tabulario eiusdem Sacrae Congregationis deprompta. Rome: Typographia Polyglotta, 1893.

Collingnon, James A. "The Catholic Church in Taiwan: An Interpretive Essay." In Allen J. Swanson, *The Church in Taiwan: Profile 1980.*

Congress of Asian Theologians (1997; Suwon, Korea). *Proceedings of the Congress of Asian Theologians (CATS).* Dhyanchand Carr and Philip Wickeri, eds. Hong Kong: Continuation Committee of the Congress of Asian Theologians, 1997–1998.

Copleston, Frederick Charles. *A History of Philosophy.* New York: Image Books, 1993.

Couplet, Philippe. *Confucius Sinarum philosophus, sive, Scientia Sinensis Latine exposita. Studio & opera Prosperi Intorcetta, Christiani Herdtrich, Francisci Rougemont, Philippi Couplet, patrum Societatis Jesu. Jussu Ludovici magni eximio missionum orientalium & litterariae reipublicae bono e Bibliotheca Regia in lucem prodit. Adjecta est tabula chronologica Sinicae monarchiae ab hujus exordio ad haec usque tempora.* Paris: apud Danielem Horthemels, 1687.

——. *Tabula chronologica monarchiae sinicae juxta cyclos annorum LX, ab anno ante Christum 2592 ad annum post Christum 1683; nunc primùm in lucem prodità Bibliotheca regia.* Paris, 1686.

Couplet, Philippe, ed. "Pröemialis Declaratio." In *Confucius Sinarum Philosophus.* Paris, 1687.

Covell, Ralph. *Confucius, the Buddha, and Christ: A History of the Gospel in Chinese.* Maryknoll, NY: Orbis Books, 1986.

——. *The Liberating Gospel in China: The Christian Faith Among China's Minority Peoples.* Grand Rapids, MI: Baker Books, 1995.

——. *Pentecost of the Hills in Taiwan: The Christian Faith Among the Original Inhabitants.* Pasadena, CA: Hope Publishing House, 1998.

Criveller, Gianni. *Preaching Christ in Late Ming China: The Jesuits Presentation of Christ from Matteo Ricci to Giulio Aleni.* (Series: *Variétés sinologiques*; n.s. 86.) Taipei; Brescia: Taipei Ricci Institute in collaboration with Fondazione Civiltà Bresciana, 1997.

Cronin, Vincent. *The Wise Man from the West.* London: Fount, 1955.

Da Qing lichao shilu: Shengzu. Tokyo: Daizo shupan kaisha; Xinjing: Da Manzhou Diguo Guowuyuan, 1937. Reprint: Beijing, Zhonghua shuju, 1985.

Dai Zhen. *Mengzi ziyi shuzheng* (Meaning of Mencius Corrected). Beijing: Zhonghua shuju, 1982.

Dawson, Christopher. *Mission to Asia: Narratives and Letters of the Franciscan Missionaries in Mongolia and China in the Thirteenth and Fourteenth Centuries.* New York: Harper & Row, 1966.

Dean, Kenneth. "Ritual and Space: Civil Society or Popular Religion?" In Timothy Brook and B. Michael Frolic, eds., *Civil Society in China.*

De Bary, William T. *Self and Society in Ming Thought.* New York: Columbia University Press, 1970.

——. *The Unfolding of Neo-Confucianism: The Conference on Seventeenth-Century Chinese Thought.* New York: Columbia University Press, 1975.

Dehergne, Joseph. "L'Eglise de Chine au tournant." *Bulletin de l'Université L'Aurore*, 10 (1949).

——. *Répertoire des jésuites de Chine de 1552 à 1800.* Rome: Institutum Historicum S.I., 1973.

D'Elia, Pasquale M. "Le Generalità sulle Scienze Occidentale di Giulio Aleni." *Revista degli Studi Orientali* 25 (1950). Rome: Scuola orientale della Università di Roma; G. Bardi, 1907–1950.

——. *The Triple Demism of Sun Yat-sen.* New York: AMS Press, 1974

D'Elia, Pasquale M., ed. *Fonti Ricciane: documenti originali concernenti Matteo Ricci e la storia delle prime relazioni tra l'Europa e la Cina (1579–1615). Vol. I. Matteo Ricci, Storia dell'introduzione del crisianesimo in*

Cina. Pte. I: libri 1–3. Da Macao a Nanciam (1582–1597). Vol. 2., Pte. II, libri 4–5, Da Nanciam a Pechino (1597–1610–1611). Vol. 3, pte. III Appendici e indici. Rome: Libreria dello Stato, 1942–1949.

———. *Il mappamondo cinese del P. Matteo Ricci S.J.: conservato presso la Bibliotca Vaticana.* [3.ed., Pechino, 1602]. *Commentato, tradotto e annotato.* Vatican City: Biblioteca apostolica Vaticana, 1938.

Delumeau, Jean. *Sin and Fear: The Emergence of a Western Guilt Culture, 13th –18th Centuries.* New York: St. Martin's Press, 1990.

Demarchi, Franco, and Riccardo Scartezzini, eds. *Martino Martini: a Humanist and Scientist in Seventeenth-Century China.* Proceedings of the International Symposium on Martino Martini and Cultural Exchanges Between China and the West, Beijing, 1994. Trento: Università degli Studi di Trento, 1996.

De Meyer, Jan M., and Peter M. Engelfriet, eds. *Linked Faiths: Essays on Chinese Religions and Traditional Culture in Honour of Kristofer Schipper.* Leiden: Brill, 1999.

Digan, Parig. *The Christian China Watchers: A Post-Mao Perspective.* Brussels: Pro Mundi Vita, 1978.

Ding Liwei and Zhang Qifeng. "Taiwan yuanzhumin de shehui wenti (I–II)." *Shenxue lunji* 111–112 (1997).

Ding Mingnan. "Guanyu Zhongguo jindaishishang jiao'an de kaocha" (An Investigation Concerning Religious Cases in Modern Chinese History). *Jindai shi yanjiu* (January 1990).

Dochy, Filip. "Assessment of Prior Knowledge as a Determinant for Future Learning." Ph.D. dissertation. Heerlen Open University, 1992.

Dopolneniia k Aktam istoricheskim. St. Petersburg: Arheograficheskaia kommissiia, 1846–1872.

Draskóczy, László. *A Magyar keresztyénség külmissziói szolgálata* (The Foreign Mission Service of Hungarian Christianity). Budapest: Református traktátus sorozat, 1940.

Du Shiran and Han Qi. "The Contribution of French Jesuits to Chinese Science in the Seventeenth and Eighteenth Centuries." *Impact of Science on Society* 167. Paris: UNESCO, 1992.

Duan Qi. "Contextualization in the Contemporary Chinese Church." In Philip L. Wickeri and Lois Cole, eds., *Christianity and Modernization: A Chinese Debate.*

Duara, Prasenjit. "Knowledge and Power in the Discourse of Modernity: The Campaigns Against Popular Religion in Early Twentieth-Century China." *Journal of Asian Studies* 50:1 (1991).

Dudink, Ad. "*Nangong shudu* (1620), *Poxie ji* (1640) and Western Reports on the Nanking Persecution (1616/1617)." In "Christianity in Late-Ming China: Five Studies." Ph. D. dissertation. Leiden, 1995.

———. "The Religious Works Composed by Johann Adam Schall von Bell, Especially His *Zhuzhi qunzheng* and His Efforts to Convert the Last Ming emperor." In Roman Malek, ed., *Western Learning and Christianity in China: The Contribution and Impact of Johann Adam Schall von Bell, S.J. (1592–1666)*.

Du Hamel, Jean-Baptiste. *Regiae scientiarum academie historia*. Paris: Joannem-Baptistani Delespine, 1701.

Dujardin, Carine. "Historiography and Christian Missions in China." In Jerome Heyndrickx, ed., *Historiography of the Chinese Catholic Church*. Leuven: Ferdinand Verbiest Foundation, 1994.

Dulles, Avery. *Models of Revelation*. Maryknoll, NY: Orbis Books, 1992.

———. *Models of the Church*. New York: Macmillan, 1974.

Duman, L. I., ed. *Russko-kitaiskie otnosheniia, 1689–1916. Ofitsial'nyie dokumenty*. Moscow, 1958.

Dunch, Ryan. *Fuzhou Protestants and Making of a Modern China, 1857–1927*. New Haven: Yale University Press, 2001.

———. "Protestants and the State in Post-Mao China." M.A. thesis, University of British Columbia, 1991.

Duosheng. Taibei: Shuiniu tushu chuban.

"The Eastern Lightning Sect: A Recent Threat to the Church in China." *Amity News Service* 6.11/12 (1997).

Eber, Irene, Sze-kar Wan, Knut Walf, and Roman Malek, eds. *Bible in Modern China: The Literary and Intellectual Impact*. (*Monumenta Serica Monograph Series*, 43.) St. Augustin: Institut Monumenta Serica, 1999.

Echanges culturels et religieux entre la Chine et l'Occident: Actes du VIIe colloque international de sinologie (Chantilly: 1992). Edward J. Malatesta, Yves Raguin, and Ad Dudink, eds. (*Variétés sinologiques-nouvelle série; 83*.) San Francisco: Ricci Institute for Chinese-Western Cultural History; Paris: Institut Ricci, 1995.

"Les écoles catholiques en Chine." *Collectanea Commissionis Synodalis*. Peking: Commission Synodalis in Sinas 2 (1929).

Edgar, J. Houston. "The Exploration and Occupation of the Centres on the Tibetan Marches." *Chinese Recorder* 50 (September 1919).

Efimov, A. B. "Novyie materaly po istorii Pekinskoi Duchovnoi Misii." Conference paper presented at *Evangeliie v kontekste mirovoi kul'tury*. Moscow, 1997.

Eglises d'Asie. Paris: Agence d'information des missions étrangères de Paris, 1994–.

Elman, Benjamin A. *From Philosophy to Philology: Intellectual and Social Aspects of Change in Late Imperial China*. Cambridge, MA: Harvard University Press, 1984.

Elvin, Mark. "The Collapse of Scriptural Confucianism." *Papers on Far Eastern History* 41 (1990).

Elwood, Douglas J., ed. *Asian Christian Theology: Emerging Themes*. (Revised edition of *What Asians Christians Are Thinking*). Philadelphia: Westminster Press, 1980.

Entenmann, Robert B. "Catholics and Society in Eighteenth-Century Sichuan." In Daniel H. Bays., ed., *Christianity in China: From the Eighteenth Century to the Present.*

——. "Chinese Catholic Clergy and Catechists in Eighteenth-Century Szechwan." In *Images de la Chine: Contexte occidental de la sinologie naissante: Actes de VIe colloque international de sinologie.*

——. "Chinese Catholic Communities in Early Ch'ing Szechwan." In *Echanges culturels et religieux entre la Chine et l'Occident: Actes du VIIe colloque international de sinologie.*

——. "Christian Virgins in Eighteenth-Century Sichuan." In Daniel H. Bays, ed., *Christianity in China: From the Eighteenth Century to the Present.*

——. "The Establishment of Chinese Catholic Communities in Early Ch'ing Szechwan." In *Echanges culturels et religieux entre la Chine et l'Occident: Actes du VIIe colloque international de sinologie.*

Etiemble. *L'Europe chinoise. II: De la sinophile à la sinophobie.* Paris: Gallimard, 1989.

Evangelische Missionsgesellschaft in Basel. China: Berichte und Korrespondenz, 1846–1900. Document: Hamberg to Inspector. Pukak, 14 May 1853 (BMG A–1.2:31).

Fairbank, John K., ed. *The Missionary Enterprise in China and America.* Cambridge: Harvard University Press, 1974.

Fan Hongye. *Yesuhuishi yu Zhongguo kexue* (The Jesuits and Chinese Science). Beijing: Zhongguo renmin daxue chubanshe, 1992.

Fang Hao. "Tianzhujiao gen Zhongguo wenhua de guanxi" (The Relationship Between Chinese Culture and Catholicism). *Hengyi* (September 1968).

——. *Zhong Xi jiaotong shi* (History of Chinese-Western Communication). Taibei: Zhonghua wenhua chubanshe, 1953–1954.

——. *Zhongguo Tianzhujiao shi renwuzhuan* (Biographies in the History of Chinese Christianity). Taizhong: Guangqi chubanshe, 1967–1973.

——. *Zhongguo Tianzhujiao shi luncong* (Discussions on the History of Christianity in China). Chongqing: Shangwu yinshuguan, 1944.

——. *Zhongwai wenhua jiaotong shi luncong* (Discussions on the History of Sino-Foreign Cultural Communications). Chongqing: Duli chubanshe, 1944.

Fang Litian. "Zhongguo zongjiao shinian" (Ten Years of Chinese Religion). *Shijie zongjiao yanjiu* (April 1990).

Fang, Mark. "The Church in Post-'97 Hong Kong." *Shenxue lunji* 113 (Fall 1997).

Farkas, Ildikó. "A turánizmus." *Magyar Tudomány*, 1993/7.

Ferguson, Sinclair B., David F. Wright, and J. I. Packer, eds. *New Direction of Theology.* Downers Grove, IL: Inter-Varsity Press, 1988.

Fernandex, Pablo. *One Hundred Years of Dominican Apostolate in Formosa (1859–1958): Extracts from the Sino-Annamite Letters, Dominican Missions and Ultramar.* Taipei: SMC Publishing Co., 1994.

Fernöstliche Kultur: Wolf Haenisch zugeeignet von seinem Marburger Studienkreis. [hrsg. u. bearb. von Helga Dressler-Wormit]. Marburg: Elwert, 1975.

The Field Afar. Boston: Catholic Foreign Mission Society of America.

The Fifty Most Unreached People Groups of China and Tibet. Chiang Mai, Thailand: Asian Minorities Outlook,1996.

Flannery, Austin, ed. "The Constitution of the Church." In *Vatican II: The Conciliar and Postconciliar Documents.* Collegeville, MN: Liturgical Press, 1975.

————. "Pastoral Constitution on the Church in the Modern World." In *Vatican II: The Conciliar and Postconciliar Documents.* Collegeville, MN: Liturgical Press, 1975.

Foreign Affairs Committee Report of the British Parliament 1994. See: Great Britain. Parliament. Foreign Affairs Committee. *FAC Report.*

Forte, Antonino. "The Edict of 638 Allowing the Diffusion of Christianity in China." In Paul Pelliot, *L'Inscription Nestorienne de Si-ngan-fou.*

Foucquet, Jean-François. "Richan." In *Lifa wenda.* London: British Library.

Fourmont, Étienne. *Linguae Sinarum Mandarinicae hieroglyphicae grammatica duplex, Latinè, et cum characteribus Sinensium: Item Sinicorum Regiae Bibliothecae librorum catalogus, denuò, cum notitiis amplioribus et charactere Sinico, editus.* Paris: Chez Hippolyte-Louis Guerin, Rollin Fils, Joseph Bullot, ex typograhiâ Josephi Bullot, 1742.

————. *Meditationes sinicae, inquibus 1o consideratur linguae philosophicae atque universalis natura . . . 20 lingua sinarum mandarinica, tum in hieroglyphis, tum in monosyllabis suis . . . talis esse ostenditur datur eorundum hieroglyphorum . . . lectio et intellectio.* Paris: Musier, 1737.

Foust, Clifford M. *Muscovite and Mandarin: Russia's Trade with China and Its Setting, 1727–1805.* Chapel Hill: University of North Carolina Press, 1969.

Fraser, J. O. "Mass Movements Among the Aborigines." *China's Millions* (November 1937).

Friends of Moslems: The Quarterly Newsletter of the Society of Friends of the Moslems in China. Hankow, Hupei, China: Pickens, 1928–1951.

Fuchs, Walter. "Der russisch-chinesische Vertrag von Nertschinsk aus dem Jahre 1689." *Monumenta Serica* 4 (1939–1940).

Furen daxue shenxue lunji (Collectanea Theologica Universitatis Fujen). Xinzhuang: Fushe shenxueyuan. See also *Shenxue lunji.*

Fuzhou Jidujiao wenshi ziliao xuanji (Selected Historical Sources on Christianity in Fuzhou). Fuzhou, 1987–.

Fuzhou Meiyimei nianhui shi (History of the Foochow Conference of the Methodist Episcopal Church). Edited by Lin Xianfang et al. Fuzhou: [Methodist Church], 1936.

Ganss, George E., ed. *Ignatius of Loyola: The Spiritual Exercises and Selected Works.* New York: Paulist Press, 1991.

Gao Junming. "Christianity and the Modernization of Formosa." *Asian Cultural Studies* 4 (September 1967).

Gaubil, Antoine. *Correspondance de Pékin, 1722–1759*. Geneva: Librarie Droz, 1970.

Geffré, Claude, and Joseph Spae. *China as a Challenge to the Church*. New York: Seabury Press, 1979.

Gernet, Jacques. *China and the Christian Impact: A Conflict of Cultures*. Cambridge. Cambridge University Press, 1985.

———. *Chine et christianisme: Action et réaction*. Paris: Gallimard, 1982.

———. "Christian and Chinese Visions of the World in the Seventeenth Century." *Chinese Science*, 4:8 (1980).

———. *Le monde chinois*. Paris: Armand Colin, 1990.

Giovagnoli, Agostino, ed. *Roma e Pechino: la svolta extraeuropea di Benedetto XV*. (Series: *Religione e società*; 33). Rome: Studium, 1999.

Glanzer, Perry L. "International Persecution of Christians." Report dated March 1, 1998, at http://www.family.org/cforum/research/papers/a0001409.html.

Golvers, Noël. *The* Astronomia Europaea *of Ferdinand Verbiest, S.J. (Dillingen, 1687): The Text, Translation, Notes and Commentaries*. (*Monumenta Serica Monograph series*, XXVIII.) Nettetal: Steyler Verlag, 1993.

Gonzáles, José María. *Historia de las misiones dominicanas in China*. Madrid: Juan Bravo, 1955–1960. Vol. 5 (*Bibliografías*) reprinted 1966.

Gonzales de Mendoza, Juan. *Historia de las cosas, mas notables ritos y costvmbres, del gran Reyno del China, sabidas assi por los libros de los mesmos Chinas, como por relacion de religiosos y otras personas que an estado en el dicho Reyno*. Rome: A costa de Bartholome Grassi, 1585.

Gospel in the Context of World Culture. A Commemoration of Moscow Metropolitan Innokenti Veniaminov at the Conference on Orthodox Missiology, Moscow, June 11–13, 1997. *See*: http://www.russian-orthodox-church.org.ru/nr180772.htm

Gourdin, F. *Catalogus cleri indigenae in Provincia Se-Tchouan, 1702–1858*. Chongqing: Typis Missionis Catholicae, 1919.

Graham, Angus C. "China, Europe, and the Origins of Modern Science: Needham's *The Grand Titration*." *Asia Major* 16, 1971. Reprinted in Nakayama Shigeru, ed., *Chinese Science: Explorations of an Ancient Tradition*.

Grantham, Alexander. *Grantham to SofS*. 311 *secret*, 1 April 1949, file 0537/4824. Hong Kong Public Records Office.

———. *Grantham to SofS*. 384 *secret*, 30 April 1949, file 0371/5839. Hong Kong Public Records Office.

Great Britain. Parliament. Foreign Affairs Committee. *FAC Report 1994*.

Grimm, Tilemann. "China und das Chinabild von Leibniz." In *Systemprinzip und Vielheit der Wissenschaften*. Wiesbaden, 1969.

Gruzinski, Serge. *La pensée métisse*. Paris: Fayard, 1999.

Gu Changsheng. *Chuanjiaoshi yu jindai Zhongguo* (Missionaries and Modern China). Shanghai: Renmin chubanshe, 1981.

——. *Cong Malixun dao Situ Leideng: lai Hua xinjiao chuanjiaoshi pingzhuan* (From Morrison to Leighton Stuart: Critical Biographies of Protestant Missionaries in China). Shanghai: Renmin chubanshe, 1985.

Gu Weimin. *Jidujiao yu jindai Zhongguo shehui* (Christianity and Recent Chinese Society). (*Jindai Zhongguo shehuishi congshu.*) Shanghai: Shanghai renmin chubanshe, 1996.

Gu Yulu. *Zhongguo Tianzhujiao de guoqu yu xianzai* (Chinese Catholicism Past and Present). Shanghai: Shehui kexue, 1989.

Guignes, Joseph de. *Histoire générale des Huns, des Turcs, des Mogols, et des autres Tartares occidentaux, &c. avant et depuis Jésus-Christ jusqu'à présent.* Paris: Desaint & Saillant, 1756–1758.

Guiot, Léonide. *La mission de Su-tchuen au XVIIIme siècle: Vie et apostolat de Mgr. Pottier, son fondateur.* Paris: Téqui, 1892.

Gumilevskii, Dimitrii Grigorévich (Abp. Filaret of Chernogov). *Istoria russkoi tserkvi: Sochinenie Filareta Gumilevskago, arkhiepiskopa Chernigovskago.* St. Petersburg: Tuzova, 1894.

Guo Xiwei. "Zhongguo Jidujiao shi yanjiu" (Studies in the History of Chinese Christianity). *Zhongguo zongjiao yanjiu nianjian 1996* (Year Book of Religious Studies in China 1996). Beijing: Zhongguo shehui kexue chubanshe, 1998.

Gutian Jidujiao zhi (Gazetteer of [Protestant] Christianity in Gutian). Edited by Gutian xian Jidujiao sanzi aiguo yundong weiyuanhui (Gutian County Committee of the Protestant Three-Self Patriotic Movement). [Gutian]: n.p., n.d.; preface 1989.

Habermas, Jürgen. *The Structural Transformation of the Public Sphere: An Inquiry into a Category of Bourgeois Society.* Thomas Burger, trans. Cambridge: MIT Press, 1989.

Hahn, Roger. *The Anatomy of a Scientific Institution: the Paris Academy of Sciences, 1666–1803.* Berkeley: University of California Press, 1971.

Hajnal (Dawn). Mission Journal of the Hungarian Reformed Church. 1909–.

Hall, David, and Roger Ames. *Anticipating China: Thinking Through the Narratives of Chinese and Western Culture.* Albany: State University of New York Press, 1995.

Han Lin. *Duoshu.* [JapSin I,144]. Rome: Archivum Romanum Societatis Iesu.

Han Lin and Zhang Geng. *Shengjiao xinzheng* (Reliable Evidence Regarding the Holy Spirit). In *Tianzhujiao dongchuan wenxian sanbian*, v. 1. Taibei: Taiwan xuesheng shuju, 1972.

Han Qi. "Europeans' Views on the Backwardness of Chinese Sciences in the 17th and 18th Centuries." *Ziran kexue shi yanjiu* (Studies in the History of Natural Science). 11.4 (1992). Beijing: Kexue chubanshe.

———. "Joachim Bouvet's Study of the Yijing and the Theory of the Chinese Origin of Western Learning in the Kangxi Period." Unpublished paper from conference *Europe in China III, Between Ming and Qing*, Berlin, 1998.

———. "Kangxi shidai chuanru de Xifang shuxue jiqi dui Zhongguo shuxue de yingxiang" (The Introduction of Western Mathematics During the Kangxi Period (1689–1723) and Its Influence on Chinese Mathematics). Ph.D. dissertation. Beijing: Institute for the History of the Natural Sciences, Chinese Academy of Sciences, 1991.

———. "The Role of the French Jesuits in China and the Académie Royale des Sciences in the Development of the 17th and 18th Century French and Chinese Sciences." In Hashimoto Keizo et al., eds., *East Asian Science: Tradition and Beyond*.

———. "Sino-British Scientific Relations Through Jesuits in the Seventeenth and Eighteenth Centuries." In *La Chine entre amour et haine: Actes du VIIIe colloque de sinologie de Chantilly*.

———. "Shuli jingyun duishu zaobiaofa yu Dai Xu de erxiang zhankaishi yanjiu" (Briggs' Method for Calculating Common Logarithm in the *Shuli jingyun* and Its Influence on Dai Xu's Study of Binomial Theorem). *Ziran kexueshi yanjiu* (Studies in the History of Natural Science). 11.2 (1992).

Hanson, Eric O. *Catholic Politics in China and Korea.* Maryknoll, NY: Orbis Books, 1980.

Harris, George L. "The Mission of Matteo Ricci, S.J.: A Case Study of an Effort at Guided Culture Change in China in the Sixteenth Century." *Monumenta Serica* 25 (1966).

Hashimoto Keizo and Catherine Jami. "Kepler's Laws in China: A Missing Link? J.-F. Foucquet's *Lifa wenda.*" *Historia Scientiarum* 6.3 (1997). Tokyo: History of Science Society of Japan.

Hashimoto Keizo, Catherine Jami, and Lowell Skar, eds. *East Asian Science: Tradition and Beyond.* Osaka: Kansai University Press, 1995.

Hatch, Nathan O. *The Democratization of American Christianity.* New Haven: Yale University Press, 1989.

Havret, Henri. *La Mission du Kiang-nan: Les trois dernières années, 1899–1901.* Zikawei: Imprimerie de la mission catholique, 1902.

Hayes, Victor C., ed. *Identity Issues in World Religions: Selected Proceedings of the Fifteenth Congress of the International Association for the History of Religions.* Bedford Park, S. Australia: Australian Association for the Study of Religions, 1986.

Hayhoe, Ruth. "Catholics and Socialists: The Paradox of French Educational Interaction with China." In Ruth Hayhoe, and Marianne Bastid, eds., *China's Education and the Industrialized World.* Armonk, NY: M.E. Sharpe, 1987.

———. "A Chinese Catholic Philosophy of Higher Education in Republican China." *Tripod* 48 (1988).

Hayhoe, Ruth, and Marianne Bastid, eds. *China's Education and the Industrialized World: Studies in Cultural Transfer.* Armonk, NY: M.E. Sharpe, 1987.

Hayhoe, Ruth, and Lu Yongling. *Ma Xiangbo and the Mind of Modern China (1840–1939).* Armonk, NY: M.E. Sharpe, 1996.

He Guichun. "Guanyu Ming-Qing Yesuhuishi zai Hua huodong pingjia de jige wenti" (A Few Questions Concerning the Assessment of Jesuit Activities During the Ming-Qing Era). *Xueshu yuekan* (November 1992).

He Zhaowu. "Tianzhujiao chuanru de shidai beijing he Yesuhuishi de zuoyong" (Background of the Age of the Catholic China Mission and the Function of the Society of Jesus). In Hou Wailu, *Zhongguo sixiang tongshi.*

Hembeye, E. R. "Tibet." In *New Catholic Encyclopedia.* New York: McGraw-Hill, 1967.

Henderson, John B. *Scripture, Canon, and Commentary: a Comparison of Confucian and Western Exegesis.* Princeton: Princeton University Press, 1991.

Herskovits, Melville J. *Man and His Works: The Science of Cultural Anthropology.* New York: Alfred A. Knopf, 1979.

Heynrickx, Jerome, ed. *Philippe Couplet S.J. (1623–1693): The Man Who Brought China to Europe.* (*Monumenta Serica Monograph series* 22.) Nettetal: Steyler Verlag, 1992.

Hírek a Provinciából (Province News).

Hirschfield, John Milton. *The Académie royale des sciences, 1666–1683.* New York: Arno Press, 1981.

Hong Kong. Office of Public Records. *Hong Kong Records Series.* Document 147 2/2 (2).

Hood, George A. *Mission Accomplished? The English Presbyterian Mission in Lingtung, South China: A Study of the Interplay between Mission Methods and Their Historical Context.* (*Studien zur interkulturellen Geschichte des Christentums*; Bd. 42.) Frankfurt am Main; New York: Verlag Peter Land, 1986.

Hou Jie and Fan Lizhu. *Zhongguo minzhong zongjiao yishi* (Concepts of Popular Chinese Religions). Tianjin: Tianjin renmin chubanshe, 1994.

Hou Wailu. *Zhongguo sixiang tongshi* (A Popular History of Chinese Thought). Beijing: Renmin chubanshe, 1957–1963.

Hsiung, James Chieh, ed. *Hong Kong the Super Paradox: Life After Return to China.* New York: St. Martin's Press, 2000.

Hsu, Immanuel C. Y. *The Rise of Modern China.* Cambridge: Oxford University Press, 1970.

Hu Shih. *The Chinese Renaissance: The Haskell Lectures in Comparative Religion, 1933.* Chicago: University of Chicago Press, 1934.

Huang, Chün-chieh, and Erik Zürcher, eds. *Time and Space in Chinese Culture.* Leiden: Brill, 1995.

Huang Wudong. *Huang Wudong huiyi lu.* Taibei: Qianwei chubanshe, 1988.

Huang Yilong. "Court Divination and Christianity in the K'ang-hsi Era." In Nathan Sivin, *Chinese Science* 10.

Huang Zhiji. *Jian dao ji* (Discovered Truths Compiled). Fuzhou: Methodist Publishing House, 1903.

———. *Ye Mo henglun* (Comparison of Jesus and Mozi). Fuzhou: Methodist Publishing House, 1912.

Huang Zongxi. *Mingru xue'an.* Beijing: Zhonghua shuju, 1985.

———. *The Records of Ming Scholars: A Selected Translation Edited by Julia Ching and . . . Chaoying Fang.* Honolulu: University of Hawaii Press, 1987.

Human Rights Watch/Asia. *China: Religious Persecution Persists.* New York: Human Rights Watch, 1995.

———. *China: State Control of Religion.* New York: Human Rights Watch, 1997.

———. *Continuing Religious Repression in China.* New York: Human Rights Watch, 1993.

Humphrey, Delos A. *The Catholic Church in Taiwan.* Taipei: Wisdom Press, 1974.

Hung Ming-shui. "Yüan Hung-tao and the Late Ming Literary and Intellectual Movement." Ph.D. thesis, University of Wisconsin, 1974.

Hunter, Alan. "A Sociological Perspective on Chinese Christianity." *Bridge* 44 (1990).

Hunter, Alan, and Kim-Kwong Chan. *Protestantism in Contemporary China.* Cambridge: Cambridge University Press, 1993.

Huonder, Anton. *Deutsche Jesuitenmissionäre des 17. und 18. Jahrhunderts: Ein Beitrag zur Missionsgeschichte und zur deutschen Biographie.* Freiburg: Herder, 1899.

Hutchinson, William R. *Errand to the World: American Protestant Thought and Foreign Missions.* Chicago: University of Chicago Press, 1987.

Ignatius, of Loyola, Saint. *Ignatius of Loyola: The Spiritual Exercises and Selected Works.* George E. Ganss, ed. New York: Paulist Press, 1991.

Images de la Chine: Contexte occidental de la sinologie naissante: Actes de VIe colloque international de sinologie (Chantilly: 1989). Edward J. Malatesta et Yves Raguin, eds. (*Variétés sinologiques-nouvelle série*; 78.) San Francisco: Ricci Institute for Chinese-Western Cultural History; Paris: Institut Ricci, 1995.

"Inculturation of the Gospel and Hymn Singing in China." *Amity News Service* 7.5/6 (1998).

Index biographique de l'Académie des sciences du 22 décembre 1666 au 1er octobre 1978. Paris: Gauthier-Villars, 1979.

International Symposium on Chinese-Western Cultural Interchange in Commemoration of the 400th Anniversary of the Arrival of Matteo Ricci, S.J. in China. Collected Essays / Jinian Li Madou lai Hua 400 zhounian Zhong Xi wenhua jiaoliu guoji xueshu huiyi. Lunwen ji. Taiwan, Xinzhuang: Furen daxue chubanshe, 1983.

"Is the Church a Help or a Hindrance to China's Development?" *Amity New Service* 8.3/4 (1999).

Isten Dalosai (Singers of God). Franciscan Mission Association, 1931–1944.

Istoricheskii ocherk khristianskoi propovedi v Kitae. Trudy Kievskoi Dukhovnoi Akademii. Kiev, 1860.

Ivanov, P. M. "K istorii vozniknoveniia Moskovskogo podvoria Pekinskoi Duchovnoi Missii." Conference paper presented at *Evangeliie v kontekste mirovoi kul'tury.* Moscow, 1997.

Jami, Catherine. "From Euclid to Pardies: The Geometry Transmitted to China by Jesuits (1607–1723)." In Federico Masini, ed., *Western Humanistic Culture Presented to China by Jesuit Missionaries (XVII–XVIII Centuries).*

———. "From Louis XIV's Court to Kangxi's Court: An Institutional Analysis of the French Jesuit Mission to China (1662–1722)." In Hashimoto Keizo et al., eds., *East Asian Science: Tradition and Beyond.*

Jensen, Lionel. *Manufacturing Confucianism: Chinese Traditions & Universal Civilization.* Durham: Duke University Press, 1997.

Ji Tai. "Hermeneutics in the Chinese Church." *Chinese Theological Review* 12 (1998).

———. "Preaching in the Church in China." *China Study Journal* 12 (1997).

Jian Youwen. *Zhongguo Jidujiao de kaishan shiye* (Pioneers of the Protestant Church in China). Hong Kong: Jidujiao fuqiao chubanshe, 1960.

Jiang Fangzhen. *Ouzhou wenyi fuxing shi* (History of the European Renaissance). Shanghai: Shangwu yinshuguan, 1947.

Jiang Wenhan. *Ming Qing jian zai Hua de Tianzhujiao Yesuhuishi* (The Catholic Society of Jesus in China During the Ming and Qing Era). Shanghai: Zhishi chubanshe, 1987.

"Jiaozong xiang Zhongguo zhujiaotuan zhici quanwen." *Hengyi* 35.6 (January 1986).

Jidujiao luntan. Taibei: Jidujiao luntanshe, 1999.

Johnson, David, Andrew J. Nathan, and Evelyn S. Rawski, eds. *Popular Culture in Late Imperial China.* Berkeley: University of California Press, 1985.

Jordan, David K., and Daniel L. Overmeyer. *The Flying Phoenix: Aspects of Chinese Sectarianism in Taiwan.* Princeton, NJ: Princeton University Press, 1986.

Josselin de Jong, P. E. de. *Contact der continenten.* Leiden: University of Leiden Press, 1978.

Journal des savants (Le iovrnal des sçavans). Paris: L'Institute de France, Académie des inscriptions et belles-lettres.

Journal de Trévoux (ou, Mémoires pour servir à l'histoire des sciences et des arts). Paris: Chéz Chaubert, 1731.

Jullien, François. *Procès ou création: une introduction à la pensée des lettrés chinois: essai de problématique interculturelle.* Paris: Editions du Seuil, 1989.

Kan Baoping. "Theology in the Contemporary Chinese Context." *Chinese Theological Review* 11:2 (1997).

Kaplan, Steven, ed., *Indigenous Responses to Western Christianity*. New York: New York University Press, 1995.

Katolikus Hitterjesztés Lapjai (Journal of Catholic Propagation of the Faith). Nagyvárad, 1881–1918.

Katolikus Missziók (Catholic [Jesuit] Missions). n.p., 1925–1948

Kinnear, Angus I. *Against the Tide: The Story of Watchman Nee*. Wheaton, IL: Christian Literature Crusade, 1978.

Kircher, Athanasius. *La Chine d'Athanase Kirchere . . . illustrée de plusieurs monuments tant sacrés que profanes, et de quantité de recherchés de la nature et de l'art. A quoy on à adjousté de nouveau les questions curieuses que le serenissime grand duc de Toscane a fait dépuis peu au P. Jean Grubere touchant ce grand empire. Avec un dictionnaire chinois & françois, lequel est tres-rare, & qui n'a pas encores paru au jour.* Amsterdam: Ches J. Jansson à Waesberge & les heritiers d'Elizé Weyeratraet, 1670.

———. *Oedipus Aegyptiacus: Hoc est Vniuersalis hieroglyphicæ veterum doctrinæ temporum iniuria abolitæ instauratio. Opus ex omni orientalium doctrina & sapientia conditum, nec non viginti diuersarium linguarum authoritate stabilitum, felicibus auspicijs Ferdinandi III. Austriaci sapientissimi & inuictissimi Romanorum Imperatoris semper Augusti è tenebris erutum, atque bono reipublicae literariae consecratum.* Romae, ex typographia Vitalis Mascardi, 1652–1654.

Knapp, Keith Nathaniel. "The *Ru* Interpretation of *Xiao*." *Early China* 20 (1995).

Kong Xiangtao. "Xinyang, renmin he zuguo: zaoqi Jidujiaohui de Huaren budaoyuan qun." *Nanjing shenxue zhi* (August 1998).

Kool, A. M. (Anna Maria). *Az Úr csodásan működik I–II*. Budapest, 1995–1997.

———. *God Moves in a Mysterious Way: the Hungarian Protestant Foreign Mission Movement, 1756–1951*. Zoetermeer: Uitgeverij Boekencentrum, 1993.

Kouduo richao. [JapSin I 81]. Rome: Archivum Romanum Societatis Iesu.

Koyama, Kosuke. "What Makes a Missionary: Toward a Crucified Mind Not a Crusading Mind." In Gerald H. Anderson, and Thomas F. Stransky, eds., *Crucial Issues in Mission Today*.

Kuan Hsin-chi et al., ed. *The 1995 Legislative Council Elections in Hong Kong*. Hong Kong: Hong Kong Institute of Asia-Pacific Studies of Chinese University of Hong Kong, 1996.

Kühn, Margarete. "Leibniz und China." In *China und Europa: Chinaverständnis und Chinamode im 17. und 18. Jahrhundert*.

Kraft, Charles. "Ideological Factors in Intercultural Communication." *Missiology* 2 (July 1974).

Kraft, Eva. "Die chinesische Büchersammlung des Großen Kurfürsten und seines Nachfolgers." In *China und Europa*.

———. "Christian Mentzel, Philippe Couplet, Andreas Cleyer und die chinesische Medizin: Notizen aus Handschriften des 17. Jahrhunderts." In *Fernöstliche Kultur: Wolf Haenisch zugeeignet von seinem Marburger Studienkreis*.

———. "Frühe chinesische Studien in Berlin." *Medizinhistorisches Journal* 11 (1976).

Krivtsov, V. *Otets Iakinf: roman*. Leningrad: Khudozhestvennaia, 1988.

Külmisszió (Foreign Mission). Hungarian Lutheran mission periodical.

Kung Kao Po (Chinese Catholic Weekly). Hong Kong.

Kwok, Puilan. *Chinese Women and Christianity, 1860–1927. (American Academy of Religion Academy Series*, no. 75.) Atlanta: Scholar's Press, 1992.

Kwok, Rowena, ed. *Votes Without Power: the Hong Kong Legislative Council Elections*. Hong Kong: Hong Kong University Press, 1992.

Lach, Donald F. *The Preface to Leibniz' Novissima Sinica*. Honolulu: University of Hawaii Press, 1957.

Lai, Tse-han, Ramon Myers, and Wou Wei. *A Tragic Beginning: The Taiwan Uprising of February 28, 1947*. Stanford: Stanford University Press, 1990.

Lam, Wing-hung (Lin Ronghong). *Chinese Theology in Construction*. Pasadena, CA: W. Carey Library, 1983.

———. *Fengchaozhong fenqi de Zhongguo jiaohui*. Hong Kong: Tiandao shulou, 1980.

Lamalle, Edmond. "La tour du propagande du P. Nicolas Trigault en faveur des missions de Chine (1616)." *Archivum Historicum Societatis Iesu* IX (1940).

Lambert, Anthony P.B. "Counting Christians in China: Who's Right?" *News Network International* (April 14, 1989).

———. "Modern Sects and Cults in China." *China Study Journal* 13:3 (1989).

———. *The Resurrection of the Chinese Church*. London: Hodder and Stoughton, 1991.

Lancashire, Douglas. "Anti-Christian Polemics in the Seventeenth-Century China." *Church History* 38 (1969).

Landry-Deron, Isabelle. *Les leçons des sciences occidentales de l'empereur de Chine Kangxi (1662–1722): Texte des Journal des Pères Bouvet et Gerbillon*. Paris: E.H.E.S.S., 1995.

Latourette, Kenneth Scott. *A History of Christian Missions in China*. London: Society for Promoting Christian Knowledge, 1929; reprint Taipei: Ch'eng-wen, 1973.

Launay, Adrien. *Histoire des missions de Chine. Mission du Se-Tchouan*. Paris: P. Téqui, 1920.

———. *Mémorial de la Société des Missions-Etrangères*. Paris: Séminaire des Missions-Etrangères, 1912–1916.

Laurentin, René. *Chine et Christianisme: Après les occasions manquées.* Paris: Desclée de Brouwer, 1977.

Lee, Peter K.H., ed. *Confucian-Christian Encounters in Historical and Contemporary Perspective.* Edwin Mellen Press, 1992.

Lee, Thomas H.C., ed. *China and Europe: Images and Influences in Sixteenth to Eighteenth Centuries.* Hong Kong: Chinese University Press, 1991.

Legge, James. *The I Ching: The Book of Changes.* Oxford, 1899.

Leibniz, Gottfried Wilhelm. *Novissima Sinica: Historiam nostri temporis illustratura in quibus de christianismo publica nunc primum autoritate propagato missa in Europam relation exhibetur . . .* u.p.: n.p., 1697.

———. *Sämtliche Schriften und Briefe. Erste Reihe, Allgemeiner politischer und historischer Briefwechsel.* Berlin: Akademie Verlag, 1993, 1998.

Lettres édifiantes et curieuses des missions étrangères. Toulouse: N. E. Sens et Gaude, 1811.

Leung, Beatrice. "The Catholic Voters." In Rowena Kwok, et al., eds., *Votes Without Power: The Hong Kong Legislative Council Elections, 1991.* Hong Kong: Hong Kong University Press, 1992.

———. "A Fragile Balance: Relations of the Vatican with China and Hong Kong." *Shenxue lunji* 113 (Fall 1997).

———. "The Uneasy Balance: Sino-Vatican-Hong Kong Relations After 1997." In Beatrice Leung and Joseph Cheng, eds., *Hong Kong SAR: In Pursuit of Domestic and International Order.*

———. "Strategic Development of the Hong Kong SAR: Social Policy, EIB Model and Implications." Paper presented at the conference "Hong Kong: A Year After Reversion" organized by the Centre for Asian Pacific Studies, Lingnan College, June 2–3, 1998. In James Chieh Hsiung, ed., *Hong Kong the Super Paradox: Life After Return to China.*

Leung, Beatrice, and Joseph Cheng, eds. *Hong Kong SAR: In Pursuit of Domestic and International Order.* Hong Kong: Chinese University Press, 1997.

Lexikon für Theologie und Kirche. Freiburg: Herder, 1986.

Leyssen, Jacobus. *The Cross Over China's Wall.* Peking: Lazarist Press, 1941.

Li Donghai. *Xianggang Donghua Sanyuan 125 nian shilue.* Beijing: Zhongguo wenshi chubanshe, 1998.

Li Guangliang. "Lüetan Yunnan Miaozu diqu de Jidujiao" (A Brief Discussion of Christianity in the Area of the Miao People of Yunnan). *Yunnan zongjiao yanjiu:* 1 (1990). Kunming: Yunnan renmin chubanshe.

Li Jingpo. "Jidujiao Taiwan Xinyihui fazhan jianshi." *Tongxin heyi.* Taibei, 1990.

Li Jiugong. *Shensi lu.* [JapSin I, 34/37]. Rome: Archivum Romanum Societatis Iesu.

———. "Wenda huichao" (A Compilation of Questions and Answers). Manuscript. Rome: Archivum Romanum Societatis Iesu.

Li Shiyue. "Fan yangjiao douzheng de xingzhi ji qita" (Characteristics of the Anti-foreign Religion Struggle and Others). *Jindai shi yanjiu* (May 1986).
———. *Jindai Zhongguo fanyangjiao yundong* (The Modern Chinese Anti-Foreign Religion Movement). Beijing: Renmin chubanshe, 1958.
———. *Fan Yangjiao yundong* (The Anti-Foreign Religion Movement). Chinese pamphlet, n.p., n.d..
Li Sixuan. *Siji Ai xiansheng xingji.* 1649. [Courant 1017]. Paris: Bibliothèque Nationale.
Li Tiangang. *Wan'guo gongbao wenxuan* (Documents from the *International Gazette*). [Hong Kong]: Sanlian shudian, 1998.
———. *Zhongguo liyi zhi zheng: lishi, wenxian he yiyi* (The Chinese Rites Controversy: History, Documents, and Significance). Shanghai: Shanghai guji chubanshe, 1998.
Li Tseng Hsiu. "The Sacred Mission: An American Missionary Family in the Lahu and Wa Districts of Yunnan, China." M.A. thesis, Baylor University, 1987.
Li Zhen. "Fuyin Zhongguohua de jiqiexing." *Jianzheng* 14.7 (April 1984).
Li Zhi. *Cang shu* (A Book Which Should Be Hidden). China: n.p., 1621.
———. *Fen shu* (A Book Which Should Be Burnt). Beijing: Zhonghua shuju, 1961.
Li Zhigang. *Jidujiao yu jindai Zhongguo wenhua lunwenji* (Collected Articles on Christianity and Recent Chinese Culture). (*Xueshu congshu.*) Taibei: Yuzhouguang chubanshe, 1989–1993.
———. *Jidujiao zaoqi zai Hua chuanjiaoshi.* Taibei: Taiwan shangwu yinshuguan, 1985.
Li Zhizao et al., eds. *Tianxue chuhan* (First Correspondence on the Heavenly Religion). Taibei: Taiwan xuesheng shuju, 1965.
Li Zubai. *Tianxue chuan'gai* in *Tianzhujiao dongchuan wenxian xubian.* Taibei: Xuesheng shuju, 1966.
Liang Jiamian. *Xu Guangqi nianpu* (Chronology of Xu Guangqi). Shanghai: Shanghai guji chubanshe, 1981.
Liang Jinwen. "Tai-Gang-Ao sandi jiaohui chutan (II)." *Shenxue lunji* 114 (Winter 1997).
Liang Kalun (Liang Jialin). *Gaige kaifang yilai de Zhongguo nongcun jiaohui.* Hong Kong: Alliance Bible Seminary, 1999.
Liang Qichao. *Qingdai xueshu gailun* (An Outline of Scholarship of the Qing Era). Shanghai: Fudan daxue chubanshe, 1986.
———. "Xiongjiali aiguozhe Gasushi zhuan (Biography of the Hungarian Patriot Lajos Kossoth)." In Liang Qichao, *Yinbingshi heji.*
———. *Yinbingshi heji* (Collected Works from the Ice-Imbibers Chamber). Beijing: Zhonghua shuju, 1989.
Liao Guangsheng. *Antiforeignism and Modernization in China, 1860–1980.* Hong Kong: Chinese University Press, 1986.
———. *Paiwai yu Zhongguo zhengzhi.* Taibei: Sanmin shuju, 1988.

Lin Benxuan. *Taiwan de zhengjiao chongtu*. Taibei: Daoxiang, 1990.

Lin Jinshui. "Christian Literati and the Rites Controversy." In D. E. Mungello, ed., *The Chinese Rites Controversy: Its History and Meaning*.

———. *Li Madou yu Zhongguo* (Matteo Ricci and China). Beijing: Zhongguo shehui kexue chubanshe, 1996.

Lin Zhiping. *Jidujiao zai Zhongguo zhi chuanbo yu jindai Zhongguo* (Modern China and the Dissemination of Protestant Christianity). Taibei: Taiwan shangwu yinshuguan, 1970.

Lippiello, Tiziana, and Roman Malek, eds. *Scholar from the West: Giulio Aleni S.J. (1582–1649) and the Dialogue Between Christianity and China*. (*Monumenta Serica Monograph series* XLII; *Fondazione civiltà bresciana annali* IX). Brescia: Fondazione civiltà bresciana; St. Augustin: Monumenta Serica Institute, 1997.

Litzinger, Charles A. "Rural Religion and Village Organization in North China: The Catholic Challenge in the Late Nineteenth Century." In Daniel H. Bays, *Christianity in China: From the Eighteenth Century to the Present*.

Liu Dingyin. "Jidujiao xundao gonghui zai Zhaotong diqu de zaoqi chuanbo." *Yunnan zongjiao yanjiu:* 2 (1988). Kunming: Yunnan renmin chubanshe.

Liu Jinchang. "Taiwan Tianzhujiao benweihua gaikuang." *Furen daxue shenxue lunji* 111 (Spring 1997).

Liu Ning. *Juesi lu*. Rome: Archivum Romanum Societatis Iesu.

Liu Wenzhou. "Jiaoyou ruhe yi wenhua chuanjiao." *Hengyi* 17.1 (August 1967).

Liu Xiaofeng. *Dao yu yan: Huaxia wenhua yu Jidu wenhua xiangyu* (The Way and the Word: The Encounter Between Chinese and Christian Cultures). Shanghai: Shenghuo, dushu, xinzhi Shanghai sanlian shudian, 1995.

———. "Xiandai yujingzhong de Hanyu Jidu shenxue." *Logos and Pneuma, Chinese Journal of Theology* 2 (Spring 1995).

Lo Guang. "The Present Situation of Evangelization in Taiwan." In Delos A. Humphrey, ed., *The Catholic Church in Taiwan*.

Lo Xianglin. "Zhongguo zupu suoji Jidujiao zhi chuanbo yu jindai Zhongguo zhi guangxi." *Journal of Oriental Studies* 7 (1969).

Lodwick, Kathleen, comp. *The Chinese Recorder Index: A Guide to Christian Missions in Asia, 1867–1941*. Wilmington, DE.: Scholarly Resources Inc., 1986.

Lowenthal, Rudolph. *The Religious Periodical Press in China*. Peking: Synodal Commission in China, 1940.

Lozada, Eriberto. "God Aboveground: Catholicism and Transnationalism in a Chinese Village." Ph.D. dissertation, Harvard University, 1998.

Lü Shiquang. *Zhongguo guanshen fanjiao de yuanyin, 1860–1874* (The Origin and Cause of the Anti-Christian Movement by Chinese Officials and Gentry, 1860–1874). (Series: *Zhongyang yanjiuyuan jindaishi yanjiusuo zhuankan*: 16.) Taibei: Zhongyang yanjiuyuan jindaishi yanjiusuo, 1966.

Lu Yao. "Lun jindai Zhongguo jiawu zhanzhengqian de jiao'an yu fanyangjiao douzheng" (About the Struggle Against Foreign Religions and Religious

Cases Before the Sino-Japanese War of 1895). *Shandong daxue xuebao* (January 1990).

Lu Yunfeng. "Report on an Investigation into the Illegal Organisation, the 'Disciples Sect.'" *China Study Journal* 13:3 (1989).

Lu Zhongwei. "Xiangshen yu fanyangjiao douzheng (The Rural Gentry and the Anti-foreign Religion Struggle). *Jindai shi yanjiu* (January 1986).

Luk, Bernard Hung-kay. "Aleni Introduces the Western Academic Tradition into Seventeenth Century China: A Study of the *Xixue fan.*" In Tiziana Lippiello and Roman Malek, eds., *Scholar From The West: Giulio Aleni S.J. (1582–1649) and the Dialogue Between Christianity and China.*

———. "And Thus the Twain Did Meet? The Two Worlds of Giulio Aleni." Ph. D. dissertation. Bloomington: Indiana University, 1977.

———. "A Study of Giulio Aleni's *Chih-fang wai-chi.*" *Bulletin of the School of Oriental and African Studies*, 40 (1977).

Lundbæk, Knud. "Chief Grand Secretary Chang Chü-cheng and the Early China Jesuits." *China Mission Studies (1550–1800) Bulletin* 3 (1981).

———. "Dr. Mentzel's kinesiske Börnbog." *Danmark-Kina* (December 1982).

———. "The First Translation from a Confucian Classic in Europe." *China Mission Studies (1550–1800) Bulletin* 1 (1979).

———. "The Image of Neo-Confucianism in *Confucius Sinarum Philosophus.*" In Julia Ching, and W. G. Oxtoby, eds., *Discovering China: European Interpretations in the Enlightenment.*

———. "Imaginary Ancient Chinese Characters." *China Mission Studies Bulletin* 5 (1983).

———. *T. S. Bayer (1694–1738): Pioneer Sinologist.* London, Malmö: Curzon Press, 1986.

Luo Guang. *Jiaoting yu Zhongguo shijie shi* (A History of Vatican Diplomatic Relations with China). Taizhong: Guangqi chubanshe, 1961.

———. *Li Madou zhuan* (The Biography of Matteo Ricci). Taizhong: Guangqi chubanshe, 1960.

———. *Tianzhujiao zai Hua chuanjiao shi ji* (Collected Works on the History of Catholic Missions to China). Tainan, Taizhong: Zhengxiang chubanshe, Guangqi chubanshe, 1967.

———. *Xu Guangqi zhuan* (The Biography of Xu Guangqi). Hong Kong: Xianggang gongjiao zhenli xuehui chuban, 1953.

Luo Shugang. *Zongjiao gongzuo fangmian de yixie redian wenti* (Some Popular Issues in Religious Work). Internally circulated document, 1996, no. 5.

Luo Weihong. "The Facts About the Activities of the Heterodox Sect 'The Established King.'" *China Study Journal* 13:3 (1989).

Luo Zhufeng, ed. *Religion Under Socialism in China.* Donald E. MacInnis and Zheng Xi'an, trans. Armonk, NY: M.E. Sharpe, 1991.

Lutz, Jessie G. *China and the Christian Colleges, 1850–1950.* Ithaca, NY: Cornell University Press, 1971.

———. *Chinese Politics and Christian Missions: The Anti-Christian Movements of 1920–28.* (Series: *The Church and the World*; 3; *The West and the Wider World*; 2.) Notre Dame, IN: Cross Cultural Publications, Cross Roads Books, 1988.

———. "The Chinese Student Movement of 1945–1949." *Journal of Asian Studies* 31 (1971).

Lutz, Jessie G., and Rolland Ray Lutz. *Hakka Chinese Confront Protestant Christianity, 1850–1900: With the Autobiographies of Eight Hakka Christians, and Commentary.* (Series: *Studies on Modern China*). Armonk, NY: M.E. Sharpe, 1998.

———. "The Invisible Missionaries: The Basel Mission's Chinese Evangelists, 1847–1866." *Mission Studies* 12.2 (October 1995).

———. "Karl Gützlaff's Approach to Indigenization: The Chinese Union." In Daniel H. Bays, ed., *Christianity in China: From the Eighteenth Century to the Present.*

Luzbetak, Louis J. *The Church and Cultures: An Applied Anthropology for the Religious Worker.* Techny, IL: Divine Word Publishing, 1963.

Ly, André. *Journal d'André Ly, prêtre chinois, missionaire et notaire apostolique 1746–1763. Texte Latin.* Introduction by Adrien Launay. Paris: Alphonse Picard et Fils, 1906.

Lyall, Leslie T. *John Sung: Flame for God in the Far East.* London: Overseas Missionary Fellowship, 1954.

Ma Xisha and Han Bingfang. *Zhongguo minjian zongjiao shi* (A History of Chinese Folk Religions). Shanghai: Shanghai renmin chubanshe, 1992.

MacInnis, Donald E. *Religion in China Today: Policy and Practice.* Maryknoll, NY: Orbis Books, 1989.

Madsen, Richard. *China's Catholics: Tragedy and Hope in an Emerging Civil Society.* (*Comparative Studies in Religion and Society*; 12.) Berkeley: University of California Press, 1998.

———. "Hierarchichal Modernization: Tianjin's Gong Shang College as a Model for Catholic Community in North China." Unpublished paper, 1996.

———. "The Public Sphere, Civil Society, and Moral Community: A Research Agenda for Contemporary China Studies." *Modern China* 19:2 (1993).

Magalhães, Gabriel de. *Doze exceléncias da China.* London: Printed for Thomas Newborough, 1688.

———. *Nouvelle relation de la Chine, contenant la description des particularitez les plus considerables de ce grand empire. Composée en l'année 1668 par le R. P. Gabriel de Magaillans, de la Compagnie de Jésus, missionaire apostolique.* Paris: C. Barbin, 1688.

Magyar Református Egyház Zsinati Levéltára (Archives of the Council of the Hungarian Reformed Church). Document 12f/15d.

Magyar Tudomány (Hungarian Science). Budapest: Akadémiai Kiadó.

Mairan, Dortous de. "Extrait des observations sur la comète qui a paru aux mois de mars & d'avril de cette année 1742, faites à Pekin par le P. Pereyra jésuite." *Mémoires de l'Académie royale des sciences*. Paris: Mémoires de l'Académie royale des sciences de Paris, 1742.

——. *Lettres des M. de Mairan, au R. P. Parrenin, missionaire de la Compagnie de Jesus, à Pekin: contenant diverses questions sur la Chine*. Paris: Desaint & Saillant, 1759.

——. *Remarques sur une comète observée à Pekin*. u.p.: n.p., 1701(?).

Malatesta, Edward, and Yves Raguin. "Chinese Catholic Clergy and Catechists in Eighteenth-Century Szechuan." In *Images de la Chine: le Contexte Occidental de la Sinologie Naissante: Actes de VIe colloque international de sinologie*.

Malek, Roman, ed. *Western Learning and Christianity in China: The Contribution and Impact of Johann Adam Schall von Bell, S.J. (1592–1666)*. (*Monumenta Serica Monograph series XXXV*.) St. Augustin: China-Zentrum: Monumenta Serica Institute; Nettetal: Steyler, 1998.

Mao Ruizheng. *Huang Ming xiangxu lu* (Record of the Imperial Ming Court Interpreter), 1629 ed. Reprinted in *Zhonghua wenshi congshu*, 3rd series, no. 17. Taibei: Taiwan huawen shuju, 1968.

Martiliat, Joachim Enjobert de. *Journal*, vol. 434. Paris: Archives des Missions Étrangères.

Martin, David. *Forbidden Revolutions: Pentecostalism in Latin America and Catholicism in Eastern Europe*. London: SPCK, 1996.

——. *Tongues of Fire: The Explosion of Protestantism in Latin America*. London: Basil Blackwell, 1990.

Martin, Robert Montgomery. *China: Political, Commercial, and Social; in an Official Report to Her Majesty's Government*. London: J. Madden, 1847.

Martini, Martino. *Sinicæ historiæ decas prima: res à gentis origine ad Christum natum in extrema Asia, sive magno Sinarum imperio gestas complexa*. Monachii: L. Straubii, 1658.

Martinson, Paul Varo. "The Protestant Church in Post-Mao China: Two Paradigms." *Ching Feng* 31:1 (1988).

Martzloff, Jean-Claude. "A Glimpse of the Post-Verbiest Period: J.-F. Foucquet's *Lifa Wenda* (Dialogue on Calendrical Techniques) and the Modernization of Chinese Astronomy, or, Urania's Feet Unbound." In John W. Witek, *Ferdinand Verbiest (1623–1688): Jesuit Missionary, Scientist, Engineer and Diplomat*.

Maryknoll Mission Archives.

Masini, Federico. "Aleni's Contribution to the Chinese Language." In Tiziana Lippiello and Roman Malek, eds., *Scholar from the West: Giulio Aleni S.J. (1582–1649) and the Dialogue Between Christianity and China*.

——. "L'Italia descritta nel *Qingchao wenxian tongkao*." *Revista degli Studi Orientali* 63 (1989).

Masini, Federico, ed. *Western Humanistic Culture Presented to China by Jesuit Missionaries (XVII–XVIII Centuries)*. Rome: Institutum Historicim Societatis Iesu, 1996.

Matzinger, Polly. "Tolerance, Danger, and the Extended Family." *Annual Review of Immunology* (1994:12).

McCarthy, John, David Britt, and Mark Wolfson. "The Institutional Channelling of Social Movements by the State in the United States." *Research in Social Movement, Conflict and Change* 13:45 (1991).

McManners, John, ed. *The Oxford Illustrated History of Christianity.* Oxford; New York: Oxford University Press, 1990.

McWhirter, Norris and Ross McWhirter, ed. *Guinness Book of World Records.* New York: Sterling Publishing Company, 1976.

Mémoires de l'Académie Royale des Sciences. Paris: L'Académie.

Mémoires de l'Académie Royale des Sciences de l'Institut de France, Année 1817. Paris: Compagnie des libraries.

Mémoires de mathématics et de physique. Paris: Imprimerie royale, 1692–1693.

Menegon, Eugenio. "Yang Guangxian's Opposition to Johann Adam Schall: Christianity and Western Science in his Work *Budeyi.*" In Roman Malek, ed., *Western Learning and Christianity in China: The Contribution and Impact of Johann Adam Schall von Bell, S.J. (1592–1666).*

Meng Ssu-ming. "The E-lo-ssu kuan (Russian hostel) in Peking." *Harvard Journal of Asiatic Studies* 23 (1960–1961).

Mentzel, Christian. *Kurtze chinesische Chronologia, oder Zeit-Register, aller chinesischen Kàyser, von ihrem also vermeinten Anfang der Welt bis hieher zu unsern Zeiten, des nach Christi unsers Seligmachers Gebuhrt 1696sten Jahres, in einer richtigen Ordnung von Jahren zu Jahren, mit ihren rechten Characteren, Nahmen und Beschreibungen, auch mit zween chinesischen erklèahrten Tafeln der vornehmsten Geschichten von ihrem Anbeginn der Welt, bezogen aus der chineser Kinder-Lehre SIAO UL HIO oder LUN genande. Nebst einem kurtzen Anhang einer moscowitischen Reise-Beschreibung zu Lande nach China, in den 1693/94 und 95sten Jahren, von dem moscowitischen Abgesandten. Isbrand gehalten.* Berlin: J. M. Rèudiger, 1696.

———. *Sylloge minutiarum lexici latino-sinico-characteristici: observatione sedulâ ex auctoribus & lexicis chinensium characteristicis eruta, inâque specimen primi laboris ulteriùs exantlandi erudito & curioso orbi exposita.* Nuremburg: n.p., 1685.

Merwin, Wallace C. *Adventure in Unity: The Church of Christ in China.* Grand Rapids, MI: Eerdmans, 1974.

Miklósi, László. *Magyar hősök öt világrészen* (Hungarian Heroes on Five Continents). Budapest, 1936.

Minamiki, George. *The Chinese Rites Controversy: From Its Beginnings to Modern Times.* Chicago: Loyola University Press, 1985.

Mish, John L. "Creating an Image of Europe for China: Aleni's *Hsi-fang ta-wen.*" *Monumenta Serica* 23 (1964). Los Angeles: Monumenta Serica Institute, University of California at Los Angeles, 1964.

Misszioi Lapok (Mission Pages). Hungarian Lutheran mission periodical successor to *Kulmisszio.*

"Modern Sects and Cults in China." *China Church Quarterly* 38 (Spring 1999)

Montgomery, Robert. "Some Research Directions for the Sociology of Missions." Presented at the annual meeting of the Religious Research Association, Pittsburgh, November 8–10, 1991.

Müller, Andreas. *Hebdomas observationum de rebus Sinicis...quibus adjunguntur tria capita examinis Monumenti Sinici.* Berlin: Ex Officina Georgi Schultzi, 1674.

Mungello, D. E. "Confucianism and Enlightenment." In Thomas H. Lee, ed., *China and Europe: Images and Influences in Sixteenth to Eighteenth Centuries.*

———. *Curious Land: Jesuit Accommodation and the Origins of Sinology.* Wiesbaden: F. Steiner Verlag, 1985.

———. "The Jesuits Use of Chang Chü-cheng's Commentary in Their Translation of the Confucian Four Books." *China Mission Studies (1550–1800) Bulletin* 3 (1981).

———. *Leibniz and Confucianism: The Search for Accord.* Honolulu: University of Hawaii Press, 1977.

———. "The Seventeenth-Century Jesuit Translation Project of the Confucian Four Books." In Charles E. Ronan, and Bonnie B. C. Oh, eds., *East Meets West: The Jesuits in China, 1582–1773.*

Mungello, D. E., ed. *China Mission Studies (1500–1800) Bulletin.* (Numbers 1–X). 1979–1988. After 1989 (Number 11–) see under D.E. Mungello, ed., *Sino-Western Cultural Relations Journal.*

———. *The Chinese Rites Controversy: Its History and Meaning.* (*Monumenta Serica Monograph series*; 33.) Netettal: Steyler Verlag, 1994.

———. *Sino-Western Cultural Relations Journal.* Waco, TX: Department of History, Baylor University, 1989–.

Munro, Robin, ed. "Syncretic Sects and Secret Societies: Revival in the 1980s." *Chinese Sociology and Anthropology* 21:4 (1989).

Murr, Christoph Gottlieb von. *Litterae patentes Imperatoris Sinarvm Kang-Hi sinice et latine.* Nuremburg: Monathi et Kvssleri, 1802.

Nagata, Judith. "Chinese Custom and Christian Culture: Implications for Chinese Identity in Malaysia." In Leo Suryadinata, ed., *Southeast Asian Chinese: The Socio-Cultural Dimension.* Singapore: Singapore Society of Asian Studies, 1995.

Nakayama Shigeru, ed. *Chinese Science: Explorations of an Ancient Tradition.* (*MIT East Asian Science series* II.) Cambridge, MA: MIT Press, 1973.

Naquin, Susan. *Millenarian Rebellion in China: The Eight Trigrams Uprising of 1813.* New Haven, CT: Yale University Press, 1976.

———. "The Transmission of White Lotus Sectarianism in Late Imperial China." In David Johnson et al., eds., *Popular Culture in Late Imperial China.*

N.C.W.C. News Service (Fides). Washington DC: National Catholic Welfare Conference, 1932–1966.

Neckebrouck, Valeer. *Paradoxes de l'inculturation: Les nouveaux habits des Yanomani*. Leuven: Leuven University Press, 1995.

Needham, Joseph. "The Roles of Europe and China in the Evolution of Oecumenical Science." In Joseph Needham, *Clerks and Craftsmen in China and the West*. Cambridge: Cambridge University Press, 1970.

———. *Science and Civilization in China*. Cambridge: Cambridge University Press, 1954–.

Needham, Joseph, and Li Guohao, eds. *Explorations in the History of Science and Technology in China*. Shanghai: Shanghai Chinese Classics Publishing House, 1982.

Némethy, Sándor. *Pagodák árnyékában* (In the Shadows of Pagodas). Budapest: Magyar Református Külmissziói Szövetség Kiadása, 1944.

Neue Zeitschrift für Missionswissenschaft. Nouvelle revue de science missionaire. Immensee: Verein zur Förderung der Missionswissenschaft, 1945–.

Noël, François. *Sinensis imperii libri classici sex: nimirum Adultorum schola, Immutabile medium, Liber sententiarum, Memcius, Filialis observantia, Parvulorum schola , e sinico idiomate in latinum traducti a Francisco Noël.* Prague: Typis Universitatis Carolo-Ferdinandeae, in Collegio Soc. Jesu ad S. Clementem, per Joachimum Joannem Kamenicky p. t. factorem, 1711.

Noël, François, ed. *Les livres classiques de l'empire de la China, recueillis par le pére Noel, précédés d'observations sur l'origine, la nature & les effets de la philosophie morale & politique dans cet empire.* Paris: Chez De Bure, Barrois ainé & Barrois jeune, 1754–1786.

Nouvelles lettres édifiantes des missions de la Chine et des Indies orientales. Paris: A. le Clere, 1818–1823.

"O nachale torgovych i gosudarstvennykh snoshenii Rossii s Kitaem i o dukhovnoi missii v Pekine." *Sibirskii Vestnik* 18–19 (1822).

Olichon, Armand. *Aux origines du clergé chinois: Le Prêtre André Ly: missionaire au Se-tchoan (1692–1775)*. Paris: Bloud & Gay, 1933.

O'Malley, John W. *The First Jesuits*. Cambridge: Harvard University Press, 1993.

100 Roman Documents Concerning the Chinese Rites Controversy (1645–1941). Translations by Donald F. St. Sure and Edward J. Malatesta; edited with introductions and summaries by Ray R. Noll (*Studies in Chinese-Western Cultural History*; 1). San Francisco: Ricci Institute for Chinese-Western Cultural History, 1992.

Origen. *Contra Celsum*. Translated with an introduction and notes by Henry Chadwick. Cambridge, NY: Cambridge University Press, 1980.

Overmyer, Daniel L. "Alternatives: Popular Religious Sects in Chinese Society." *Modern China* 7:2 (1981).

——. *Folk Buddhist Religion: Dissenting Sects in Late Traditional China.* Cambridge: Harvard University Press, 1976.

Pantoja, Diego de, and Sabatino de Ursis. *Jujie* (Memorial of Defense). 1616. [Courant 7321] Paris: Bibliothèque Nationale.

Parish, William L., and Martin King Whyte. *Village and Family in Contemporary China.* Chicago: University of Chicago Press, 1978.

Pelliot, Paul. *L'Inscription Nestorienne de Si-ngan-fou.* Edited with supplements by Antonino Forte. Kyoto: Scuola de studi sull'Asia orientale; Paris: Collège de France, Institut des Hautes Etudes Chinoises, 1996.

Pepper, Suzanne. *Civil War in China: The Political Struggle, 1945–1949.* Berkeley: University of California Press, 1978.

Percy, Martin. "The City on a Beach: Future Prospects for Charismatic Movements at the End of the Twentieth Century." In *Charismatic Christianity: Sociological Perspectives.*

Persson, C. "Christianity in the Tarim Basin," *Friends of Moslems* (April 1940).

Pfister, Aloys. *Notices biographiques et bibliographiques sur le Jésuites de l'ancienne mission de Chine, 1552–1773.* Shanghai: Imprimerie de la mission catholique, 1932–1934.

Pfister, Lauren. "A Transmitter but Not a Creator: Ho Tsun-sheen (1817–1871), the First Modern Chinese Protestant Theologian." In Irene Eber, Sze-kar Wan, Knut Walf, and Roman Malek, eds., *Bible in Modern China: the Literary and Intellectual Impact.*

——. "From the Golden Light Within: Reconsideration of James Legge's Account of Ch'ëa Kam Kwong, the Chinese 'Proto-Martyr'." Paper presented at the International Conference on James Legge, Aberdeen, April 1997.

Pingxintu (pseud.) "Dui yuanzhumin zhujiao zhusheng dadian de ruogan lianxiang."*Jiaoyou shenghuo zhoukan* 2284 (October 4, 1998).

Piolet, J.-B. *La France en dehors: Les missions catholiques françaises au XIXe siècle.* Paris: Librarie Armand Colin, 1900.

Pó Léung Kuk (Hong Kong). *Po Leung Kuk Hong Kong 110th Anniversary Report.* Hong Kong: Po Leung Kuk, 1988.

Poggi, Vincenzo. "Cristologia e Chiesa Sirorientale." *Coscienza: Fatti, Idee, Dialogo* 12 (1989).

Polnoe sobranie postanovlenii i rasporiazhenii po vedomstvu pravoslavnogo ispovedaniia Rossiiskoi imperii. Series 1–3. St. Petersberg, 1879–1910.

Polnoe sobranie zakonov Rossiiskoi imperii s 1649 goda. First series. 1649, 1825. St. Petersburg: Gosudarstvennoi Tipografii, 1830–1884.

Popper, Karl Raimund. *Of Clouds and Clocks: An Approach to the Problem of Rationality and the Freedom of Man.* St. Louis: Washington University, 1966.

Poxie ji. See Xu Changzhi, *Shengchao poxie ji.*

Pozdniaev, Dionisii. *Pravolslavie v Kitae (1900–1997 gg.).* Moscow: Izdatelstvo Sviato-Vladimirskogo Bratstva, 1998.

Pray, Georg. *Annales veteres Hunnorum, Avarum et Hungarorum.* Vienna: Typis Georgii Ludovici Schulzii, 1761.

Prigogine, Ilya. *Les lois du chaos.* Paris: Flammarion, 1994.

Procès verbaux. Paris: Académie des Sciences.

Pyenson, Lewis. *Civilizing Mission: Exact Sciences and French Overseas Expansion, 1830–1940.* Baltimore, MD: Johns Hopkins University Press, 1993.

Qi Qizhang. "Jindai jiao'an he Yihetuan yundong de xingqi" (Modern Religious Cases and the Rise of the Boxer Movement). *Guizhou shehui kexue* (January 1991).

Qin Heping. "Dianxi bufen shaoshu minzu diqu Jidujiao lishi wenti chutan" (An Initial Investigation into Questions About the History of the Christian Church in the Minority Areas of Western Yunnan). *Shijie zongjiao yanjiu* 3 (1987).

Qin Shenglan. "Three-Self Education for Theological Students." *China Study Project Journal* 5:3 (1990).

Qingchao wenxian tongkao. [Qing Gaozong chizhuan]. Reprint: Shanghai: Shangwu yinshuguan, 1936.

Qing mo jiao'an (Late Qing Religious Cases). Beijing: Zhonghua shuju, 1998–.

Qiu Sheng. *Shuwen pian.* [JapSin I,40/4]. Rome: Archivum Romanum Societatis Iesu.

Qu Haiyuan. "Taiwan diqu Jidujiao fazhan zhi chubu tantao." In *Proceedings of the First Conference of the History and Chinese Social Transformation.* Taibei: Institute of Ethnography, 1981.

——. "Taiwan diqu Tianzhujiao fazhan qushi zhi yanjiu." *Journal of the Institute of Ethnography* 51 (Spring 1982).

——. "Woguo zongjiao bianqian de shehuixue fenxi" (A Sociological Analysis of the Religious Transformation in Our Country). In Zhu Cenglou, ed., *Woguo shehui de bianqian yu fazhan.*

——. "Zongjiao pian." In Qu Haiyuan, ed., *Chongxiu Taiwan sheng tongzhi.* Nantou: Taiwan sheng wenxianhui, 1992.

Qu Haiyuan, ed. *Chongxiu Taiwan sheng tongzhi.* Nantou: Taiwan sheng wenxianhui, 1992.

Rabe, Valentin H. "Evangelical Logistics: Mission Support and Resources to 1920." In John K. Fairbank, ed., *The Missionary Enterprise in China and America.*

Raber, Dorothy A. *Protestantism in Changing Taiwan: A Call to Creative Response.* Pasadena, CA: William Carey Library, 1978.

Rachewiltz, Igor de. *Papal Envoys to the Great Khans.* Stanford: Stanford University Press, 1971.

Rafael, Vicente L. *Contracting Colonialism: Translation and Christian Conversion in Tagalog Society Under Early Spanish Rule.* Durham; London: Duke University Press, 1993.

Regent Chinese Journal (Weizhen xuekan). Vancouver: Chinese Studies Program at Regent College.

Reil, Sebald. *Kilian Stumpf, 1655–1720: Ein Würzburger Jesuit am Kaiserhof zu Peking*. Münster: Aschendorff, 1978.

Reinhard, Wolfgang. "Akkulturationsprozesse und Missionsstrategien in Asien." In *Geschichte der europäischen Expansion*. Stuttgart: Kohlhamer, 1983.

Ren Yanli. "Repubblica Popolare Cinese e Santa Sede." In Agostino Giovagnoli, ed., *Roma e Pechino: la svolta extraeuropea di Benedetto XV*.

Ren Zhongxiang. *Shanghai Jidutu juhui chujianshi*. Shanghai: n.p., 1996.

Revue d'histoire des missions. Paris: Amis de Missions, 1924–1940.

Ricci, Matteo. *China in the Sixteenth Century: The Journals of Matthew Ricci, 1583–1610*. Translated by Louis J. Gallagher. New York: Random House, 1953.

———. *Ershiwu yan* (Twenty-five Sayings). 1604. Reprinted in *Tianxue chuhan*. Taibei: Taiwan xuesheng shuju, 1965.

———. *Jiren shipian* (Ten Chapters on an Extraordinary Man). 1608. Reprinted in *Tianxue chuhan*. Taibei: Taiwan xuesheng shuju, 1965.

———. *Li Madou Zhongguo zhaji* (The China Journal of Matteo Ricci). Translated by He Gaoji, Wang Zunzhong, and Li Shen. (Series: *Zhongwai guanxishi mingzhu yicong*.) Beijing: Zhonghua shuju, 1983.

———. *Il mappamondo cinese del P. Matteo Ricci S.J.: conservato presso la Bibliotca Vaticana*. Pasquale M. D'Elia, ed. Vatican City: Biblioteca apostolica Vaticana, 1938.

———. *The True Meaning of the Lord of Heaven (T'ien-chu Shih-i)*. Translated with an introduction and notes, by Douglas Lancashire and Peter Hu Kuo-chen; edited by Edward J. Malatesta. (*Variétés sinologiques*; *nouvelle sér.* 72.) Taipei: Institut Ricci, 1985.

Richardson, William J. "Christianity in Taiwan Under Japanese Rule, 1895–1945." Ph.D. dissertation, St. John's University, 1972.

Robert, Dana Lee. *American Women in Mission: Social History of Their Thought and Practice*. (Series: The Modern Mission Era, 1792–1992.) Macon, GA: Mercer University Press, 1996.

Roh, Lupus Seong-key. "Research into the First Christian Evangelization of China: The Theological Ideas Expressed in the Stele of the Luminous Religion." Ph.D. dissertation. Rome: Pontificia Universitas Lateranensis, 1999.

Ronan, Charles E., and Bonnie B. C. Oh, eds. *East Meets West: The Jesuits in China, 1582–1773*. Chicago: Loyola University Press, 1988.

Rosenthal, A.M. "On My Mind: Persecuting Christians." *New York Times*, February 11, 1997.

Rouleau, Francis A. "Chinese Rites Controversy." In *The New Catholic Encyclopedia*. New York: McGraw-Hill, 1967.

Ruan Yuan. *Chouren zhuan*. Shanghai: Shangwu yinshuguan, 1935.

Rubinstein, Murray A. "American Evangelicalism in the Chinese Environment: Southern Baptist Convention Missionaries in Taiwan, 1949–1981." *American Baptist Quarterly* II.3 (September 1983).

———. *The Protestant Community on Modern Taiwan: Mission, Seminary, Church.* Armonk, NY: M.E. Sharpe, 1991.

———. *Taiwan: A New History.* Armonk, NY: M.E. Sharpe, 1999.

Ruland, Vernon. "The Inflated Catholic Difference." *America* (June 4, 1994).

Rule, Paul. "Neo-Confucianism: Theism, Atheism or Neither?" In Victor C. Hayes, ed., *Identity Issues in World Religions: Selected Proceedings of the Fifteenth Congress of the International Association for the History of Religions.*

Santangelo, Paolo. *Il peccato in Cina: bene e male nel nepconfucianesimo dalla metà del XIV alla metà del XIX secolo.* Bari: G. Laterza, 1991.

Sawatsky, Sheldon. "State-Church Conflict in Taiwan: Its Historical Roots and Contemporary Manifestations." *Missiology: An International Review*, IX.4 (October 1981).

Sayers, Dorothy L. *Creed or Chaos?* Manchester: Sophia Institute Press, 1995.

Schaible, David. "A-Kwui, einer der Erstlinge von Nyenhangli, in seinem Leben und Sterben." Nyenhangli (2 May 1893). Evangelische Missionsgesellschaft in Basel. China: Berichte und Korrespondenz, 1846–1900 (BMG A–1.27:95).

Schipper, Kristofer. *The Taoist Body.* Berkeley: University of California Press, 1993.

Schlatter, Wilhelm. *Geschichte der Basler Mission 1815–1915: Mit besonderer Berücksichtigung der ungedruckten Quellen.* Bd. 2 *Die Geschichte der Basler Mission in Indien und China.* Basel: Verlag der Basler Missionsbuchhandlung, 1916.

Schneider, Laurence A. *Ku Chieh-kang and China's New History: Nationalism and the Quest for Alternative Traditions.* Berkeley: University of California Press, 1971.

Scholtz, Ödön. "Az evangélikus missziói egyesületek, s ezek között is elsősorban az egyetemes jellegű Lipcsei Evangélikus-Lutheránus Misszíoegyesület áldásos munkakörébe kell szervesen belekapcsolódnia." In Scholtz, Ödön. *Az evangélikus missziós ügy fejlodése Magyarországon kezdettol fogva az Országos Misszióegyesület megalapításáig.* Budapest, 1940.

———. *Az evangélikus missziós ügy fejlodése Magyarországon kezdettol fogva az Országos Misszióegyesület megalapításáig* (The Development of the Lutheran Mission Cause in Hungary from the Beginning to the Establishment of the National Mission Association). Budapest, 1940.

Schultze, Otto. "Geschichte der Basler Missionsstation Tschongtshun." Tschongtshun (27 October 1889). Evangelische Missionsgesellschaft in Basel. China: Berichte und Korrespondenz, 1846–1900 (BMG A–1.23:120).

Schwartz, Benjamin I. "Culture, Modernity, and Nationalism—Further Reflections." *Daedalus* 122:3 (1993).

Scott, Ian. *Political Change and Crisis of Legitimacy in Hong Kong.* Hong Kong: Oxford University Press, 1989.

"Seeking College Diploma: Private University Is Seen as an Expensive Place for Second Best." *Shanghai Daily*, November 22, 1999.

Segal, Gerald. "Does China Matter?" *Foreign Affairs* (September–October 1999).

Selznick, Philip. *The Organizational Weapon: A Study of Bolshevik Strategy and Tactics.* New York: McGraw-Hill, 1952.

Semedo, Álvaro. *Histoire universelle du grand royaume de la Chine.* Paris: S. et G. Cramoisy, 1645.

———. *Histoire universelle de la Chine.* Lyon: Hierosme Prost, 1667.

———. *Relatione della grande monarchia della Cina.* Rome: Sumptibus H. Scheus, 1643.

Serruys, Henry. "Andrew Li, Chinese Priest, 1692 (1693?)–1774." *Neue Zeitschrift für Missionswissenschaft* 32.2 (1976).

Shehui zhuanxing yu jiaohui daxue (Social Transformation and Christian Colleges). Wuhan: Hubei jiaoyu chubanshe, 1998.

Shen Que. *Nangong shudu* (Memorials from the Southern Palace). 1616. In Xu Changzhi, *Poxie ji.* Japanese edition, 1639.

Shen Yifan. "Zhongguo Jidujiao de zili yundong" (The Self-Supporting Movement of Chinese Christianity). *Shanghai shehui kexue* (March 1982).

Shengchao poxie ji. See Xu Changzhi. *Shengchao poxie ji.*

Shengjiao ru Chuan ji. Chongqing: Shengjia shuju, 1918. Reprinted in the series: *Sichuan lishi ziliao congshu.* Chengdu: Sichuan renmin chubanshe, 1981.

Shenxue lunji (Collectanea Theologica Universitatis Fujen). Xinzhuang shi: Fushe shenxueyuan. See also *Furen daxue shenxue lunji.*

Shijie zongjiao wenhua (Religious Cultures in the World). Beijing: Zhongguo shehui kexue chubanshe, 1995–.

Shijie zongjiao yanjiu (Studies of World Religions). Beijing: Zhongguo shehui kexue chubanshe, 1979–.

Shue, Vivienne. *The Reach of the State: Sketches of the Chinese Body Politic.* Stanford: Stanford University Press, 1988.

Sichuan jiao'an yu Yihe quan dang'an (Sichuan Religious Cases and Boxer Documents). Chengdu: Sichuan renmin chubanshe, 1985.

Sino-Western Cultural Relations Journal. See under D. E. Mungello, ed.

Sivin, Nathan, ed. *Chinese Science.* Cambridge, MA: International Society for the History of East Asian Science, Technology, and Medicine; Los Angeles: Center for Chinese Studies, Center for Pacific Rim Studies, University of California Los Angeles, 1993–1994.

————. "Why the Scientific Revolution Did Not Take Place in China—Or Did It?" In Joseph Needham, and Li Guohao, eds., *Explorations in the History of Science and Technology in China*.

Smith, Carl. *Chinese Christians: Elites, Middlemen and the Church in Hong Kong*. Hong Kong: Oxford University Press, 1985.

So, Alvin, and Ludmilla Kwitko. "The New Middle Class and the Democratic Movement in Hong Kong." *Journal of Contemporary Asia* 20.3 (1990).

"Some Thoughts About the State of Contextualization in Chinese Christian Art." *Amity News Service* 7.11/12 (1998).

Song Guangyu. "Sishinian lai Taiwan de zongjiao fazhan qingkuang." In Song Guangyu, *Zongjiao yu shehui* (Religion and Society).

————. *Zongjiao yu shehui* (Religion and Society). Taibei: Dongda, 1995.

Song Yingxing. *Tiangong kaiwu*. u.p.: Langhua shulin, Ming Chongzhen dingchou (1637).

Spence, Jonathan D. *God's Chinese Son: The Taiping Heavenly Kingdom of Hong Xiuquan*. New York: W. W. Norton, 1996.

Spitzel, Gottlieb. *De re literaria sinensium commentarius: in quo scripturae pariter ac philosophiae sinicae specimina exhibentur, et cum aliarum gentium, praesertim Aegyptiorum, Graecorum, et Indorum reliquorum literis atque placitis conferuntur*. Leiden: Ex Officina Petri Hackii, [M] [D] CLX [1660].

Standaert, Nicolas. "The Christian Fragment in the Chinese Fractal: Towards Chinese Culture in the 21st Century." *Ching Feng* 35:2 (1992).

————. "The Classification of Science and the Jesuit Mission in Late Ming China." In Jan M. de Meyer, and Peter M. Engelfriet, eds., *Linked Faiths: Essays on Chinese Religions and Traditional Culture in Honour of Kristofer Schipper*.

————. "Confucian-Christian Dual Citizenship in the Chinese Context." *China Notes*, XXIX 2 and 3 (1991).

————. *Yang Tingyun, Confucian and Christian in Late Ming China*. Leiden: Brill, 1988.

Standaert, Nicolas, et al., eds. *Handbook of Christianity in China*. (series: *Handbook of Oriental Studies*.) Leiden: E. J. Brill, 2000.

————. *Xujiahui cangshulou Ming Qing Tianzhujiao wenxian* (Chinese Christian Texts from the Zikawei Library). Taibei: Furen daxue shenxueyuan, 1996.

Stewart, Charles, and Rosalind Shaw, eds. *Syncretism/Anti-Syncretism: the Politics of Religious Synthesis*. London; New York: Routledge, 1994.

Streit, Robert and Josef Dindinger, eds. *Bibliotheca Missionum*. Freiburg: Herder, 1916.

Stroup, Alice. *A Company of Scientists: Botany, Patronage, and Community at the Seventeenth-Century Parisian Royal Academy of Sciences*. Berkeley: University of California Press, 1990.

Stücken, Christian. "Der Astronom des Kaisers: Vom Leben des Chinamissionars Ignaz Kögler S.J. (1680–1746)." *Sammelblatt des Historichen Vereins Ingolstadt* 102–103 (1994).

Sturdy, David J. *Science and Social Status: The Members of the Academie des Sciences, 1666–1750.* Woodbridge, Suffolk, UK; Rochester, NY: Boydell Press, 1995.

Stursberg, Peter. *The Golden Hope.* Toronto: United Church Publishing House, 1987.

Swanson, Allen J. *The Church in Taiwan: Profile 1980.* Pasadena: William Carey Library, 1981.

———. *Taiwan: Mainline Versus Independent Church Growth: A Study in Contrasts.* South Pasadena: William Carey Library, 1973.

Sweeten, Alan Richard. "Catholic Converts in Jiangxi Province: Conflict and Accomodation, 1860–1900." In Daniel H. Bays, *Christianity in China: From the Eighteenth Century to the Present.*

Taiwan Jidu zhanglao jiaohui bainian shi (A One Hundred Year History of the Presbyterian Church in Taiwan). Taibei: Presbyterian Church of Formosa Centennial Publications Committee, 1965.

Taiwan shenxue lunkan (Taiwan Journal of Theology). Taibei: Taiwan shenxueyuan.

"Taiwan Tianzhujiao de jianglai" (The Future of Taiwanese Catholicism). *Dousheng,* 10.7 (July 1972).

Tang, Edmond, and Jean-Paul Wiest, eds. *The Catholic Church in Modern China.* Maryknoll, NY: Orbis Books, 1993.

Tang Lisan. *Shandong jiao'an shiliao* (Shandong Reliogious Cases Source Documents). Jinan: Qilu shushe, 1980.

Tang Rongtao. "Refresher Courses in Guizhou." *China Study Project Journal* 3:2 (1988).

Tang Shoulin and Ren Zhongxiang. "Jianjue dizhi Li Changshou de yiduan xieshuo" (Firmly Resist Li Changshou's Heretical Teachings). *Jiaocai* (Teaching Materials) (April 1983).

Tang Yi. "Chinese Christianity in Development." *China Study Journal* 6:2 (1991).

Tao Feiya. "Jindai guonei de Jidujiao shi (Xinjiao) yanjiu jianping" (Brief Critical Review of Recent Chinese Studies on the History of (Protestant) Christianity in China"). In Zhu Weizheng, ed., *Jidujiao yu jindai wenhua.*

Tao Feiya and Liu Tianlu. *Jidujiaohui yu jindai Shandong shehui* (Protestantism in Modern Shandong). Jinan: Shandong daxue chubanshe, 1995.

Taylor, Howard, Mrs. *Pastor Hsi of North China: One of China's Christians.* London: Morgan & Scott; China Inland Mission, 1905.

"Teaching English in China." In *China and Ourselves* 48 (Winter 1986). Toronto, Ontario: Canada China Programme.

Thelin, Mark C. "Propagation of the Gospel, Prophesy, and Prosperity: Some Sociological Reflections on the Role of the Presbyterian Church on

Taiwan." Paper presented at the Symposium on American Missionaries and Social Change in China: Collision and Confluences. Linfield College, Oregon, 1994.

Thomas, Aquinas, Saint. *Summa Theologiae.*

Thomas, W. H. Griffith. "Modernism in China." *Princeton Theological Review* XIX (1921).

Thompson, Roger R. "Twilight of the Gods in the Chinese Countryside: Christians, Confucians, and the Modernizing State." In Daniel H. Bays, ed., *Christianity in China: From the Eighteenth Century to the Present.*

Thoraval, Joel. "Pourquoi les 'religions chinoises' ne peuvent-elles apparaître dans les statistiques occidentales?" *Perspectives chinoises* 1 (1992).

Thun, Albin. *A magyar misszió végnapjai Kinában* (The Last Days of the Hungarian Mission in China). Budapest, 1997.

Tian Feng. Shanghai: Zhongguo Jidujiao xuehui, 1981–.

Tianxue chuhan. See Li Zhizao. *Tianxue chuhan.*

Tianzhujiao dongchuan wenxian xubian (Documents Concerning the Spread of Christianity to the East). (Series: *Zhongguo shixue congshu.*) Taibei: Taiwan xuesheng shuju, 1965.

Tianzhujiao haiwai dongtai ziliao (Materials on the Activities of the Overseas Catholic Church). Shanghai: Guangqi Press.

"Tianzhujiao Taiwan diqu zhujiaotuan shengmin." *Jiaoyu shenghuo zhoukan* 2254 (May 3, 1998).

Tianzhujiao zai Taiwan xiankuang zhi yanjiu. Taibei: Guangqi chubanshe, 1987.

Tianzhujiao yanjiu ziliao huibian (Collected Research Materials on the Catholic Church). Shanghai: Guangqi Press (biweekly).

T'ien Ju-k'ang. "Cementations of Segregatory Tribes—The Protestant Church Among Minority Nationalities in Yunnan." Unpublished paper, 1990.

———. *Peaks of Faith: Protestant Mission in Revolutionary China.* (Series: *Studies in Christian mission,* 8.) Leiden: E. J. Brill, 1993.

Timkovskii, Egor. *Puteshestvie v Kitai chrez Mongoliiu v 1820 i 1821 godakh.* St. Petersburg: Tip. Meditsinskago departamenta Ministerstva vnutrennikh diel, 1824.

Ting, K.H. "Discussion with Members of the Yeller Sect." *Religion in the People's Republic of China: Documentation* 15 (October 1984).

———. Letter to the Religious Affairs Bureau. *Baixing* 187 (March 1, 1989). Hong Kong.

Ting, K.H., and Wang Weifan. "Recent Developments in the Study of Religion." *Chinese Theological Review* (1988).

Todorov, Tzvetan. *La conquête de l'Amérique: La question de l'autre.* Paris: Seuil, 1982.

Tong, Hollington. *Christianity in Taiwan: A History.* Taipei: China Post, 1961.

Towery, Britt E., Jr. *The Churches of China: Taking Root Downward, Bearing Fruit Upward.* Waco, TX: Baylor University, 1990.

Trigault, Nicolas. *De Christiana expeditione apvd Sinas svscepta ab Societate Jesv, ex P. Matthµi Ricij eiusdem Societatis com[m]entarijs. Libri V ad S.D.N. Pavlvm V in quibus Sinensis Regni mores, leges atq. instituta & novæ illius Ecclesiæ difficillima primordia accurate & summa fide describuntur / auctore Nicolao Trigavtio Belga, ex eadem Societate.* Augsburg: Christoph. Mangium, 1615.

Tripod [*Ding*]. Hong Kong: Holy Spirit Study Centre, 1981–.

Tu, Wei-ming. *Centrality and Commonalty: An Essay on the Chung-yung.* Honolulu: University of Hawai'i Press, 1976.

Tu Youguang. "Cultural Graft and Higher Education." In Ruth Hayhoe, ed., *East-West Dialogue in Knowledge and Higher Education.*

Tung Chee-hwa. "Future of Excellence and Prosperity for All." Speech of July 1, 1997.

———. "Preparing Hong Kong for a New Era." Address at the Provisional Legislative Council Meeting, October 8, 1997.

Übelhör, Monika. "Geistessrömungen ser späten Ming-Zeit die das Werken der Jesuiten in China begünstigten." *Saeculum* 23 (1972).

———. "Hsü Kuang-ch'i und seine Einstellung zum Christentum." *Oriens Extremus* 15, Part I (1968), 16, Part II (1969).

Vagnoni, Alfonso. *Qijia xixue* (Regulating the Family According to Western Science). 1631.

———. *Tongyou jiaoyu* (On the Education of Children). c. 1620.

———. *Xiushen xixue* (Self-Perfection According to Western Science). c. 1631. Reprint: Shanghai: Tushanwan yinshuguan, 1923.

———. *Zhiping xixue* (Governing [the Country] and Pacifying [the Realm] According to Western Science). date unknown.

Vámos, Péter. "The Hungarian Jesuit Mission in Daming, Hebei Province." Paper delivered at the 35th ICACNS. Budapest, 1997.

———. *Két kultúra ölelésében Magyar misszionáriusok a Távol-Keleten* (Embracing Two Cultures: Hungarian Missionaries in the Far East). Budapest: Jésus Társasága Mayaroszági Rendtartománya, 1997.

Van Engen, John. "The Christian Middle Ages as an Historiographical Problem." *American Historical Review* 91 (1986).

Varo, Francisco. *Arte de la lengua mandarina; compuesto por el M. R[everend]o P[adr]e Fr. Francisco Varo . . . ; acrecentado y reducido a mejor forma por N[uestr]o H[onoros?]o Fr. Pedro do [i.e. de] la Piñuela , por y Comissario prov. de la Mission Serafica de China; añadiose un confesionario muy vtil y provechoso para alivio de los nueõs ministros.* Impreso en Canton: n.p., año de 1703.

Väth, Alfons. *Johann Adam Schall von Bell SJ: Missionar in China, kaiserlicher Astronom und Ratgeber am Hofe von Peking 1592–1666* (*Monumenta Serica Monograph series* 25). St. Augustin: Steyler Verlag, 1991.

Verbiest, Ferdinand. *Kunyu tushuo* (Explanation of the World Map). 1674. Reprint (Series *Congshu jicheng chu bian*, 3266). Shanghai: Shangwu yinshuguan, 1937.

Verhaeren, H. *Catalogue de la Bibliothèque du Péi-t'ang: Mission catholique des Lazaristes à Pekin*. Pékin: Imprimerie des Lazaristes, 1949.

Wakeman, Frederic E. *The Great Enterprise: the Manchu Reconstruction of Imperial Order in Seventeenth-Century China*. Berkeley: University of California Press, 1985.

Waldron, Arthur. *From War to Nationalism: China's Turning Point, 1924–1925*. Cambridge: Cambridge University Press, 1995.

Waley-Cohen, Joanna. "China and Western Technology in the Late Eighteenth Century." *American Historical Review* 98 (1993).

Walker, Andrew. "Thoroughly Modern: Sociological Reflections on the Charismatic Movement from the End of the Twentieth Century." In *Charismatic Christianity: Sociological Perspectives*.

Wallace, Anthony F. C. *Religion: An Anthropological View*. New York: Random House, 1966.

Wallis, Arthur. *China Miracle: A Voice to the Church in the West*. Eastbourne: Kingsway, 1985.

Walls, Andrew F. *The Missionary Movement in Christian History: Studies in the Transmission of Faith*. Maryknoll, NY: Orbis Books, 1996.

Walravens, Hartmut. *China illustrata: Das europäische Chinaverständnis in Spiegel de 16. bis 18. Jahrhunderts*. Weinheim: Acta Humaniora VCH, 1987.

Wang Meixiu. "Jidujiao de Zhongguohua jiqi nandian" (Indigenization of Chinese Christianity and its Difficulties). *Shijie zongjiao yanjiu* (January 1996).

Wang Minglun. *Fan Yangjiao shuwen jietiexuan* (A Selection of Anti-Foreign Religion Documents and Notices). Jinan: Qilu shushe, 1984.

Wang, Peter Chen-main [Wang Chengmian]. "A Bastion Created, A Regime Reformed, An Economy Reengineered, 1949–1970." In Murray A. Rubenstein, ed., *Taiwan: A New History*.

———. "Taiwan Jidujiao gaodeng jiaoyu de jiantao." *Fokuang Journal* 1 (1996).

———. *Wenshe de shengshuai—erling niandai Jidujiao bensehua zhi ge'an yanjiu*. Taibei: Caituan faren Jidujiao Yuzhouguang chuanbo zhongxin chubanshe, 1993.

Wang Shixing. *Guang zhu yi* (Comprehensive Gazeteer Explained), 1597. Reprint (Series: *Yuan Ming shiliao biji congkan*). Beijing: Zhonghua shuju, 1981.

Wang Weifan. "Chinese Theology and Its Cultural Sources." *Chinese Theological Review* 11:2 (1997).

Wang Zhixin. *Zhongguo Jidujiao shigang* (An Outline History of Christianity in China). Shanghai: Qingnian xiehui shuju, 1940.

Watson, Burton, trans. and ed. *The Basic Writings of Hsun-tzu*. New York: Columbia University Press, 1964.

Webb, John. *An Historical Essay: Endeavoring a Probability that the Language of the Empire of China is the Primitive Language*. London: N. Brook, 1669.

Wei Jiahua. "Fuchuan yu difang jiaohui zhi jianli." *Jiaoyou shenghuo zhoukan* 2290 (November 11, 1998).

Weizhen xuekan See *Regent Chinese Journal*.

Wenhua chuanbo yu jiaohui daxue (Cultural Communication and the Christian Colleges). Hubei jiaoyu chubanshe, 1996.

West China Missionary News. Chungking, West China: West China Missions Advisory Board, 1899–1943.

Whyte, Bob. *Unfinished Encounter: China and Christianity*. London: Fount, 1988.

Whyte, Martin King, and William L. Parish. *Urban Life in Contemporary China*. Chicago: University of Chicago Press, 1984.

Wickeri, Janice K. "Creating a Chinese Christian Idiom: Cultural Receptivity and Bible Translation." Unpublished conference paper, 1998.

Wickeri, Philip Lauri. *Seeking the Common Ground: Protestant Christianity, the Three-Self Movement, and China's United Front*. Maryknoll, NY: Orbis Books, 1988.

Wickeri, Philip Lauri, and Lois Cole, eds. *Christianity and Modernization: A Chinese Debate*. Selected conference proceedings from *Jidujiao wenhua yu xiandaihua guoji yantaohui* (International Conference on Christian Culture and Modernization), October 1994, Beijing. Hong Kong: DAGA Press, 1995.

Widmaier, Rita. *Die Rolle der chinesischen Schrift in Leibniz' Zeichentheorie*. Wiesbaden: Franz Steiner, 1983.

Widmaier, Rita. ed. *Leibniz korrespondiert mit China: Der Briefwechsel mit den Jesuitenmissionaren 1689–1714*. Frankfurt: Vittorio Klostermann, 1990.

Widmer, Eric. *The Russian Ecclesiastical Mission in Peking During the Eighteenth Century*. Cambridge, MA: East Asian Research Center, Harvard University; Harvard University Press, 1976.

Wiest, Jean-Paul. "Bringing Christ to the Nations: Shifting Models of Missions in China." *The Catholic Historical Review* (October 1997).

———. "The Legacy of Vincent Lebbe." *International Bulletin of Missionary Research* 23 (1999).

———. *Maryknoll in China*. Armonk, NY: M. E. Sharpe, 1988.

Wilders, N. M. *The Theologian and His Universe: Theology and Cosmology from the Middle Ages to the Present*. New York: Seabury Press, 1982.

Wills, John E. "From Manila to Fuan: Asian Contexts of Dominican Mission Policy." In D. E. Mungello, ed., *The Chinese Rites Controversy: Its History and Meaning*.

———. "Maritime Asia, 1500–1800: The Interactive Emergence of European Domination." *American Historical Review* 98 (1993).

Witek, John W. *Controversial Ideas in China and in Europe: A Biography of Jean-François Foucquet, S.J. (1665–1741)*. Rome: Institutum Historicum S.I., 1982.

——. *Ferdinand Verbiest (1623–1688): Jesuit Missionary, Scientist, Engineer and Diplomat*. (*Monumenta Serica* monograph series: 30). Nettetal: Steyler Verlag, 1994.

——. "Principles of Scholasticism in China: a Comparison of Giulio Aleni's *Wanwu zhenyuan* with Matteo Ricci's *Tianzhu shiyi*." In Tiziana Lippiello and Roman Malek, eds., *Scholar from the West: Giulio Aleni S.J. (1582–1649) and the Dialogue Between Christianity and China*.

Wolff, Christian. *Oratio de Sinarum philosophia practica. Christiani Wolfii . . . Oratio de Sinarum philosophia practica in solemni Panegyri recitata: cum in ipso Academiae Halensis natali XXVIII. d. XII. Julii A.O.R. 1721: fasces prorectorales successori traderet: notis uberioribus illustrata*. Frankfurt am Main: Apud Joh. B. Andreae & Henr. Hort., 1726.

——. *Rede über die praktische Vernunft der Chinesen*. Edited by Michael Albrecht. Hamburg: Felix Meiner, 1985.

Wong, Wai-ching. "Asian Theology in a Changing Asia: Towards an Asian Theological Agenda for the 21st Century." In *Proceedings of the Congress of Asian Theologians (CATS)*, Part I. Hong Kong: Continuation Committee of the Congress of Asian Theologians, 1997–1998.

Worley, Harry Westcott. *The Central Conference of the Methodist Episcopal Church: A Study in Ecclesiastical Adaptation, or a Contribution of the Mission Field to the Development of Church Organization*. Foochow: Christian Herald Mission Press, 1940.

Wu Fei. "Maimangshangde shengyan: yige xiangcun Tianzhujiaohuizhongde xinyang he shenghuo." M.A. thesis. Beijing: Beijing University, 1999.

Wu, John Cardinal. "March into the Bright Decade: Pastoral Exhortation of Cardinal John Baptist Wu on the Pastoral Commitment of the Catholic Diocese of Hong Kong." n.p., 1989.

Wu, Pei-yi. "Self-Examination and Confession of Sins in Traditional China." *Harvard Journal of Asiatic Studies* 39 (1979).

Wu Wenxiong. "Taiwan Jidu Zhanglao jiaohui bentuhua zhi yanjiu" (Studies on the Indigenization of the Presbyterian Church in Tiawan). *Taiwan shenxue lunkan* 9 (March 1987).

Wurth, E., ed. *Papal Documents Related to the New China, 1937–1984*. Maryknoll, NY: Orbis Books, 1985.

Wuthnow, Robert. *Christianity in the Twenty-first Century: Reflections on the Challenges Ahead*. New York: Oxford University Press, 1993.

——. *The Restructuring of American Religion: Society and Faith Since World War II*. Princeton: Princeton University Press, 1988.

Xi Lian. "No Earthly Salvation: Wang Mingdao, John Sung, Watchman Nee, and the Rise of Indigenous Christianity in China." Paper delivered at the annual meeting of the Association for Asian Studies, Boston, March 1999.

Xia Guiqi. "Lun wo guo 1922–1927 nian jian de fei Jidujiao yundong" (Discussion of Our Nation's Anti-Christian Movement of 1922–1927). *Hangzhou daxue xuebao* (February 1988).

Xia, Mathias. *Jili paozhi*. [JapSin I 39/4]. Rome: Archivum Romanum Societatis Iesu.

Xiang Da. *Zhong Xi jiaotong shi* (A History of Chinese-Western Communication). Shanghai: Zhonghua shuju, 1934.

Xie Sufen. "Serving a Changing Society: Catholicism in the Republic of China on Taiwan." *Sinorama*, 22.3 (March 1997).

Xianggang jiaoqu huiyi wenxian (Documents from the Hong Kong Diocesan Convention). Hong Kong: Xianggang jiaoqu shiduo daibiao huiyi, 1974.

Xin Weixi (pseud.). *Xin Weixi zhenlunji*. Hong Kong: Ming Po Press, 1987.

Xinde (Faith). Hebei: Xinde Press, 1991–.

Xinshiqi zongjiao gongzuo wenxian xuanbian (Selected Documents on Religious Work for a New Age). Zhonggong zhongyang wenxian yanjiushi zonghe yanjiuzu, Guowuyuan zongjiao shiwuju zhengce faguisi, eds. Beijing: Zongjiao wenhua chubanshe, 1995.

Xiong Yuezhi. *Xixue dongjian yu wan Qing shehui* (The Dissemination of Western Learning into China and Late Qing Society). Shanghai: Renmin chubanshe, 1994.

Xu Baoqian. *Jidujiao yu Zhongguo wenhua* (Christianity and Chinese Culture). Shanghai: Qingnian xiehui shuju, 1934.

Xu Changzhi. *Shengchao poxie ji*. Hong Kong: China Alliance Press, 1996.

Xu Guangqi. *Bianxue shugao* (alternatively *Bianshui zhangshu*) in *Xu Guangqi ji* (Collected Works of Xu Guangqi). Beijing: Zhonghua shuju, 1963.

———. *Da xiangren shu*. In Xu Maoxi, ed., *Zengding Xu Wending Gong ji* (Collected Works of the Venerable Xu Wending). Taibei, 1962.

———. *Xu Guangqi ji* (Collected Works of Xu Guangqi). Beijing: Zhonghua shuju, 1963.

———. *Xu Wending Gong ji* (Collected Works of the Venerable Xu Wending). Edited by Xu Zongze. Shanghai: Xujiahui Tianzhu Tang cangshulou, 1933.

———. *Zaowuzhu huaxiang lueshuo* in *Tianzhujiao dongchuan wenxian sanbian*. Taibei: Taiwan xuesheng shuju, 1972.

———. *Zengding Xu Wending Gong ji* (Collected Works of the Venerable Su Wending, Revised and Enlarged). [Li Di edited, Xu Zengze supplemented] Taibei: Xu Maoxi, 1962.

Xu Jiatun. *Xu Jiatun Xianggang huiyilu* (Xu Jiatun's Hong Kong memoir). Taibei: Lianjing chuban shiye gongsi; [Hong Kong]: Xianggang Lianhe Bao, 1995.

Xu Shen. *Shuowen jiezi*. n.p.: Chen Dake Bailang shushe, Wanli *wuxu* [1598].

Xu Shuming. "Guanyu Shun Kang Yong Qian shiqi de Yesuhuishi pingjia wenti" (Concerning the Question of Evaluation of the Jesuits During the Shunzhi, Kangxi, Yongzheng, and Qianlong Reigns). *Zhongguoshi yanjiu dongtai* (October 1985).

Xu Yihua. "Jidujiao zai Hua gaodeng jiaoyu chutan" (Initial Inquiry into Christian Higher Education in China). *Fudan Journal*, no. 5 (1986).

Xue Bozan. "Qishiniandai yihou Taiwan xuanjiao shigong zhi texing yu yiyi." *Taiwan shenxue lunkan* 9 (March 1987).

Xueshu yuekan (Academic Monthly Journal).

Xunzi. see Burton Watson.

Yahuda, Michael. *Hong Kong: China Challenge*. London: Routledge, 1996.

Yamamori Tetsunao and Kim-Kwong Chan. "Missiological Ramifications of the Social Impact of Christianity on the Lisu of China." *Missiology* (October 1998).

Yang, Fenggang. *Chinese Christians in America: Conversion, Assimilation, and Adhesive Identities*. University Park, PA: Pennsylvania State University Press, 1999.

Yang Senfu. *Zhongguo Jidujiao shi* (History of [Protestant] Christianity in China). Taibei: Taiwan shangwu yinshuguan, 1968.

Yang Tianhong. *Jidujiao yu jindai Zhongguo, A Study of the Anti-Christian Movement in China*. Chengdu: Sichuan renmin chubanshe, 1994.

———. "Zhongguo fei Jidujiao yundong (1922–1927)" (The Anti-Christian Movement in China,1922–1927). *Lishi yanjiu* (August 1993).

Yang Tingyun. *Dai yi pian* (Instead of Doubting), 1621. Later edition with added title *Quæstiones Diversæ de Religione Christiana*. Shanghai: Tushanwan yinshuguan, 1935.

———. *Dai yi xubian* (Instead of Doubting, Further Essays). Revised by Zhang Geng, 1635. [Courant 7111] Paris: Bibliothèque Nationale.

———. *Tian Shi ming bian* (The Clear Distinction Between [the Doctrine of] Heaven and Buddhism), 1628. In *Zhongguo shixue congshu*. Taibei: Taiwan xuesheng shuju, 1965.

Yao Minquan. "Indigenization in China in the First Half of the Twentieth Century." *Chinese Theological Review* 11:1 (1996).

Ye Delu, ed. *Min yuan yilai Tianzhujiao shi luncong* (Collection on the History of Catholicism Since the Begiinning ot the Republic). Beiping: Furen daxue tushuguan, 1943.

Ye Xiaowen. "Dangqian woguo de zongjiao wenti" (Contemporary Religious Questions of the Motherland). In *Zhonggong zhongyang dangxiao baogao* (Selected Reports of the Party Central School), vol. 191, no. 5, 1996. Internally circulated document.

———. "Speech to the Chinese Catholic Sixth National Representatives' Conference, 17th January, 1998." *China Study Journal* 13:1 (1998).

Yeo Khiok-Khng. *What Has Jerusalem to do with Beijing: Biblical Interpretation From a Chinese Perspective*. Harrisburg, PA: Trinity Press International, 1998.

Yihetuan yanjiu tongxun (Boxer Studies Newsletter). Jinan: Yihetuan yanjiuhui: Shandong daxue lishi xi, 1981–.

Yihetuan yanjiuhui huikan (Boxer Study Group Notices). Jinan: Yihetuan yanjiuhui: Shandong daxue lishi xi, 1981–.

Ying Fuzang. *Wenhua shiying yu Zhongguo Jidujiao (1860–1911)*. Hong Kong, 1995.

Yip, Ka-che. *Religion, Nationalism, and Chinese Students: The Anti-Christian Movement of 1922–1927*. Bellingham, WA: Center for East Asian Studies, Western Washington University, 1980.

Young, John D. *Confucianism and Christianity: The First Encounter*. Hong Kong: Hong Kong University Press, 1983.

Yuen, Mary. "Hong Kong Catholics Recent Participation in Social Movements." In *Hong Kong Social Movements: Forces from the Margins*. Hong Kong July 1 Link & Hong Kong Women's Christian Council, 1997.

Yunnan zongjiao yanjiu (Research on the Religions of Yunnan). Kunming: Yunnan renmin chubanshe.

Zacher, Hans. *Die Hauptschriften zur Dyadik von G. W. Leibniz*. Frankfurt: Vittorio Klostermann, 1973.

Zha Shijie. "Sishiniande Taiwan Jidujiaohui." In *Zhonghua minguo shi zhuanti lunwenji*. Taibei: Guoshi guan, 1992.

———. *Zhongguo Jidujiao renwu xiaozhuan* (Concise Biographies of Important Chinese Christians). Taibei: Zhonghua fuyin shenxueyuan chubanshe, 1983.

Zhang Chunshen. "Jiaohui benweihua de zhengjie." *Shenxue lunji* 33 (October 1977).

———. "Qiaoliang jiaohui yu jiemei jiaohui." *Shenxue lunji* 113 (Fall 1997).

———. "Tianzhujiao zai Taiwan chuan fuyin de xiankuang yu weilai fangxiang." *Shenxue lunji* 74 (Winter 1987).

———. "Tianzhujiao zai Taiwan weisheme jizu?" *Xinshizhe* 20 (February 1994).

———. "Zhongguo jiaohui de benweihua shenxue." *Shenxue lunji* 42 (January 1980).

Zhang Dawei. "The 'Calendar Case' in the Early Qing Dynasty Re-Examined." In Roman Malek, ed., *Western Learning and Christianity in China: the Contribution and Impact of Johann Adam Schall von Bell, S.J. (1592–1666)*.

Zhang Fengzhen. *Fuyin liuchuan Zhongguo shilue* (A Brief History of the Evangelization of China). Taibei: Furen daxue, 1970–1971.

Zhang, John B. "Catholic Press in Contemporary China." In *Print Media: the Media of the Future*. Paris: Union catholique internationale de la presse, 1997.

Zhang Kaiyuan, ed. *Shehui zhuanxing yu jiaohui daxue*. Wuhan: Huazhong shifan daxue, 1998.

Zhang Kaiyuan and Arthur Waldron, eds. *Zhong Xi wenhua yu jiaohui daxue: shoujie Zhongguo jiaohui daxueshi xueshu yantaohui lunwenji* (Christian Universities and Chinese-Western Cultures: Selected Works of the First International Symposium on the History of Pre-1949 Christian Universities in China. Wuhan: Hubei jiaoyu chubanshe, 1991.

Zhang, Richard X.Y. "Doing Theology in Chinese." *Chinese Theological Review* 11:2 (1996).

Zhang Tan. *Zhaimenqiande shimenkan: Jidujiao wenhua yu Chuan Dian Qian Bian Miaozu shehui* (The Stone Threshold in Front of the Narrow Door: Christian Culture and Miao People's Society of the Border Regions of Sichuan, Yunnan and Guizhou Provinces" (Series: *Xi'nan yanjiu shuxi*). Kunming: Yunnan jiaoyu chubanshe, 1992.

Zhang Weihua. *Mingshi Folangji Lüsong Helan Yidaliya si zhuan zhushi* (A Commentary of the Four Chapters on Portugal, Spain, Holland and Italy in the History of the Ming Dynasty). *Yenching Journal of Chinese Studies* Monograph Series, no. 7. Beijing: Havard-Yenching Institute, 1934. Reprinted in *Zhongguo shixue conshu xubian* 22. Taibei, 1972.

Zhang Weihua and Sun Xi. "Shiliu shiji Yesuhuishi zai Hua chuanjiao zhengce de yanbian" (The Evolution of the Jesuits Evangelical Policies in the Sixteenth Century China). *Wen shi zhe* (January 1985).

Zhang Xie. *Dong Xi yang kao* (A Study About the Eastern and Western Oceans), 1617. *Congshu jicheng chubian* 3259–3261. Reprinted Beijing: Zhonghua shuju, 1985.

Zhang Xinglang. *Ouhua dongjian shi* (The History of European Cultural Dissemination into China). Shanghai: Shangwu yinshuguan, 1934.

———. *Zhong Xi jiaotong shiliao huibian* (A Compilation of Source Materials on the History of Chinese-Western Communication). Beijing: Furen daxue tushuguan, 1930.

Zhang, Yunqiu. "From State Corporatism to Social Representation: Local Trade Unions in the Reform Years." In Timothy Brook and B. Michael Frolic, eds., *Civil Society in China*.

Zhao Binshi. "Zhongguo daotong yu chuanjiao." *Hengyi* (May 1967).

Zhao Chunchen. "Wan Qing yangwupai yu jiao'an" (Late Qing Westernizers and Religious Cases). *Lishi yanjiu* (April 1988).

Zhao Qiusheng. "The Old Testament Commentaries of Jia Yuming." *Chinese Theological Review* 9 (1994).

Zhao Tian'en and Zhuang Wanfang. *Dangdai Zhongguo Jidujiao fazhan shi, 1949–1997* (A History of Christianity in Socialist China, 1949–1997). Taibei: China Ministries International, 1997.

Zhongguo jiaohui daxue shi yanjiu tongxun (Newsletter for Historical Research on China Christian Colleges). Wuhan, Hong Kong: Central China Normal University, 1995–.

Zhongguo jiaohui daxue wenxian mulu (A Catalog of Documents on Chinese Christian Colleges). Hong Kong: Chung Chi College, 1998.

Zhongguoshi yanjiu dongtai (Development of the Study of Chinese History). Beijing: Zhongguo shehui kexue yuan lishi yanjiusuo, Zhongguo shehui kexue chubanshe, 1979–.

Zhongguo Tianzhujiao (Catholic Church in China). Beijing: Zhongguo Tianzhujiao bianjibu, 1980–.

Zhongguo wenhua yu Jidujiao (Chinese Culture and Christianity). Shanghai: Qingnian xiehui shuju, 1927.

"Zhonghua minguo Taiwan diqu Tianzhujiao jiaowu jianbao." *Hengyi* 35.6 (January 1986).

Zhonglian. Singapore: China Catholic Communication.

Zhu Cenglou, ed. *Woguo shehui de bianqian yu fazhan.* Taibei: Sanmin, 1981.

Zhu Qianzhi. *Zhongguo Jingjiao* (Chinese Nestorianism). Beijing: Wenhuabu yinshuachang, 1982.

———. *Zhongguo Jingjiao: Zhongguo gudai Jidujiao yanjiu* (Chinese Nestorianism: Studies in China's Ancient Christianity). Beijing: Dongfang chubanshe, 1993.

Zhu Sancai. *1995 nian Taiwan Jidujiaohui jiaoshi baogao.* Taizhong, 1995.

Zhu Weizheng, ed. *Jidujiao yu jindai wenhua* (Christianity and Modern Culture). Shanghai: Renmin chubanshe, 1994.

Zhu Zongyuan. *Da kewen* (Answers to the Questions of a Guest). [Courant 7036]. Paris: Bibliothèque Nationale, 1697.

———. *Zhengshi lueshuo* (An Outline of Salvation). Rome: Archivum Romanum Societatis Iesu, JS I.145.

Zhuang Tianci. "Zhanglao jiaohui yu 2.28 pingfan yundong (1987–1990)." *Taiwan shiliao yanjiu* 12 (November 1998).

Zhuo Xinping. "Jidujiao yanjiu gaishuo" (Survey of Research on Christianity). *Zhongguo zongjiao yanjiu nanjian 1996* (Year Book of Religious Studies in China 1996). Beijing: Zhongguo shehui kexue chubanshe, 1998.

Zürcher, Erik. "Aleni in Fujian, 1630–1640: the Medium and the Message." In Tiziana Lippiello and Roman Malek, eds., *Scholar from the West: Giulio Aleni S.J. (1582–1649) and the Dialogue Between Christianity and China.*

———. "Bouddhisme et christianisme." In *Bouddhisme, christianisme et société chinoise.* Paris: Conférences, essais et leçons du Collège de France, 1990.

———. "Confucian and Christian Religiosity in Late Ming China." *The Catholic Historical Review* 83 (1997).

———. "Giulio Aleni's Chinese Biography." In Tiziana Lippiello and Roman Malek, eds., *Scholar From the West: Giulio Aleni S.J. (1582–1649) and the Dialogue Between Christianity and China.*

———. "In the Beginning: 17th Century Chinese Reactions to Christian Creationism." In Huang Chun-chieh and Erik Zürcher, eds., *Time and Space in Chinese Culture.*

———. "Jesuit Accommodation and the Chinese Cultural Imperative." In D. E. Mungello, D.E., ed., *The Chinese Rites Controversy: Its History and Meaning.*

———. "The Jesuit Mission in Fukien in Late Ming Times: Levels of Response." In E. B. Vermeer, ed., *Development and Decline of Fukien Province in the 17th and 18th Centuries.* Leiden: Brill, 1990.

———. "The Lord of Heaven and the Demons: Strange Stories Froma Late Ming Christian Manuscript." In G. Naundorf, K.-H. Pohl, and H. H. Schmidt, eds., *Religion und Philosophie in Ostasien: Festschrift für H. Steiniger.* Würzburg: Königshausen & Neumann, 1985.

——. "The Spread of Buddhism and Christianity in Imperial China: Spontaneous Diffusion Versus Guided Propagation." In *China and the West. Proceedings of the International Colloquium held in the Koninklijke Academie voor Wetenschappen, Letteren en Schone Kunsten van België, Brussels, November 23–25, 1987.* Brussels: Paleis der Academiën, 1993.

Glossary

Ai Rulüe 艾儒略
Aidi 哀帝
Aijin xingquan 哀矜行詮
Alopen 阿羅本
An Lushan 安祿山
An Wensi 安文思
Anhui 安徽

bao 報
Baoding 保定
Baoqing 寶慶
Beifang jinde 北方進德
Beiguan 北館
Beijing 北京
beili 背理
Beitang 北堂
benweihua 本位化
bian 貶
Bianxue shugao 辨學疏稿
Bianxue zhangshu 辨學章疏
Bogeli 柏格理
bu Ru 補儒
bu Ru yi Fo 補儒易佛
Budeyi 不得已
Buluo 博羅
Bencao 本草
Budeyi bian 不得已編
Buyi 布依

buyi wanghua zuoyou rushu mizheng fofa 補益王化左右儒術敉正佛法

Cai Sanxiong 蔡三雄
Cangshu 藏書
Chang'an 長安
changping cang 常平倉
Changsha 長沙
Changyuan 長垣
Chao, Jonathan T'ien-en 趙天恩
Chaoxian 朝鮮
chaoxing zhi gui 超性之規
Che Jinguang 車金光
Chen Chuanzheng 陳川正
Chen Dake bailang shushe 陳大科白狼書社
Chen Duxiu 陳獨秀
Chen Houguang 陳侯光
Chen Manhong 陳滿鴻
Chen Minxiu 陳敏秀
Chen Shenru 陳申如
Chen Suli 陳素梨
Chen Yuan 陳垣
Cheng Jingyi 誠靜怡
Cheng Shiguang 成世光
Cheng Yi 程頤
chongjiao 寵敎
Chongsheng pai 重生派

Chongxiu Taiwan sheng tongzhi
    重修台灣省通志
Chongzhen 崇禎
Chongzhen Lishu 崇禎曆書
chouren 疇人
Chouren zhuan 疇人傳
Chuanjiaoshi yu jindai Zhongguo
    傳教士與近代中國
chujia 出家
Cong Malixun dao Situ Leideng: lai
    Hua xinjiao chuanjiaoshi
    pingzhuan 從馬利遜到司徒
    雷登：來華新教教士評傳
Congshu jicheng 叢書集成

da fumu 大父母
Da Gong Bao 大公報
Da kewen 答客問
Da Ming huidian 大明會典
Da Qing lichao shilu: Shengzu
    大清歷朝實錄：聖祖
datong 大同
Da xiangren shu 答鄉人書
Dai (People) 傣
Dai Qifeng 戴起鳳
Dai yi pian 代疑篇
Dai yi xubian 代疑續編
Daming 大名
Dang Huairen 黨懷仁
dangchu Tianzhu huasheng zhiyou
    yinan yinü 當初天主化生止
    有一男一女
dao 道
Dao yu yan: Huaxia wenhua yu
    Jidujiao wenhua xiangyu 道與
    言：華夏文化與基督教文化相遇
daoke 道科
daoli 道理
Daxue 大學
Deng Yuzhi 登裕志
di 帝
Ding Guangxun 丁光訓
Ding Liwei 丁立偉
Ding Mingnan 丁名楠
Ding Wenjiang 丁文江

Dong (people) 侗
Dong Conglin 董叢林
Dong Li 董黎
Dong Xi yang kao 東西洋考
Donghai Xihai xintong litong
    東海西海心同理同
Donglin Dang 東林黨
Dongming 東明
duanque 短缺
Dui yuanzhumin zhujiao zhusheng
    dadian de ruogan lianxiang 對原
    住民主教祝聖大點的若干聯想
Dumen yulu 都門語錄
Duosheng 鐸聲
Duoshu 鐸書

Eluosi Beiguan 俄羅斯北館
Eluosi guan 俄羅斯館
Eluosi Nanguan 俄羅斯南館
Eluosi Wenguan 俄羅斯文館
Eluosi xue 俄羅斯學
en 恩
enjiao 恩教
Ershiwu yan 二十五言

fa 法
fake 法科
Falun gong 法輪功
falü zhi xiang 法律之庠
Fan Hongye 樊洪業
Fan Lizhu 范麗珠
fan Tianzhu ming 犯天主命
Fang Hao 方豪
Fang Litian 方立天
Fang Yizhi 方以智
Fanyangjiao douzheng de xingzhi ji
    qita 反洋教斗爭的性質及其他
Fanyangjiao shuwen jietie xuan
    反洋教書文揭帖選
Fanyangjiao yundong 反洋教運動
Fenshu 焚書
Feng Chengjun 馮承鈞
Feng Congwu 馮從吾
Feng Youlan 馮友蘭

*Fengchaozhong fenqi de Zhongguo
    jiaohui* 風潮中奮起的中國教會
Fengtian 奉天
Fojiaotu 佛教徒
Folangji 佛郎機
Fu Xi 伏羲
Fuchuan yu difang jiaohui zhi jianli
    福傳與地方教會之建立
Fujian 福建
Funeng 傅能
Furen daxue 輔仁大學
Furen daxue shenxue lunji 輔仁
    大學神學論集
fuxing 復興
Fuyin liuchuan Zhongguo shilüe
    福音流傳中國史略
Fuyin Zhongguohua de jiqiexing
    福音中國化的急切性
Fuyong 福永
Fuzhou Jidujiao wenshi ziliao xuanji
    福州基督教文史資料選集

*Gaige kaifang yilai de Zhongguo
    nongcun jiaohui* 改革開放以來
    的中國農村教會
Gansu 甘肅
Gao Junming 高俊明
Gao Yizhi 高一志
Gaoxiong 高雄
gewu 格物
gewu qiongli 格物窮理
gewu zhizhi 格物致知
geyi 格義
Gongshang Xueyuan 工商學院
Gu Changsheng 顧長聲
Gu Weimin 顧衛民
Gu Yaowen 谷耀文
Gu Yulu 顧裕祿
guan 官
Guang zhi yi 廣志繹
Guangqi She 光啓社
Guangqi Xuexiao 光啓學校
Guangxi 廣西
Guangzhou 廣州

*Guanyu Ming Qing Yesuhuishi zai
    Hua huodong pingjia de jige
    wenti* 關於明清耶穌會士在華
    活動評價的幾個問題
*Guanyu Shun Kang Yong Qian shiqi
    de Yesuhuishi pingjia wenti* 關於
    順康雍乾時期的耶穌會士評價
    問題
*Guanyu Zhongguo jindai shi shang
    jiao'an de kaocha* 關於中國
    近代史上教案的考察
gudian 古典
Guizhou 貴州
Guizhou shehui kexue
    貴州社會科學
Guluodong 古洛東
Guo Xiwei 郭熹微
Guofu 國父
Guomindang 國民黨
guoshi 國史
Guowuyuan Zongjiao Shiwuju
    Zhengce Faguisi 國務院宗教
    事務局政策法規司

Hani 哈尼
Hai pian 海篇
Hainan Dao 海南島
Han Bingfang 韓秉方
Hanhui 漢會
Han Lin 韓霖
Han Qi 韓琦
Hangzhou daxue xuebao
    杭州大學學報
Hankou 漢口
Hanyu shenxue 漢語神學
Hao'an xianhua 蒿庵閒話
He Guichun 何桂春
He Jinshan 何進善
He Zhaowu 何兆武
Hebei 河北
*Hedongtang chang lidai zhaomu
    Zhushen* 河東堂常歷代昭穆
    主神
Hei Yi 黑彝
Hengyi 恆毅

Heshang 河殤
Hong Xiuquan 洪秀全
hongmao 紅毛
Hou Jie 候杰
houtian 後天
Hou Wailu 侯外廬
houru 後儒
Hu Shi 胡適
Huang Di 黃帝
Huang Ming xiangxu lu 皇明象胥錄
Huang Wudong 黃武東
Huang Wudong huiyi lu
    黃武東回憶錄
Huang Yong'an 黃永安
Huang Zhen 黃貞
Huang Zongxi 黃宗羲
Huangyu quanlantu 皇輿全覽圖
Huayang 華陽
Huazhong Shifan Daxue
    華中師範大學
Hui (Islamic people) 回
hui 會
huifu guxue 恢復古學
huiguo zixin 悔過自新
huitong 會通
huizhang 會長
hun 魂
Hunan 湖南

ji du Tianxue zhushu 及睹天學諸書
Ji Zhiwen 計志文
jia (family) 家
jia (to marry) 嫁
jia jia Xu Zheng, renren Jia Ma
    家家許鄭，人人賈馬
Jia Yuming 賈玉銘
Jiading 嘉定
Jiajing 嘉靖
Jiali 家禮
jian shu yamen 鑑書衙門
Jian Youwen 簡又文
Jiang Dejing 蔣德璟
Jiang Falin 江發琳
Jiang Fangzhen 蔣方震

Jiang Jiaoren 江覺仁
Jiang Yong 江永
Jiang Wenhan 江文漢
Jiangsu 江蘇
Jianzheng 見證
Jianzhou 簡州
jiaohua 教化
jiaohua huangdi 教化皇帝
Jiaohuang 教皇
Jiaohui benweihua de zhengjie
    教會本位化的癥結
Jiaohui dui Taiwan minjian sangli de
    shiying 教會對台灣民間喪禮
    的適應
jiaoke 教科
Jiaoting yu Zhongguo shijie shi
    教庭與中國使節史
jiaotou 教頭
jiaowang 教王
Jiaowu jiao'an dang 教務教案檔
jiaoyi eryi 教一而已
Jiaoyou ruhe yi wenhua chuanjiao
    教友如何以文化傳教
Jiaoyou shenghuo zhoukan
    教友生活周刊
Jiaozong 教宗
Jiaozong xiang Zhongguo
    zhujiaotuan zhujiao zhici
    quanwen 教宗向中國主教團
    主教致詞全文
Jidujiao de Zhongguohua ji qi
    nandian 基督教的中國化及其
    難點
Jidujiao luntan 基督教論壇
Jidujiao Taiwan Xinyihui fazhan
    jianshi 基督教台灣信義會發展
    簡史
Jidujiao xundao gonghui zai
    Zhaotong diqu de zaoqi chuanbo
    基督教循道公會在昭通地區的
    早期傳播
Jidujiao yanjiu gaishuo
    基督教研究概說
Jidujiao youyi Zhongguo, jiushi jiao
    chengquan Rujiao 基督教有益

中國,救世教成全儒教
Jidujiao yu jindai wenhua
　基督教與近代文化
Jidujiao yu jindai Zhongguo shehui
　基督教與近代中國社會
Jidujiao yu Zhongguo wenhua
　基督教與中國文化
Jidujiao zai Hua gaodeng jiaoyu
　chutan
　基督教在華高等教育初探
Jidujiao zai Zhongguo zhi chuanbo
　yu jindai Zhongguo 基督教在中
　國之傳播與近代中國
jihe 幾何
Jili paozhi 祭禮泡製
Jin Nige 金尼閣
Jindai guonei de Jidujiao shi
　(Xinjiao) yanjiu jianping 近代
　國內的基督教史(新教)研究簡評
Jindai jiao'an he Yihe Tuan yundong
　de xingqi 近代教案和義和團運
　動的興起
Jindaishi yanjiu 近代史研究
jing 經
jingdian 經典
Jingjiao 景教
Jingjiao beiwen 景教碑文
Jingpo 景頗
jingshi zhi yong 經世致用
jingtang 經堂
jingtian 敬天
jing wu zhen shi 經無眞實
jingxue 經學
jingzhuan 經傳
jingzuo 靜坐
Jiren shipian 畸人十篇
jiupin 九品
Jiutian shuo 九天說
jizu 祭祖
juan 卷
Juesi lu 覺斯錄
Jujie 具揭

Kang Qian shengshi 康乾盛世
Kang Youwei 康有爲

Kangding 康定
Kangxi 康熙
Kangxi shidai chuanru de Xifang
　shuxue jiqi dui Zhongguo shuxue
　de yingxiang 康熙時代傳入的
　西方數學機器對中國數學的影
　響
kaozheng 考證
Kashe 喀什
Ke jihe yuanben xu 刻幾何原本序
keguan guina 客觀歸納
Kongjiao hui 孔教會
kongtan xingli 空談性理
Kouduo richao 口鐸日抄
Kunyu tushuo 坤輿圖說

Lahu 拉枯
Lam Wing-hung 林榮洪
Lama jiao 喇嘛教
Lhasa 拉薩
Li (People) 黎
li 理
Li Ande 李安德
Li Di 李杕
Li Donghai 李東海
Li Erqu 李二曲
Li Jingpo 李靜波
Li Jiubiao 李九標
Li Jiugong 李九功
Li Leisi 利類思
Li Madou 利瑪竇
Li Madou Zhongguo zhaji
　利瑪竇中國札記
Li Madou zhuan 利瑪竇傳
Li Madou yu jindai Zhongguo
　利瑪竇與近代中國
Li Shiyin 李世音
Li Shiyue 李時岳
Li Sixuan 李嗣玄
Li tiandi zhi zhuzai 立天地之主宰
Li Tiangang 李天綱
Li Zhen 李震
Li Zhenggao 李正高
Li Zhi 李贄

Li Zhigang 李志剛
Li Zhizao 李之藻
Li Zubai 李祖白
Liang Fa 梁發
Liang Jiamian 梁家勉
Liang Jinwen 梁錦文
Liang Kalun (Jialin) 梁家麟
Liang Qichao 梁啓超
liangzhi 良知
Liao Guangsheng 廖光生
Libu 禮部
Lifa wenda 曆法問答
Lifan yuan 理藩院
Liji 禮記
Liju 曆居
like 理科
Lilang 李郎
lin 林
Lin Benxuan 林本炫
Lin Jinshui 林金水
Lin Ronghong *see* Lam Wing-hung
Lin Zhiping 林治平
linghun 靈魂
lingwei 靈位
lingxing 靈性
Lishi yanjiu 歷史研究
Lisu 傈僳
Liu Dingyin 劉鼎寅
Liu Jinchang 劉錦昌
Liu Ning 劉凝
Liu Tianlu 劉天路
Liu Tingfang 劉廷芳
Liu Wenzhou 劉文周
Liu Xiaofeng 劉小楓
Liu Zijian 劉子健
liuke 六科
liuyi 六藝
Lixue 理學
liyun 禮運
Lizhi 曆志
Long yu Shangdi: Jidujiao yu
Zhongguo chuantong wenhua
龍與上帝: 基督教與中國傳統
文化

Lu Jiuyuan 陸九淵
Lü Shiqiang 呂實强
Lu Yao 路遙
Lu Zhongwei 盧仲維
Lüetan Yunnan Miaozu diqu de
Jidujiao 略談雲南苗族地區
的基督教
Lujiabang 陸家浜
Lun jindai Zhongguo jiawu
zhanzheng qian de jiao'an yu
fanyangjiao douzheng 論近代
中國甲午戰爭前的教案與反洋
教斗爭
Lun woguo 1922–1927 nianjian de
fei Jidujiao yundong 論我國
1922–1927年間的非基督教運動
Lunyu 論語
Luo Guang 羅光
Luo Shugang 雒樹剛
Luo Yage 羅雅各

Ma Xiangbo 馬相伯
Ma Xisha 馬西沙
Maimangshang de shengyan: yige
xiangcun Tianzhujiaohuizhong de
xinyang he shenghuo 麥芒上的
聖言: 一個鄉村天主教會中的
信仰和生活
Manzhouli 滿洲里
Mao Ruizheng 茅瑞徵
Maoping 毛坪
Mei Wending 梅文鼎
Meizhou 梅州
Menggu 蒙古
Menggu ren 蒙古人
Mengzi ziyi shuzheng 孟子字義疏證
Miandian 緬甸
mianfenjiao 麵粉教
Miao 苗
Ming 明
Ming Bao 明報
Mingmo Tianzhujiao yu Ruxue de
jiaoliu yu chongtu 明末天主教
與儒學的交流與沖突

*Ming Qing jian zai Hua de
    Tianzhujiao Yesuhuishi* 明清間
    在華的天主教耶穌會士
Ming Ruxue'an 明儒學案
Mingshi 明史
mingde 明德
Mingli tan 名理探
mingshi 明示
*Mingshi Folangji Lüsong Helan
    Yidaliya si zhuan zhushi* 明史
    佛郎機呂宋和蘭意大里亞四傳
    注釋
*Minyuan yilai Tianzhujiao shi
    luncong* 民元以來天主教史論叢
minzu 民族
mixin 迷信
mizheng 密證
moyou 默牖
mu 木
Musilin 穆斯林
naifenjiao 奶粉教

Nan Huairen 南懷仁
Nangong shudu 南宮署牘
Nanguan 南館
Nanjing 南京
Nanle 南樂
Naxi 納西
*Neidi, Gang, Tai sandi jiaohui de
    shehui jiaose* 內地，港，台
    三地教會的社會角色
Ni Tuosheng 倪柝聲
Ningxia 寧夏
nü 女

Ouhua dongjian shi 歐化東漸史
Ouluoba 歐羅巴
Ouzhou wenyi fuxing shi
    歐洲文藝復興史
Paiwai yu Zhongguo zhengzhi
    排外與中國政治
Pang Diwo 龐迪我
piao 票
ping Tianxia 平天下
pingfan 平反

Pingxintu 平信徒
Pixie ji 闢邪集
po 魄
Posi 波斯
Poxie ji 破邪集
Puyang 濮陽

Qi Qizhang 戚其章
qi yao yi (jing) zhengzi
    其要已（經）正（字）子
Qian Daxin 錢大昕
Qiaoliang jiaohui yu jiemei jiaohui
    橋樑教會與姊妹教會
Qie li wu er shi 且理無二是
qijia 齊家
Qijia xixue 齊家西學
qian 簽
Qianlong 乾隆
Qianwei 犍爲
Qin Heping 秦和平
Qinbao Tianxue 欽裦天學
Qing 清
Qing Gaozong 清高宗
Qing Lifan yuan 清理藩院
Qing mo jiao'an 清末教案
Qingchao wenxian tongkao
    清朝文獻通考
Qingdai xueshu gailun
    清代學術概論
Qingfeng 清豐
Qinghai 青海
Qingxue 清學
qinlai jiushi 親來救世
qiongli 窮理
Qiqiha'er 齊齊哈爾
*Qishiniandai yihou Taiwan xuanjiao
    shigong zhi texing yu yiyi* 七十
    年代以後台灣宣教事工之特性
    與意義
Qiu Sheng 丘昇
Qu Haiyuan 瞿海源
Qu Qiubai 瞿秋白
Qu Taisu 瞿太素
Quanzhou 泉州

Quanfanwei jiaohui 全範圍教會

ranqi 然啓
ren (benevolence) 仁
ren (human being) 人
Ren Yanli 任延黎
rendao 人道
renxing 人性
renxing qi benshan 人性其本善
renyi eryi yi 仁義而已矣
Richan 日躔
Ru 儒
Ruan Yuan 阮元
rujiao 儒教

Saideke 賽德克
sanjiao 三教
San min zhuyi 三民主義
saze'erduode 撒則爾鐸德
sen 森
Shandong daxue xuebao
    山東大學學報
Shandong jiao'an shiliao
    山東教案史料
Shangdi 上帝
Shang Di suo jiangsheng
    上帝所降生
shang Tian zhi you Zhu 上天之有主
Shanghai shehui kexue
    上海社會科學
shanshu 善書
Shaozhou 韶州
Shehui zhuanxing yu jiaohui daxue
    社會轉型與教會大學
shen 神
Shen Nong 神農
Shen Yifan 沈以藩
Shen Que 沈潅
shenfu 神父
sheng 生
Shengchao Poxie ji 聖朝破邪集
shenghou zhi xue 生後之學
Shengjia shuju 聖家書局
Shengjiao ru Chuan ji 聖教入川記
Shengjiao xinzheng 聖教信證

Shengjing 聖經
shengqian zhi xue 生前之學
Shengren 聖人
Shengshen 聖神
Shengshui jiyan 聖水紀言
shengxian 聖賢
Shengxue 聖學
shenjiao 身教
Shensi lu 慎思錄
shenwei 神位
Shenyang 沈陽
shenzu 神祖
Sheshan 佘山
Shi Jinghuan 史靜寰
shijiao 示教
Shijie zongjiao wenhua
    世界宗教文化
Shijie zongjiao yanjiu
    世界宗教研究
Shiliu shiji Yesuhuishi zai Hua
    chuanjiao zhengce de yanbian
    十六世紀耶穌會士在華傳教政
    策的演變
Shilun Ming mo Qing chu Yesuhuishi
    de lishi zuoyong 試論明末清初
    耶穌會士的歷史作用
shixue 實學
Shizijia yu long 十字架與龍
shu 熟
shujiao 書教
Shuli jingyun 數理精蘊
Shuli jingyun dui shuzao biaofa yu
    Dai Xu de erxiang zhankaishi
    yanjiu 數理精蘊對數造表法
    與戴煦的二項展開式研究
Shundefu 順德府
Shuowen jiezi 說文解字
Shuwen bian 述聞編
Shuwen pian 述文篇
shuyuan 書院
shuzui 贖罪
Sichuan 四川
Sichuan jiao'an yu Yihequan
    dang'an 四川教案與義和拳
    檔案

Siji Ai xiansheng xingji
思及艾先生行蹟
Sishinian de Taiwan Jidujiaohui
四十年的台灣基督教會
*Sishinian lai Taiwan de zongjiao
fazhan qingkuang*
四十年來台灣的宗教發展情況
Sishu 四書
Song Shangjie 宋尚節
Song Yingxing 宋應星
Su Hongxiao 蘇宏孝
Sun Jiang 孫江
Sun Shangyang 孫尚揚
Sun Xi 孫西
Sun Xueshi 孫學詩
Sun Zhongshan (Sun Yat-sen)
孫中山
suoyiran 所以然

Tai Gang Ao sandi jiaohui chutan
台港澳三地教會初探
Taiji 太極
Tainan 台南
taiping 太平
Taiwan de zhengjiao chongtu
台灣的政教衝突
*Taiwan diqu Jidujiao fazhan zhi
chubu tantao* 台灣地區基督
發展之初步探討
*Taiwan diqu Tianzhujiao fazhan
qushi zhi yanjiu* 台灣地區
天主教發展趨勢之研究
*Taiwan Jidu Zhanglao jiaohui
bainian shi*
台灣基督長老教會百年史
*Taiwan Jidu Zhanglao jiaohui beijia
yundong de tantao jiqi shenxue
yiyi* 台灣基督長老教會倍加
運動的探討及其神學意義
*Taiwan Jidu Zhanglao jiaohui
bentuhua zhi yanjiu*
台灣基督長老教會本土化
之研究
*Taiwan Jidujiao gaodeng jiaoyu de
jiantao* 台灣基督教高等教育

的檢討
Taiwan shiliao yanjiu
台灣史料研究
*Taiwan Tianzhujiao benweihua
gaikuang*
台灣天主教本位化概況
Taiwan Tianzhujiao de jianglai
台灣天主教的將來
*Taiwan yuanzhu minzu de shehui
wenti* 台灣原住民族的社會問題
Taixi 太西
Taixi shuifa 泰西水法
Taizong 太宗
Tajike 塔吉克
Tang 唐
Tang Lisan 唐立三
Tao Feiya 陶飛亞
Tian 天
Tian di jun fu shi 天地君父師
Tian di jun qin shi 天地君親師
Tian di ren wu zhen shen
天地人物貞神
Tianfeng 天風
Tian Rukang *see* T'ien Ju-k'ang
Tian Shi mingbian 天釋明辨
Tian zhi shang biyou zhuzhi shu
天之上必有主之書?
Tian Zi 天子
tiandao 天道
Tiangong kaiwu 天工開物
Tianjin Gongshang Xueyuan
天津工商學院
tianli 天理
tianli tang 天理堂
Tianwen 天文
Tianwenxue Gong 天文學宮
Tianxue 天學
Tianxue chuangai 天學傳概
Tianxue chuhan 天學初函
Tianxue: Tianzhujiaoxue ye
天學：天主教學也
Tianzhu 天主
Tianzhu jing 天主經
Tianzhu qintai zhengjing
天主親胎正經

Tianzhu shiji 天主實蹟
Tianzhu shiyi 天主實義
Tianzhu zhi jingdian 天主之經典
Tianzhujiao chuanru de shidai
    beijing he Yesuhuishi de zuoyong
    天主教傳入的時代背景和耶穌
    會士的作用
Tianzhujiao dongchuan wenxian
    天主教東傳文獻
Tianzhujiao dongchuan wenxian
    sanbian 天主教東傳文獻三編
Tianzhujiao dongchuan wenxian
    xubian 天主教東傳文獻續編
Tianzhujiao gen Zhongguo wenhua
    de guanxi 天主教跟中國文化
    的關係
Tianzhujiao haiwai dongtai ziliao
    天主教海外動態資料
Tianzhujiao Taiwan diqu zhujiaotuan
    shengmin 天主教台灣地區主教
    團聲明
Tianzhujiao xue 天主教學
Tianzhujiao yanjiu ziliao huibian
    天主教研究資料匯編
Tianzhujiao zai Hua chuanjiao shi ji
    天主教在華傳教史集
Tianzhujiao zai Taiwan chuan fuyin
    de xiankuang yu weilai fangxiang
    天主教在台灣傳福音的現況與
    未來方向
Tianzhujiao zai Taiwan weisheme
    jizu? 天主教在台灣為什麼
    祭祖?
Tianzhujiao zai Taiwan xiankuang
    zhi yanjiu 天主教在台灣現況
    之研究
Tianzhuxue 天主學
T'ien Ju-k'ang 田汝康
Tongliang 銅梁
Tongxin heyi 同心合一
Tongyou jiaoyu 童幼教育
Tu'er yuxi 土耳語系
Tujia 土家

Wa 佤

Wan'guo gongbao wenxuan
    萬國公報文選
Wan Qing yangwupai yu jiao'an
    晚清洋務派與教案
wang 王
Wang Chengmian 王成勉
Wang Meixiu 王美秀
Wang Mingdao 王明道
Wang Minglun 王明倫
Wang Shixing 王士性
Wang Weifan 汪維藩
Wang Yangming 王陽明
Wang Yuchu 王煜初
Wang Yuanshen 王元深
Wang Zheng 王徵
Wang Zhixin 王治心
Wang Zhongmin 王重民
Wanli 萬曆
wanwu 萬物
wanwu yiti 萬物一體
Wanwu zhenyuan 萬物眞原
wei 位
Wei Jiahua 魏嘉華
wei Xiren suo yong 為西人所用
Weiwu'er 維吾爾
Weiwu'er zu 維吾爾族
Wen shi zhe 文史哲
Wenda huichao 問答彙抄
Wenhua chuanbo yu jiaohui daxue
    文化傳播與教會大學
wenke 文科
Wenshe de shengshuai 文社的盛衰
wenshi ziliao 文史資料
wenyi zhi xue 文藝之學
wenzhang 文章
Woguo shehui de bianqian yu fazhan
    我國社會的變遷與發展
Woguo zongjiao bianqian de
    shehuixue fenxi 我國宗教變遷的
    社會分析
wokou 倭寇
Wu Leichuan 吳雷川
Wu Baiyi 吳百益
Wu Fei 吳飛

Wu Wenxiong 吳文雄
Wu Yaozong 吳耀宗
Wujing 五經
wulun 五倫
wu ri sanxing wushen
　　吾日三省吾身
Wuhua 五華
Wusheng laomu 無生老母
Wushi wuzhong ziyou zhi zhushen
　　無始無終自有之主神
wuxu bianfa 戊戌變法

Ximing 西銘
Xi Shengmo 席勝魔
Xia Guiqi 夏瑰琦
Xia Madiya 夏瑪第亞
Xiamen 廈門
xiantian 先天
Xiang Da 向達
Xianggang Donghua Sanyuan 125
　　nien shilüe 香港東華三院125年
　　史略
xianggong 相公
Xiangshen yu fanyangjiao douzheng
　　鄉紳與反洋教斗爭
xiangshi 庠師
xianru 先儒
Xianxian 獻縣
xiao 孝
Xiaocheng Fojiao 小乘佛教
Xiaojing 孝經
xiaoxue 小學
xie 邪
xiejiao 邪教
Xifa 西法
Xifang dawen 西方答問
Xifang yaoji 西方要記
Xihai Ai xiansheng yulü
　　西海艾先生語綠
Xi'nan yanjiu shuxi 西南研究書系
Xin Weisi 辛維思
Xin Weisi zhenglunji 辛維思政論集
Xinde 信德
Xinde she 信德社
Xindu 新都

xinfa 新法
xingjiao 性教
Xinhua 新華
Xinhui 新會
Xinjiang 新疆
Xinshiqi zongjiao gongzuo wenxian
　　xuanbian 新時期宗敎工作文獻
　　選編
Xinshizhe 新使者
xinxue 心學
xinxue 新學
xing 性
xingqing 性情
Xiong Sanba 熊三拔
Xiong Yuezhi 熊月之
Xiongjiali aiguozhe Gasushi zhuan
　　匈加利愛國者噶蘇士傳
Xiongnu 匈奴
Xiongyali 匈牙利
Xiongjialirenzhe Yazhou
　　Huangzhong er gu Xiongnu zhi
　　yiyi ye 匈加利人者亞洲黃種
　　而古匈奴之遺裔也
xiru 西儒
xiseng 西僧
xiushen 修身
Xiushen xixue 修身西學
Xixue 西學
Xixue dongjian yu wan Qing shehui
　　西學東漸與晚清社會
Xixue fan 西學凡
Xixue Zhongyuan 西學中源
Xizang ren 西藏人
Xu Baoqian 徐寶謙
Xu Changzhi 徐昌治
Xu Dashou 許大受
Xu Fuguang 徐復光
Xu Guangqi 徐光啓
Xu Guangqi ji 徐光啓集
Xu Guangqi nianpu 徐光啓年譜
Xu Guangqi zhuan 徐光啓傳
Xu Jiatun 許家屯
Xu Jiatun Xianggang huiyilu
　　許家屯香港回憶錄
Xu Maoxi 徐懋禧

Xu Shen 許慎
Xu Shuming 許淑明
Xu (Stephanus) 徐
Xu Tian yue 吁天約
Xu Wending Gong ji 徐文定公集
Xu Xinliu 徐新六
Xu Yihua 徐以驊
Xu Zongze 徐宗澤
Xue Bozan 薛伯讚
Xueshu yuekan 學術月刊
Xujiahui 徐家匯
Xujiahui cangshulou Ming Qing Tianzhujiao wenxian 徐家匯藏書樓明清天主教文獻
Xunzi 荀子
Xuting mishi suojing 序廳迷詩所經
Xuzhou 徐州

Yan Maoyou 顏茂猷
Yan Wenhui 宴文輝
Yan Yangchu 晏陽初
yang 陽
Yang Guangxian 楊光先
Yang Senfu 楊森富
Yang Tianhong 楊天宏
Yang Tingyun 楊廷筠
Yangzhou 揚州
Yao 瑤
Ye Xianggao 葉向高
Ye'erqiang 葉爾羌
Yesu 耶穌
Yesu jiating 耶穌家庭
Yesuhuishi yu Zhongguo kexue 耶穌會士與中國科學
yi 義
Yi Shi Bao 益世報
yi ziyou suo cong aimingzhe sanjiao baijia 亦自有所從愛命者三敎白家
yiduan 異端
Yiguan dao 一貫道
Yihetuan yanjiu tongxun 義和團研究通訊
Yijing 易經

Yijiujiuwunian Taiwan Jidujiao jiaoshi baogao 一九九五年台灣基督敎敎勢報告
yike 醫科
yilun 議論
yin 陰
Yin-Ou 印歐
Yinbingshi heji 飲冰室合集
Ying Lianzhi 英斂之
Ying-Hua shuyuan 英華書院
yong Xi 用西
Yongzheng 雍正
Yongzhou 永州
Youguan shenxue benweihua de jijuhua 有關神學本位化的幾句話
Yu Rizhang 余日章
Yuan 元
Yuan Ming shiliao biji congkan 元明史料筆記叢刊
Yuanben lun 原本論
Yuanmingyuan 圓明園
Yuanyelikewen kao 元也里可溫考
yuanzu min 原族民
Yulan Xifang yaoji 御覽西方要記
Yunnan 雲南
Yunnan zongjiao yanjiu 雲南宗敎研究
Yuzhi Lüli yuanyuan 御製律曆淵源

zaijia jushi 在家居士
Zang-Mian 藏緬
zaowuzhe 造物者
Zaowuzhu huaxiang lüeshuo 造物主華象略說
zaoqi sixiang qimeng 早期思想啓蒙
Zengding Xu Wending gong ji 增訂徐文定公集
Zha Shijie 查時傑
Zhaimenqian de shimenkan: Jidujiao wenhua yu Chuan Dian Qian bian Miaozu shehui 窄門前的石門坎：基督敎文化與川滇黔邊苗族社會
Zhang Chunshen 張春申

Zhang Erqi 張爾岐
Zhang Fengzhen 張奉箴
Zhang Fuxing 張復興
Zhang Geng 張賡
Zhang Guangtian 張廣湉
Zhang Junmai 張郡勱
Zhang Juzheng 張居正
Zhang Kaiyuan 章開沅
Zhang Qifeng 張起鳳
Zhang Taiyan 章太炎
Zhang Tan 張坦
Zhang Weihua 張維華
Zhang Xie 張燮
Zhang Xinglang 張星烺
Zhang Xingyao 張星曜
Zhang Zai 張載
Zhanglao jiaohui yu ererba pingfan yundong (1987–1990) 長老教會與二二八平反運動 (1987–1990)
Zhao Binshi 趙賓時
Zhao Chunchen 趙春晨
Zhao Tian'en *see* Chao, Jonathan T'ien-en
Zhao Zichen 趙紫宸
Zhejiang 浙江
Zhen Yesu jiaohui 眞耶穌教會
Zheng Xuan 鄭玄
Zhendan daxue 震旦大學
Zhengdao tigang 正道提綱
zhengming 正名
Zhengshi lüeshuo 拯世略說
Zhen'guan 貞觀
zhiguo 治國
Zhifang waiji 職方外紀
Zhiping xixue 治平西學
zhixing heyi 知行合一
zong 宗
Zhong Mingren 鐘鳴仁
Zhong Xi jiaotongshi 中西交通史
Zhong Xi jiaotong shi ziliao huibian 中西交通史資料匯編
Zhong Xi wenhua yu jiaohui daxue 中西文化與教會大學
Zhongyong 中庸

Zhonggong zhongyang wenxian yanjiushi zonghe yanjiuzu 中共中央文獻研究室綜合研究組
Zhongguo daotong yu chuanjiao 中國道統與傳教
Zhongguo fei Jidujiao yundong 1922–1927 中國非基督教運動1922–1927
Zhongguo guanshen fanjiao de yuanyin, 1860–1874 中國官紳反教的原因, 1860–1874
Zhongguo jiaohui daxue shi yanjiu tongxun 中國教會大學史研究通訊
Zhongguo jiaohui daxue wenxian mulu 中國教會大學文獻目錄
Zhongguo jiaohui de benweihua shenxue 中國教會的本位化神學
Zhongguo Jidujiao de kaishan shiye 中國基督教的開山事業
Zhongguo Jidujiao de zili yundong 中國基督教的自立運動
Zhongguo Jidujiao renwu xiaozhuan 中國基督教人物小傳
Zhongguo Jidujiao shi 中國基督教史
Zhongguo Jidujiao shigang 中國基督教史綱
Zhongguo Jidujiao shi yanjiu 中國基督教史研究
Zhongguo Jidujiao sishinian 中國基督教四十年
Zhongguo Jingjiao 中國景教
Zhongguo liyi zhi zheng: lishi, wenxian he yiyi 中國禮儀之爭：歷史, 文獻和意義
Zhongguo minjian zongjiaoshi 中國民間宗教史
Zhongguo minzhong zongjiao yishi 中國民眾宗教意識
Zhongguo shengwang: Yi meng Tianzhu kaiqi qi xin 中國聖王：亦蒙天主開啓其心
Zhongguo shixue congshu xubian 中國史學叢書續編

Zhongguo sixiang tongshi
中國思想通史
Zhongguo Tianzhujiao 中國天主教
*Zhongguo Tianzhujiao de guoqu yu
xianzai* 中國天主教的過去與
現在
Zhongguo Tianzhujiaoshe
中國天主教社
Zhongguo Tianzhujiaoshi luncong
中國天主教史論叢
*Zhongguo Tianzhujiaoshi
renwuzhuan* 中國天主教史
人物傳
Zhongguo wenhua yu Jidujiao
中國文化與基督教
Zhongguo Yesujiao zilihui
中國耶穌教自立會
Zhongguo Zhujiaotuan 中國主教團
Zhongguo zongjiao shinian
中國宗教十年
Zhongguo zongjiao yanjiu nianjian
中國宗教研究年鑑
Zhongguoshi yanjiu 中國史研究
Zhongguoshi yanjiu dongtai
中國史研究動態
*Zhonghua minguo Taiwan diqu
Tianzhujiao jiaowu jianbao* 中華
民國台灣地區天主教教務簡報
*Zhonghua minguo shi zhuanti
lunwenji*
中華民國史專題論文集
Zhonghua Renmin Gongheguo
中華人民共和國
Zhonghua Shuju 中華書局
zhongshi shehui 重視社會
*Zhongwai wenhua jiaotongshi
luncong* 中外文化交通史論叢
zhongxue 中學
Zhongxue wei ti, Xixue wei yong
中學爲體西學爲用
zhongzu 種族
Zhou 周

Zhou Dunyi 周敦頤
Zhu Cenlou 朱岑樓
Zhu Qianzhi 朱謙之
Zhu Sancai 朱三才
Zhu Shichang 朱世昌
Zhu Xi 朱熹
Zhu Weizheng 朱維錚
Zhu Zhengyi 朱正誼
Zhu Zongyuan 朱宗元
Zuanji 專集
Zhuang 莊
Zhuang Tianci 莊天賜
Zhujiao yuanqi 主教緣起
zibenzhuyi mengya 資本主義萌芽
zheng 正
zhengchang 正常
zhengdao 正道
Zhuo Xinping 卓新平
Zihui 字彙
Zikawei *see* Xujiahui
Ziran kexueshi yanjiu
自然科學史研究
zixiu 自修
ziyou (as incorrectly written by Ly)
自有
ziyou 自由
*Zongjiao gongzuo fangmian de yixie
redian wenti* 宗教工作方面的
一些熱點問題
Zongjiao pian 宗教篇
Zongjiao yu shehui 宗教與社會
zonglun 總論
zongshuo 總說
*Zuzhi rentong celüe yu fei yingli
zhuzhi de guanxi: dui Jidujiao
jiaohui de xibao xiaozu moshi
jiaohui yundong zhi yanjiu*
組織認同策略與非營利組織的
關系：對基督教教會的細胞小
組模式教會運動之研究

List of Participants

LAUREN ARNOLD
Arnold is an art historian and research associate of the USF Ricci Institute. She has just completed and published her book entitled *Princely Gift and Papal Treasures: The Franciscan Mission to China and Its Influence on the Art of the West, 1250–1350* (1999).

DANIEL H. BAYS
Bays chairs the History Department at the University of Kansas. He is the author of four books and many publications on the history of Christianity in China. His most recent edited book is *Christianity in China, the Eighteenth Century to the Present* (1996).

JUDITH A. BERLING
Berling is professor of history of religions at the Graduate Theological Union in Berkeley, California. A specialist in religious studies, she is most recently the author of *A Pilgrim in Chinese Culture: Negotiating Religious Diversity* (1997).

PAUL BERNADICOU, SJ
Bernadicou serves as chair of the Theology and Religious Studies Department at the University of San Francisco. He also serves as chair of the American Academy of Religion and the Society of Biblical Literature. Most of his recent research and publications are on Jesuit spirituality.

CLAUDIA VON COLLANI
Von Collani is assistant to the chair of missiology at the University of Würzburg. She is a researcher in the study of the China mission (1580–1780) with over 120 publications on the Chinese Rites Controversy, Figurism, Leibniz and China, and the history of European sciences in China.

Her most recent publication is entitled *The Dialogue between Christianity and China* (1997).

RALPH R. COVELL
Covell is senior professor of world Christianity at Denver Seminary. He has published five books and many articles. His most recent publication is *Pentecost of the Hills in Taiwan. The Christian Faith among the Original Inhabitants* (1998).

WM. THEODORE DE BARY
De Bary is the John Mitchell Mason Professor Emeritus and Provost Emeritus at Columbia University. He is also the founder of several institutions, including the University Seminars in Asian Thought and Religion and Neo-Confucian Studies. He has published numerous influential books and articles, including *Asian Values and Human Rights* (1998).

DONG LI
Dong Li is director of the Department of Architecture at South China College of Architecture in Guangzhou, China. His most recent publication is *A Study of the Christian University Architecture of China* (1998).

DINARA V. DOUBROVSKAIA
Doubrovskaia is senior research scientist at the Russian Academy of Science, Institute of Oriental Studies in Russia. Her research publication on the *First Jesuit Mission in China in the Late 16th–18th Centuries: Matteo Ricci and Others* is forthcoming.

RYAN DUNCH
Dunch is assistant professor of history at the University of Alberta. His forthcoming book is entitled *Fuzhou Protestants and Making of a Modern China, 1857–1927* (2001).

ROBERT E. ENTENMANN
Entenmann is professor of history at Saint Olaf College. He is the author of many publications, including a recently published paper, "Andreas Ly on the First Jinchuan War in Western Sichuan, 1747–1749" (1997), and an entry on "The Scene: After the Time of Persecution (1720)," in the *Handbook of Oriental Studies: Christianity in China* (1999).

HAN QI

Han serves as professor at the Institute for the History of Natural Sciences at the Chinese Academy of Sciences in China. His area of specialty is the history of Chinese-Western scientific and cultural relations in the seventeenth and eighteenth centuries. His most recent publication is "Li Shanlan and Chinese Theorem," in *Ziran Kexueshi Yanjiu* (*Study of the History of Natural Sciences*) (1999).

RUTH HAYHOE

Hayhoe is director of The Hong Kong Institute of Education. Both a sinologist and a specialist in comparative education, she is currently president-elect of the Comparative and International Education Society in the United States. Her recent publication is *Education and Society in Twentieth-Century China* (forthcoming).

BEATRICE LEUNG, SPB

Leung is associate professor in the Department of Politics and Sociology at Lingnan College in Hong Kong. A writer of over thirty articles and chapters in journals and books, one of her most recent publications is "The Sino-Vatican Negotiations: Old Problems in a New Context," in *The China Quarterly* (1998).

LI TIANGANG

Li is professor at the Institute of History at the Academy of Social Sciences in Shanghai, China. Currently he is a visiting scholar at the Harvard Yenching Institute. An author of many books and articles, Li's most recent book is entitled *Chinese Rites Controversy: Its History, Documents and Significance* (1998).

KATHLEEN L. LODWICK

Lodwick is professor of history at Pennsylvania State University. She has taught courses on traditional, modern, and twentieth-century China. Lodwick is also the author of several books and articles. Her recently published book is entitled *Crusaders Against Opium: Protestant Missionaries in China, 1880–1917* (1996).

ERIBERTO P. LOZADA
Lozada is assistant professor of anthropology at Butler University. He has conducted extensive fieldwork on religion, ethnicity, and transnational processes in various villages in China. His most recent publication is entitled "A Hakka Community in Cyberspace: Diasporic Ethnicity and the Internet," in *The Future of Anthropology* (1999).

THOMAS LUCAS, SJ
Lucas is the founding chair of the University of San Francisco's Fine and Performing Arts Department. He was active in Rome from 1988 to 1991 where he designed and supervised the architectural restoration of the sixteenth-century rooms of St. Ignatius of Loyola, curated the Ignatian year exhibit at the Vatican Library, and edited the exhibit catalog, *Saint, Site, and Sacred Strategy* (1990).

JESSIE G. LUTZ
Lutz is professor of history emeritus at Rutgers University. She is the author/editor of several books on Christian missions to China and co-authored a recent publication entitled, *Hakka Chinese Confront Protestant Christianity* (1998).

RICHARD P. MADSEN
Madsen is professor of sociology at the University of California at San Diego. His area of specialty includes, among others, sociology of ideas/culture, political sociology, sociology of religion, and moral anthropology. His most recent book is *China's Catholics: Tragedy and Hope in an Emerging Civil Society* (1999).

EUGENIO MENEGON
Menegon is pursuing a doctorate in Chinese history at the University of California at Berkeley. He is currently researching the Dominican community of Fuan (Northern Fujian, China) in the seventeenth and eighteenth centuries and recently authored a biography of the Jesuit missionary Giulio Aleni, entitled *Un solo Cielo. Giulio Aleni S.J., (1582–1649): Geografia, arte, scienza, religione dall'Europa alla Cina* (1994).

PETER TZE MING NG
Ng is associate professor and chair of the Religion Department at the Chinese University of Hong Kong. His major area of research is on the Christian Colleges in China. His most recent publication is entitled *Chinese*

Studies Programs at Christian Colleges in China—A Study of Christian Colleges in Modern China, 1900–1950 (1998).

ELIZABETH ROCHAT DE LA VALLÉE
Rochat de la Vallée is secretary general of the Institut Ricci in Paris. She has held various teaching positions throughout Europe teaching ancient Chinese philosophy and classical Chinese medicine. She is also the author of many translations, books, booklets, and articles on the above subjects.

PAUL A. RULE
Rule is senior lecturer in history and director of the Religious Studies Program at La Trobe University in Melbourne, Australia. He teaches courses on Chinese and aboriginal religions, religious theory, and modern Catholicism. Among his numerous works is a recent publication entitled "The Negotiation of Religious Diversity in Christian Theology," in *Australian Religion Studies Review* (1999).

SHI JINGHUAN
Shi is professor of education in the Department of Education at Beijing Normal University, China. Her major fields of teaching and research include international education development, Chinese history of education, comparative education, and women's education. Her most recent publication is *Christian Education and Chinese Intellectuals* (1997).

NICOLAS STANDAERT, SJ
Standaert has been professor of Chinese Studies at Catholic University of Leuven, Belgium, since 1993. Among many of his publications in Chinese-Western cultural history is an edited book entitled *Handbook of Christianity in China* (2000).

R. G. TIEDEMANN
Tiedemann is lecturer in the modern history of China at the School of Oriental and African Studies, University of London. He was a distinguished fellow of the EDS-Stewart Chair for Chinese-Western Cultural History at the Ricci Institute, University of San Francisco in 1999-2000. His recent published research is entitled "China and Its Neighbours," in *A World History of Christianity* (1999).

STEPHEN UHALLEY, JR.
Uhalley is a distinguished fellow of the EDS-Stewart and Kiriyama Chairs, Ricci Institute/Center for the Pacific Rim, University of San Francisco;

research associate, Center for Chinese Studies, University of California at Berkeley; and professor of history emeritus, University of Hawaii. Among his numerous publications are a biography of Mao Zedong and a history of the Chinese Communist Party.

PÉTER VÁMOS
Péter Vámos is lecturer in history and Chinese at the Karoli Gaspar University of Sciences in Budapest, Hungary. His research is focused on Sino-Hungarian relations. His most recent book is entitled *The Destruction of the Hungarian Jesuit Mission in China. The Diary of Fr. Istvan Koch, S.J.* (forthcoming).

BENOÎT VERMANDER, SJ
Vermander is director of the Ricci Institute for Chinese Studies in Taipei. His paintings and calligraphy have been exhibited in China, Taiwan, and Europe. He has published three collections of paintings and calligraphy and several books and articles on political philosophy and social problems in China today.

PETER CHEN-MAIN WANG
Wang is professor of history at the Department of History, the National Chung-Cheng University in Taiwan and the author of several publications. His recent research article entitled "Contextualizing Protestant Publishing in China: The Wenshe, 1924–1928," is included in *Christianity in China: From the Eighteenth Century to the Present* (1996).

EVELYN EATON WHITEHEAD
Whitehead is a distinguished fellow of the EDS/Stewart Chair for Chinese-Western Cultural History at the Ricci Institute, University of San Francisco. She has co-authored with James Whitehead ten cross-disciplinary books. In the last three years, James and Evelyn Whitehead have been lecturing on Christian theology and spirituality at several universities in China.

PHILIP L. WICKERI
Wickeri is the Flora Lamson Hewlett Professor of Evangelism and Mission at the San Francisco Theological Seminary. For over two decades, he served in pastoral and educational ministries in Taiwan, Hong Kong, and China. One of his recent works is *Christianity and Modernization: A Chinese Debate* (1995).

JEAN-PAUL WIEST

Wiest is senior research fellow at the Center for Mission Research and Study at Maryknoll. His primary field of research is in the history of the Roman Catholic Church in modern and contemporary China with an emphasis on Sino-Western cultural and religious interactions. His most recent book is *Popular Catholicism in a World Church: Seven Case Studies in Inculturation* (1999).

JOHN E. WILLS

Wills is professor of history at the University of Southern California. His main research interests include the Ming-Qing transition in seventeenth-century China; pre-modern Chinese foreign relations; and the maritime interconnections of Europeans and Asians in early modern times. His forthcoming book is entitled *China and Maritime Europe, (1500–1800): Trade, Settlement, Diplomacy, and Missions*.

JOHN W. WITEK, SJ

Witek is associate professor of history at Georgetown University. He is the author of over twenty-five articles and essays in books. Currently, he serves as chairman of the International Ricci Association for Chinese Studies. His most recent publication is entitled *Monumenta Sinica I* (forthcoming).

WU XIAOXIN

Wu is the director of the Ricci Institute at the University of San Francisco. In addition to his research work on the history of Christian higher education and archival sources on Christian missionaries in China, he also directs the Ricci 21st Century Roundtable project at the Ricci Institute.

ZHANG KAIYUAN

Zhang is director of the Center for Chinese Christian Colleges Historical Studies and professor at the Central China Normal University. His most recent publications include "Christianity and the May Fourth Movement" (1996), and "The Historical Value of Bates' Papers" (1998).

ZHUO XINPING

Zhuo is the director of the Institute of World Religions at the Chinese Academy of Social Sciences. He is the author of over eighty publications on theology, Christianity, and China, and comparative religious studies. His recent publication is entitled *Catholic Theology in the Contemporary Western Countries* (1998).

ERIK ZÜRCHER
Zürcher is professor of Chinese history and former director of the Sinologisch Institut of Leiden University. His special fields of research include Buddhism in early medieval China, early Chinese Buddhist iconography, the late Ming and early Qing Jesuit mission in China, and pre-modern Chinese reactions to Christianity and other elements of European culture. He is also the author of extensive publications in these fields.

Index